Divine *Mania*

'Our greatest blessings come to us by way of *mania*, provided it is given us by divine gift,' – says Socrates in Plato's *Phaedrus*. Certain forms of alteration of consciousness, considered to be inspired by supernatural forces, were actively sought in ancient Greece. Divine *mania* comprises a fascinating array of diverse experiences: numerous initiates underwent some kind of alteration of consciousness during mystery rites; sacred officials and inquirers attained revelations in major oracular centres; possession states were actively sought; finally, some thinkers, such as Pythagoras and Socrates, probably practiced manipulation of consciousness. These experiences, which could be voluntary or involuntary, intense or mild, were interpreted as an invasive divine power within one's mind, or illumination granted by a super-human being.

Greece was unique in its attitude to alteration of consciousness. From the perspective of individual and public freedom, the prominent position of the divine *mania* in Greek society reflects its acceptance of the inborn human proclivity to experience alteration of consciousness, interpreted in positive terms as god-sent. These mental states were treated with cautious respect, and in contrast to the majority of complex societies, ancient and modern, were never suppressed or pushed to the cultural and social periphery.

Yulia Ustinova is Associate Professor at the Department of General History, Ben-Gurion University of the Negev, Israel. Her research focuses on ancient Greek religion and its role within the society. In addition to the study of textual and archaeological sources, her approach is based on the application of results of cognitive neuroscience, anthropology, and sociology to the interpretation of historical phenomena.

Divine *Mania*

Alteration of Consciousness in Ancient Greece

Yulia Ustinova

Routledge
Taylor & Francis Group

LONDON AND NEW YORK

First published 2018 by Routledge

2 Park Square, Milton Park, Abingdon, Oxfordshire OX14 4RN
52 Vanderbilt Avenue, New York, NY 10017

Routledge is an imprint of the Taylor & Francis Group, an informa business

First issued in paperback 2020

British Library Cataloguing-in-Publication Data
A catalogue record for this book is available from the British Library

Library of Congress Cataloging-in-Publication Data
Names: Ustinova, Yulia, author.
Title: Divine mania : alteration of consciousness in ancient Greece /
    Yulia Ustinova.
Description: New York : Routledge, 2017.
Identifiers: LCCN 2017025464 | ISBN 9781138298118
    (hardback : alk. paper) | ISBN 9781315098821 (ebook)
Subjects: LCSH: Altered states of consciousness—Greece.
Classification: LCC BF1045.A48 U88 2017 | DDC 154.4—dc23
LC record available at https://lccn.loc.gov/2017025464

ISBN: 978-1-138-29811-8 (hbk)
ISBN: 978-0-367-59426-8 (pbk)

Typeset in Goudy
by Apex CoVantage, LLC

Contents

Preface

Dame Folly and us

> There is being; but by what name
> To call it? It's neither sleep nor waking;
> It's between them, and in man through it
> Saneness borders on insanity.
>
> He is in the fullness of his reason,
> But at the same time visions, like waves,
> Run against him from all sides,
> Each one more rebellious and willful than the last,
> As if he were given to the elemental
> Bewilderment of his ancient homeland.
> But sometimes, set on fire by a dream,
> He sees a light not revealed to others.[1]

Yevgeny Baratynsky, a Russian poet who lived in 1800–1844, began his poem *The Last Death* (1827) with these words. Half a century later, in 1885, Alfred Tennyson portrayed a seer talking about his visions in *The Ancient Sage*:

> And more, my son! for more than once when I
> Sat all alone, revolving in myself
> The word that is the symbol of myself,
> The mortal limit of the Self was loosed,
> And past into the Nameless, as a cloud
> Melts into Heaven. I touch'd my limbs, the limbs
> Were strange not mine – and yet no shade of doubt,
> But utter clearness, and thro' loss of Self
> The gain of such large life as match'd with ours
> Were Sun to spark – unshadowable in words,
> Themselves but shadows of a shadow-world.

In this poem, Tennyson appears to render in verse his own experiences. In his later years, he recalled states of illumination that occurred to him throughout his life:

> A kind of waking trance I have frequently had, quite from boyhood, when
> I have been all alone. This has generally come upon me thro' repeating my

own name two or three times to myself silently, till all at once, as it were out of the intensity of the consciousness of individuality, the individuality itself seemed to dissolve and fade away into boundless being, and this not a confused state, but the clearest of the clearest, the weirdest of the weirdest, utterly beyound words, where death was an almost laughable impossibility, the loss of personality (if so it were) seeming no extinction but the only true life.[2]

Experiences depicted by the two 19th-century poets can hardly be dismissed as merely reflecting Romantic literary conventions, exaggerated, imaginative, or irrelevant for the comprehension of their work. In the age of reason, these – and other – educated and sane people lived through mental states that were completely different from their usual awareness, and attributed revelatory and artistic significance to these sensations. Admittedly, not every creative individual visited the 'shadow-world' where 'saneness borders on insanity.' However, Yevgeny Baratynsky, Alfred Tennyson, and others who knew this elation on the brink of folly lead us into the strange realm of deviation from the ordinary consciousness, a state that is not a psychiatric disorder to be treated medically, but one of the sources of our praised cultural assets. This realm is not in some exotic country or faraway past; it is our world, here and now.

Nevertheless, the reluctance to acknowledge that being in a non-ordinary state of consciousness is not synonymous to being mad is characteristic of our culture, which tends to medicalise the nonconformities, especially behavioural deviance. In historical and cultural situations different from the modern Western norm, people take for granted that a person may be out of his or her mind, but not crazy; for instance, in the traditional Inuit society a shaman while healing is not deemed mad.[3] In our society, the idea that deviation from the normal state of consciousness may be beneficial is still considered by many extravagant, if not preposterous.

Even allowing that artists, who are eccentric by definition,[4] may sometimes indulge in follies, many modern Westerners still believe that regular law-abiding citizens usually think rationally. Yet even in most practical spheres, including economy and finances, irrational biases and intuitions are deeply involved in decision-making. Behavioural economics, particularly the prospect theory of Amos Tversky and the Nobel prize laureate Daniel Kahneman, demonstrate that in real life, people tend to make choices that are neither logical nor consistent.[5] Furthermore, many psychiatrists and neuroscientists are convinced that 'normal' people are positively biased, due to an endogenic release of euphoriants; only the moderately depressed judge the world realistically, their brain lacking the required amounts of these drug-like substances.[6] In a word, our optimism is a device to cope with the gloomy realities of life. This idea is not new: in Erasmus' *Praise of Folly* Dame Folly says that not only does she make life bearable, but she is at the origins of life, since without the intervention of madness nobody would ever care to produce offspring.[7]

If indeed most people make irrational decisions on important matters, our confidence in our own rationality[8] seems to be a culturally supported illusion rather than a logical inference from facts. This illusion is cherished by individuals and by the society in general, perpetuating patterns of behaviour and attitudes that are considered positive or adequate. One of its expressions is the still dominant Hegelian vision of the world as steadily progressing from ignorance to rationality. Scientific writing is part of this tendency, providing ample examples of the auto-censored concept of intellectual history. As A. Thiher observes, 'Newton's obsessive mysticism or Paracelsus' demented cosmology are left aside in writing the history of physics, mechanics, medicine. . . . The erroneous and the irrational have been excluded from the pantheon.'[9]

Dame Folly rules the modern Western world in multiple ways. The unreasonable believe that they are guarded by pure reason, and those who are endowed with moments of illumination usually either keep silent or compare them to madness. We misunderstand our own culture, and attempt to apply the yardstick of our illusions to other cultures.

Ancient Greek culture is treated along these lines: non-rational is more often than not categorised as aberrant and pathological, and consequently disregarded, played down, or explained away. For example, *From Myth to Logos* is the title of two different books on the development of Greek thought, one written by an influential German philologist Wilhelm Nestle, and the other by a Russian historian of ancient philosophy F. H. Kessidi. B. Snell called a chapter in his *The Discovery of the Mind* 'From Myth to Logic.' For these scholars, as well as for many others, 'the Greek achievement' was the rationalistic world view and logical scrutiny: the zenith of the Greek civilisation was the Age of Reason.[10] Nowadays, the concept of a clear-cut movement from myth to reason is questioned: in a collection entitled *From Myth to Reason?* eminent classicists emphasise the complexity of the familiar trajectory.[11] However, a paradigm shift has not yet happened. E. Rohde, the pioneer in the study of the Greek *psyche*, followed F. Nietzsche's sharp distinction between the Apollonian intellectualism and the Dionysian frenzy.[12] E. R. Dodds, the author of the ground-breaking *The Greeks and the Irrational*, stopped short at admitting that prominent Greek intellectuals had faith in divine revelation: 'We need not assume that Plato believed the Pythia to be verbally inspired.'[13] R. Padel, who wrote two books on madness in tragedy, is convinced that Plato's concept of certain kinds of madness as a blessing 'did not represent [Greek] culture's beliefs.'[14]

This book is an attempt at demonstrating that, in fact, this was exactly the case.

Notes

1 Есть бытие; но именем каким |Его назвать? Ни сон оно, ни бденье; |Меж них оно, и в человеке им |С безумием граничит разуменье. |Он в полноте понятья своего, |А между тем, как волны, на него, |Одни других мятежней, своенравней, |Видения бегут со всех сторон, |Как будто бы своей отчизны давней |Стихийному смятенью отдан он; |Но иногда, мечтой воспламененный, |Он видит свет, другим не откровенный (Baratynsky 1957: 129; my translation makes use of the version by Brown [1986: 3, 323]).

2 Hallam Tennyson, *Alfred Lord Tennyson: A Memoir of his Son* (London, 1897), vol. 1, p. 320, quoted after Nichols (1986: 132). The most often cited instance of Tennyson's 'trances' or 'epiphanies' is Section XCV of *In Memoriam*, depicting a visitation by a

soul of his dead friend or an otherworldly reality (Nichols 1986: 140, with further referencess.).

3 Wiley and Allen (2009: 361); Ward (1989: 26).
4 'We of the craft are all crazy,' as Lord Byron remarked (Jamison 1993: 2).
5 Kahneman (2011).
6 Burton (2009: 118, 121); Sharot (2011).
7 Thiher (2004: 52).
8 Whatever everyone means by the term 'rational': Harris (2006: 387). See Davidson (2004) for 'problems of rationality'; Stoller (1995) for an overview of different concepts of rationality tailored for a student of religion; Lloyd (1987) on rationality in Greece; Winkelman (2000: 3) for the European tradition of depreciating altered states of consciousness and emphasising rational thought.
9 Thiher (2004: 8).
10 Nestle (1940); Kessidi (1972); Snell (1960).
11 Buxton (1999); Gill (1996: 252) on B. Snell's progressivism.
12 Rohde (1925) (the German original published in 1894).
13 Dodds (1973: 222, 217–218) (first published in 1951)
14 Padel (1995: 82); Padel (1992). Cf. J.M. Rhodes' thesis that the 'prophetic-poetic beginning' of Plato's discussion of the divine *mania* 'is entirely mythical' (Rhodes 2003: 474).

References

Baratynsky, Y. A. 1957. *Complete Poems (Polnoye sobraniye stikhotvoreniy)*. Leningrad: Sovetskiy Pisatel.

Brown, W. E. 1986. *A History of Russian Poetry of the Romantic Period*. Ann Arbor: Ardis.

Burton, N. 2009. *The Meaning of Madness*. Oxford: Acheron.

Buxton, R., ed. 1999. *From Myth to Reason? Studies in the Development of Greek Thought*. Oxford: Oxford University Press.

Davidson, D. 2004. *Problems of Rationality*. Oxford: Oxford University Press.

Dodds, E. R. 1973. *The Greeks and the Irrational*. Berkeley-Los Angeles: University of California Press.

Gill, C. 1996. "Mind and madness in Greek tragedy." *Apeiron* 29 (3):249–267.

Harris, J. P. 2006. "Divine madness and human sanity in Plato's *Phaedrus*." *Mouseion* 6:387–406.

Jamison, K. R. 1993. *Touched With Fire: Manic-Depressive Illness and the Artistic Temperament*. New York: The Free Press.

Kahneman, D. 2011. *Thinking, Fast and Slow*. London: Allen Lane.

Lloyd, G. E. R. 1987. *The Revolutions of Wisdom: Studies in the Claims and Practice of Ancient Greek Science*. Berkeley-Los Angeles: University of California Press.

Nestle, W. 1940. *Vom Mythos zum Logos, die Selbstentfaltung des griechischen Denkens von Homer bis auf die Sophistik und Sokrates*. Stuttgart: Kröner.

Nichols, A. 1986. "The epiphanic trance poem: Why Tennyson is not a mystic." *Victorian Poetry* 24 (2):131–148.

Padel, R. 1992. *In and Out of the Mind: Greek Images of the Reagic Self*. Princeton: Princeton University Press.

Padel, R. 1995. *Whom Gods Destroy: Elements of Greek and Tragic Madness*. Princeton: Princeton University Press.

Rhodes, J. M. 2003. *Eros, Wisdom, and Silence: Plato's Erotic Dialogues*. Columbia: University of Missouri Press.

Rohde, E. 1925. *Psyche*. London: Routledge & Kegan Paul.

Sharot, T. 2011. *The Optimism Bias: A Tour of the Irrationally Positive Brain*. New York: Pantheon Books.

Snell, B. 1960. *The Discovery of the Mind: The Greek Origins of the European Thought*. New York: Harper & Row.

Stoller, P. 1995. *Embodying Colonial Memories: Spirit Possession, Power, and the Hauka in West Africa*. London: Routledge.

Thiher, A. 2004. *Revels in Madness: Insanity in Medicine and Literature*. Ann Arbor: University of Michigan Press.

Ward, C. A., ed. 1989. *Altered States of Consciousness and Mental Health: A Cross-Cultural Perspective*. Newbury Park: Sage.

Wiley, A. S., and J. S. Allen. 2009. *Medical Anthropology: A Biocultural Approach*. Oxford: Oxford University Press.

Winkelman, M. 2000. *Shamanism: The Neural Ecology of Consciousness and Healing*. Westport: Bergin & Garvey.

Acknowledgements

While working on this book, I was blessed with generous help and support of many people and institutions. The research was funded by the Israel Science Foundation (grant No. 1077/12). Ben-Gurion University of the Negev provided a stimulating intellectual environment, as well as resources for my sabbatical leaves and research trips. I am very grateful to my colleagues at the Department of History, particularly to Elisheva German and Merav Haklai; my debt to the late Lucien (Uri) Posnanski will always remain enormous. Expert editing by Carolyn Gross-Baruch greatly improved the text of the book.

The manuscript began to take shape and was completed while I was a Visiting Fellow at the Institute of Classical Studies of the University of London. The Institute and the Joint Library of the Hellenic and Roman Societies offer exceptional conditions for research on Classical antiquity, and I cannot overstate how privileged I was to spend my days in London there. It is a pleasure to thank the successive directors of the Institute of Classical Studies, John North and Greg Woolf, for their cordial welcome at the Institute. The help, friendly advice, and consideration of the members of the staff, especially Sue Willetts, made the institute and the library even more inviting.

I was fortunate to participate in many scientific meetings, which greatly benefitted this book. The workshops of CAARE, a project on Cognitive Approaches to Ancient Religious Experience, initiated and headed by Esther Eidinow and Armin Geertz, were especially important. Another long-standing source of inspiration was provided by the conferences of Centre International d'Étude de la Religion Grecque Antique, with their candid and genial discussions. I am very grateful to friends and colleagues who shared with me their knowledge on various occasions, and by supporting or questioning my ideas played an important role in formulating, developing, or modifying them. In particular, I wish to thank Peter Agosc, Pierre Bonnechere, Joe Banks, Etzel Cardeña, Michael Crawford, Christopher Faraone, Gabriel Herman, Vayos Liapis, Irad Malkin, Robert Parker, and Richard Seaford. Ralph Anderson, Erica Angliker, Ariadne Konstantinou, and Amir Yerucham kindly allowed me to use their yet unpublished work.

Portions of discussion laid out in this book in an extended and modified form were first presented in previously published papers. I am grateful to the editors and publishers of the journals where these papers have appeared:

Scripta Classica Israelica (Ustinova, Y. 2012. "Madness into memory: *Mania* and *mnêmê* in Greek culture." *SCI* 31: 109–132.);

Kernos (Ustinova, Y. 2013. "Modes of prophecy, or modern arguments in support of the ancient approach." *Kernos* 26: 25–44.);

Bulletin of the Institute of Classical Studies (Ustinova, Y. 2013. "To live in joy and die with hope: Experiential aspects of ancient Greek mystery rites." *BICS* 56 (2): 105–123.);

Psychological Trauma: Theory, Research, Practice, and Policy (Ustinova, Y. and E. Cardeña. 2014. "Combat stress disorders and their treatment in Ancient Greece." *Psychological Trauma: Theory, Research, Practice, and Policy.* June 6 (6): 739–748). My co-author E. Cardeña gracefully agreed that I use our joint work in this book.

I am very grateful to the staff at Routledge, who saw this book to its completion. Greatest thanks go to Michael Greenwood, Editor in Classical Studies, for his engagement with my project and constant encouragement, and to Michael Bourne, Senior Editorial Assistant who supervised the producing of the book. I am indebted to the anonymous readers who reviewed the manuscript for Routledge for their thoughtful comments.

My gratitude to the two most important people in my life, my mother Elvira Cherniak, and my husband Isaac Gilead, is more profound than words can express.

Abbreviations

Abbreviations of ancient authors and works follow the *Greek-English Lexicon* of H.G. Liddell and R. Scott, revised by H.S. Jones, and *Oxford Latin Dictionary* for the Classical authors, and *Année Philologique* for the periodicals.

ANET: Pritchard, J.B. 1969. *Ancient Near Eastern Texts Relating to the Old Testament*. Princeton: Princeton University Press.

CIL: *Corpus Inscriptionum Latinarum*. Berlin: Reimer-De Gruyter, 1863–

DK: Diels, H. and W. Kranz. 1951. *Die Fragmente der Vorsokratiker*. Berlin: Weidmann.

FGH: Jacoby, F. 1923–1958. *Die Fragmente der griechischen Historiker*. Leiden: Brill.

IErythr.:   Engelman, H. and R. Merkelbach. 1972–1973. *Die Inschriften von Erythrai und Klazomenai*. Bonn: Habelt.

IG: *Inscriptiones Graecae*. Berlin: Reimer-De Gruyter, 1903–

IMagn.:   Kern, O. 1900. *Die Inschriften von Magnesia am Meander*. Berlin: Spemann.

ISM: Pippidi, D.M. and I. Stoian, eds. 1970–1987. *Inscriptiones Scythiae Minoris Graecae et Latinae*. *Series Altera*. Bucharest: Editura Academiei Republicii Socialiste Românîa.

IStratonikeia: Şahin, M.Ç. 1982. *Die Inschriften von Stratonikeia*. Bonn: Habelt.

Janko: Janko, R. 2010. *Philodemus, On Poems, Books 3–4, with the Fragments of Aristotle, On Poets*. Oxford: Oxford University Press.

Körte-Thierfelder: Körte, A. and A. Thierfelder. 1959. *Menandri quae supersunt*. Leipzig: Teubner.

LIMC: *Lexicon Iconographicum Mythologiae Classicae*. Zurich: Artemis, 1997–

Lobel-Page: Lobel, E. and D.L. Page. 1968. *Poetarum Lesbiorum fragmenta*. Oxford: Clarendon Press.

LSAM: Sokolowski, F. 1955. *Lois sacrées de l'Asie Mineure*. Paris: de Boccard.

LSAM Suppl.:   Sokolowski, F. 1962. *Lois sacrées des cités grecques. Supplément.*
                    Paris: de Boccard.
LSCG: Sokolowski, F. 1969. *Lois sacrées des cités grecques.* Paris: de
                    Boccard.
Maehler: Maehler, H. 1984–1989. *Pindari carmina cum fragmentis.*
                    Leipzig: Teubner.
Merkelbach-West: Merkelbach, R. and M.L. West. 1977. *Fragmenta Hesiodea.*
                    Oxford: Clarendon Press.
OF: Kern, O. 1922. *Orphicorum fragmenta.* Berlin: Weidemann.
Page: Page, D. 1962. *Poetae melici Graeci.* Oxford: Clarendon Press.
PMG: Preisendanz, K. 1973–1974. *Papyri Graecae magicae.* Stuttgart:
                    Teubner.
RE: *Paulys Real-Encyclopadie der classischen Altertumswissen-
                    schaft.* Stuttgart: Metzler-Druckenmuller, 1903–
Rose: Rose, V. 1886. *Aristotelis qui ferebantur librorum fragmenta.*
                    Leipzig: Teubner.
Sandbach: Sandbach, F.H. 1967. *Plutarchi Moralia.* Leipzig: Teubner.
SEG: *Supplementum Epigraphicum Graecum.* Leiden-Amsterdam:
                    Brill-Gieben, 1923–
TGF: Kannicht, R., B. Snell, and S. Radt. 1971–2004. *Tragicorum
                    Graecorum fragmenta.* Göttingen: Vanderhoek & Ruprecht.
ThCRA: *Thesaurus Cultus et Rituum Antiquorum.* Los Angeles, J. P.
                    Getty Museum, 2005–2012.
TLG: *Thesaurus Linguae Graecae: A Digital Library of Greek Litera-
                    ture.* http://www.tlg.uci.edu.
Wehrli: Wehrli, F. 1944–1969. *Die Schule des Aristoteles.* Basel:
                    Schwabe.
West: West, M.L. 1972. *Iambi et elegi Graeci.* Oxford: Clarendon
                    Press.
Wimmer: Wimmer, F. 1964. *Theophrasti Eresii opera quae supersunt
                    omnia.* Frankfurt am Main: Minerva.

Introduction

Socrates on divine *mania*

In Plato's *Phaedrus*, Socrates says that *mania* is not always an evil, because 'in reality, the greatest of blessings come to us through *mania*, when it is sent as a gift of the gods.'[1] This statement is followed by a discourse on different kinds of *mania*, and I will return to each of them in due course. At the moment, I will focus on the notion of god-sent insanity. Did Socrates mean that it could be positive?

The divine gift of *mania* is inspiration, *epipnoia*, which unites all the four kinds of *mania* that Socrates considers:[2] having briefly mentioned prophetic, telestic (initiatory), and poetic madness, he discusses in detail the gifts of erotic *mania*. For Socrates, *mania* can be an evil or a blessing:

> There are two kinds of madness, one arising from human diseases, and the other from a divine release from the customary habits. . . . And we made four divisions of the divine madness, ascribing them to four gods, saying that prophecy was inspired by Apollo, the telestic madness by Dionysus, the poetic by the Muses, and the madness of love, inspired by Aphrodite and Eros, we said was the best.[3]

From this dichotomy, by means of a brilliant dialectic argument,[4] Plato proceeds to the idea that some kinds of *mania* cannot be easily tagged as either good or bad:

> As our two discourses just now assumed one common principle, unreason, and then, just as the body, which is one, is naturally divisible into two, right and left, with parts called by the same names, so our two discourses conceived of madness as naturally one principle within us.[5]

In reality, Socrates argues, just as the body has two hands, many phenomena possess dual traits. His favourite example is erotic *mania*, which may be either beneficial or harmful.[6] This statement paves the way to the possibility that possession by other gods, and not only by Eros, can be ambivalent.

The initial sharp opposition between the negative madness, which is a human disease, and the positive one, which is the divine gift to humanity, is not questioned, but nuanced: divine *mania* is complex, and it is only as 'aids to speech and thought' that this multifarious phenomenon is 'collected into one and divided into many.'[7]

For the most part, a student of Plato is required to switch from the normal world of real things to the ideal world of concepts. This book is essentially an attempt at doing the opposite; namely, it suggests a return from the Platonic notions to the perception of the actual world by ancient Greeks. To this purpose, I will try to see whether the concept of god-sent *mania* corresponds to phenomena noticed and described by other writers.

I will contend that this correspondence exists – in a broad sense and with caveats, but nevertheless consistently. People from different walks of life thought, or felt intuitively, and most importantly, acted in accordance with the belief that certain abnormal mental states were beneficial to the person who experiences them, and to his or her community. They also knew that *mania* was not static, but multifarious and multileveled. Notwithstanding the awareness that attaining the state of *mania* might be difficult and dangerous, many Greeks valued it and sought to experience it in various contexts.

It has been argued that the idea of madness as a blessing did not represent the Greek culture's beliefs,[8] belonged to Plato alone, and that this Platonic invention became one of the cultural constructs determining modern Western world view.[9] It is obvious that Plato's universe was profoundly different from the world of ordinary men; in the Platonic dialogues, the line between Plato's own mind and Socrates' mind is blurred, and there is no doubt that Plato's reader is often left perplexed as to whether a certain idea is put forward earnestly or ironically.[10] Nevertheless, not all the Platonic statements are idiosyncratic, and some of them reflect opinions of his contemporaries. It is significant that the passages on divine *mania*, attributed to Socrates, deal with the most intimate kind of contact between mortals and immortals, visitation of a human by a god and its value. Although Socrates' behaviour was overtly eccentric, and his peculiarity will be discussed in detail in Chapter 8, regarding the realm of the gods he was usually 'a man of his time.'[11] Plato had never questioned his piety, and attributing the notion of divine *mania* to Socrates hinted at its embeddedness in traditional values.

Plato was the first to define the general concept of divine *mania*, listing its sub-forms and bringing together their rewards: he transformed the mosaic of discrete cases into a beautiful system (ignoring or casting away a few facts and experiences that he considered of minor importance). His classification is theoretical and schematic – but this is the essence of abstraction. I argue that this abstraction was not an invention, but a concise presentation of his reflection on the contemporary cultural reality.[12]

Mania: words and images

The word *mania* refers to a range of multifarious conditions, which cannot be concisely described by the words 'madness' or 'frenzy' used in modern English translation. In Greek, *mania* also implies divine inspiration or revelation. Any deviation from an ordinary baseline state of consciousness, whether achieved voluntarily or involuntarily, deliberately sought or resulting from a disease, seen as a god-sent blessing or a curse could be dubbed *mania*. This variety of meanings reflects a wide range of experiences, from ecstatic prophesying to violent frenzy. The word *mania* derives from the Indo-European root *men-*, meaning 'active mental force' which includes in its scope thought accompanied by effort; excited thought, raving, or being in a special or differentiated state of consciousness; and finally the action of remembering or reminding.[13] In Greek, *mania*, *menos*, and *mnêmê* – madness, mental force, and memory – are cognate words.[14] As this grouping is unique, I prefer to use the Greek term encompassing manifold meanings, rather than the English word 'madness.'

While the word *mania* covered a vast semantic sphere, several other terms denoted abnormal mental states explicitly attributed to divine intervention. A mortal could be possessed by a god (*theolêptos* or *katochos*), and her or his state would be described as possession, *katôchê*.[15] The name of the god was sometimes specified; for instance, *phoibolêptos* was seized by Apollo and *numpholêptos* by the nymphs. Apparently, these expressions implied the sensation of outside control, being taken or held by an external power. People who called themselves *bakchoi* or *bakchai* indicated complete abandon of their regular self and identification with Dionysus.[16] One could also have the god inside, literally 'be engodded' (*entheos*); in this case, the super-human compulsion was supposedly felt as an invasive power within one's body or mind.[17] Every god could enthuse a mortal with *enthousiasmos*, 'engoddedness' or *epipnoia*, 'inspiration.'[18] However, the difference between 'possession from the outside' and 'invasion from the inside' was subtle and inconsistent, and the word usage hardly reflects a contrast in the human experience of approaching the divine: the same deities, in particular Apollo and the Muses, could both 'seize' and 'inspire' mortals, and quite often the words *katochos* and *entheos* were used synonymously.[19]

The ambiguity of the word *entheos* is similar to that of *mania*: on the one hand, Plato's poets, seers, and true lovers are 'engodded,' and this state is regarded as a blessing, but on the other hand, Euripides' agonised Phaedra looks like *entheos*, invaded by malicious gods.[20] This usage persisted into later periods: Plutarch describes Cato's course of action as *arethês enthousiasmos*, '(religious) frenzy for virtue,' meaning that obsession, even with virtue, is pure madness.[21] The dichotomy *emphrôn-ekphrôn*, describing a person in and out of his or her mind (*phrên*),[22] could be applied to the contrast between the sane and either divinely inspired or mad individuals. People belonging to the latter category could be described as 'disturbed,' the idea rendered by the verb *ekplêttô* (to strike out) and cognate words.[23] I will return to the language of madness on multiple occasions; at the moment it will suffice to call attention to the fact that in Greek discourse on *mania* and *enthousiasmos*, danger and achievement, super-human and deranged, were often intertwined.

These two phenomena looked quite similar to an outside observer. In *The Sacred Disease*, a fifth-century Hippocratic physician scorns the witch-doctors that attribute different kinds of fits to different gods:

> If the patient imitate a goat, if he roar, or suffer convulsions in the right side, they say that the Mother of the Gods is to blame. If he utter a piercing and

loud cry, they liken him to a horse and blame Poseidon. . . . If he foam at the mouth and kick, Ares has the blame.[24]

The same outward symptoms are often attributed to individuals possessed by divine powers. Roaring and goat-like leaping were characteristic of the bacchants, seers were often represented as shouting, great heroes in a state of combat fury were depicted as foaming at the mouth, and the most ancient account of the Sibyl refers to her mouth as 'mad.' Like Xenophon, everyone knew that 'all who are under the influence of any of the gods seem well worth gazing at; . . . those who are possessed . . . have a tendency to be sterner of countenance, more terrifying of voice, and more vehement.'[25] Nevertheless, all these manifestations were often regarded as god-given gifts. Even today, alterations of consciousness sought by various cult groups and individuals are not always easy to discern from symptoms of psychiatric disorders. For instance, the difference between depersonalisation and false memories as symptoms of dissociation identity disorder, and the detachment from the body and modified awareness of the past in spiritual seekers and sect members is far from self-evident.[26] In antiquity, the spectrum between derangement and divine inspiration was perceived as a continuum, and the ambiguity of *mania*, even as a god-given gift, is one of the main themes to be explored in this book.

In Greece, madness could be personified as an anthropomorphic deity, although rather rarely. Lyssa, a goddess of rabid, literally wolfish, frenzy driving mortals into hideous madness, appeared in the Athenian theatre more than once.[27] In the fifth century, this goddess was portrayed as a frightening female, sometimes with canine heads emerging above her head and snakes coiling around her hands.[28] The goddess of madness could also be simply named Mania. She is depicted on an early fourth-century crater by Asteas from Paestum as a serene and attractively looking woman watching the scene of Heracles slaughtering his children – her name indicated under her image.[29]

Remarkably, an area in Arcadia was called Maniai, Madnesses, and in the second century AD a sanctuary of goddesses by the same name was situated there.[30] In Pausanias' opinion, this name was the epiclesis of the Eumenides, and in fact local people said that it was there that Orestes was seized with madness after the matricide. Not far from this sanctuary was a mound with a stone finger on it, called Finger's Tomb; this was believed to be the place where Orestes, feeling the surging frenzy, bit off one of his fingers as a sin-offering and gave it to the Eumenides. This act averted their wrath; therefore the nearby area was called Akê (Quiet),[31] and there was a sanctuary of the Eumenides: while chasing Orestes they appeared to him black, but after they had accepted his finger they became white, and seeing that sight Orestes recovered his sanity.[32] This landscape forcefully symbolises the duality of *mania*: a place called Tranquility, with its own deities of insanity who are emphatically dual and combine hellish and heavenly aspects, neighbours a place called Madnesses, in which a sanctuary of the madnesses exists. In Arcadia, insanity and peace of mind were tangibly adjacent, and goddesses of madness appeared as plural, changeable and elusive: it's a pity that the early history of this locality can only be guessed about.

The autonomous existence of madness in tragedy and art underscores its perception as an external irresistible force, invading the human mind from the outside. The only instance of a real-life cult of the *Maniai* is late, but probably derives from much more ancient notions, and is focused on the ambiguity of *mania* and close proximity of madness and serenity.

Mania as mental disorder: its definition and characteristics

As we have just seen, god-sent and human madness shared some common ground; therefore before we turn to the discussion of the divine *mania*, a few remarks on the popular attitude to abnormal behaviour and mental disorders are called for.[33] The viewpoint of the Greek medical professionals will interest us within the context of its influence on the opinions of the laymen; therefore I will touch upon specialists' writings on the subject only occasionally, focusing on the evidence representing the outlook of the general public.

Defining madness was a great challenge to the Greek thinkers, and fifth-century intellectuals known as the Sophists painstakingly strove to comprehend its nature. The anonymous author of *Dissoi Logoi* (*Debated Questions*), perplexed by the lack of a clear-cut gap between the behaviour of mad and sane, even argued that only judging upon the situation one can assume understanding of right and wrong, which will allow discerning between the sane and the mad.[34]

In the Hippocratic literature, with its emphasis on fits of florid madness and lack of interest in borderline mental states,[35] mild deviations from the norm are seldom noted. It is sometimes difficult to discern how grave certain behaviour was in the physician's view and whether it would be categorised as madness or merely a temporary peculiarity. People who talked too much or kept silent, exhibited sudden unexplained mood changes or were improperly aggressive and rude were often diagnosed with a disease involving disturbance of the mind, but then strange behaviour was not the only symptom of pathology.[36] There was a range of possible deviations from the norm, the norm itself was not crystal clear, and individual features were taken into account.[37]

Hippocratic texts appear to offer a clue to the problem of the definition of madness in Greece. Generally, psychological disturbances are expressed in terms referring to the intellect; patients who are aware of their surroundings, and react coherently to external stimuli, are considered sane: they are 'within themselves';[38] those who are unable to recognise people and places, and do not react coherently, are 'outside themselves.'[39] Thus, the ability to relate to one's environment correctly, meaning recognition of people and understanding their speech, is the major criterion of sanity in the Hippocratic corpus.

This understanding was shared by some laymen, intellectuals interested in people's inner life. Euripides created an array of images of women who were described as 'mad,' such as Medea, Phaedra, and Agave. Medea commits a shocking crime of infanticide, and she does so in cold blood, of her own free will and conscious of her deeds.[40] Phaedra is struck by a deity with erotic *mania* (the subject of Chapter 7), but she is still capable of perceiving her physical surroundings and social norms in the same manner as other people do. Agave (in the *Bacchae*, discussed in detail in Chapter 3) in her Bacchic *mania* mistakes her son for a lion whelp, tears him asunder, and returns home carrying his head as a trophy. The difference between Medea and Phaedra, on the one hand, and Agave, on the other hand, is that the latter is not aware of her actions: she perceives the world incorrectly, not in the way sane people do. A person acting contrary to current ethics was a transgressor, to be punished by gods and men – but he or she was not literally mad. A person committing a crime and aware of it could (and still can) be called mad metaphorically, but a person committing a crime and not aware of this action was mad in literal sense.

Even modern psychiatrists and psychologists find it sometimes very difficult to pinpoint the difference between idiosyncrasy and mental disorder. However, perception – physical and social – was and still is crucial.[41] In Greece, conditions that today would be treated by psychiatrists were not necessarily considered as needing particular care, especially when they were not accompanied by violent attacks. In addition, the distinction between the socially unacceptable behaviour of a sane person and insanity as a clinical state cannot be defined precisely in any culture,[42] and the Greeks were not an exception.

Plato's approach to mental illness was innovative: contrary to the opinions prevailing in his age, Plato defines illnesses of the soul (*nosêmata psuchês*) as dementia (*anoia*), and claims that the latter can be of two types, *mania* and *amathia* – madness and ignorance.[43] Thus, Plato articulates the notion of 'illness of the soul,' contrary to the Hippocratic opinion that that an illness of the soul may be due to an illness of the body,[44] and contends that *anoia* is not necessarily derangement, ensuing from somatic reasons, but can ensue from ignorance. Plato's definition of the notion of the health of the soul as a moral concept had most important consequences for both medicine and philosophy.[45]

Although Aristotle did not leave a systematic treatment of mental disorders, he seems to have believed in their physical nature, and put an emphasis first and foremost on the blatantly deviant behaviour of deranged persons, often associated with violence.[46] The most radical examples of insanity would be a person who sacrificed and ate his own mother and a slave who devoured his friend's liver, cited by Aristotle, who argued that cannibalism resulted from *mania*.[47]

Obviously, not every individual who was considered mad by his or her environment went as far as cannibalism. Most people had an obscure idea as to what madness was, but labelled abnormal conduct as 'mad' or 'insane.' Xenophon's down-to-earth rendering of Socrates' depiction of mad behaviour is typical:

> Some madmen have no fear of danger and others are afraid where there is nothing to be afraid of, as some will do or say anything in a crowd with no sense of shame, while others shrink even from going abroad among men, some respect neither temple nor altar nor any other sacred thing, others worship stocks and stones and beasts.[48]

Some traits of madmen's behaviour immediately call to mind manifestations of divine possession, such as the fearlessness of valiant warriors in the grip of Lyssa,

or the violence of the maenads when they follow Dionysus' call. The circumstances of each case of abnormal behaviour allowed taking decisions upon its
nature, but the incidence of borderline situations was probably not negligible.

Mania could be intense and short termed or persistent. An Athenian named
Thrasyllus, who considered all the ships arriving at Piraeus as his own, was
described as mad; having been healed, he complained that he was most happy in
his delusion (*mania*), when he 'did not know any sorrow, but enjoyed numerous
pleasures.'[49] This anecdote, even if invented by Heraclides, indicates that the
word *mania* designated not only florid frenzy, but also quiet enduring disorders. An
important twist is added: delusion may be pleasurable. This case is not exceptional: Aristotle as well was aware of the 'marvellous pleasures' that madmen
(*paraphronountes*) sometimes enjoy.[50] Thus, on the one hand, the diversity of madness was clear to everyone, but on the other hand, any behaviour that did not
match reality was regarded as madness, even when enchanting and inoffensive.

In the Homeric poems and fifth-century drama, madness-words (*atê*, *mainomai*,
margos, *margainô*) quite often imply deviation from socially acceptable patterns of
behaviour, with harmful consequences either for the agent or for other people.[51]
For instance, Penelope asked the nurse, who had brought her astounding news,
whether the gods have deprived the old woman of her mind:[52] the queen is represented as thinking that the nurse imagined the impossible, which was Odysseus'
homecoming. In Aeschylus' *Persians* Xerxes' mother describes her son's daring
ambitions as 'a disease of the mind': being 'out of one's *phrenes*' does not necessarily mean 'being mad' literally.[53] Some early Greek sages even associated bad man-
ners with madness: for Chilon, moving arms when speaking, and for Bias, quick
speech, were signs of *mania*.[54]

In this respect, comedy followed everyday parlance: Aristophanes' frequent
comparisons of socially unacceptable behaviour with madness are usually no more
than a common idiom.[55] In court speech, an absurd decision could be called 'crazy,'
and a man who took it was 'not in his right mind.'[56] Gorgias put an emphasis on
moral and practical judgment, saying in his *Defence of Palamedes*: 'For it is madness
(*mania*) to undertake works that are impossible, unprofitable, disgraceful, by
which one will harm one's friends and benefit one's enemies, and expose one's own
life to reproaches and snares.'[57] In all these instances, the authors are clearly aware
of the fact that the individuals described as 'mad' were, in fact, clinically sane.[58]

It is difficult or impossible to perform a statistical analysis of the Greek vocabulary of madness. K. J. Dover observed that 'the Greeks used all their words for
insanity much more freely in warning, reproach and vilification than we use our
corresponding words.'[59] Perhaps that was correct for the British English of K. J.
Dover's milieu in the 1970s; I am not sure whether his remark still holds true, but
in any case ancient Greeks used words implying madness rather freely. However,
this lack of clarity – which modern Westerners share with the Greeks – discloses
perhaps the socially convenient attitude to dissident behaviour as a pathology to
be treated and eradicated, rather than just loose terminology characteristic of
non-professional parlance. Definition of 'real madness' remains extremely controversial even today, and it is conditioned by social and political ideas current in
the society.[60] Categorising various kinds of marginal behaviour as mad,

inacceptable, dangerous, and punishable all at once reflects the conformist stance of the majority.

In Greece, psychotic behaviour was usually envisaged as an illness, resulting from either a divine or organic cause. Almost a hundred years ago A. O'Brien-Moore argued that 'there is a medical, a popular, and a poetic conception of madness' and that, accordingly, the medical notion connected madness with a superfluity of black bile, the common people with possession by daemons and tragedy with the divine world.[61] Nowadays, many are still convinced that

> the most prominent difference [between literary and philosophic texts and medical writings] was that from the 5th century BC physicians ascribed illness almost exclusively to biological-organic causes, while literature consistently held it to be of supernatural origin and in particular a result of divine intervention.[62]

This idea oversimplifies the reality which was more complex: in literature, history, and philosophy, indications of psychological and organic reasons of mental disorders were quite common. Referring to the real world, Herodotus declined to decide on the aetiology of Cambyses' mental disorder, ready to accept that it was caused either by an inborn illness or by the anger of the gods.[63] Referring to a myth, Euripides has the chorus ask love-sick Phaedra whether some god possessed her; as an alternative, the chorus supposes two natural causes, Phaedra's distress or the weak constitution of women.[64] Ultimately, the cause of Phaedra's ailment was Aphrodite's wrath. Similarly, in the *Bacchae* Tiresias guesses that Pentheus could have been maddened by a drug (*pharmakon*).[65] Any *mania* could be attributed to a god's intervention and consequently regarded as divine: in Sophocles' *Ajax* the chorus declares that he is 'dwelling with divine madness,' which is 'hard to cure.'[66] The gods were certainly prominent in tragedy and punished heroes and heroines with madness, but dramatists and their audience realised that other factors could also cause mental disorders.

Madness could of course be believed to follow possession by malicious daemons, even if sometimes possession was only alluded to metaphorically. The verb *kakodaimonan*, 'to be possessed by an evil spirit,' may simply mean 'be mad, out of one's wits.'[67] People who were infatuated with political or sexual desire, which drove them absolutely out of their mind, could be described as 'possessed by evil spirit' (*kakodaimonôsi*).[68]

Divine vengeance could strike every transgressor. In Greek mythology, florid madness was a common expression of the gods' wrath, which might manifest as a justified penalty for a transgression, but quite often fell on innocent victims. The Greeks were not very resourceful in imagining methods that their gods could use to punish mortals while they were still alive – the realm of the dead had customs of its own. In addition to death and various forms of disgrace, the gods were limited to choosing a disease from a rather short list: they could inflict blindness, or make happen one of the misfortunes awaiting transgressors that are listed by Aeschylus in Apollo's oracle to Orestes: ulcers, sores, and madness.[69] These plagues were certainly visible and fatal enough to serve as a proper punishment, but most significantly, they seem to have been associated with the sphere of the sacred. Ulcers and sores symbolised pollution, whereas blindness and madness were almost equivalent, meaning blocked perception of reality and often inflicted by gods as punishment for the gravest infringements.[70] If madness was by far more popular than ulcers as a divine penalty in mythology and on the scene, the reason was much deeper than mere appropriateness: damage to one's mind seems to have been feared more than damage to one's body.

The focus of Greek mythology on madness reflects a deep apprehension for one's sanity felt by many. This anxiety seems to correspond to the fear of oblivion: throughout the *Odyssey* the danger of forgetting one's origins amounts to loss of identity; the most horrible characteristic of the souls in Hades in *Song Eleven* is their loss of memory – and the resulting vanishing of self. Absence of mind, *nous*, was insanity, *anoia*, or *paranoia*. It equalled physical death, because it was the possession of *nous* that defined human beings and distinguished them from animals. In Homer, animals may have other mental organs, such as *psuchê* or *phrenes*, but they never possess *nous*.[71] When Odysseus' companions are turned into pigs by Circe, their appearance is changed, but their human essence remains unaffected: Homer makes that clear by saying that they retain their *nous*.[72] Most Greeks feared losing their mind more than losing their life. The chorus in Sophocles' *Ajax* bitterly states that 'for a sufferer of a useless illness (i.e. madness), it is better to lie in.'[73]

Ostensibly, there are two sorts of divine punishment with madness: madness that is the punishment by itself (e.g. of Io and Orestes) and madness that is instrumental in causing other disasters (e.g. of Ajax and Heracles).[74] In fact, in the world of myth and its representations in tragedy, these varieties of madness frequently intermingle. In addition, sometimes the mad personage is an instrument bringing destruction on a third party: as we will see in Chapter 3, Dionysus maddens guilty Pentheus in order destroy him, while the almost innocent Agave is destined to be an instrument of destruction. Even more significant is the fact of choice of madness as the method of punishment. Choosing derangement as an instrument leading to ultimate devastation means more than an aggravation of the final ruin, because together with the self-awareness it wipes away the dignity and the personality of the victim. Only a few mythological figures, such as Heracles, were believed to have survived the humiliation and retain the forces needed to return to a respectable life.

There was no sharp contrast between the condition of madmen in ordinary life and in tragedy. The core of the madmen's situation was their inner alienation and isolation from the society of the sane, in both their own corrupted perception of the real world and the attitude of the world to them.[75] The estrangement of madmen was voiced in the myths associating madness with wandering. In the myth, the Proetids, Io, Bellerophon, and Orestes are physically distanced from their home; in polis communities, as we will see shortly, mentally deranged were to be physically isolated from the sane, and alienated from some of their rights. In many respects, madness approached or was associated with pollution.[76] Tragic madmen were separated from their self, they were 'out of [their] mind,'[77] or their minds (*phrenes*) were 'ungovernable';[78] insane women were frequently compared to maenads or *thuiades*,[79] who were both mad and roaming in the wild.[80] Dread, disgust, and anxiety caused by insanity were projected upon the attitude to people pronounced divinely possessed, such as the maenads, literally 'mad women': they also aroused fear. In addition, distinguishing between the two was not always easy.

Physicians belonging to various schools considered insanity as a disease or a symptom of a disease, produced by physiological disturbances.[81] Aristotle associated anger with boiling of the blood around the heart.[82] The Hippocratic school assumed that mental diseases were no different from other afflictions and resulted from the misbalance of humours.[83] The health of the entire body was important for mental health,[84] but according to the Hippocratic physicians, the brain was held primarily responsible for perception and thought, its normal state meant health, and thus the disruption of its activities was the cause of insanity. For instance, epilepsy was associated with superfluity of phlegmatic humours in the brain: the phlegm obstructs the passage of the air (*pneuma*) in the blood vessels, and causes attacks of the disease.[85] Excess of fluids in the brain could bring about other afflictions, such as derangement and *mania*.[86] The nature of the excessive humour, phlegm considered cold and bile hot, defined the nature of *mania*.[87] In addition, brain injuries were known to affect mental function.[88]

Natural causes of mental diseases are asserted quite frequently in historical texts and in comedy, and in the fifth and the fourth centuries, medical ideas gained wide currency among the general public.[89] Xenophon attributes to Socrates an opinion that 'forgetfulness, depression, discontent and madness' ensue from bad health, and Aristophanes uses the phrase 'to be in good health' as synonymous with sanity.[90] In his narrative of Cambyses' frenzy, Herodotus observes that the mind (*nous*) cannot be healthy when the body is seriously afflicted.[91] Psychological reasons of mental afflictions were considered quite common. Pindar already knew that 'unattainable desires cause acute (or sharp) madnesses.'[92] Herodotus had Amasis, the wise king of Egypt, remark when reproached for his frequent revels, that a man, like a bow, cannot be constantly strung up, but needs relaxation; otherwise 'before he knew that, he would be mad or get a stroke.'[93]

Madmen were stereotyped as extremely aggressive. The Hellenistic author of the *Second Alcibiades* mentions as a matter of fact that those consorting with madmen normally 'get knocks and blows,' and Plutarch makes a man 'mad with happiness' remark that one should wonder why he did not throw stones at people.[94] It is not surprising that comedy made the most of the image of the violent madman.[95] People who have lost their minds were not regarded as entirely human. Even in medical writings madness was sometimes be associated with bestiality. The Hippocratic author of *Prorrhetic 1* stated that 'of madness, characterised by boldness, are bestial.'[96] Euripides' mad Heracles is compared to 'a bull ready to charge'[97] and loses his human characteristics.[98] However, the same playwright compares maenads possessed by Dionysus to hounds and birds, while Homer likens Achilles' fearless soldiers to wolves:[99] even bestiality could be ambivalent.

The insane were ridiculed and despised. During Socrates' lifetime, laughing at madmen was so common that an eccentric person feared being insulted by public laughter, as if he were mad.[100] Mentally deranged people were feared so much that every means of driving them away was deemed acceptable, including stoning.[101] These casual references to violence towards the mentally ill and their relations demonstrate that their mistreatment was quite common in Greece.[102] Stoning, a rare method of execution employed in scapegoat rituals and against particularly impure or hated individuals, hints at the connection of madness with pollution.[103]

Given the stigmas associated with madness, it is only natural that the mentally ill were considered a disgrace to their families and communities. In Plato's imaginary well-governed city, madmen were not seen in the streets and fines were to be imposed on their relatives if they failed to keep them away from the public.[104] People who were violently mad had to be placed under the constant watch of an attendant or a family member, and in most acute cases, like that of the mad Spartan king Cleomenes, even be kept in the stocks.[105] The madman's physical freedom was limited not only in Sparta: it was considered the obvious practice in the fifth-century Athens.[106] Having a mad relative was a shame, preferably to be hidden.

The alienation felt by many towards the insane was, to a large degree, rooted in ignorance in matters of mental disorders. Some even considered madness a contagious evil: Theophrastus' superstitious man shudders or spits in his own bosom when he sees a madman or an epileptic, believing in the prohibitive qualities of human spittle, which was deemed to keep away the gods and daemons inflicting the dreaded diseases.[107] Mentally deranged people were feared, and even their relatives might avoid them, especially if they were abusive or violent.[108] This dread did not entirely disappear even when a person was convinced that the derangement he or she witnessed was of divine origin.[109]

Tragic *topoi* reflected the stereotype image of madman's behaviour. Throughout the fifth century, the same symptoms appear time and again in tragedies by different dramatists: a shaking head,[110] fiercely rolling and bloodshot eyes,[111] a foaming mouth,[112] mad laughter,[113] and silence or inarticulate speech.[114] Raging lunacy, self-damnation, as well as bloodshot and overwrought eyes, are the signs of madness diagnosed as *melancholia* in Menander's *Arbitration*.[115] All these symptoms fit also the Hippocratic descriptions of hysteria and *mania*.[116] According to Xenophon, symptoms of possession included excessive movement, the possessed becoming a frightening sight, resembling the Gorgons.[117] The standard set of symptoms remained the same for both mentally deranged and divinely inspired.[118]

This congruity seems to indicate that the most dreadful characteristics of the appearance of real-life insane were singled out and combined to create a cumulative image of the frightening madman, and the image of the madman presented at the theatre was what the audience expected to see. Furthermore, as some modern psychiatrists argue, once a stereotype of insanity has developed, it structures the attitude of the society toward deviation and even shapes the behaviour of individuals labelled as deviant, who tend to conform to the pattern of expectations.[119] Returning to Greece, it is plausible that the socially shared image represented on the stage could become a self-fulfilling prophecy and mould the behaviour of real-life madmen – insane and divinely inspired alike.

While stereotypes of madman's behaviour were quite common, and included loss of spatial orientation and other aberrations of perception, bizarre appearance, and proclivity to violence, it is noteworthy that 'hearing voices,' one of the common symptoms listed today in Western psychiatry,[120] is almost absent in Greek evidence. Moreover, individuals who claimed to have experienced such sensations were often regarded as receiving messages from gods and *daimonia*, as seers, nympholepts, or 'divine men.'[121] This acceptance of deviance as divine seems to ensue from the respect for god-sent messages: veneration of prophetic *mania* prevented the Greeks from including 'hearing voices' in the pattern of typical madman's behaviour. Thus, not only the opinions on insanity were projected on divine possession: the connection worked both ways.

In exceptional cases, fear of a madman could transform into awe and even lead to heroisation and develop into a cult. A fascinating example of the ambivalent attitude towards a dreaded madman is provided by Pausanias. At the seventy-first Olympiad, at 495 BC, Cleomedes of Astypalea killed his opponent at a boxing competition, was accused of unfair play and deprived of his prize. Driven mad (*ekphrôn*) by this misfortune, Cleomedes returned home, entered a school where sixty children were studying, and pulled down the pillar that supported the roof, causing a disaster. Pelted with stones by the citizens, he found refuge at the sanctuary of Athena and disappeared miraculously. When asked for advice, the Pythia commanded the people of Astypalea to 'honour him with sacrifices, as no more mortal.'[122] Even until Pausanias' time, the murderous boxer enjoyed a hero cult on the island. A cult of a mad murderer might seem strange, but Heracles himself in a fit of insanity committed horrible deeds, slaying his own children.[123] Thus, Cleomedes' cult was not unique and did not lack impressive precedents, like the one provided by Heracles. However, Cleomedes' success did not even approach the extraordinary achievements of far more accomplished athletes, such as Theagenes of Thasos, who had also been heroised,[124] and Cleomedes' fame was mostly due to mad violence and an inexplicable disappearance. A pelted mad outcast turned into an honoured hero: fear and despise were distilled into awe. Here, we are touching upon a very important point regarding the attitude to madmen and madness: the ambiguity of the condition, the anxiety it caused, and the ensuing easy oscillation between loathing fear and pious trepidation. The supposition that apparently insane behaviour was, in fact, divinely inspired, influenced the popular attitude to abnormal conduct: the case of Cleomedes demonstrates that *mania* could easily provoke apprehension of a deity's intervention.

Thus, regular human insanity was not only described by basically the same set of words as divine possession: it involved similar behaviour which unsuspecting people could easily confuse with divine madness, with the ensuing danger of gods' punishment for them and their community. Divine presence and divine vengeance were manifested in similar signs, and when a visitation of one of these was believed to have occurred, the other one most probably lurked in the background.

Madness in context: the importance of historicism

A historian of the ancient mind has to define his or her own path between Scylla of ascribing absolute cultural specificity to states of mind and Charybdis of seeing the ancients and us as sharing basically the same emotions, states of mind, and attitudes towards mental activity. This controversy is ongoing. For instance, D. Konstan contends that 'there is reason to think that the ancient Greek concept [of anger] is in fact significantly different from the modern.'[125] In contrast, K. Kalimitzis regards anger among the Greeks as characteristic 'not of the Athenians of Spartans, but anger *qua human.*'[126] Assuming a balanced position in his studies of shame and other emotions in Greece, D. Cairns argues that 'we must dispense with simplistic polarities of "biology" *versus* "culture,"'[127] and that a 'possibility for dialogue between ancient cultures and our own exists; we must attempt it in a way which avoids both the naïve assumption of shared humanity and unsuccessful strategies of alienation.'[128]

A dominant ideology of a society shapes the attitude towards social, political, and cultural issues prevalent at a certain moment.[129] Such ideology determines the behaviour expected or accepted from an individual belonging to a certain group. These norms, in their turn, guide the ideas about deviance: in each culture, people think about, experience, and treat their own and other people's nonconformity in different ways.[130] The historically conditioned environment is perhaps the most significant factor determining the society's attitude to voluntary and involuntary alterations of consciousness and their categorisation as illness, depravity, or privilege.

This awareness has been sharpened by modern research, but it is not a modern construct. Dionysius of Halicarnassus discerned the chasm between Greek and Roman attitude to ecstatic practices:

> And no festival is observed among them [the Romans] as a day of mourning or by the wearing of black garments and the beating of breasts and the lamentations of women because of the disappearance of deities, such as the Greeks perform in commemorating the rape of Persephone and the misfortunes of Dionysus and all the other things of like nature. And one will see among them, even though their manners are now corrupted, no ecstatic transports, no Corybantic frenzies, cultic gatherings, no Bacchic rites or secret mysteries, no all-night vigils of men and women together in the temples, nor any other mummery of this kind; but alike in all their words and actions with respect to the gods a reverence is shown such as is seen among neither Greeks nor barbarians. And . . . notwithstanding the influx into Rome of innumerable nations . . . the city has never officially adopted any of those foreign practices. . . . But, even though it has, in pursuance of oracles, introduced certain rites from abroad, she celebrates them in accordance with her own traditions, after banishing all fabulous clap-trap.[131]

Clearly, in Dionysius' eyes, ecstatic behaviour was considered normal in Greece and repulsive in Rome. There is no reason to suppose that it was only his personal opinion.[132] In 213 BC, after the battle of Cannae, Roman citizens demanded that the Senate intervene and put an end to boisterous rites which appeared as incompatible with the ancestral piety.[133] When Bacchic celebrations reached Rome and an audacious minority dared to try the taste of the liberating foreign rites, the Senate showed zero tolerance towards the practice that undermined patriarchal values and authority, and in 186 prohibited it throughout Italy.[134] In particular, the Romans were anxious about the dignity of their women. In his discussion of good order during mystery rites, Cicero is ready to admit that the Eleusinian nocturnal ceremonies were beneficent for the civilisation, but in his opinion, the modesty of the female participants was even more important:

> Assuredly we must make most careful provision that the reputation of our women be guarded by the clear light of day, when they are observed by many eyes, and that initiations into the mysteries of Ceres be performed only with those rites which are in use in Rome (*quo Romae initiantur*). The strictness of our ancestors in matters of this character is shown by the ancient decree of the Senate with respect to the Bacchanalia, and the investigation and punishment conducted by the consuls with the assistance of specially-enrolled military force.[135]

Cicero admittedly presented an idealised picture of the Roman life, but his main message is clear: whatever the advantages of nocturnal mystery rites, for the Greeks and for humanity, they do not belong with traditional Roman religion and should be prohibited at any cost. The Greeks were no less protective towards their womenfolk, but preventing a woman from participating in nocturnal mystery initiations or Bacchic roaming in the wild would be considered sacrilegious and thus unthinkable: ecstatic celebrations belonged to the venerated tradition, sanctified by its age.[136]

Here lies the chasm between the Greek and the Roman attitudes to ecstatic cults: in Rome, they were suppressed, and at least the upper classes avoided them until the Imperial age, whereas in Greece numerous rites involving frenzy – Dionysius listed a few examples only – flourished throughout its history. Since the Romans were not biologically different from the Greeks, and when under the Empire were given an opportunity to abandon themselves to emotionally charged cults, happily did so, it is clear that the reasons for the divergence between the two cultures are of historical nature.

In modern research, the predominant opinion is that human societies are divided into two groups regarding their attitude towards manipulation of consciousness. 'Polyphasic' cultures value altered states of consciousness experienced principally in ritual contexts; they are for the most part pre-industrial. 'Monophasic,' mainly post-industrial, cultures marginalise these experiences as unorthodox or even criminalise them, and alteration of consciousness in such societies is limited to the secular sphere.[137] It is also argued that with increasing inequality, altered states become a domain of particular practitioners, gender- or otherwise specialised; in highly stratified societies cults focused on such states are expected to play a peripheral role.[138] Furthermore, social complexity is expected to bring about an emphasis on mediumistic activities, at the expense of other types of alteration of consciousness.[139] The contrast between Greece and Rome demonstrates that the divergence does not follow the division between pre- and post-industrial societies; we will also see that Greece differed from other Mediterranean societies in its attitude towards cults involving alteration of consciousness. The aim of this book is to explore how these phenomena corresponded with other aspects of Greek civilisation.

The dissimilarity between Greece and Rome, as well as between Archaic and Classical Greece and the Hellenistic world, is seldom reflected in modern writing on alterations of consciousness and mental disorders: many authors treat the Graeco-Roman world as a cultural entity and downplay the changes in attitudes towards these phenomena. This approach is misleading. The developing discipline of medical anthropology insists that medicine as a field of knowledge is shaped historically and socially: 'medicine formulates the human body and disease in a culturally distinctive fashion.'[140] Turning to ethno-psychiatry, it is clear that while every disease has multiple social aspects, in mental disorders these aspects acquire paramount significance.[141] Behavioural norms are defined by the society, or even by social strata or groups within larger communities, and as a result, the notion of deviant behaviour is a social convention. Contemporary psychiatry regards both organic and social factors as crucial for understanding and treating mental illness.[142] Non-pathological alterations of consciousness, that are very often associated with religious beliefs and practices, are even more emphatically culture-dependent. Since the attitude towards behavioural areas changed together with the socio-cultural environment, sweeping generalisations about mental disorders and alteration of consciousness in the Greco-Roman world are anachronistic and therefore distorted. Even the meaning of the words has evolved,[143] hence close attention to the cultural background is essential at all the stages of the research, beginning from the reading of primary sources. This is not to say that sources on Hellenistic phenomena cannot be applied in a study of the Classical world, but each time evidence from a different period is used, we have to examine its applicability.

The perspective of our own culture is not easy to define. Obviously, nowadays no less than in antiquity, individuals and groups of people differ in their views on such issues as behavioural norm and abnormality, as well as manipulation and alteration of consciousness. Furthermore, these views evolve. During the last fifty years, more and more people, members of the general public as well as the academic and medical establishment, have ceased to regard alteration of consciousness exclusively as either a pathology or part of primitive rites, engage with them personally (by means of meditation, psychedelic drugs, or hypnosis), and learn about them.[144] Homosexuality is another example. In the 1970s and '80s, research on mental disorders in Greece still referred to homosexuality as a malady: the psychoanalyst and ethnologist G. Devereux labelled Sappho's feelings as 'inversion' in his otherwise brilliant analysis of her 'seizure.' In his book on mental disorders in antiquity, J. Pigeaud included a sub-chapter on homosexuality in a chapter entitled 'Maladies.'[145] The nature of mental disorders is constantly contested: for instance, a few years ago, the journal *Culture, Medicine, Psychiatry* devoted an issue to a debate on the question of whether post-traumatic stress disorder was a cultural construction or a naturally occurring mental disorder.[146] The *Diagnostic and Statistical Manual of Mental Disorders* (*DSM*), published by the American Psychiatric Association, was first compiled in 1952.[147] Now in its fifth edition (*DSM-5*, 2013), it has changed most substantially, but the disagreements between clinicians on many issues, especially on the diagnostic criteria, demonstrate that even among Western medical professionals, there is no consensus on the crucial question of the definition of mental health and disorder.[148]

As D. Hershkowitz observes, 'historicism runs the risk of not taking into account its own historical situatedness and implications this has on its readings of the past, and so of being subject . . . to positivistic fallacy.'[149] The examples just cited demonstrate how fluid modern views are, which implies that our perspective on past cultures is bound to evolve constantly. Since this cannot be changed, at least we should be aware of the historical embeddedness of our own perspective. Furthermore, we can only talk about the majority opinion, legal situation, and idiosyncrasies at a given moment in a certain community. With all good intentions to discern between historical periods, social environments, and even individual mind frames in antiquity, historians of the ancient mind must be aware of their limitations in appreciating the contemporary state of affairs, and appropriately modest in their ambition to arrive at an adequate comprehension of the past.

Throughout the book, I will try to discern, when possible, between the views of different people or usually groups of people, and to be aware of their historical background.[150] Unfortunately, very often this level of resolution is not possible, and we are left with just a few dispersed pieces of evidence. In other cases a certain view is taken for granted by an ancient source, and I assume that it was shared by many contemporaries of the author, but we may never know whether they formed the majority of the community. Even more perilous is drawing conclusions founded upon renderings of myths, such as the epic, drama, or later mythography. Conscious of all these obstacles, I believe that a careful analysis of different kinds of sources may lead to some reasonably grounded notions on what many Greek individuals thought about alteration of consciousness, and how some basic ideas shared by most members of the communities evolved during the Archaic and Classical periods. *Mania* as a distinct cultural phenomenon has never been studied as an integral part of its social environment, and it is the interaction of various aspects of *mania* that expounds some unique features of the Greek culture. This book will survey various kinds of culturally approved alterations of consciousness, examine their advantages and dangers for the experiencers and society, and explore multiple manifestations of *mania* in the context of the Greek way of life.

Alterations of consciousness between unity and diversity: aspects of methodology and terminology

The aim of this book is to explore Greek cultural phenomena involving alteration of consciousness, which requires elucidating mechanisms and processes behind individual experiences and behaviours, as well as setting them against their historical background. In practical terms, my approach to the study of Greek *mania* is based on combining the traditional historical methods with the results of neuroscience, cognitive science, and psychology. For decades, these disciplines have worked in conjunction with anthropology.[151] Conceptual integration between the humanities and biology and neuroscience in the study of religion is known as neurotheology or neurophenomenology.[152] The pioneer in the field of Classical studies is W. Burkert, whose book *Creation of the Sacred: Tracks of Biology in Early Religions* not only deals with the psychology of religious phenomena, but rather endeavours 'to tie historical and philological research to biological anthropology.'[153] Theoretical foundations of the cognitive approach to the study of religion began to be formulated during the recent decades,[154] and the interaction between cognition and cultural phenomena is explored by experts on cognition, as well as philosophers, historians, and linguists.[155] This approach to the study of ancient religion has already been endorsed by several Classical scholars.[156] Tremendous opportunities presented by such integrated inquiry are forcefully put forward by E. Slingerland who demonstrates how general models based on the theory of evolution and embodied cognition, alongside domain-specific methodologies and approaches, allow the humanities a breakthrough into the modern intellectual community.[157] The study of the alteration of consciousness is still an emerging area of research, and many issues are far from being resolved by the experts. Some of these will be mentioned shortly.

My approach is largely phenomenological: I try to understand how multifarious phenomena stemming from alteration of consciousness were felt and perceived by the people who experienced them and their communities and in what way they interacted with the Greek culture. M. Bitbol has recently aptly defined this manner of tackling the phenomena of consciousness: 'Disclosing how objectivity is elaborated out of finite and transient episodes of phenomenal consciousness is considered by phenomenology as more relevant than asking, reciprocally, how phenomenal consciousness arises from certain objective processes.'[158] I have allowed myself to skip past the neurocognitive mechanisms directly to cultural experiences, since my task as a historian is to situate phenomena of consciousness in their temporal and cultural framework.

Methodologically, it is imperative to separate different classes of evidence at the initial stages: for each Greek cultural phenomenon, I will first examine the historical evidence (literary, epigraphical, and archaeological), offer its interpretation, and only at a later stage juxtapose my historical analysis with other classes of evidence, such as the results of neurocognitive and anthropological research. When discussing subjects beyond my expertise, I made every effort to follow mainstream opinions. I often use cable-like methods of argumentation, which intertwine several stands of reasoning, as opposed to chain-like arguments that progress link-by-link. The methodological foundation of this approach is expounded by D. Lewis-Williams.[159] Whereas in the 'chain method,' one absent or faulty link can invalidate the entire chain, the 'cabling' method permits compensation for gaps in extant records, by enabling the researcher to seek an explanation of a certain phenomenon in a different field and employ congruous data in an explanatory model. An example of the successful use of the 'cabling' method is the widespread acceptance of the anthropological perspective in the study of the Greek society.[160] In a study of ancient Greek cultural phenomena, first the links firmly based on Greek evidence are to be established, and then they may be connected by additional links, created from materials supplied by other disciplines. My emphasis will always remain on Greek culture. However, I do make use of insights from other disciplines for the initial definition of questions to be asked when exploring ancient evidence, subsequently bringing together distinct manifestations of *mania*, and finally attempting the comprehension of its role in Greece.

Writing on alteration of consciousness, it is paramount that the author first define what, in their opinion, the term 'consciousness' denotes. The question is one of the most contended in contemporary philosophy, psychology, and neuroscience.[161] I adopt the most basic definition based on the intuitive understanding of the phenomenon and offered by the *Blackwell Companion to Consciousness*: 'Anything that we are aware of at a given moment forms part of our consciousness';[162] this awareness includes our surroundings, ourselves, and the recognition that we are aware of the awareness.[163] Using the terms 'mind' and 'cognition,' I include emotions as well, following neuropsychologists who maintain that reasoning and emotions are not antithetical, but interact in numerous intricate ways.[164] In recent years the term 'neuropsychology' has gradually been replaced by 'cognitive neuroscience,' with an extra emphasis on the biological aspect in this vast field of knowledge;[165] I will use the two terms interchangeably.

People are biological and cultural creatures at the same time.[166] The categories of 'biological' and 'cultural' were, and still are, often regarded as equal to the dichotomy of phenomena determined by nature, inborn, and as such, common to all humans *versus* those conditioned by historical situation, fluid and therefore culturally specific. It becomes increasingly clear that although this dichotomy is valid in most cases and useful epistemologically, it is far from being absolute. The brain is not exactly 'hardware' that is determined and shared by every individual belonging to the species of *Homo sapiens*: the anatomy of the brain can be modified during an individual lifetime, and affected by social components, which means that neuroplasticity is a factor of major importance for every student of past human societies.[167] On the other hand, culture is not entirely 'software': gender is cultural, but it is ultimately a reaction to the principle of sexual reproduction; feasting customs are cultural, but the need for nutrition is biologically determined, etc. The psychologist E. Cardeña defines the relations between biological and cultural factors: 'A substrate of human potentials and limitations informs the selection of cultural choices, and cultural processes, in turn, reinforce particular manifestations and provide them with specific interpretations.'[168] In this perspective, voluntary and involuntary alterations of consciousness and attitudes to these phenomena feature sets of characteristics of divergent nature that are constantly interrelating, and it is the interface between them that the cognitive approach to the study of religious phenomena seeks to explore.[169] Neurological and culturally specific manifestations are disentangled for the purposes of discussion, and in this section I'll review some basic evidence on alteration of consciousness that is relevant to the study of this phenomenon in Greece.

Every historian will readily agree that our mind is 'embedded,' meaning that cognition, that is, the way the mind represents and processes information and defines accordingly thoughts and actions, is dependent on historical context.[170] Many scholars tend to disregard the fact that our mind is also moulded by its being embodied, i.e. shaped by bodily experiences, limitations of the body, and physical factors of the surrounding world influencing various physiological processes.[171] However, it has been compellingly demonstrated that cognition is 'embodied and embedded'[172] or even 'embrained, embodied, encultured, extended and distributed.'[173] The debate between the embodied cognitive science and the conservative view of mind and cognition is beyond the scope of my study. Remaining in the boundaries of mainstream cognitive psychology, I adopt the most basic assumption that various factors acting on the human body influence the person's mind and may alter his or her consciousness.[174] The practical corollary is that a student of any culture, ancient Greek culture included, cannot regard human agents as solely cultural entities.[175] Our cognitive functions, through the brain and the nervous system, are affected by a plethora of bodily processes: manipulation of the body influences our mental states.[176] We have to be aware of the factors affecting human cognition, and be particularly attentive to the mental states of people engaged in potentially mind-altering practices. Only seldom have we found accounts of such practices, but even allusions to their elements (sometimes by mere choice of words and metaphors) may be indicative.

The normal spectrum of consciousness is subdivided into stages.[177] As we pass from stage to stage, we disengage from environmental stimuli and move on to imagery, visual and auditory, gradually disconnecting from the external reality. Even in the waking state, our consciousness is 'fragmented': we oscillate between outwardly directed to inwardly directed states, completing about a hundred such cycles every day.[178]

Waking consciousness, considered the only one normal by most modern Westerners, is merely one state of consciousness inside a much broader range, a 'continuum of consciousness.'[179] Characteristically, states other than the waking consciousness are dubbed 'altered states of consciousness.'[180] Their systematic study was launched by W. James;[181] the classical definition of these forms of consciousness was given by A. M. Ludwig:

> any mental state(s), induced by various physiological, psychological, or pharmacological maneuvers or agents, which can be recognised subjectively by the individual himself (or by objective observer of the individual) as representing a sufficient deviation in subjective experience or psychological

functioning from certain general norms for that individual during alert, waking consciousness.[182]

Altered states of consciousness can be attained by different methods, and involve different experiences, but they share a most important common characteristic: temporary and reversible changes in perception and cognition, which can range from minor to deep. When sufficiently profound, these changes silence the waking consciousness and free the mind from the limitations of the alert ego, allowing self-transcendence and an awareness undisturbed by the external world.[183] For an observer, the behaviour of a person in an altered state of consciousness looks very much like dissociation, including such characteristics as depersonalisation, derealisation, identity alteration, and amnesia.[184] Pathological and non-pathological conditions involving alteration of consciousness also share another important common characteristic, namely disruption in the relationship between the individual's consciousness and the world, which results in an altered representation of the surrounding context.[185]

According to the psychologist J. F. Kihlstrom, altered states of consciousness can be regarded in four perspectives:

> An altered state of consciousness can be defined by four features: (1) operationally, as the product of a particular induction technique; (2) phenomenologically, as an individual's subjective report of altered awareness or voluntary control; (3) observationally, as changes in overt behavior corresponding to a person's self-report; and (4) physiologically, as a particular pattern of changes in somatic functioning.[186]

As to the term, D. Lewis-Williams observes:

> The states towards the end of the intensified trajectory – visions, and hallucinations that may occur in any of the five senses – are generally called 'altered states of consciousness.' The phrase can apply equally to dreaming and 'inward' states on the normal trajectory, though some people prefer to restrict its use to hallucinations and trance states. By now it will be obvious that this commonly encountered phrase is posited on the essentially Western concept of the 'consciousness of rationality.' It implies that there is 'ordinary consciousness' that is considered genuine and good, and then perverted, or 'altered,' states. But, as we have seen, all parts of the spectrum are equally 'genuine.' The phrase 'altered states of consciousness' is useful enough, but we need to remember that it carries a lot of cultural luggage.[187]

Phenomena involving alteration of consciousness are often overlapping, and various terms connected to them are often employed interchangeably. Altered states of consciousness are sometimes called mystical phenomena; however, it is useful to classify mystical experiences as a sub-category inside the broader category of altered states of consciousness: every mystical experience involves altered states of consciousness, but not every hallucination, which is an altered state of consciousness, is necessarily a mystical experience.[188] As to the notions of ecstasy and trance, also often used synonymously with mystical states, they are only partially intersecting: ecstatic experiences of euphoria are not always mystical or trance-like.[189] Some researchers insist on a clear distinction between trance and ecstasy. In the opinion of G. Rouget, ecstasy is characterised by silence, solitude, sensory deprivation, and vivid imagery, whereas a trance is defined by energetic movement, group practices, sensory overstimulation, and lack of vivid imagery.[190] The difference is hardly universal, and shamans may be engaged both in soul flight (associated by G. Rouget with ecstasy) and mediumistic activities (which he associates with trance and possession).[191] For practical purposes, it may be useful to distinguish between modalities in alteration of consciousness,[192] one based on quiescence and another on excitement – although these modalities can be interconnected even in the experiences of one person.[193]

In this book, the term 'possession' will be applied to a range of phenomena involving dissociation and similar symptoms.[194] In contrast to mental disorders, possession is abnormal behaviour that is enacted in conformity with social norms.[195] Recently, it has been suggested that the term 'patterned dissociative identity' be used, as it designates culturally patterned manifestations of temporary identity change. Patterned dissociative identity differs from dissociative identity disorder (formerly called multiple personality disorder) in three respects: it is not considered an illness, is induced by wish of the individual or community, and the *alters* are entities belonging to one's cultural system, such as gods, spirits, etc.[196] These differences cannot be absolute, and leave an ambiguous area between desirable or socially acceptable cases of patterned dissociative identity and dissociation *par excellence*, which is considered a mental disorder. The mutual penetrability of the characteristics of mental disorders and alterations of consciousness illuminates the flexibility of their definition and assessment inside different cultures, and underscores the wide range of meanings covered by the Greek terms designating possession by a god.

Perplexed by the lack of uniformity in defining alterations of consciousness, some researchers prefer to call these states peak, acute, or intense experiences.[197] It has recently been contended that since it is not the consciousness itself, i.e. awareness, but rather its content that is altered, the correct term should be 'altering phenomenology' rather than 'altering consciousness.'[198] In order to avoid misunderstanding I prefer to employ the traditional terms, even if inexact.

Altered states of consciousness are cross-cultural. About one-third of randomly sampled Americans and Europeans report having experienced psychic and faith phenomena that can be identified as mystical;[199] and 2–3% of the polled population claim to have had an intensely emotional mystical experience, such as the feeling of oneness with the world.[200] In other polls, 10% of the general population report having deep mystical experience and 30% a superficial one – though the term 'mystical experience' is not uniformly defined.[201] Between 10% and 25% of the non-clinical population in the West report having had at least one hallucinatory experience.[202] No less impressive than these statistics is the account of a class studying a university course on mysticism by W. Harmless, in which several participants recognised their own experiences in the biographies of the mystics: 'These mystics were talking about things that they [the students] themselves had tasted, that they too had felt.'[203] A survey of approximately five hundred traditional societies around the globe, conducted by E. Bourguignon, demonstrates the presence of culturally patterned institutionalised forms of altered states of consciousness in 90% of sampled societies.[204] This is 'a striking finding and suggests that we are dealing with a matter of major importance, . . . a psychobiological capacity available to all societies.'[205] The ability to experience alterations of consciousness is, so it seems, a part of human biological potential.[206]

The use of concepts like 'human biological potential' requires caution and must be based on sound empirical evidence. I adopt the 'pragmatic stance' put forward by E. Slingerland:

> Against post-modern relativism, we can maintain that there *are* structures of cognition common to all human beings regardless of their culture, language, or particular history. Against objectivism, we can argue that these commonalities are not reflections of some a priori order existing independently of humans, . . . but rather out of interactions of biological systems with a fairly stable physical world over the course of both evolutionary and personal time, which makes the presence of certain cognitive structures inevitable for creatures like ourselves.[207]

The cross-cultural nature of alteration of consciousness has two corollaries that are important for this study. First, it presents a fascinating challenge to a historian: if experiencing these states is part of being human, the variety of cultural phenomena involving these states ensues from culture-specific conditions, exactly like gender norms *versus* sex and feasting arrangements *versus* nutrition. The function and status of alteration of consciousness in a given society are indicative of its important characteristics.[208] My intention is to examine the role of alteration of consciousness in ancient Greece.

Second, the ubiquity of this phenomenon allows a cautious application of evidence on the manipulation of consciousness in other cultures, ancient and modern, to the research of Greek civilisation. The potential of using the results of cognitive studies and neuroscience cannot be overestimated: existing testimonies on Greek religion and culture contain very limited direct evidence on the mental experiences of those involved in various cultic activities. These accounts cannot be explained solely inside their cultural context. What is called for in order to fill in the gaps in the knowledge of humans of the past is the application of facts and explanatory models based on the study of humans of the present, provided by modern science.

This is the moment to summarise some most important characteristics of alteration of consciousness, as assessed by modern anthropology, neuroscience, and psychology, which suggest a fresh look at some well-known aspects of Greek culture. No generally agreed classification of altered states of consciousness has been established, so far.[209] Altered states of consciousness are characterised by several common denominators, present in individual experiencers to a greater or lesser degree, and include alterations in thinking, disturbed time sense, perceptual distortion, changes of body image, as well as changes in the feeling of control and in emotional expression.[210] Some researchers single out alteration 'in the informational or representational relationships between consciousness and the world.'[211] These states often involve hallucinations, which can be visual, auditory, olfactory, tactile, gustatory, or a combination of these.[212] The senses and emotions may be intensified: sounds seem louder, colours are more vivid, and emotions disinhibited, creating the feeling of immense joy – or sometimes distress.[213]

A change in bodily awareness, which is often a component of alteration of consciousness, can lead to a set of paradoxically related phenomena, all of them ensuing from a disruption in the basic definition of the physical self as opposed to the world.[214] One of the hallmarks of alteration of consciousness is the feeling of oneness with the world, known as the oceanic experience. The *unio mystica* of the Christian religion, the Hindu *samadhi*, the Buddhist Nirvana, or the Absolute of some philosophical schools, are but a few examples of this state of mind.[215] In this state, no sense of time and space exist, and absolute reality is attained. It has an extensive spectrum, starting at its lower end with an insight into the world of the mysterious and reaching at its extreme end the supreme mystical feat of union with the God or the Absolute.[216]

Common and culturally almost invariant phenomenon is the out-of-body experience, sometimes called an ecsomatic state, transport, soul flight, soul journey, or astral projection.[217] An out-of-body experience is 'a waking experience combining disembodiment, elevated perspective, and autopsy.'[218] These experiences are reported by 5 to 10% of the general population, and range from brief, 'everyday' sensations of watching oneself from a distance, which can be felt while quite awake, to a deep mystical state involving a sensation of separation of the consciousness (or soul) from the body and its independent movement and perception.[219] Another variety of alteration of consciousness is the near-death experience, 'the psychological experience of alternative reality actually reported by . . . a minority of people who survive' 'physical circumstances of being near death,'[220] which often comprise sensations of separation from the body, travelling through darkness to light, meeting a kindly presence, and other features.[221]

All these states share a common characteristic: when in an altered state of consciousness, the individual perceives his or her inside and outside world in a manner different from the usual, and consciousness produces misrepresentations, such as hallucinations, delusions, and memory, body image, and time distortions.[222] Until half a century ago, the age-old question had been 'Why do people hallucinate?' This question implies that the normal state is the baseline waking state, and it has to be manipulated in some way in order to be modified and allow hallucinations to occur. In the 1960s, the Polish neuropsychologist J. Konorski was the first to put forth the opposite question, 'Why do people not hallucinate constantly?' He demonstrated that the connections between our brain and the sense organs work in both directions. Under normal circumstances, 'retro' connections from the brain to the sense organs, which produce hallucinations, are suppressed, but when for whatever reason the sensory input is crucially limited, the backflow from the cortex to the periphery produces hallucinations which are subjectively impossible to differentiate from the perceived world. This insight, revolutionary half a century ago, has been abundantly corroborated by the neurological research and at present is considered fundamental and almost self-evident.[223] It is of critical importance for my study, because it explains, economically and elegantly, several basic characteristics of the altered states of consciousness: the wide range of the experiences ensuing from a wide range of conditions, and the reality of images and sensations from the viewpoint of the experiencing person.

It is fundamental to understand the vast variety of experiences amassed under the label 'alteration of consciousness' in order to properly study Greek *mania*, which encompasses an entire range of phenomena. Furthermore, the word 'state' may produce an erroneous impression that altered consciousness is a distinct stable modality, while it is fluid and changes throughout its duration.[224] In reality, altered states of consciousness are multifarious, can involve various subjective and objective manifestations, and may be induced by many methods. While undiscerning attribution of the same behavioural pattern to various individuals whose mental state is described as abnormal in ancient sources is unwarranted and misleading, we will see that it is still common among the scholars.

Alteration of consciousness is associated with physiological processes in the human brain.[225] During recent years, owing to the progress in research technology, physiological correlations of altered states of consciousness are being intensively explored. For instance, neuroimaging of an LSD-induced alteration of consciousness recorded considerable physiological changes accompanying hallucinations and other experiences.[226] Although the study of physiological responses requires laboratory conditions which are usually unavailable when alteration of consciousness is spontaneous or reached in a particular cultural or cultic context, this restriction is not absolute: experienced Zen monks are able to meditate while various parameters of their brain activities are recorded, and research of the effects of meditation on brain has been taking place for several decades.[227]

Comprehensive approaches are based on theories claiming that phenomenologically different kinds of alteration of consciousness all ensue from deregulation in a certain brain structure.[228] In contrast, other scientists argue that altered states may result from divergent neural mechanisms that produce them.[229] It is noteworthy that similar experiential, cognitive, and phenomenological results can be obtained by means of chemical manipulation of the consciousness, most familiar to modern Westerners and relatively easy to study in the laboratory, and non-chemical techniques, known chiefly from anthropological and historical sources.[230] Whether this happens because different methods tap the same brain circuit[231] is irrelevant for the purposes of my research. It is, however, of great consequence that congruent experiences can arise in different circumstances and be induced in different ways. Furthermore, as no physiological pattern has been established for many alterations of consciousness, the emphasis in the investigation of this field still remains on the individual's subjective experience of a dramatic change in the consciousness state.[232]

Overall, mental states of humans can be manipulated by similar methods cross-culturally, notwithstanding differences between societies. These methods are broadly divided into two groups, those based on excessive stimulation, and those following its opposite, that is sensory deprivation. They include extensive motor behaviour, auditory driving, activation of endogenous euphoriant releases, ingestion of psychotropic substances, meditation, and hypnotic suggestion.[233] Techniques of consciousness alteration can be learnt, and although their effect is greatly enhanced by a belief in the reality of supernatural agents that the experiencer seeks to approach, even total non-believers can have visions of such entities if they follow the traditional procedure.[234] Whatever particular technique is used, the emphasis on absorption training, such as meditation, isolation, visualisation, etc., is common to various traditions of vision quest.[235]

Sensory deprivation is one of the common techniques of inducing altered states of consciousness; elimination of external stimuli forces the human mind to concentrate within itself, and brings about an intensive discharge of inner imagery. Visions appearing in a dreamlike autistic state are often perceived as more real than everyday experience. In contemporary traditional societies and in the past, sensory deprivation was attained in caves and artificial grottos, and prolonged sojourns in monastic cells and other retreats are known to produce the same effect.[236] Even restricted environmental stimulation in controlled experiments results in visual anomalies in many subjects, uncanny emotions, and other altered-state-like experiences.[237] Hallucinations of different sorts occur even in open spaces, when the environment is monotonous and does not supply sufficient stimulation to the perceptual systems of the brain.[238] Sensory stimulation, by means of whirling movement or other intensive physical activities, is no less common; the best-known examples of this technique are Sufi dancing and trance possession. Sensory stimulation can bring about sensations of ecstatic joy, which may develop into a mystical experience, accompanied by an orgasm-like sense of catharsis.[239]

Music, singing, and dancing are time-honoured techniques which serve to manipulate consciousness, used by many cultures around the globe.[240] As R. Jourdain observes, 'Music seems to be the most immediate of all the arts, and so the most ecstatic. . . . It really is as if some "other" has entered not just our bodies, but our intentions, taking us over.'[241] The power of melody, rhythm, and especially their combination creates the sensation of an invasion of one's mind and body from the outside, often defined as possession.[242] Music can induce enormous emotional arousal, and with it a spectrum of feelings from pleasure to anxiety to painful sadness, all of them compelling; this arousal also creates potent memory associations, as well.[243] Sounds bring about physical sensations and create an impetus towards moving, and music is often accompanied by dancing which amplifies its impact. On the neurophysiological level, music boosts pleasure by triggering the release of endorphins in the body; it is enhanced by a combination of auditory impact with kinaesthetic engagement.[244] These reactions are contagious, making music even more powerful when experienced in groups.[245] In addition, auditory perception operates in conjunction with other channels, and the 'soundscape' of an experience includes its multiple modalities.[246] Finally, music, and especially its rhythm, is a potent bonding factor, and communal marching, chanting, and dancing create a powerful sense of self-reinforcing unity that may culminate in the entire group experiencing a shifting of consciousness.[247]

Hypnosis, including autosuggestion, is a very efficient method of consciousness manipulation.[248] A change in the focus of attention, for instance by means of meditation, is commonly acknowledged, particularly in religious and therapeutic contexts.[249] Drug consumption is probably the most prominent technique used for this purpose for millennia.[250] Self-inflicted mortification, such as fatigue, fasting, sleeplessness, and pain can also shift the consciousness from its baseline state.[251] Fasting, which leads to hypoglycaemia, and dehydration are commonly used by ascetics in combination with other methods to induce an alteration of consciousness.[252] These techniques are often used in combinations that significantly amplify their effects, and are intensified when a person is culturally and cognitively prepared for the alteration of consciousness.[253]

The intensity of altered states of consciousness can vary, from conditions in which the individual remains aware of his or her environment to deep unconscious states.[254] A quantitative shift in mental functioning is subjectively perceived as a qualitative shift in the overall pattern of experience, which we label as alteration of consciousness, yet as with many other human conditions, the difference between 'normal' and 'altered' is not dichotomic, but rather a continuum.[255] When studying Greek culture, it is essential to be aware of the subjectivity of assessing a certain state of consciousness as altered, and the spectrum of manifestations covered by this term.

Altered states of consciousness can be cultivated, and their depth can be controlled. It may vary for the individual from occasion to occasion, and can develop or decrease with time. The ability to attain mental concentration, intense visual imagery and altered states of consciousness differs among individuals. It defines their 'measure of absorption proclivity,' and may be enhanced by training.[256] People labelled as 'hypnotic virtuosos' consistently experience alterations of consciousness, even when unsuggested, and are in general prone to anomalous experiences.[257] A person who experiences altered states of consciousness more frequently, in a culturally patterned institutionalised framework, will have greater control over the process.[258] In laboratory experiments, the 'suggestiveness of the context' and the background of the participants influenced their ability to have mystery experiences.[259] Thus, suitable preparation, including knowledge of lore, rituals, and a unique environment, are of paramount importance. The focus on the 'core' procedure of alteration of consciousness, while ignoring its cultural background and induction process, is misleading.[260]

As observed above, cultures differ in the manner in which they construe altered states of consciousness: the range of states perceived as divergent from the norm may be narrow and rigid, or wide and allowing for a variety of subjective and objective expressions.[261] These data are crucial when evaluating the nature and significance of evidence on alteration of consciousness in Greece, and in particular when rendering Greek terms, such as *mania*, *bakcheia*, and *enthousiasmos*, by means of common words like 'madness' or 'frenzy.' The cultural reality behind these terms and the context in which they are used may be much more flexible and rich than that prompted by the researcher's notions of modern Western behavioural norms and diversions.

Alterations of consciousness can be experienced individually or in a group. In the later case, shared expectations are essential.[262] When combined with collective driving behaviour, they generate continuous focus and sustained shifts of consciousness.[263] This observation is significant for the understanding that several people may experience similar visions, and that these visions may be accepted as divine by other members of the community. Evidence on collective excitement and bonding resulting from performing identical actions (fasting, rhythmical music, etc.) and endorsed by common beliefs must be taken into account when assessing group ecstatic behaviour of the Greeks.

Altered states of consciousness create 'an enhanced sense of reality.'[264] A major characteristic of these states is suppression of 'objective relativistic framework' that allows an experience to be evaluated as real or unreal. Disconnection from 'consensus reality' generates the feeling that the alternative reality created inside one's mind truly exists.[265] Some experts even argue that 'a visionary or transcendental state must be perceived as completely real for it to be considered authentic.'[266] The corollary of this conviction is the belief in the genuineness of mental representations experienced by a person in a dissociative state, their interpretation as stemming from the supernatural beings possessing this individual, and therefore having supernatural force (e.g. healing) or disclosing supernatural knowledge (e.g. prophecy).

The noetic quality of these experiences manifests itself in feelings of illumination and ultimate salience, and they may change the person's attitude towards life. Obviously, these deductions are of utmost importance for the study of religious phenomena in general, and Greek in particular. For the individual who has experienced alteration of consciousness, the truth attained in hallucinations is purer than mundane knowledge and immutable. During these states, people often feel that they are in contact with supreme reality, and everything in the world becomes salient and deeply meaningful. These experiences are much more valid for them than percepts, feelings or thoughts when in the alert state.[267] Perhaps here lies the reason for the great persuasive power of visionaries and prophets: the phantoms created by their brain are completely real to them. Hence, in communicating their revelations to the society, they can speak in all sincerity of apparitions as actually existing. Their own straightforward belief persuades the audience, often believers yearning for super-human pronouncement, to accept every word as the uttering of the truth.

Intense alterations of consciousness, such as mystical and near-death experiences, which I discuss below, are not easily dismissed and can cause *metanoia* – 'a change of mind, that alters the direction and orientation in life.'[268] Such *metanoia* is sometimes compared to conversion, but it can be much more significant for a person than a change of religious denomination, and involve a remarkable transformation of one's personality. These alterations affect the individual's way of life and his or her relationships with the environment; they cannot remain concealed. In the chapters that follow, I will discuss the impact of mystical experiences, epiphanies, and possession on individuals and communities in ancient Greece.

Alterations of consciousness involve wordless comprehension, and are thus difficult to describe, and as a consequence, experiencers and their community often regard them as ineffable.[269] The abnormality of the experience makes giving its account in ordinary language almost impossible.[270] Verbalisation of such an experience is easier in a supporting cultural environment,[271] but even an inexact verbal reconstruction of the 'indescribable' usually develops from a long reflection on the nature of the experience and a painful struggle with words.

Subjective feelings of experiencers of alteration of consciousness range from happiness and euphoria to distress.[272] In most cases, the experience is pleasurable, the reason being its association with the introduction of opiates produced by the brain, such as endorphin and encephalin, together with an alteration of consciousness.[273] Sensory deprivation, intense motor activities, emotional excitement, and other kinds of stimulation inducing consciousness alteration trigger the discharge of these substances, which act in the human body as natural euphoriants.[274] As a result, for instance, mystical experiences involve 'an extraordinary strong affective tone, again of various kinds (e.g. sublime joy, utter serenity, great fear, incomparable pleasure, etc. – often an unusual combination of these).'[275] During out-of-body experiences, many individuals feel fantastic delight, which may be of brief or prolonged duration.[276] The intrinsic joy often associated with alteration of consciousness is a very powerful factor to be taken into consideration when evaluating the reasons of the tremendous popularity of ecstatic cults or the readiness of many people to undergo various austerities in order to attain mystical states.

New knowledge or experience acquired in an altered state may be of a disparate character. Altered states of consciousness can be sources of creativity for artists and scientists. These states involve changes in mental functioning, including attention, imagery and fantasy, perception, memory, and high-level thought processes. The combination of images and ideas may be dramatically different from the baseline state of mind, with the resulting heightened ability to innovate and create exceptional works of art and music, or generate scientific ideas. Some of these creations and ideas may prove worthless and be discarded after being deliberated in a regular state of mind, but other insights may be truly brilliant.[277] Furthermore, changes in attention, perception, emotional feeling and responsiveness can sharpen reactions to music, art, and nature.[278]

It is important to emphasise that in most cases, various altered states are manifested in individuals who are mentally healthy from the point of view of their own culture and modern Western psychiatry.[279] Modern psychological research demonstrates that people who experience mystical states enjoy higher-than-average levels of overall psychological health, measured by standard scales evaluating interpersonal relationships, anxiety, and general outlook on life.[280] Despite the similarity of some shamanic states to pathological states,[281] shamans are generally among the healthiest members of their communities.[282] Mental imagery cultivation is the deliberate fostering of visionary experience by healthy people, who learn to use the potential offered by their brains to manipulate their state of consciousness.[283] Moreover, people who report transcendent experiences usually have particular personality characteristics,[284] which could hint at their propensity to visions and suggest their choice by the community as 'mediators of the divine.'

Nonetheless, the boundary between pathological and non-pathological alteration of consciousness is often blurred. As stated above, there are three main types of alteration of consciousness: physiological, pharmacological, and pathological.[285] Their symptoms overlap to a considerable extent, and in many cases differentiation between these types is not evident even to experts. The evolution of the medical and social construct of psychiatric pathology makes this distinction even more elusive. Thus, with all the knowledge accumulated during the last two thousand years, our 'alteration of consciousness' broadly corresponds to Greek *mania*, both terms denoting a variety of phenomena that share one common characteristic, deviation from a baseline state of consciousness.

The scope of this book and its sources

This study covers mostly the late Archaic-Classical periods, roughly the sixth to fourth centuries. These three centuries also share some fundamental characteristics, such as the organisation of social life in full-fledged poleis, politically independent but dynamically interconnected. At this time, the Greek civilisation had already come of age, but had not yet entered the period of profound changes brought about with the beginning of the Hellenistic period. Even during this time span, Greek society constantly changed in many important respects,[286] and their pace was varied in different spheres. As far as the sources allow high viewing resolution, I try to offer diachronic representations of phenomena and discuss their development.

On multiple occasions I discuss evidence from earlier periods, such as epic poetry, and much later texts, especially Hellenistic historiography and inscriptions. This evidence is mostly used to the extent that it sheds light on the attitude to *mania* in the Greek polis society. I treat later evidence with due caution. In order to escape anachronistic projection of Hellenistic and Roman ideas onto the Classical past, I make very limited use of testimonies provided by later sources, and only when they are compatible with earlier accounts.

What philosophers said or wrote does not necessarily reflect the opinion of the 'man in the street,' quite often the opposite, as I will try to demonstrate in Chapter 8. Their testimonies have to be juxtaposed with evidence on the notions current in various walks of the Greek society; only when congruous with views of less eccentric people, or at least other thinkers, can philosophers' ideas, including those of Plato, be taken as representing an outlook of a certain group. In particular, Socrates was odd in the opinion of the majority of the Athenians. Furthermore, whatever we know about him comes from the writings of his disciples or later tradition. I will not dwell on the highly controversial question discussing whether Socrates of the early Platonic dialogues is a historical figure and Socrates of the middle dialogues is the mouthpiece of Plato. Thus, although many of Socrates' features are unique and I believe that his biographers did not invent them, almost always when I refer to Socrates it is Plato's Socrates that I have in mind, unless a particular biographical detail is specifically attributed to Socrates by a different author.[287]

Mythology and drama are widely used as a source on ancient cultural norms and notions. They are obviously a very complex source: on the one hand, myths reflect aspirations and fears of real people, and their quotation and re-enactment on stage during the Classical period ensue from their relevance to the mental world of generations of Greeks. On the other hand, the motives and actions of mythological heroes did not faithfully mirror the behaviour of ordinary mortals, and these mortals could hold widely different world views.

Unless a quotation presents philological or textual problem, I use TLG texts and cite standard editions of Greek and Latin authors. For the most part, Loeb translations are quoted. When the existing translation seemed to me imprecise, I either translated the text myself or modified the existing version. Given the width of the audience that this book addresses, Greek expressions are transliterated and confined to a minimum, and Greek names are rendered in their Latinised form, familiar to the reading public.[288] Biblical quotations are from the *Revised Standard Version*.[289] For epigraphic evidence I consulted a range of sources, and when I cite an inscription the publication is indicated. All the dates of ancient events are BC, unless indicated otherwise.

Notes

1 *Phdr.* 244A: νῦν δὲ τὰ μέγιστα τῶν ἀγαθῶν ἡμῖν γίγνεται διὰ μανίας, θείᾳ μέντοι δόσει διδομένης (translation H. N. Fowler). For this passage and its context see Linforth (1946); Rowe (1986: 168–171); Morgan (1990: 158–187); Harris (2006); Werner (2011).
2 *Phdr.* 265B; Naddaf (2013): 301.
3 *Phdr.* 265AB, translation H. N. Fowler, slightly modified: Μανίας δέ γε εἴδη δύο, τὴν μὲν ὑπὸ νοσημάτων ἀνθρωπίνων, τὴν δὲ ὑπὸ θείας ἐξαλλαγῆς τῶν εἰωθότων νομίμων γιγνομένην. . . . Τῆς δὲ θείας τεττάρων θεῶν τέτταρα μέρη διελόμενοι, μαντικὴν μὲν ἐπίπνοιαν Ἀπόλλωνος θέντες, Διονύσου δὲ τελεστικήν, Μουσῶν δ᾽ αὖ ποιητικήν, τετάρτην δὲ Ἀφροδίτης καὶ Ἔρωτος, ἐρωτικὴν μανίαν ἐφήσαμέν τε ἀρίστην εἶναι.
4 For this passage, see Brisson (1992: 63).
5 *Phdr.* 265E, translation H. N. Fowler: ἀλλ᾽ ὥσπερ ἄρτι τὼ λόγω τὸ μὲν ἄφρον τῆς διανοίας ἕν τι κοινῇ εἴδος ἐλαβέτην, ὥσπερ δὲ σώματος ἐξ ἑνὸς διπλᾶ καὶ ὁμώνυμα πέφυκε, σκαιά, τὰ δὲ δεξιὰ κληθέντα, οὕτω καὶ τὸ τῆς παρανοίας ὡς <ἓν> ἐν ἡμῖν πεφυκὸς εἴδος ἡγησαμένω τὼ λόγω.
6 Dodds (1973: 64); Harris (2006); see below, Chapter 7.
7 *Phdr.* 266B. In the comparison to the human body, divine madness is associated with the right and human insanity with the left. Since the left hand is inferior to the right hand by definition (Lloyd 1962; Sassi 2001: 90–93), there can be no doubt about the superiority of the divine madness in comparison to its human counterpart (Harris 2006: 403).
8 Padel (1995: 82): 'It is not fifth-century. Tragedy spectators and poets would not have felt it.'

9 Padel (1995: 94–95).

10 Findlay (1974: 2–5).

11 Vlastos (1991: 158); consensus on Socrates' traditional piety: Morgan (1990: 9); McPherran (2011). For Socrates as a religious figure see the recent book by Périllié (2015), emphasizing this truly important and unduly neglected aspect of the great thinker, although it may be contested on many subjects.

12 These attitudes were discussed by thinkers before and after Plato. In the late sixth–early fifth century Heraclitus associated prophecy with madness in his description of the Sibyl (*DK* fr. B92, discussed below, Chapter 1). Democritus wrote on divine inspiration of the poets (below, Chapter 6), and discussed veridical visions – unfortunately, the fragments at our disposal allow only general conjectures regarding his views (*DK* A77–78, B166; Delatte 1934: 46; Dodds 1936: 369–370). Although Aristotle showed less interest in alteration of consciousness than Plato, he analysed the experience of alteration of consciousness, defined it, and sometimes attributed it to an outside physical factor (Arist. *Pol.* 1342b1–5 and in the Introduction). Aristotle's interest in hypnosis is reflected in Clearchus' story of a boy whose soul was drawn out of his body and travelled to faraway places (fr. 7 Wehrli, Procl. In *R*. 122; Lewy 1938: 208–209).

13 Giangrande (1987); cf. Watkins (1995: 68); Simondon (1982: 19); Ustinova (2012).

14 Frisk (1973–1979); Chantraine (1983–1984), s.v. *mainomai, mimnêskô*; Pokorny (1994: 726–728); Simondon (1982: 19).

15 For a discussion of the term see Skoda (1998).

16 Santamaría (2013: 38–42); below, Chapter 3.

17 The word used by Hoffmann (1997: 30). G. Rouget called this state 'endieué' (Rouget 1990: 346). For the term *entheos* see Briand (2003).

18 The earliest attested occurrence of *enthousiasmos* is in Democritus (*DK* B18). For this passage see below, Chapter 6.

19 For instance, in Pl. *Ion* 536B some poets are described as inspired by Orpheus or Musaeus, while others are possessed by Homer. Apollo, the Muses, and mind of the mortals: Chapters 2 and 6. Graf (2009: 592) suggesting that *katochos* and *entheos* represent two different 'templates' seems to put too much emphasis on subjective nuances of meaning.

It is noteworthy that in terms of modern neuroscience, internal and external personal control are associated with similar brain activities (Deeley et al. 2014).

20 Pl. *Phdr.* 244B; *Ion* 534B; *Smp.* 179A; E. *Hipp.* 141–144, 241–248.

21 Plu. *Cat.* 26. 5.

22 Beginning from Homer, *phrenes* was considered by many, including Aristotle and his school, as the seat of the intellect: Langholf (1990: 40); Byl (2004: 46–47); Padel (1995: 14, 121–122).

23 E.g. Pl. *Phdr.* 250A; 255B; 259B; *Smp.* 192B; Capra (2014: 72); Byl (2004: 49–50). Hippocratic physicians used an assortment of terms to describe various mental disorders, and modern attempts to sort out this disarray often lead to even greater confusion. For an analysis of the subject, see Pigeaud (1987: 15–27); Thumiger (2013).

24 Hp. *Morb. Sacr.* 4; translation W.H.S. Jones. See Laskaris (2002) for *The Sacred Disease* as a polemic text aiming at contesting popular appreciation of traditional healers.

25 πάντες μὲν οὖν οἱ ἐκ θεῶν του κατεχόμενοι ἀξιοθέατοι δοκοῦσιν εἶναι, . . . οἱ μὲν . . . πρὸς τὸ γοργότεροί τε ὁρᾶσθαι καὶ φοβερώτερον φθέγγεσθαι καὶ σφοδρότεροι εἶναι φέρονται, X. *Smp.* 1. 9. 10, translation O. J. Todd.

26 Luhrmann (2005: 135–136).

27 In Aeschylus' *Xantriae*, Dionysus seizes the goddess of madness Lyssa and makes her join the bacchants, suffering the paroxysms of madness herself (*TGF* fr. 169, cited below, Chapter 3). In Euripides' *Heracles*, Lyssa appears on the scene in person and is described as 'Gorgon of Night with the hissing of a hundred snakes . . . with the petrifying

gaze' (Νυκτὸς Γοργὼν ἑκατογκεφάλοις ὄφεων ἰαχήμασι Λύσσα μαρμαρωπός, E. *FH* 882–883 translation M.R. Halleran). The horrible creature seizes Heracles; in line 865 she uses the feminine participle ἀποκτείνασα referring to herself as the killer of Heracles' children (Franzino 1995: 62). While in her possession, Heracles commits unspeakable atrocities, but Lyssa also has some touchingly human features, and is portrayed making an effort to prevent wronging the hero (lines 842–861). For Lyssa see Chapter 4.

28 Duchemin (1967); Kossatz-Deissmann (1992).

29 At Museo Arqueológico Nacional in Madrid, Inv. 11094; Trendall (1987: No. 2/127, pl. 46); Boardman 1992.

30 The place cannot be located precisely, but M. Jost indicates that the toponyme 'Maniai' is attested elsewhere in Arcadia, and the finger memorial was perhaps an ancient burial with a betyl on its top (Jost 1985: 528). After the foundation of Megalopolis in 371 and given the popularity of Orestes there, Maniai merged with the Eumenides, inseparable from Orestes in literature and especially in Attic drama (Jost 1985: 188).

31 Chantraine (1983–1984: s.v. *akos*); Frisk (1973–1979: s.v. *akos*). Beekes (2010: s.v. *akos*) pronounces the etymology of *akos* and *akeomai* unknown. The noun ἀκή, meaning 'cure, remedy,' occurs only once in the Hippocratic Corpus (*Mochl.* 21).

32 Paus. 8. 34. 1–4. Orestes' sacrifice of his finger, which allows him to regain sanity, can be viewed in the perspective of *pars pro toto*, dedication/sacrifice of a substitute (in this case a digit) for one's self (in Orestes' case identity): Borgeaud (1996: 53); Burkert (2001: 37).

33 Several important works deal with various aspects of madness in Greece. E. Rohde (1925) and E.R. Dodds (1973) launched the modern research on psyche in Greece, especially on its ecstatic states and their importance in religion. The books by A. Vaughan (1919) and A. O'Brien-Moore (1924) present useful summaries of the sources, but their general viewpoint, rooted in the early twentieth-century approach to madness, is outdated today. J. Mattes (1970) surveys Greek myths regarding madmen, using poetry as his main source. R. Padel (1992, 1995) focuses on madness and tragedy. The book of G. Rosen (1968) is a diachronic study of madness as a social phenomenon, from ancient Israel to modern times, and contains a thought-provoking chapter on Greece and Rome, but quite naturally such research gives a general overview, and does not distinguish between Greek and Roman attitudes to mental disorder. B. Simon (1978) limits his research to three models, the poetic, the philosophical, and the medical, and analyses his sources to a large extent from the viewpoint of modern psychoanalysis. J. Pigeaud (1987, 1989, 2005) examines philosophic and medical attitudes to the body–mind connection and the treatment of madness throughout antiquity, drawing mainly on Hellenistic and Roman texts.

  During the recent years, several books on madness in antiquity have been published. A monograph by G. Guidorizzi (2010) calls attention to the ambivalence of madness in the cultural universe of the Greeks; it is based mostly on epic poetry and drama, with sections on Plato and Hippocratic medicine. A collective volume on mental disorders, edited by W.V. Harris (2013), deals with concepts, diagnosis, and therapy of mental afflictions in Classical antiquity. A recent monograph by M. Ahonen (2014) focuses on the attitude of ancient philosophers to madness.

34 *Dissoi Logoi* 5. 6–10.

35 Hippocratic texts almost entirely ignore enduring mental disorders, regarding acute frenzy as the only expression of mental pathology: O'Brien-Moore (1924: 9); van Hooff (1990: 99); Garland (2010: 137); Gill (1985: 316).

36 E.g. *Epid.*1. 2; 8; 11; *Epid.* 3. 14; 15; *Epid.* 7. 1; 7; 10; 25; 85.

37 E.g. *Epid.* 4. 15: foul language used by a young man who became mad (ἐξεμάνη) and eventually died, was one of the symptoms of disease because he 'was not of that type.'

38 ἐν ἑωυτῷ, e.g. *Epid.* 1, case 4; 7. 3; 11.

39 ἐξ ἑωυτοῦ. This opposition is argued in detail by Gundert (2000: 34–35), who emphasizes that these expressions are not to be taken in the spatial sense that the soul leaves the body or returns to it.

40 For Medea's deed as Euripidean invention and other versions of the myth see Mastronarde (2002: 50–57).

41 It is noteworthy that some modern researchers single out the incapability to interact with the environment as the main criterion of the alteration of consciousness: Revonsuo, Kallio, and Sikka (2009).

42 See below in the Introduction.

43 *Ti.* 86B; Pigeaud (1989: 52); Ostenfeld (1987: 37); Robinson (1995: 107–110); Goodey (1992: 39–40); Ahonen (2014: 46–51). Plato does not always follow his own nuanced definitions: for instance, in *R.* 382C he refers to causing 'harm through madness or ignorance' (μανία ἤ . . . ἄνοια).

44 Jouanna (2013: 104); Simon (2008: 178).

45 In the *Gorgias* and *Republic*, Plato discusses conditions for mental health, *euexia*, and claims that it is maintained by the skills of the lawgiver and the judge: diseases of an unwell soul are cured by good judges, similar to the diseases of an unwell body that are cured by skilled physicians; mental health is justice, vice is madness, and those whose mind is incurably corrupt are to die (*R.* books 4 and 10, e.g. 444DE; Robinson 1995: 119–125; Robinson 2000; Goodey 1992 on the diachronic evolvement of Plato's views on this cluster of topics). This approach is the opposite of the Hippocratics' position, who held that the well-being of the soul depended on the good health of the body, rather than the other way around. Whatever the case may be, Plato's dialogues are often interpreted as 'medicinal works,' intended to cure or mitigate the disease of thoughtlessness and to serve as *therapeia psuchês*, 'tendance of soul' (Pl. *La.* 185E; Guthrie 1971: 231; Rosen, S. 1968: xv; Kahn 1992: 46).

46 E.g. *EN* 1147a15; *PA* 651b1–8; Ahonen (2014: 70–77).

47 *EN* 1148b; Ahonen (2014: 81–82).

48 X. *Smp.* 1.1.14, translation E. C. Marchand: μαινομένοις ὁμοίως διακεῖσθαι πρὸς ἀλλήλους. τῶν τε γὰρ μαινομένων τοὺς μὲν οὐδὲ τὰ δεινὰ δεδιέναι, τοὺς δὲ καὶ τὰ μὴ φοβερὰ φοβεῖσθαι, καὶ τοῖς μὲν οὐδ' ἐν ὄχλῳ δοκεῖν αἰσχρὸν εἶναι λέγειν ἢ ποιεῖν ὁτιοῦν, τοῖς δὲ οὐδ' ἐξιτητέον εἰς ἀνθρώπους εἶναι δοκεῖν, καὶ τοὺς μὲν οὔθ' ἱερὸν οὔτε βωμὸν οὔτ' ἄλλο τῶν θείων οὐδὲν τιμᾶν, τοὺς δὲ καὶ λίθους καὶ ξύλα τὰ τυχόντα καὶ θηρία σέβεσθαι. For Socrates' opinion on madness in Xenophon see Ahonen (2014: 45).

49 Ath. 12. 544EF, Ael. *VH* 4. 25, based on Heraclides Ponticus (fr. 56 Wehrli, fourth century).

50 Arist. *Protrepticus* fr. 98; *Mir.* 832b20; 847b7–10; Ahonen (2014: 79–80).

51 Saïd (2013: 265–377).

52 *Od.* 23. 11: μάργην σε θεοὶ θέσαν.

53 A. *Pers.* 750: νόσος φρενῶν; for 'out of one's *phrenes*' see Padel (1992: 19–23).

54 D. L. 1. 70; 86.

55 E.g. Ar. *Ra.* 564; *Av.* 13–14; 427–430; *Pax* 65–67. For the sake of the comic effect, Aristophanes sometimes used even semi-medical terms, employed by contemporary physicians, for instance παραφρονέω in *Ec.* 250 and 1001; *Pl.* 2. On Hippocratic vocabulary in Aristophanes see Miller (1945); Byl (1990).

56 Is. 1. 19–21 (a phrase 'my opponents . . . should accuse him of greatest madness,' ὅτι παράνοιαν αὐτοῦ τὴν μεγίστην οὗτοι κατηγοροῦσι, followed by opposition of 'being in one's right mind,' εὖ φρονῶν and 'be crazy,' παραφρονῶν; D. 35. 40 (μαινοίμην, 'I should be mad'), cf. 93. 24: ὑπερβάλουσιν ἀνοίᾳ; Aeschin. 3. 156 ('do not convict the Athenians of insanity,' παρανοίας); cf. Dover (1974: 128).

57 *Pal.* 25, fr. B11A *DK*, translation D. W. Graham. This usage persisted into later periods: Plutarch describes Metellus' policy as *mania* and Cato's course of action as *arethês enthousiasmos*, '(religious) frenzy for virtue' (Plu. *Cat.* 26. 5).

58 R. Padel thinks that 'hyperbolic' and 'real' madness are not to be differentiated (Padel 1995: 194–196, 205) and therefore broadens her subject unwarrantedly, including in her two books (Padel 1992, 1995) numerous episodes in which *thumos* or *phrēn* are damaged, or *atē* is at work. I believe that despite the existence of a broad 'grey zone,' not every case of uncontrollable anger, psychological trauma, or reckless behaviour belong to the sphere of madness, as perceived by us – and by the Greeks.

59 Dover (1974: 129).

60 This notion was developed to *nec plus ultra* by the antipsychiatrist movement in the second half of the twentieth century, started most notably by T. Szasz, who argued that psychiatry cooperates with the oppressive society, labelling dissidents as mentally ill (Szasz 1971; for a reassessment of Szasz's ideas see Bentall [2003: 176–177]). In the humanities this was one of the main theses of M. Foucault (1978). During the recent decades neuroscience has revealed that on a structural and biochemical level, mental disease is a biological phenomenon, as well. Many psychiatrists, philosophers, and historians would agree that 'our invention and use of such concepts [as madness] are grounded in reality that in some sense justifies them' (Thiher 2004: 6, 320–321); for the position of contemporary psychiatry see Bentall (2003: 118–145); Burton (2009).

61 O'Brien-Moore (1924: 10).

62 Cilliers and Retief (2009: 130); Jouanna (2012: 55–79).

63 Hdt. 3. 33–34.

64 *Hipp.* 141–147, 159, 161.

65 E. *Ba.* 327.

66 609–611: δυσθεράπευτος (the word used by Hippocratic writers; Finglass [2011: 318]); θεία μανία ξύναυλος.

67 O'Brien-Moore (1924: 16–18). Aristophanes even makes a pun on the similarity of *mania* and *kakodaimonia*: 'madness or a sport of a malicious *daimôn*,' and uses *kakodaimonan* as a synonym of 'to be (mentally) ill and melancholic,' that is, to say nonsense (Ar. *Pl.* 501, 364–372).

68 D. 8. 16; *Mem.* 2. 1. 5

69 A. *Ch.* 278–96. Although Aeschylus gives a plastic depiction of the plagues and even uses expressions from the Hippocratic vocabulary, exact identification of the diseases is hardly possible, cf. Headlam and Thomson (1938: 2: 182); Tucker (1901: 79); Grmek (1989: 164).

70 Buxton 1980: 33. In some cases, madness and blindness are interchangeable, the most conspicuous example being Lycurgus, who was said to have been either driven mad, or blinded by the gods (below, Chapter 3).

71 Harrison (1960: 74); animals having mental organs: *Il.* 17. 111; *Od.* 14. 426.

72 *Od.* 10. 240; Harrison (1960: 74).

73 *Aj.* 635: κρείσσων γὰρ Ἅιδα κεύθων ὁ νοσῶν μάταν; μάταιος may also mean 'vain' or even 'foolish,' 'insane' (Garvie 1986: 117).

74 Parker (1983: 246); against this view: Padel (1995: 192).

75 In nineteenth century English, psychiatrists were called alienists, from French *aliéniste*, deriving from *aliéné*, 'alien,' and eventually 'insane.' The word comes from the Latin *alienatus*, meaning 'estranged,' and one could be 'deprived' of reason, among other things, *alienatio mentis* (Plin. *NH* 21. 89 [155]; *Dig.* 18. 18. 4) or simply *alienatio* (Sen. *Ep.* 78. 9; Caelius Aurelianus *TP* 1. 146) being 'aberration of mind.' The combination of the two senses reflects the gloom of a madman's existence, designating a person separated from the common sense and from the community (Weiner 2008: 284; Rosen, G 1968: ix).

76 Parker (1983: 243–248).

77 E. *Tr.* 414.

78 E. *Or.* 1023–1024.

79 E.g. E. *Tr.* 417; A. *Suppl.* 564.

80 Padel (1995: 104–109); Montiglio (2005: 37).

81 Lloyd (1987: 23–24).
82 *De anima* 403b1. Following the same logic, Praxagoras of Cos and Diocles of Carystus regarded inflammation of the heart or the diaphragm as the cause of *phrenitis* (Anonymus Parisinus, *De morbis acutis et chroniis* 1; Steckerl 1958: fr. 72; van der Eijk 2000: No. 72; 2: 144–148).
83 Pigeaud (1989: 70).
84 van der Eijk (2005: 124–125).
85 *Morb. Sacr.* 15. In another Hippocratic tract, *Breaths*, epilepsy was caused by the perturbation of the blood's movements (*Flat.* 14; Jouanna 2012: 100).
86 *Gland.* 12; 15; *Morb. Sacr.* 17; Gundert (2000: 26).
87 Jouanna (2013: 99–102); cf. *Vict.* 1. 35.
88 Effects of brain injuries, especially concussion, on patients' behaviour: *Coac.* 489, 490; *Aph.* 7. 58. Blows and wounds were known as potentially dangerous and capable of affecting rational powers (*Aph.* 7. 14; *Loc. hom.* 32; *Prorrh.* 2. 14).
89 For instance, Aristophanes' Strepsiades, having attacked his creditor with a colloquial suggestion that he had fallen off a donkey, continues by using learnt medical language, and says that the man is in bad health and his brain had a shaking (*Ar. Nu.* 1273–1276). Together with the term, Aristophanes' hero apparently adopted the Hippocratic notion of aberrant behaviour being an illness resulting from brain damage. Two comedies of Menander, the *Arbitration* and the *Shield*, contain scenes depicting melancholic bouts, demonstrating that the Athenian public was familiar with enduring depression, called it *melancholia*, associated this condition with natural bitterness, and knew that such people were prone to illnesses of organic nature (Jacques 1998: 227–234; Most 2013: 395–397).
90 X. *Mem.* 3. 12. 6: λήθη δὲ καὶ ἀθυμία καὶ δυσκολία καὶ μανία; Ar. *Pl.* 364–366 (ὑγιαίνειν); Dover (1974: 127).
91 Hdt. 3. 33.
92 ἀπροσίκτων δ' ἐρώτων ὀξύτεραι μανίαι; Pi. *N.* 11. 49.
93 Hdt. 2. 173: μανεὶς ἢ ὅ γε ἀπόπληκτος γενόμενος.
94 [Pl.] *Alc.* 2 139C; Plu. *Pomp.* 36; cf. Vaughan (1919: 40); O'Brien-Moore (1924: 58–59).
95 In Aristophanes' *Frogs*, Dionysus' slave avoids paying for his feast by pretending to be mad, bellowing and brandishing a sword: the frightened tavern-keeper immediately flees without getting her money (*Ra.* 564).
96 *Prorrh.* 1. 26: αἱ ἐπ' ὀλίγον θρασέως παρακρούσιες θηριώδεες; Jouanna (2012: 84–85).
97 E. *HF* 869.
98 Provenza (2013).
99 E. *Ba.* 748, 731, 977; Hom. *Il.* 16. 156–157; below, Chapters 3 and 4.
100 Pl. *Euthphr.* 3C.
101 Orestes was stoned during a fit of madness, together with Pylades, in Tauris, and in the *Ajax* even the madman's brother is threatened with pelting, along with the madman (E. *IT* 310; S. *Aj.* 748; Simon 1978: 153). Simon (1992: 33, 153) believes that the abrupt way in which Athena hits the mad Heracles with a large stone and thus puts an end to his frenzy in Euripides' play (*HF* 1003) alludes to the practice of the stoning of madmen.
102 Ar. *Av.* 524; *V.* 1491; *Ach.* 1166; S. *Aj* 252; O'Brien-Moore (1924: 59–60).
103 Rosen, G. (1968: 87); Padel (1995: 101); on stoning and its connotations see Rosivach (1978: 234–237); Parker (1983: 194–196).
104 *Lg.* 11. 934CD; Ahonen (2014: 62).
105 Hdt. 6. 75; for his life and death see Devereux (1995).
106 *Epid.* 7. 11; X. *Mem.* 1. 2. 50; Ar. *V.* 69, 111. The myth of Cassandra's imprisonment reflects the same pattern of thinking: even a non-violent madman was a dishonour to his family and was to be hidden (Lycophr., *Alex.* 1461–71).

107 Thphr. *Char.* 16; Pliny mentions a similar Roman prejudice, *NH* 10. 69; 28. 35; for spitting in order to avert evil as a development of a belief in deadly qualities of human saliva see Nicolson (1897: 30–31); Diggle (2004: 374–375).

108 Lucian's depiction of members of a madman's family not daring to even approach him (*Abd.* 14) can hardly be a late development.

109 Contempt and disgust towards the insane square well with the stereotype content model of social cognition, explaining avoidance, and even expulsion of extreme out-groups, viewed as less human (Fiske and Taylor 2013: 287).

110 E. *IT* 282; *HF* 867.

111 E. *HF* 932–933; *Or.* 219–220; 253–254; *Ba.* 1123; S. *Aj.* 447.

112 E. *HF* 934; *IT* 307–308.

113 S. *Aj.* 303; E. *HF.* 935.

114 A. A. 1050–71; *PV* 885; Papadopoulou (2005: 64–65).

115 *Epit.* 878–881; 893; 900–901.

116 Smith (1967: 294); von Staden (1992: 139).

117 X. *Smp.* 1. 10

118 As discussed in Chapters 1, 3, and 4.

119 Scheff (1966: 32, 88); Thiher (2004: 162).

120 Murphy (1978: 252).

121 As discussed in Chapters 1, 5, and 8.

122 Paus. 6. 9. 6–8.

123 In addition to Euripides' *Heracles*, the story was narrated by Stesichorus and Pher-ecydes as early as in the sixth century, alongside many later sources: Paus. 9. 11. 2, Pherecyd. *FGH* 58 fr. 14 (Schol. Pi. *I.* 4. 104); Dicaearch. fr. 101 Wehrli; D.S. 4. 11. 1; Apollod. 2. 4. 12; 2. 6. 1–2 ; von Staden (1992: 136); Gantz (1993: 1: 380).

124 Theagenes emulated Heracles and Achilles, won more than a thousand victories, and received a heroic cult following the Pythia's reply (Paus. 6. 11. 1–9).

125 Konstan (2006: 41); cf. Muellner (1996: 4).

126 Kalimitzis (2012: 3).

127 Cairns (2001: 28).

128 Cairns (1993). A similar position on a balance between naïve realism of unqualified universalism and cultural relativism is assumed by several scholars studying ancient cultures: Lada (1993: 95); Lloyd (2011). From the perspective of neuropsychology, the cross-cultural ability of individuals from divergent cultural backgrounds to clas-sify musical excerpts demonstrates that the perception of basic emotions is innate to us as humans (Peretz 2010: 101–102).

129 I don't think the term 'mentality,' used by many, e.g. Padel (1992: 5, 7) and else-where, is helpful: Greeks differed in their education, social status, and natural pro-clivities more or less as we do. For an assessment of the term see Lloyd (1990: 1–14).

130 Rosen, G. (1968: 90); Kleinman (1980: 8); J. Cassaniti and T. Luhrmann (2014) talk about 'cultural kindling of spiritual experiences.'

131 D.H. 2. 19. 2–3: ἑορτή τε οὐδεμία παρ᾽ αὐτοῖς μελανείμων ἢ πένθιμος ἄγεται τυπετοὺς ἔχουσα καὶ θρήνους γυναικῶν ἐπὶ θεοῖς ἀφανιζομένοις, ὡς παρ᾽ Ἕλλησιν ἐπιτελεῖται περὶ τε Φερσεφόνης ἁρπαγὴν καὶ τὰ Διονύσου πάθη καὶ ὅσα ἄλλα τοιαῦτα· οὐδ᾽ ἂν ἴδοι τις παρ᾽ αὐτοῖς, καίτοι διεφθαρμένων ἤδη τῶν ἐθῶν, οὐ θεοφορήσεις, οὐ κορυβαντιασμούς, οὐκ ἀγυρμούς, οὐ βακχείας καὶ τελετὰς ἀπορρήτους, οὐ διαπαννυχισμοὺς ἐν ἱεροῖς ἀνδρῶν σὺν γυναιξίν, οὐκ ἄλλο τῶν παραπλησίων τούτοις τερατευμάτων οὐδέν, ἀλλ᾽ εὐλαβῶς ἅπαντα πραττόμενά τε καὶ λεγόμενα τὰ περὶ τοὺς θεούς, ὡς οὔτε παρ᾽ Ἕλλησιν οὔτε παρὰ βαρβάροις·... καίπερ μυρίων ὅσων εἰς τὴν πόλιν ἐληλυθότων ἐθνῶν ... οὐδενὸς εἰς ζῆλον ἐλήλυθε τῶν ξενικῶν ἐπιτηδευμάτων ἡ πόλις δημοσία ... , ἀλλὰ καὶ εἴ τινα κατὰ χρησμοὺς ἐπεισηγάγετο ἱερά, τοῖς ἑαυτῆς αὐτὰ τιμᾷ νομίμοις ἅπασαν ἐκβαλοῦσα τερθρείαν μυθικήν (translation E. Cary, modified).

132 Some ecstatic elements were present in Roman cults of matronal goddesses, but these were limited to female devotees (Scheid 2012: 299); the frantic rites of the Luperci and the Salii (Varr. *LL* 5. 85) 'were the exceptions rather than the rule' (Beard 2012: 324).

133 Liv. 25. 1; Scheid (2016: 117).
134 *CIL* I² 2, 581; Liv. 39. 8–18; North (1979); Rüpke 2016: 15–17.
135 Cic. *Leg.* 2. 37, translation C. W. Keyes.
136 Cf. Gragg (2009: 118) on the danger of the 'socio-political form' of the ecstatic cult of Bacchus that was sensed by Roman senators who prohibited it in 186 (D.S. 39. 8–19), and Scheid 2012: 299–301 on male citizens being excluded from the cult of the Roman matronal deities.
137 Laughlin, McManus, and D'Aquili (1992); cf. Lewis (1989) on central and peripheral possession.
138 Whitehead (2011: 190–191).
139 Cohen (2007: 87), following the research of M. Winkelman, e.g. Winkelman (2000).
140 Good (1994: 65); Kleinman (1980); Ward (1989); Jacobson-Widding and Westerlund (1989); Wiley and Allen (2009).
141 Romanucci-Ross and Tancredi (1991); Helman (1990: 214–266).
142 Bentall (2003: 118–145); Burton (2009).
143 For instance, D. Hershkowitz observes that 'the reassignment, through a Romanized reading, of words such as *mênis* or *atê* to the complex of language associated with madness depends in large part on a reassessment of the behaviours these words describe' (Hershkowitz 1998: 156).
144 Beischel, Rock, and Krippner (2011).
145 Devereux (1970); Pigeaud (1989: 120–122).
146 Issue 28, June 2004.
147 https://en.wikipedia.org/wiki/Diagnostic_and_Statistical_Manual_of_Mental_Disorders, viewed March 26, 2016.
148 https://en.wikipedia.org/wiki/DSM-5, viewed March 26, 2016; Hughes (2013).
149 Hershkowitz (1998: 15).
150 Cf. Lloyd (1990: 14–38) on such notions as styles of discourse and reasoning, alongside status and tradition, as crucial to a study of ideas and behaviours.
151 Boyer (2001); McCauley and Lawson (2002).
152 D'Aquili and Newberg (1999: 4); Joseph (2003b); Andresen (2001b: 258); Winkelman (2011: 176); Winkelman (2004). For a critical reassessment of the approach developed by E. D'Aquili and A. Newberg, see Atran (2002: 182–186).
153 Burkert (2001: xi).
154 Lawson (2000); Boyer (2001); McCauley and Lawson (2002); Pyysiäinen and Anttonen (2002); Atran (2002); Geertz (2004).
155 Tremlin (2006); McCauley (2011); Bulbulia and Slingerland (2012); Geertz (2013); Martin and Sørensen (2011); Slingerland (2014).
156 Martin and Pachis (2009); Martin and Sørensen (2011); Larson (2016). *Journal for the Cognitive Study of Religion*, edited by A. W. Geertz, R. McKay, K L. Nielbo, and D. Xygalatas, *Journal of Cognitive Historiography*, edited by E. Eidinow and L. Martin, and the project *Cognitive Approaches to Ancient Religious Experience*, launched by E. Eidinow and A. Geertz, attest to this growing interest. For an overview of the earlier research on the subject see Martin (2014); Larson (2016: 378–384).
157 Slingerland (2008).
158 Bitbol (2015: 104).
159 Lewis-Williams (2002: 102–104). I used this method in my previous research (Ustinova 2009: 11).
160 Jeanmaire (1939); Gernet (1981); Vidal-Naquet (1986); Whittaker (1965).
161 Vol. 16 (5) (2009) of *Journal of Consciousness Studies* is dedicated to the problem of the definition of consciousness; see in particular Velmans (2009); Vimal (2009) refers to no less than forty meanings of the term.
162 Schneider and Velmans (2008: 1); Farthing (1992: 6).
163 Hobson (2007: 101).
164 Damasio (2000).
165 Peretz (2010: 99–100).

166 Romanucci-Ross and Tancredi (1991: x–xii). For the dichotomy of 'nature *versus* culture' as a Western category see Lloyd (2005: 131–132).
167 Chiao (2009); Slingerland (2008: 151–218); Laughlin (2015); Thompson, Kirbyb, and Smith (2016).
168 Cardeña (1996: 368).
169 E.g. Cohen (2007: 86); Geertz (2010).
170 Definition of cognition: McCauley (2011: 3); its embeddedness: McCauley (2011: 17).
171 A hotly discussed sphere in cognitive science, the theory of embodied cognition, contends that processes in a person's mind are dependent on the body beyond the brain (Varela, Thompson, and Rosch 1991; Clark 1997; Gallagher 2005). This direction of research is criticized by many; see for instance Adams and Aizawa (2009). For an updated discussion see vol. 22 (3–4) (2015) of *Journal of Consciousness Studies*, dedicated to various aspects of extended consciousness.
172 McCauley (2011: 17).
173 Geertz (2010: 304).
174 Atran (2002: 181).
175 Research on embodiment in the study of ancient religion is already being carried out: Rüpke (2011: 198–199); Martin (2014).
176 Geertz (2010: 307).
177 For instance, C. Martindale assumes six stages between waking and sleeping: waking, problem-oriented thought; realistic fantasy; autistic fantasy; reverie; hypnagogic (falling asleep) states; dreaming (Martindale 1981: 311–314; cf. Wulff 1997: 109).
178 Laughlin, McManus, and D'Aquili (1992: 132–138).
179 Bitbol (2015: 107); Farthing (1992: 170–200).
180 For a recent multidisciplinary assessment of the phenomenon, see Cardeña and Winkelman (2011). Some researchers regard sleep as an altered state of consciousness: Farthing (1992: 202).
181 James (1961, first published in 1902: 298).
182 Ludwig (1972: 11); Ludwig (1968: 69).
183 For a comparison between different modes of consciousness see Winkelman (2000: 113–124).
184 Geertz (2004: 368–369).
185 Revonsuo, Kallio, and Sikka (2009: 194–198).
186 Kihlstrom (1994: 207).
187 Lewis-Williams (2002: 125).
188 The work that introduced this term is W. James' 1902 book: James (1961). On mystical experiences see Ellwood (1980: xi); Streng (1978: 142–143); Austin (1998: 19–20); Bishop (1995a); Paper (2004); Harmless (2008); on hallucinations in general: Siegel and West (1975); Bentall (2000). On different mystical traditions see: Zaehner (1961); Stace (1960); Bishop (1995b); Dierkens (2005). For an up-to-date popular overview of the subject, see Horgan (2003).
189 Björkqvist (1982); Siikala (1982: 104); Laski (1990).
190 Rouget (1990: 39–84, table on p. 52).
191 Lewis (1989).
192 Cardeña (1996).
193 Examples given in Rouget (1990: 54).
194 For an anthropological overview see Bourguignon (1976); Lambek (1989); Stoller (1995); a recent treatment: Cohen (2007); neuroscientific perspective: McNamara (2009: 167–192); Deeley et al. (2014).
195 Helman (1990): 217; Lambek (1989: 48–49).
196 Klass (2003: 119); for a critical appraisal of the dichotomy between dissociation as pathology and institutionalised/accepted dissociation, see Cohen (2007: 83–84); Geertz (2004: 366–367).
197 Laski (1990); Geels (1982: 48); Atran (2002: 168–169).

198 Beischel, Rock, and Krippner (2011: 128).
199 Ellwood (1980: 1); Hood (1997: 227); Geels (1982: 48); Austin (1998: 20); D'Aquili and Newberg (1999: 195).
200 Atran (2003: 195).
201 Noyes Jr. et al. (2009: 61); cf. the polls cited by Horgan (2003: 82–83).
202 Bentall (2000).
203 Harmless (2008: x).
204 Bourguignon (1968); Bourguignon (1973). Cf. Lewis (1989: 9); Holm (1982).
205 Bourguignon (1968: 11).
206 Winkelman (2000).
207 Slingerland (2008: 24), italics in the original. For a similar approach see Fagan (2011: 39–41).
208 Lambek (1989: 46).
209 Cardeña (2011b: 4–5).
210 Ludwig (1968: 77–81); Farthing (1992: 207–212).
211 Revonsuo, Kallio, and Sikka (2009: 187).
212 Siegel and West (1975); West (1975); Bentall (2000). Different kinds of hallucinations are strongly correlated: Atran (2002: 191).
213 Martindale (1981: 334–335).
214 Martindale (1981: 326).
215 Martindale (1981: 326); James (1961: 329); Nieto (1997: 143–154); Stace (1960: 21–25); Idel and McGinn (1999); especially Dupré (1999); Merkur (1993: 11–35).
216 For theories explaining this experience, see D'Aquili and Newberg (1998: 196); D'Aquili and Newberg (1999: 112–113); cf. Lex (1979: 124–125).
217 Winkelman (2000: 88–92); Metzinger (2005). See Chadwick (1942: 71–73, 90–105); Eliade (1956) for a comparative anthropological perspective; Carlsson (2004) for 'heavenly journeys' in early Judaism and Christianity.
218 Dieguez and Blanke (2011: 249).
219 Green (1968); Gabbard and Twemlow (1984); Blackmore (1993: 170–171); Metzinger (2005); Dieguez and Blanke (2011: 249).
220 Holden, Greyson, and James (2009: 1–2); Greyson (2000). Near-death experiences are discussed in detail in Chapter 2.
221 Zingone and Alvarado (2009: 19–21); Dieguez and Blanke (2011: 250).
222 Revonsuo, Kallio, and Sikka (2009).
223 Sacks (2007: 77–78) for the exposition of J. Konorski's work and its assessment based on present-day research.
224 Cardeña (2011b: 8–9).
225 For instance, see the analysis of neurological changes involved in shamanic altered states of consciousness: Krippner and Combs (2002); Winkelman (2000).
226 Carhart-Harrisa et al. (2016). See also Strassman (2001) for the laboratory study of experiences induced by DMT, a psychedelic chemical endogenously produced in the human brain. Mystical experiences were also explored in a controlled environment without use of hallucinogens: Andersen et al. (2014: 222).
227 Austin (1998).
228 E.g. Dietrich (2003): prefrontal cortex; Persinger (1987); Persinger (2003); Ramachandran and Blakeslee (1998: 174–198): temporal lobes; Strassman (2001: 56–85): pineal gland.
229 E.g. D'Aquili and Newberg (1999: 164–176); Beauregard (2011); McNamara (2009: 133–144). An overview of the discussion: Atran (2002: 174–198).
230 McNamara (2009: 138–139).
231 McNamara (2009: 140–141) contends that that they involve dopaminergic and serotoninergic activity affecting the prefrontal, frontal, and temporal lobes, which mediate religious cognitive processes.
232 Farthing (1992: 206).

233 Lex (1979: 122–130); Ludwig (1968); Martindale (1981: 316–320); Hood (1997: 228); Wulff (1997: 188–199); Winkelman (2000: 148–152); Winkelman (2002: 1878); Winkelman (2004: 198); Pearson (2002: 74); Geertz (2004); Cardeña and Krippner (2010); Cardeña and Winkelman (2011).

234 E.g. the anthropologist T. Luhrmann (2005: 140) recounts how she participated in groups practicing magic as part of her research, and had 'the darnedest experiences' herself.
    Learning and repetitive practice of alteration of consciousness enhancing mystical experiences: Andersen et al. (2014: 222).

235 Luhrmann (2005: 144).

236 Ustinova (2009). For the neurophysiological mechanism of hallucination in the state of sensory deprivation see: D'Aquili and Newberg (1998: 194); Newberg, d'Aquili, and Rause (2001: 40); Lex (1979: 132–147); Newberg and D'Aquili (2000: 56); Andersen et al. (2014: 224); cf. Andresen (2001a: 260–261).

237 Farthing (1992: 191); Andersen et al. (2014).

238 Sacks (2007: 74–75); prolonged journey in an open sea or in a desert, and monotonous music are examples of such environments.

239 Atran (2002: 181–182), with a discussion of the neurophysiological mechanism of this phenomenon.

240 Rouget (1990); Fachner (2011); Atran (2002: 171–172).

241 Jourdain (1997: 328).

242 This sensation is common even in the most sober and mentally balanced individuals. As a result of various factors, from environmental and chemical to psychiatric pathology, many individuals feel, temporarily or constantly, that a certain tune or different kinds of music are constantly playing in their minds (Sacks 2007: 30–88, 279–282). This condition could hardly be defined otherwise than possession in most pre-modern cultures.

243 Scherer and Coutinho (2013); Jourdain (1997: 309–324).

244 Jourdain (1997: 325); Peretz (2010); Koelsch (2013).

245 Scherer and Coutinho (2013: 138).

246 For the theoretical foundations and methodology of this approach, see Emerit (2015); Yerucham (2016).

247 Sacks (2007: 246–247).

248 Cognitive and neural nature of hypnosis: Oakley and Halligan (2013); Cardeña (2005); Cardeña and Krippner (2010). Deep hypnosis as alteration of consciousness: Revonsuo, Kallio, and Sikka (2009: 198–199).

249 Farthing (1992: 421–448); Austin (1998).

250 Iversen (2001); Presti (2011); Ustinova (2011).

251 Lewis (1989: 34). On pain in religious rituals see: Fischer and Xygalatas (2014).

252 Ludwig (1968: 74); Wulff (1997: 70–75). Ordeals and privation preceding a mythic hero's spiritual journey in proto-Indo-European times and in different Indo-European cultures: Allen (2005).

253 La Barre (1980: 39); Wulff (1997: 76); Geels (1982: 44); Siikala (1982: 105); Merkur (1985: 172); Austin (1998: 102, 494); Joseph (2003a: 9).

254 Siikala (1982); Lewis-Williams (2002: 134); Harner (1990: 48–49); Austin (1998: 21).

255 In their definitions of altered states of consciousness, Tart (1969: 1) and Farthing (1992: 205) underscore the importance of subjective experience, while Revonsuo, Kallio, and Sikka (2009), as mentioned above, insist on an objective representational definition based on the assessment of informational relationship.

256 Luhrmann (2005: 142).

257 Cardeña (2005: 51); correlation between hypnotic susceptibility and intense religious experiences: McNamara (2009: 139); Dieguez and Blanke (2011: 251).

258 Bourguignon (1976: 55); Ellwood (1980: 119–139); Aune (1983: 86); Winkelman (2000: 124); Rouget (1990: 89); Shanon (2002: 302–303).

259 Andersen et al. (2014: 226, 237).

260 Tart (2011: xiv).

261 Cardeña and Krippner (2010).
262 West (1997: 502).
263 Cardeña and Krippner (2010).
264 Shanon (2002: 265).
265 Klass (2003: 124).
266 Nichols and Chemel (2011: 128–129).
267 D'Aquili and Newberg (1998: 195); Ellwood (1980: 20); Shanon (2002: 264–266); Streng (1978: 146).
268 Sacks (2007: 15).
269 Austin (1998: 515–516); Ahlberg (1982: 68–72); Martindale (1981: 323); Farthing (1992: 210).
270 Sargant (1973: 74).
271 Geels (1982: 52).
272 Ramachandran and Blakeslee (1998: 179).
273 Geertz 2004: (372–373).
274 Lewis (1989: 10, 34); Blackmore (1993: 107); Winkelman (2004: 208).
275 Gimello (1978: 178), cited by D'Aquili and Newberg (1998: 193–194); cf. Wulff (1997: 188).
276 Gabbard and Twemlow (1984: 22–23): in 68% of cases individuals report having felt freedom, 72% calm, and 55% joy. For 85% their out-of-body experience was 'very pleasant,' to 73% it granted 'lasting benefits,' and 43% characterized it as 'the greatest thing ever happened to them.'
277 Farthing (1992: 204, 208–209).
278 Farthing (1992: 204, 210–211). For an opposite position, namely that creativity is entirely based on conscious activities, see Rothenberg (1990).
279 Lewis (1989: 166); Merkur (1985: 10–40); Cardeña and Krippner (2010).
280 Newberg, d'Aquili, and Rause (2001: 108); Winkelman (2000: 78); Lewis (1989: 163–165); Lukoff (2011: 306). For a comparison between 'the mystical path' and schizophrenic reactions see Austin (1998: 30–34).
281 For a critical survey of these opinions see Lewis (1989: 161–163).
282 Newberg, d'Aquili, and Rause (2001: 108); Winkelman (2000: 78); Lewis (1989: 163–165); Lukoff (2011: 306).
283 Geyson (2000). Retrospective studies of modern people who report near-death experiences (discussed in Chapter 2) compellingly demonstrate that they are psychologically sound, and their experiences are unrelated to clinical disorders.
284 Persinger (1988); Hood (1991).
285 Ludwig (1972: 11), cited above; Noirhomme and Laureys (2011: 265); Cardeña (2011a); McNamara (2009: 80–130).
286 Cf. Parker (1983: 12) on the grave difficulty to pinpoint a study of *miasma* on a particular period. The reasons listed by R. Parker are valid, *mutatis mutandis*, for the case of *mania*.
287 For an overview of this discussion see Graham (1992); Bussanich (1999: 31); Prior (2006: 137–141). Cf. Kahn (1992: 46): 'As far as we are concerned, the Socrates of the dialogues *is* the historical Socrates.'
288 When citing Greek words in transliteration, I follow their Greek spelling, e.g. *bakchoi, lussa*, but when the same words are names, e.g. Bacchus, Lyssa, or common terms deriving from them, e.g. bacchant, I use Latinised forms.
289 http://quod.lib.umich.edu/r/rsv/browse.html, viewed on May 4, 2017.

References

Adams, F. and K. Aizawa. 2009. "Why the mind is still in the head." In *The Cambridge Handbook of Situated Cognition*, edited by P. Robbins and M. Aydede, 78–95. Cambridge: Cambridge University Press.

Ahlberg, N. 1982. "Some psycho-physiological aspects of ecstasy in recent research." In *Religious Ecstasy*, edited by N. G. Holm, 63–73. Stockholm: Akmqvist & Wiksell.

Ahonen, M. 2014. *Mental Disorders in Ancient Philosophy*. Heidelberg-New York: Springer.

Allen, N. 2005. "Asceticism in some Indo-European traditions." *Studia Indo-Europaea* 2:37–51.

Andersen, M., U. Schjødt, K. L. Nielbo, and J. Sørensen. 2014. "Mystical experience in the lab." *Method & Theory in the Study of Religion* 26 (3):217–245.

Andresen, J. 2001a. "Conclusion: Religion in the flesh: Forging new methodologies for the study of religion." In *Religion in Mind: Cognitive Perspectives on Religious Belief, Ritual, and Experience*, edited by J. Andresen, 257–287. Cambridge: Cambridge University Press.

Andresen, J. 2001b. "Introduction: Towards a cognitive science of religion." In *Religion in Mind: Cognitive Perspectives on Religious Belief, Ritual, and Experience*, edited by J. Andresen, 1–44. Cambridge: Cambridge University Press.

Atran, S. 2002. *In God We Trust: The Evolutionary Landscape of Religion*. Oxford: Oxford University Press.

Atran, S. 2003. "The neuropsychology of religion." In *NeuroTheology: Brain, Science, Spirituality, Religious Experience*, edited by R. Joseph, 147–166. San Jose: University Press.

Aune, D. E. 1983. *Prophecy in Early Christianity and the Ancient Mediterranean World*. Grand Rapids: Eerdmans.

Austin, J. 1998. *Zen and the Brain: Toward an Understanding of Meditation and Consciousness*. Cambridge, MA-London: MIT Press.

Beard, M. 2012. "The cult of the 'Great Mother' in Imperial Rome." In *Greek and Roman Festivals*, edited by J. R. Brandt and J. W. Iddeng, 323–362. Oxford: Oxford University Press.

Beauregard, M. 2011. "Transcendent experiences and brain mechanisms." In *Altering Consciousness: Multidisciplinary Perspectives*, edited by E. Cardeña and M. Winkelman, vol. 2, 63–84. Santa Barbara: Praeger.

Beekes, R. 2010. *Etymological Dictionary of Greek*. 2 vols. Leiden: Brill.

Beischel, J., A. J. Rock, and S. Krippner. 2011. "Reconceptualizing the field of altered consciousness: A 50-year perspective." In *Altering Consciousness: Multidisciplinary Perspectives*, edited by E. Cardeña and M. Winkelman, vol. 1, 113–135. Santa Barbara: Praeger.

Bentall, R. P. 2000. "Hallucinatory experiences." In *Varieties of Anomalous Experience: Examining the Scientific Evidence*, edited by E. Cardeña, S. J. Lynn, and S. Kripper, 85–120. Washington, DC: American Psychological Association.

Bentall, R. P. 2003. *Madness Explained: Psychosis and Human Nature*. London: Penguin.

Bishop, D. H. 1995a. "Introduction." In *Mysticism and the Mystical Experience: East and West*, edited by D. H. Bishop, 11–37. London-Toronto: Associated University Presses.

Bishop, D. H., ed. 1995b. *Mysticism and the Mystical Experience: East and West*. London-Toronto: Associated University Presses.

Bitbol, M. 2015. "When 'altered' states of consciousness become fundamental. A review of: E. Thompson, *Waking, Dreaming, Being: Self and Consciousness in Neuroscience, Meditation, and Philosophy*. New York: Columbia University Press, 2014." *The Journal of Mind and Behavior* 36:101–112.

Björkqvist, K. 1982. "Ecstasy from a physiological point of view." In *Religious Ecstasy*, edited by N. G. Holm, 74–86. Stockholm: Akmqvist & Wiksell.

Blackmore, S. 1993. *Dying to Live: Near-Death Experiences*. Buffalo, NY: Prometheus Books.

Boardman, J. 1992. "Mania." In *LIMC* 6 (1):353.

Borgeaud, P. 1996. *Mother of the Gods: From Cybele to the Virgin Mary*. Baltimore: Johns Hopkins University Press.

Bourguignon, E. 1968. "World distribution and patterns of possession states." In *Trance and Possession States*, edited by R. Prince, 3–35. Montreal: R. M. Bucke Memorial Society.

Bourguignon, E., ed. 1973. *Religion: Altered States of Consciousness, and Social Change*. Columbus: Ohio State University Press.

Bourguignon, E. 1976. *Possession*. San Francisco: Chandler & Sharp.

Boyer, P. 2001. *Religion Explained: The Human Instincts That Fashion Gods, Spirits, and Ancestors*. London: Heinemann.

Briand, M. 2003. "Inspiration, enthousiasme et polyphonies: *entheos* et la performance poétique." *Noesis* 4:97–154.

Brisson, L. 1992. "L'inité du Phèdre de Platon. Rhétorique et philosophie dans le Phèdre." In *Understanding the Phaedrus: Proceedings of the II Symposium Platonicum*, edited by L. Rossetti, 61–76. Sankt Augustin: Academia Verlag.

Bulbulia, J. and E. Slingerland. 2012. "Religious studies as a life science." *Numen* 59 (5):564–613.

Burkert, W. 2001. *Creation of the Sacred: Tracks of Biology in Early Religions*. Cambridge, MA: Harvard University Press.

Burton, N. 2009. *The Meaning of Madness*. Oxford: Acheron.

Bussanich, J. 1999. "Socrates the mystic." In *Traditions of Platonism: Essays Presented to John Dillon*, edited by J. Cleary, 29–51. Alershot-Brookfield: Ashgate.

Buxton, R.G.A. 1980. "Blindness and limits: Sophocles and the logic of myth." *JHS* 100:22–37.

Byl, S. 1990. "Le vocabulaire hippocratique dans les comédies d'Aristophane et particulièrement dans les deux dernières." *RPh* 64:151–162.

Byl, S. 2004. "Le délire, symptôme cnidien ou coaque?" In *La médecine grecque antique*, edited by J. Jouanna and J. Leclant, 45–52. Paris: de Boccard.

Cairns, D. L. 1993. *Aidos: The Psychology and Ethics of Honour and Shame in Ancient Greek Literature*. Oxford: Oxford University Press.

Cairns, D. L. 2001. "Anger and the veil in ancient Greek culture." *GR* 48:18–32.

Capra, A. 2014. *Plato's Four Muses: The Phaedrus and the Poetics of Philosophy*. Washington, DC: Center for Hellenic Studies.

Cardeña, E. 1996. "'Just floating in the sky': A comparison of hypnotic and shamanic phenomena." In *6th Jahrbuch für Transkulturelle Medizin und Psychotherapie*, edited by R. Quekelbherge and D. Eigner, 367–380. Berlin: Verlag für Wissenschaft und Bildung.

Cardeña, E. 2005. "The phenomenology of deep hypnosis: Quiescent and physically active." *Journal of Clinical and Experimental Hypnosis* 51 (3):37–59.

Cardeña, E. 2011a. "Altered consciousness in emotions and psychopathology." In *Altering Consciousness: Multidisciplinary Perspectives*, edited by E. Cardeña and M. Winkelman, vol. 2, 279–300. Santa Barbara: Praeger.

Cardeña, E. 2011b. "Altering consciousness: Setting up the stage." In *Altering Consciousness: Multidisciplinary Perspectives*, edited by E. Cardeña and M. Winkelman, vol. 1, 1–21. Santa Barbara: Praeger.

Cardeña, E. and S. Krippner. 2010. "The cultural context of hypnosis." In *Handbook of Clinical Hypnosis*, edited by S.J. Lynn, J.W. Rhue, and I. Kirsch, 743–771. Washington, DC: American Psychological Association.

Cardeña, E. and M. Winkelman, eds. 2011. *Altering Consciousness: Multidisciplinary Perspectives*. Santa Barbara: Praeger.

Carhart-Harrisa, R. L., S. Muthukumaraswamy, L. Roseman, M. Kaelen, W. Droog, K. Murphy, E. Tagliazucchi, E. E. Schenberg, T. Nest, C. Orban, R. Leech, L. T. Williams, T. M. Williams, M. Bolstridge, B. Sessa, J. McGonigle, M. I. Sereno, D. Nichols, P. J.

Hellyer, P. Hobden, J. Evans, K. D. Singh, R. G. Wise, H. V. Curran, A. Feilding, and D. J. Nutt. 2016. "Neural correlates of the LSD experience revealed by multimodal neuroimaging." *Proceedings of the National Academy of Sciences* 113 (17):4853–4858. www.pnas.org/cgi/doi/10.1073/pnas.1518377113.

Carlsson, L. 2004. *Round Trips to Heaven: Otherwordly Travelers in Early Judaism and Christianity.* Stockholm: Almqvist & Wiksell.

Cassaniti, J. L., and T. M. Luhrmann. 2014. "The cultural kindling of spiritual experiences." *Current Anthropology* 55 (10):333–343.

Chadwick, N. K. 1942. *Poetry and Prophecy.* Cambridge: Cambridge University Press.

Chantraine, P. 1983–1984. *Dictionnaire étymologique de la langue grecque.* Paris: Klincksieck.

Chiao, J., ed. 2009. *Cultural Neuroscience: Cultural Influences on Brain Function.* Amsterdam-Boston: Elsevier.

Cilliers, L., and F. P. Retief. 2009. "Mental illness in the Greco-Roman era." In *Mania: Madness in the Greco-Roman World,* edited by P. R. Bosman, 130–140. Pretoria: Classical Association of South Africa.

Clark, A. 1997. *Being There: Putting Brain, Body, and World Together Again.* Cambridge, MA: MIT Press.

Cohen, E. 2007. *The Mind Possessed: The Cognition of Spirit Possession in Afro-Brazilian Religious Tradition.* Oxford: Oxford University Press.

Damasio, A. R. 2000. *The Feeling of What Happens: Body and Emotion in the Making of Consciousness.* London: Heinemann.

D'Aquili, E. and A. B. Newberg. 1998. "The neuropsychological basis of religions, or why God won't go away." *Zygon* 33 (2):187–201.

D'Aquili, E. and A. B. Newberg. 1999. *The Mystical Mind: Probing the Biology of Religious Experience.* Minneapolis: Fortress Press.

Deeley, Q., D. A. Oakley, E. Walsh, V. Bell, M. A. Mehta, and P. W. Halligan. 2014. "Modelling psychiatric and cultural possession phenomena with suggestion and fMRI." *Cortex* 53 (April):107–119.

Delatte, A. 1934. *Les conceptions de l'enthousiasme chez les philosophes présocratiques.* Paris: Les Belles Lettres.

Devereux, G. 1970. "The nature of Sappho's seizure in Fr. 31 LP as evidence of her inversion." *CQ* 20:17–31.

Devereux, G. 1995. *Cléomène le roi fou.* Paris: Aubier.

Dieguez, S. and O. Blanke. 2011. "Altered states of bodily consciousness." In *Altering Consciousness: Multidisciplinary Perspectives,* edited by E. Cardeña and M. Winkelman, vol. 2, 237–262. Santa Barbara: Praeger.

Dierkens, J. 2005. "Les techniques de méditation et les inductions théurgiques vers les états mystiques." In *Mystique: la passion de l'Un, de l'Antiquité à nos jours,* edited by A. Dierkens and B. Beyer de Ryke, 25–46. Bruxelles: Editions de l'Université de Bruxelles.

Dietrich, A. 2003. "Functional neuroanatomy of altered states of consciousness: The transient hypofrontality hypothesis." *Consciousness and Cognition* 12 (2):231–256.

Diggle, J. 2004. *Theophrastus: Characters, Edited With Introduction, Translation and Commentary.* Cambridge: Cambridge University Press.

Dodds, E. R. 1936. "Telepathy and clairvoyance in classical antiquity." In *Greek Poetry and Life: Essays Presented to G. Murray on His Seventieth Birthday,* edited by C. Bailey, E. A. Barber, C. M. Bowra, J. D. Denniston, and D. L. Page, 364–385. Oxford: Clarendon Press.

Dodds, E. R. 1973. *The Greeks and the Irrational.* Berkeley-Los Angeles: University of California Press.

Dover, K. J. 1974. *Greek Popular Morality in the Time of Plato and Aristotle*. Oxford: Clarendon Press.

Duchemin, J. 1967. "Le personnage de Lyssa dans l'Héraclès Furieux d'Euripide." *RÉG* 80:130–139.

Dupré, L. 1999. "Unio mystica: The state and the experience." In *Mystical Union in Judaism, Christianity, and Islam*, edited by M. Idel and B. McGinn, 3–23. New York: Continuum.

Eliade, M. 1956. "Symbolisme du 'vol magique.'" *Numen* 3:1–13.

Ellwood, R. S. 1980. *Mysticism and Religion*. Englewood Cliffs: Prentice-Hall.

Emerit, S., S. Perrot, and A. Vincent, eds. 2015. Le paysage sonore de l'Antiquité. Méthodologie, historiographie et perspectives. Paris: Le Caire: Institut Français d'Archéologie Orientale.

Fachner, J. C. 2011. "Time is the key: Music and altered states of consciousness." In *Altering Consciousness: Multidisciplinary Perspectives*, edited by E. Cardeña and M. Winkelman, vol. 1, 355–376. Santa Barbara: Praeger.

Fagan, G. G. 2011. *The Lure of the Arena. Social Psychology and the Crowd at the Roman Games*. Cambridge: Cambridge University Press.

Farthing, G. W. 1992. *The Psychology of Consciousness*. Englewood Cliffs: Prentice-Hall.

Findlay, J. N. 1974. *Plato: The Written and Unwritten Doctrines*. London: Routledge & Kegan Paul.

Finglass, P. J. 2011. *Sophocles: Ajax. Edited With Introduction and Commentary*. Cambridge: Cambridge University Press.

Fischer, R. and D. Xygalatas. 2014. "Extreme rituals as social technologies." *Journal of Cognition and Culture* 14:245–355.

Fiske, S. T. and S. E. Taylor. 2013. *Social Cognition: From Brains to Culture*. Los Angeles: Sage.

Foucault, M. 1978. *Histoire de la folie à l'âge classique*. Paris: Gallimard.

Franzino, E. 1995. "Euripides' *Heracles* 858–73." *ICS* 20:57–63.

Frisk, H. 1973–1979. *Griechisches etymologisches Wörterbuch*. Heidelberg: C. Winter.

Gabbard, G. O. and S. W. Twemlow. 1984. *With the Eyes of the Mind: An Empirical Analysis of Out-of-Body States*. New York: Praeger.

Gallagher, S. 2005. *How the Body Shapes the Mind*. Oxford: Oxford University Press.

Gantz, T. 1993. *Early Greek Myth*. Baltimore: The Johns Hopkins University Press.

Garland, R. 2010. *The Eye of the Beholder: Deformity and Disability in the Graeco-Roman World*. Bristol: Bristol Classical Press.

Garvie, A. F. 1986. *Aeschylus, Choephori*. Oxford: Clarendon Press.

Geels, A. 1982. "Mystical experience and the emergence of creativity." In *Religious Ecstasy*, edited by N. G. Holm, 27–62. Stockholm: Akmqvist & Wiksell.

Geertz, A. W. 2004. "Cognitive approaches to the study of religion." In *New Approaches to the Study of Religion. Vol. 2: Textual, Comparative, and Cognitive Approaches*, edited by P. Antes, A. W. Geertz, and R. R. Warne, 347–400. Berlin-New York: de Gruyter.

Geertz, A. W. 2010. "Brain, body, and culture: A biocultural theory of religion." *Method and Theory in the Study of Religion* 22:304–321.

Geertz, A. W., ed. 2013. *Origins of Religion, Cognition and Culture*. Durham: Acumen.

Gernet, L. 1981. *The Anthropology of Ancient Greece*. Baltimore: Johns Hopkins University Press.

Geyson, B. 2000. "Dissociation in people who have near-death experiences: Out of their bodies or out of their minds?" *The Lancet* 355:460–463.

Giangrande, L. 1987. "A note on the roots Ma(-n)-, Mna- and Men-." *CB* 63 (4):104.

Gill, C. 1985. "Ancient psychotherapy." *JHI* 46:307–325.

Gimello, R. M. 1978. "Mysticism and meditation." In *Mysticism and Philosophical Analysis*, edited by S. T. Katz, 170–199. London: Sheldon Press.

Good, B. J. 1994. *Medicine, Rationality, and Experience: An Anthropological Perspective*. Cambridge: Cambridge University Press.

Goodey, C. F. 1992. "Mental disabilities and human values in Plato's late dialogues." *Archiv für Geschichte der Philosophie* 74 (1):26–42.

Graf, F. 2009. "Apollo, possession, and prophecy." In *Apolline Politics and Poetics: International Symposium*, edited by L. Athanassaki, R. P. Martin, and J. F. Miller, 587–607. Athens: Hellenic Ministry of Culture; European Cultural Centre of Delphi.

Gragg, D. L. 2009. "'Another people': Understanding the Roman senate's suppression of the Bacchanalia." In *Imagistic Traditions in the Graeco-Roman World: A Cognitive Modeling of History of Religious Research*, edited by L. H. Martin and P. Pachis, 137–151. Thessaloniki: Equinox.

Graham, D. W. 1992. "Socrates and Plato." *Phronesis* 37 (2):141–165.

Green, C. 1968. *Out-of-the-Body Experiences*. London: Hamish Hamilton.

Greyson, B. 2000. "Near-death experiences." In *Varieties of Anomalous Experience: Examining the Scientific Evidence*, edited by E. Cardeña, S. J. Lynn, and S. Krippner, 315–352. Washington, DC: American Psychological Association.

Grmek, M. D. 1989. *Diseases in the Ancient Greek World*. Baltimore: Johns Hopkins University Press.

Guidorizzi, G. 2010. *Ai confini dell' anima: I Greci e la follia*. Milano: Raffaelo Cortina.

Gundert, B. 2000. "Soma and psyche in Hippocratic medicine." In *Psyche and Soma: Physicians and Metaphysicians on the Mind-Body Problem From Antiquity to Enlightenment*, edited by J. P. Wright and P. Potter, 13–36. Oxford: Oxford University Press.

Guthrie, W.K.C. 1971. "Plato's views on the nature of the soul." In *Plato: A Collection of Critical Essays*, edited by G. Vlastos, 230–243. Notre Dame: University of Notre Dame Press.

Harmless, W. 2008. *Mystics*. Oxford: Oxford University Press.

Harner, M. 1990. *The Way of the Shaman*. San Francisco: Harper.

Harris, J. P. 2006. "Divine madness and human sanity in Plato's *Phaedrus*." *Mouseion* 6:387–406.

Harris, W. V., ed. 2013. *Mental Disorders in the Classical World*. Leiden: Brill.

Harrison, E. L. 1960. "Notes on Homeric psychology." *Phoenix* 14:63–80.

Headlam, W. G. and G. Thomson. 1938. *The Oresteia of Aeschylus*. Cambridge: Cambridge University Press.

Helman, C. G. 1990. *Culture, Health and Illness*. Oxford: Oxford University Press.

Hershkowitz, D. 1998. *The Madness of Epic: Reading Insanity From Homer to Statius*. Oxford: Oxford University Press.

Hobson, J. A. 2007. "Normal and abnormal states of consciousness." In *The Blackwell Companion to Consciousness*, edited by M. Velmans and S. Schneider, 141–153. Malden, MA-Oxford: Blackwell.

Hoffmann, H. 1997. *Sotades: Symbols of Immortality on Greek Vases*. Oxford: Oxford University Press.

Holden, J. M., B. Greyson, and D. James. 2009. "The field of near-death studies: Past, present, and future." In *The Handbook of Near-Death Experiences*, edited by J. M. Holden, B. Greyson and D. James, 1–16. Santa Barbara: Praeger.

Holm, N. G., ed. 1982. *Religious Ecstasy*. Stockholm: Almqvist & Wiksell.

Hood Jr., R. W. 1991. "Religious orientation and the experience of transcendence." In *Psychology of Religion: Personalities, Problems, Possibilities*, edited by H. N. Maloney, 87–98. Grand Rapids: Baker.

Hood Jr., R. W. 1997. "The empirical study of mysticism." In *The Psychology of Religion*, edited by B. Spilka and D. N. McIntosh, 222–232. Boulder: Westview Press.

Horgan, J. 2003. *Rational Mysticism: Dispatches From the Border Between Science and Spirituality*. Boston: Houghton Mifflin.

Hughes, J. C. 2013. "If only the ancients had had DSM, all would have been crystal clear: Reflections on diagnosis." In *Mental Disorders in the Classical World*, edited by W. V. Harris. Leiden: Brill.

Idel, M. and B. McGinn, eds. 1999. *Mystical Union in Judaism, Christianity, and Islam*. New York: Continuum.

Iversen, L. 2001. *Drugs: A Very Short Introduction*. Oxford: Oxford University Press.

Jacobson-Widding, A. and D. Westerlund, eds. 1989. *Culture, Experience and Pluralism: Essays in African Ideas of Illness and Healing, Uppsala Studies in Cultural Anthropology 13*. Uppsala: Almquist & Wiksell.

Jacques, J.-M. 1998. "La bile noire dans l'antiquité grecque: médecine et littérature." *REA* 100:217–234.

James, W. 1961. *The Varieties of Religious Experience*. London: Collier-MacMillan.

Jeanmaire, H. 1939. *Couroi et Courètes*. Lille: Bibliothèque Universitaire.

Joseph, R. 2003a. "Mythologies of modern science." In *NeuroTheology: Brain, Science, Spirituality, Religious Experience*, edited by R. Joseph, 9–22. San Jose: University Press.

Joseph, R., ed. 2003b. *NeuroTheology: Brain, Science, Spirituality, Religious Experience*. San Jose: University Press.

Jost, M. 1985. *Sanctuaires et cultes d'Arcadie*. Paris: Vrin.

Jouanna, J. 2012. *Greek Medicine From Hippocrates to Galen: Selected Papers*. Leiden: Brill.

Jouanna, J. 2013. "The typology and aetiology of madness in ancient Greek medical and philosophical writing." In *Mental Disorders in the Classical World*, edited by W. V. Harris, 97–118. Leiden: Brill.

Jourdain, R. 1997. *Music, the Brain, and Ecstasy: How Music Captures Our Imagination*. New York: Harper.

Kahn, C. H. 1992. "Did Plato write Socratic dialogues?" In *Essays on the Philosophy of Socrates*, edited by H. H. Benson, 35–52. Oxford: Oxford University Press.

Kalimitzis, K. 2012. *Taming Anger: The Hellenic Approach to the Limitations of Reason*. London: Bristol Classical Press.

Kessidi, F. K. 1972. *From Myth to Logos (Ot mifa k logosu)*. Moscow: Mysl' (in Russian).

Kihlstrom, J. F. 1994. "Altering states of consciousness." In *Learning, Remembering, Believing: Enhancing Human Performance*, edited by D. Druckman and R. A. Bjork, 207–248, 351–364. Washington, DC: The National Academies Press.

Klass, M. 2003. *Mind Over Mind: The Anthropology and Psychology of Spirit Possession*. Lanham: Rowman & Littlefield.

Kleinman, A. 1980. *Patients and Healers in the Context of Culture: An Exploration of the Borderline Between Anthropology, Medicine, and Psychiatry*. Berkeley-Los Angeles: University of California Press.

Koelsch, S. 2013. "Striking a cord in the brain: Neurophysiological correlates of music-evoked positive emotions." In *The Emotional Power of Music: Multidisciplinary Perspectives on Musical Arousal, Expression, and Social Control*, edited by T. Cochrane, B. Fantini, and K. R. Scherer, 227–249. Oxford: Oxford University Press.

Konstan, D. 2006. *The Emotions of the Ancient Greeks: Studies in Aristotle and Classical Literature*. Toronto: University of Toronto Press.

Kossatz-Deissmann, A. 1992. "Lyssa." In *LIMC* 6 (1):322–329.

Krippner, S. and A. Combs. 2002. "The neurophenomenology of shamanism: An essay review." *Journal of Consciousness Studies* 9 (3):77–82.

La Barre, W. 1980. *Culture in Context*. Durham, NC: Duke University Press.

Lada, I. 1993. "'Emphatic understanding': Emotion and cognition in classical dramatic audience-response." *PCPhS* 39:93–140.

Lambek, M. 1989. "From disease to discourse: Remarks on the conceptualization of trance and spirit possession." In *Altered States of Consciousness and Mental Health: A Cross-Cultural Perspective*, edited by C. A. Ward, 36–61. Newbury Park: Sage.

Langholf, V. 1990. *Medical Theories in Hippocrates: Early Texts and the 'Epidemics.'* Berlin-New York: De Gruyter.

Larson, J. 2016. *Understanding Greek Religion: A Cognitive Approach*. London-New York: Routledge.

Laskaris, J. 2002. *The Art Is Long: On the Sacred Disease and the Scientific Tradition*. Leiden: Brill.

Laski, M. 1990. *Ecstasy in Secular and Religious Experiences*. Los Angeles: J. P. Tarcher.

Laughlin, C. D. 2015. "Neuroarchaeology." *Time and Mind* 8 (4):335–349.

Laughlin, C. D., J. McManus, and E. D'Aquili. 1992. *Brain, Symbol, and Experience: Toward a Neurophenomenology of Human Consciousness*. New York: Columbia University Press.

Lawson, E. T. 2000. "Towards a cognitive science of religion." *Numen* 47:338–349.

Lewis, I. M. 1989. *Ecstatic Religion: A Study of Shamanism and Spirit Possession*. London-New York: Routledge.

Lewis-Williams, D. 2002. *The Mind in the Cave*. London: Thames & Hudson.

Lewy, H. 1938. "Aristotle and the Jewish sage according to Clearchus of Soli." *HThR* 31:205–235.

Lex, B. W. 1979. "The neurobiology of ritual trance." In *The Spectrum of Ritual*, edited by E. D'Aquili, C. D. Laughlin, and J. McManus, 117–151. New York: Columbia University Press.

Linforth, I. M. 1946. "The Corybantic rites in Plato." *University of California Publications in Classical Philology* 13 (5):121–162.

Lloyd, G.E.R. 1962. "Right and left in Greek philosophy." *JHS* 82:56–66.

Lloyd, G.E.R. 1987. *The Revolutions of Wisdom: Studies in the Claims and Practice of Ancient Greek Science*. Berkeley-Los Angeles: University of California Press.

Lloyd, G.E.R. 1990. *Demystifying Mentalities*. Cambridge: Cambridge University Press.

Lloyd, G.E.R. 2005. *Cognitive Variations: Reflections on the Unity and Diversity of the Human Mind*. Oxford: Oxford University Press.

Lloyd, G.E.R. 2011. "The Greeks and Chinese on the emotions and the problem of cross-cultural universals and cultural relativism." In *How Should One Live? Comparing Ethics in Ancient China and Greco-Roman Antiquity*, edited by R.A.H. King and D. Schilling, 241–258. Berlin: de Gruyter.

Ludwig, A. M. 1968. "Altered states of consciousness." In *Trance and Possession States*, edited by R. Prince, 69–95. Montreal: R. M. Bucke Memorial Society.

Ludwig, A. M. 1972. "Altered states of consciousness." In *Altered States of Consciousness*, edited by C. T. Tart, 11–24. New York: Wiley.

Luhrmann, T. 2005. "The art of hearing God: Absorption, dissociation, and contemporary American spirituality." *Spiritus* 5:133–157.

Lukoff, D. 2011. "Visionary spirituality and mental disorders." In *Altering Consciousness: Multidisciplinary Perspectives*, edited by E. Cardeña and M. Winkelman, vol. 2, 301–326. Santa Barbara: Praeger.

Martin, L. H. 2014. "Introduction to the issue." *Journal of Cognitive Historiography* 1 (1):10–14.

Martin, L. H., and P. Pachis, eds. 2009. *Imagistic Traditions in the Graeco-Roman World: A Cognitive Modeling of History of Religious Research*. Thessaloniki: Equinox.

Martin, L. H., and J. Sørensen, eds. 2011. *Past Minds: Studies in Cognitive Historiography*. London: Routledge.

Martindale, C. 1981. *Cognition and Consciousness*. Homewood, IL: Dorsey Press.

Mastronarde, D. J. 2002. *Euripides: Medea*. Cambridge: Cambridge University Press.

Mattes, J. 1970. *Der Wahnsinn im griechischen Mythos und in der Dichtung bis zum Drama des fünften Jahrhunderts*. Heidelberg: Winter.

McCauley, R. N. 2011. *Why Religion Is Natural and Science Is Not*. Oxford: Oxford University Press.

McCauley, R. N. and E. T. Lawson. 2002. *Bringing Ritual to Mind: Psychological Foundations of Cultural Forms*. Cambridge: Cambridge University Press.

McNamara, P. 2009. *The Neuroscience of Religious Experience*. Cambridge: Cambridge University Press.

McPherran, M. L. 2011. "Socratic religion." In *The Cambridge Companion to Socrates*, edited by D. R. Morrison, 111–137. Cambridge: Cambridge University Press.

Merkur, D. 1985. *Becoming Half Hidden: Shamanism and Initiation Among the Inuit*. Stockholm: Almqvist & Wiksell.

Merkur, D. 1993. *Gnosis: An Esoteric Tradition of Mystical Visions and Unions*. Albany: State University of New York Press.

Metzinger, T. 2005. "Out-of-body experiences as the origin of the concept of a 'soul.'" *Mind and Matter* 3 (1):57–84.

Miller, H. W. 1945. "Aristophanes and medical language." *TAPhA* 76:74–83.

Montiglio, S. 2005. *Wandering in Ancient Greek Culture*. Chicago: The University of Chicago Press.

Morgan, M. L. 1990. *Platonic Piety: Philosophy and Ritual in Fourth-Century Athens*. New Haven: Yale University Press.

Most, G. W. 2013. "The madness of tragedy." In *Mental Disorders in the Classical World*, edited by W. V. Harris, 395–410. Leiden: Brill.

Muellner, L. 1996. *The Anger of Achilles: Menis in Greek Epic*. Ithaca: Cornell University Press.

Murphy, J. M. 1978. "Psychiatric labelling in cross-cultural perspective." In *Health and the Human Condition: Perspectives on Medical Anthropology*, edited by M. H. Logan and E. E. Hunt Jr., 248–270. Belmont: Wadsworth.

Naddaf, G. 2013. "Philosophic and poetic inspiration in the *Republic*." In *Dialogues on Plato's Politeia (Republic)*, edited by N. Notomi and L. Brisson, 301–306. Sankt Augustin: Academia.

Newberg, A. B. and E. D'Aquili. 2000. "The creative brain/The creative mind." *Zygon* 35 (1):53–68.

Newberg, A. B., E. D'Aquili, and V. Rause. 2001. *Why God Won't Go Away? Brain Science and the Biology of Belief*. New York: Ballantine Books.

Nichols, D. E. and B. R. Chemel. 2011. "LSD and the serotonin system's effects on human consciousness." In *Altering Consciousness: Multidisciplinary Perspectives*, edited by E. Cardeña and M. Winkelman, vol. 2, 121–146. Santa Barbara: Praeger.

Nicolson, F. W. 1897. "The saliva superstition in classical literature." *HSCPh* 8:23–40.

Nieto, J. C. 1997. *Religious Experience and Mysticism: Otherness as Experience of Transcendence*. Lanham: University Press of America.

Noirhomme, Q. and S. Laureys. 2011. "Altering consciousness and neuropathology." In *Altering Consciousness: Multidisciplinary Perspectives*, edited by E. Cardeña and M. Winkelman, vol. 2, 263–278. Santa Barbara: Praeger.

North, J. A. 1979. "Religious toleration in Rome." *PCPhS* 25:85–103.

Noyes Jr., R., P. Fenwick, J. M. Holden, and S. R. Christian. 2009. "Aftereffects of pleasurable Western adult near-death experiences." In *The Handbook of Near-Death Experiences*, edited by J. M. Holden, B. Greyson and D. James, 41–62. Santa Barbara: Praeger.

Oakley, D. A. and P. W. Halligan. 2013. "Hypnotic suggestion and cognitive neuroscience." *Trends in Cognitive Sciences* 13 (6):264–270.

O'Brien-Moore, A. 1924. *Madness in Ancient Literature*. Weimar: Wagner.

Ostenfeld, E. 1987. *Ancient Greek Psychology and the Modern Mind-Body Debate*. Aarhus: Aarhus University Press.

Padel, R. 1992. *In and Out of the Mind: Greek Images of the Tragic Self*. Princeton: Princeton University Press.

Padel, R. 1995. *Whom Gods Destroy: Elements of Greek and Tragic Madness*. Princeton: Princeton University Press.

Papadopoulou, T. 2005. *Heracles and Euripidean Tragedy*. Cambridge: Cambridge University Press.

Paper, J. 2004. *The Mystic Experience: A Descriptive and Comparative Analysis*. Albany: State University of New York Press.

Parker, R. 1983. *Miasma: Pollution and Purification in Early Greek Religion*. Oxford: Oxford University Press.

Pearson, J. L. 2002. *Shamanism and the Ancient Mind: A Cognitive Approach to Archaeology*. Walnut Creek: Altamira Press.

Peretz, I. 2010. "Towards a neurobiology of musical emotions." In *Music and Emotion: Theory, Research, Applications*, edited by P. N. Juslin and J. A. Sloboda, 99–126. Oxford: Oxford University Press.

Périllié, J.-L. 2015. *Mystères socratiques et traditions orales de l'eudémonisme dans les dialogues de Platon*. Sankt Augustin: Academia.

Persinger, M. A. 1987. *Neuropsychological Bases of God Beliefs*. New York: Praeger.

Persinger, M. A. 1988. "Temporal lobe signs and personality characteristics." *Perceptual and Motor Skills* 66:49–50.

Persinger, M. A. 2003. "The temporal lobe: The biological basis of the God experience." In *NeuroTheology: Brain, Science, Spirituality, Religious Experience*, edited by R. Joseph, 273–278. San Jose: University Press.

Pigeaud, J. 1987. *Folie et cures de la folie chez les médicins de l'Antiquité gréco-romaine*. Paris: Les Belles Lettres.

Pigeaud, J. 1989. *La maladie de l'âme: étude sur la relation de l'âme et du corps dans la tradition médico-philosophique antique*. Paris: Les Belles Lettres.

Pigeaud, J. 2005. *De la mélancolie: Fragments de poétique et d'histoire*. Paris: Éditions Dilecta.

Pokorny, J. 1994. *Indogermanisches etymologisches Wörterbuch*. Tübingen: Francke.

Presti, D. 2011. "Neurochemistry and altered consciousness." In *Altering Consciousness: Multidisciplinary Perspectives*, edited by E. Cardeña and M. Winkelman, vol. 2, 21–41. Santa Barbara: Praeger.

Prior, W. J. 2006. "The portrait of Socrates in Plato's *Symposium*." *OSAPh* 31:137–166.

Provenza, A. 2013. "Madness and bestialization in Euripides' *Heracles*." *CQ* 63:68–93.

Pyysiäinen, I. and V. Anttonen, eds. 2002. *Current Approaches in the Cognitive Science of Religion*. London-New York: Continuum.

Ramachandran, V. S. and S. Blakeslee. 1998. *Phantoms in the Brain*. London: Fourth Estate.

Revonsuo, A., S. Kallio, and P. Sikka. 2009. "What is an altered state of consciousness?" *Philosophical Psychology* 22 (2):187–204.

Robinson, T. M. 1995. *Plato's Psychology*. Toronto: University of Toronto Press.

Robinson, T. M. 2000. "The defining features of mind-body dualism in the writings of Plato." In *Psyche and Soma: Physicians and Metaphysicians on the Mind-body Problem From Antiquity to Enlightenment*, edited by J. P. Wright and P. Potter, 37–56. Oxford: Oxford University Press.

Rohde, E. 1925. *Psyche*. London: Routledge & Kegan Paul.

Romanucci-Ross, L. and L. R. Tancredi. 1991. "Psychiatry, the law, and cultural determinants of behavior." In *The Anthropology of Medicine: From Culture to Method*, edited by L. Romanucci-Ross, D. E. Moerman, and L. R. Tancredi, 267–300. Westport: Bergin & Garvey.

Rosen, G. 1968. *Madness in Society: Chapters in Historical Sociology of Mental Illness*. Chicago: The University of Chicago Press.

Rosen, S. 1968. *Plato's Symposium*. New Havens: Yale University Press.

Rosivach, V. J. 1978. "Execution by stoning in Athens." *CA* 6:232–248.

Rothenberg, A. 1990. *Creativity and Madness*. Baltimore: Johns Hopkins University Press.

Rouget, G. 1990. *La musique et la trance*. Paris: Gallimard.

Rowe, C. J. 1986. *Plato: Phaedrus, Edited With Translation and Commentary*. Warminster: Aris & Phillips.

Rüpke, J. 2011. "Lived ancient religion: Questioning 'cults' and 'polis religion.'" *Mythos* 5:191–203.

Rüpke, J. 2016. *Religious Deviance in the Roman World*. Cambridge: Cambridge University Press.

Sacks, O. 2007. *Musicophilia: Tales of Music and the Brain*. London: Picador.

Saïd, S. 2013. "From Homeric *ate* to tragic madness." In *Mental Disorders in the Classical World*, edited by W. V. Harris, 363–393. Leiden: Brill.

Santamaría, M. A. 2013. "The term *bacchos* and Dionysos Bacchios." In *Redefining Dionysos*, edited by A. Bernabé, M. Herrero de Jáuregui, A. I. Jiménez San Cristóbal, and R. Martín Hernández, 38–57. Berlin: de Gruyter.

Sargant, W. 1973. *The Mind Possessed: A Physiology of Possession, Mysticism and Faith Healing*. London: Heinemann.

Sassi, M. M. 2001. *The Science of Man in Ancient Greece*. Chicago: The University of Chicago Press.

Scheff, T. 1966. *Being Mentally Ill: A Sociological Theory*. Chicago: Aldine.

Scheid, J. 2012. "The festivals of the Forum Boarium area. Reflections on the construction of Roman identity." In *Greek and Roman Festivals*, edited by J. R. Brandt and J. W. Iddeng, 289–304. Oxford: Oxford University Press.

Scheid, J. 2016. *The Gods, the State, and the Individual*. Philadelphia: University of Pennsylvania Press.

Scherer, K. R. and E. Coutinho. 2013. "How music creates emotion: multifactorial process approach." In *The Emotional Power of Music: Multidisciplinary Perspectives on Musical Arousal, Expression, and Social Control*, edited by T. Cochrane, B. Fantini, and K. R. Scherer, 121–145. Oxford: Oxford University Press.

Schneider, S. and M. Velmans. 2008. "Introduction." In *The Blackwell Companion to Consciousness*, edited by M. Velmans and S. Schneider, 1–6. Oxford: Blackwell.

Shanon, B. 2002. *The Antipodes of the Mind: Charting the Phenomenology of the Ayahuasca Experience*. Oxford: Oxford University Press.

Siegel, R. K. and L. J. West, eds. 1975. *Hallucinations: Behavior, Experience, and Theory*. New York: Wiley.

Siikala, A.-L. 1982. "The Siberian shaman's technique of ecstasy." In *Religious Ecstasy*, edited by N. G. Holm, 103–121. Stockholm: Almqvist & Wiksell.

Simon, B. 1978. *Mind and Madness in Ancient Greece: The Classical Roots of Modern Psychiatry*. Ithaca: Cornell University Press.

Simon, B. 1992. "Shame, stigma, and mental illness in ancient Greece." In *Stigma and Mental Illness*, edited by P. J. Fink and A. Tasman, 29–39. Washington, DC: American Psychiatric Press.

Simon, B. 2008. "Mind and madness in Classical antiquity." In *History of Psychiatry and Medical Psychology*, edited by E. R. Wallace and J. Gach, 175–197. New York: Springer.

Simondon, M. 1982. *La mémoire et l'oublie dans la pensée grecque jusqu'à la fin du Ve siècle avant J.-C.* Paris: Le Belles Lettres.

Skoda, F. 1998. "Sens et histoire de deux dénominations de la catalepsie (*katoche, katalepsis*) dans les texts médicaux grecs." In *Nommer la maladie: Recherches sur le lexique gréco-latin de la pathologie*, edited by A. Debru and G. Sabbah, 21–38. Saint-Étienne: Publications de l'Université de Saint-Etienne.

Slingerland, E. 2008. *What Science Offers the Humanities: Integrating Body and Culture.* Cambridge: Cambridge University Press.

Slingerland, E. 2014. "Toward a second wave of consilience in the cognitive scientific study of religion." *Journal of Cognitive Historiography* 1 (1):121–130.

Smith, W. D. 1967. "Disease in Euripides' Orestes." *Hermes* 95:291–307.

Stace, W. T. 1960. *The Teachings of the Mystics.* New York: New American Library.

Steckerl, F. 1958. *The Fragments of Praxagoras of Cos and His School.* Leiden: Brill.

Stoller, P. 1995. *Embodying Colonial Memories: Spirit Possession, Power, and the Hauka in West Africa.* London: Routledge.

Strassman, R. 2001. *DMT: The Spirit Molecule: A Doctor's Revolutionary Research Into the Biology of Near-Death and Mystical Experiences.* Rochester: Park Street Press.

Streng, F. J. 1978. "Language and mystical awareness." In *Mysticism and Philosophical Analysis*, edited by S. Katz, 141–169. London: Sheldon Press.

Szasz, T. 1971. *The Manufacture of Madness: A Comparative Study of the Inquisition and the Mental Health Movement.* London: Routledge & Kegan Paul.

Tart, C. T. 1969. "Introduction." In *Altered States of Consciousness: A Book of Readings*, edited by C. T. Tart, 1–6. New York: Wiley.

Tart, C. T. 2011. "Preface: Extending our knowledge of consciousness." In *Altering Consciousness: Multidisciplinary Perspectives*, edited by E. Cardeña and M. Winkelman, vol. 1, ix–xx. Santa Barbara: Praeger.

Thiher, A. 2004. *Revels in Madness: Insanity in Medicine and Literature.* Ann Arbor: University of Michigan Press.

Thompson, B., S. Kirby, and K. Smith. 2016. "Culture shapes the evolution of cognition." *Proceedings of the National Academy of Sciences* 113 (16):4530–4535.

Thumiger, C. 2013. "The early Greek medical vocabulary on insanity." In *Mental Disorders in the Classical World*, edited by W. V. Harris, 61–95. Leiden: Brill.

Tremlin, T. 2006. *Minds and Gods: The Cognitive Foundation of Religion.* Oxford: Oxford University Press.

Trendall, A. D. 1987. *The Red-Figure Vases of Paestum.* Rome: British School at Rome.

Tucker, T. G. 1901. *The Choephori of Aschylus.* Cambridge: Cambridge University Press.

Ustinova, Y. 2009. *Caves and the Ancient Greek Mind: Descending Underground in the Search for Ultimate Truth.* Oxford: Oxford University Press.

Ustinova, Y. 2011. "Consciousness alteration practices in the West from prehistory to late antiquity." In *Altering Consciousness: Multidisciplinary Perspectives*, edited by E. Cardeña and M. Winkelman, vol. 1, 45–71. Santa Barbara: Praeger.

Ustinova, Y. 2012. "Madness into memory: Mania and mnêmê in Greek culture." *SCI* 31:109–132.

van der Eijk, P. J. 2000. *Diocles of Carystus: A Collection of Fragments With Translation and Commentary.* Leiden: Brill.

van der Eijk, P. J. 2005. *Medicine and Philosophy in Classical Antiquity: Doctors and Philosophers on Nature, Soul, Health and Disease.* Cambridge: Cambridge University Press.

van Hooff, A.J.L. 1990. *From Autothanasia to Suicide: Self-killing in Classical Antiquity.* London: Routledge.

Varela, F. J., E. Thompson, and E. Rosch. 1991. *The Embodied Mind: Cognitive Science and Human Experience.* Cambridge, MA: MIT Press.

Vaughan, A. C. 1919. *Madness in Greek Thought and Custom.* Baltimore: J. H. Furst.

Velmans, M. 2009. "How to define consciousness and how not to define consciousness." *Journal of Consciousness Studies* 16 (5):139–156.

Vidal-Naquet, P. 1986. *The Black Hunter.* Baltimore: Johns Hopkins University Press.

Vimal, R. 2009. "Meanings attributed to the term 'consciousness': An overview." *Journal of Consciousness Studies* 16 (5):9–27.

Vlastos, G. 1991. *Socrates: Ironist and Moral Philosopher.* Cambridge: Cambridge University Press.

von Staden, H. 1992. "The mind and skin of Heracles: Heroic diseases." *Hautes Études Médiévales et Modernes* 70:131–150.

Ward, C. A., ed. 1989. *Altered States of Consciousness and Mental Health: A Cross-Cultural Perspective.* Newbury Park: Sage.

Watkins, C. 1995. *How to Kill a Dragon: Aspects of Indo-European Poetics.* Oxford: Oxford University Press.

Weiner, D. B. 2008. "The madman in the light of reason. Enlightenment psychiatry: Part II. Alienists, treatises, and the psychologic approach in the era of Pinel." In *History of Psychiatry and Medical Psychology*, edited by E.R. Wallace and J. Gach, 281–303. New York: Springer.

Werner, D. 2011. "Plato on madness and philosophy." *AncPhil* 31 (1):47–72.

West, L. J. 1975. "A clinical and theoretical overview of hallucinatory phenomena." In *Hallucinations: Behavior, Experience, and Theory*, edited by R.K. Siegel and L.J. West, 287–311. New York: Wiley.

West, L. J. 1997. "Perception." In *Encyclopaedia Britannica* 25:481–502.

Whitehead, C. 2011. "Altered consciousness in society." In *Altering Consciousness: Multi-disciplinary Perspectives*, edited by E. Cardeña and M. Winkelman, vol. 1, 181–202. Santa Barbara: Praeger.

Whittaker, C. R. 1965. "The Delphic oracle: Belief and behaviour in ancient Greece – And Africa." *HThR* 58:21–47.

Wiley, A. S. and J. S. Allen. 2009. *Medical Anthropology: A Biocultural Approach.* Oxford: Oxford University Press.

Winkelman, M. 2000. *Shamanism: The Neural Ecology of Consciousness and Healing.* Westport: Bergin & Garvey.

Winkelman, M. 2002. "Shamanism as neurotheology and evolutionary psychology." *American Behavioral Scientist* 45 (12):1873–1885.

Winkelman, M. 2004. "Shamanism as the original neurotheology." *Zygon* 39 (1):193–217.

Winkelman, M. 2011. "Shamanism and the alteration of consciousness." In *Altering Consciousness: Multidisciplinary Perspectives*, edited by E. Cardeña and M. Winkelman, vol. 1, 159–180. Santa Barbara: Praeger.

Wulff, D. M. 1997. *Psychology of Religion*. New York: Wiley.

Yerucham, A. 2016. "Cultic soundscapes in Euripides' *Bacchae*." *RCCM* 14:138–154.

Zaehner, R. C. 1961. *Mysticism Sacred and Profane*. Oxford: Oxford University Press.

Zingone, N. L., and C. S. Alvarado. 2009. "Pleasurable Western adult near-death experiences: Features, circumstances, and incidence." In *The Handbook of Near-Death Experiences*, edited by J. M. Holden, B. Greyson, and D. James, 17–40. Santa Barbara: Praeger.

1 Prophetic *mania*

In Socrates' list of the blessings of madness, prophetic *mania*[1] holds a place of honour: madness of prophetic priestesses is mentioned first, discussed at length and praised as the noblest of arts:

> For the prophetess at Delphi and the priestesses at Dodona when they have been mad have conferred many splendid benefits upon Greece both in private and in public affairs, but few or none when they were in their right minds; and if we should speak of the Sibyl and all the others who by prophetic inspiration have foretold many things to many persons and thereby made them fortunate afterwards. . . . And it is worth while to adduce also the fact that these men of old who invented names thought that madness (*mania*) was neither shameful nor disgraceful; otherwise they would not have connected the very word *mania* with the noblest of arts, that which foretells the future, by calling it the manic art. No, they gave this name thinking that *mania*, when it comes as a gift of the gods, is a noble thing, but nowadays people call prophecy the mantic art, tastelessly inserting a T in the word. So also, when they gave a name to the investigation of the future which the rational persons conduct through observation of birds and by other signs, since they furnish mind and investigation to human thought from the intellect, they call it oionoistic art, which modern folks now call oionistic. . . . The ancients, then testify that a proportion as inspired prophecy (*mantikê*) is superior to augury (*oiônistikê*), both in name and in fact, in the same proportion madness (*mania*) which comes from god, is superior to sanity (*sôphrosunê*), which is of human origin.[2]

Not only does Plato have Socrates say that prophecy uttered in the state of *mania* is superior to that given by sober-headed people, but he also claims that etymologically, the words *mania* and *manteia*, inspired prophecy, are cognate.[3] In Socrates' opinion, god-induced prophecy is a quintessential expression of divine *mania*, the greatest gift of the immortals to mortals.

Inspired prophecy: definitions, ancient and modern

In the ancient world, there were two ways to ascertain the will of the gods: either directly, by means of pronouncements by a person believed to serve as a transmitter of the divine truth or will, or indirectly, by the interpretation of signs or omens.[4] In the *Timaeus*, the distinction between inspired seers, *manteis*, and diviners, *prophêtai*, is pronounced and explained in detail:

> No man achieves true and inspired divination (*mantikê*) when in his rational mind, but only when the power of his intelligence is fettered in sleep or when it is distraught by disease or by reason of some divine inspiration (*enthousiasmos*). But it belongs to a man when in his right mind to recollect and ponder both the things spoken in dream or waking vision. . . . But it is not the task of him who has been in a state of frenzy, and still continues therein, to judge the apparitions and voices seen or uttered by himself; for it was well said of old that to do so and to know one's own and oneself belongs only to him who is sound of mind. Wherefore also it is customary to set the tribe of prophets (*prophêtai*) to pass judgment upon these inspired divinations (*entheoi manteiai*); and they, indeed, themselves are called 'diviners' (*manteis*) by certain who are wholly ignorant of the truth that they are not diviners but interpreters of the mysterious voice and apparition, for whom the most fitting name would be 'prophets of things divined' (*prophêtai*).[5]

This passage asserts that true *mantikê* is possible only in an altered state of consciousness, and never in the regular waking condition.[6] The exact nature of the alteration of consciousness, whether dream or vision, induced by illness or divine inspiration, is irrelevant to Plato. In any case, the message may be interpreted only by a sober man, either the person who experienced the vision, after he has emerged from this abnormal state, or another person. Finally, Plato's contemporaries did not always observe the terminological precision required by the philosopher, and confused *manteis* and *prophêtai* in their speech.[7]

The later Greek tradition is reconstructed mostly on the basis of *On Divination* by Cicero who refers to the Peripatetic philosophers Dicaearchus and Cratippus as his authorities on the subject.[8] Following the Greeks, Cicero states that

> You divided divination into two modes, artificial (*artificiousum*) and natural (*naturale*). Artificial divination is based partially on conjecture, and partially on prolonged observation. Natural divination comes from the spirit seizing and obtaining information from an external source, from the god. . . . You will refer to the artificial divination almost all the existing techniques: extispicy, prediction of the future by the lightning and other prodigies, augury and the use of signs and omens. Natural divination, on the contrary, . . . is incited or induced by the exaltation of the spirit, or produced in sleep by the soul liberated from sensations and troubles.[9]

Thus, Plato and Cicero discerned between two kinds of divination, one based on observation of signs and the other, ensuing from divine inspiration, which could be obtained only in a state other than regular waking consciousness, that is, while in the grip of a deity, in an attack of frenzy, or in sleep.

Since A. Bouché-Leclercq first published his research in 1879,[10] most Classical scholars have maintained that in the Greco-Roman world, the will of the gods could be ascertained in two ways: either directly, by means of pronouncements by a person believed to serve as a transmitter of the divine truth or will, or indirectly, by interpretation of signs or omens. Transmission was a natural or divine gift, hence *mantikê atechnos* for the Greeks and *divinatio naturalis* for the Romans, whereas interpretation could be learnt as an art, therefore defined *mantikê entechnos* and *divinatio artificiosa* respectively.[11] Terms used by modern Classical scholars differ: direct, intuitive, inspired, or enthused on the one hand, indirect, inductive or deductive on the other. Most studies of Greek divination still adhere to the ancient division.[12] This division, and particularly the communicative aspect, is emphasised in ancient Near Eastern studies: prophecy is defined as 'human transmission of allegedly divine messages,'[13] in sharp contrast to divination, which is based on observation of facts or events and their interpretation. The focus is on the experience of intermediation between the divine and the human, which results in the revelation delivered by the prophet to his audience.

In ancient Greece, indirect divination comprised numerous methods. In addition to extispicy, which was the most common technique, there were ornithomancy, cleromancy, pyromancy, lecanomancy, etc. These were crafts to be learnt: 'many ways of divination' (*mantikê*), such as extispicy, ornithomancy, as well as interpretation of dreams and unspecified sound omens (*klêdones*) and signs (*sumboloi*) are listed by Prometheus in Aeschylus' *Prometheus Bound* as skills that he taught to humankind.[14] Interpretation of written oracles assembled in books ascribed to Orpheus, Musaeus, and Bacis,[15] and distributed by itinerant and sedentary oracle-mongers, could be a prosperous business.[16] Many oracular sanctuaries focused on various methods of interpretation of signs, such as arbitomancy, cleromancy, empyromancy, inductive hydromancy, and theriomancy.[17] Although sometimes adverse omens could be very troublesome,[18] on the whole these methods, regarded as routine procedures, seem to have been managed smoothly. Paradoxically, the art of divination can be regarded as quite rational: having assumed the only irrational postulation, namely the primary statement that the gods declared their will by non-verbal signs, one could proceed with the interpretation of these signs as a sophisticated logical procedure, in an entirely rational fashion.

In contrast, direct or inspired prophecy was always associated with special conditions. As stated in the *Phaedrus*, prophetic *mania* was caused by *epipnoia*, inspiration, granted by Apollo.[19] In practice, although Apollo was the oracular god par excellence, other deities could also inspire prophecy-giving. To gain inspiration, the seer (*mantis*) or prophet (*prophêtês*) had to become *entheos* or *katochos*, inspired or seized by a god: they served as mediums, conveying superhuman knowledge by means of their bodies.[20] When in the grip of the god, the medium could display a wide range of abnormal behaviour, from mere detachment to violent paroxysms. These mental states, which today would be referred to as 'altered states of consciousness,' were *enthousiasmos* ('engoddedness') or *mania* for the Greeks.

Some mythological seers, such as Helenus, Theoclymenus, and Amphiaraus,[21] were equally skilled at indirect and direct prophecy. A conjunction of inspired and technical modes of divination was not unusual. The most famous example is Delphi, where cleromancy coexisted with inspired prophecy.[22] The great Corycian cave served as a seat of a lot oracle, but cases of nympholepsy occurred there, as well.[23] Different modes of prophecy perhaps coexisted in Dodona.[24] Collaboration between an ecstatic mouthpiece of the gods and sober officials recording the divine messages existed in several oracular centres, including Delphi, Didyma, and Claros.[25] The lack of terminological consistency condemned by Plato, and the ongoing scholarly dispute on the functions of ecstatic and non-ecstatic personnel in several sanctuaries,[26] indicate that the time-honoured dichotomy needs to be fine-tuned. It is quite evident that both methods of divination were considered divine: they were aids granted to the mortals by the immortals.[27] For a modern researcher, the two modes of divination are 'two sides of the same coin,' triggered by the human urge to overcome insecurity by ascertaining the divine will.[28] Yet even if the ancient dichotomy between direct and indirect prophecy is not absolute, discarding this distinction altogether would be a major methodological error.[29] After all the caveats have been taken into consideration, it is still very important to consider inspired prophecy and divination by signs separately, since they involve quite distinct cognitive activities and require that the practitioners possess different abilities.

Inspired divination in Greece

In Greece, prophecy inspired by a divinity was believed to be more ancient than the decipherment of signs and superior to it.[30] The vast array of methods used in direct divination can be classified in various ways, all of them doomed to be inexact. For instance, W. Friese bases her classification on mechanisms that induced prophecy-giving: self-suggestion, comprised of dream-oracles and oracles of the dead, and external suggestion, induced by factors such as drinking water or blood of a sacrificial animal and the inhalation of vapours.[31] This is a valuable approach, for it puts an emphasis on driving agents that triggered alteration of consciousness of the prophetic individual, but it inescapably downplays other essential factors, such as the environment, preparatory procedures, and the lifestyle and status of the person receiving the message. My discussion will focus on subjective experiences of people who prophesied. Accordingly, individuals who could be endowed with divinely inspired revelation can be subdivided into three main categories: religious personnel of established oracular shrines, unaffiliated seers, and enquirers in oracular centres based on direct communication between the consulter and the deity.

Prophetic priests

The most famous example of a prophetic individual holding a post in an oracular sanctuary is the Pythia, who is also listed first in Socrates' list of the people blessed with madness. By the eighth century, the oracle at Delphi had become famous across Greece.[32] During the period when the Delphic sanctuary was at its zenith, the procedure of oracle-giving there was familiar to everyone: when Herodotus wished to describe an oracle unknown to the general public, he stated plainly that the responses were given there 'just as at Delphi.'[33] Prophecy was delivered by a woman from Delphi, known as the Pythia. She had to be chaste, either a virgin or a woman who no longer engaged in marital relations.[34]

Unfortunately, no details are known regarding the criteria that guided the choice of the candidates for the post of the Pythia. It may be noteworthy that the women of Delphi practiced alteration of consciousness on a regular basis as *thuiades* in the service of Dionysus, and it was thus possible to discern which women were more apt to become 'engodded,' a factor that could be taken into account during the selection of the prophetic priestess. The importance of the Delphic *thuiades* was emphasised symbolically by sculpturing them on one of the gambles of the fourth-century temple of Apollo:[35] was this a hint at the fact that the divine half-brothers shared not only the temple, but also patronised similar activities?

Furthermore, the Pythia had to live in isolation, refrain from all contact with strangers, and to curb any emotion that would interfere with her function as a mouthpiece of the god.[36] Having drunk some water from the sacred Cassotis spring, the Pythia entered the holy of holies in the innermost part of the temple known as the *aduton* (adyton, 'space not to be entered'), *manteion* ('prophetic chamber'), or *chrêstêrion* ('seat of an oracle'), which was probably an artificial construction above a fissure reaching down to the bedrock.[37] During the oracular session, the priestess mounted a tripod, the symbol of Delphic divination,[38] and inspired by Apollo, responded to the questions posed by enquirers.[39]

After the Pythia had been asked the question, she entered an altered state of consciousness, known to the Greeks as prophetic *mania*.[40] Her utterance, heard by the consulters present in the adyton, was articulate and could be rendered in verse or in prose,[41] to be put in writing by male priests.[42] The meaning of Pythia's words often remained obscure: the oracular Apollo was *Loxias*, 'the ambiguous.' 'The lord whose *manteion* is in Delphi neither reveals nor conceals, but indicates,' says Heraclitus.[43] As opposed to the Bacchic ecstasy, the Pythia's *enthousiasmos* did not manifest itself in agitation or hyper-excitement. Although possessed by the god, she was neither frenzied nor hysterical: in both painted and verbal depictions, she appears calm and concentrated. While Greek pottery normally portrays the bacchants in twisted attitudes, in the depictions of the Delphic ritual, notably the famous fifth-century Vulci cup,[44] the prophetess is serene and composed. The Pythia's mental state was described by the Greeks as *enthousiasmos*, 'engoddedness' or divine inspiration.[45] Modern researchers usually define it as possession, and it has recently been proposed to classify it as 'patterned dissociative identity.'[46]

The strain of prophecy-giving was considerable, and the Pythia had to rest after a prophetic séance. Originally, one Pythia gave oracular responses once a year, on Apollo's birthday, but due to the increasing popularity of the oracle, during the Classical period three priestesses dispensed oracles nine times a year.[47] Presumably even these efforts did not meet the growing demand, and in the fourth century, the casting of lots at Delphi apparently became a common method of oracle-giving,[48] possibly because of the dearth of inspired seers. The Corycian cave, sacred to the nymphs and located just about 18 kilometres from the temple of Apollo, became an annex to the sanctuary at Delphi, intended as it seems for humbler people who left numerous but cheap offerings in acknowledgement of responses obtained by cleromancy.[49]

The traditional procedure ensured the priestess that she followed the divine will; when it was violated, the Pythia believed that vaticination was unwarranted, and could be physically destroyed by the wrench of prophecy-giving. Thus, in the cases depicted by Plutarch and Lucan, the priestesses who were compelled to speak on an inauspicious day, raged in torments caused by this coercion, and died as a consequence.[50] Only when the Pythia was forced to act was her behaviour described as frantic.

The earliest explicit accounts of the prophetic séance in Delphi are rather late: on the eve of the first century AD, Strabo attributed Pythia's oracles to the breath of inspiration (*pneuma enthousiastikon*) raising from beneath the prophetic cave, *antron*, in the temple, above which the Pythia was perched on her tripod.[51] This was a most unusual seat, as it consisted of a cauldron for boiling sacrificial meat attached to a three-legged support. Earlier sources do not refer specifically to the *pneuma* as a source of prophetic inspiration, but beginning from the fifth century various authors located Apollo's mantic chamber in a cavern or nook (*stomion* or *muchos*), and described the Pythia as physically going down there from the main space in the temple.[52] It is important to note that for almost a millennium the written accounts describing the layout of the Delphic adyton and the procedure of oracle-giving contain no apparent contradictions and draw a coherent picture of the ceremony and its environment.[53]

Divine *pneuma* seems to be the most enigmatic element in the mysterious process of prophecy-giving at Delphi.[54] Until the beginning of the twentieth century, ancient tradition had never been questioned.[55] The archaeological excavations in Delphi, which yielded no substantial remains of the adyton, brought about a completely different approach to the reconstruction of the prophetic séance: the prevailing opinion now was that neither subterranean hollows nor gases affecting the mental state of the Pythia ever existed in the adyton.[56] As a result, the entire ancient tradition had to be explained away, and this task was ingeniously carried out by several scholars.[57] Their hypercritical attitude is indeed paradoxical, since early in the twentieth century F. Courby had already taken note of the fact that only meagre traces of the adyton had been preserved, and that these remains did not contradict the traditional image of the temple. Although there was no trace of a natural cleft below the temple floor, indications of the existence of an artificial construction were discovered.[58]

Recent geological discoveries in the area of Delphi have succeeded in demonstrating that both fracturing and emissions of intoxicating gases occurred under the temple of Apollo.[59] Thus, after a hundred years of disbelief, the ancient tradition declared 'unsatisfactory' has been proven to offer a rather accurate account of the layout of the temple and ritual at Delphi. Notwithstanding the reassessment of the ancient tradition on *pneuma*, testimonies regarding the existence of a submerged vault in the Delphic adyton are still questioned. Nowadays, there are three main lines of argument: methodological, toxicological, and archaeological.

The fundamental opposition is based mainly on the opinion that any attempt to account for ancient religious phenomena using results obtained by modern science[60] is methodologically erroneous. This approach, based on the understanding of human beings as social actors separated from their biological nature, limits historical research. Although at present the exact composition of the 'oracular breath' at Delphi has not been established exactly, it is essential that geological and physiological aspects of oracle-giving in Delphi be studied along with written and archaeological evidence: as argued in the Introduction, humans are both cultural and biological beings, and deliberately ignoring their embodiment and interaction with the physical environment is erroneous. Another important methodologic problem is questioning a thousand-year-long written tradition which is basically coherent. Such an endeavour has to be grounded on solid facts: *onus probandi* lies on those who contend that from Aeschylus to Plutarch, dozens of ancient authors deliberately misled their audiences, each for his own reasons, but all proclaiming the same lie and placing Apollo and his main oracular chamber into a lowly nook.

It is also argued that the concentration of a particular gas, namely ethylene, was insufficient to induce the Pythia's trance.[61] However, two other gases detected by chemical analyses of travertine deposits from the Delphic springs, ethane and methane, can also alter human consciousness.[62] The concentration of the intoxicating gas needed to alter the consciousness of a highly hypnotisable individual, firmly believing in the sacredness of the rite, and after a day of fasting is much lower than that needed to induce such changes in the consciousness of an average person.[63] Moreover, the gas could serve as a trigger, a driving factor that put into action the Pythia's autosuggestion, and in this case even a low concentration would have been sufficient. It is noteworthy that in various cultural practices around the globe, patterned dissociative identity can be precipitated by a combination of consciousness-altering substances with one or several other methods, or even be induced without any psychotropic substances.[64] The Greeks seem to have been aware of the psychoactive qualities of *pneuma*, although they did not rely on it alone.

In the recent re-evaluation of the archaeological remains, two most prominent experts on Delphic archaeology, P. Amandry and E. Hansen, contend that the inner part of the cellar has deliberately never been paved and that there was no descent to a lower level, but rather in this part of the cellar the ground remained uncovered.[65] The plan they publish indicates with an interrogation mark the lack of clarity concerning this locale.[66] It is hard to imagine that the most important part of the most important temple in the Greek world, the place of its navel, would deliberately be left incomplete for centuries without a good reason. The most logical reason must have been the need to assure immediate contact between the Pythia and the ground. P. Amandry argues that there was no subterranean space because the stones of the foundations below the floor level remained rough, and the descent would not be pleasing aesthetically. However, the prophetic nook did not have to be very deep, in fact, G. Roux suggested that the depression was no more than 2 metres deep, and was separated from the rest of the cellar by a light construction, rather than stone walls.[67] Most significantly, there is no doubt that the fourth-century temple was constructed in an absolutely unique manner, leaving a part of the bedrock below it unsealed.[68] The whole building seems to have been erected in order to enable access to a strip of prophetic ground.[69]

It appears now that the inner sanctum at Delphi was an artificial enclosure above an opening in the ground allowing the Pythia to be in physical contact with the soil underlying the temple.[70] A growing number of authors acknowledge the role of *pneuma* in Pythia's inspiration.[71] Hydrocarbon gases issuing from the bedrock could reach the Pythia and act alongside other factors of religious and psychological nature, such as fasting, drinking the water from the Cassotis, sitting on the tripod in the sacred nook, and being inside the adyton.[72] Of course, the personality of the Pythia was of crucial importance: people differ in their reactivity to suggestion,[73] and a candidate for the role of the god's mouthpiece must have been chosen carefully.[74] The accumulated interaction of all these factors enabled successful induction of the Pythia into a state of possession by Apollo – prophetic *mania*.

Delphi is not unique: the precinct of Apollo in Hierapolis resembles the Delphic sanctuary in several respects. In Hierapolis, in the Hellenistic period the autochthon cult of Gaia was superimposed by Apollo.[75] This association was articulated by the connection between the temple of Apollo and a hole emitting gases (until present-day) known as Plutonium, and the position of the temple above an active fault.[76] It is noteworthy that in imperial times cleromancy was also practiced in the Hierapolis sanctuary.[77] Poisonous gases are reported to have been present in oracular caves along the Meander valley, most notably the medical oracle at Acharaca and in the cave of Apollo at Hieracome, where the enquirers or priests experienced visions or obtained extraordinary physical abilities.[78]

At Claros near Colophon in Asia Minor, inspired prophecy was probably delivered in the Archaic period: the sanctuary then included a closed courtyard focused on a well, which seems to have been used as a source of prophetic insight, similar to the later temple in Didyma, discussed below.[79] From the fourth century onward, the mantic session was also held in an artificial grotto, which has been discovered by L. Robert. The water source inside the grotto was not visible from the surface.[80] At a later stage, the procedure took place at night and included 'numerous ceremonies.'[81] Most enquirers seem to have awaited a response in the temple: Tacitus says that the prophesying priest heard only the names of the enquirers, apparently leaving them behind when he descended into the grotto. A few were honoured and allowed to enter the grotto together with the medium and the cult officials. In the underground darkness, an intricate passage to the prophetic vault, with no less than seven turns, must have given the impression of a maze.[82]

The staff of the temple included a prophet (*prophêtês*) and a secretary who were appointed for a year, as well as a priest and a *thespiôdos* ('inspired singer'), who held their offices for a long period or even for life. It is likely therefore that it was the *thespiôdos* who served as an inspired medium, as this function demanded special personality traits, and that the prophet only recorded and edited them.[83] The medium alone entered the innermost sanctum, invisible to those present at the ceremony.[84] Influenced by his faith, the long passage through the maze, and by purification ceremonies undergone before entering the grotto, he drank the sacred water. The medium sang his response in verse which was probably revised by the prophet; many of these oracles were carved on stelae and are still in existence today. The prophetic séance was an ordeal for the medium; while in the grip of the god he was 'neither himself nor has any consciousness of what he says and where on earth he is, so that even after prophesying, he sometimes scarcely gets control of himself.'[85]

The diviner at Claros had to abstain from food for a day and a night before descending into the underground chamber, where he drank from the sacred source. The medium, usually a man possessing no special education, distanced himself from ordinary mortals. According to Iamblichus, he withdrew from human affairs, lived in an inaccessible place, and prepared for possession by the god with a day and night of fasting.[86] The strain of prophesying was considerable: Pliny notes that drinking from the sacred pool inspired wonderful oracles, but shortened the life of the drinker. In fact, drinking water could be lethal for prophets: the legend of the seer Tiresias, who died after having drunk water from the spring of Telphusa, may reflect this belief.[87] Aristotle compares the drinking of water at Claros to the practice of Thracian prophets of Dionysus who uttered their prophecies having drunk unmixed wine, which in Greece was considered toxic and dangerous;[88] in any case, the belief in the prophetic qualities of water was widely spread in the Greek world.[89]

Drinking the sacred water was certainly not a life-shortening factor on its own, but was only a part of the strenuous lifestyle of the medium, comprised of seclusion, purifications, fasting and other austerities, and indeed the strain of possession by the god.[90] It might be this strain that made it necessary to introduce an additional technique of oracle-giving at Claros: from the late fifth or early fourth century, divination by lot was probably used at the sanctuary.[91]

In modern terms, the medium at Claros, an individual endowed with a proclivity for alteration of consciousness, attained this state due to the effect of his descent into the underground grotto, enhanced by earlier preparations. Drinking of the water could have served as an immediate driving factor, triggering prophetic singing. For the Greeks, this prophetic *mania* was Apollo's gift, transmitted by the water and bestowed upon the selected few, carefully safeguarding their purity.

Another great centre of Apolline prophecy in Asia Minor was the sanctuary at Didyma or the Branchidae, near Miletus. The sanctuary was active by the seventh century, perhaps from pre-Hellenic times,[92] and oracles were given by male prophets chosen by lot from the Branchidae clan; this tradition is echoed in the foundation myth that attributed the prophetic power of the Branchidae to a gift bestowed on their forefather, Branchus, by Apollo, in compensation for yielding to his love.[93] Judging by the scant Archaic evidence, even at an early date the god in Didyma spoke by means of mediums, who uttered the replies in a state of trance.[94]

After the destruction of Miletus by the Persians in 494 the cult continued in a modified form;[95] the restoration of the sanctuary on a grand scale was begun in 334 by Alexander and remained unfinished five centuries later. Both the sacked Archaic and the Hellenistic-Roman Didymaea featured an extremely unusual layout: the temple was essentially a roofed enclosure surrounding an open-air courtyard that served as the temple's adyton. Beginning from the earliest times, it contained a sacred spring, a small temple-like structure known as *naiskos*, and a grove of laurel trees; a depression around the spring defined the floor level of the courtyard, which was several metres below that of the external construction.[96] The location of the temple is unimpressive, and appears to be dictated by the cultic importance of the spring on which the oracular procedure was focused.[97] Although the basic design of the temple remained unchanged from the Archaic age onwards,[98] as of the fourth century the male *prophêtês* was substituted by a female *promantis*, following perhaps the practice at Delphi.

The procedure of oracle-giving in the new temple can be tentatively reconstructed on the basis of the archaeological remains of the Hellenistic-Roman temple and literary evidence. After preliminary sacrifices, the enquirers could enter the temple and remain in the *pronaos*: in this case, they would wait for the proclamation of the response from the central window in the blind wall separating the entrance of the temple from its inner parts, and would never witness the ceremony of prophecy uttering – like in Claros.[99] It is also suggested that at least several properly purified enquirers accompanied the temple officials, descended into the underground chamber and could observe the procedure in the courtyard – similar to the practice at Delphi.[100]

From a chamber beyond the *pronaos*, the so-called eastern chamber, a priest called *prophêtês* (with or without the consulters), descended through one of the two sloping vaulted passages that led into small unroofed rooms, and continued downward, this time by a flight of steps, into the enormous adyton. These dark narrow passages provide the only access from the majestic *pronaos* to the imposing adyton; the architects of the Didymaeum must have had good reasons for this bizarre arrangement, and it seems to hint at murky underground passages, such as in Claros.[101]

The *prophêtês* proceeded to a sacred spring that was near the small temple (*naiskos*) housing Apollo's statue; the prophetic priestess (*promantis*) would then sit above the spring on an axle or pivot called *axôn*, the hem of her garment dampened by the water. Inspired by the god, she uttered oracular responses either in prose or in hexametres that were written down, supposedly edited by the male prophet, announced to the enquirers and finally handed to them in the office of the temple at its entrance. A large number of these responses, sometimes preceded by questions, are still in existence.[102]

The procedure of oracle-giving at Didyma is described in detail only by Iamblichus, in his long passage on inspired prophecy. Inspiration of the prophetic priestess is attributed to inhalation of vapours from the sacred spring:

> And as for the woman at Branchidae who gives oracles (literally, *chresmôdos*, 'one who sings oracles'), it is either by holding the staff first given by a certain

god that she is filled with the divine radiance; or else when sitting on the axle she predicts the future; or whether dipping her feet or skirt in the water, or inhaling vapour from the water, at any rate, she receives the god: prepared and made ready by any or all of these preliminaries for his reception from without, she partakes of the god. This is what is shown by the abundance of sacrifices, the established custom of the whole ritual, and everything that is performed with due piety prior to divination: also the baths of the prophetess, her fasting for three whole days, abiding in the innermost sanctuary, already possessed by light, and rejoicing in it for a long time.[103]

The staff was granted by Apollo to Branchus and may be compared to the sceptre given by the Muses to Hesiod in the scene of his initiation as a poet: in both cases, it embodied the divine gift of truthful speech, poetic or prophetic.[104] The axle or pivot on which the prophetess sat is reminiscent of the Pythia's tripod, which was considered so essential for prophecy-giving that it became a symbol of inspired vaticination; the pivot could be swung over the spring in order to place the medium immediately above the sacred water that corresponded to the chasm in Delphi. In both cases, the emanation, from the spring or from the fissure in the earth, was considered responsible for the prophetic trance.[105] It is noteworthy that the opening of the spring in Didyma was possibly not fixed, and the source could sometimes shrink or look no more impressive than a puddle:[106] these fluctuations in the water level are reminiscent of the changes in the gas emissions at Delphi. Similar to Delphi and Claros, the temple at Didyma was built to encompass a natural source that was believed to enable prophetic inspiration. The temple and procedure at Branchidae seem to combine Delphic elements, such as a chaste female medium and the inhalation of vapours emanating from the earth, and Clarian ones, including the use of water and an intricate descent to its source.

The secluded way of life of the priestess and the ascetic preparations for the oracular séances resemble the regimes followed by the Pythia and the prophet at Claros, but three-days-long fasting is exceptional.[107] In addition, at Didyma the prophetess probably had to be a virgin.[108] She must have lived in the temple, at least during the days of purifications and fasting. The austerities rendered the priestess 'otherworldly' even before she actually began prophecy-giving: Iamblichus speaks of her 'rejoicing' and being 'possessed by light,' both sensations occurring during alterations of consciousness.[109] In Iamblichus' time, the consultation could not take place more often than every fifth day, but in practice it probably occurred once a month, as in Delphi,[110] especially given the need to allow the *promantis* to recover from the exhaustion of fasting and trance. The finds of knucklebones in the sanctuary indicate that cleromancy was probably practiced in Didyma, alongside inspired prophecy,[111] as a less venerable, but affordable method of divination.

Apollo appears to have used male prophets in mainland Greece, as well. In Boeotia, the sanctuary of Apollo at Ptoion had been active since the seventh century, and was prominent as an oracular centre in Pindar's days.[112] The subsequent sacred compound, dated to the fourth century, included a temple and a natural spring from which water was conveyed to an artificial grotto.[113] Herodotus recounts the story of the consultation of the oracle by Mys in the early fifth century, according to which the prophet (called *promantis* and *prophêtês*) gave his response in the enquirer's presence, and in the Carian language. Whatever language he really used,[114] it is clear that the prophet's words could be recorded. Most significant, he appears to have acted by direct inspiration, probably induced by entering the grotto and drinking the sacred water.[115] The fact that the prophet's language was identified by the Persian enquirers as Carian, which he could hardly have known, also hints at the prophet's ecstatic state: his entranced performance in the local Boeotian dialect was perhaps so confusing that to the foreigners it sounded like Carian. An early third-century hexametre dedication from the sanctuary addresses Apollo as 'nocturnal' (*ennuchos*) and describes a direct encounter between the dedicant and the god: 'according to the promise you gave me in the darkness, when you uttered your words (in response) to my voice and smiled.'[116] It is probable that at Ptoion, Apollo appeared to his mouthpiece, the male prophet, as a vision inside the gloomy grotto, and the prophet attained his hallucinations in an altered state, which affected his articulation, at least on some occasions.

In his discussion of divine transport (*theophoria*), Iamblichus enumerates several methods of attaining prophetic inspiration by mediums acting as temple officials:

> Another kind of divination, famous and most splendid, is that of the inspired oracle, which takes diverse forms. About this you [Porphyry] declare the following: 'Some are inspired while drinking water, like the priest of Clarian Apollo in Colophon; others while sitting near apertures like the women who prophesy at Delphi; others while inhaling vapours from waters, like the prophetesses of the Branchidai.' You have mentioned three of these far-famed oracles, not because there are only three, for those omitted are much more numerous, but since these take precedence over the others.[117]

In the prophetic sanctuaries enumerated by Iamblichus, as well as in other places, the prophetic person needed a set of ritual actions, often including exposure to various substances, in order to change his or her state of consciousness. A common prerequisite was a solitary and ritually pure way of life in general, as well as isolation for a fast and ceremonies of purification immediately preceding oracle-giving.[118] Setting prophetic séances in dark underground chambers, grottos, and natural caves supposedly resulted in complete or partial sensory deprivation, which could induce visions and hallucinations.[119] The list of substances includes various gases in different concentrations, from a considerable one at Hierapolis to a debatable amount at Delphi, and liquids, water first and foremost, as well as unmixed wine (at the oracle of Dionysus)[120] and bull's blood (at the oracle of Gaia at Aegira).[121] While mind-altering gases in high concentration, as well as pure wine, could influence the state of consciousness of the medium, drinking water or blood and inhaling psychoactive gases in low concentration could serve as triggers activating an autosuggestive chain leading to prophetic trance. It is significant that inspired vaticination was induced by a complex process involving several factors: in an easily hypnotisable person, isolated way of life and fasting, appropriate driving behaviour, and faith in one's vocation in most cases resulted in alteration of consciousness. Unfortunately, we have no information on the selection methods of prophetic priests, but it was well-known in antiquity that individuals differed in their ability to attain alteration of consciousness, and one can a priori assume that mediums were chosen among people who entered the state of engoddedness relatively easily.[122]

The presence of a sober temple official writing down the utterings of an ecstatic prophet, female or male, in Delphi, Claros, and Didyma, is noteworthy. This arrangement seems to have permitted prophetic words to be corrected or modified. At Delphi, the possibilities of interfering with the general message of the Pythia were limited, since the enquirers were allowed into the adyton; the fact that at Claros and at Didyma the consultants could hear the prophecy only on rare occasions probably reflects an attempt at controlling the contents of the announced prophecy.[123]

Another notable point is the use of cleromancy in or close to sanctuaries providing ecstatic prophecy, such as Delphi, Claros, and Didyma: in terms of human effort required for the consultation, divination by lot is immensely less demanding, and therefore served as a relatively cheap and easy way to consult the gods. A Greek proverb which says, 'Many are lot-throwers (*thrioboloi*), prophets (*manteis*) are few,'[124] may refer to this fact.

Laymen who received oracular messages in sanctuaries

In many cases, inspired divination was based on direct contact between the god and the consulter. The most striking and well-documented example is the oracle of Trophonius in Lebadeia (Boeotia), which was active in the sixth century.[125] Trophonius supposedly vanished beneath the earth and lived in a cave under a hill as an oracular god.[126] In both literary and epigraphic sources, the act of consultation of the oracle is described as descent (*katabasis*) to the god's underground dwelling.[127]

Luckily, Pausanias left behind a detailed description of the procedure there: the preparation for the consultation took several days and included not only preliminary sacrifices, but also secluded lodging, cold baths, prayers, a special diet, and sexual abstinence, as well as music and dancing.[128] Only when well prepared for the tremendous experience, i.e. exhausted, tense with anticipation, and disposed to hallucinations,[129] did the consulter descend to Trophonius' cave. The symbolism of the Trophonium was that of the netherworld: at night two boys called *Hermae*, personifying Hermes the conductor of the souls to Hades, led the enquirer to the oracular cave.[130] The prophetic adyton was most probably an artificial circular hole, several metres deep: the enquirer lay on the ground, and then, according to Pausanias, he was swiftly drawn into another hole, as if by an eddy (*dinê*).[131] In fact, the image of the whirl could derive from the vortex experienced by the enquirers at the beginning of their prophetic trance, and could have been the result of an altered state of consciousness, induced by the immersion into the dark coolness of the grotto. Immediately after his stay in the underground cave, the consulter took a seat on the chair of Mnemosyne and recounted his experience to the priests. Only after this procedure was the suppliant, semi-conscious and paralyzed with terror, allowed to be taken away by his relatives.[132] The underground experiences of the enquirers were so awesome that they lost the ability to smile, which prompted the proverb 'He consulted the Trophonium.'[133]

Trophonius was believed to appear to the enquirers in person.[134] The consulter's experience in the Trophonium is described by Plutarch in *The Daimonion of Socrates*.[135] This is a fascinating account of the communication of a young man named Timarchus, who spent two nights and a day in the cave, in a world beyond normal experience. Either asleep or in trance, Timarchus' soul flew above an ocean with shining isles, and in a mixture of joyfulness and awe he heard voices that explained to him the mystery of metempsychosis and predicted his imminent death:

> He said that on descending into the oracular crypt his first experience was of profound darkness; next, after a prayer, he lay a long time not clearly aware whether he was awake or dreaming. It did seem to him, however, that at the same moment he heard a crash and was struck on the head, and that the sutures parted and released his soul. As it withdrew and mingled joyfully with air that was translucent and pure, it felt in the first place that now, after long being cramped, it had again found relief . . . ; and next it faintly caught the whir of something revolving overhead with a pleasant sound. . . . He saw islands illuminated by one another with soft fire, taking on now one colour, now another, like a dye. . . . All this he viewed with enjoyment of the spectacle. But looking down he saw a great abyss . . . most terrible and deep it was. . . . From it could be heard innumerable roars and groans of animals . . . the mingled lamentations of men and women, and noise and uproar of every kind. . . . After an interval someone he did not see addressed him: 'Timarchus, what would you have to explain?'
>
> 'Everything,' he answered. . . .
>
> 'Nay,' the voice relied, 'in the higher regions we others have but little part, as they belong to gods; but you may, if you wish, inquire into the portion of Persephone [the Netherworld], administrated by ourselves. . . . Of these matters . . . you will have better knowledge, young man, in the third month from now; for the present, depart.'
>
> . . . Once more [Timarchus] felt a sharp pain in his head, as though it had been violently compressed, and he lost all recognition and awareness of what was going on around him; but he presently recovered and saw that he was lying in the crypt of Trophonius near the entrance, at the very spot he had first laid himself down. . . . When he had come back to Athens and died in the third month, as the voice had foretold, we were amazed.[136]

For the purposes of the present discussion, Timarchus' historicity as a person is insignificant.[137] The most substantial inference from Plutarch's description is that an enquirer in the sanctuary of Trophonius lived through an out-of-body experience: lack of awareness of the surroundings, passage through darkness to translucent and pure light, flight over a magnificent country, visual and auditory hallucinations, a mixture of joyfulness and awe when he heard voices that explained to him the mystery of metempsychosis, and the final gift of clairvoyance which allowed the prediction of his imminent death. Unsurprisingly, Timarchus' altered state of consciousness was accompanied by culturally patterned visions, reflecting Greek religious and philosophical ideas, such as the mythical geography of the netherworld, as well as the notions of the soul, its liberty and need for purification.

The variance in the kind of hallucinations experienced in Trophonius' cave was known to Pausanias, who observed that different enquirers visiting the prophetic chamber learn the future in different ways, sometimes by sight and other times by hearing.[138] Much earlier, fifth- and fourth-century references to prophetic séances at the Trophonium include the opposition of memory and oblivion, independence of soul, and its levitation. It is therefore reasonable to assume that altered states of conscience were experienced in the Trophonium as early as in the fifth century.[139]

To achieve an altered state of consciousness, the suppliant did not need other influences in addition to his being alone in awe-inspiring surroundings, isolated from the world, its fresh air, light, sounds, human society, and other distractions.[140] Even if we assume that at the sanctuary of Trophonius enquirers who did not appear likely candidates for surrendering into a state of trance were segregated at preliminary ceremonies' stage, their number remained limited. Cases of alteration of consulters' consciousness and ensuing reports of divine revelations must have been common enough to allow institutions like this oracular centre to operate smoothly. The evidence on Trophonius' oracular shrine suggests that under similar conditions, namely cultic preparations, isolation inside a cave, and religious awe, ancient Greek consulters would have attained similar experiences and interpreted them in a similar way, as a revelation disclosed by the god.

A different method of manipulating the consciousness of consulters, who also believed that they received an oracular response from the gods, was practiced in a cave sacred to Charon at Acharaca,[141] the most famous among several caves emitting mephitic gases and located along the Meander valley in Asia Minor.[142] Sick people were brought to the Charonium and left on their own and without food for many days, 'like (animals) in a den.' In certain cases, the diseased themselves were blessed with visions sent by the gods, and heeded to their prescriptions, or the priests slept in the Charonium on behalf of the suppliants, and through dreams learnt their cure. The place was forbidden and deadly to everybody but the sick and the priests. The enquirers usually received guidance from the priests, who initiated them into the mysteries. Acharaca was also the site of an annual festival: in a nocturnal ceremony, the participants could see and hear 'all these things,' and at noon nude boys and young men would lead a bull into the cave and leave it there to die.

A medical oracle (*iatromanteion*) seems to have been situated at Acharaca, where at least some of the enquirers seeking cures experienced direct contact with the divinity, obviously in a state of delusion brought on by the poisonous gas, the frightening surroundings and the long fast, and enhanced by their malady. Presumably all the sick were initiated into the mysteries, which were also celebrated in the annual nocturnal rite.[143]

Numerous other medical oracles, first and foremost of Asclepius, but also of Amphiaraus and other deities, were based on incubation: the consultant saw the healer god or hero in a dream.[144] We can only guess how the encounters with the dead at the oracles of the dead at Taenarum, Heracleia Pontica, and Acheron were envisaged, but the possibility of incubation there cannot be excluded.[145] Thus, direct encounters between mortals and immortals in oracular sanctuaries did not always require that the consulter undergo a full-fledged alteration of consciousness, and mere sleep was often deemed to suffice.

However, genuine alterations of consciousness are amply attested to, and must have occurred to dozens, if not hundreds, of enquirers. Even if not dubbed as *mania* in antiquity, they doubtlessly belong to the same realm. Ordinary people could attain visions interpreted as instructions from the gods either during encounters with divine beings in their established sanctuaries, or in other locations, mostly in places considered numinous, such as caves and thick forests.[146] One such experience is attested to by an inscription left in the Corycian cave, a seat of a lot oracle, by a simple woman who 'heard the nymphs and Pan,'[147] that is, experienced auditory hallucinations. We will never know, of course, how many similar numinous experiences have not been commemorated in writing. In any case, visions thus attained were highly valued and left a profound impact – I will return to imagined encounters with the nymphs in Chapter 5. In the antiquity, communications prompted by such uncanny encounters were considered divinely inspired prophecy; nowadays these experiences cannot be regarded otherwise than alterations of consciousness.

It is noteworthy that at the Trophonium and at the Acharaca cave, achievement of oracular visions was associated with initiatory elements, and the conditions created for the enquirers were essentially an enhanced – i.e. tougher – version of the complex of ritual requirements, environment and triggers that drove oracular priests in established prophetic centres to their *enthousiasmos*. Elaborate preparations and allusions to a journey to the netherworld, or initial sickness and poisonous gases, in addition to a long solitary sojourn in an underground space, were the 'heavy artillery' which was employed in order to enable unexperienced laymen to achieve altered states of consciousness – in an apparent contrast to cult officials who needed gentler mechanisms to attain similar results. The reason for this disparity ensues from the fact that an experienced and trained person can manipulate his or her consciousness in a more efficient fashion: professional mediums from Delphi, Claros, and other sanctuaries needed much less in terms of environment, duration of the session, and driving factors. In addition, exposure to the strain of the oracular trance was bad enough to strip a person of the ability to laugh; such an awesome experience could be afforded once in a lifetime or very rarely. Like modern exceptionally efficient and dangerous medical proceedings that cannot be administered often, the extreme conditions of the Trophonium or

Acharaca provided assured results, but could not be imposed upon people who had to attain prophetic visions on a regular basis.

In summary, laymen – at least some of them – could achieve one or more episodes of prophetic *mania*, which were significant enough to be commemorated in inscriptions, and discussed by later writers with no less awe than utterings of prophetic priests. This arrangement, allowing rank-and-file people of both sexes a possibility of a publicly acknowledged and esteemed direct encounter with the divine in an institutionalised context, with a restricted and optional correction of their accounts by the priests of the cult, is another form of social accommodation of the powerful preference for ecstatic communication with the gods. This urge could not be blocked – and alongside oracular centres focused on professional mediumship, sanctuaries where laypeople received prophetic responses throve due to the fact that they provided conditions for personal direct contact between the enquirer and the deity, by means of inducing visions and apparitions.

Unaffiliated seers

In contrast to prophetic priests, seers were much more independent. They could be itinerant or live permanently in a certain place, consider a certain god their patron *par excellence* or be entirely self-reliant: the only characteristic many of them shared was a certain eccentricity of behaviour. Self- or god-chosen, they knew the future, the hidden past and the present, and – most importantly – received this knowledge from the gods in the state of possession, defined in ancient sources as *enthousiasmos* or *mania*.

Among Greek legendary seers, the Sibyl is the most intriguing figure.[148] The earliest appearance of the Sibyl in Greek literature is thrilling. She is introduced dramatically in a fragment of Heraclitus, cited by Plutarch: 'The Sibyl, uttering with mad mouth cheerless, unembellished, unperfumed words, reaches to a thousand years with her voice given by the god.'[149]

This is the core of the prophetess' personality. The Sybil is inspired by the god to whom her voice belongs, which makes her mouth 'mad.' The Sibyl's madness indicates that the utterances are delivered in a state of prophetic trance. The application of the participle *mainomenos* to the description of the Sybil is very significant: while the Pythia's inspiration had not been explicitly called *mania* before Plato, Heraclitus' phrase dates the association of prophecy with *mania* to the late sixth–early fifth century.[150] It also proves that prophetic *mania* was not Plato's invention.

While Sibylline prophecies are also attested to on Samos in the late eighth–early seventh centuries,[151] the origin of the word 'sibyl' remains obscure.[152] In the sixth and the fifth centuries, the Sibyl is referred to in the singular.[153] Multiple Sibyls make their appearance in the fourth century BC,[154] numbering as many as ten in the first century.[155] The problem of the early Sibyl's historicity is insoluble,[156] and the lack of clarity as to whether she really lived does not affect the appreciation of the Sibyl as a type of prophetic figure, an image that was created in the cultural context of the Archaic period, most probably in west Asia Minor.[157]

Collections of Sibylline oracles are reported in the fifth century at the latest, and perhaps a century earlier: by the sixth century the tradition has already arrived in Italy.[158] Attempts to systematise the increasing number of these books and their wide circulation may explain the splitting of one Sibyl into several entities.[159]

The Sibyl's lifestyle as itinerant prophet was not unknown in Archaic Greece, where purifiers, prophets, bards, and healers wandered from city to city.[160] Pausanias reports that the first Sibyl made her proclamations in the state of *mania*, seized by Apollo.[161] The words of Heraclitus' Sibyl are unpolished and her predictions gloomy. They encompass inconceivably long periods, stretching into the distant future: it is quite possible that Heraclitus was already familiar with the collections of Sibylline oracles, predicting faraway events.[162] The Sibyl's prophecies were spontaneous and unsolicited: we never hear about enquirers posing questions to the Sibyl, and receiving responses.[163] Unlike the Pythia who was the mouthpiece of the god and spoke as if she were Apollo, the Sibyl preserved her personality and sometimes even addressed the god in her prophesies: 'She is essentially a clairvoyante rather than a medium.'[164] The early Sibyl emerges as an inspired prophetess, whose vatic talent is usually ascribed to her possession by Apollo.

Heraclitus' portrait of the Sibyl is almost identical to Aeschylus' description of Cassandra, tortured by her visions of the future, frantic when putting them in words.[165] Cassandra was a Trojan princess, whereas Marpessus in the Troad claimed to be the home of the first Sibyl.[166] Both Cassandra and the Sibyl were wooed by Apollo, but preferred to preserve their chastity. Like the Sibyl, who was granted longevity by Apollo, but denied eternal youth,[167] Cassandra also received a gift from him, but was denied the means to profit from it: she predicted the truth, but nobody believed her.[168]

In *Agamemnon*, she is constantly hovering between madness and divine inspiration. The chorus in the tragedy is aware of her 'prophetic glory.'[169] Though a slave, she still preserves 'the divine in her mind,'[170] and this divine vision comes from Apollo. Her powers are divine skills, her words inspired by the god.[171] However, when Cassandra begins to prophesy, the same chorus immediately becomes doubtful, and wonders whether her possession is indeed of divine nature, or she is simply frenzied.[172] Although the chorus eventually decides that she is truly possessed by a god, this god is an anonymous malicious daemon rather than the venerated Apollo.[173]

Cassandra is also portrayed as mad by Euripides. In the *Trojan Women*, the herald describes her plainly as 'out of her mind' and 'maenad.'[174] Cassandra herself and other characters realise that she is a 'bacchant of the maiden,' but her knowledge supposedly comes from Apollo, rather than Dionysus.[175] Uttering predictions of horrible future, Cassandra seems to her mother and the chorus out of her mind: what else could these women think, when the royal maiden, destined to become Agamemnon's concubine, rejoices in her wedding with the enemy.[176] However, contrary to the Trojan women, in her prophetic vision Cassandra is able to see the destruction of the hated house of Agamemnon, hence her preparation for the nuptials – in fact rape – is a celebration of self-sacrifice leading to the longed-for vengeance. In the *Trojan Women*, all of her visions contain truthful prophecies, but some seem to Hecuba and the other women to be no more than hallucinations. In contrast, in *Hecuba* Cassandra's divine inspiration is referred to unequivocally, when she is called 'inspired singer' and 'prophetic maenad.'[177] However, Cassandra only seems mad – when in reality she is constantly aware of the hidden future and behaves in accordance with her superior knowledge; her *mania* is god-given.

The myth of Cassandra reflects the widespread awareness of the perils of prophecy. Attributing to a clairvoyant women an inability to persuade and mad behaviour that is appallingly embarrassing,[178] the myth highlights the sorrows of the seer, which join the anguish of prophecy-giving. The destiny of an independent seer could be arduous, especially when the seer was female. This was perhaps one of the reasons for the gradual disappearance of unaffiliated seers from the records by the end of the Archaic period.

Cassandra's prophetic visions in *Agamemnon* are reminiscent of the revelation of the seer Theoclymenus in the *Odyssey*.[179] In the midst of a feast, after the entrance of Odysseus, when the insolent suitors were driven mad by Athena, Theoclymenus stood up and reported a complex auditory and visual apparition: he heard the suitors' moaning and saw their blood-stained bodies, blood flowing from the ceiling, and ghosts filling the space, which was gradually covered by darkness; having said that and being ridiculed as a madman, Theoclymenus left the palace, where the suitors went on debauching in their derangement. The seer's vision, horrible but sober, is juxtaposed with the insanity of suitors, who refuse to believe his prophecy: not only are they unable to perceive their own madness, but they misperceive Theoclymenus' uttering as words of a madman, while in reality he alone clearly sees the future. The contrast between the divine blessing of a pious seer with a truthful vision and the divine punishment of transgressors with horrible derangement is also emphasised in this episode. Thus, a seer could be regarded as a madman by his environment, especially if the environment was reluctant to accept the validity of predictions, and in some cases truthful prophecy was uttered by people who were in fact deranged.

As mentioned previously, mythological seers are sometimes portrayed as equally good in indirect and direct prophecy. For instance, Helenus 'the best of the ornithomancers' was also able to hear 'the voice of the gods.'[180] The insight of blind Tiresias is not only greater than that of other mortals – it is almost divine, 'most like . . . Apollo.'[181] Tiresias' descendants were endowed with talent for either direct or indirect divination: his daughter Manto was also famous for her inspired oracles and even called a Sybil. According to the written tradition, Manto's son Mopsus was an expert in ornithoscopy, but seems to have been regarded by the people of Mallos, a city that he founded, as capable in soul travelling and inspired insight, to judge by the coins where Mopsus is portrayed wearing wings and holding a mirror.[182] Melampous, the inventor of divination and an expert in extispicy, understood the language of animals, purified, cured, and founded a dynasty of seers.[183] His descendants, Theoclymenus and Amphiaraus, interpreted signs and predicted the future by divine inspiration.[184] Halitherses was both an ornitomancer ('knew the birds') and uttered mantic pronouncements.[185] Significantly,

Herodotus emphasises the contrast between the two gifts of Melampous, who acquired his mantic arts 'by himself,' while divination from sacrificed victims, in Herodotus' opinion, originated from abroad.[186]

Musaeus, a friend of Orpheus, not only prophesied, but also healed with his music[187] and was ascribed the ability to fly.[188] Abaris, a Hyperborean holy man, wandered all over the earth, possessed by the god (*entheos*), Apollo's arrow in his hand, curing sicknesses, purifying pestilence, and predicting earthquakes.[189] The invention of flying is sometimes attributed to Onomacritus, and the idea in general reflects the popular opinion that great ecstatics knew to fly, which was probably based on the accounts of out-of-body journeys in the state of altered consciousness by real-life seers.

Bacis, a Boeotian seer (*chrêsmologos*), was also credited with purifying the women of Sparta when they suffered an outbreak of madness.[190] Many of the Greek ecstatics were attributed written texts, either collections of prophecies, as Manto, Bacis, Euclus the Cyprian, and Lycus,[191] or poems, as Orpheus. Musaeus the *chrêsmologos* was believed to be the author of poems and books of prophecies.[192] The conjunction of prophetic, poetic, and telestic activities in the biographies of the Archaic quasi-historical seers indicates that at this stage, the three spheres had not yet been differentiated entirely: all types of super-human knowledge were deemed to emanate from the divine, and the mortals could approach the gods only when possessed by them, that is, in the state of *mania*. Another common feature of early Greek inspired seers is their aristocratic or even royal origin: Amphiaraus, Mopsus, Helenus, Cassandra, Calchas, Tiresias, Manto, and Theoclymenes were all high born.

The activities of some prophets seem to be attested historically.[193] Amphilytus (or Amphitrytus) the Acarnanian, who acted by 'providence of heaven' (*theia pompê*), is reported by Herodotus to have welcomed Peisistratus in a state of possession (*entheazôn*).[194] Evenius, a simple-minded man, allegedly blinded by the gods who bestowed on him the mantic gift, lived sometime in the late sixth century.[195] However, the greatest Greek seers are mythical or quasi-historical: the age of freelance *chrêsmologoi* ended with the Archaic period, and during the later times inspired prophecy was limited to oracular sanctuaries, whereas historical *chrêsmologoi* collected and published oracles pronounced in the past. Even in cases in which they forged new pronouncements, this principle did not change: they never dared to claim authorship of these creations.[196]

As a rule, seers maintained a special relationship with the source of their inspiration: for instance, the Sibyl, Cassandra, Melampous, Orpheus, and Abaris were endowed with their gift by Apollo, while Bacis prophesied when possessed by the nymphs in a cave sacred to them. The clairvoyants needed very few triggers in order to encompass the past, the present, and the future in their mind: their visions came spontaneously, unsuggested, unsolicited, and uncontrolled. Such freedom could barely be tolerated in a developed polis society, hence the images of a clairvoyant who was disbelieved (Cassandra) or naive (Evenius), and the tendency to appropriate their prophetic reputation by attributing to them collection of written predictions or associating their names with oracular sanctuaries.

Inspired prophets as instruments of the gods

To attain true knowledge in the state of god-sent *mania* is the greatest challenge, and the path to this knowledge is perilous and excruciating. Descriptions of divination séances as painful ordeals are found in the literatures of many cultures. The Greek and Roman accounts tell us of the exhaustion of the Pythia in Delphi, the frenzy of the Sibyl, and the health risks faced by the prophets at Claros, and they are joined by similar examples from beyond the Mediterranean world. In a Norse saga, a wise prophetess, who was posed two questions by the same person, says: 'I will not undergo this great strain again, for it has been of no small cost to me, and neither threads nor fair words will be of any avail.'[197] While these scenes can hardly be taken for candid descriptions of actual oracular practices, they convey their authors' ideas on ecstatic prophecy-giving. Even at present, the prophetic trance consumes all the energies of the medium known as the Kuden at the Nechung oracle in Tibet.[198]

Due to the anguish which it entailed, the inspired seer could not enter the state of *enthousiasmos* frequently. The proverb contrasting the accessibility of cleromancy and the exclusivity of inspired prophecy cited above[199] demonstrates that many Greeks took the distinction between the two modes of prophecy for granted. The same point is made in *On the Sign of Socrates* by Plutarch's Theocritus, himself a *mantis*[200] and therefore an expert on the subject:

> Homer, it is evident, knew the distinction of which we others speak, as he calls some diviners 'consultants of birds' and 'priests,' but thinks that others indicate the future from an understanding and awareness of the actual conversation of the gods. . . . So heaven consorts directly with but few, and rarely, but to the great majority gives signs, from which arises the art called divination (*mantikê*).[201]

Obtaining a response from a prophetic sanctuary was a troublesome and costly enterprise.[202] It was obviously much easier to look into a collection of oracles or inspect the entrails of sacrificial animals. Yet there was a clear tendency to seek divinely induced predictions at Delphi, Didyma, and other centres of ecstatic prophecy, whenever important issues had to be resolved. Even the anti-Athenian position, adopted by Delphi more than once, did not discourage Athenians from consulting the Pythia.[203] The consultants paid considerable sums for access to the Pythia, and left in Delphi precious dedications.[204] This preference for a kind of prophecy which was much more costly in material resources and human effort can be explained only if the obtained predictions were valued more highly. 'The less the human being participates in prophecy, the more divine it is,' to quote A. Piñero:[205] prophetic *mania* was treasured because it enabled messages to be transmitted directly from the gods.

Given the scant availability of direct prophecy, it is easy to understand the demand for indirect divination, especially by armies on the move, in situations when an immediate response was required: no army could wait for a seer to attain ecstasy and start to prophesy. Diviners accompanying military contingents often belonged to families of *manteis* and formed guilds, tracing their origins to mythical ancestors prominent in the same craft, similar to other intellectuals, such as physicians.[206] The engagement of many military seers in the regular aristocratic lifestyle[207] highlighted the profound difference between diviners and ecstatic prophets; the latter were often of humble origin and female, and their lifestyle could be secluded and peculiar in many respects.[208] In a word, diviners were professionals blessed with inborn talents and acquired skills, while the main distinction of ecstatics was to be chosen by the gods as their mouthpiece.[209]

A great gap separated diviners, whose aptitude was unlimited in time, from inspired seers, whose prophecy was directly initiated and sustained by the will of the gods at the very moment when the immortals used a human being as a mouthpiece. Plato has Socrates relate to this issue several times. In the *Apology*, Socrates maintains that the poets, like soothsayers (*chrêsmôdoi*) and seers of the divine (*theomanteis*), are driven by their nature and inspiration (*enthousiazontes*). In the *Meno*, he says the seers and soothsayers 'say many truthful things, but don't realise anything they say.'[210] In the *Ion*, in the middle of his discourse on poets who can create only when inspired by the Muse (to which I return in Chapter 6), Socrates compares poetry to prophecy:

> And for this reason God takes away the mind of these men [poets] and uses them as his ministers, just as he does soothsayers and godly seers, in order that we who hear them may know that it is not they who utter these words of great price, when they are out of their wits, but that it is God himself who speaks and addresses us through them.[211]

In this respect, Xenophon's position was very similar. Writing on Socrates' *daimonion*, 'divine sign,'[212] he states that in order to get a counsel from the god, most people needed such instruments as birds or sacrifices, whereas Socrates perceived the divine guidance directly, by means of his *daimonion*. Xenophon's point is that the god was using Socrates in the same way as he used 'birds, utterances, coincidences, and sacrifices':[213] all these were instruments by means of which the god communicated his will.

Aristotle adhered to this view. In the *Eudemian Ethics*, discussing involuntary acts, caused by overpowering motives, he observes:

> On this account also in the case of persons who are inspired (*enthousiôntes*) and utter prophecies (*prolegontes*), although they perform an act of thought, nevertheless we do not say that saying what they said and doing what they did rested with themselves.[214]

Several centuries later Plutarch compared the soul of the Pythia to a musical instrument, which produced music through interaction between its own nature and an exterior force, and emphasised the communication between the Pythia's soul and the external (divine) force in the process of prophecy-giving.[215] This contact is envisioned as a whirl created by two movements, one imparted by the god and the other one by the soul of the priestess.[216] Concerning the Pythia's *enthousiasmos*, Plutarch gives the following definition:

> The voice is not that of the god, not the utterance of it, nor the diction, nor the metre, but all these are the woman's; he puts into her mind only the visions (*phantasiai*), and creates the light in her soul in regard to the future; for inspiration (*enthousiasmos*) is precisely this.[217]

Dio Chrysostom agrees with this view of the Pythia: she merely translates the divine message, being a medium or transmitter.[218] Iamblichus takes this idea even further, and groups together all the intermediate instruments sent forth by the gods to mortals in order to guide them, inanimate objects as well as human seers:

> For if this divine power extends in its predictions to inanimate objects, such as little pebbles, rods, or certain woods . . . it gives life to inanimate things and motion to things motionless, and makes all clear, knowledgeable, and participating in reason . . . and yet having no reason in themselves. . . . And just as he makes some simple-minded human being utter statements full of wisdom, by which it becomes clear to all that this is not some human but a divine accomplishment, so through beings deprived of knowledge he reveals thoughts which surpass all knowledge. At the same time, the god manifests to humans that the signs shown are worth of credence, and that they are superior to nature, and god is exalted above it.[219]

Elsewhere, Iamblichus plainly says that the god uses the prophet at Claros 'as an instrument.'[220] In his view, the divine is primarily responsible for the oracular message, but the medium must be properly prepared and pure in order to serve as an instrument of the gods.[221]

Plutarch's idea that the Pythia's soul possessed the inborn ability to prophesy probably reflects the Platonic perception, which was also adopted by later philosophers, such as Aristotle and the Stoics,[222] of souls acquiring this ability in certain states, such as sleep or imminent death; Iamblichus' thought combined Neoplatonism with theurgy;[223] both Iamblichus and Plutarch may have been influenced by Plato's statements in the *Apology, Meno* and elsewhere; and both Plato and Xenophon were disciples of Socrates. All that does not change the fact that for these thinkers, an inspired seer was an instrument used by the gods, more akin to a bird directed by the divine will than to an interpreter of its flight. In their opinion, inspired prophecy emanated from the gods directly, the seer being a divine instrument, while interpretation of signs involved human explanation of actions of divine instruments (such as birds, prodigies, etc.).[224] Indirect or artful methods of prophecy introduced an additional stage, an agent separating the divine from the human.

Homer is the earliest source of evidence that direct contact with the gods was considered as superior to interpretation of signs. For instance, Priam assures Hecabe that if they were advised to ransom Hector's body by mortals,

> seers divining from sacrifices or priests, we would consider it false and turn away from it still more; but now that I heard the goddess myself and I looked at her, I will go, and her word will not be wasted.[225]

Priam's words affirm that in Homer's time, the difference between direct and indirect prophecy was extremely important from the enquirer's point of view.[226] Unmediated contact with a god, in a dream or when awake, is quite common in the Homeric epos;[227] in addition, seers, such as Helenus, and other characters refer to insights that come straight from the gods, and firmly believe that they are truthful. Thus, Helen says in the Odyssey: 'Hear me, I will prophesy (*manteusomai*) as the immortals put it into my heart (*thumos*), and I think it will be brought to pass.'[228] More than two hundred years after Homer, and a hundred years before Plato, Aeschylus has the Pythia say: 'I prophesy in a way that the god leads me.'[229] Consequently, the idea of the supremacy of direct communication from the gods, appearing as early as in Homer, cannot be dismissed as an ideologically prompted Platonic invention.[230]

Furthermore, these views are congruent with the position of other cultures on spirit mediums and possession. The anthropologist E. Cohen suggests 'the displacement principle' in the perception of possession: 'whatever the case may be, at any moment, there is only one intentional agency represented – one mind and not two.'[231] Following this logic, in ancient Greece, as long as a prophetic individual was possessed by a deity, it was the deity's mind – rather than the mortal's – that was considered to be active. Thus, the Greek point of view makes sense in terms of the 'default cognitive mechanism' of prophecy-giving: a person whose mind was perceived to be invaded by an external supernatural agent was considered superior to the intellectual capacity of any human, limited by definition. However, the human and divine components were not completely isolated, the human medium had to be worthy of serving as an instrument of the gods, and the interpreter had to decipher divine signs.

Inspired prophecy in Greece as compared to other cultures

Inspired prophecy was comparatively rare in the ancient Mediterranean. In the ancient Near East, the usual method of learning the gods' will was by deciphering the language of signs, most commonly extispicy or haruspicy, divination by reading of the entrails of sacrificial animals.[232] In pharaonic Egypt, direct prophecy did not exist: deities announced their will by movements, to be interpreted and recorded by the priests.[233] In Italy, imported oracles, mostly of Greek origin, were based on divine inspiration, while the normal indigenous mode of divination was by lots.[234] Roman traditional divination was based on the taking of the auspices, interpretation of prodigies, and extispicy.[235] As for the Etruscans, prophetic figures were prominent in their mythical past, but absent from real-life divinatory practices.[236] Thus, although direct communication with the gods through mediums, or through visions and dream-visions, is known in the Near East, in Mesopotamia (Old Babylonian and Neo-Assyrian texts to be discussed below), in the Syro-Phoenician area,[237] as well as in Anatolia (Hittites),[238] it seems to have played a minor role in these civilisations.[239] In ancient Israel, in contrast to other Near Eastern cultures, inspired prophecy was prominent.[240] In the modern world, examples of divinatory trance are known in Africa and Asia, in Cameroon (Mofu), and in Tibet.[241]

Prophecy in Mesopotamia in comparison with Greece

There are some exceptions to the rule stating that ecstatic prophecy in the ancient Near East was no more than incidental. In Mesopotamia, these exceptions are recorded on approximately sixty tablets, dated ca. 1800–1750 BC, discovered at Mari,[242] in addition to several dozen texts from Assyria, dated a millennium later.[243]

Prophetic pronouncements were given by cult officials and laypeople, some of them spontaneously and others as responses to queries. Among the diviners were both women and men. Some prophetic figured are dubbed *āpilums*, 'respondents,' while others are *muhhūms*, 'ecstatics.'[244] 'The informal acquiring of the word of god' is rare in Mesopotamia, and the Mari practices are the earliest manifestation of inspired prophecy in the Near East.[245] Alongside the direct prophecy, traditional methods of divination by signs continued to flourish, and played a main role in the prediction of the future.[246] Divination was also used to control the veracity of prophetic oracles: in order to represent the mediums during the authenticating of the uttering, their hair or hem were sometimes attached to tablets containing the oracle.[247]

Mari tablets attest to three main modes of inspired prophecy. Some prophetic figures were honoured by an oracular visitation of a deity in unspecified places. Several individuals among them were designated as either *muhhūm* or *āpilum*,[248] whereas others seem to be laypeople. Some of them moved from town to town;[249] in certain cases mediums were undoubtedly laymen, even married women.[250] Several tablets mention their names, indicate their connection to a particular deity and the fact that they received a payment or gift from the court, occasionally specifying that these were awards for oracles delivered.[251] The messages, received in a state of trance or in dream, were coherent and could later be reported in articulate texts.

Many laypersons received messages from the gods in the temples, in various ways, including dreams,[252] later reporting their visions to the king.[253] This mode of contact with the deity closely resembles that of the enquirers in the Greek oracular centres.

Finally, some respondents of both sexes were temple officials who recounted their oracular visions. They did not receive divine messages in dreams, and in most cases *āpilum* replied to questions put to the deities.[254] Other temple officials were occasionally reported to receive prophetic messages, for instance, transvestite or eunuch functionaries called *assinnum*.[255] It is noteworthy that the behaviour of ecstatics, even those participating in elaborate ceremonies performed in temples, was unpredictable. Two texts describing rituals in the temple of Ishtar allow for two possibilities: either that male and female *muhhūms* remained sane, or that they entered a state of frenzy and prophesied.[256]

We do not know much of the background and personal qualities of Mari prophets, but some details indicate that their behaviour was considered bizarre. At least one category of mediums is described as 'madmen' or 'ecstatics.' Their trances presumably did not affect their ability to speak coherently – or to be interpreted by scribes. In one case, a *muhhūm* of Dagan devoured a lamb raw, and later described his act as a sign of pestilence.[257] Androgynous *assinnum* differed from general population by definition, but Mari texts provide no detailed references to their function and behaviour.[258] All the mediums, both cultic personnel and laypersons, seem to have played peripheral roles in the society and cult, but in some cases received remuneration from higher social groups.[259]

The Mari texts attest to a situation that in many respects is broadly congruent to the Greek modes of direct prophecy. Divinely inspired mediums at Mari were male and female, and they acted in three kinds of setting: as cult officials in temples, as people associated with a particular god who received a divine message, or as laypersons visited by a deity in temples or elsewhere. In some sanctuaries the god's communication could be received by more than one category of mediums. Several gods used ecstatic mediums, both *muhhūms* and *āpilums*, as their mouthpieces, most often the god Dagan and the goddess Annunitum, a manifestation of the warrior aspect of Ishtar.[260] Mediums, including laypeople, usually received messages pertaining to the king and the state, rather than to themselves – though this information may be biased by the nature of our sources, which are records of oracles reported to the king. These oracles refer to the material, military, and political affairs of the king, as well as his personal safety. The prophecy is reported to have been given to the medium directly, implying immediate contact between the deity and the mortal.

Mari prophecy records are usually compared with the Old Testament.[261] As a corpus, they appear to have much less in common with the Old Testament prophecy,[262] independent from the temple worship, than with the world of ancient Greek prophecy. The similarity between the three modes of inspired prophecy-giving in Greece and in Mari is remarkable. Furthermore, the subjects of the Mari vatic utterings were earthly concerns, both political and everyday matters. This is characteristic of Greek oracles, in contrast to the ancient Israelite prophecy with its socio-ethical emphasis.[263]

Ecstatic prophecy in Greece and at Mari differs in several respects. Contrary to the Greek practice of ambiguous utterances, Mari texts are never obscure, though this is perhaps due to editing by scribes. Most experts regard direct divination at Mari as peripheral in comparison to the traditional divination by signs, whereas in Greece the correlation was reverse.

Before the discoveries at Mari, the Greek culture was unique in its liberal recognition of cult officials, freelance seers and laypeople as legitimate mediums. The

Mari tablets demonstrate that in this respect the Greeks were not alone in the Mediterranean-Near Eastern *oikoumene*. I would like to stress that I am not assuming derivation of any kind, either by the Greeks from Mari or by both from some third party: it was structural, rather than genetic proximity.[264]

Neo-Assyrian words for 'prophet' were *mahhû*, meaning 'mad' or 'frenzied,' and *raggimu*, deriving from 'to cry, to proclaim.' Several texts explicitly indicate that persons described as *mahhû* or *raggimu* transmitted divine words while in a state of frenzy. Ecstatic prophets could be male, female or transgender, and many were affiliated with the worship of Ishtar.[265] As in Mari, the behaviour of ecstatics in Assyria was unpredictable: a *raggimu* could 'lack a vision' and be unfit to perform.[266]

Ecstatic prophecy, a precious commodity dependent on the will of the gods, was open-ended and hard to manipulate. In contrast, inductive divination was performed by scholars, representing a long tradition of expert erudition.[267] M. Nissinen highlights the difference between rational interpretation of signs by male intellectuals, and ecstatic prophets, mainly women, acting as direct mouthpieces of gods and never writing themselves: 'in Assyria, the roles of scholar and prophet are not interchangeable. The inductive and non-inductive methods of divination never mixed.'[268] It is evident why soothsaying by indirect methods was preferred: it was more available, relatively easy to control and did not require the extraordinary states of consciousness indispensable for ecstatic prophecy. Small wonder that most experts consider direct divination at Mari and in Assyria to have been peripheral to the traditional divination by signs: it is the situation in Greece, where the reverse was true, that calls for explanation.

Prophecy in ancient Israel in comparison with Greece

In Israel of the monarchical period (ca. 1000–586),[269] the tradition of inspired prophecy played a unique role. For those used to the study of ancient Greek prophecy, the Old Testament tradition is fascinating, because it is rich in descriptions and details lacking in Greek literature. As a result, the Old Testament allows a glimpse into the experience of an ancient inspired prophet, filling in the gaps left by the meagre bits and pieces we can find in the Greek evidence on the activities of unaffiliated seers. Following is a brief overview of several aspects of the Old Testament prophecy, to be compared with the activities of Greek seers.

The key to the discussion of the modalities of prophetic experience in ancient Israel is a verse in 1 *Samuel* 28. 6: 'And when Saul inquired of the Lord, the Lord did not answer him, either by dreams, or by Urim, or by prophets,'[270] Thus, in ancient Israel there were three customary ways to learn the god's will: by signs,[271] by dreams that the heavenly beings may send to anyone, or by utterings of god-inspired prophets.[272]

The *Urim and Thummim* was a priestly form of divination, witnessed during the early monarchy.[273] These objects, kept inside the priest's garment (*ephod*),[274] are never described in detail. The majority opinion is that they were used as lots, giving binary responses.[275]

Dreams were considered an important channel used by the god to announce his will to the mortals of all walks of life.[276] Perhaps this is the reason why dreams were considered inferior to pronouncements by prophets. Although *Deuteronomy* does not discriminate between dreams and prophecies as means of communication with the heavenly forces, Jeremiah puts forward the following claim: 'Let the prophet who has a dream tell the dream, but let him who has my word speak my word faithfully. What has straw in common with wheat? says the Lord.'[277]

Finally, there were prophets. Before we discuss their activities, I would like to stop for a moment and compare – in most general lines – between the modes of Old Testament divination, on the one hand, and the divination at Mari and in Greece, on the other hand. Indirect divination based on interpretation of signs thrived in all these cultures. Hebrew prophets acted alongside or in competition with prophets of pagan gods, such as Baal and Asherah.[278] However, at Mari and in Greece gods' pronouncements were also revealed in temples – by inspired temple officials or even by laymen. In ancient Israel, a prophet was usually independent of the temple. Some (exceptional) prophets were of priestly origin, yet even their prophecy was not reliant on the temple.[279] Thus, out of the three modes of inspired prophecy known at Mari and in Greece, only one, that of independent seers, was practiced in Israel.

The Old Testament prophet (*nabi'*) or seer (*hozeh*)[280] is an intermediary between the human and divine worlds. The intermediary is sometimes called a 'man of god' and described as a 'dreamer of dreams.' The experience is usually referred to as a 'vision,' even when it comprises speech, and is clearly auditory.[281] It is noteworthy that this ability is attested to not only by the text of the Bible, heavily edited during the post-exilic period, but also by an inscription discovered at Deir Alla in Jordan, datable to 840–760, which states in its first line that the pagan prophet Balaam, known from the Biblical tradition, was a 'seer of the gods.'[282] The revelation could include mental pictures of the future, or sights of the other world, such as encounters with divine councils, heavenly armies and awesome god-sent apparitions. Historically, most experts differentiate between Moses, the early prophets, such as Samuel, Elijah, and Elisha, and the classical prophets, such as Jeremiah and Ezekiel. The divergences between Hebrew and pagan prophets, and between true and false prophets, are also very important.[283] Female prophets were exceptional, but seem to perform in the same manner as male seers.[284] Israelite prophets resemble Greek seers, and especially the Sibyl, in several respects: they were also repeatedly depicted as wanderers, their prophecy was unsolicited, and they received the god's messages irrespective of their own will.[285]

Revelation is often ascribed to the 'hand of Yahweh' or 'spirit of Yahweh' coming upon the prophet, which clearly indicates possession by Yahweh. In many cases the text only states that a certain message is 'the word of Yahweh,'[286] and the idea that the god uses the prophet as his mouthpiece is apparent.[287] Yahweh charges the prophet with a message: the wish of the prophet to speak or of the audience to listen is irrelevant.[288] One wonders whether the subjective feeling of being 'seized' by a god (being *theolêptos* or *katochos*), often attributed to Greek seers, is a way to refer to the same experience which is described in Hebrew as 'Yahweh's hand pressed hard on me' or simply 'was on me.'[289]

Only to Moses did the god speak clearly and face to face, whereas other prophets, beginning with Miriam who dared to claim equality with Moses, received vague messages by means of visions or dreams.[290] Prophetic utterings of Greek seers were notoriously obscure: the ambiguity of ecstatic prophecy seems to be its universal characteristic.

In the Deuteronomic tradition, the Mosaic prophetic mediator (such as Samuel and Elijah) was the only accepted intermediary between Israel and its god.[291] The message could be a reply to an inquiry – common people and kings came to prophets to seek the word of Yahweh, – or an unsolicited oracle delivered by the divine inspiration.[292] The idea of annulation of the mental abilities of the prophet, who becomes a mere instrument used by the deity to communicate his message, is central to Hebrew prophecy and emphasised no less than in Greece; this idea was later adopted by the Christian apologetic.[293]

The revelatory trance of 'men of god' could be spontaneous and uncontrolled or deliberately induced by various methods, such as rhythmical music, dancing, and even the use of hallucinogens.[294] In many cases, the seer's trance is clearly referred to. For instance, Balaam is described as 'falling down' while prophesying: he 'who hears the words of God, and knows the knowledge of the Most High, who sees the vision of the Almighty, falling down, but having his eyes uncovered.'[295]

The oracles were normally given in the form of oral poetry, and while they were written down later and edited during the subsequent centuries, these texts doubtlessly reflect historical reality.[296] Prophetic messages are often rendered in a rather stereotypical language, which may ensue either from the distinctive vocabulary of the prophets or from later editing.[297] Sometimes the urge to preserve a revelation forever is ascribed to the god: a prophet may claim that Yahweh himself commanded him to write down a prophecy.[298] Some prophets recited laments and sang on various subjects.[299] The association of prophecy and poetry and attribution of written texts to seers are prominent in Greece, as well.

Receiving the divine message and uttering prophecy could be both a joy and a torture. Jeremiah said that 'Thy words were found, and I ate them, and thy words became to me a joy and the delight of my heart,' but also 'My anguish, my anguish! I writhe in pain! Oh, the walls of my heart! My heart is beating wildly; I cannot keep silent; for I hear the sound of the trumpet, the alarm of war.'[300] Cassandra's agony in *Agamemnon*[301] and the Sybil's compulsion to speak[302] are reminiscent of the suffering (which can be as sweet as honey) of Jeremiah and Ezekiel.

Such figures as Samuel, Elijah, and Elisha combined the characteristics of sages, sorcerers, medicine men, and seers. They multiplied oil, flour, and other substances, called fire or water from the heaven, purified lands, healed leprosy, and performed the supreme feat of resurrecting the dead.[303] Isaiah caused the sun go back ten grades on the sun dial.[304] Elijah's demise was no less miraculous than his life: he was taken to the heaven by a fiery whirlwind.[305] It seems that some prophets were capable of reaching out-of-body states at will: Elisha followed his servant in spirit form, and Ezekiel was seized by a spirit and carried away.[306] These personages are classified as belonging to the 'shamanistic type,'[307] exactly like the Greek Archaic sages, such as Hermotimus and Aristeas, who travelled in spirit to remote lands, and Abaris who cured pestilences and droughts, moved by a magic means of transportation, performed miracles, and prophesied. Once again, we are talking about generic rather than genetic proximity: neither the Greek nor Hebrew ecstatics had to import techniques of manipulation of consciousness from abroad, but rather freely developed their natural inclinations.

Groups of ecstatics, known as 'sons of the prophets' or 'bands of prophets' worshipping Yahweh or Baal and pagan gods, experienced collective alterations of consciousness and are reported to number hundreds. They could sometimes even live together,[308] but normally the seer attained illumination individually. The behaviour of many seers was so manifestly abnormal, that hostile sources branded them as 'mad.'[309] This divergence from the custom could often follow stereotypical behaviour patterns, reflecting social expectations from an inspired prophet, who was both venerated and feared.[310]

In the Old Testament, the verb 'to prophecy' has an additional meaning 'to rage,' 'to be deranged.'[311] The Greeks were hesitant to determine whether Cassandra was mad or inspired,[312] and this ambiguity seems to lurk in the background constantly, in cases of ordinary people facing the awesome phenomenon of ecstatic prophecy. Furthermore, it was often very convenient to claim that a madman pronounced a disturbing prediction, rather than a divinely inspired prophet.

While the deeds of the Old Testament prophets were deemed worthy of record, their subjective experiences usually remain concealed. We are fortunate to have detailed accounts of Ezekiel's multiple harrowing visions of unearthly force, among them the overwhelming experience described in minor detail.[313] The prophet is entirely overpowered by the god, whose speech is divinely commanded; in fact, some scholars regard him as 'the god's marionette.'[314] The book of *Ezekiel* provides a formidable account of a complex multi-stage experience, which comprises visual, auditory, tactile, gustatory, and kinaesthetic hallucinations.[315] It starts as an apparition of a fiery vortex, consisting of winged man-like burning creatures that are elsewhere defined as cherubs.[316] The vision is accompanied by the noise of their wings, and it grows into the magnificent picture of the Lord enthroned and talking to the prophet. This tremendous encounter leads Ezekiel to the next stage of his experience, the feeling that the spirit entered him. Overridden with awe, he falls prostrated before the god, but the spirit supported him from the inside, forcing him to stand up and heed to the words of the god. At this stage, two more feelings became involved in the hallucination: Ezekiel not only sees the scroll given by the god, but feels its touch and sweet taste in his mouth. Until this moment, the prophet felt that he remained in the same place where his experience started. Then suddenly the spirit lifted him into the air, and he sensed himself flying, the fiery creatures surrounding him. After the return from his flight, Ezekiel remained torpid for seven days. Ezekiel's intricate experience comprises hallucinations involving all his senses, or perhaps synaesthesia with one sensation altering into another, as well as possession by a spirit and an out-of-body flight. No wonder that this exquisite passage inspired Jewish mystics ever since.[317] This description is unique not only in ancient Israel, but in the entire ancient world. Obviously, alterations of consciousness as profound as Ezekiel's were exceptional, but they are likely to have been present, usually in less intense form, in all the prophetic experiences.

Conclusions

In Greece, unaffiliated 'impresarios of the gods' were less limited by cultic traditions and autonomous in many of their choices. In contrast, prophetic priests in institutionalised centres were usually selected by the authorities and had to abide to a strict code of behaviour. Finally, enquirers in the oracles based on direct encounter with the divine had to respect the rules of the shrine and prepare for the awesome experience according to custom, but almost everyone could apply. Due to the accessibility of these oracular centres, many Greeks of both sexes either lived through or witnessed prophetic *mania* ensuing from direct contact with a deity, at least once in their lifetime.

From the point of view of the diviner, indirect divination required technical knowledge, sensitivity to the social environment, and astuteness, qualities that are inborn or acquired by the seer and may be retained throughout his or her life. In contrast, inspired prophecy involved not only a general predisposition, but also the ability to induce vatic trance spontaneously or upon request, and endure its strain – an ability not entirely controllable even by experienced ecstatics. Lifestyles of ecstatic prophets were usually abnormal, contrary to that of diviners by signs, who adhered to social norms.[318] Preparations for a session of direct and indirect divination were completely different. Most significant disparity was between mental states of inspired and artful diviners: the latter were sober and their normal personality unchanged, while the former's condition was anomalous. This abnormality was perceived both subjectively and objectively: an ecstatic diviner felt led or possessed by an outside power and in many cases was oblivious of his or her behaviour and speech during a prophetic séance or a fit of clairvoyance. Those observing this individual could clearly see that only the outer shell remained the same, while other elements of the personality, such as the contents of speech, even the voice, manner of movement, and facial expression, changed dramatically. These characteristics of alteration of consciousness, as we have seen, are conditioned by neuropsychological mechanisms and therefore cross-cultural. It is therefore not surprising that in various cultures such individuals were considered instruments used by higher powers: the 'other,' prophetic personality was visibly animated by a source different from one's regular human nature. Furthermore, encounters with these phenomena were overwhelming and produced a numinous sensation of divine presence, both in the prophetic individual and in his or her community.

Turning to the point of view of the public, technical divination was accessible: extispicy could be performed anywhere and other methods were also almost always at hand. Indirect divination could be controlled, even though with some effort.[319] In contrast, the mere fact of ecstatic prophecy-giving was not guaranteed, and obtaining the right to seek a god's advice in an oracular centre consumed much time, energy, and resources. Finally and most significantly, the result of the endeavour was open-ended. All these troubles were endured because direct prophecy came from a different level than the indirect divination: the latter was a product of human mind, whereas the former came from the gods, an ultimate source of authority. Since during the Archaic and Classical periods cities and individuals sought oracles in order to 'obtain certainty in an uncertain world,'[320] due to the belief in its divine source, direct prophecy was a far more forceful factor in the social life of individuals and communities: divine inspiration was passed over to the community, and an inspired prophet was a better provider of assurance and self-confidence.

Connections between cultures brought about a diffusion of various techniques of deductive divination, arts that were to be learnt, from the Near East to Greece.[321] However, in the case of alteration of consciousness, we don't need to look for proof of diffusion in order to account for similar phenomena: these phenomena were and remain cross-cultural, and are present in almost every culture around the globe.[322] The typological proximity I suggest allows two corollaries. First, descriptions of the behaviour of Old Testament prophets open a possibility of cautious reconstruction of the experiences of Greek seers, or the ideas of their contemporaries and later generations about activities appropriate to seers. Second and most important, the question to be asked is why was ecstatic prophecy highly appreciated in some cultures and considered a supplementary way of divination in others. According to extant sources, most ancient cultures preferred divination by signs, for an apparent reason: it could be controlled[323] and did not impose much physical strain on the diviner. Only two cultures, ancient Israel during pre-exilic period[324] and Greece throughout its history, put an emphasis on inspired divinations. In Israel, prophecy was uttered by independent seers only; in Greece, the age of such seers ended with the Archaic period, and in later times mediums acquired indications of divine will mostly in temples.

My attempt at interpretation is tentative and schematic, for it is supposed to account for a broad picture. Prophecy is a social phenomenon, so attempts at its comprehension are bound to be based on interpretation of its social context, which includes the involvement of the audience in the acts of prophecy-giving.[325] Inspired prophecy is also a neuropsychological phenomenon, ensuing from the human predisposition toward alteration of consciousness. In order to construe ecstatic prophecy, we are to be aware of the interaction between the social and the biological. Hallucinations and visions are ubiquitous and common to all the human societies; they produce the feeling of coming from the outside, hence invite attribution to an external supernatural agent. These revelations, hunches or intuitions are exciting and awe-inspiring, but their human source may be humble, look abnormal or outlandish, and the entire phenomenon is difficult to manage and control. The most natural way to overcome the difficulty is to suppress ecstatic soothsaying and boost society's vigour and stamina by means of artful technical divination, and this solution was adopted by most ancient Mediterranean societies. The more rigid and ubiquitous the state and/or priestly authority, the less place is left for open-ended ecstatic prophecy. There is a good reason for that. To cite T. Overholt, an expert on cross-cultural studies of prophecy: 'The people choose their prophets.'[326] In order to be able to do that, considerable segments of society must enjoy enough liberty for their opinion on the revelations of the prophet to matter. Moreover, prophetic figures usually emerge in times of crisis,[327] when many people feel most vulnerable and seek solutions, which the established cults fail to provide.

Egypt would not tolerate almost any divination unless performed in the temples. Most Near Eastern cultures dealt well with divination by signs, with infrequent occasions of direct prophecy given in temples, and therefore open, to a certain degree, to management. Rendering the prophetic uttering in writing seems to have been a crucial component. In addition, the Mari knew unsolicited prophecy by private persons, but its extent seems to be modest, at least judging by the surviving documents. They all belong to the period immediately preceding the invasion of Babylon by Hammurabi, when the level of anxiety was probably high. Other ancient Near Eastern cultures left isolated testimonies of unique cases of this type of prophecy. The monarchical period in the history of Israel was extremely turbulent, and there is ongoing discussion of the reality of the centralised state:[328] in the midst of instability, in an ambivalent interaction with the royalty and with the temple authorities, independent prophecy flourished.[329] In Etruria prophetic figures were prominent in the mythical past, but absent from the real life as attested by the extant sources. This transformation was perhaps due to the domination of political and religious life by aristocratic families who controlled haruspication: this social structure could not accommodate the liberty of inspired prophecy[330]

In Greece, independent prophecy-giving comparable in some respects to the activities of Biblical prophets was characteristic of mythological or quasi-historical figures of the pre-Archaic and early Archaic period, when in many places the monarchy disappeared, and intensive innovation brought about apprehension. Beginning from the early Archaic period, oracular centres, such as Delphi and Didyma, grew rapidly, and in the Classical period inspired prophecy, given either by temple officials or laymen, was further institutionalised, and could be supervised and influenced by various interested parties, while freelance clairvoyants almost entirely disappeared. As a consequence, in the Classical period divine messages received in sanctuaries either by temple officials or laymen became the predominant channel of communication with the gods. This was the maximum the polis society could do to keep an eye on the mysterious sphere of the prophetic *mania*.

The respect of the Greeks for the inspired prophecy is often regarded as an embarrassing superstition; even E. R. Dodds felt a need to play down the reverence of intellectuals towards the source of the Pythian oracles.[331] However, it is clear that almost all the Greeks regarded inspired divination as communication with the gods, close to revelation.[332] From the perspective of individual and public freedom, the prominent position of prophetic *mania* in the Greek society reflects its openness and acceptance of the inborn human propensity to experience alterations of consciousness which was interpreted in positive terms as god-sent. This drive was handled with cautious respect; it could be harnessed to a certain extent by institutionalisation, but never suppressed or pushed to the cultural and social periphery.

Notes

1 This chapter draws on my article: Ustinova (2013).
2 Pl. *Phdr.* 244AD: ἥ τε γὰρ δὴ ἐν Δελφοῖς προφῆτις αἵ τ' ἐν Δωδώνῃ ἱέρειαι μανεῖσαι μὲν πολλὰ δὴ καὶ καλὰ ἰδίᾳ τε καὶ δημοσίᾳ τὴν Ἑλλάδα ἠργάσαντο, σωφρονοῦσαι δὲ βραχέα ἢ οὐδέν· καὶ ἐὰν δὴ λέγωμεν Σίβυλλάν τε καὶ ἄλλους, ὅσοι μαντικῇ χρώμενοι ἐνθέῳ πολλὰ δὴ πολλοῖς προλέγοντες εἰς τὸ μέλλον ὤρθωσαν. . . . τόδε μὴν ἄξιον ἐπιμαρτύρασθαι, ὅτι καὶ τῶν παλαιῶν οἱ τὰ ὀνόματα τιθέμενοι οὐκ αἰσχρὸν ἡγοῦντο οὐδὲ ὄνειδος μανίαν· οὐ γὰρ ἂν τῇ καλλίστῃ τέχνῃ, ᾗ τὸ μέλλον κρίνεται, αὐτὸ τοῦτο τοὔνομα ἐμπλέκοντες μανικὴν ἐκάλεσαν. ἀλλ' ὡς καλοῦ ὄντος, ὅταν θείᾳ μοίρᾳ γίγνηται, οὕτω νομίσαντες ἔθεντο, οἱ δὲ νῦν ἀπειροκάλως τὸ ταῦ ἐπεμβάλλοντες μαντικὴν ἐκάλεσαν. ἐπεὶ καὶ τήν γε τῶν ἐμφρόνων, ζήτησιν τοῦ μέλλοντος διά τε ὀρνίθων ποιουμένων καὶ τῶν ἄλλων σημείων, ἅτ' ἐκ διανοίας ποριζομένων ἀνθρωπίνῃ οἰήσει νοῦν τε καὶ ἱστορίαν, οἰονοϊστικὴν ἐπωνόμασαν. . . . ·ὅσῳ δὴ οὖν τελεώτερον καὶ ἐντιμότερον μαντικὴ οἰωνιστικῆς, τό τε ὄνομα τοῦ ὀνόματος ἔργον τ' ἔργου, τόσῳ κάλλιον μαρτυροῦσιν οἱ παλαιοὶ μανίαν σωφροσύνης τὴν ἐκ θεοῦ τῆς παρ' ἀνθρώπων γιγνομένης (translation H. N. Fowler, modified). On this passage see Hackforth (1972: 60); Rowe (1986: 168–173); Morgan (1990: 163–167). Morgan (1990: 164) emphasizes the lack of hierarchy of the types of madness.
3 The etymological connection is clear to modern scholars, as well: Frisk (1973–1979); Chantraine (1983–1984): s.v. *mainomai*. Both words derive from the Indo-European root *men-* meaning 'to be in a special, or differentiated, state of consciousness' (West 2007: 29; Nagy 1990: 60; Manetti 1993; Watkins 1995: 73; Ustinova 2009b; Ustinova 2012: 109). An attempt to divorce *mantis* from *mania* by Casevitz (1992) is convincingly rebutted by González (2013: 222–223).
4 The most comprehensive account of divination still remains Bouché-Leclercq 1879–1882. W. R. Halliday (1913) introduced an anthropological approach into the study of divination. Since then, studies of major oracles and related phenomena have greatly increased our knowledge, but there are still few synthetic studies of Greek oracles (e.g. Parke 1967; Vernant 1974; Burkert 2005a). Recent years witness renewed interest in the subject, as several books (Rosenberger 2001; Rosenberger 1998; Flower 2008; Johnston 2008; Friese 2010; Stoneman 2011), as well as collections of articles (Heintz 1997; Ciraolo and Seidel 2002; Johnston and Struck 2005; Georgoudi 2012) demonstrate.
5 Ti. 71E–72B: οὐδεὶς γὰρ ἔννους ἐφάπτεται μαντικῆς ἐνθέου καὶ ἀληθοῦς, ἀλλ' ἢ καθ' ὕπνον τὴν τῆς φρονήσεως πεδηθεὶς δύναμιν ἢ διὰ νόσον, ἢ διά τινα ἐνθουσιασμὸν παραλλάξας. ἀλλὰ συννοῆσαι μὲν ἔμφρονος τά τε ῥηθέντα ἀναμνησθέντα ὄναρ ἢ ὕπαρ ὑπὸ τῆς μαντικῆς τε καὶ ἐνθουσιαστικῆς φύσεως . . . τοῦ δὲ μανέντος ἔτι τε ἐν τούτῳ μένοντος οὐκ ἔργον τὰ φανέντα καὶ φωνηθέντα ὑφ' ἑαυτοῦ κρίνειν, ἀλλ' εὖ καὶ πάλαι λέγεται τὸ πράττειν καὶ γνῶναι τά τε αὑτοῦ καὶ ἑαυτὸν σώφρονι μόνῳ προσήκειν. ὅθεν δὴ καὶ τὸ τῶν προφητῶν γένος ἐπὶ ταῖς ἐνθέοις μαντείαις κριτὰς ἐπικαθιστάναι νόμος· οὓς μάντεις αὐτοὺς ὀνομάζουσίν τινες, τὸ πᾶν ἠγνοηκότες ὅτι τῆς δι' αἰνιγμῶν οὗτοι φήμης καὶ φαντάσεως ὑποκριταί, καὶ οὔτι μάντεις, προφῆται δὲ αντευομένων δικαιότατα ὀνομάζοιντ' ἄν (translation R. G. Bury). Cf. Nagy (1990: 60–61); Manetti (1993: 16); Struck (2016: 73–85).
6 On alteration of consciousness see above, Introduction.
7 Georgoudi (1998: 328–334); Dillery (2005: 171).

8 Cic. *Div.* 1. 49. 113. Aristotle (Aristotle, *De philosophia* fr. 10 Rose) maintains that when the soul is 'on its own' in sleep, it returns to its proper nature and divines the future; thus, the notion of gods ensues from the cases of (divine) inspiration and prophecy in sleep or close to death, when the soul is leaving the body (Aristotle's views on prophecy in sleep: *Div. somn.* 463a5; van der Eijk 1995). The Peripatetics shared perhaps the (Pythagorean) idea of the soul dormant in the waking body, attached to its organs (D.L. 8. 30; Ael. *VH* 3. 11; Vernant 1983: 101). In the Hippocratic Book IV of the *Regimen*, discussing iatromantic qualities of dreams, the author claims that dreams are divine (*theia*), and in sleep the soul acquires powers of perception it does not have when the body is awake; therefore the one who knows to interpret dreams acquires great wisdom (Detienne 1963: 73–76; Jones 1923: 1: xlv–xlvi; van der Eijk 2004: 190; Hulskamp 2013: 42–47).

9 Cic. *Div.* 2. 11. 26: *Duo enim genera divinandi esse dicebas, unum artificiosum, alterum naturale; artificiosum constare partim ex coniectura, partim ex observatione diuturna; naturale, quod animus adriperet aut exciperet extrinsecus ex divinitate. . . . Artificiosa divinationis illa fere genera ponebas: extispicum eorumque qui ex fulgoribus ostentisque praedicerent, tum augurum eorumque qui signis aut ominibus uterentur, omneque genus coniecturale in hoc fere genere ponebas. Illud autem naturale aut concitatione mentis edi et quasi fundi videbatur aut animo per somnum sensibus et curis vacuo provideri.* Cf. *Div.* 1. 6. 10; 1. 18. 34.

10 Bouché-Leclercq (1879–1882: 1: 107–110).

11 Bouché-Leclercq (1879–1882: 1: 62); Nilsson (1961–1967: 1: 164).

12 Bouché-Leclercq (1879–1882: 1: 107–110); Flacelière (1972); Dodds (1973: 70); Manetti (1993: 19); Karp (1998: 13); Dietrich (1990); Rosenberger (2001); Burkert (2005b); Belayche and Rüpke (2005: 80); Johnston (2008: 8–9); Friese (2010: 73–105).

13 Nissinen (2003: 1); cf. Gurney (1981: 142); Overholt (1989: 17–25); Petersen (2000). M. Nissinen insists that 'The prophetic process of transmission consists of the divine sender of the message, the message itself, the human transmitter of the message and the recipient(s) of the message. These four components should be transparent in any written source to be identified as a specimen of prophecy' (Nissinen 2003: 2).

14 *Pr.* 484–499; cf. Flower (2008: 90–91); Johnston (2008: 125–141).

15 Dillery (2005: 179–180); West (1983: 40–41); Parke (1988: 180).

16 E.g. Isoc. 19; Pl. *R.* 364B–365A; for itinerant seers see Burkert (1983); Eidinow (2011: 10).

17 Friese (2010: 93–103, with refs.).

18 As before the battle of Plataea (Hdt. 9. 61), or during the march of the Ten Thousand (*X. An.* 6. 4. 22); Powell (2009).

19 *Phdr.* 265B; cf. *Lg.* 738C; Naddaf (2013: 302).

20 On cult officials in oracular shrines, see Georgoudi (1998).

21 Discussed below in this chapter.

22 Parke and Wormell (1956: 1: 18); Rosenberger (2001: 56); Larson (2001: 235).

23 Ustinova (2009c: 65–68).

24 Gartziou-Tatti (1990); Friese (2010: 93–94); Georgoudi (2012); Stoneman (2011: 62–63). On the one hand, Plato (*Phdr.* 244A cited above) suggests that priestesses in Dodona were ecstatic, like the Pythia, Herodotus gives an account of three priestesses called doves, and Strabo (9. 2. 4) narrates a story of a prophetess who gave an oracular prediction; on the other hand, lead plaques attest to some system of lot-drawing. The evidence from the Classical and Hellenistic periods is further complicated by the Archaic references to oracles given by Zeus by means of an oak tree, and male priests who slept on the ground and never washed their feet (Hom. *Il.* 16. 235; *Od.* 14. 327; 19. 296; Hes. fr. 134 Merkelbach-West). S. Johnston suggests that in Dodona signs of different nature, such as the words of dove priestesses, as well as sounds produced by doves, cauldrons, and oak trees, were 'interpreted by women, while in an altered state

of consciousness, to be messages from Zeus' (Johnston 2008: 72). However, there is no clear evidence for the existence of ecstatic interpreters in Dodona (Georgoudi 2012: 70–71). Moreover, ecstatic interpretation of signs implies a contradiction in terms – interpretation is bound to be rational – and since no detail of this procedure is known, S. Johnston's 'single model' remains unsubstantiated. In any case, even the exact technique of lot-drawing in Dodona cannot be established with any certainty, and the method of inspired divination, if at all practiced in Dodona in historical times, remains a mystery.

25 Below in this chapter.

26 Georgoudi (1998: 348–355); Dillery (2005: 169–172); Ustinova (2009c: 111).

27 Pl. *Ti.* 71DE; *Smp.* 188BD; X. *Mem.* 1. 4. 14–15.

28 Allen (2010).

29 I discuss this issue elsewhere (Ustinova 2013), arguing against the position of scholars who disregard the divergence between inspired and technical divination. For instance, M. A. Flower (2008) refutes the ancient classification, mainly because the social function of the prediction was the same. His own suggestion is amorphous: either to regard any distinction between different types of divination as misleading, and 'rather think in terms of spectrum or range of activities,' or to assume a three-fold classification, comprising possession divination, technical divination, and intuitive divination. L. Maurizio (1995) adopts a typology based on Chinese materials: divination is divided into non-interpersonal (lacking interaction between the diviner and the spirits, e.g. horoscopy) and interpersonal (including spirit possession along with augury, and regarding devices, such as stones and birds, as possessed by spirits). In his book on oracles, R. Stoneman (2011) devotes a chapter to definitions of various oracular practices, but does not distinguish clearly between inspired and technical divination. Many scholars suggest that the contrast between direct and indirect divination was more superficial than previously thought (Annus 2010; Georgoudi, Koch Piettre, and Schmidt 2012), or that interpretation of signs was to a considerable extent based on intuition (Struck 2016: 17–18). A. Winitzer (2010) even asserts that signs obtained by extispicy or other modes of divination were envisaged by Mesopotamians as 'divinely inspired in some transcendental fashion,' deducing that 'divination . . . is nothing less than a source of revelation, its product tantamount to the divinely related word.'

30 Bouché-Leclercq (1879–1882: 1, 49–55).

31 Friese (2010: 74–92).

32 Hom. *Od.* 8. 79; *Il.* 9. 404–405; Hes. *Theog.* 498; Price (1985: 131); Dietrich (1990: 170).

33 Hdt. 7. 111; Parke (1939: 18); Ustinova (2009b: 121–153); Ustinova (2009c).

34 D.S. 16. 26. 6; Plu. *Mor.* 405C; Parke (1939: 32); Parke and Wormell (1956: 1, 34–40); Flacelière (1938: 79); Roux (1976: 64–69, 147); Latte (1940: 17); Sissa (1990: 33); Maurizio (1998); Scott (2014: 20–24).

35 Paus. 10. 19. 4; Villanueva Puig (1986: 38–40); on *thuiades* see Chapter 3.

36 Plu. *Mor.* 438C.

37 Roux (1976: 134–135); for a discussion of the layout of the adyton see Ustinova (2009b: 142–146, with refs.). The spring: Cassotis (Paus. 10. 24. 7) or Castalian (Euseb. *PE* 5. 28. 9); Amandry (1950: 135–139).

38 Str. 9. 3. 5; Paus. 10. 8. 6–32. 1; cf. Flacelière (1938: 81–85); Roux (1976: 121–149); Suárez de la Torre (2005: 23–27).

39 The conception of the Pythia's enthusiasm as a marital union between the priestess and the god, and her inspiration as resulting from 'her willingness to couple with the god,' (Sissa 1990: 32; Maurizio 1998: 155; cf. Latte 1940) cannot be extended to the enthusiasm of male prophets, at Claros, for instance. Thus, the requirement of chastity and a secluded life is not related to the goddess' sex; alongside other restrictions, it is a precondition for the individual's ability to experience *mania* necessary to attain the divine revelation.

40 Rohde (1925: 312–313); Dodds (1973: 65–101); Maurizio (1995: 76–79).
41 Str. 9. 3. 5; Amandry (1950: 164); Delcourt (1981: 54–55); Roux (1976: 157); Maurizio (1995: 70); for a different approach see Parke and Wormell (1956: 1, 39); Whittaker (1965: 26).
42 Str. 9. 3. 5; Plu. *Mor.* 397BC; Graf (2009b: 590).
43 *DK* fr. 93; cf. Parke (1939: 28–31); Whittaker (1965: 24–28); Serra (1998).
44 The cylix by Codrus Painter represents Themis as Pythia seated on the tripod, with Aegeus as enquirer in front of her. It was manufactured in Athens in 440–430 (Berlin Mus. No. F 2538; Beazley 1963: 1269. 5). It is reproduced in almost every work on Greek prophecy.
45 Str. 9. 3. 5; Plu. *Mor.* 397C.
46 Possession: Maurizio (1995); Arnott (1989); patterned dissociative identity: Flower (2008: 226); Chalupa (2014: 42–43).
47 Flacelière (1938: 72); Roux (1976: 70–75); Parke (1939: 15); Amandry (1950: 81).
48 Amandry (1950: 25–36); Parke and Wormell (1956: 1: 18); Whittaker (1965: 27); Grottanelli (2005: 130); Rosenberger (2001: 56); Larson (2001: 235).
49 Amandry (1984: 401); Larson (1995: 348).
50 Luc. 5. 147–196; *Mor.* 438AB; Dodds (1973: 72); Bayet (1946); Fontenrose (1978: 204–212); Ustinova (2009c: 140–141).
51 Str. 9. 3. 5; see also Ps.-Longin. *Subl.* 13. 2; Plu. *Mor.* 437CD. In 45 Cicero already referred to *vis illa terrae* 'that force of the earth,' which enthused the soul of the Pythia with divine inspiration (*De div.* 1. 37–38; cf. 1. 115).
52 A. *Ch.* 797, 803–805; *Eu.* 180; E. *Ion* 226–229; cf. *Ion* 220, 233, 245, *Andr.* 1093; *Ph.* 237; the descent of the Pythia: Hdt. 5. 92; Plu. *Mor.* 397A; 405C; 438B; *Tim.* 8; Ustinova (2009b: 133–139).

     According to a myth told in Delphi, the 'power' (*dunamis*) which caused ecstasy was first manifested 'when a shepherd by chance fell in and later gave inspired utterances' (Plu. *Mor.* 433CD; D.S. 16. 16).
53 A niche with a statue of Apollo, carved into a rock adjoining the temple of Apollo Pythios on the island of Ceos (Angliker forthcoming), hints perhaps at the association of the Pythian Apollo with dark nooks. I owe the information on this sanctuary to the kindness of E. Angliker.
54 I discuss the subject in detail in Ustinova (2009b: 121–153).
55 Bouché-Leclercq (1879–1882: 1: 350, 3: 75–102); Rohde (1925: 290).
56 Oppé (1904).
57 Many scholars consider the ancient evidence of its existence to be false (Will 1942–1943; Amandry 1950: 215–230; Fontenrose 1978: 197; Parke 1939: 21; Nilsson 1961–1967: 1, 172; Dietrich 1978: 6; Rosenberger 2001: 53). Those tending to rely on the ancient tradition interpret it as evidence of religious and psychological, rather than natural, phenomena (Poulsen 1920: 22–23; Will 1942–1943: 174; Flacelière 1965: 51; Roux 1976: 156–157; Schefer 1996: 28; Dodds 1973: 73; Lloyd-Jones 1976: 67; Parke 1967: 80). The lack of reference to *pneuma* in accounts of other oracles is explained as due to the exceptional popularity of Delphi (Roux 1976: 156–157). It has recently been suggested that the exhalations and the cavern resulted from a projection of practices prevailing in other oracular centres onto Delphi (Rosenberger 2001: 53, 132). Finally, some scholars are reluctant to propose any explanation of ancient accounts of vapours in Delphi (Price 1985: 141). See Ustinova (2009b: 122, 132) for an overview.
58 Courby (1927: 47–80); Roux (1976: 94); Vallois (1931: 319–321); Parke (1939: 20, 27–28); Parke and Wormell (1956: 1, 21); Green (1989: 110); Sissa (1990: 14).
59 de Boer and Hale (2001); de Boer, Hale, and Chanton (2001); Spiller, Hale, and de Boer (2002). These gases, methane, ethane, and ethylene, are colourless and can produce mild narcotic effects. Ethylene in particular was used as a surgical anaesthetic till the 1970s, and in light doses it allows full control of the body, but creates a sensation of

euphoria (Hale et al. 2003; de Boer, Hale, and Chanton 2001). A different approach to the location of the geological faults and the nature of gaseous emissions is suggested by Etiope et al. (2006) and Piccardi et al. (2008), who suppose that it was not ethylene but hydrogen sulphide (L. Piccardi) or methane and carbon dioxide (G. Etiope). However, the three approaches agree on two major points, that there are fissures under the temple, and that they emitted gases that affect human consciousness.

60 Lehoux (2007); Foster and Lehoux (2007). This position is endorsed by González (2013: 273). Brouillette (2014: 182–191) insists on philosophical roots of Plutarch's *pneuma*, but does not even mention modern geological research and their assessment by the historians of Greek religion.

61 Foster and Lehoux (2007: 87); Flower (2008: 226); Chalupa (2014: 38).

62 Spiller, Hale, and de Boer (2002: 193).

63 Which provides an explanation for the fact that the state of consciousness of the enquirers and priests remained unchanged, an argument raised by Chalupa (2014: 39).

64 Klass (2003: 121–123).

65 Amandry and Hansen (2010: 79, 473).

66 Amandry and Hansen (2010: 80, fig. 2).

67 Roux (1976: 134–135); Roux (2000: 195); Courby (1927: 59–69); Delcourt (1981: 42); Green (1989: 110).

68 J. Z. de Boer's suggestion, that the *omphalos* discovered in the adyton, featuring a funnel-shaped axial hole, was used as a stopper for ethylene, covering the vent in the floor, and was opened during prophetic sessions (de Boer 2007), remains to be proven: the hole could serve for a different purpose.

69 Roux (1976: 109).

70 Ustinova (2009b: 150–153).

71 Mikalson (2005: 106); Ogden (2001: 245); Curnow (2004: 56); Bowden (2005: 19); Graf (2009a: 71); Friese (2010: 90, 131); Scott (2014: 24); Green (2009).

72 Graf (2009b: 602); Johnston (2008: 49–50).

73 Cardeña (2005).

74 For this choice, see also Chapter 3.

75 Oesterheld (2014: 213, 216). I discuss the subject of Gaia's superimposing by Apollo in Delphic myth and cult in Ustinova (2009b: 151).

76 Str. 13. 4. 14; Bean (1989b: 202–204); Negri and Leucci (2006); Ustinova (2009b: 84–86); Friese (2010: 91–92); D'Andria (2013); Semeraro (2014).

77 Oesterheld (2014: 213).

78 Acharaca: see below in this chapter; Hieracome: Paus. 10. 32. 6; Ustinova (2009b: 120–121).

79 Moretti et al. (2014: 34).

80 Robert (1967: 309–310, fig. 117); Bean (1989a: 158–159); Parke (1985: 138); Wujewski (2001); Ferrary (2005); Ustinova (2009b: 109–112); a most recent discussion of the temple and the procedure: Moretti et al. (2014).

81 Iamb. *Myst.* 3. 11. A reconstruction of the procedure in its development from the Hellenistic to Roman period: Parke (1985: 222–223).

82 Robert (1967: 311); Wujewski (2001: fig. 9).

83 Robert (1967: 310); Stoneman (2011: 95); Moretti et al. (2014: 41). Bouché-Leclerq demonstrates that *theispiôdos* belongs to the category of mediums, 'instruments of revelation' (Bouché-Leclercq 1879–1882: 1, 351). Most other scholars ascribe the function of the medium to *prophêtês*, and that of rendering the utterance in verse to *theispiôdos* (Picard 1922: 208–213; Bean 1989a: 159; Parke 1967: 139; Parke 1985: 220–223; Aune 1983: 31; Burkert 1985: 115; Merkelbach and Stauber 1996: 3; Georgoudi 1998: 352).

84 Iamb. *Myst.* 3. 11; Parke (1985: 219–220).

85 Iamb. *Myst.* 3. 11: οὔτε ἑαυτοῦ ὄντι οὔτε παρακολουθοῦντι οὐδὲν οἷς λέγει ἢ ὅπου γῆς ἐστιν· ὥστε καὶ μετὰ τὴν χρησμῳδίαν μόγις ποτὲ ἑαυτὸν λαμβάνει (translation E. C. Clarke, J. M. Dillon, and J. P. Hershbell).

86 Iamb. *Myst.* 3. 11; Tac. *Ann.* 3. 54; Robert (1967); Parke (1985: 219–224); Busine (2002); Busine (2005: 48).

87 Plin. Nat. 2.232; Paus. 9. 33. 1; Apollod. 3. 7. 3.

88 Arist. ap. Macr. *Sat.* 1. 18. 1; Bouché-Leclercq (1879–1882: 2: 381).

Greek wine probably contained toxic substances, and although its alcoholic content hardly exceeded 14%, various plants added to the wine could render it not merely intoxicating, but plainly toxic. Some wines, in particular the mythic Marron's wine, were believed to be extremely potent (*Od.* 9. 209; addition of plants to wine in Roman times: Plin. *Nat.* 14. 19. 107–112; 24–25. 120–130; Ruck 1976: note 20). In fact, immoderate drinking was believed to lead to madness and loss of sound mind as early as in Homeric poetry; Herodotus suggests that Cleomenes' frenzy might result from this reason (Hom. *Od.* 21. 295–304; Hdt. 6. 75; [Arist.] *Pr.* 953a–954a (30.1); Philo *De plantatione* 36. 148; cf. *VH* 13. 6). Drinking of unmixed wine was considered as sufficient to cause madness (Diod. 4. 3. 4) or even death (Ath. 10. 437).

89 On prophetic qualities of water, see Ustinova (2009b: 131–132); sanctuaries applying inspired hydromancy: Friese (2010: 86–87).

90 Plin. *Nat.* 2. 232; Iamb. *Myst.* 3. 11.

91 This practice is demonstrated by the attachment of bronze astragals to the crepis of the Hellenistic temple, juxtaposing of astragals with Apollo and his attributes on the coins of Colophon in the late fifth–fourth centuries, and is hinted at by Lucian (*Alex.*43: ἐκπίπτοντες χρησμοί; Amandry 1950: 30; Moretti et al. 2014: 34).

92 Paus. 7. 2. 6; Gorman (2001: 187–187); Greaves (2002: 110).

93 Callimachus fr. 174, 229 Pfeiffer; for mythology and Didyma see Parke (1985: 2–12).

94 Parke (1985: 32).

95 Fontenrose (1988: 14–15). The date of destruction is debated: most scholars accept 494, as given by Hdt. 6. 19, but Paus. 8. 46. 3 suggests 479.

96 A detailed archaeological report: Wiegand and Knackfuss (1941); for a less specialised concise description of the temple and its history see Tuchelt (1991); the history of the Didymaeum: Günther (1971).

97 Greaves (2002: 109–110).

98 Fontenrose (1988: 40).

99 Günther (1971: 119–122); Stoneman (2011: 84–90).

100 Haussollier (1920); Flacelière (1965: 30–31); Fontenrose (1988: 80). Parke (1985: 214–218) suggests a change in the procedure some time in the third century, from the original admittance of the enquirers to the adyton to the Egyptian model.

101 Montegu (1976). From the eastern chamber staircases decorated with a very impressive meander pattern, called in temple accounts 'labyrinths' and presumably associating these passages with mazes, led to an upper room, attic or terrace; their function remains undefined (Wiegand and Knackfuss 1941: 71–79; Fontenrose 1988: 37–38). The striking decoration would look strange on staircases if they had led to rooms of secondary importance, therefore Parke (1985: 217) suggests that the prophetess stayed there when she underwent her preparations for the prophetic séance. In any case, the 'labyrinths' descending into the eastern chamber seem to be symbolically connected with the dark passages leading from this chamber to the adyton, and it's a pity that the picture of the *promantis* descending by the 'labyrinth' to the eastern chamber and thence to the adyton cannot be more than a plausible hypothesis.

102 Catalogue: Fontenrose (1988: 177–244).

103 Iamb. *Myst.* 3. 11: Καὶ μὴν ἥ γε ἐν Βραγχίδαις γυνὴ χρησμῳδός, εἴτε ῥάβδον ἔχουσα τὴν πρώτως ὑπὸ θεοῦ τινος παραδοθεῖσαν πληροῦται τῆς θείας αὐγῆς, εἴτε ἐπὶ ἄξονος καθημένη προλέγει τὸ μέλλον, εἴτε τοὺς πόδας ἢ κράσπεδόν τι τέγγουσα τῷ ὕδατι ἢ ἐκ τοῦ ὕδατος ἀτμιζομένη δέχεται τὸν θεόν, ἐξ ἁπάντων τούτων ἐπιτηδεία παρασκευαζομένη πρὸς τὴν ὑποδοχὴν ἔξωθεν αὐτοῦ μεταλαμβάνει. Δηλοῖ δὲ καὶ τὸ τῶν θυσιῶν πλῆθος καὶ ὁ θεσμὸς τῆς ὅλης ἁγιστείας καὶ ὅσα ἄλλα δρᾶται πρὸ τῆς χρησμῳδίας θεοπρεπῶς, τά τε λουτρὰ τῆς προφήτιδος καὶ ἡ τριῶν ὅλων ἡμερῶν

ἀσιτία καὶ ἡ ἐν ἀδύτοις αὐτῆς διατριβὴ καὶ ἐχομένης ἤδη τῷ φωτὶ καὶ τερπομένης ἐν πολλῷ χρόνῳ (translation E.C. Clarke, J.M. Dillon, and J.P. Hershbell). For an analysis of this passage see Parke (1985: 210–219); Fontenrose (1988: 81–83).

104 *Th.* 22–34; Parke (1985: 211). On the proximity of poetry and prophecy see also below, Chapter 6.

105 Parke (1985: 212–213).

106 Wiegand and Knackfuss (1941: 36, 46–47); Günther (1971: 114–115); Fontenrose (1988: 40); Tuchelt (1991: 18); Parke (1985: 212–213).

107 Parke (1985: 216).

108 Stoneman (2011: 87).

109 Above, Introduction.

110 Parke (1985: 216).

111 Greaves (2002: 117).

112 Strabo 9. 2. 34; Pind. fr. 51b Maehler; Schachter (1967: 1); Ducat (1971: 451); Kowalzig (2007: 368–371). I discuss Ptoion in Ustinova (2009b: 113–116).

113 Guillon (1943: 96, 137, 140, pl. 14); Friese (2010: 153).

114 Her 8. 135, cf. Paus. 9. 23. 6, Plu. *Mor.* 411F. For the discussion of the language see Robert (1950); Laumonier (1958: 23); Schachter (1981–1994: 1: 66).

The existence of male prophets is confirmed in a series of inscriptions discovered on the site and dating from the fourth century BC to the third century AD: Schachter (1967: 2); Schachter (1981–1994: 1: 67).

115 Schachter (1967: 2); Guillon (1943: 22).

116 τά μοι ἔννυχος αὐτὸς ὑπέσχου, φωνὴν φθεγξάμενος πρὸς ἐμὴν ὄπα προσγελάσας τε; Guillon (1943: 109–110, 144); Guillon (1946); cf. Schachter (1981–1994: 1: 67).

117 Iamb. *Myst.* 3. 11: ἕτερον δὲ τὸ τῶν χρηστηρίων διαβόητον καὶ ἐναργέστατόν ἐστι πολυμερὲς ἔνθεον μαντεῖον, περὶ οὗ τὰ τοιαῦτα ἀποφαίνει· οἱ δὲ ὕδωρ πιόντες, καθάπερ ὁ ἐν Κολοφῶνι ἱερεὺς τοῦ Κλαρίου, οἱ δὲ στομίοις παρακαθήμενοι, ὡς αἱ ἐν Δελφοῖς θεσπίζουσαι, οἱ δ' ἐξ ὑδάτων ἀτμιζόμενοι, καθάπερ αἱ ἐν Βραγχίδαις προφήτιδες. Τριῶν δὲ τουτωνὶ διωνύμων χρηστηρίων ἐμνημόνευσας, οὐχ ὅτι μόνα ἐνταῦθα, πολὺ γὰρ πλείονα ὑπῆρχε τὰ παραλειπόμενα (translation E.C. Clarke, J.M. Dillon, and J.P. Hershbell).

118 On the importance of fasting in manipulation of consciousness see the Introduction.

119 Ustinova (2009a: 53–155).

120 Arist. ap. Macr. *Sat.* 1. 18. 1; on drinking pure wine see above in this chapter.

121 Plin. *Nat.* 28. 41. 147; Paus. 7. 25. 13; Ustinova (2009a: 88).

122 Differences in the ability to manipulate consciousness: see the Introduction; awareness of these differences in antiquity is discussed in detail in Chapter 2.

123 Graf (2009b: 590) cites the case of the Muslim Laujé of Sulawesi, where the words of an ecstatic female medium are 'translated' to the public by a male healer, and interprets this practice, as well as that attested to at Delphi, as following the enactment of traditional gender roles. The case of all-male prophecy at Claros demonstrates that it was not the gender of the medium that was of primary importance.

124 St. Byz. s.v. *Thria*.

125 The most systematic and profound research on Trophonius was conducted by P. Bonnechere: Bonnechere (2003a), as well as a series of papers: Bonnechere and Bonnechere (1989); Bonnechere (1998b, 1998a, 1999, 2003b, 2010). See also Schachter (1967, 1984); Schachter (1981–1994: 3, 66–89); Clark (1968); Ustinova (2002: 269–274); Ustinova (2009b: 90–96).

126 Paus. 9. 37. 3; Schol. Ar. *Nu.* 508; cf. Schachter (1981–1994: 3, 71); Bonnechere (2003a: 358).

127 Ar. *Nu.* 508; Hdt. 8. 134; Semus of Delos, *FGH* 396 F10 (in Ath. 14. 614A); Paus. 9. 39; *IG* VII. 4136. Dicaearch. fr. 13–22 Wehrli; Ath. 13. 594 EF and 14. 641 EF; cf. Schachter (1981–1994: 3, 80); Bonnechere (1998a: 445); Clark (1968); Clark (1979: 56).

128 Paus. 9. 39. 4–5, cf. Philostr. VA 8. 19. For the ceremony at the Trophonium, see Deubner (1900: 17–28); Bonnechere (2003a: 32–61, esp. 40–41; 139–164; 236–248); Bonnechere (2007: 34–36). For the site, see Schachter (1981–1994: 3, 72–79); Bonnechere (1998b: 91–96); Bonnechere (2003a: 7–26).

129 Bonnechere (2003a: 150–153).

130 Bonnechere (2003a: 246–248).

131 Paus. 9. 39. 11. On the shape of the prophetic cavern and the position of the consulter, see Bonnechere (2003a: 159–163). A different reconstruction: Rosenberger (2001: 37–38, fig. 2).

132 Paus. 9. 39. 13; Bonnechere (2003a: 249–271).

133 Ath. 614 B.

134 Max. Tyr. 8. 2; Origenes *Cels.* 3. 34, cf. Rohde (1925: 105); Bonnechere and Bonnechere (1989: 291); Bonnechere (2003a: 185); Schachter (1981–1994: 3, 80).

135 Plu. *Mor.* 590B–592F; Corlu (1970).

136 590B–592F, translation by Ph. D. De Lacy and B. Einarson.

137 Cf. Bonnechere (1998a: 449, with bibliography).

138 Paus. 9. 39. 11; Clark (1968: 70).

139 Babut (1984: 51, 72); Bonnechere (1998a: 452–453); Bonnechere (2003a: 132–138, 192–196).

140 P. Bonnechere (Bonnechere 2003a: 154–164; Bonnechere 2002) describes the experience of enquirers at Trophonium as 'altered state of consciousness'; Hani (1975) suggests self-inflicted trance. For a different approach, see Hamilton (1906: 89), Clark (1968: 73), and Schachter (1981–94: 3, 83).

141 14. 1. 44.

142 Ustinova (2009b: 84–87); Ustinova (2002).

143 For the gods worshipped at Acharaca and the archaeological research on the site and its vicinity see Cook (1914–1940: 1, 503–504); Laumonier (1958: 507–508).

144 Edelstein and Edelstein (1948); Sineux (2007); Ustinova (2009b: 96–99). For the cognitive aspects of the experience of incubation in the Asclepaea, see Panagiotidou (2014).

145 Ogden (2001: 68–81).

146 Ustinova (2009b: 68).

147 SEG 3. 406.

148 I treat this subject in detail elsewhere: Ustinova (2009b: 156–168). I focus on earlier pagan evidence and don't refer to the extant books of Sibylline oracles that are late and/or stem from Jewish and Judeo-Christian circles, using however some pagan *topoi* (Lightfoot 2007: esp. 19–21).

149 Plu. *Mor.* 397A; *DK* fr. 92: Σίβυλλα δὲ μαινομένωι στόματι καθ' Ἡράκλειτον ἀγέλαστα καὶ ἀκαλλώπιστα καὶ ἀμύριστα φθεγγομένη χιλίων ἐτῶν ἐξικνεῖται τῆι φωνῆι διὰ τὸν θεόν. While estimations of the length of the authentic fragment of Heraclitus in this passage range from the whole sentence to the words 'the Sibyl with mad mouth' only, the latter judgment appears too radical: Parke (1988: 63); cf. Delatte (1934: 6); Kahn (1979: 124–126).

150 If we disregard the very late (predating the eighth century AD) reference by Audax to Hesiod as an author who maintained that Phemonoe, the first prophet (*vates*) of Apollo, uttered oracles *per insaniam*, because of insanity (fr. 327 Merkelbach-West).

151 FGH 241 F26; Parke (1988: 53–64).

152 Aune (1983: 37).

153 Heraclit. *loc. cit.*, Ar. *Pax* 1095, 1116, Pl. *Phdr.* 244B; *Thg.* 124D; Parke (1988: 23).

154 Clement. Alex. *Strom.* 1. 21. 108; Heraclid. Pont. fr. 130 Wehrli.

155 Lactant. *Div. inst.* 1. 6; Schol. in Pl. *Phdr.* 244B; Suid s.v. *Sibulla*; Parke (1988: 24–50); Potter (1990: 473–474).

156 Potter (1990: 475).

157 Graf (1985: 346); Parke (1988: 51–70); Potter (1990: 475); Mazzoldi (2001: 103).

158 Ar. *Pax* 1095; Parke (1988: 103–104); Potter (1990).
159 Aune (1983: 37); Potter (1990: 478); Parke (1988: 1–22).
160 Burkert (1983); Bremmer (2008: 133–151). Lightfoot (2007: 13) suggests that motifs and conceptions of poetic inspiration were applied to the Sybil.
161 10. 12. 1–11.
162 Aune (1983: 37).
163 Virgil's depiction of the Sibyl (A. 6. 42) is historically suspect, being the only instance of a Sibyl uttering responses, Aune (1983: 355).
164 Parke (1988: 10); Mazzoldi (2001: 99–114); Lightfoot (2007: 10).
165 A. A. 1035–1330; Mazzoldi (2001: 94–97); Mazzoldi (2002).
166 Paus. 10. 12. 4–6; Parke (1988: 25–26, 37–39).
167 Ov. *Met.* 14. 130.
168 Nikiprowetsky (1970: 3); Parke (1988: 55–58); Clark (1979: 206); Graf (1985: 338–339); Mazzoldi (2001: 19–23, 107–110); Cusset (2004).
169 A. A. 1098: κλέος μαντικόν.
170 μένει τὸ θεῖον δουλίαι περ ἐν φρενί, A. A. 1084.
171 τέχναι ἐνθέοι, θέσφατοι, A. A. 1210, 1113, 1030.
172 φρενομανής τις εἶ θεοφόρητος, A. A. 1140.
173 *Ag.* 1174–1177; O'Brien-Moore (1924: 83, 100–101).
174 E. *Tr.* 414, 417.
175 E. *Tr.* 342, 428, 348. 252, 255, 366
176 E. *Tr.* 310–352.
177 E. *Hec.* 676, 121: θεσπιῳδός, μαντίπολος Βάκχη.
178 One myth even has her father Priam imprison the wretched maiden in a cave, in order to hide her madness from the public eye: Lycophr., *Alex.* 1461–1471, Ustinova (2009b: 158).
179 *Od.* 350–379; Russo, Fernández-Galiano, and Heubeck (1992: 124); Burkert (2005b: 34); Guidorizzi (1997); Guidorizzi (2010: 108); Saïd (2013: 382–383).
180 *Il.* 6. 76, 7. 53.
181 Hes., fr. 162 Merkelbach-West; Apollod. 3. 6. 7; Phleg. *FGH* 257 F36; Hygin. *Fab.* 75; Halliday (1913: 78); S. *OT.* 284–285; Bouché-Leclercq (1879–1882: 2: 30–34); Buxton (1980: 28).
182 D.S. 4. 66; Pi. *P.* 4. 336; Bouché-Leclercq (1879–1882: 2: 34–36). Coins, beginning from the Classical period: Metzler (1990); Stoneman (2011: 80 and fig. 18).
183 Hdt. 2. 49, 9. 34; Apollod. 2. 2. 2; Paus. 5. 5. 10; Bouché-Leclercq (1879–1882: 2: 16–18); Hoessly (2001: 149–151).
184 Paus. 5. 13. 6; Apollod. 3. 6. 4; A. *Th.* 276; Hom. *Od.* 20. 351–355; Dillery (2005: 173–176); Vicaire (1979); Sineux (2007).
185 *Od.* 2. 159.
186 Hdt. 2. 49; 2. 58. Hesiod attributed Melampous' arts either to Apollo or to licking of his ears by snakes (Hes. fr. 261 Merkelbach-West); on Melampous the seer see Dowden (1989: 100–115); Hoessly (2001: 149–151).
187 Suid. s.v. *Musaios*; Paus. 10. 7. 2; founder of the Eleusinian mysteries: D.S. 4. 25. 1; cf. Kern (1922: Nos. 166–172); Dillery (2005: 179).
188 Paus. 1. 22. 7.
189 Abaris' legend was known in the fifth century to Pindar (Harp. s.v. *Abaris*) and to Herodotus (4. 36); cf. Pl. *Chrm.* 158CD; Iamb. *VP* 91, 136, 141, Porph. *VP* 29; Rohde (1925: 300, 328); Corssen (1912); Baudy (1996).
190 Theopomp. in Schol. Ar. *Av.* 962; Moulinier (1952: 57); Parker (1983: 209). On Bacis see also below, Chapter 5.
191 D.S. 4. 66; Paus. 10. 12. 11; Bouché-Leclercq (1879–1882: 2: 104–106).
192 Pl. *Prt.* 316D. Musaeus' prophecies collected (and tampered with) by Onomacritus: Hdt. 7. 6; cf. Ar. *Ra.* 1033; Paus. 10. 9. 11; poems: Paus. 1. 14. 3; 1. 22. 8; 10. 5. 6. For the scanty evidence on early written oracles see Dillery (2005: 225–226).

193 See Dillery (2005: 183–185) for a historical analysis from a different viewpoint.
194 Hdt. 1. 62; Pollard (1965: 108); Dillery (2005: 186).
195 Hdt. 9. 93–95; Grottanelli (1994–1995, 2003); Burkert (1997).
196 Bouché-Leclercq (1879–1882: 1: 348–349, 2: 95, 108); Flower (2008: 60–65); for *chrêsmologos* as soothsayer see Paus. 1. 34. 4; Dillery (2005: 170). Forgery: Onomacritus: Hdt. 7. 6; Dillery (2005: 167–168, 189–192).
197 *Ljosvetninga Saga* 11, cited after Davidson (1981: 135).
198 Arnott (1989); Sidky (2011: 84–89).
199 St. Byz. s.v. *Thria*.
200 Corlu (1970: 15–16).
201 Plu. *Mor.* 593CD, translation P. H. de Lace and B. Einarson.
202 Amandry (1950: 86–103).
203 E.g. during the Persian war: Parke (1967: 97–106); Parker (2000: 98) doubts that Delphi medized; in 432: Parker (2000: 107). See Bowden (2005) for Delphi's prestige, and Parker (2000) for the political authority of the major oracles, almost all of them focused on inspired prophecy.
204 Green (2009: 42–44) on the belief in the validity of the oracles given at Delphi.
205 Piñero (1991: 17).
206 Dillery (2005: 175, 200–207); Johnston (2008: 110).
207 Trampedach (2008: 229); Johnston (2008: 117). However, some diviners were itinerant figures of doubtful status: Dillery (2005: 223).
208 See above for the code of behaviour of prophetic priests, such as the Pythia and the prophet at Claros.
209 Dillery (2005: 172).
210 *Ap.* 22BC; *Men.* 99CD. Here again, one would have preferred Plato to respect his own rules of word usage, rather than carelessly adopt the popular parlance. Cf. *Euthphr. passim*; Mikalson (2010: 126–129).
211 *Ion* 534CD: διὰ ταῦτα δὲ ὁ θεὸς ἐξαιρούμενος τούτων τὸν νοῦν τούτοις χρῆται ὑπηρέταις καὶ τοῖς χρησμῳδοῖς καὶ τοῖς μάντεσι τοῖς θείοις, ἵνα ἡμεῖς οἱ ἀκούοντες εἰδῶμεν ὅτι οὐχ οὗτοί εἰσιν οἱ ταῦτα λέγοντες οὕτω πολλοῦ ἄξια, οἷς νοῦς μὴ πάρεστιν, ἀλλ' ὁ θεὸς αὐτός ἐστιν ὁ λέγων, διὰ τούτων δὲ φθέγγεται πρὸς ἡμᾶς (translation W.R.M. Lamb).
212 Discussed in detail in Chapter 8.
213 X. *Mem.* 1. 1. 4–5.
214 *EE* 1225a22: διὸ καὶ τοὺς ἐνθουσιῶντας καὶ προλέγοντας, καίπερ διανοίας ἔργον ποιοῦντας, ὅμως οὔ φαμεν ἐφ' αὑτοῖς εἶναι, οὔτ' εἰπεῖν ἃ εἶπον, οὔτε πρᾶξαι ἃ ἔπραξαν (translation H. Rackham).
215 414E; 431B, cf. Johnston (2008: 10); Jaillard (2007); Brouillette (2014: 194–196).
216 *Mor.* 404F; Graf (2009b: 594).
217 *Mor.* 397C, translation F.C. Babbitt.
218 D. Chr. *Or.* 10. 23; Graf (2009b: 589).
219 *Myst.* 3. 17, translation E. C. Clarke, J. M. Dillon, and J. P. Hershbell.
220 *Myst.* 3. 11: ὡς ὀργάνῳ.
221 Addey (2013).
222 Arist. *Div. somn.* 463a5; Plu. *Mor.* 432C-D; Pl. *Ti.* 71E, cf. Cic. *Div.* 1. 30. 62; Amandry (1950: 222–224); Schröder (1990: 24–59); Schröder (1994–1995); Holzhausen (1993); Brouillette (2014: 200–206).
223 Shaw (1998).
224 The oracle at Pharae described by Pausanias (7.22. 2–3) and discussed by D. Jaillard (Jaillard 2012: 99–101) is very unusual: the first word the enquirer hears, after he had completed a complex rite, is considered the divine response. In this case, the word was believed to be inspired by Hermes. However, it was the action of the person who pronounced the word that was produced by divine will, like a sign given by means of a flying bird or a rustling tree. The enquirer received a god-sent sign: he was not

inspired. It can hardly be just chance that this unique oracle belonged to Hermes, traditionally the patron of lot oracles.

225 *Il.*, 24. 221–224: εἰ μὲν γάρ τίς μ' ἄλλος ἐπιχθονίων ἐκέλευεν, |ἢ οἳ μάντιές εἰσι θυοσκόοι ἢ ἱερῆες, |ψεῦδός κεν φαῖμεν καὶ νοσφιζοίμεθα μᾶλλον· | νῦν δ,' αὐτὸς γὰρ ἄκουσα θεοῦ καὶ ἐσέδρακον ἄντην, | εἶμι καὶ οὐχ ἅλιον ἔπος ἔσσεται.

226 Contrary to M. A. Flower's opinion that the client could be indifferent to the method of divination (Flower 2008: 87).

227 E.g. *Il.*, 1. 193–218; 3. 396–418, 14. 361–378. On epiphanies in Homer see Dietrich (1983).

228 *Od.* 15. 172–173, translation A. T. Murray; *Il.* 7. 44: Helenus 'understood in his heart' the plan of the gods.

229 A. *Eu.* 33: Μαντεύομαι γὰρ ὡς ἂν ἡγῆται θεός.

230 As argued by Flower (2008: 85).

231 Cohen (2007: 139).

232 Gurney (1981); Bottéro (1974: passim, esp. 190); Stökl (2012).

233 Assmann (2001: 154); Ray (1981); Grabbe (1995: 86); Wilson (1980: 124–128). The only exception is the account of a seizure of a person by Amon, left by the Egyptian priest Wenamon, but it refers to the latter's stay in Byblos sometime between 1080 and 1070 BC; the individual 'seized' by Amon was presumably a local, and the term used in the original is 'big youth': the term 'seer' adopted in some translations in based on the context only (Ritner 2003). The entire episode may reflect Semitic rather than Egyptian tradition (Grabbe 1995: 85).

234 Champeaux (1990a: 271); Guittard (2007: 223–224).

235 North (2000).

236 Briquel (1990: 74); cf. Pairault-Massa (1985); Jannot (2005: 33) convincingly argues that the few cases of consulting oracles by Etruscans (mirrors depicting Etruscans consulting an oracle of Orpheus and the consultation of Delphi (Hdt. 1. 167) are associated with Greek practices, very different from *disciplina etrusca* (see also Pairault-Massa (1985: 66); Guittard (2007: 289–341). Briquel (1990) demonstrates a sharp contrast between the conspicuous role of prophetic figures in mythology and the absence of inspired divination in real-life cultic practices. De Grummond (2006: 23–40) regards consultation of books attributed to mythological figures as prophecy, but in this case the authority is derived from the scripture, and is not directly inspired by a god. Even more problematic is de Grummond's interpretation of haruspication as prophecy. On music, magic, and inspiration in Etruria, see Bagnasco Gianni (2011).

237 Seow (2003) cites three non-Hebrew texts, the Amman citadel inscription (ninth century BC), the Zakkur stela from the vicinity of Aleppo (eighth century BC), and most notably, the inscription discovered at Deir Alla in Jordan (Seow 2003: Nos. 136–138; Wilson 1980: 129–133).

238 *ANET*, No. 395; Bryce (2002: 150).

239 Gurney (1981: 146); Piñero (1991: 15).

240 See below in this chapter.

241 Rouget (1990: 84).

242 About fifty of ca. 20,000 texts, Durand (1997); *ANET* 623–626; Nissinen (2003: 13–77).

243 Of ca. 30,000 texts unearthed, Nissinen (2003: Nos. 68–118); Nissinen (2000a: 89), cf. Parpola (1997); Gurney (1981).

244 *āpilum*: Nissinen (2003: Nos. 1–5, 8); *muhhûm*: Nissinen (2003: Nos. 10, 12, 16, 25, 31, 32). The translation of these words is based on etymology and normal usage; the texts themselves do not give details on the state of consciousness of these individuals. The verb is also used in its literal meaning in descriptions of prophetic activities (*ANET*: 624; Malamat 1989: 85; Nissinen 2003: 6).

245 Malamat (1989: 81); cf. Nissinen (2003: 179), No. 119.

246 A mansion of a haruspex or *barūm* has been unearthed at Mari: Malamat (1989: 80, 82).

247 E.g. Nissinen (2003: Nos. 2, 8, 10, 11, etc., esp. 36); Huffmon (2000: 50).

248 Nissinen (2003: Nos. 1–4, 6, 18, 19, 29, 34, 47, 48: *āpilum*; Nos. 10, 11, 30–32, 46, 49, 50: *muhhūm*).

249 E.g. Nissinen (2003: No. 9).

250 E.g. Nissinen (2003: Nos. 20, 27, 35, 45).

251 E.g. Nissinen (2003: No. 9, 16). Some administrative documents refer to remuneration received by prophets: Nissinen (2003: 79, Nos. 53–63).

252 E.g. Nissinen (2003: Nos. 38, 41).

253 E.g. Nissinen (2003: No. 12); Malamat (1989: 90–94). An oracle received by an ecstatic in the assembly of the elders: Nissinen (2003: No. 16); pronounced near the palace gate: (No. 47).

254 Nissinen (2003: Nos. 5, 43).

255 Literally 'man-woman,' Nissinen (2003: 7; Nos. 7, 8, 22, 23); Malamat (1989: 85).

256 Nissinen (2003: Nos. 51, 52).

257 Nissinen (2003: No. 16); Grabbe (2000: 22); Huffmon (2000: 49).

258 On other documents on the *assinnum* see Wilson (1980: 106–107).

259 Several *āpilums* were associated with cults in towns not governed by the ruler of Mari, and the reports of their prophetic utterings reached the court in a haphazard way: Wilson (1980: 110, 101–102).

260 Nissinen (2003: 16).

261 For the historiography see Wilson (1980: 98–110); Barstad (1993: 49); Malamat (1989: 79–96).

262 Notwithstanding common origins: West Semitic (Amorite) elements were quite prominent in Mari (Malamat 1989: 2, 27, 70).

263 Especially later or classical prophets, such as Amos, Isaiah, Jeremiah, Ezekiel, and others (Lindblom 1962: 108–122; Overholt 1989: 21). The claim that this emphasis ensues from the editorial impact of scribes and priests rather than from the message of the prophets (Grabbe 1995: 117) contradicts the principle of using the Old Testament as the main source for the reconstruction of the prophetic tradition, if there is no unequivocal evidence indicating its untrustworthiness.

264 Suggestions to establish historic-genetic connections between the Mari and the Old Testament prophecy (notwithstanding the gap dividing the two phenomena) lack factual and methodological foundations. Cf. Wilson (1980: 90).

265 Parpola (1997: il–l); Nissinen (2000b: 91–93).

266 Huffmon (2000: 61).

267 Lloyd (2005: 38–41).

268 Nissinen (2000b: 109).

269 The historical books of the Old Testament received their definite form only after the Babylonian exile, hence the ongoing debate on the accuracy of the data on early prophecy. Thus, the text of these books is challenging in many respects, mainly because we deal with a written record of oral pronouncements, and also because the Old Testament had been edited and re-edited, making the version in our disposal extremely problematic as a source (Caroll 1989; Barstad 1993).

270 וישאל שאול ביהוה לא ענהו יהוה גם בחלונות וגם באורים וגם בנביאים
Cf. *Deut.* 13. 1–2: 'If a prophet arises among you, or a dreamer of dreams, and gives you a sign or a wonder . . . כי-יקום בקרבך נביא או חולם חלום ונתן אליך אות או מופת. It is to be indicated that King Saul tried the three standard methods of divination before he turned to a necromancer, which was deemed abnormal.

271 Some prophets condemn divination by signs, e.g. *Jes.* 2. 6, 8. 19, 19. 3, 44. 25, 47. 13; *Jer.* 27. 9, 29. 9; Overholt (1989: 126).

272 The same tripartite division of manifestations of the divine will is attested to in a Hittite text recording *Plague Prayers of Mursilis*. The king asks the gods to uncover the reason of their anger: 'Either let it be established by an omen, or let me see it in

a dream, or let a prophet declare it!' (No 2, *ANET* 395, about a third quarter of the fourteenth century BC).

273 E.g. *Exod.* 28. 30; *Lev.* 8. 8; *Num.* 27.21; *Deut.* 33. 8; *Esra* 2. 63; *Neh.* 7. 65.

274 *Exod.* 28. 30; *Lev.* 8. 8.

275 Grabbe (1995); Porter (1981: 206). It has also been suggested that the priest received a revelation which had to be confirmed by means of *Urim and Thummim*.

Divination by signs existed in early Israel, and is alluded to and criticized more than once (e.g. *2 Sam.* 5. 24; *Deut.* 13. 2–6); necromancy is also clearly attested to (*1 Sam.* 28), although the evidence of these practices seems to have been suppressed in the Old Testament tradition (cf. Lindblom 1962: 88–89; Porter 1981: 203–204, 208).

276 E.g. *Gen.* 28. 11–20; 46. 1. Spending the night in a holy place in the hope to receive divine illumination through a dream, resembles incubation attested elsewhere in the Near East, as well as in Greece: *1 Reg.* 3; *1 Sam.* 3. 5–14; Porter (1981: 202).

277 *Deut.* 13; *Jer.* 27. 9; Malamat (1989: 92).

278 *1 Reg.* 18; Huffmon (2000: 63).

279 Without doubt, Jeremiah, Ezekiel, and Zechariah; Samuel's augural vision (*1 Sam.* 3) took place in the temple but the presentation of some prophets as performing some functions in the temple is insufficient for the isolation of 'cultic prophets' into a separate type: Lindblom (1962: 80–82, 208); Petersen (2000: 35); Grabbe (1995: 112–113); Caroll (1989: 211–212); Overholt (1989: 75).

280 איש האלוהים, חולם חלומות, רואה, חוזה Huffmon (2000: 63–69); Haldar (1945: 108–126); Grabbe (1995: 82–84, 108–112). For the words see Wilson (1980: 136–140, 256–257). It is noteworthy that the *Septuagint* usually translates נביא as *prophêtês*, rather than *mantis*. The word נביא is used in several Hebrew ostraca from Lachish (sixth century BC; Seow 2003: Nos. 139–141), alluding to the activities of a prophet at a time of a great calamity.

281 חזון or 2 מראה *Sam.* 7. 17; *Jes.* 1. 1; 2. 1; *Ez.* 7. 13; *1 Sam.* 9. 15; Lindblom (1962: 112–137).

282 *Num.* 22–24; van Kooten and van Ruiten (2008).

Other prophets dubbed seer (חוזה or רואה) Iddo, *2 Chron.* 9. 29; Elisha (*2 Reg.* 8. 13); Isaiah (*Jes.* 1. 1; 21. 2); Zechariah (*Zach.* 1. 8), and most conspicuously Ezekiel (*Ez.* 7. 13; 8. 4).

283 Grabbe (1995: 113).

284 Huldah in *2 Reg.* 22. 11–20; *2 Chr.* 34. 22–28; Deborah in *Jud.* 4–5

285 Given the Sibyl's provenance from Asia Minor and solid evidence for the presence of Assyrian divination techniques (hepatoscopy) and 'seers of an Eastern type' in Greece about 800 (Burkert 1983: 118), the possibility that the emergence of the Sibyl-like prophetesses was influenced by Levantine examples cannot be ruled out.

286 *Jes.* 22. 2; *Jer.* 37. 2; *Zach.* 7. 7.

287 Grabbe (1995: 111); Wilson (1980: 144); Lindblom (1962: 55, 109–115); Piñero (1991: 7–10); Tiemeyer (2011). For the historiography of association of Old Testament prophets with ecstasy, which is the dominant approach at present, see Wilson (1980: 5–8).

288 *Ez.* 3. 10; *Jes.* 6. 9; *Jer.* 20. 8; Lindblom (1962: 109–110, 148–165).

289 E.g. *Ez.* 3. 14, 3. 22, 8. 1, 37.1.

290 *Num.* 12. 6–8: 'If there is a prophet among you, I Yahweh make myself known to him in a vision (במראה), I speak with him in a dream (בחלום)… With him I speak mouth to mouth, clearly, and not in dark speech (לא בחידת); and he beholds the form (תצונת יהוה) of Yahweh'.

291 *Deut.* 18; prophet as intermediary: Tiemeyer (2011); Wilson (1980: 155–166, with refs.).

292 Inquiries: *1 Reg.* 14. 3, 22. 5; *2 Reg.* 1. 3, 8. 7, *Jer.* 21. 2; *Jes.* 30. 2; unsolicited oracles: *1 Reg.* 11–13; *1 Sam.* 2. 27; *Jes.* 21. 10; *Jer.* 37. 20; Lindblom (1962: 71–72, 110–111).

293 Piñero (1991: 17, cf. 29).

294 E.g. 1 *Sam*.10. 5–6, 10; 1 *Reg.* 20. 36-38; 2 Reg. 3. 15; *Zach.* 13. 6; 4 *Esra* 14. 39–41. Servants of the pagan god Baal practicing self-flagellation are nevertheless called prophets (*1 Kings* 18: 29). The Levitical families of Asaph, Heman and Jeduthun are described as engaged in prophesying, playing music and singing (הנביאים בכנרות בנבלים ובמצלתים) – and in temple service (*1 Chron.* 25. 1). See Lindblom 1962: 59–60.

295 *Num.* 24. 15–16, verse 16: נפל וגלוי עינים; Lindblom 1962: 93; Wilson 1980: 147–150.

296 Barstad (1993: 59). This reality is corroborated by the Lachish ostraca mentioned above.

297 Wilson (1980: 144). The book of Ezekiel may serve an excellent example: notwithstanding the ongoing controversy on the exact discrimination between the prophet's own words and the later editions, it is clear that the book is essentially a sixth-century creation, 'profoundly influenced, both in content and in style, by Ezekiel himself' (Joyce 2007: 16).

298 *Jes.* 30. 8; *Jer.* 30. 2, 41. 60; *Ez.* 43. 11; Lindblom (1962: 163–164).

299 E.g. *Jes.* 5; Lindblom (1962: 154–155).

300 *Jer.* 15. 16: מעי מעי אחולה קירות:19 .4 *Jer.*; נמצאו דבריך ואכלם ויהי דבריך לי לששון ולשמחת לבבי, cf. *Jer.* 20. 7-9; Lindblom, 1962: 179, 195. לבי המה-לי לבי לא אחריש כי קול שופר שמעתי נפשי תרועת מלחמה

301 δεινός ὀρθομαντείας πόνος, A. A. 1215.

302 Lightfoot (2007: 10).

303 *1 Reg.* 17–38, 2 *Reg.* 1. 2–12, 2. 19–22, 4. 8–37, 42–44.

304 2 *Reg.* 20. 8–11.

305 2 *Reg.* 2. 11.

306 2 *Reg.* 5. 26; *Ez.* 3. 12, cf. 8. 1–3, 11. 24.

307 Aune (1983: 83, 86–87); Grabbe (1995: 149); cf. Lindblom (1962: 47–104, 197–202); Overholt (1989: 89–111). For 'shamanism' in ancient Israel, see Miller II (2014).

308 חבל הנביאים, להקת הנביאים e.g. *1 Sam.* 10. 5, 10; 19. 20; 1 *Reg.* 20. 35; 2 *Reg.* 2. 3; Huffmon 2000: 64. The term usually refers to prophetic activities in the time of Samuel and to Elijah and Elisha (Wilson 1980: 141; Lindblom 1962: 65, 69–70).

309 *Jer.* 29. 26; *Hos.* 9. 7; 2 *Reg.* 9. 1; cf. Saul's stripping off his clothes (*1 Sam.* 19. 2–24); Isaiah's remaining naked for three years (*Jes.* 20. 3); Ezekiel remaining on his side for 430 days (*Ez.* 4–5).

310 Wilson (1980: 87); Lindblom (1962: 74).
   It is noteworthy that derivatives from the word נביא could not necessarily designate uttering a prophecy, but also being chosen by the god. Thus, the seventy elders chosen to share the leadership with Moses, when the spirit rested upon them, 'acted like a prophet,' ויתנבאו (*Num.* 11. 25, cf. *1 Sam.* 10. 5–6), which implies that being a prophet involved stereotypical and recognisable abnormal behaviour (Wilson 1980: 153, 177; Lindblom 1962: 102).

311 E.g. *Jer.* 29. 26: לכל-איש משגע ומתנבא, 'each man mad and prophesying;' cf. 1 *Sam* 10. 10: הגם שאול בנביאים.

312 A. A. 1140.

313 *Ez.* 1–3; cf. the visions of Isaiah, esp. *Jes.* 6.
   For the Ezekiel tradition see Clements (1996: 145–169, with refs.); Joyce (2007).

314 Tiemeyer (2011: 177).

315 The author of the *Apocalypse* of John also claimed that he had received a scroll from an angel and eaten it (10. 9).

316 *Ez.* 10. 16–22.

317 'Merkabah literature,' Sholem (1987: 19–24); Joyce (2007: 56).

318 Nissinen (2010: 343–345); Dillery (2005).

319 Dillon (1996: 119).

320 Bowden (2013: 46); Eidinow (2007: 10–25).

321 West (1997); Burkert (2004); on diviners see in particular Burkert (1983).

322 See the Introduction above.
323 The possibility of manipulation of the diviner's responses seems to be assumed in *Num*. 22. 6.
324 The *Book of Daniel*, referring to the Antiochene persecutions, is obviously much later, which makes it exceptional.
325 Overholt (1989: 17–25, 86–115).
326 Overholt (1989: 71).
327 Overholt (1989: 81, 112–113).
328 For an overview see Finkelstein and Mazar (2007: 99–180).
329 Cross (1973) even argues that Israelite prophecy was embedded in the royal institutions. For criticism see Petersen (2000: 36).
330 Briquel (1990: 74); cf. Pairault-Massa (1985).
331 Dodds (1973: 222).
332 Parker (2011: 13–16), esp. on Pl. *Lg.* 738BC, where Plato insists that 'tradition ultimately rests on communication from the gods, whether that came from oracles or through visual or auditory epiphany' (Parker 2011: 16), not to be altered in his ideal state.

References

Addey, C. 2013. "Ecstasy between divine and human: Re-assessing agency in Iamblichean divination and theurgy." In *Literary, Philosophical and Religious Studies in the Platonic Tradition*, edited by J. F. Finamore and J. Phillips, 7–24. Sankt Augustin: Academia.

Allen, J. 2010. "Greek philosophy and signs." In *Divination and Interpretation of Signs in the Ancient World*, edited by A. Annus, 26–40. Chicago: The University of Chicago Press.

Amandry, P. 1950. *La mantique apollinienne à Delphes*. Paris: de Boccard.

Amandry, P. 1984. "Le culte des nymphes et de Pan à l'antre Corycien." *BCH* Suppl. 9:395–425.

Amandry, P. and E. Hansen. 2010. *Le temple d'Apollon du IVe siècle, Fuilles de Delphes: Topographie et architecture 14*. Paris: de Boccard.

Angliker, E. forthcoming. "Worship and stones on the Cycladic Islands: A case study of the aniconic cult of Apollo and Zeus." In *Cycladic Archaeology: New Approaches and Discoveries*, edited by E. Angliker and J. Tully. Oxford: Archeopress.

Annus, A., ed. 2010. *Divination and Interpretation of Signs in the Ancient World*. Chicago: The University of Chicago Press.

Arnott, W. G. 1989. "Nechung: A modern parallel to the Delphic oracle?" *G&R* 36:152–157.

Assmann, J. 2001. *The Search for God in Ancient Egypt*. Ithaca: Cornell University Press.

Aune, D. E. 1983. *Prophecy in Early Christianity and the Ancient Mediterranean World*. Grand Rapids: Eerdmans.

Babut, D. 1984. "Le dialogue de Plutarque 'Sur le démon de Socrate.' Essai d'interprétation." *BAGB*:51–76.

Bagnasco Gianni, G. 2011. "Lettere eimagini: esempi etruschi di parola ispirata." In *Corollari: Scritti di antichità etrusche e italiche in omaggio all'opera di Giovanni Colonna*, edited by D. F. Maras, 185–192. Pisa-Roma: Fabrizio Serra.

Barstad, H. M. 1993. "No prophets? Recent developments in Biblical prophetic research and ancient near Eastern prophecy." *Journal for the Study of the Old Testament* 57:39–60.

Baudy, G. 1996. "Abaris." In *Der Neue Pauly*, 5–6.

Bayet, J. 1946. "La mort de la Pythie: Lucain, Plutarque et la chronologie delphique." In *Mélanges dédiés à la mémoire de Félix Crat*, vol. 1, 53–76. Paris: Droz.

Bean, G. E. 1989a. *Aegean Turkey*. London: J. Murray.

Bean, G. E. 1989b. *Turkey Beyond the Meander*. London: J. Murray.

Beazley, J. D. 1963. *Attic Red-Figure Vase-Painters*. Oxford: Clarendon Press.

Belayche, N. and J. Rüpke. 2005. "Divination romaine." In *ThCRA*, 79–104.

Bonnechere, P. 1998a. "La scène d'initiation des Nuées d'Aristophane et Trophonios: nouvelles lumières sur le culte lébadéen." *RÉG* 111 (2):436–480.

Bonnechere, P. 1998b. "Les dieux du *Trophonion* lébadéen: panthéon ou amalgame?" *Kernos* Suppl. 8:91–108.

Bonnechere, P. 1999. "La personalité mythologique de Trophonios." *RHR* 216 (3):259–297.

Bonnechere, P. 2002. "Mantique, transe et phénomènes psychiques à Lébadée: entre rationnel et irrationel en Grèce et dans la pensée moderne." *Kernos* 15:179–186.

Bonnechere, P. 2003a. *Trophonios de Lébadée*. Leiden: Brill.

Bonnechere, P. 2003b. "Trophonios of Lebadea. Mystery aspects of an oracular cult in Boeotia." In *Greek Mysteries: The Archaeology and Ritual of Ancient Greek Secret Cults*, edited by M. B. Cosmopoulos, 169–192. London-New York: Routledge.

Bonnechere, P. 2007. "The place of the sacred grove (*alsos*) in the mantic rituals of Greece: The example of the oracle of Trophonios at Lebadeia (Boeotia)." In *Sacred Gardens and Landscapes: Ritual and Agency*, edited by M. Conan, 17–41. Washington, DC: Dumbarton Oaks Research Library and Collection.

Bonnechere, P. 2010. "Notes trophoniaques, IV: avancées, retours, mises au point." *LEC* 78:57–72.

Bonnechere, P. and M. Bonnechere. 1989. "Trophonios à Lebadée. Histoire d'un oracle." *Etudes classiques* 67 (4):289–302.

Bottéro, J. 1974. "Symptômes, signes, écritures." In *Divination et rationalité*, edited by J.-P. Vernant, 70–197. Paris: Seuil.

Bouché-Leclercq, A. 1879–1882. *Histoire de la divination dans l'Antiquité*. Paris: E. Leroux.

Bowden, H. 2005. *Classical Athens and the Delphic Oracle*. Cambridge: Cambridge University Press.

Bowden, H. 2013. "Seeking certainty and claiming authority: The consultation of Greek oracles from the classical to the Roman Imperial periods." In *Divination in the Ancient World*, edited by V. Rosenberger, 41–60. Stuttgart: Franz Steiner.

Bremmer, J. N. 2008. *Greek Religion and Culture, the Bible and the Ancient Near East*. Leiden: Brill.

Briquel, D. 1990. "Le paradoxe étrusque: une parole inspirée dans oracles prophétiques." *Kernos* 3:67–75.

Brouillette, X. 2014. *La philosophie delphique de Plutarque*. Paris: Les Belles Lettres.

Bryce, T. 2002. *Life and Society in the Hittite World*. Oxford: Oxford University Press.

Burkert, W. 1983. "Itinerant diviners and magicians: A neglected element in cultural contacts." In *The Greek Renaissance of the Eighth Century* BC: *Tradition and Innovation*, edited by R. Hägg, 115–119. Stockholm: Paul Åströms Förlag.

Burkert, W. 1985. *Greek Religion*. Cambridge, MA: Harvard University Press.

Burkert, W. 1997. "Euenios der Seher von Apollonia und Apollon Lykeios: Mythos jensits der Texte." *Kernos* 10:73–81.

Burkert, W. 2004. *Babylon, Memphis, Persepolis: Eastern Contexts of Greek Culture*. Cambridge, MA: Harvard University Press.

Burkert, W. 2005a. "Mantik in Griechenland." In *ThCRA* 3:1–51.

Burkert, W. 2005b. "Signs, commands, and knowledge: Ancient divination between enigma and epiphany." In *Mantikê: Studies in Ancient Divination*, edited by S. I. Johnston and P. T. Struck, 29–49. Leiden: Brill.

Busine, A. 2002. "La consultation de l'oracle d'Apollon dans le discourse de Jamblique." *Kernos* 15:187–198.

Busine, A. 2005. *Paroles d'Apollon: Pratiques et traditions oraculaires dans l'Antiquité tardive (IIe-VIe siècles).* Leiden: Brill.

Buxton, R.G.A. 1980. "Blindness and limits: Sophocles and the logic of myth." *JHS* 100:22–37.

Cardeña, E. 2005. "The phenomenology of deep hypnosis: Quiescent and physically active." *Journal of Clinical and Experimental Hypnosis* 51 (3):37–59.

Caroll, R. N. 1989. "Prophecy and society." In *The World of Ancient Israel*, edited by R. E. Clements, 203–225. Cambridge: Cambridge University Press.

Casevitz, M. 1992. "Mantis: le vrai sens." *RÉG* 105:1–18.

Chalupa, A. 2014. "Pythiai and inspired divination in the Delphic oracle: Can cognitive sciences provide us with an access to 'dead minds'?" *Journal of Cognitive Historiography* 1 (1):24–51.

Champeaux, J. 1990a. "*Sors oraculi*: les oracles en Italie sous la république et l'empire." *MEFRA* 102 (1):271–302.

Chantraine, P. 1983–1884. *Dictionnaire étymologique de la langue grecque.* Paris: Klincksieck.

Ciraolo, L. and J. Seidel, eds. 2002. *Magic and Divination in the Ancient World.* Leiden: Brill.

Clark, R. J. 1968. "Trophonios: The manner of his revelation." *TAPhA* 99:63–75.

Clark, R. J. 1979. *Catabasis: Vergil and the Wisdom-Tradition.* Amsterdam: Grüner.

Clements, R. E. 1996. *Old Testament Prophecy: From Oracles to Canon.* Louisville: West-minster John Knox Press.

Cohen, E. 2007. *The Mind Possessed: The Cognition of Spirit Possession in Afro-Brazilian Religious Tradition.* Oxford: Oxford University Press.

Cook, A. B. 1914–40. *Zeus.* Cambridge: Cambridge University Press.

Corlu, A. 1970. *Plutarque, Le démon de Socrate: Texte et traduction avec une introduction et des notes.* Paris: Klincksieck.

Corssen, P. 1912. "Der Abaris des Heraklides Ponticus." *RhM* 67:21–47.

Courby, F. 1927. *Fouilles de Delphes. Vol. II: La terrasse du temple.* Paris: de Boccard.

Cross, F. 1973. *Canaanite Myth and Hebrew Epic.* Cambridge, MA: Harvard University Press.

Curnow, T. 2004. *The Oracles of the Ancient World.* London: Duckworth.

Cusset, C. 2004. "Cassandre et/ou la Sibylle: les vois dans l'Alexandra de Lycophron." In *La sibylle: Parole et représentation*, edited by M. Bouquet and F. Morzadec, 53–60. Rennes: Presses universitaires de Rennes.

D'Andria, F. 2013. "Il Ploutonion a Hierapolis di Frigia." *IstMitt* 63:157–217.

Davidson, H.R.E. 1981. "The Germanic world." In *Divination and Oracles*, edited by M. Loewe and C. Blacker, 115–141. London: Allen & Unwin.

de Boer, J. Z. 2007. "Delphi's small 'omphalos': An enigma." *SyllClass* 18:81–104.

de Boer, J. Z. and J. R. Hale. 2001. "The geological origins of the oracle at Delphi, Greece." In *The Archaeology of Geological Catastrophes*, edited by W. G. McGuire, D. R. Griffiths, P. L. Hancock, and O. S. Stewart, 399–412. London: Geological Society.

de Boer, J. Z., J. R. Hale, and J. Chanton. 2001. "New evidence for the geological origins of the ancient Delphic oracle (Greece)." *Geology* 29 (8):707–710.

de Grummond, N. T. 2006. *Etruscan Myth, Sacred History, and Legend.* Philadelphia: University of Pennsylvania Museum of Archaeology and Anthropology.

Delatte, A. 1934. *Les conceptions de l'enthousiasme chez les philosophes présocratiques.* Paris: Les Belles Lettres.

Delcourt, M. 1981. *L'oracle de Delphes*. Paris: Payot.

Detienne, M. 1963. *La notion de daïmôn dans le pythagorisme ancien*. Paris: Les Belles Lettres.

Deubner, L. 1900. *De incubatione*. Leipzig: Teubner.

Dietrich, B. C. 1978. "Reflections on the origins of the oracular Apollo." *BICS* 25:1–18.

Dietrich, B. C. 1983. "Divine epiphanies in Homer." *Numen* 30:53–79.

Dietrich, B. C. 1990. "Oracles and divine inspiration." *Kernos* 3:157–174.

Dillery, J. 2005. "Chresmologues and *manteis*: Independent diviners and the problem of authority." In *Mantikê: Studies in Ancient Divination*, edited by S. I. Johnston and P. T. Struck, 167–231. Leiden: Brill.

Dillon, M. 1996. "The importance of oionomantheia in Greek divination." In *Religion in the Ancient World*, edited by M. Dillon, 99–121. Amsterdam: Hakkert.

Dodds, E. R. 1973. *The Greeks and the Irrational*. Berkeley-Los Angeles: University of California Press.

Dowden, K. 1989. *Death and the Maiden: Girls' Initiation Rites in Greek Mythology*. London-New York: Routledge.

Ducat, J. 1971. *Les kouroi du Ptoion*. Paris: de Boccard.

Durand, J.-M. 1997. "Les prophéties des textes de Mari." In *Oracles et prophéties dans l'antiquité*, edited by J.-G. Heintz, 115–134. Paris: de Boccard.

Edelstein, L. and E. J. Edelstein. 1948. *Asclepius*. Baltimore: Johns Hopkins University Press.

Eidinow, E. 2007. *Oracles, Curses, and Risk Among the Ancient Greeks*. Oxford: Oxford University Press.

Eidinow, E. 2011. "Networks and narratives: A model for ancient Greek religion." *Kernos* 24:9–38.

Etiope, G., G. Papatheodorou, D. Christodoulou, M. Geraga, and P. Favali. 2006. "The geological links of the ancient Delphic Oracle (Greece): A reappraisal of natural gas occurrence and origin." *Geology* 10 (34):821–824.

Ferrary, J.-L. 2005. "Les mémoriaux de délégation de sanctuaire oraculaire de Claros et leur chronologie." *CRAI*: 149 (2):717–765.

Finkelstein, I. and A. Mazar. 2007. *The Quest for the Historical Israel: Debating Archaeology and the History of Early Israel (Archaeology and Biblical Studies)*. Leiden: Brill.

Flacelière, R. 1938. "Le fonctionnement de l'oracle de Delphes au temps de Plutarque." *Annales de l'École des Hautes Études de Gand* 2:69–107.

Flacelière, R. 1965. *Greek Oracles*. London: Elek.

Flacelière, R. 1972. *Devins et oracles grecs*. Paris: Presses Universitaires de France.

Flower, M. A. 2008. *The Seer in Ancient Greece*. Berkeley-Los Angeles: University of California Press.

Fontenrose, J. 1978. *The Delphic Oracle*. Berkeley-Los Angeles: University of California Press.

Fontenrose, J. 1988. *Didyma: Apollo's Oracle, Cult, and Companions*. Berkeley-Los Angeles: University of California Press.

Foster, J. and D. Lehoux. 2007. "The Delphic oracle and the ethylene-intoxication hypothesis." *Clinical Toxicology* 45 (1):85–89.

Friese, W. 2010. *Den Göttern so nah: Architektur und Topographie griechischer Orakelheiligtümer*. Stuttgart: Franz Steiner.

Frisk, H. 1973–1979. *Griechisches etymologisches Wörterbuch*. Heidelberg: C. Winter.

Gartziou-Tatti, A. 1990. "L'oracle de Dodone. Mythe et rituel." *Kernos* 3:175–184.

Georgoudi, S. 1998. "Les porte-parole des dieux: réflexions sur le personel des oracles grecs." In *Sibille e languaggi oracolari*, edited by I. Chirassi Colombo and T. Seppilli, 315–365. Pisa-Rome: Istituti Editoriali e Poligrafici Internazionali.

Georgoudi, S. 2012. "Des sons, des signes et des paroles: la divination à l'oeuvre dans l'oracle de Dodona." In *Présages, rites, destin dans les sociétés de la Méditerranée ancienne*, edited by S. Georgoudi, R. Koch Piettre, and F. Schmidt, 55–90. Leiden: Brill.

Georgoudi, S., R. Koch Piettre, and F. Schmidt, eds. 2012. *Présages, rites, destin dans les sociétés de la Méditerranée ancienne*. Leiden: Brill.

González, J. M. 2013. *The Epic Rhapsode and His Craft*. Washington, DC: Center for Hellenic Studies.

Gorman, V. B. 2001. *Miletos, the Ornament of Ionia*. Ann Arbor: University of Michigan Press.

Grabbe, L. L. 1995. *Priests, Prophets, Diviners, Sages: A Socio-Historical Study of Religious Specialists in Ancient Israel*. Valley Forge: Trinity Press International.

Grabbe, L. L. 2000. "Ancient Near Eastern prophecy from an anthropological perspective." In *Prophecy in Its Ancient Near Eastern Context*, edited by M. Nissinen, 13–32. Atlanta: Society of Biblical Literature.

Graf, F. 1985. *Nordionische Kulte*. Rome: Schweizerisches Institut in Rom.

Graf, F. 2009a. *Apollo*. London: Routledge.

Graf, F. 2009b. "Apollo, possession, and prophecy." In *Apolline Politics and Poetics: International Symposium*, edited by L. Athanassaki, R. P. Martin and J. F. Miller, 587–607. Athens: Hellenic Ministry of Culture; European Cultural Centre of Delphi.

Greaves, A. M. 2002. *Miletos: A History*. London-New York: Routledge.

Green, P. 1989. *Classical Bearings: Interpreting Ancient History and Culture*. London: Thames and Hudson.

Green, P. 2009. "Possession and *pneuma*: The essential nature of the Delphic oracle." *Arion* 17 (2):27–47.

Grottanelli, C. 1994–1995. "L'Événios d'Hérodote, IX 92–95." *Métis* 9–10:79–98.

Grottanelli, C. 2003. "Evenius becomes a seer (Herodotus 9. 93–5). A paradoxical initiation?" In *Initiation in Ancient Greek Rituals and Narratives*, edited by D. B. Dodd and C. A. Faraone, 203–218. London-New York: Routledge.

Grottanelli, C. 2005. "*Sorte unica pro casibus pluribus enotata*. Literary texts and lot inscriptions as sources for ancient cleromancy." In *Mantikê: Studies in Ancient Divination*, edited by S. I. Johnston and P. T. Struck, 129–146. Leiden: Brill.

Guidorizzi, G. 1997. "The laughter of the suitors: A case of collective madness in the *Odyssey*." In *Poet, Public, and Performance in Ancient Greece*, edited by L. Edmunds and R. W. Wallace, 1–8. Baltimore: Johns Hopkins University Press.

Guidorizzi, G. 2010. *Ai confini dell' anima: I Greci e la follia*. Milano: Raffaelo Cortina.

Guillon, P. 1943. *Les trépieds du Ptoion. 2: Depositif matériel. Signification historique et religieuse*. Paris: École française d'Athènes.

Guillon, P. 1946. "L'offrande d'Aristichos et la consultation de l'oracle du Ptoion au début du IIIe s. av. J.-C." *BCH* 70:216–232.

Guittard, C. 2007. *Carmen et prophéties à Rome*. Turnhout: Brepols.

Günther, W. 1971. *Das Orakel von Didyma in hellenistischeer Zeit*. Tübingen: E. Wasmuth.

Gurney, O. R. 1981. "The Babylonians and Hittites." In *Divination and Oracles*, edited by M. Loewe and C. Blacker, 142–173. London: Allen & Unwin.

Hackforth, R. 1972. *Plato's Phaedrus: Translated With an Introduction and Commentary*. Cambridge: Cambridge University Press.

Haldar, A. 1945. *Associations of Cult Prophets Among the Ancient Semites*. Uppsala: Almqvist & Wiksell.

Hale, J. R., J. Z. de Boer, J. P. Chanton, and H. A. Spiller. 2003. "Questioning the Delphic oracle." *Scientific American*, August:66–73.

Halliday, W. R. 1913. *Greek Divination: A Study of Its Methods and Principles*. London: Macmillan.

Hamilton, M. 1906. *Incubation*. London: Henderson & Son.

Hani, J. 1975. "Le mythe de Timarque chez Plutarque et la structure de l'exstase." *RÉG* 88:105–120.

Haussollier, B. 1920. "Inscriptions de Didymes." *RPh* 44:248–277.

Heintz, J.-G., ed. 1997. *Oracles et prophéties dans l'Antiquité*. Paris: de Boccard.

Hoessly, F. 2001. *Katharsis: Reinigung als Heilverfahren. Studien zum Ritual der archaischen und klassischen Zeit sowie zum Corpus Hippocraticum*. Göttingen: Vandenhoeck & Ruprecht.

Holzhausen, J. 1993. "Zur Inspirationslehre Plutarchs in De Pythiae oraculis." *Philologus* 137:72–91.

Huffmon, H. B. 2000. "A company of prophets: Mari, Assyria, Israel." In *Prophecy in Its Ancient Near Eastern Context*, edited by M. Nissinen, 47–70. Atlanta: Society of Biblical Literature.

Hulskamp, M.A.A. 2013. "The value of dream diagnosis in the medical praxis of the Hippocratics and Galen." In *Dreams, Healing, and Medicine in Greece: From Antiquity to the Present*, edited by S. M. Oberhelman, 33–68. Farnham: Ashgate.

Jaillard, D. 2007. "Plutarque et la divination: la piété d'un prêtre philosophe." *RHR* 224:149–169.

Jaillard, D. 2012. "Hermès et la mantique grecque." In *Présages, rites, destin dans les sociétés de la Méditerranée ancienne*, edited by S. Georgoudi, R. Koch Piettre, and F. Schmidt, 91–107. Leiden: Brill.

Jannot, J.-R. 2005. *Religion in Ancient Etruria*. Madison: The University of Wisconsin Press.

Johnston, S. I. 2008. *Ancient Greek Divination*. Oxford: Oxford University Press.

Johnston, S. I. and P. T. Struck, eds. 2005. *Mantikê: Studies in Ancient Divination*. Leiden: Brill.

Jones, W.H.S. 1923. *Hippocrates*. Cambridge, MA: Harvard University Press.

Joyce, P. M. 2007. *Ezekiel: A Commentary*. New York: T & T Clark.

Kahn, C. H. 1979. *Art and Thought of Heraclitus*. Cambridge: Cambridge University Press.

Karp, A. 1998. "Prophecy and divination in Archaic Greek Literature." In *Mediators of the Divine: Horizons of Prophecy, Divination, Dreams and Theurgy in Mediterranean Antiquity*, edited by R. M. Berchman, 9–44. Atlanta: Society of Biblical Literature.

Kern, O. 1922. *Orphicorum Fragmenta*. Berlin: Weidmann.

Klass, M. 2003. *Mind Over Mind: The Anthropology and Psychology of Spirit Possession*. Lanham: Rowman & Littlefield.

Kowalzig, B. 2007. *Singing for the Gods: Performances of Myth and Ritual in Archaic and Classical Greece*. Oxford: Oxford University Press.

Larson, J. 1995. "The Corycian Nymphs and Bee Maidens of the Homeric Hymn to Hermes." *GRBS* 36 (4):341–357.

Larson, J. 2001. *Greek Nymphs*. Oxford: Oxford University Press.

Latte, K. 1940. "The coming of the Pythia." *HThR* 33:9–18.

Laumonier, F. 1958. *Les cultes indigènes de Carie*. Paris: de Boccard.

Lehoux, D. 2007. "Drugs and the Delphic oracle." *CW* 101 (1):41–56.

Lightfoot, J. L. 2007. *The Sibylline Oracles*. Oxford: Oxford University Press.

Lindblom, J. 1962. *Prophecy in Ancient Israel*. Oxford: Blackwell.

Lloyd, G.E.R. 2005. *The Delusions of Invulnerability: Wisdom and Morality in Ancient Greece, China and Today*. London: Duckworth.

Lloyd-Jones, H. 1976. "The Delphic oracle." *G&R* 23:60–73.

Malamat, A. 1989. *Mari and the Early Israelite Experience*. Oxford: Oxford University Press.

Manetti, G. 1993. *Theories of the Sign in Classical Antiquity*. Bloomington-Indianapolis: Indiana University Press.

Maurizio, L. 1995. "Anthropology and spirit possession: A reconstruction of the Pythia's role at Delphi." *JHS* 115:69–86.

Maurizio, L. 1998. "Narrative, biographical and ritual conventions at Delphi." In *Sibille e linguaggi oracolari*, edited by I. Chirassi Colombo and T. Seppilli, 133–158. Pisa-Rome: Istituti Editoriali e Poligrafici Internazionali.

Mazzoldi, S. 2001. *Cassandra, la vergine e l'indovine*. Pisa-Rome: Istituti Editoriali e Poligrafici Internazionali.

Mazzoldi, S. 2002. "Cassandra's prophecy between ecstasy and rational mediation." *Kernos* 15:145–154.

Merkelbach, R. and J. Stauber. 1996. "Die Orakel des Apollon von Klaros." *EA* 27:1–53.

Metzler, D. 1990. "Der Seher Mopsos auf den Münzen der Stadt Mallos," *Kernos* 3:235–250.

Mikalson, J. D. 2005. *Ancient Greek Religion*. Oxford-Malden: Blackwell.

Mikalson, J. D. 2010. *Greek Popular Religion in Greek Philosophy*. Oxford: Oxford University Press.

Miller II, R. D. 2014. "Shamanism and totemism in ancient Israel." *Journal of the Washington Academy of Sciences* 100:21–58.

Montegu, J. C. 1976. "Note on the *labyrinths* of Didyma." *AJA* 80:304–305.

Moretti, J.-C., N. Bresch, I. Bonora, D. Laroche, and O. Riss. 2014. "Le temple d'Apollon et le fonctionnement de l'oracle." In *Le sanctuaire de Claros et son oracle*, edited by J.-C. Moretti and L. Rabatel, 33–50. Lyon: Maison de l'Orient et de la Méditerranée-Jean Pouilloux.

Morgan, M. L. 1990. *Platonic Piety: Philosophy and Ritual in Fourth-Century Athens*. New Haven: Yale University Press.

Moulinier, L. 1952. *Le pur et l'impur dans la pensée des Grecs*. Paris: Klincksieck.

Naddaf, G. 2013. "Philosophic and poetic inspiration in the *Republic*." In *Dialogues on Plato's Politeia (Republic)*, edited by N. Notomi and L. Brisson, 301–306. Sankt-Augustin: Academia.

Nagy, G. 1990. "Greek poetry, prophecy, and concepts of theory." In *Poetry and Prophecy: The Beginnings of a Literary Tradition*, edited by J. L. Kugel, 56–64. Ithaca: Cornell University Press.

Negri, S. and G. Leucci. 2006. "Geophysical investigation of the temple of Apollo (Hierapolis, Turkey)." *Journal of Archaeological Science* 33:1505–1513.

Nikiprowetsky, V. 1970. *La troisième Sibylle*. Paris: La Haye.

Nilsson, M. P. 1961–1967. *Geschichte der griechischen Religion*. 2 vols. Munich: C. H. Beck.

Nissinen, M., ed. 2000a. *Prophecy in Its Ancient Near Eastern Context*. Atlanta: Society of Biblical Literature.

Nissinen, M. 2000b. "The socioreligious role of the Neo-Assyrian prophets." In *Prophecy in Its Ancient Near Eastern Context*, edited by M. Nissinen, 89–114. Atlanta: Society of Biblical Literature.

Nissinen, M. 2003. *Prophets and Prophecy in the Ancient Near East*. Atlanta: Society of Biblical Literature.

Nissinen, M. 2010. "Prophecy and omen divination: Two sides of the same coin." In *Divination and Interpretation of Signs in the Ancient World*, edited by A. Annus, 341–351. Chicago: Oriental Institute of the University of Chicago.

North, J. A. 2000. *Roman Religion*. Oxford: Oxford University Press.

O'Brien-Moore, A. 1924. *Madness in Ancient Literature*. Weimar: Wagner.

Oesterheld, C. 2014. "La parole salvatrice transformée en remèdie perpétuel: l'oracle d'Apollon de Claros rendu à la ville de Hiérapolis en Phrygie." In *Le sanctuaire de Claros et son oracle*, edited by J.-C. Moretti and L. Rabatel, 211–226. Lyon: Maison de l'Orient et de la Méditerranée-Jean Pouilloux.

Ogden, D. 2001. *Greek and Roman Necromancy*. Princeton: Princeton University Press.

Oppé, A. P. 1904. "The chasm at Delphi." *JHS* 24:214–240.

Overholt, T. W. 1989. *Channels of Prophecy*. Minneapolis: Fortress Press.

Pairault-Massa, F.-H. 1985. "La divination en Etrurie. Le IVe siècle, période critique." *Caesarodunum* Suppl. 52:56–115.

Panagiotidou, O. 2014. "The Asklepios Cult: Where brains, minds and bodies interact with the world creating new realities." *Journal of Cognitive Historiography* 1 (1):14–23.

Parke, H. W. 1939. *A History of the Delphic Oracle*. Oxford: Blackwell.

Parke, H. W. 1967. *Greek Oracles*. London: Hutchinson.

Parke, H. W. 1985. *The Oracles of Apollo in Asia Minor*. London: Croom Helm.

Parke, H. W. 1988. *Sibyls and Sibylline Prophecy in Classical Antiquity*. London-New York: Routledge.

Parke, H. W. and D.E.W. Wormell. 1956. *The Delphic Oracle*. Oxford: Blackwell.

Parker, R. 1983. *Miasma: Pollution and Purification in Early Greek Religion*. Oxford: Oxford University Press.

Parker, R. 2000. "Greek states and Greek oracles." In *Oxford Readings in Greek Religion*, edited by R. Buxton, 76–108. Oxford: Oxford University Press.

Parker, R. 2011. *On Greek Religion*. Ithaca: Cornell University Press.

Parpola, S. 1997. *Assyrian Prophecies*. Helsinki: Helsinki University Press.

Petersen, D. L. 2000. "Defining prophecy and prophetic literature." In *Prophecy in Its Ancient Near Eastern Context*, edited by M. Nissinen, 33–44. Atlanta: Society of Biblical Literature.

Picard, C. 1922. *Éphèse et Claros*. Paris: de Boccard.

Piccardi, L., C. Monti, O. Vaselli, F. Tassi, K. Gaki-Papanastassiou, and D. Papanastassiou. 2008. "Scent of a myth: Tectonics, geochemistry and geomythology at Delphi (Greece)." *Journal of the Geological Society* 165 (1):5–18.

Piñero, A. 1991. "A Mediterranean view of prophetic inspiration: On the concept of inspiration in the *Liber Antiquitatum Biblicarum* by Pseudo-Philo." *MHR* 6 (1):5–34.

Pollard, J. 1965. *Seers, Shrines and Sirens*. London: Allen & Unwin.

Porter, J. R. 1981. "Ancient Israel." In *Divination and Oracles*, edited by M. Loewe and C. Blacker, 191–214. London: Allen & Unwin.

Potter, D. 1990. "Sibyls in the Greek and Roman World." *JRA* 3:471–483.

Poulsen, F. 1920. *Delphi*. Edited and translated by G. S. Richards. London: Gyldendal.

Powell, A. 2009. "Divination, royalty and insecurity in Classical Sparta." *Kernos* 22:35–82.

Price, S. 1985. "Delphi and divination." In *Greek Religion and Society*, edited by P. E. Easterling and J. V. Muir, 128–154. Cambridge: Cambridge University Press.

Ray, J. F. 1981. "Ancient Egypt." In *Divination and Oracles*, edited by M. Loewe and C. Blacker, 174–190. London: Allen & Unwin.

Ritner, R. K. 2003. "Report of Wenamon." In *Prophets and Prophecy in the Ancient Near East*, edited by M. Nissinen, 219–220. Atlanta: Society of Biblical Literature.

Robert, L. 1950. "Le Carien Mys et l'oracle du Ptôon." In *Hellenica VIII*, 23–38. Paris.

Robert, L. 1967. "L'oracle de Claros." In *La civilisation grecque*, edited by C. Delvoye and G. Roux, 305–312. Brussels: La Renaissance du livre.

Rohde, E. 1925. *Psyche*. London: Routledge & Kegan Paul.

Rosenberger, V. 1998. *Gezähmte Götter: Das Prodigienwesen der römischen Republik*. Stuttgart: F. Steiner.

Rosenberger, V. 2001. *Griechische Orakel: Eine Kulturgeschichte*. Darmstadt: WBG.

Rouget, G. 1990. *La musique et la trance*. Paris: Gallimard.

Roux, G. 1976. *Delphes: Son oracle et ses dieux*. Paris: Les Belles Lettres.

Roux, G. 2000. "L'architecture à Delphes: un siècle de découvertes." In *Delphes: Cent ans après la Grande fouille. Essai de bilan*, edited by A. Jacquemin, 181–199. Paris: de Boccard.

Rowe, C. J. 1986. *Plato: Phaedrus, Edited With Translation and Commentary*. Warminster: Aris & Phillips.

Ruck, C. 1976. "Duality and the madness of Heracles." *Arethusa* 9 (1):53–75.

Russo, J., M. Fernández-Galiano, and A. Heubeck. 1992. *A Commentary on Homer's Odyssey, Books XVII-XXIV*. Oxford: Oxford University Press.

Saïd, S. 2013. "From Homeric *ate* to tragic madness." In *Mental Disorders in the Classical World*, edited by W. V. Harris, 363–393. Leiden: Brill.

Schachter, A. 1967. "A Boeotian cult type." *BICS* 14:1–16.

Schachter, A. 1981–1994. *Cults of Boeotia*. 4 vols. BICS Suppl. 38. 1–4. London: Institute of Classical Studies.

Schachter, A. 1984. "A consultation of Trophonios (IG 7. 4136)." *AJPh* 105:258–270.

Schefer, C. 1996. *Platon und Apollon*. Sankt Augustin: Academia.

Schröder, S. 1990. *Plutarchs Schrift De Pythiae Oraculis: Text, Einleitung und Kommentar*. Stuttgart: Teubner.

Schröder, S. 1994–1995. "Platon oder Chrysipp: zur Inspirationstheorie in Plutarchs Schrift De Pythiae oraculis." *WJA* 20:233–256.

Scott, M. 2014. *Delphi: A History of the Center of the Ancient World*. Princeton: Princeton University Press.

Semeraro, G. 2014. "Archaeology of the cult in the sanctuary of Apollo in Hierapolis." *Scienze dell'Antichità* 20 (2):11–29.

Seow, C.-L. 2003. "West Semitic sources." In *Prophets and Prophecy in the Ancient Near East*, edited by M. Nissinen, 201–218. Atlanta: Society of Biblical Literature.

Serra, M. 1998. "Il frammento 93 B DK.: Eraclito e la rivelazione delfica." In *Sibille e linguaggi oracolari*, edited by I. Chirassi Colombo and T. Seppilli, 191–208. Pisa-Rome: Istituti Editoriali e Poligrafici Internazionali.

Shaw, G. 1998. "Divination in the Neoplatonism of Iamblichus." In *Mediators of the Divine: Horizons of Prophecy, Divination, Dreams and Theurgy in Mediterranean Antiquity*, edited by R. M. Berchman, 225–267. Atlanta: Society of Biblical Literature.

Sholem, G. 1987. *Origins of the Kabbalah*. Philadelphia: Jewish Publication Society.

Sidky, H. 2011. "The state oracle of Tibet, spirit possession, and shamanism." *Numen* 58:71–99.

Sineux, P. 2007. *Amphiaraos: Guerrier, devin et guérisseur*. Paris: Les Belles Lettres.

Sissa, G. 1990. *Greek Virginity*. Cambridge, MA: Harvard University Press.

Spiller, H. A., J. R. Hale, and J. Z. de Boer. 2002. "The Delphic oracle: A multidisciplinary defense of the gaseous vent theory." *Clinical Toxicology* 40 (2):189–196.

Stökl, J. 2012. "Ancient Near Eastern prophecy." In *Dictionary of the Old Testament Prophets*, edited by M. J. Boda and J. G. McConville, 16–24. Downers Grove: InterVarsity Press.

Stoneman, R. 2011. *The Ancient Oracles: Making the Gods Speak*. New Haven: Yale University Press.

Struck, P. T. 2016. *Divination and Human Nature: A Cognitive History of Intuition in Classical Antiquity*. Princeton: Princeton University Press.

Suárez de la Torre, E. 2005. "Delphes." In *ThCRA*, 16–31.

Tiemeyer, L.-S. 2011. "Ezekiel: A compromised prophet in reduced circumstances." In *Constructs of Prophecy in the Former and Latter Prophets and Other Texts*, edited by L. L. Grabbe and M. Nissinen, 175–195. Atlanta: Society of Biblical Literature.

Trampedach, K. 2008. "Authority disputed: The seer in Homeric epic." In *Practitioners of the Divine: Greek Priests and Religious Officials From Homer to Heliodorus*, edited by B. Dignas and K. Trampedach, 207–230. Cambridge, MA: Harvard University Press.

Tuchelt, K. 1991. *Branchidai-Didyma*. Mainz am Rhein: von Zabern.

Ustinova, Y. 2002. "'Either a daimon, or a hero, or perhaps a god': Mythical residents of subterranean chambers." *Kernos* 15:267–288.

Ustinova, Y. 2009a. "Apollo Iatros: A Greek god of Pontic origin." In *Die Griechen und ihre Nachbarn am Nordrand des Schwarzen Meeres*, edited by K. Stähler and D. Metzler, 245–298. Münster: Ugarit-Verlag.

Ustinova, Y. 2009b. *Caves and the Ancient Greek Mind: Descending Underground in the Search for Ultimate Truth*. Oxford: Oxford University Press.

Ustinova, Y. 2009c. "Caves and the ancient Greek oracles." *Time and Mind* 2 (3):265–286.

Ustinova, Y. 2012. "Madness into memory: Mania and mnêmê in Greek culture." *SCI* 31:109–132.

Ustinova, Y. 2013. "Modes of prophecy, or modern arguments in support of the ancient approach." *Kernos* 26:25–44.

Vallois, R. 1931. "Les strophes mutilées du péan de Philodamos." *BCH* 55:241–364.

van der Eijk, P. J. 1995. "Aristotle on 'distinguished physicians' and on the medical significance of dreams." In *Ancient Medicine in its Socio-Cultural Context*, edited by Ph. J. van der Eijk, H.E.J. Horstmanshoff and P. H. Schrijvers, 447–459. Amsterdam-Atlanta, GA: Rodopi.

van der Eijk, P. J. 2004. "Divination, prognosis and prophylaxis: The Hippocratic work 'On Dreams' (*De Victu* 4) and its Near Eastern background." In *Magic and Rationality in Ancient Near Eastern and Graeco-Roman Medicine*, edited by H.E.J. Horstmanshoff and M. Stol, 187–218. Leiden: Brill.

van Kooten, G. H. and J. van Ruiten, eds. 2008. *The Prestige of the Pagan Prophet Balaam in Judaism, Early Christianity and Islam*. Leiden: Brill.

Vernant, J.-P., ed. 1974. *Divination et rationalité*. Paris: Éditions du Seuil.

Vernant, J.-P. 1983. *Myth and Thought Among the Greeks*. London: Routledge & Kegan Paul.

Vicaire, P. 1979. "Images d'Amphiaraos dans la Grèce archaïque et classique." *BAGB*:2–45.

Villanueva Puig, M.-C. 1986. "À propos des thyiades de Delphes." In *L'association dionysiaque dans les sociétés anciennes*, 31–51. Rome: L'École française de Rome.

Watkins, C. 1995. *How to Kill a Dragon: Aspects of Indo-European Poetics*. Oxford: Oxford University Press.

West, M. L. 1983. *The Orphic Poems*. Oxford: Oxford University Press.

West, M. L. 1997. *The East Face of Helicon*. Oxford: Oxford University Press.

West, M. L. 2007. *Indo-European Poetry and Myth*. Oxford: Oxford University Press.

Whittaker, C. R. 1965. "The Delphic oracle. Belief and behaviour in ancient Greece – And Africa." *HThR* 58:21–47.

Wiegand, T. and H. Knackfuss. 1941. *Didyma. Teil 1: Die Baubeschreibung*. Berlin: Mann.

Will, E. 1942–1943. "Sur la nature du pneuma delphique." *BCH* 66/67:161–175.

Wilson, R. R. 1980. *Prophecy and Society in Ancient Israel*. Philadelphia: Fortress.

Winitzer, A. 2010. "The divine presence and its interpretation in early Mesopotamian divination." In *Divination and Interpretation of Signs in the Ancient World*, edited by A. Annus, 177–197. Chicago: The University of Chicago Press.

Wujewski, T. 2001. "Sanktuarium w Klaros (in Polish, with a German abstract)." *Eos* 88:95–126.

2 Telestic *mania* and near-death experiences

Telestic,[1] or initiatory, *mania* makes a striking personified appearance in Socrates' list of blessings of madness:

> When diseases and the greatest troubles have been visited upon certain families through some ancient guilt, madness (*mania*) has entered in and by prophecy found a way of release for those in need, taking refuge in prayers and in the service of the gods, and so, by purifications (*katharmoi*) and sacred rites (*teletai*) brought him who has this madness to safety for the present and future time, and found for him who is rightly (*orthôs*) mad a release from present evils.[2]

One is tempted to spell the word *mania* in this passage with capital M, and envisage madness as an anthropomorphic deity.[3] Do we hear an echo of a phenomenon similar to the Arcadian cult of the Maniai?[4] In any event, Socrates speaks here of the power of the god-sent *mania* to heal illnesses, mostly mental disorders, and avert other troubles, by means of purifications and initiations. He refers not only to cults involving the cure of mental disorders or relief from the stress of everyday life, such as the Corybantic and Bacchic rites.[5] At the beginning of the sentence both diseases (*nosoi*) and troubles (*ponoi*) are listed as punishments for some ancient transgressions, and at its end they are referred to as evils (*kakoi*) in general. No particular god is mentioned, no specific myth cited, and the beneficial *mania* is represented as release from every distress. Thus, in this passage Socrates probably refers to rites (*teletai*) which cure disease and assuage human condition, *kakoi* as a whole.

When later in the dialogue Plato assigns one god to every kind of divine madness, telestic *mania* is attributed to Dionysus, who is chosen as the divine patron of initiation rites *par excellence*, like Apollo, who is selected as the symbol of prophetic *mania*.[6] The choice of Dionysus provides perhaps a clue to the obscure allusion to the ancient guilt of some families: Plato might have in mind foundation myths of Bacchic rites, such as the stories of Pentheus and Lycurgus.[7] An echo of these ideas may be reflected in a poem attributed to Orpheus and cited by the

Neoplatonic Damascius, which refers to the healing powers of Dionysus *Lyseus* (Liberator):

> People . . . perform rites (*orgia*), seeking deliverance from unlawful ancestors.
> But you (Dionysus), having powers over them, whomever you wish
> You will deliver from difficult suffering and limitless frenzy (*oistros*).[8]

This text correlates with Plato's words referring to families suffering great troubles because of an ancient guilt, and release for the mad by means of 'purifications and *teletai.*'[9] Both passages allude to the effectiveness of the ceremonies in averting 'present evils' and 'difficult suffering,' meaning the burden of human existence in general. The rich evidence on the Dionysiac rites, and other mystery rites as well, indicates that they were not limited to healing mental disorders, but promised happiness and bliss at large.

Some scholars argue that Plato 'invented' telestic (initiatory) *mania* as it had never been mentioned before him.[10] However, although extant testimonies predating the *Phaedrus* do not mention telestic *mania* explicitly, alteration of consciousness among initiates is implicitly referred to in several texts, most notably in the *Bacchae.*[11] In one of the earliest pieces of evidence on bacchants, Heraclitus of Ephesus juxtaposed mystery initiates with bacchants.[12] Aeschylus presented to the Attic spectators the 'thrill' and 'rapture of the mystic rite.'[13] If indeed Plato was the first to frame the notion of telestic *mania*, the cited passage from the *Phaedrus* attests to the perspicacity of the great philosopher in recognising the abandonment of normality by the initiates, and defining this phenomenon as *mania*: his 'invention' was actually labelling behaviour that must have been quite familiar.

Plato refers to various kinds of telestic *mania* on multiple occasions, sometimes using comparisons to this phenomenon in elaborate arguments, as a starting point based on common knowledge, easily understandable to his readers. For instance, in the *Symposium* Diotima *Mantinikê* (a woman from Mantinea) suggests that she leads Socrates into the mysteries of Eros.[14] Socrates' remarks on etymology clarify the full appellation of his mentor: Diotima means 'honoured by Zeus,' hence wise,[15] and her Mantinean origin indicates that she is an expert in *mantikê*, that is, divination, as well as alteration of consciousness, *manikê*, which is *mantikê* in its pristine and pure form.[16] Diotima's mysteries aim beyond love, to eternal beauty and immortality,[17] and *mania* leads to the revelation of the ultimate truth – a subject which will be discussed in detail in Chapter 8. The perspective is that of real-life initiatory rites: Diotima the mystagogue is not sure whether Socrates is able to follow her, and asks him to try to proceed correctly (*orthôs*)[18] – exactly like *mania* in the passage just cited requiring that the participants in the rites be 'rightly mad.' In the *Symposium* and *Phaedrus*, Plato emphasises that initiation is a test, and success must not be taken for granted. In both cases, Plato uses the same terms, but refers to different kinds of *teletai* and different *Maniai*; nevertheless, the conjunction of the two notions remains constant. It is plain for Plato that the personages of his dialogues and his readers are familiar with initiatory madness. The experience was apparently well-known, but it may have been Plato who coined its designation, *telestikê mania*.

This chapter discusses the embodied mystery experiences of individual initiates. Greek authors from Plato to Plutarch often refer to *teletai* in general, alluding perhaps to their essential congruity. It is underscored by the fact that their most prominent varieties, the Eleusinian and the Orphic-Bacchic mysteries, were focused on the same two gods, Dionysus and Core.[19] The compatibility of divergent mystery cults may be illustrated by a fragment from Euripides' *Cretans*, combining initiations into the mysteries of Idaean Zeus, the Mountain Mother, and Bacchus, with a special way of life.[20] Mystery rites presumably involved more than one kind of alteration of consciousness, and I suggest their division into two categories, based on the nature and function of telestic *mania* in various initiations, those focused on an ecstatic state as their primary goal, and those aiming at enlightenment and featuring manipulation of consciousness as a method of its attainment or one of its characteristics.

Mystery initiations

Mysteries, or mystery initiations,[21] were secret cults intended to bestow happiness in this world and often a better life in the hereafter on their adherents, usually called *mustai*. 'Mystery initiations' is a common rendering of the Greek word *teletê* (rite of fulfilment); however, it is not the only meaning of this word.[22] The term 'initiations' can be applied to mystery rites and is in my opinion hermeneutically useful,[23] although each cult described as *teletê* possessed its own distinct characteristics, and the word *teletê* could sometimes designate ceremonies of a different nature. This terminological chaos reflects a reality that resists classification and good order, but invites questions that may disclose the way the Greeks perceived *teletai* and associated phenomena.

An additional complication ensues from the fact that the word *bakcheia*, Bacchic or Dionysiac *mania*, could denote cultic phenomena focused mainly on mystery initiations or ecstatic worship of the god, and these phenomena frequently overlapped. Precise categorisation of some cults is impossible or even misleading, and this and the following chapter will provide examples of such mixed rites. Nevertheless, it is my opinion that discrimination between the varieties of Dionysiac cults involving ecstatic constituents (and splitting the discussion into two chapters) is heuristically justified.

By the sixth century (or perhaps earlier), several mystery cults were in existence, including the Eleusinian mysteries, celebrated in Eleusis in Attica and dedicated to Demeter, the mysteries of the Cabiri, conducted on the island of Samothrace, and the Dionysian mysteries, which could be performed everywhere. There is firm evidence for the existence of many lesser mysteries in the subsequent period, some of them of local importance, others renowned throughout the Greek world.[24] Various mystery initiations were very popular: the majority of adult Athenians were Eleusinian *mustai*.[25] On the small island of Mykonos, all the women of the citizen community were admitted to the local mysteries of Demeter.[26] The Orphic or Bacchic mysteries spread all over the Mediterranean, their mendicant priests knocking on every door in Athens. To Plato's dismay, in many cases these itinerants were welcome.[27] There is no uniformity in the organisation of mystery cults: several among them allowed very vast membership, and many dispensed with permanent organisation, although in certain cases adherence to mystery cult congregations could endow their members with a feeling of exclusiveness.[28]

The most famous mystery cults of the Classical era, such as the Eleusinian and the Orphic-Bacchic mysteries,[29] promised the initiates a blissful existence in present and future, particularly after death. Other *teletai*, notably the Corybantic rites, did not deal with salvation after the death, but reformed the earthly lives of the adherents. However, while mystery initiations focused on different gods, and seem to have had a different aim, they still had some basic characteristics in common.

In the course of the central ceremony of initiation into a mystery cult, a great secret was imparted to the *mustai*. All the details of the eye-opening life-changing disclosure of the ultimate secret were ineffable.[30] At the peak of the ceremonies the initiates witnessed certain objects and heard certain uttering. In many cases, something hidden in a closed chest was displayed to the initiates. A winnowing basket filled with fruit from which a phallus arose remained the symbol of the Dionysiac mysteries until their eclipse in late antiquity,[31] and ears of grain were presumably prominent in the Eleusinian cult.[32] Scenes and actions together forming a sacred drama were probably staged at Eleusis and on Samothrace.[33] In several places the priests participating in the drama or the initiates wore masks.[34] Sacred formulae, *sunthêmata*, were pronounced in various mystery cults.[35] Some items, such as masks, phalli, and baskets, were used in many rites open to the public. Moreover, stripped of their secrecy, mystery initiations appeared dull and bleak. Even the awesome rites of Eleusis,[36] when divulged in the streets by the atheist Diagoras, lost their gripping force.[37] In any case, these objects, words and actions do not seem to have contained any life-changing revelation or knowledge that could potentially provide participants in the ceremonies with a release from the earthly evils, as Socrates said.

In addition to the precious gifts listed by Socrates, some mysteries offered further privileges. Cicero affirms that in Eleusis the initiates 'get the idea not only how to live in joy, but also how to die with hope for the best.'[38] In both the Eleusinian and Bacchic mysteries, initiates are often described as 'happy and blessed,' this dual designation seemingly indicating two distinct kinds of happiness that they obtained through the initiations.[39] Plutarch restates the ancient idea, expressed in the *Homeric Hymn to Demeter*,[40] and reiterated by Plato in *Phaedo*: those who arrive in Hades uninitiated would wallow in the mud, while those initiated (into the Eleusinian mysteries) would dwell with the gods.[41] The same notion is repeated time and again in the texts inscribed on gold tablets discovered mainly in South Italy, the Northern Balkans, and on Crete, which accompanied *mustai*, Dionysiac or Orphic, to the grave, and were believed to guide their souls on their last journeys.[42] The destiny of the *mustês* underwent so dramatic a transformation that it could be perceived as an apotheosis: 'Once human, you have become a god,' is the inscription on one of the gold tablets.[43] Thus, through initiation rites mortals could hope to attain renewal and be spared the 'senselessness of Hades' – but only after their bodily demise.[44] Euripides has Heracles say that he succeeded in bringing Cerberus from Hades because 'he was blessed with seeing the rites of *mustai*,' implying that a *mustês*, presumably Eleusinian, could fight the powers of the netherworld.[45] Hope is the precious gift of the Eleusinian mysteries to humanity: Isocrates praises the Athenians for allowing the rest of the world to partake of 'sweeter hopes concerning both the end of life and all time.'[46]

Most mysteries transformed the initiate's personality through changing his or her attitude to life, and the Eleusinian and Bacchic-Orphic rites delivered much more, altering the initiate's feelings about death.[47] The *mustai* were aware of their *metanoia*, and described it as 'becoming a different person.'[48] This chapter offers an analysis of the two major categories of mystery cults, focusing on the nature of the initiate's experiences in each group, and especially on the connection between these experiences and their impact on the lives of the *mustai*. I will argue that although alteration of consciousness is conspicuous in both categories, its nature, function, and consequences were quite different.

The nature of the initiate's experience I: *mania* for *mania's* sake or for its treatment

Mania is the distinguishing characteristic of the Corybantic, as well as the Bacchic rites, which are sometimes mentioned together, almost as synonymous notions. A passage from Plato's *Laws* provides a telling example:

> This course is adopted and its usefulness recognized both by those who nurse small children and by those women who in rites administer Corybantic cures (*iamata*). Thus when mothers have children suffering from sleeplessness, and want to lull them to rest, the treatment they apply to give them, not quiet, but motion, for they rock them constantly in their arms; . . . and thus they literally cast a spell (*kataulousi*) upon the children, as one cures frantic bacchants by movement and dance and music. . . . So whenever one applies an external shaking to affections of that kind, the external motion thus applied overpowers the internal motion of fear and frenzy, and by thus overpowering it, it brings about a manifest calm in the soul and a cessation of the grievous palpitation of the heart which had existed in each case. . . . The children are put to sleep; the bacchants, who are awake, it brings into a sound state of mind instead of frenzied condition, by means of dancing and playing.[49]

The word *kataulousi* is noteworthy; it means 'to enaulise,' that is, to enchant by means of an *aulos*.[50] Mothers and nurses obviously did not play flute to the children, but women – presumably men as well – who performed the Corybantic rites did so, and by using this word Plato creates a forceful association between the two settings, the nursery and the locale of an ecstatic celebration. While it is clear that the passage refers to the Corybantic cure of frenzy, the Corybantic devotees are likened to the bacchants, which implies that the word 'bacchant' could be, at least sometimes, synonymous to 'madman,' and many aspects of Corybantic rites resembled bacchic ecstasy.

Evidence on the Corybantic initiations is sufficiently rich to allow an attempt at reconstruction of the central ceremony of this cult. Regrettably, our knowledge of Dionysiac and Sabaziac initiations is vague and largely based on the example of the Corybantes. Plato's association of the Corybantic devotees with bacchants in the *Laws* hints at the possibility that when he has Socrates talk about cathartic initiations in the passage in the *Phaedrus* which opens this chapter, he is in fact referring to ceremonies similar to the Corybantic *teletai*. Therefore, this section begins with an overview of the Corybantic rites, and proceeds to other initiations based on ecstatic experiences.

The Corybantic rites

The Corybantic rites appear in Plato's dialogues on several occasions. Heart palpitations among the Corybantic devotees are mentioned by Alcibiades who claims in the *Symposium* that when he listens to Socrates he feels like a participant in Corybantic rites: his heart pounds and tears pour from his eyes.[51] In the *Crito*, Socrates remarks that in the tumult of their rites the *korubantiôntes* hear only the sound of the flutes, which re-echoes within them, rending them deaf to other sounds.[52] In the *Ion*, poets who are possessed by a divinity are compared to people possessed by the Corybantes: both are in a state of special excitement. As rhapsodes are inspired by one poet only, similar Corybantic devotees react to one tune only, that of the god who possesses them.[53]

Corybantic rites are defined as initiations: in the *Euthydemus*, the verb *telein* is used:

> They are acting just like the celebrants of the Corybantic rites, when they perform the enthronement of the person whom they are about to initiate (*telein*). There, as you know, if you have been initiated, they have dancing and merry-making: so these two are merely dancing about you and performing their sportive gambols with a view to your subsequent initiation.[54]

These observations are made in comparisons, apropos other ideas, and cannot possibly be intentionally misleading, which modern interpreters often suspect when Plato's texts are used as sources of historical information. In fifth-century Athens, Corybantic rites were regarded as initiations, well-known to the upper classes.[55] The rites involved deafening music as well as dancing, and produced a powerful effect on the participants: music resounded in their bodies, their heart rate increased, and they wept of excitement. This physical and mental condition is certainly not the normal baseline state and can be appropriately described as alteration of consciousness.

While their power to inflict mental disorders was shared with other deities and daemons, the Corybantes were believed to be endowed with this ability *par excellence*. Euripides' Phaedra is asked whether she is possessed by the *semnoi*

Korubantes, and a comic response to someone uttering a strange phrase would have been: 'are you mad or possessed by the Corybantes?' The scholia to both passages explain that the Corybantes caused madness.[56] They were considered to be capable of healing frenzy as well, and Aristophanes refers to this fact as common knowledge in the *Wasps*; the scholiast explains that a comic hero performed their mysteries 'as means of purifying of madness.'[57]

This evidence implies that Corybantism was, *inter alia*, a technique of healing mental disorders.[58] Both healers and madmen were called *korubantiôntes*. These people could belong to various social classes, including men of considerable social standing and wealth.[59] The common manifestation of Corybantism was ecstatic dancing at the state of collective violent frenzy, and in Strabo's days the dancers were frequently armed.[60] However, women were apparently not only admitted, but could play a leading role in the initiations: Plato mentions women 'who administer Corybantic cures,' while fourth- and second-century inscriptions from Erythrae and Macedonia refer to priestesses of the Corybantes.[61] Corybantic *mania* was collective and easily transmitted from one participant to another.[62] The ceremonies could be performed even in private homes: a dedication to *Kurbantes* on a crater was discovered in a bathroom in a fourth-century house in the town of Toumba in Macedonia.[63]

Corybantic treatment of mental disorders, *korubantismos*, was based on the idea that madness may be cured by means of madness: a cathartic paroxysm could release a person from possession by a daemon or a divinity.[64] The main Corybantic ceremony may be reconstructed as follows: after offering a sacrifice,[65] and perhaps cleansing by bathing,[66] the leader of the initiation, who was also the healer, drove the patient into a state of excitement.[67] The healer asked questions, gave orders, and sang incantations to intensify the suggestive influence on the patient. This procedure was called *thronôsis*, and is described by Plato.[68] The patient sat on a chair, while other participants danced and sang, raising a great din around him and playing tambourines, flutes, and other musical instruments. Wine seems to have been used during the rites, although the nature of the 'rite of crater' (*kratêrismos*) remains unclear.[69] As a result of the participation in the ceremony, the patient was driven to frenzy, gradually losing consciousness of all but the whirling rhythm, and began dancing and singing. Presumably many of the participants wept and experienced violent heartbeats.[70] Afterwards the patient might return to the former pathological condition, but usually the new balanced state was maintained by means of participation in the rites. During the *thronôsis* ceremony the psychological state which caused the mental disorder was 'polarised,' the result being an intensification of religious feelings leading to ecstasy – *mania* – during the rites, on the general background of normal behaviour: the frenzy attacks were regulated, and madness received 'telestic orientation.'[71] Thus an ex-madman became initiated or 'Corybanted,' which is the literal translation of the word *kekorybantismenos*, appearing in a second-century inscription, probably from Erythrae.[72] Other participants, once initiated in the same way, also returned to the normal tranquil state – until the next gathering. The majority of participants did not suffer from a particular mental ailment, and simply enjoyed the excitement caused by the ritual tunes. In the passage cited below, Aristotle mentions 'enthusiastic excitement' caused by ecstatic ritual tunes, which brings about cure and purification (*katharsis*), as well as feelings of relief and delight.[73]

Corybantic rites are first described in the fifth century, but probably came into existence much earlier.[74] In any case, this cult was perceived as Phrygian,[75] and remained popular during the Hellenistic period. In the surviving fragments of Menander's *The Girl Possessed* (*Theophoroumene*),[76] the girl who is demonically possessed is put to test by having the tune of the Mother of the Gods and a Corybantic hymn played to her; she performs such a hymn herself, mentioning Cybele with her train of the Corybantes and worshippers playing cymbals.[77]

Historical and anthropological parallels allow some insights into the composition, organisation and ritual of Corybantic associations. In mediaeval and early modern Europe, periodic cure of patients suffering from epilepsy and psychiatric ailments by means of compulsive dances gave rise to annual dancing festivals, some of them surviving well into the twentieth century.[78] Modern anthropology is familiar with a great number of healing techniques similar to Corybantism, notably *zar* and *bori*, used in some regions of modern Africa and Arabia.[79] Cognitively, these healing techniques are based on the representativeness heuristic, which is attested cross-culturally and consists of the tendency to associate similar objects or phenomena, and believe that an effect is to resemble the cause. This way of thinking is prominent in the history of medicine. The best-known example in the West is homeopathy based on the 'law of similars,' which remains popular notwithstanding its pseudo-scientific foundations.[80]

Most significantly, homeopathy and participation in possession cults heal. Ecstatic possession is beneficial for people suffering from mental afflictions: observing such people during and after voodoo ceremonies in Haiti, the psychiatrist W. Sargant noted that they felt better, and did not suffer from any adverse effects. The primary condition for the success of this treatment was of course sincere faith in its fundamental validity.[81] Therapeutic methods used by native practitioners in their séances combining exorcism, persuasion, shock, suggestion, and hypnotic-like techniques have been found to be effective in the treatment of a variety of mental and other disorders.[82]

The exorcist him- or herself was usually formerly possessed, and in order to keep health had to practice trancing.[83] Symptoms associated with spirit possession often include depression, guilt feelings, and dissociation, reported by patients who had suffered a period of acute or chronic stress.[84] The aim of these and similar therapeutic methods is not to abolish possession-trance behaviour, but to impart a new direction and thus to control it: illness and cure constitute a form of initiation. The anthropologist E. Bourguignon presumes that

> the ability to work through a personal psychological crisis in a culturally acceptable way makes the experience one of personality growth and reorganization. . . . The rituals of therapy and the acquisition of new ritual status by the new cult member . . . thus are methods of social adaptation.[85]

Repeated participation in rituals of exorcism is often necessary for the mainte-nance of the balanced state: ritualised possession provides 'periodic release of tension by catharsis of damned-up and socially unacceptable impulses.'[86] The depth of the trance and the degree of dissociation vary considerably in different individuals, and even in the same individual it fluctuates from occasion to occasion; besides, in mod-ern possession-trance rituals there is much play acting.[87] Cultural and even physical environment where the healing takes place are of crucial importance and affect the patients so much, that the same traditional healers who are successful in their home shrines do not attain similar results when invited into psychiatric wards.[88]

A number of people must participate in the assembly in order for it to provide a setting conductive to successful healing and preservation of sanity of the initiated. The communal nature of the healing procedure offers the patient social reinforce-ment achieved in the process of ritual or symbolic manipulation.[89] This requires the development of some institutionalised organisation of the believers, headed by one or several cult leaders. Thus, people with abnormal behavioural features, who have been treated by a certain ecstatic technique and obtained a state which is recognised in a given society as sanity, can maintain it only if they experience that same altered state of consciousness from time to time. These alterations of con-sciousness are often considered to be inspired by the same divinity or spirit who had inflicted the illness in the first place. The ceremony serves as an initiation to the cult of this divinity, and the victim is liberated from the illness as a result of an ecstatic rite. The particular nature of the cult demands that the people subjected to the divine madness unite in an organised manner which provides them with the framework necessary for the periodic participation in the ecstatic rites.

The anthropological studies of possession-trance behaviour suggest a plausible model for understanding of the Corybantic rites. People cured by means of a Coryban-tic initiation needed to experience telestic *mania* over and over, as means of maintain-ing both their mental health and the order of the ceremonies. They performed their rites in associations, which had to meet more or less regularly and were focused on a charismatic exorcist, who had probably been healed of insanity him- or herself.

If, however, only former madmen participated in the Corybantic initiations, this phenomenon would not have been so widespread. The majority of the *korubantiôntes* must have been quite sane. In this connection, it is noteworthy that Socrates' remarks on the selective reaction of the Corybantic devotees to one tune only and their strong physiological reaction are endorsed by modern research on the effects of music on the brain. On the one hand, pathological manifestations, such as seizures in patients suffering from musicogenic epilepsy, are provoked by a certain kind of music, either a particular quality of sound or the emotional impact of a specific style.[90] On the other hand, healthy individuals with special sensitivity to music display different physiological reactions to different musical performances. J. C. Fachner observes that

a study on religious and deep listeners (people who have strong emotional reactions, like goosebumps or crying or are otherwise deeply moved when listening to their favourite music) in comparison to controls showed stronger responses in heart rate and galvanic skin response when listening to self-selected, preferred music. . . . Deep listeners described their experiences in transcendent terms and responses occurred parallel to differing parts of the music that were of high subjective valence for the listeners.[91]

This study suggests that the Corybantic initiates who did not suffer from any mental problem reacted to the tunes performed during the ceremonies in a way that ensured their excitement was apparent to all, enjoyed this sensation immensely, and developed emotional connection bordering on addiction to the rites.[92]

From the anthropological viewpoint, as a result of a large-scale research embracing both urbanised and traditional societies, E. Bourguignon reached the conclusion that though pathology may be evident in some individuals seeking possession-trance, it is not a necessary precondition for the development of the behaviour.[93] The cultural framework and social environment determine that certain kinds of alteration of consciousness and associated behaviour are encouraged as desirable; this socially accepted behaviour is controlled and never leads to pathological disability. On the contrary, it apparently has a wholesome effect on the sane majority who benefit from the resolution of personal stress and other salutary consequences of the ecstatic experience.[94]

Bacchic and Sabaziac initiations

Not only adepts of Corybantism, but also participants in other ecstatic cults could be attracted by the emotional influence of the initiations. Many rites sacred to Dionysus comprised alteration of consciousness, but we have no means of evaluating these elements in each particular cult: the evidence only indicates that there was no single pattern of Bacchic rites, which were often dubbed *teletai* or *orgia*.[95] To further confuse the modern researcher, rites sacred to Dionysus, the Corybantes, and Cybele are grouped together quite often by Euripides, Plato, Strabo, and other writers.[96] The most impressive example is a late fourth–early third-century gold tablet from a tomb in Pherae, referring to a *thiasos* of *mustai*, *orgia* of Bacchus and *telê* (*teletê*) of Demeter Chthonia and of the Mountain Mother.[97] Besides, it is quite probable that there were substantial differences between Dionysiac *teletai* throughout their history, perhaps even inside the same polis.[98]

Heraclitus, as mentioned above, wrote about 'night-wanderers, mages, male and female bacchants, and *mustai*, some of them he threatens with [what happens] after death, for others prophesies fire, because the *musteria* customary celebrated by men are enacted in an unholy way.'[99] This text is far from being clear, but it attests to a late sixth–early fifth-century association of bacchants, ideas on the holy or correct way of performing mysteries, and posthumous punishment for the violation of these rules. It is tempting to suppose that the mysteries were interpreted as dealing with afterlife, but this obscure passage would then be stretched too far: we are told what the punishment for incorrect ritual practice would be, but not a word alludes to rewards for correct actions.

The term *teletai* could be used rather loosely. For instance, Herodotus relates the story of the ill-fated Scythian king Scyles, who was initiated into the mysteries (*telesthênai*) of the Bacchic Dionysus in the Greek city of Borysthenes (later Olbia) on the Northern Black Sea littoral.[100] One of the citizens, offended by the Scythians ridiculing the Greeks who 'submitted to *bakcheia* while possessed by the god,' secretly showed them their own king with his *thiasos*, 'who has been seized by the same deity, and is revelling, maddened by the god.'[101] Since the rites took place in public and could hardly be secret, the verb *telesthênai* is probably applied by Herodotus to another aspect of Dionysiac rites: Scyles could both be initiated and participate in ecstatic congregations. This word usage seems to reflect the proximity of initiatory and ecstatic rites, as well as the lack of clear discrimination between facets of the Bacchic cult.[102] In any event, Bacchic rites in the Greek city of Olbia could be dubbed *teletê* and celebrated in a *thiasos* in the streets of the city.

In Euripides' *Bacchae*, the *thiasos* of Dionysus praises the man who is 'happy in in his knowledge of the god's sacred rites (*teletai*), lives pure life, and joins his soul to the *thiasos*, performing Bacchic rites in the mountains.'[103] In another passage, Dionysus tempts the doomed Pentheus with the benefits of secret knowledge forbidden to the uninitiated, yet does not disclose details.[104] Like Herodotus in the passage on Scyles, Euripides juxtaposes *teletai* with Bacchic rites, but neither equates the two nor represents one as a precondition for the other; furthermore, the nature of the *teletai* remains obscure.[105] The main emphasis in the *Bacchae* is on the overwhelming ecstatic drive of the maenadic *thiasos*, while allusions to telestic rites remain peripheral to this central theme. This perspective is very different from other plays by the same dramatist, where Bacchic initiations are associated with vegetarianism, purity laws, and Orphic texts or other mysteries:[106] we are dealing with conjoining but distinct phenomena.

Plato mentions Bacchic ecstasy more than once, and usually associates it with initiations.[107] In a discussion of dance styles in the *Laws*, he refers to '*bakcheia* cultivated by those who indulge in drunken imitations of the nymphs, Pans, Sileni and Satyrs, as they call them, when performing certain rites of purification and initiation (*teletai*).'[108] Plato repeatedly associated Bacchic ecstasy with initiations, ritual cleansing, and expiation, but while in his earlier work he was neutral or even positive about these practices, in his old age he voiced disapproval of this 'questionable dancing' and declared it unfitting for the citizens of his ideal state.

Archaic and Classical evidence on Dionysiac *teletai* aiming primarily at alteration of consciousness is not abundant. These rites seem to have been based on personal initiative, they maintained considerable privacy, were focused on ecstatic union with Dionysus, and admitted both sexes. During this period, the most powerful expression of Bacchic ecstasy was maenadism. Maenadic festivals, discussed in detail in the next chapter, were usually described by the word *orgia*, 'rites,'[109] celebrated by the cities or on their behalf, and attracted mostly women; their telestic aspect, noted from time to time, was subordinate to the pure *enthousiasmos*. Bacchic ecstatic elements were important in another category of cults, classified as Orphic-Bacchic initiations, but the ambitions of their devotees, as we will see shortly, went beyond merely experiencing the liberating and cleansing joy of *bakcheia*. Most probably there was some overlap between these phenomena, and its extent could vary from place to place.

In addition to the Dionysiac and Corybantic rites, ecstatic initiations honouring other deities throve, at least in Athens. Demosthenes describes *teletai* performed by Aeschines' mother Glaucothea:

> On arriving at manhood, you assisted your mother in her initiations, you read the book and helped generally with other things. At night you clothed the participants in fawn-skins, mixed wine (literally 'performed *kratêrismos*, rites around the crater'), purified the initiates scouring them with the loam and the bran, and when their purification was duly performed, set them on their legs and instruct them to say 'I escaped evil, I found the better.' . . . In day-time you marshalled your gallant *thiasos* through the streets, their heads crowned with fennel and white poplar on their heads; and as you went you squeezed the fat-cheeked snakes and brandished them above your head, now shouting *Euoi Saboi*, and footing it to the measure of *Hyes Attes! Attes Hyes!* – saluted by all the old women as leader and instructor and ivy-bearer and basket-bearer.[110]

Ceremonies performed by Aeschines' mother were both cathartic and telestic,[111] and combined elements of secret nocturnal initiations and ecstatic parading of *thiasoi* through the city during daytime. This combination allows perhaps a better understanding of Herodotus' passage on Scyles and other seemingly paradoxical references to *teletai* that could be observed by all. Not only Bacchic rites, but considerable stretches of Eleusinian and other mystery rites were also conducted in public places. The word *teletai* and its derivatives were malleable, and could designate a wide spectrum of celebrations, of which only a certain stage was secret or quasi-secret.

The rites described by Demosthenes were celebrated in honour of the Phrygian Sabazius.[112] This cult had much in common with the Greek cult of Dionysus, including such elements as the use of ivy and snakes and even the terms *thiasos* and *liknophoros*.[113] It is significant to bear in mind that the Greeks considered Dionysus as a foreign god.[114] The Corybantic rites also shared with the Bacchic ritual the emphasis on wine-drinking, symbolised by *kratêrismos*.[115] The majority of ancient sources maintain that the Corybantic sources diffused from Asia Minor, and the cult of the Corybantes was often associated with that of Cybele, another foreign deity.[116] Euripides' portrayal of the Dionysiac *thiasos* praising Corybantic drums and the Phrygian pipes of the Mother, that mingle in accompaniment to ecstatic dances of the bacchants, is symbolic of the amalgamation of these cults.[117] The attribution of foreign origins to ecstatic rites seems to ensue from a combination of embarrassment and an ardent wish to join them, felt by many of the participants.

In any event, many people obviously sought (as they seek nowadays) the violent kaleidoscope of sharp emotions, produced during the state of *enthousiasmos*. Aristotle comments on the allure of various ecstatic rites:

> For any experience that occurs violently in some souls is found in all, though with different degrees of intensity – for example pity and fear, and also

religious excitement (*enthousiasomos*); for some persons are very liable to this form of emotion, and under the influence of sacred music we see these people, when they use tunes that violently arouse the soul, being thrown into a state as if they had received medicinal treatment and taken a purge (*katharsis*); the same experience then must come also to the compassionate and the timid and the other emotional people generally in such degrees as befalls each individual of these classes, and all must undergo a purgation and a pleasant feeling of relief; and similarly the purgative melodies afford harmless delight to people.[118]

This state, which granted release from psychological tensions and brought about cathartic rejoicing, was vividly described by the physician Aretaeus of Cappadocia in the first century AD:

Some people slash their limbs, with the pious notion that they are doing something pleasing their gods, who, they believe, expect this of them. Their madness is limited to this assumption on their part, because they are sane in all other respects. They are roused by pipes and gladness of the heart or drunkenness, under the instigation of other persons who are present. This madness (*mania*) is what is called enthusiasm (*entheos*). If they endure to the end, they are happy and free of distress, believing that they have been initiated into the mysteries of the god.'[119]

Aretaeus' passage refers to a generic ecstatic experience, reminiscent of the similar attitude of Plato and Aristotle, cited above. From the point of view of the enlightened physician, people participating in these cults are sane, the only manifestation of their *mania* being their passion for ecstatic rites, which they regard as initiations. A century later, Iamblichus distinguished between different kinds of divine inspiration, maintaining that possession by a deity is the god's gift to mortals, and discussing in the same passage the inspiration by the Corybantes, the life-engendering power of the Mother of the Gods, and the *bakcheia* of Sabazius.[120]

The attitude of the Greek polis communities to violent initiatory frenzy is noteworthy. In fifth- and fourth-century Athens, the Corybantic rites were popular, and even aristocrats like Socrates' friends, Alcibiades and his cousin Cleinias, were acquainted with their details; when referring to these rites, Plato never expressed a word of disapproval.[121] Although Demosthenes claims that the rites managed by Aeschines' mother Glaucothea were loathed by respectable Athenians, Glaucothea belonged to a famous mantic family, and the ceremonies she performed may have been no less popular than the Corybantic initiations.[122] Demosthenes, who does his best to denigrate Aeschines, fails to indicate the social status of the *thiasoi* members: if they had been largely foreigners and freedmen, Demosthenes would not have omitted this detail.

In Erythrae, the state regulated at least some aspects of the Corybantic rites: Corybantic city *orgia* were celebrated, and the priests and priestesses of voluntary

Corybantic associations – at least three were active in the city – were granted the right to participate in the city *orgia*, and perform ablutions and other rites.[123] A parallel is provided by a detailed sacred law from Miletus, establishing formal relations between the city and the Bacchic *thiasoi*: these organisations were headed by their own priests and priestesses, who were subordinate to priests and priestesses of the polis.[124] In general, the policy of Greek cities was not to interfere with the affairs of voluntary cult associations.[125] In the cases of both Corybantic and Bacchic voluntary associations, the existence of a state festival of these deities may have encouraged the introduction of state control, but the reasons for these changes are unclear. They could have been purely financial,[126] or perhaps some accidents connected to the fierce nature of both Dionysiac ecstasy and the Corybantic possession may have urged Erythrae and Miletus to impose control on these rites.

In summary, *mania* of the initiates in the Corybantic and Bacchic rites was visible and well-known; *thiasoi* marching through cities in broad daylight could hardly maintain secrecy, but nevertheless such terms as *teletai* and *mustai* were employed in contemporary references to these events. The reason was perhaps the splitting of these rites into two stages, the first one concealed from the uninitiated, and the other one conducted in public places. Corybantic or Bacchic *mania* might at times be regarded as excessive, therefore in need of some state control. However, ecstatic initiations were respectable enough for Athenian aristocrats to be familiar with the sensations felt by participants in the rites. Ecstatic initiatory cults shared a number of significant elements, and unbounded telestic *mania* seems to have often been associated with gods whom the Greeks regarded as foreigners. Fifth- and fourth-century authors, as well as later sources, repeatedly list various ecstatic *teletai* together, and in their opinion the resemblance between these cults in many respects outweighed the differences. In particular, the prominence of *mania* in ecstatic initiation rites appeared very significant to ancient authors. They put an emphasis on possession by a deity, *enthousiasmos*, as the core experience of these rites: the encounter with the divine was perceived as mingling with the god, and this temporal unity with the divine was the aim of the initiation.

The nature of the initiate's experience II: *paradosis* and *epopteia*

In the second century AD the Neoplatonist Theon of Smyrna summed up the stages of initiation rites (*muêsis*):

> Initiation has five parts: the preliminary part is the purification (*katharmos*). For not everyone who wishes may participate in the mysteries, but some people are told in advance that they are excluded, like those whose hands are impure or whose speech is unintelligible. And those who are not excluded must first be purified in some way. Second, after the purification, is the *paradosis* of the rite. The third stage is called *epopteia*. Fourth, and the completion of the *epopteia*, is the *anadesis* (binding of) and laying on wreaths, so that a

person who has received the initiation may pass it to the others, if he holds the office of torch-bearer or hierophant or some other priesthood. Fifth is the blessedness of being loved by the gods and living with them.[127]

Theon's trajectory comprises preparations, rational understanding, the core experience known as *epopteia* ('beholding,' discussed in detail below), and the supreme joy attained as the result of the participation in the mystery rites.

The impact of *teletê* on the participants appears to have been very different from an array of myths or prescriptions: instead, the extant sources suggest the attainment of an awareness of a sort.[128] Synesius, a Neoplatonic philosopher and later bishop of Cyrenaica, cites Aristotle, who 'states that the participants of initiations into mysteries do not have to learn anything, but rather to experience and to be inclined, that is to say, to become fit (for the purpose).'[129] Aristotle seems to refer to a generic mystery experience, disregarding particularities, such as divine patrons of cults or locations of ceremonies. In his view, the most important objective of the Greek initiations is to ensure that the participants undergo a certain experience.

Clement of Alexandria also distinguished between stages of pagan initiations and stressed the importance of the experience of *epopteia* and *perinoia*, non-rational, holistic contemplation and comprehension, at the consummation of the mystery rites:

> It is not then without reason that in the Greek mysteries, there are purifications in the beginning. . . . After these are the minor mysteries, which give some foundation of instruction and of initial preparation for what is about to happen; and the great mysteries, in which nothing remains to be learned, but only to contemplate (*epopteuein*) and comprehend (*perinoein*) nature and things.[130]

Instruction, often called *paradosis*, covers the intellectual part of the preparation, acquaintance with the myths associated with the particular mystery rite.[131] The lore of mystery cults was revered as their sacred stories, *hieroi logoi*. Some cults made use of books,[132] while others were based on oral transmission of this secret knowledge. This *sacrorum traditio*[133] provided the contents for the rites. For instance, the initiate was supposed to feel the anguish of Demeter, live with her through bereavement, and shudder when he learnt about the sufferings of Dionysus cunningly murdered by the Titans.[134]

This information is a verbalised symbolic representation,[135] intended to prepare the *mustai* for the apprehension of a different kind of knowledge: doctrines seem to have been subordinate to the living experience of the rites.[136] Hidden or true meanings of images and rites were revealed to them as an experience shared with the deity rather than perceived as a result of systematic teaching. For instance, in Plato's *Symposium* Diotima clearly dismisses as insignificant all those myths and interpretations she had disclosed to Socrates at the beginning of their conversation, her equivalent of the *paradosis*.[137] The author of Derveni papyrus also emphasises that simply learning a set of myths or prescriptions will not lead an initiate to enlightenment,[138] which means that most initiates did not proceed beyond superficial acquaintance with the sacred lore and mere attendance at the ceremonies.

The focus of various mysteries was revelation of the hidden truth, *epopteia*, 'beholding,' a direct encounter with the divinely imparted exclusive knowledge, which elevated the initiate to his new blessed state.[139] In his treatise on the Isiac mysteries, Plutarch states that *epopteia* is the end of a mystery initiation and contains its fundamental truth:

> The knowledge of what is knowable, pure, and simple, that illuminates the soul like a thunderbolt and for this only time allows it to touch and see. For which reason Plato and Aristotle termed this part of philosophy 'epoptic' because they pass by ostensible, heterogeneous, and manifold notions, and leap up towards the primal, the simple, and the immaterial, and when they really touch the pure truth concerning these matters they think that, just as in mystery initiations (*teletê*), they reached the end (*telos*) of philosophy.[140]

The initiate had to be prepared for the *teletê* properly, and meticulously follow the prescribed stages of initiation; quite often the primary initiation, *muêsis*, was a requirement for proceeding to the culmination of the *teletê*.[141] In several cults, the *mustês* was blindfolded at the beginning of the ceremony, the veil removed only towards the climax of the rite, presumably when the initiate was ready to witness the awesome sight.[142] The contrast between sightlessness and sight was apparently reflected in the terminology of the mystery cults. The word *mustês* is derived from the verb *muein*, 'to close' (the lips or the eyes).[143] Moreover, in the Eleusinian and Samothracian mysteries *mustês* contrasts with *epoptês*, 'beholder,' the two terms designating respectively the first-time and second-time participants in the rites: during the primary stage of initiation, the *mustês* remained in darkness. Thus, the first stage of initiation is characterised by darkness and ritual blindness, while the subsequent stage is focused on light and sight.[144]

We are unable to define exactly what *epopteia* is.[145] In Plato's *Symposium*, Diotima contrasts *muêsis* as the initial stage of the search for supreme wisdom, and *epoptika* as the ultimate stage.[146] The trajectory of initiation, as outlined in the *Symposium*, is from experiencing particulars to learning laws and contemplation, to attaining a vision of the ultimate beauty, which makes the mortal dear to the gods (that is, happy) and close to immortality.[147] The highest point of this trajectory to immortality is 'neither reason nor knowledge,'[148] but rather 'seeing' the pure essence of a phenomenon, divine revelation corresponding to the mystic *epopteia*.

Another indication is given by Plato in the *Phaedrus*: those who experience *epopteia* are mentioned by Socrates in his explanation of the capability of unembodied souls in the distant past to see the shining beauty, 'the blessed sight and vision of the most blessed of the mysteries,' and unite with the divine.[149] By recollecting his soul's perceptions during its past travels with god, 'always initiated into perfect mysteries, he alone becomes truly perfect.'[150] Interpreting the Platonic ideas, Plutarch records the following view:

> [Plato] praised geometry since it draws us away from concentration on the perception by the senses and brings us back to mentally conceived and eternal nature, the sight of which is the end of philosophy, like *epopteia* is the end of mystery initiation (*teletê*).[151]

In the *Symposium* as well as in the *Phaedrus*, *epopteia* is mental vision rather than actual perception of a sight. It is unclear whether in real-life mystery initiations *epopteia* was limited to physical observation of objects and actions, or this sight, awesome as it might be, was only inductive to the numinous experience of inner vision, the supreme *epopteia* which changed one's attitude to life and death. Plutarch's interpretation indicates that the latter was considered the genuine *epopteia*, Platonic as well as actually achieved in mystery rites. It is impossible to determine how many of the participants truly attained this supreme *epopteia* as compared to those who were simply excited by the music and other background effects and the actions of the sacred officials and other initiates.

Mystery rites involved no conflict between doctrines and experiences: sensation and knowledge lead to illumination, and their interaction resulted in approaching the god.[152] The divinely given effect was 'knowing beyond knowledge,'[153] wordless comprehension which promised salvation and had to be remembered forever. This experience is repeatedly described as ultimate joy, harmony, and bliss.[154]

The core experience in the 'great mysteries,' *mania,* and alteration of consciousness

The most fascinating description of a mystery experience from the point of view of the initiate is given by Plutarch. He refers to the 'great mysteries,' probably meaning mysteries in general:

> At first there was wandering, and wearisome roaming, and some fearful journeys through unending darkness, and just before the end (*telos*), every sort of terror, shuddering and trembling and sweat and amazement. Out of these emerges marvellous light, and pure places and meadows follow after,[155] with voices and dances and solemnities of sacred utterances and holy visions. Among these the completely initiated [*mustês*], walks freely and without restraint; crowned, he takes part in rites, and joins with pure and pious people; he observes the crowd of people living at this very time uninitiated and unpurified, who are driven together and trample each other in deep mud and darkness, and continue in their fear of death, their evils and their disbelief in the good things in the other world. Then in accordance with nature the soul stays engaged with the body in close union thereafter.[156]

This account depicts a long movement through the darkness, with a marvellous light in its end, visions, happiness, and meetings with kindly people, as well as the soul's reunification with the body, which implies that they were conceived as temporarily separated during the experience. In modern terms, the report is a description of the initiate's alteration of consciousness. For the Greeks, this was *telestikê mania*.

Modern research demonstrates that altered states of consciousness often generate a subjective sensation of contact with a transcendent spiritual world. As observed in the Introduction, during these states, people feel that they are in contact with a higher reality, a sensation that brings about illumination and profound meaningfulness. These feelings remain very vivid for a long time, sometimes triggering changes in the attitude to other people, life, and death. Speaking about an altered state of consciousness is so difficult that in many traditions they are considered ineffable.[157] The access of the Greeks who experienced these sensations to the tradition of initiations provided them with specific patterns of articulating their memories.

At present, individuals who have experienced profound alterations of consciousness, recurrently claim to feel a sense of renewed hope, rejuvenation, or rebirth.[158] This aspect of altered states of consciousness is especially significant for assessing the impact of participation in ancient Greek mystery initiations on the lives of those who experienced them: it explains recurrent comparisons of mystery rites to rebirth and allusions to bliss and hopefulness felt during and after the ceremonies. Another important characteristic is the vision of shining light, illumination in the literal sense of the word. It is significant that ritual *epopteia* was perceived as quintessential light, and Plato depicted the initiatory experience as culminating in a vision of pure light.[159] I will return to this subject shortly.

Alterations of consciousness vary in their intensity, from deeply unconscious to less dramatic states, which still may be responsible for visions or hallucinations. The broad range of altered states of consciousness is vital: even if Greek mystery initiations did not involve a deep trance, milder conditions could also involve sensations of contact with the divine, and feelings of bliss and enlightenment.

The Greeks were aware of the fact that the ability to manipulate consciousness varies among individuals. Plato notes: 'as they say concerning mystery rites (*teletai*), many bear the Bacchic rod, but few are bacchants (*bakchoi*),' implying that only a small fraction of numerous people attracted to ecstatic rites actually experienced real self-abandonment and merger with the god.[160] Aristotle discusses variations in the impact of *enthousiasmos*, divine possession in his lengthy excursus on music.[161] In his opinion as well, people differed in their ability to attain altered states of consciousness.

The core element of Plutarch's account is the separation of the initiate's soul from the body, or in modern terms, out-of-body experience. During such experience, an individual feels great delight, which may be of brief or prolonged duration.[162] As is the case with other altered states of consciousness, the person is left with a conviction that the experience was real, but he or she is unable to put it in words. Out-of-body experiences were known in Greece: several archaic semi-legendary personages, such as Aethalides, Abaris, and Hermotimus of Clazomenae, were ascribed this ability.[163] For the purposes of the present discussion, it is unimportant whether these particular individuals experienced out-of-body states; it is crucial that the Greek public was acquainted with this phenomenon and thought that it occurred to (enlightened) mortals in the past and in present.[164]

These outstanding figures practiced manipulation of consciousness and their experiences were known to many and became paradigmatic. It goes without saying that most people could hardly attain this level of intensity. However, many initiates endeavouring to attain illumination could live through an alteration of consciousness, its depth determined by his or her personality, preparation, environment during the ceremony, and other factors. In any case, all the elements of Plutarch's account are in perfect accord with descriptions of altered states of consciousness by modern experiencers. It appears to attest to authentic experiences of some *mustai*, which less gifted or fortunate initiates probably strove to emulate.

Not all the people who described themselves as *mustai* necessarily experienced or pretended to have experienced out-of-body sensations. The gold leaf from Hipponium, South Italy, dated to ca. 400, promises that the initiate joins 'glorious *mustai* and *bakchoi*'; another one, from Pelinna (Thessaly), about a hundred years later, is even more forthright, instructing the initiate to tell Persephone that 'Bacchius himself released you'; a contemporary gold leaf from Amphipolis in Macedonia pronounces the initiate 'sacred to Bacchius.'[165] The experience that these initiates lived through comprised *bakcheia*, ecstatic feeling of 'engoddedness,' or being one with the god. In contrast to the maenads and people like Scyles and his Olbian *thiasos*, ecstatic liberation of the '*mustai* and *bakchoi*' was not the primary aim of the rites, but rather a method of transforming their identity and world view, particularly their perception of death. The overpowering sensation of temporarily, or even momentarily, partaking in the god's divinity was for many *mustai* the physical and irrefutable proof of the great secret truth of the origin of the human race from a heavenly spark, alluded to in many Orphic-Bacchic tablets:[166] myth coalesced with ecstatic experience.

The value of participation in festivals, sacrifices, and other rites enacted inside the community and directed towards the deity, did not depend on the participant's memory of his or her feelings, what mattered most was the mere fact of attendance. In contrast, the impact of a mystery initiation was lost if the initiated forgot the sensation itself and the resulting illumination.[167] A life-long memory of the initiation rites was exceptional and was created by special methods, above all by inducing telestic *mania*.

Several Bacchic tablets refer to the work or gift of memory when one is about to die, and to the request to drink from the lake of memory when one arrives in the netherworld: the marvel of initiation was to be remembered forever.[168] Actually, the impact of a mystery initiation was lost if the initiated forgot the sensation itself and the resulting illumination.[169] In one case, the initiate is called 'the hero who remembers.'[170] In order 'to live in joy and to die with hope' after the ceremony – to use Cicero's phrase cited above, – the initiates had to remember it every day of their lives. To preserve the memory of the rite, the initiated learnt cryptic *sumbola* or *sunthêmata* of their distinction; in some cases they kept material tokens of it.[171] The peculiarities of their behaviour could also serve a sort of reminder: for instance, the Orphics did not eat eggs, and Eleusinian initiates avoided red mullet.[172] However, it seems that not the material symbols, but rather the profound emotional involvement of the initiate during the initiation ceremonies was the reason and guarantee of the persistence of their memory. Conversely, the awesome experience was rendered worthwhile solely by its perpetual memory: if the feeling of well-being during the rites had been forgotten, *teletai* would have been useless.[173] Recurrent participation in mystery rites of those already initiated apparently boosted the memory of the experience. Memory formation was probably a complex process: a multidisciplinary study of high-arousal rituals has recently demonstrated that they promote memory formation, but also allow ample space for cultural representations to interfere and adjust individual perceptual memories to social expectations.[174] Therefore, what Greek initiates remembered after having participated in mystery rites could be to a considerable extent a result of the adaptation of an individual's memories to his or her conscious or unconscious efforts to feel, perceive, and learn in accordance with the standard current in their community.

To recuperate, *mania* is attested to in various mystery initiations, and interpreted as encounter with the divine or at least approaching such an encounter. However, the nature and function of the telestic *mania* are not always the same. Life-changing revelation attained in the state of telestic *mania* was the core element of the Eleusinian and Orphic-Bacchic mysteries. In the Corybantic initiations, sometimes regarded as similar to Bacchic ecstasy, ecstatic *mania* was the main element of the ceremony, aiming at *enthousiasmos*, possession by the god. Dionysiac initiations seem to oscillate between rites aiming at revelation and rites focusing on alteration of consciousness as a spiritual aim. Based upon the role of *mania*, mystery initiations are divided into two categories. The first one is comprised of ecstatic initiations seeking alteration of consciousness as their primary aim, for instance the Corybantic and some Dionysian rites. The second category includes principally the Eleusinian and Orphic-Bacchic mysteries: at these initiations, alteration of consciousness was much more complex and versatile. There, it was both a means of 'becoming fit' to attain illumination, and a part of the core experience, which included visions or sensations of contact with the divine, out-of-body states and other phenomena associated with altered states of consciousness. In all the initiations, due to its tremendous emotional impact, the sensation of alteration of consciousness was remembered during the entire lifetime of the initiates, whose memory was enhanced by means of *mania*.

Techniques of 'getting ready' for the core experience of mystery initiations and *mania*

The initiates had to make efforts to become 'fit for the purpose' (*epitêdeioi*). This requirement is emphasised in Socrates' account of the telestic madness: by means of purifications and *teletai* mentally disturbed individuals who suffer from 'ancestral illness' may attain release from their disease, provided they are 'possessed and mad in a correct manner.'[175] Heraclitus prophesied fiery punishment after death to bacchants of both sexes and *mustai*, and claimed that people performed 'the customary initiations in an unholy way,' implying that in contrast to the unrefined crowd, a wise man knew how to celebrate these rites piously.[176]

This stipulation is crucial: the preparations for the rite were to be accomplished meticulously. The initiate was neither an observer nor a conscious learner: his or her state of mind was an important precondition for achieving a sense of contact with the divine. Only when well-prepared for the tremendous experience, that is, acquainted with the myth, and most significantly, exhausted, tense with anticipation and over-reactive, the initiate was allowed to participate in the central rites of a mystery cult.

Mystery rites were intended to unsettle, disturb, and horrify, as only in absolute contrast to the initial terror could the initiate arrive at profound modification of his attitude to life. This characteristic of mystery rites is articulated by Aeschylus: 'I shudder with the erotic rapture of this mystery rite.'[177] Shudder, fear, erotic rapture, and awe mixed together is Socrates' comparison of erotic and philosophical initiations.[178] In Plutarch's description of the mystery experience cited above, 'terror, shuddering and trembling and sweat and amazement' are listed as its initial or preliminary stage; 'fear,' as well as 'consternation and shudder' are mentioned as self-evident by several authors in their references to mystery rites.[179] W. Burkert stresses the importance of the anthropologically attested archaic methods of 'shaking the foundations of the personality,' such as extreme pain and terror, in the Greco-Roman initiations.[180] Violent 'striping' of the initiate's personality could be achieved by various kinds of physical suffering, even by flagellation, regarded as a form of purification.[181]

Initiation rites often included various austerities attested to in descriptions of Greek mysteries, among them fasting, exhaustion, fear, pain, sensory deprivation, rhythmic noises, and uproar. Fasting and thirst, used by ascetics of various denominations in order to attain visions, are prominent at the priming stage of Greek mystery rites.[182] Most notable is the example of the Eleusinian mysteries: after a day's march from Athens to Eleusis, having covered 22 kilometres on foot, the initiates abstained from food during the entire day before the great ceremony.[183] Fasting and abstinence are prominent in the cult and mysteries of Isis.[184] The combination of exhaustion and subsequent fast enhanced the initiates' sensitivity to the awesome rites.

Purification rites,[185] often complex and intimidating, in addition to preliminary sacrifices,[186] prepared the initiate for participation in the central ceremony of a mystery rite. The stage of the Greater Mysteries in Eleusis began with the *thronôsis* ceremony, during which the initiate was seated blindfolded on a low stool, and purified by the fire of a burning torch.[187] In the Corybantic rites *thronôsis* was probably the most important stage of the initiation.[188]

Consumption of psychotropic substances during initiation rites has also been assumed by some scholars.[189] However, the recipe of *kukeôn*, the sacred beverage of the Eleusinian mysteries, remains controversial.[190] Depictions of Demeter with poppies[191] do not prove that poppies were used in her cult for the manipulation of consciousness: this plant was used in Greece for medicinal purposes and as a somnifer, so its appearance as an attribute could symbolise the deity's healing powers (as in the case of Asclepius and Apollo) or allude to her connection to the chthonic world.[192] Poppy-capsules are represented on a plate in a depiction of the purification ceremony preceding the Eleusinian initiation on the Lovatelli urn,[193] but again, poppy was often portrayed on funerary monuments and could indicate the association of the rite with the netherworld; it is significant that the capsules are not notched, therefore the relief conveyed no hint at opium sap. Thus, *kukeôn* was probably just a simple potion used to break the fast.[194] So far, there is no unequivocal evidence for the use of mind-altering substances other than wine in mystery initiations.

The power of music to induce *mania* was common knowledge,[195] and dancing and music were prominent in many mystery rites.[196] Lucian is confident that no ancient mystic rite (*teletê*) was celebrated without dance.[197] Whirlers (*rhomboi*), instruments whirled around on a string, were known to be used often in mystery rites.[198] Percussion instruments, such as clappers, metal finger cymbals and tambourines (*krotala* and *tumpana*), are usually associated with Cybele or Dionysus, and Dionysiac connections are probably the reason for the use of the tambourines by Orphic initiates.[199] Whirlers together with drums produced roaring sounds resembling thunder, both deafening and frightening, and this effect was exploited in various mystery rites.[200]

Double flutes, *auloi*, are especially noteworthy: these instruments were so unanimously considered trance-inducing, that their name produced a verb, *kataulein*, 'to cast a spell,' literally 'to cause trance by means of an *aulos*.' Aristotle observes that *auloi* are appropriate for enthusing the listener with ecstasy.[201] Instruments resembling Greek *auloi*, called *ney*, are still used by ecstatic dervishes in Turkey, Iran, and Pakistan.[202]

Satyrs, maenads, and mortals playing string and wind instruments, as well as dancing in Bacchic rapture, are prominent on Apulian funerary vases, and their ecstasy is perhaps indicative of the state of initiates whose happiness in the netherworld is the main concern of the Italian gold tablets.[203] In a rare unequivocal portrayal of a mystery scene on a mid-fifth century crater, its context is indicated by the presence of a *liknon*-bearer, approaching two gods, presumably Dionysus and Ariadne (or Sabazius and Cybele). The vase features an array of musical activities: there are two flute players, a group of girls dancing wildly, one of them holding a tambourine, and a boy with cymbals.[204]

On Samothrace, the Hall of Choral dancers was decorated with a frieze featuring dancers and musicians, which depicted the rite enacted there.[205] The mysteries of the Cabiri on Lemnos and in Thebes involved ecstatic dancing, as well as heavy drinking.[206] Participants in the Eleusinian procession who marched from Athens to Eleusis on the day preceding the great night-time ceremony sang and danced.[207] Swift dancing leading to ecstasy were central in the Corybantic rites and probably in the Eleusinian mysteries, as well.[208] The name of Eumolpus, the mythical forefather of the Eumolpidae, one of the three Athenian clans in charge of the

Eleusinian cult, implies the importance of *molpê*, choral performance combining dance and song.[209]

As observed in the Introduction, music and dancing are used for manipulation of consciousness worldwide. Neuropsychological research demonstrates that music activates a cascade of brain regions involved in arousal and pleasure; furthermore, music is a more effective tool than language for arousing feelings and emotions.[210] During mystery initiations, music could be used to 'tune' the mind of the participants to the mood desired at each stage of the ceremonies, make them feel sorrow or joy, and finally enhance their feeling of bliss. Choral dancing and singing fostered the sense of cohesion among the selected, who sensed in unison and felt that their selves were fused together, and united with the deity.

It is fascinating that the Greeks were quite aware of the ability of music to alter consciousness: Plato took for granted the use of music in mystery rites, and explicitly stated that Dionysiac initiations involved violent dancing.[211] Aristotle was convinced that the Phrygian mode brought about *enthousiasmos*, and the Phrygian mode, of all the musical modes, influenced the audience in the same manner as *aulos* among the musical instruments; both were in his opinion 'exciting (*orgiastika*) and passionate.'[212] It is hardly surprising that Orpheus, the quintessential musician, was considered the inventor of the mysteries.[213] In addition, folk etymologies associated the words 'mysteries' and 'Muses' from the fifth century onwards,[214] this relationship indicating that the Greeks were aware of the role of music in mystery rites.

Moving between extremities was essential in mystery rites and was one of their central motifs: initiates following Aeschines' mother exclaimed 'I escaped from evil, I found the better.'[215] This opposition is reflected in various aspects of the mystic ritual. Centuries later, Aelius Aristides described Eleusis as 'the most frightening and the most resplendent of all that is divine for men.'[216]

Degrees of spiritual enlightenment were intrinsically connected with the contrast between darkness and light.[217] Demetrius states that in the context of mysteries, darkness and night are allegories of consternation and trembling: 'Therefore the mysteries are allegorically represented as if in darkness and at night, in reference to consternation and shudder. The allegory seems to be to the darkness and night.'[218] In the reflection on initiation ceremonies of Dio Chrysostom, 'a mystical recess (*muchos*)' is presented as an obvious and necessary part of the environment, where the initiate 'hears many mystic voices and sees many mystic sights while light and darkness appear to him alternately.'[219] In the Eleusinian mysteries, the central ceremony was illuminated by the sacred light, in striking contrast to the preceding darkness.[220] Euripides' *Bacchae*, which is infused with mystery symbolism, contains allusions to sacred darkness and blessed light, and the god himself is addressed as 'greatest light' (in the darkness).[221] In the *Frogs*, Iacchus-Dionysus is called 'light-bearing star of the nightly *teletê*.'[222] A recently published epitaph of an initiate in the Samothracian mysteries mentions 'the sacred light of the two Cabiri,' thus attesting to the existence of a ritual similar to that of Eleusis on Samothrace.[223]

Dionysiac rites, and mystery initiations in particular, were often performed at night.[224] The function of the natural and artificial caves that frequently served as spaces of mystery rites, in terms of their physical impact on the mind of the initiates, was either to enhance the effect of normal vision of outer surroundings, or to induce an altered state of consciousness.[225] Dramatic transition from darkness to light, from being blinded to seeing great sights was intended to alter the initiate's perception of his surroundings. Moreover, darkness was not merely functional, but also profoundly symbolic: K. Clinton observes that 'the loss of sight, seeing only darkness in a kind of death, was like an experience of the Underworld.'[226]

In sum, the Greeks were familiar with various techniques of manipulation of consciousness, and many of these methods were used in preparation and during mystery rites: fasting, sensory deprivation, enduring physical pain and exhaustion, dancing and singing to the sounds of stimulating music, contrast of darkness and bright light and other devices are frequently mentioned in ancient accounts of mystery rites. These techniques were not employed together in every mystery initiation, but each of them by itself was sufficient to alter the initiate's state of consciousness (slightly or considerably) and make him or her hyper-sensitive to whatever he perceived. In this condition, seeing the sacred symbols, even if they were in fact very trivial objects, could become a life-changing experience. The personality of the beholder and his or her state of mind were of crucial importance. Attaining the desirable state of mind, minor or obvious *mania*, was therefore the most important prerequisite for a successful initiation.

Mystery rites and near-death experiences

Mystery cults did not only promise the initiate's bliss after death.[227] Hints scattered through the works of various authors indicate that the aim of the initiate was to attain harmony and serenity by enduring death and learning not to fear it.[228] Plutarch compares mystery initiations to death, noting the resemblance of the Greek words 'to die' (*teleutan*) and 'to be initiated' (*teleisthai*), and alleges that at the moment of death, the soul experiences an emotion similar to the act of being initiated:

> Therefore we say that the soul that has passed there has died, due to its complete change and conversion. Here it is without knowledge, except when it is already on the threshold of death; but then it has an experience like that of people who are initiated into great mysteries. Therefore the words 'to die' (*teleutan*) and 'to be initiated' (*teleisthai*), as well as the actions, are similar.[229]

Several hundred years earlier, Plato juxtaposed the words *teletai* and *teleutan*, 'to pass away,' hinting that they were cognate.[230] A Gnostic treatise referring to the Eleusinian practice of proceeding from the Lesser to the Greater mysteries cites Heraclitus' phrase 'Greater deaths obtain greater shares' and clarifies its relevance to the Greater mysteries: 'Those who obtained these deaths obtain greater shares.'[231] Thus, the deeper the feeling of death, the greater was the blessing. Owing to this awareness, a second-century AD Eleusinian hierophant, as his epitaph states, revealed that 'to the mortals, death is no evil, but rather good.'[232]

Dionysus was associated with death very early. Heraclitus asserted: 'For were it not in Dionysus' honour that they made processions and sung hymns to phallus, the action would be most insolent, because Hades and Dionysus, for whom they become mad and maenadic, are the same.'[233] This double identity of Dionysus was reflected in the festival of Anthesteria, combining wine-drinking with the cult of the dead.[234] It is no coincidence that at Derveni, a magnificent crater decorated with Dionysiac scenes served as an urn for the ashes of a fourth-century Macedonian aristocrat,[235] while another contemporary burial in the same area contained a charred Orphic book burnt on the funeral pyre.[236] It is suggested that the words 'life-death-life,' alongside 'Dionysus' and 'Orphics' on the Olbian bone tablet refer to the juxtaposition of life and death in mystic ritual.[237]

A tangible manifestation of the funerary symbolism of the Dionysiac initiations is the construction of a shrine in the form of a tomb by a Bacchic *thiasos* in Callatis on the Thracian cost.[238] A third-century decree of this association refers to a subterranean grotto (*psalis*), a first-century BC document attests to the dedication of a cave (*antron*) to Dionysus, whereas a first-century AD inscription stipulates that an ex-voto be placed in a 'recess' (*muchos*).[239] The term *neobakchoi*, designating newly-initiated Dionysiac *mustai*, as well as the celebration of trieteric festival by the *thiasos*, indicate that the activities of the association in Callatis included mystery initiations.[240] *Psalis* is an architectural term meaning 'vault,' and many contemporary subterranean vaults were constructed in the area to serve as tombs.[241] Thus, the Dionysiac grotto of Callatis, where initiatory rites were enacted, was most probably an artificial grotto, modelled on contemporary vaulted tombs.[242]

A number of Orphic-Bacchic gold tablets refer to the initiatory experience as preparing for the death. This great experience is probably hinted to in a fourth-century gold tablet from Thurii: 'Greetings to you who have had an experience not like anything you had had before.'[243] It is as a result of this experience, having overcome death, that the *mustês* of this lamella is proclaimed a god instead of mortal.

It may further be supposed that the terrible experience of obliteration of the previous personality and almost-death might be the atonement referred to in contemporary gold leaves, from Thurii and Pherae: 'Enter the holy meadow, for the *mustês* is redeemed (*apoinos*).'[244] The retribution, *poinê*,[245] described in these tablets, is perhaps the equivalent to the horrible experience, 'not like anything you have had before.' It is followed by the supreme joy of redemption, visualised as entering the 'holy meadow' in the Pheran gold leaf, and reminiscent of Plutarch's portrayal of the *mustês*' delight in the meadow in his description of the initiatory experience.

The transformation obtained by means of initiation could be perceived as an apotheosis. In three fourth-century tablets from Thurii, the initiates proclaim that they were struck by lightning.[246] One lamella is particularly interesting. The deceased declares:

> For I also claim to be of your happy race
> But Moira overcame me and the other immortal gods and the star-flinger with lightning
> I have flown out of the heavy, difficult circle.[247]

Being struck by lightning is mentioned between the assertion of inborn divinity, and the statement that the initiate was able to leave the painful circle (of life? of reincarnations?).[248] Being smitten by lightning is symbolic of the fiery deaths of Asclepius, Semele, and Heracles: it is an apotheosis.[249] The comparison to Heracles is double: like the hero who was ignited by Zeus' bolt and then adopted by Hera, our initiate is first struck by lightning and then 'enters the bosom of the queen of the netherworld,' which means adoption or at least nursing of the initiate by the goddess.[250] Thus, in some gold tablets the transformative fiery purification of one's nature from mortality is further ratified by the goddess' acceptance, and the radical reformation of the initiate's status is symbolically represented as his or her entrance into the holy meadow, after the death of his or her earthly body, of course. These gifts are attained due to a horrible experience perceived as atonement.

What kind of experience was it? Did it include sensations of being struck and purified with lightning, accepted by a goddess and walking in a meadow? Feeling that one's mortal foundations were burnt is the strongest possible way to describe the annihilation of the man who lived before the initiation, even as a metaphor. Yet I suggest that at least some *mustai* used the image of incineration of their past self not only as a symbol, but also as a faithful description of their sensations of 'being struck by lightning' or 'seeing the great light,' and meeting with a kindly divine being, which are characteristic of revelatory or mystical experiences.[251]

Mystic initiation may be defined as ersatz-death, *imitatio mortis*.[252] Thanks to initiation rites that brought them as close to death as was permissible to the mortals, *mustai* were less fearful of the inescapable end of their life. They were confident of their renewal and rebirth as immortals, because mystic death was followed by rebirth.[253] As a consequence, real death was considered as birth and a thrice-happy event, as one of the Pelinna tablets declares.[254]

In modern terms, alteration of consciousness experienced by the initiate during the ceremony induced the feeling of rejuvenation and transformed his personality through changing his attitude to life and death. The idea of death before rebirth in a new status is indeed present in tribal initiations, one of the sources from which mystic initiations allegedly evolved.[255] The aim of approaching death in Greek mystery cults was however quite different, namely, the 'brush with death' was intended to lead to a spiritual transformation, rather than to a passage to a different status in the community.[256]

Plutarch's account of the initiate's experience immediately follows his observations on the proximity of mystery experience to death, cited above.[257] In real life, today and two thousand years ago, some people approach death very closely as a result of an illness, wound, or accident, and describe their 'brush with death' as a complex event, dubbed a near-death experience.[258] If one had tried to construct a description of an experience as close to near-death experience as possible, it is hard to imagine a more apt and vivid report than this Plutarchean fragment. Plutarch's account of the catabasis into the subterranean grotto in the Trophonium, a place imbued with the symbolism of Hades, features conspicuous elements of mystery initiations.[259] It also suggests that the enquirer's state there was almost equivalent to a near-death experience. In these two texts, Plutarch described sensations of people who were not actually dying; could he be aware of the proximity between mystery and near-death experiences?

Near-death experiences are profound subjective events reported in contemporary studies by a quarter to a third of the people who have been in extreme life-threatening danger, on the verge of death, or were believed or pronounced clinically dead – but ultimately survived. They are cross-cultural, attested in traditional and industrial societies.[260] Although their aetiology has not yet been compellingly established, and notwithstanding the position of those who proclaim near-death experiences as the proof of mind-brain dualism, the neuroscientific orthodoxy is that near-death experiences stem from neurophysiological processes.[261] In the modern (Western and non-Western) world, they are quite common: depending on the methodology of the research, incidence of near-death experiences is estimated as 35% in retrospective studies and 17% in prospective studies.[262] Near-death experiences result from enhanced cognitive functioning and include one or several of the following elements: out-of-body experiences, a sense of being in a different realm, transcending the boundaries of ego and limitations of space and time; panoramic replay of one's life and meeting in the world of beyond with other people alive or deceased, and with various fantastic creatures; and a strong positive sensation of encounter with a source of all-embracing light, wisdom, and love. These sensations are typically described as ineffable. Cultural and religious factors are significant in determining the contents and especially interpretation of near-death experiences, as well as their after-effects.[263]

Near-death experiences often lead to enduring personality transformations of individuals who have lived through them, among them

> a greater appreciation for life, a renewed sense of purpose, greater confidence and flexibility in coping with life's vicissitudes, increased value of love and service and decreased concern with personal status and material possessions, greater compassion for others, a heightened sense of spiritual purpose, and a greatly reduced fear of death.[264]

Major studies comparing changes in the perception of patients after cardiac arrest demonstrate significant, sometime twice as high, positive changes in those who had a near-death experience in comparison to those who had no such experience. Their understanding of life, acceptance of others, belief in afterlife, and sense of inner meaning of life rose dramatically, and the changes persisted for many years. Most remarkably, fear of death diminished in about half of people who had undergone near-death experiences, whereas many reported higher self-esteem and feeling specifically favoured by god. These people also mentioned a sense of estrangement from the body and the feeling that they were imprisoned in the body, as well as the notion of being reborn. Many featured 'psychic awakening,' a developing sense of being guided and a proclivity for paranormal-related activities, such as clairvoyance, telepathy, healing, out-of-body travelling, and contact with spirits.[265] From the point of view of most people who had experienced this sensation and many researchers, the key point is not the objective neurological basis of the near-death experiences, but their transformative significance.

For the purposes of this study it is crucial to emphasise that near-death experiences occur in divergent cultures and can be a priori expected to have happened in the ancient world, and many characteristics are consistently congruent with notions expressed by Greek initiates. Another important point is the resemblance of many features of near-death experiences and alteration of consciousness, in particular mystical experiences.[266] Descriptions of out-of-body experiences and drug-induced hallucinations are often so similar to near-death experiences, in structure and content, that the probability of common processes and underlying neurophysiological mechanisms has been put forward.[267]

Near-death experiences were doubtlessly known in Greece. First of all, dying is a gradual process, and sensations accompanying approaching death could be communicated to the people surrounding the deathbed. Furthermore, modern resuscitation technique is not necessary for some individuals to be considered as returning to life after having been dead: detailed accounts of what today would be named near-death experiences were published in Europe and America in the nineteenth century, and members of traditional societies around the globe report near-death experiences after having been considered dead and sometimes even prepared for burial.[268] In ancient Greece, a whole group of people was known as *deuteropotmoi*, 'those who die twice,' or *hysteropotmoi*, 'those whose destiny is postponed.'[269] *Deuteropotmoi* were people who had been pronounced dead, yet returned to their community: either those for whom a tomb was constructed on the assumption that they were dead, or those reported to have died abroad, but then reappeared at home. Given the state of medicine and of personal security in the Greek world, *deuteropotmoi* were bizarre and mysterious, but not unique. Democritus even wrote a book entitled *On Hades* about people mistakenly believed to be dead.[270] Around the turn of the era, a novel depicting late fifth–early fourth-century Syracuse, described a girl who had been buried, but 'received return to life' the day after she had been pronounced dead.[271] The novel does not touch upon supernatural elements, which means that 'return to life' was considered an actual possibility, which the readers would readily accept as a part of a plot. In Sicily in particular return from death was believed to occur from time to time: Diogenes Laertius credits Empedocles with reanimating a woman, who had been dead for thirty days, and the subject was discussed by Heraclides of Pontus, as well; Empedocles himself claimed that he healed the sick by retrieving them from the netherworld.[272] The historicity of Empedocles' ambitions does not concern us at the moment; these anecdotes illustrate that in the fifth-century Acragas, people unwell enough to be pronounced dead could recover and share their experiences.

Most remarkable are two detailed stories of *deuteropotmoi*, of Er in Plato's *Republic* and of Thespesius in Plutarch's *On the Delays of the Divine Vengeance*,[273] both fictitious, but probably modelled on real accounts of near-death experiences. In the story of Er, he died in battle; ten days later, his body, surprisingly untouched by decay, was taken home for burial. Two days later, when placed on the funeral pyre, Er came back to life, and recounted what he had seen in the netherworld. In the opening part of his story, Er says that his soul, 'after it left his body' (*ekbênai*) arrived in a marvellous meadow; unfortunately, Plato neglects to give details of its return back to the body. Although Er's story is without doubt literary fiction, a modification of Orphic and Pythagorean ideas,[274] it also includes many elements that were familiar to the public, and details of an out-of-body experience should also be recognisable to Plato's audience. Significantly, in the opinion of several experts on near-death experiences, Er's story was based on an account of a return from death.[275] This tale is intended to illustrate Plato's conception of true initiation, whose success is dependent on one's worldly achievements rather than just on ritual purity.[276] It is remarkable that Plato's quintessential initiation is straightforwardly pictured as a real journey to the realm of death and back.

Plutarch's tale of Thespesius contains quite a number of ostensibly authentic features of near-death experience, including a flight within a dark void at the beginning of the story. The story of Thespesius incorporates apparent death, the soul's separation from the body, a sense of being drawn out of the body, enhanced visual perception, a bright spot in a dark void, the presence of guiding beings, visions of the netherworld, including pictures of the divine beauty and meetings with acquaintances, the feeling of being pulled back to life, and finally a return to this world with supreme knowledge – all elements which appear consistently in the reports of modern near-death survivors. The connection between return from the netherworld and the reformation undergone by Thespesius, who not only abandoned his depraved lifestyle but even changed his name, is particularly noteworthy: many present-day people who have had near-death experiences undergo a *metanoia*, dramatically changing their attitude to life and behaviour.[277]

In the sixth century AD, Proclus, writing about Er in his *Commentary to Plato's Republic*, cited several examples of people brought to burial who were resuscitated, including the case of Cleonymus of Athens, narrated by Aristotle's disciple Clearchus of Soli. At the moment of his death, Cleonymus' soul was separated from his body, and flew above various places invisible to the men to a place where it met female *daimonia* of indescribable beauty. In particular, Proclus refers to dramatic changes in the lifestyle of another *deuteropotmos*, Eurynous of Epirus, who became much more virtuous after his resuscitation.[278]

The list of after-effects reported by people who have experienced near-death in modern times, cited above, remarkably corresponds to the blessings of mystery rites, as reflected in the ancient sources. They also find parallels in the Greek descriptions of *deuteropotmoi*, which is not surprising given the cross-cultural nature of near-death experiences. I therefore believe that it is methodologically justified to look at the characteristics of modern near-death experiences and compare them with the evidence on ancient mystery cults.[279]

The vortex, a journey through a dark void to bright light, frequently appears in anthropological accounts of altered states of consciousness as experienced by various religious practitioners and in laboratory experiments investigating such states.[280] It is also characteristic of near-death experiences, but rarely occurs among people in normal physical condition.[281] Its main feature is a tunnel-like perspective, which often terminates in a bright light appearing in the centre of the field of vision, the light sometimes described as warm or kindly, or as brightly lit human forms. In the Greek and Latin texts alluding to mystery experiences a number of passages probably hint to the vortex sensation, sometimes listing several of its characteristics. In Plutarch's account of the descent into Trophonium, the enquirer in the Trophonium lived through an out-of-body state, his soul flew above an ocean with shining isles and enjoyed a conversation with divine beings; most significantly, the enquirer's soul was 'released.'[282] In the description of a mystery experience he first passed through a dark area, and then saw 'marvellous light.' In a second to third century AD papyrus text, Heracles combines passing through darkness with seeing light and a goddess, saying that during his initiation at Eleusis, he saw 'fire and Kore' in the night.[283]

As mentioned above, the emphasis on seeing extraordinary brilliance contrasted with darkness is conspicuous in the Eleusinian and Bacchic *teletai*, and the core experience of many mystery rites was focused on a vision of 'shining beauty,' to use Plato's definition.[284] It is noteworthy that Plutarch compares *epopteia* to a thunderbolt.[285] The sensation of being struck by lightning appears in three gold tablets, as we have just seen. This encounter with great light and a benign supernatural presence in an altered state of consciousness could be perceived as equivalent to a similar sensation that is part of the near-death experience, and therefore interpreted as a form of preparation for death by means of approaching it while alive.

Near-death experiences occur to the dying or those facing a real possibility of death – and in many cases actually end in death. Prior to death, many modern subjects reported transition from anxiety and pain to an ineffable sensation of serenity and being cleansed. People who had near-death experiences are transformed, most notably they are 'not concerned about dying.'[286] For many modern survivors, near-death experiences are the most intense and happiest moments of their lives. A modern respondent described an overwhelming sensation of peace during her near-death experience: 'If you took one thousand best things in your life and multiplied it by a million, maybe . . . you could get close to this feeling.'[287]

These moments are typically remembered as 'realer than real.'[288] Many modern survivors report decreased death anxiety, an increase in psychic abilities, a higher zest for life, and viewing life as rich with purpose; they are fearless about death, and virtually fearless about life.[289] Transcendental sensations of encounter with the loving supreme being are later recalled as glimpses of direct vision of the ultimate reality and in some cases amount to deep personality change.[290]

Immediately before death, many modern subjects who did not survive their near-death experience reported transition from anxiety and pain to an ethereal sensation of peace. Perhaps most significant is the fact that information on near-death experiences, and especially witnessing them, greatly comforted the frightened and grieving relatives of the deceased.[291] A contemporary girl who saw a beautiful light on her deathbed, hours before she actually died, said to her mother:

'You can't go with me! The light is coming to get me but you can't go! I wish you could see it. . . .' Another girl, who survived her near-death experience, reflected: 'It was like I had a new life. I'm not afraid so much of dying because I know more about it now.'[292] It is possible that in ancient Greece, similar events hinted that approaching death might bring about harmony, wisdom, and liberation from fear – the blessings of mystery initiations that are alluded to by ancient authors. If we try to imagine how the Greeks could define such states, is seems that they would have used such words as *eudaimonia*, 'blessedness,' or perhaps *entheos*, 'engodded.'

The noetic quality of near-death experiences, the conviction in the reality of the encounter with a deity, the change in their attitude to life and the acceptance of death as benign left a tremendous impression on survivors and those who witnessed the process of dying,[293] and presumably forced many of them to share their illuminative knowledge with other people. The idea that alteration of consciousness is homologous to near-death experience, and therefore endows the person who has undergone the experience with the same benefits, could emerge and gain currency among people eager to be liberated from the fears of human existence.

The lore of near-death experiences, combined with the universal human propensity to manipulate consciousness, and the tradition of tribal initiations, could influence the evolution of mystery initiations. The darkness-light transition as part of the practice leading to spiritual renewal may have been chosen by individuals who had lived through a near-death experience or an introverted mystic experience, and sought a way to impart their knowledge to other people. Plato's and Plutarch's juxtaposition of mystic experiences to death discloses perhaps their intuition that the two sensations are cognate. In a later text, Heracles declares that he does not need to be initiated at Eleusis, because he 'has been initiated into much truer mysteries':[294] the Eleusinian rites – ersatz-death – were unnecessary for a person who has been to the real netherworld.

Conclusions

Alteration of the initiate's state of consciousness, *mania*, was a major element of mystery rites. All of them promised the *mustai* contact with the divine, either in the form of possession by the god or as a revelation of the divine truth about life and death. There are two categories of telestic *mania*: the first one, most obvious and straightforward, consisted of excitement or even trance interpreted by the ancients as divine possession and characteristic of ecstatic initiations. In the Corybantic, Sabaziac, and some Bacchic rites, attaining the state of divine *mania* was the main purpose for the participation in the ceremony.

The second category was more complex and is difficult to ascertain on the basis of the incomplete evidence at our disposal. It involved two stages: first, alteration of consciousness as a means of attaining revelation, the phase which could be comparable to the ecstatic telestic *mania*. This was a preparatory stage for the supreme feat of *epopteia*, rather than an independent aim. The second stage was the peak of the mystery initiation, defined by the ancients as blessedness, *eudaimonia*. The extant references to the core experience of the *mustai* leaves little place for doubt that ideally, this holistic experience included different levels of alteration of consciousness, from slight to considerable. The Bacchic-Orphic initiations belonged to this category, as well as the Eleusinian mysteries, and perhaps a few other mystery rites, which promised the initiates illumination, using various techniques of manipulation of consciousness to achieve the state of blessedness. Initiation rites belonging to the second category were meant to obtain a wordless comprehension of the mystery of life and death, and were essentially a rehearsal of the real death, modelled perhaps on near-death experiences. In any case, the brush with death which rendered the *mustai* fearless in the face of death and imperturbable to the perils of human existence seems to have been central to this category of rites.

Even in slightly altered states of consciousness, every detail of one's surroundings may take on incredible beauty and acquire supreme significance. Such states can be induced by various techniques. Mystery rites could appear unimportant or even ridiculous to people in a regular state of mind: for trivial events to be remembered by the *mustai* as revelations, they had to be brought to a state of heightened sensitivity and perhaps also suggestibility. The experience itself, undergone in an altered state of consciousness, could not be communicated in words; hence, its transcendental content was bound to remain ineffable.[295] During altered states of consciousness normal language abilities are often inhibited: the feeling of ineffability accompanying alterations of consciousness – telestic *mania* – may be one of the important reasons why mystery initiations were shrouded in secrecy. Another important feature of altered states of consciousness is the sensation of rejuvenation or rebirth reported by some modern experiencers. This feeling is strongly evident in the ideology of mystery cults, as well as in the subjective sensations of the *mustai*. Throughout the history of the mystery rites individual predisposition and environment defined the profundity of one's experience, and many initiates attended the ceremonies 'for the record,' others experienced various degrees of altered states of consciousness, while the lucky few could even attain the supreme bliss of feeling at one with the deity they worshipped.

Notes

1 This chapter draws on my article: Ustinova (2013).
2 Pl. *Phdr.* 244E–245A: ἀλλὰ μὴν νόσων γε καὶ πόνων τῶν μεγίστων, ἃ δὴ παλαιῶν ἐκ μηνιμάτων ποθὲν ἔν τισι τῶν γενῶν ἡ μανία ἐγγενομένη καὶ προφητεύσασα, οἷς ἔδει ἀπαλλαγὴν ηὕρετο, καταφυγοῦσα πρὸς θεῶν εὐχάς τε καὶ λατρείας, ὅθεν δὴ καθαρμῶν τε καὶ τελετῶν τυχοῦσα ἐξάντη ἐποίησε τὸν [ἑαυτῆς] ἔχοντα πρός τε τὸν παρόντα καὶ τὸν ἔπειτα χρόνον, λύσιν τῷ ὀρθῶς μανέντι τε καὶ κατασχομένῳ τῶν παρόντων κακῶν εὑρομένη (translation H. N. Fowler, modified); see Delatte (1934: 71); Linforth (1946b); Rouget (1990: 350–365).
3 Linforth (1946b) feels that in this phrase 'Mania is alive and active as a person'; Yunis (2011: 133) interprets the dramatic quality of the image of *mania* as indicating that it belongs to the 'imaginary archaic world of tragic poetry, though no particular drama is called to mind.'
4 Discussed in the Introduction.

5 As suggested by Linforth (1946b: 171–172).

6 *Phdr.* 265AB.

7 Discussed in detail in Chapter 3.

8 OF 350: ἄνθρωποι . . . ὄργιά τ᾽ ἐκτελέσουσι λύσιν προγόνων ἀθεμίστων | μαιόμενοι· σὺ δὲ τοῖσιν ἔχων κράτος, οὕς κε θέλῃσθα | λύσεις ἔκ τε πόνων χαλεπῶν καὶ ἀπείρονος οἴστρου (translation F. Graf).

On the sting of *oistros*, gadfly's barb, as synonymous to a sudden attack of frenzy, see below, Chapter 7.

9 Graf and Johnston (2007: 147). In the often quoted passage on the *orpheotelestai*, Plato refers to remission of sins and purification by means of *teletai*, but does not indicate specifically that these rites purge madness (*R.* 365A).

10 E.g. Rowe (1986: 168).

11 Seaford (1981) and Chapter 3 below.

12 Heraclit. fr. B14 *DK*, cited and discussed below.

13 Speaking probably of the Eleusinian mysteries; *TGF* fr. 387 ἔφριξ᾽· ἔρως δὲ τοῦδε μυστικοῦ τέλους ('I shudder with rapture of the mystic rite'); another fragment refers to 'unthinking madness for the gods' (ἀσαλὴς θεόθεν μανία, *TGF* fr. 319); regrettably, it is impossible to establish the nature of connection between the two lines.

14 For mystagogues in real-life rites, see Bremmer (2014: 3).

15 Reale and Burnett (2001: 224), citing Sophocles' fragment (247 *TGF*): 'nobody is wise but the one honoured by the god' (σοφὸς γὰρ οὐδεὶς πλὴν ὃν ἂν τιμᾷ θεός).

16 Calame (1992: 187).

17 Frede (2012).

18 *Smp.* 210A; Rowe (1998: 193); Riedweg (1987: 22–28); Morgan (1990: 86–89); Gómez Iglesias (2016).

19 For the core elements and functions shared by all the mystery cults of the Classical world, which determine their basic nature, see Burkert (1987: 4); Turcan (1998: 121). The essential characteristics of mystery initiations remained constant throughout the centuries of their history, modifications of ritual notwithstanding: Seaford (1981: 252); Clinton (1992: 131); Dunand (2000); Dunand (2000: 131); North (2000: 68).

20 *TGF* fr. 472; Bremmer (2014: 66–67); Bernabé (2016b).

21 I chose to use these terms, which cover 'mysteries in general' and are widely used, rather than retain U. Bianchi's categories of mystic, mysteriosophical, and mystery cults (Bianchi 2004; cf. Sfameni Gasparro 2011: 290; Borgeaud 2013: 143).

22 Cole (2003: 193); Versnel (1990: 150); Clinton (2003: 54–58); Graf (2003: 4, 9). The most comprehensive study of the term is Schuddeboom (2009), who demonstrates that in Archaic and Classical literature τελετή may mean ritual act in general, as well as the mystery rites; in the Hellenistic literature the latter meaning prevails; in the epigraphic evidence the word occurs in various meanings (Schuddeboom 2009: 37, 99, 224). In addition, the word ὄργια can denominate rites or objects associates with mystery rites, especially in Hellenistic inscriptions (Jaccottet 2005b: 223).

23 For a critical approach to the common use of the term see Dodd and Faraone (2003); even D. B. Dodd acknowledges that the application of the initiations paradigm to such central phenomena as Eleusinian and Samothracian mysteries is 'less controversial' (Dodd and Faraone 2003: xv).

24 Burkert (1987); Scarpi (2002); Cosmopoulos (2003); Bianchi (2004); Bottini (2005); Sfameni Gasparro (2011); Casadio and Johnston (2009b); Bowden (2010); Bremmer (2014).

25 Burkert (1983: 254); Burkert (1985: 286) argues that all or almost all of them; Bremmer (2014: 4) contends that we don't know how many Athenians were initiated; however, he is confident that in the mid-fifth century the number of initiates reached thousands (Bremmer 1995: 73, citing *IG* I³ 6 and Hdt. 8. 65). In 408/07, after the disasters of the Peloponnesian War had decimated the citizen body of Athens, about

2,200 people were initiated at Eleusis (Cavanaugh 1996: 211–212; Sourvinou-Inwood 2003: 47). Reservations: Clinton (1992: 85).

26 *LSAM* No. 96; *SIG*³ No. 1024; Burkert (1983: 253–254).

27 Plato, *R*. 364E. The identification of these rites is controversial: Burkert (1985: 300); Graf (1993); Price (1999: 119–121); Bremmer (2002: 24); Buxton (1980: 73); Graf and Johnston (2007: 142–144); Cole (2003: 207); Bowden (2010: 15); Tzifopoulos (2010: 115–121); Bremmer (2014: 55–80); Bernabé and Jiménez San Cristóbal (2008: 179–205); Edmonds III (2013); Jenner (2014: 31–53).

28 Burkert (1983: 255). The most radical case is a separate burial plot at Cumae for those who have become Bacchic, βεβαχχευμένοι, *LSAM Suppl.* No. 120; Cole (1980: 231); Turcan (1986); Parker (2011: 258); cf. Edmonds (2009) on the claims on special purity and consequently elevated status of Orphic initiates. Purity laws and vegetarian diet of initiates: E. *Hip.* 952–954; fr. 472 *TGF*; special clothes: Hdt. 2. 81; Bremmer (2014: 67).

29 A second–first century epitaph of an initiate in both Samothracian and Eleusinian mysteries, who completed eighty years of life 'without pain and trouble,' and hoped to dwell after death 'with the pious' (*eusebeis*), probably attests to the expectations of the Samothracian initiates to attain the double bliss of happiness in the two worlds (Dimitrova 2008: No. 29, p. 88; Parker 2011: 255); unfortunately, its late date doesn't allow certainty as to the prospects of the *mustai* during the earlier periods.

30 Sources: Scarpi (2002); cf. Burkert (1987: 9). For the limits of the ineffable see Burkert (1983: 252).

31 Chest (*kistê*): Burkert (1983: 272–273); winnowing basket (*liknon*): Synesius, *Dio* 7; Nilsson (1957: 21–37); Burkert (1987: 34, 96); iconographic evidence: Nilsson (1957: figs. 3, 4, 8, 10a; 15,18, 19, 35); Burkert (1987: figs. 5, 7); Kerényi (1976: fig. 135); Bianchi (1976: figs. 84, 88).

32 Hippol. *Ref.* 5. 8. 39; Burkert (1987: 91, 9–10).

33 Clinton (2003: 66–70); Clinton (2004); Sourvinou-Inwood (2003: 35); Burkert (1983: 286–288); Cosmopoulos (2015: 22).

34 In Pheneus (Paus. 8. 15. 3) and Lycosoura in Arcadia: Jost (2003: 157–161).

35 Plu. *Mor.* 611D; Delatte (1954: 699–708); Burkert (1987: 46, 94, 98); Bernabé and Jiménez San Cristóbal (2008: 151–160); Faraone (2013: 130–131).

36 Their contents remain an educated guess. Even if the hinted-at animal sacrifice, initiation of a boy by fire, and sacred marriage between the hierophant and the priestess did actually occur (for the discussion see Burkert 1983: 279–285; Clinton 1993: 118–119; Sourvinou-Inwood 2003), all these rites were enacted publicly on other occasions.

37 Crater. *FGH* 342 F16 (Schol. Ar. *Av.* 1073); Janko (1997: 88–89).

38 *Leg.* 2. 36: *neque solum cum laetitia vivendi rationem accepimus, sed etiam cum spe meliore moriendi*.

39 μάκαρες καὶ εὐδαίμονες or ὄλβιοι, E. *Ba.* 72; Pl. *Phdr.* 250B; Graf and Johnston (2007: No. 5); Riedweg (1987: 53). The gift many *mustai* expected from Dionysus and recorded in their dedications was good fortune in this life: Cole (1993: 293).

40 Plu. fr. 178 Sandbach, discussed below; *H. Car.* 480–482; A. *TGF* fr. 837; Isoc. 4. 28; Pi. fr. 137 Maehler; cf. Duchemin (1955: 100–101, 322–324); Cole (2003: 194); Bianchi (2004: 264–265).

41 Pl. *PhD.* 69C; cf. Clinton (1992: 85). Cf. E. *Ba.* 73–77 on the Bacchic *teletai*.

42 Sources: Scarpi (2002: 329–333, 421–429); cf. Zuntz (1971: 277–393); Cole (1980); Cole (1993); Cole (2003: 207–208); Riedweg (1998); Riedweg (2002); Graf and Johnston (2007); Bernabé and Jiménez San Cristóbal (2008); Dunand (2000: 138–140); Tzifopoulos (2010).

43 *IG* XIV 642, cf. 641. 1; Graf and Johnston (2007: Nos. 3, 5); Zuntz (1971: 301, 329); Cole (2003: 207); Bernabé and Jiménez San Cristóbal (2008: L. 8, 9). A mid-second or third-century AD tablet from Rome also seems to indicate transformation of the

deceased from mortal to immortal (Graf and Johnston 2007: No. 9). Cf. Tzifopoulos (2010: 129); Jiménez San Cristóbal (2009: 51–53); Edmonds (2009).

44 Empedocles, the extravagant sage who declared that the knowledge of gods' secrets had rendered him divine during his lifetime, laid claims to an extraordinary achievement: D. L. 8. 62, fr. B112 *DK*; Wright (1981: 264–266); Inwood (2001: 57–58). On similar expectations of Empedocles' contemporary Theron of Acreages, see Trépanier (2004: 122). See Burkert (2009) for the 'senselessness of Hades.'

45 E. *HF* 613; initiation at Eleusis: Apollod. 2. 5. 12; D.S. 4. 26. 1; X. *HG* 6. 3. 6; Boardman (1975); Colomo (2004).

46 Isocr. *Panegyricus* 28: περί τε τῆς τοῦ βίου τελευτῆς καὶ τοῦ σύμπαντος αἰῶνος ἡδίους τὰς ἐλπίδας. After the death of their daughter Plutarch consoled his wife by referring to the 'mystical token of the Dionysiac rites,' which supposedly reminded her that the death liberated the soul from the burden of the body (*Mor.* 611DE). Children and initiations: Cole (1993: 288–290).

47 The earthly status of the initiates remained unchanged: Waldner (2013: 217).

48 Waldner (2013: 237).

49 *Lg.* 790D–791A: ἐξ ἐμπειρίας αὐτὸ εἰλήφασι καὶ ἐγνώκασιν ὂν χρήσιμον αἵ τε τροφοὶ τῶν σμικρῶν καὶ αἱ περὶ τὰ τῶν Κορυβάντων ἰάματα τελοῦσαι· ἡνίκα γὰρ ἄν που βουληθῶσιν κατακοιμίζειν τὰ δυσυπνοῦντα τῶν παιδίων αἱ μητέρες, οὐχ ἡσυχίαν αὐτοῖς προσφέρουσιν ἀλλὰ τοὐναντίον κίνησιν, ἐν ταῖς ἀγκάλαις ἀεὶ σείουσαι . . . καὶ ἀτεχνῶς οἷον καταυλοῦσι τῶν παιδίων, καθάπερ ἡ τῶν ἐκφρόνων βακχειῶν ἰάσεις, ταύτῃ τῇ τῆς κινήσεως ἅμα χορείᾳ καὶ μούσῃ χρώμεναι. . . . ὅταν οὖν ἔξωθέν τις προσφέρῃ τοῖς τοιούτοις πάθεσι σεισμόν, ἡ τῶν ἔξωθεν κρατεῖ κίνησις προσφερομένη τὴν ἐντὸς φοβερὰν οὖσαν καὶ μανικὴν κίνησιν, κρατήσασα δέ, γαλήνην ἡσυχίαν τε ἐν τῇ ψυχῇ φαίνεσθαι ἀπεργασαμένη τῆς περὶ τὰ τῆς καρδίας χαλεπῆς γενομένης ἑκάστων πηδήσεως . . . , τοὺς μὲν ὕπνου λαγχάνειν ποιεῖ, τοὺς δ' ἐγρηγορότας ὀρχουμένους τε καὶ αὐλουμένους . . . κατηργάσατο ἀντὶ μανικῶν ἡμῖν διαθέσεων ἕξεις ἔμφρονας ἔχειν (translation R. G. Bury, modified). Cf. Str. 10. 3. 11–15.

50 Hoffmann (1997: 29); West (2000: 254).

51 215 CD; Linforth (1946a: 141–142).

52 *Cri.* 54D.

53 *Ion* 534A; 533 BC; Velardi (1989: 75–78); on this passage see also below, Chapter 6.

54 277E: ποιεῖται δὲ ταὐτὸν ὅπερ οἱ ἐν τῇ τελετῇ τῶν Κορυβάντων, ὅταν τὴν θρόνωσιν ποιῶσιν περὶ τοῦτον ὃν ἂν μέλλωσι τελεῖν. καὶ γὰρ ἐκεῖ χορεία τίς ἐστι καὶ παιδιά, εἰ ἄρα καὶ τετέλεσαι· καὶ νῦν τούτω οὐδὲν ἄλλο ἢ χορεύετον περὶ σὲ καὶ οἶον ὀρχεῖσθον παίζοντε, ὡς μετὰ τοῦτο τελοῦντε. (Translation W.R.M. Lamb, slightly modified).

55 Contrary to the opinion of Padel (1995: 135) that Athenians were not 'deeply familiar' with the Corybantic rites.

56 E. *Hipp.* 141–144; Ar. V. 8.

57 Ar. V. 119 with school: τὰ τῶν Κορυβάντων ἐποίει αὐτῷ μυστήρια ἐπὶ καθαρμῷ τῆς μανίας; Hesych. s.v. *korubantismos*.

58 For a detailed analysis of clinical and therapeutic data see Jeanmaire (1970: 105–108).

59 In addition to the evidence from Athens, an inscription on the Corybantic *teletai* from Erythrae contains regulations concerning individuals who purchased the offices of priests and priestesses, who were apparently well-to-do (*IErythr.* 206; Dignas 2002).

60 Str. 10. 3. 7.

61 Pl. *Lg.* 790D; *LSAM* 23 (*IErythr.* 206), with new readings by Dignas (2002), late fourth century, refers to priests and priestesses of the Corybantes; *LSAM* 25 (*IErythr.* 201), from the mid-third century, lists the posts of priests in three Corybantic associations. IG XII. 6. 2. 1197, a second-century *lex sacra* concerning the sale of Corybantic priesthood, mentions priestesses and *gunaikonomoi* (the inscription was discovered on Samos, but most likely originates from Erythrae: Herrmann 2002). Macedonia: Voutiras (1996). For other epigraphic evidence on the Corybantes (mostly late) see Graf (1985: 329–332).

62 Pl. *Ion* 536; *Cri*. 54D.
63 Voutiras (1996).
64 Pl. *Lg*. 790D; *Euthd*. 277DE.
65 Offering sacrifices was the duty of the priests of the Corybantes at Erythrae (*LSAM* 23), and it is most improbable that the Attic Corybantes did not deal with them.
66 Voutiras (1996); Graf (1985: 320–321); bathing is also mentioned in *LSAM* 23.
67 The invention of the tambourine was ascribed to the Corybantes (Str. 10. 3. 13) or Rhea (E. *Ba*. 55–58) with whom they were intimately associated in mythology and cult. E.g. Ar. *Vs*. 119; cf. Guidorizzi (2010: 191–192).
68 *Euthd*. 277DE; Dio Chrysostom gives a very similar description (a rite during which 'the performers of initiation seat the initiates and dance round them in circles'), attributing *thronôsis* to mystery rites in general (*Or*. 12. 33). Among Orphic poems there were *Korybantikon* and *Enthronements for the Mother* (OF 605, Graf and John-ston 2007: 147; West 1983: 27). The cult of the Corybantes and of Rhea or Mother of Gods were closely linked, at least during the Hellenistic-Roman periods (Graf 2010: 174). There is no evidence of early Athenian association of the two cults, but it becomes obvious in the fourth century, as attested to by Menander's *Theophoroumene (The Girl Possessed)*: Balme (2001: 243).
69 Bremmer (2014: 51). *Kratêrismos* is mentioned quite often in references to the Cory-bantic rites (Graf 1985: 321), including in the sacred law from Erythrae (*IEryhthr*. 206, l. 11), and wine jars were discovered in the domestic sanctuary at Toumba (Voutiras 1996: 247).
70 Pl. *Smp*. 215E.
71 Jeanmaire (1970: 138).
72 IG XII. 6. 2. 1197: l. 11, see also above in this chapter.
73 *Pol*. 1342a10.
74 Parker (1983: 247).
75 Bremmer (2014: 49). It is even suggested that the word *Korubantes* derives from *Kubabê*, the goddess identified as Cybele by the Greeks (Quattordio Moreschini 1986). Actually, the origin of both the word *Korubantes* and the phenomenon remain undetermined: Frisk (1973–1979); Chantraine (1983–1984: s.v. *Korubas*). See also Graf (1985: 329–332).
76 Gomme and Sandbach (1973: 400–407); Balme (2001: 241–245).
77 Balme (2001: 242–245). Men playing cymbals are depicted on a third-century AD mosaic from the House of Menander in Mytilene entitled 'Second Act of *Theopho-roumene*,' and probably also on a series of mosaics and frescoes illustrating this com-edy which was exceedingly popular (Nervegna 2010).
78 Most notably, dancing processions of Esternach, Dodds (1940: 158, 160, with refs.).
79 Jeanmaire (1970: 119–131). On *zar* and *bori* see Modarressi (1968); Saunders (1977); various possession cults including *zar*: Sargant (1973: 110–193).
80 Gilovich and Savitsky (2002: 618–620).
81 Sargant (1973); Cohen (2007).
82 Cardeña and Krippner (2010); McNamara (2009: 184).
83 Atkinson (1992: 309); cf. Kleinman (1980: 212, 232).
84 Atran (2002: 166).
85 Bourguignon (1976: 9); Jeanmaire (1970: 108); Cardeña and Krippner (2010).
86 Crapanzano and Garrison (1977: xiii, 15–17).
87 Bourguignon (1976: 40–41).
88 Kleinman (1980: 222).
89 Cardeña and Krippner (2010); Kleinman (1980: 205–206, 239) emphasises the con-trast between group or family treatment in traditional societies (Chinese folk heal-ing in his research) and modern Western medicine based on one-to-one medical practitioner-patient transactions.
90 Sacks (2007: 24–25).

91 Fachner (2011: 361–362).
92 See Anderson (2004: 111–145) for a different analysis of the Corybantic rites, putting an emphasis on 'objectification of mental disorder' (p. 126). I'm grateful to R. Anderson for sharing with me his unpublished Ph.D. dissertation.
93 Kleinman (1980: 212–214) arrives at similar conclusions.
94 Bourguignon (1973: 329–330).
95 For the terms see Motte and Pirenne-Delforge (1992); Schuddeboom (2009).
96 Pl. *Lg.* 790D–791A , cited above; E. *Ba.* 55–60, 120–124; *TGF* fr. 472; Str. 10. 3. 11–15, discussed below. For the connection between Cybele and the Dionysiac sphere, see Sfameni Gasparro (1985: 9–19).
97 Graf and Johnston (2007: No. 28). For frequent identification of Cybele with Demeter see Versnel (1990: 108–109).
98 Bremmer (2014: 78); Jaccottet (2005b).
99 Heraclit., fr. B14 *DK*: νυκτιπόλοις, μάγοις, βάκχοις, λήναις, μύσταις· τούτοις ἀπειλεῖ τὰ μετὰ θάνατον, τούτοις μαντεύεται τὸ πῦρ· τὰ γὰρ νομιζόμενα κατ᾽ ἀνθρώπους μυστήρια ἀνιερωστὶ μυεῦνται, cf. B15 *DK*; Seaford (1981: 19); Sfameni Gasparro (2011: 282–284); Schlesier (2011: 184–185); Most (2013: 160–161); for the authenticity of fr. 14 see Bremmer (2014: 70, with refs.). For the cult of Dionysus Bacchus or Baccheus in Asia Minor see Graf (1985: 285–291).
100 Hdt. 4. 79, Jeanmaire (1970: 88–94), discussed in Chapter 3.
101 Hdt. 4. 79. βακχεύει τε καὶ ὑπὸ τοῦ θεοῦ μαίνεται.
102 Dionysus was worshipped in Olbia in the early fifth century, as attested to by the inscribed bone tablets where the name of the god appears in conjunction with *Orphikoi*: SEG 32. 796; 42. 720; 50. 699; West (1982); Graf and Johnston (2007: 185–187). See also below, Chapter 3.
103 E. *Ba.* 67–72, cited and discussed below, Chapter 3.
104 E. *Ba.* 471–474. Whatever happens during this fateful day to Pentheus, as well as Agave, is definitely not a mystery initiation (Seaford 1996: 42–43).
105 Schuddeboom (2009: 7–33); Sfameni Gasparro (1985: 18–19).
106 E. *Hip.* 952–954; fr. 472 *TGF*; cf. Edmonds III (2013: 217–220).
107 E.g. *Phdr.* 265AB cited above and *Phd.* 69C cited below.
108 *Lg.* 815C: βακχεία τ᾽ ἐστὶν καὶ τῶν ταύταις ἑπομένων, ἃς Νύμφας τε καὶ Πᾶνας καὶ Σειληνοὺς καὶ Σατύρους ἐπονομάζοντες, ὥς φασιν, μιμοῦνται κατῳνωμένους, περὶ καθαρμούς τε καὶ τελετάς τινας ἀποτελούντων (translation R. G. Bury, modified). See Delavaud-Roux (1988: 32–33).
109 Schuddeboom (2009: 131–144); Burkert (1985: 276).
110 D. 18. 259–260: ἀνὴρ δὲ γενόμενος τῇ μητρὶ τελούσῃ τὰς βίβλους ἀνεγίγνωσκες καὶ τἆλλα συνεσκευωροῦ, τὴν μὲν νύκτα νεβρίζων καὶ κρατηρίζων καὶ καθαίρων τοὺς τελουμένους καὶ ἀπομάττων τῷ πηλῷ καὶ τοῖς πιτύροις, καὶ ἀνιστὰς ἀπὸ τοῦ καθαρμοῦ κελεύων λέγειν 'ἔφυγον κακόν, εὗρον ἄμεινον,' ... ἐν δὲ ταῖς ἡμέραις τοὺς καλοὺς θιάσους ἄγων διὰ τῶν ὁδῶν, τοὺς ἐστεφανωμένους τῷ μαράθῳ καὶ τῇ λεύκῃ, τοὺς ὄφεις τοὺς παρείας θλίβων καὶ ὑπὲρ τῆς κεφαλῆς αἰωρῶν, καὶ βοῶν 'εὐοῖ σαβοῖ,' καὶ καὶ ὑπὲρ τῆς κεφαλῆς αἰωρῶν, καὶ βοῶν 'εὐοῖ σαβοῖ,' καὶ ἐπορχούμενος 'ὑῆς ἄττης,' ἔξαρχος καὶ προηγεμὼν καὶ κιττοφόρος καὶ λικνοφόρος καὶ τοιαῦθ᾽ ὑπὸ τῶν γρᾳδίων προσαγορευόμενος (translation C. A. Vince, substantially modified); Hoessly (2001: 229–232).
111 Moulinier (1952: 137–140).
112 Jeanmaire (1970: 94–97); Versnel (1990: 114–115); Graf (1985: 322); Voutiras (1996: 248). Demosthenes mentions Aeschines' mother referring to the introduction of the Sabaziac mysteries in Dem. 19. 281, with schol.
113 Bernabé and Jiménez San Cristóbal (2008: 93).
114 See below, Chapter 3.
115 Graf (1985: 322–323).
116 Str. 10. 3. 15; Voutiras (1996: 249–250); Graf and Johnston (2007: 147); Graf (2010: 174).

117 E. *Ba.* 123–134.
118 Arist. *Pol.* 1342a5–15: ὃ γὰρ περὶ ἐνίας συμβαίνει πάθος ψυχὰς ἰσχυρῶς, τοῦτο ἐν πάσαις ὑπάρχει, τῷ δὲ ἧττον διαφέρει καὶ τῷ μᾶλλον, οἷον ἔλεος καὶ φόβος, ἔτι δ᾽ ἐνθουσιασμός· καὶ γὰρ ὑπὸ ταύτης τῆς κινήσεως κατοκώχιμοί τινές εἰσιν, ἐκ τῶν δ᾽ ἱερῶν μελῶν ὁρῶμεν τούτους, ὅταν χρήσωνται τοῖς ἐξοργιάζουσι τὴν ψυχὴν μέλεσι, καθισταμένους ὥσπερ ἰατρείας τυχόντας καὶ καθάρσεως· ταὐτὸ δὴ τοῦτο ἀναγκαῖον πάσχειν καὶ τοὺς ἐλεήμονας καὶ τοὺς φοβητικοὺς καὶ τοὺς ὅλως παθητικούς, τοὺς δ᾽ ἄλλους καθ᾽ ὅσον ἐπιβάλλει τῶν τοιούτων ἑκάστῳ, καὶ πᾶσι γίγνεσθαί τινα κάθαρσιν καὶ κουφίζεσθαι μεθ᾽ ἡδονῆς (translation H. Rackham); Croissant (1932: 4); Boyancé (1937: 190); Sifakis (2001: 83–86); Kraut (1997: 208–212); Halliwell (2011: 242–252). Halliwell (2011: 245) interprets *pathêtikoi* as 'emotionally pathological,' but he himself cites *EN* 1105b24 where this adjective 'denotes the capacity to feel emotions *tout court*,' and I see no reason to regard emotionally responsive individuals in the passage in the *Politics* as behaving abnormally.
119 Aret. *SD* 6. 11: Τέμνονταί τινες τὰ μέλεα, θεοῖς ἰδίοις ὡς ἀπαιτοῦσι χαριζόμενοι εὐσεβεῖ φαντασίῃ· καὶ ἔστι τῆς ὑπολήψιος ἡ μανίη μοῦνον, τὰ δ᾽ ἄλλα σωφρονέουσι. ἐγείρονται δὲ αὐλῷ καὶ θυμηδίῃ, ἢ μέθῃ, ἢ τῶν παρεόντων προτροπῇ. ἔνθεος ἥδε ἡ μανίη. κἢν ἀπομανῶσι, εὔθυμοι, ἀκηδέες, τελεσθέντες τῷ θεῷ (translation I. Linforth, modified).
120 *Myst.* 3. 10.
121 *Ion* 534 A; *Euthd.* 277 DE; Linforth (1946a: 162); Dodds (1973: 79).
122 Graf (1985: 321); Voutiras (1996: 248); Goff (2004: 284). On Glaucothea's status see Eidinow (2016: 17–19); on the vogue for the Corybantic rites see Linforth (1946a: 159).
123 *LSAM* 23. l. 3–4; Graf (1985: 319–334).
124 *LSAM* 48, dated to 276/75; Henrichs (1978); Villanueva Puig (1998); see also below, Chapter 3.
125 Ustinova (2005: 187–188). On blurring the border between public and private in the organisation of the Corybantic cult at Erythrae: Dignas (2002: 34–35).
126 Dignas (2002: 40).
127 *De utilitate mathematicae* 14–15: μυήσεως δὲ μέρη πέντε. τὸ μὲν προηγούμενον καθαρμός· οὔτε γὰρ ἅπασι τοῖς βουλομένοις μετουσία μυστηρίων ἐστίν, ἀλλ᾽ εἰσὶν οὓς αὐτῶν εἴργεσθαι προαγορεύεται, οἷον χεῖρας μὴ καθαρὰς καὶ φωνὴν ἀξύνετον ἔχοντας, καὶ αὐτοὺς δὲ τοὺς μὴ εἰργομένους ἀνάγκη καθαρμοῦ τινος πρότερον τυχεῖν. μετὰ δὲ τὴν κάθαρσιν δευτέρα ἐστὶν ἡ τῆς τελετῆς παράδοσις· τρίτη δὲ ἡ ἐπονομαζομένη ἐποπτεία· τετάρτη δέ, ὃ δὴ καὶ τέλος τῆς ἐποπτείας, ἀνάδεσις καὶ στεμμάτων ἐπίθεσις, ὥστε καὶ ἑτέροις, ἅς τις παρέλαβε τελετάς, παραδοῦναι δύνασθαι, δαδουχίας τυχόντα ἢ ἱεροφαντίας ἤ τινος ἄλλης ἱερωσύνης· πέμπτη δὲ ἡ ἐξ αὐτῶν περιγενομένη κατὰ τὸ θεοφιλὲς καὶ θεοῖς συνδίαιτον εὐδαιμονία.
128 For instance, in *h.Cer.* 478–479, ὄργια . . . σεμνά, τά τ᾽ οὔ πως ἔστι παρεξίμεν οὔτε πυθέσθαι, οὔτ᾽ ἀχέειν ('awful mysteries which no one may in any way transgress or pry into or utter,' translation H. G. Evelyn-White), the word πυθέσθαι emphasises, as it seems, that the mysteries could not be learnt, but be only experienced (Motte and Pirenne-Delforge 1992: 125).
129 Fr. 15 Rose, Synesius (*Dio* 8): Ἀριστοτέλης ἀξιοῖ τοὺς τελουμένους οὐ μαθεῖν τί δεῖν, ἀλλὰ παθεῖν καὶ διατεθῆναι, δηλονότι γενομένους ἐπιτηδείους; Croissant (1932: 137–161); Burkert (1987: 69); Schefer (2000: 60); Riedweg (1987: 128); Borgeaud (2013: 136); Bernabé (2016a: 34–38); Waldner (2013: 231); Larson (2016: 273). In the eleventh century, Michael Psellus alludes to this text and refers to the rites as Eleusinian, but this may be his interpretation rather than Aristotle's words.
130 Clem. Al. *Strom.* 5. 11. 71: οὐκ ἀπεικότως ἄρα καὶ τῶν μυστηρίων τῶν παρ᾽ Ἕλλησιν ἄρχει μὲν τὰ καθάρσια . . . μετὰ ταῦτα δ᾽ ἐστὶ τὰ μικρὰ μυστήρια διδασκαλίας τινὰ ὑπόθεσιν ἔχοντα καὶ προπαρασκευῆς τῶν μελλόντων, τὰ δὲ μεγάλα περὶ τῶν συμπάντων, οὗ μανθάνειν ἔτι ὑπολείπεται, ἐποπτεύειν δὲ καὶ περινοεῖν τήν τε φύσιν καὶ τὰ πράγματα. Cf. Riedweg (1987: 5); Cf. Burkert (1987: 69 n. 13).

131 Ath. 40D; D. S. 3. 65. 6; Cic. *Tusc.* 1. 29; Clem. Al. *Strom.* 7. 27. 6; Plu. *Mor.* 422C; Riedweg (1987: 6–14); Burkert (1987: 69).
132 A child reading from a scroll in the Villa of Mysteries in Pompeii (first century, Nilsson 1957: fig. 10a); a decree issued by Ptolemy IV required all the participants in Bacchic *teletai* to hand over copies of their sacred books to a representative of the authorities (Nilsson 1957: 111); 'host of books written by Musaeus and Orpheus': Pl. R. 364E, cf. E. *Hipp.* 954; *hieroi logoi* of the Samothracian mysteries: Hdt. 2. 51; Cole (1984: 28). Cf. Henrichs (2003: 205–240); Riedweg (2002); Tzifopoulos (2010: 101–115). A chest and books in the rules of the Andanian mysteries: *IG* V 1. 1390: 9; 'writings' referring to the mysteries of Demeter Kidaria at Pheneus: Paus. 8. 15. 1; Jost (2003: 156).
133 Apul. *Met.* 11. 29.
134 Demeter: Isoc. 4. 28; the Samothracian mysteries: Hdt. 2. 51; D.S. 5. 49. 1–6; (presumably) Orphic-Bacchic initiations: Pl. *Phd.* 62B, cf. Clem. Al. *Protr.* 2. 17–18; Riedweg (1987: 10–13); Bremmer (2014: 77); mysteries of Cybele: Arnob. *Adv. Nat.* 5. 5–7. Cf. Sfameni Gasparro (2011: 291–293) on the paradigm of 'god in vicissitude.'
135 Beck (2006: 62) 'that "doctrine" is an expression of the mysteries, not vice versa'; cf. Pachis (2009: 25).
136 Therefore, in terms of H. Whitehouse's theory of imagistic and doctrinal rituals (Whitehouse 2004), I tend to associate Greek mysteries of the Classical period with the imagistic mode, rather than a blending of the initial imagistic and the historically attested doctrinal mode, as suggested by J. Larson (Larson 2016: 276).
137 Pl., *Smp.* 211A.
138 Betegh (2004: col. 20).
139 Cole (1980: 233); Burkert (1987: 90).
140 Plu. *Mor.* 382DE: ἡ δὲ τοῦ νοητοῦ καὶ εἰλικρινοῦς καὶ ἁπλοῦ νόησις ὥσπερ ἀστραπὴ διαλάμψασα τῆς ψυχῆς ἅπαξ ποτὲ θιγεῖν καὶ προσιδεῖν παρέσχε. διὸ καὶ Πλάτων καὶ Ἀριστοτέλης ἐποπτικὸν τοῦτο τὸ μέρος τῆς φιλοσοφίας καλοῦσιν, καθ᾽ ὅσον οἱ τὰ δοξαστὰ καὶ μικτὰ καὶ παντοδαπὰ ταῦτα παραμειψάμενοι τῷ λόγῳ πρὸς τὸ πρῶτον ἐκεῖνο καὶ ἁπλοῦν καὶ ἄυλον ἐξάλλονται καὶ θιγόντες ἀληθῶς τῆς περὶ αὐτὸ καθαρᾶς ἀληθείας οἷον ἐν τελετῇ τέλος ἔχειν φιλοσοφίας νομίζουσι; Croissant (1932: 157–164).
141 Ar. *Pax* 375; Pl. *Grg.* 497C; des Places (1981: 86).
142 Veiled initiates: Eleusinian, Bianchi (1976: 47, 49); the Lovatelli urn, Burkert (1987: figs. 2–4); Bianchi (1976: 50); Clinton (1992: 86); Clinton (1993: 118); the mysteries of the Cabiri at Thebes: Schachter (1981–1994: 101); Bacchic: Nilsson (1957: 11, 14, 18); Kerényi (1976: fig. 135); Burkert (1987: fig. 6); Bianchi (1976: figs. 84–86); Mithraic: Merkelbach (1984: figs. 29, 30); Vermaseren (1956: No. 189); Campbell (1968: 296, 298).
143 Scarpi (2002 1: XVII). The initiates had to keep their silence with the uninitiated about the sacred rites they had seen, and hence the word *mustês* is interpreted by some as indicating the prohibition on divulging the secrets, e.g. Meyer (1987: 4); Cole (2003: 193); Simms (1990); Bremmer (2014: viii) remains undecided.
144 Dowden (1980: 414); Lehmann (1969: 2, 14–15); Burkert (1983: 268, 275); Cole (1984: 26–36); Clinton (1992: 86); Clinton (2003: 50); Schefer (2000: 67, 71–73); Scarpi (2002: 1: 160–168); Dimitrova (2008: 78); Bremmer (2014: 11–16); Gómez Iglesias (2016: 75).
145 Bremmer (2014: 11, 28).
146 210A.
147 *Smp.* 208B; esp. 212A; cf. Snell (1960: 150).
148 *Smp.* 211A: οὐδέ τις λόγος οὐδέ τις ἐπιστήμη; cf. Gómez Iglesias (2016: 72–75).
149 *Phdr.* 250BC, cf. 247DE; Riedweg (1987: 37–38, 55); des Places (1981: 93).
150 *Phdr.* 249C; note the word play: τελέους ἀεὶ τελετὰς τελούμενος, τέλεος ὄντως μόνος γίγνεται. Cf. de Vries (1969: 145–153); Hackforth (1972: 87).

151 *Mor.* 718C. See also Chapter 8.
152 Cf. the refutation of the 'reason for the wise, symbols for the vulgar' approach and the emphasis on 'induction' into mysteries rather than 'teaching' their doctrines by Beck (2006: 41–50).
153 Wulff (2000: 398), citing the words of a modern spiritual seeker.
154 des Places (1981: 90–91).
155 For the meadows of the Bacchic gold leaves, land of the pious, and Elysian fields see Cole (2003: 212).
156 Fr. 6 Dübner = fr. 178 Sandbach; Stob., *Anthologion* 4. 52. 49: πλάναι τὰ πρῶτα καὶ περιδρομαὶ κοπώδεις καὶ διὰ σκότους τινὲς ὕποπτοι πορεῖαι καὶ ἀτέλεστοι, εἶτα πρὸ τοῦ τέλους αὐτοῦ τὰ δεινὰ πάντα, φρίκη καὶ τρόμος καὶ ἱδρὼς καὶ θάμβος· ἐκ δὲ τούτου φῶς τι θαυμάσιον ἀπήντησεν καὶ τόποι καθαροὶ καὶ λειμῶνες ἐδέξαντο, φωνὰς καὶ χορείας καὶ σεμνότητας ἀκουσμάτων ἱερῶν καὶ φασμάτων ἁγίων ἔχοντες· ἐν αἷς ὁ παντελὴς ἤδη καὶ μεμυημένος ἐλεύθερος γεγονὼς καὶ ἄφετος περιιὼν ἐστεφανωμένος ὀργιάζει καὶ σύνεστιν ὁσίοις καὶ καθαροῖς ἀνδράσι, τὸν ἀμύητον ἐνταῦθα τῶν ζώντων <καὶ> ἀκάθαρτον ἐφορῶν ὄχλον ἐν βορβόρῳ πολλῷ καὶ ὁμίχλῃ πατούμενον ὑφ' ἑαυτοῦ καὶ συνελαυνόμενον, φόβῳ δὲ θανάτου τοῖς κακοῖς ἀπιστίᾳ τῶν ἐκεῖ ἀγαθῶν ἐμμένοντα. ἐπεὶ τό γε παρὰ φύσιν τὴν πρὸς τὸ σῶμα τῇ ψυχῇ συμπλοκὴν εἶναι καὶ σύνερξιν ἐκεῖθεν ἂν συνίδοις. This description is interpreted as referring to mysteries in general: Burkert (1987: 91); Riedweg (1998: 367); Bernabé (2009: 106); Eleusinian mysteries: Meyer (1987: 8); Sourvinou-Inwood (2003: 33); Orphic initiation: Mylonas (1961: 265).
157 Above, Introduction.
158 Ludwig (1968: 81–82); Persinger (1987: 38–39).
159 des Places (1981: 93).
160 *Phd.* 69C.
161 Arist. *Pol.* 1342a5–15, cited above in this chapter.
162 Gabbard and Twemlow (1984: 22–23); Green (1968: 37–41, 85–87). See also the Introduction.
163 Below, Chapter 8.
164 Hundreds of years later, Philo of Alexandria, writing on Greek and barbarian ascetic sages (*askêtai*) referred to the out-of-body experience as their standard practice and classified them as *aitherobatountes*, air-walkers (*De specialibus legibus* 2. 45). Plotinus, the 'father of Western mysticism' (Rist 1977: 86, 213; Wallis 1972: 55), wrote a powerful description of his own multiple out-of-body experiences: *Ennead* 4. 8. 1. 1–11. Porphyry witnessed Plotinus' mystical feats and admired his efforts at liberation from the bonds of the body: Porph. *Plot.* 23; Dodds (1973: 286–287).
165 Graf and Johnston (2007: Nos. 1, 26, 30); Bernabé and Jiménez San Cristóbal (2008: L. 1, 7; 66–76).
166 Graf and Johnston (2007: Nos. 1, 2, 8, 10–14, 16, 18, 25, 29); Bernabé and Jiménez San Cristóbal (2008: L. 1–6; 40–47).
167 Cf. Whitehouse (2004: 105–115); Gragg (2004); McCauley and Lawson (2002: 103).
168 Graf and Johnston (2007: Nos. 1, 2, 9); Bernabé and Jiménez San Cristóbal (2008: L1, 2, 3, 8, 2).
169 In his analysis of Roman mystery cults, D. Gragg follows the distinction between 'special-agent' and 'special-patient' rituals, put forward by R. N. McCauley and E. T. Lawson (Gragg 2004; McCauley and Lawson 2002). According to this theory, the latter rituals, characterised by passivity of the super-human figures that remain recipients of regularly performed actions, do not have a long-term impact on the worshipper, whereas the former, involving active participation of a supernatural figure, are rare or once-in-the-lifetime events for the worshipper and typically feature high levels of sensory pageantry. D. Gragg suggests that while traditional Roman cultic practice belongs to the special-patient category, mystery cults, with their permanent effect on the life of the initiate, would be special-agent rituals, hence the sense of their extraordinary importance and popularity.

170 μεμνημένος ἥρως: Bernabé and Jiménez San Cristóbal (2008: L. 2, 55).
171 See above in this chapter.
172 Burkert (1987: 47).
173 Detailed discussion in Ustinova (2012: 115–120).
174 Xygalatas et al. (2013).
175 Pl. *Phdr.* 244E. Cf. *Smp.* 210A; E. *Ba.* 79; Synesius *Dio* 8; Porph. *Abst.* 4. 5: 'accurately performing the appointed rites.'
176 Heraclit., fr. B14 *DK*, cited above in this chapter.
177 *TGF* fr. 387, cited above in this chapter; Cairns (2013: 101).
178 *Phdr.* 251A, see Chapters 7 and 8 below.
179 Plu. *Mor.* 81D; Demetr. *Eloc.* 101. Terrifying apparitions in Eleusinian and Bacchic *teletai*: Lada-Richards (1999: 91–94).
180 Burkert (1987: 102); ego-shattering effects of initiations: Atran (2002: 163–164).
181 Hsch.: καθαρθῆναι·μαστιγωθῆναι. Flogging is depicted on one of the frescoes in the Villa of the Mysteries at Pompeii (Burkert 1987: 168); for whips see also Cole (1993: 291); the scene as an allegorical allusion to initiations: Bowden (2010: 130–131). As to the mysteries of the Classical period, flagellation and torture are playfully hinted to in comedy (e.g. Ar. *Ra.* 618–622, *Nu.* 439–442; Lada-Richards 1999: 73–74, 97) and in Plato's *Euthydemus* (277E).
   The mysteries of Mithras are especially notorious in this respect: not only torture seems to have been common, but real human sacrifice probably occurred, attested not only by rumours of Commodus' act of murder during the Mithraic ceremonies, but also by the discoveries of human skulls in Mithraea: Turcan (1981: 91–97); Campbell (1968: 297); Burkert (1987: 102–104); Beck (2000: 146); Martin (2009).
   The Galli of Cybele not only castrated themselves in the grip of the sacred frenzy, but also flogged and cut themselves every year on *dies sanguinis*, splattering the goddess' image and altars with their blood: Vermaseren (1977: 97); Lucianus *Syr.d.* 50–53.
182 Burkert (1987: 77); see also the Introduction.
183 Parke (1977: 69); Bremmer (2014: 7), emphasising 'euphoric effects' of the journey from Athens to Eleusis. The fast imitated the goddess' fasting after the loss of her daughter; to break the fast, the initiates drank *kukeôn* (Clem. Al. *Protr.* 21. 2), presumably before the ceremony.
184 Apul. *Met.* 11. 23; Witt (1971: 57, 158).
185 A whole day before the initiation at Eleusis was devoted to purification, by sea-bath and by sprinkling with pig's blood, Parke (1977: 62–63).
186 Eleusis: Schol. Ar. *Ach.* 747; cf. Plu. *Phoc.* 28; Burkert (1983: 258); Andania: *IG* V. 1. 1390; Dionysiac mysteries: Tzetz, comm. to Ar. *Ra.* 338; *LSCG* No 90; Cumont (1933: 240–241); purifications and mystery rites: *LSAM* No. 48 and esp. E. fr. 472 *TGF*; Scarpi (2002: 1: 597, 607); Bremmer (1984: 274–275); Versnel (1990: 143–144); Seaford (1981: 266).
187 *Thronôsis*: Hsch., s.v.; D. Chr. 12. 33; on the Lovatelli urn Heracles is shown seated and veiled; on the sarcophagus from Torre Nova a priestess approaches the initiate from behind, holding a blazing torch close to him, Burkert (1983: 267–268).
188 Pl. *Euthd.* 277DE; Linforth (1941); Jeanmaire (1970: 131–138); Ustinova (1992–1998).
189 Kerényi (1967: 177–180); Wasson, Hofmann, and Ruch (1998); Ott (1993: 141–144); Rinella (2010).
190 The *sunthêma* mentioning *kukeôn*: Clem. Al. *Protr.* 2. 21, mentioned above in this chapter. The most detailed analysis of evidence on the recipe of *kukeôn* is by Delatte (1954: 710–726), who thinks that it was prepared from ground barley cooked with thyme, coriander, basil, etc., and that drinking *kukeôn* was the most primitive and traditional way to finish the fast. It is also suggested that it was prepared from barley contaminated with ergot (*Claviceps purpurea*), the common grain fungus and toxic

infectant of flour, containing potent hallucinogenic alkaloids similar to LSD: Was-son, Hofmann, and Ruch (1998); Ott (1993: 141–144). A case has been made for the use of opium and poppy juice (Burkert 1983: 281). See the criticism of both suggestions by Burkert (1987: 108–109), Bowden (2010: 37, 43), and Cosmopou-los (2015: 19–21), who doubt that the quantities of ergot-infested grain or opium necessary for thousands of initiates could be procured, and in addition, indicate that the consequence of poisoning with ergot is painful or even lethal. However, Rinella (2010: 134–135) argues that it is possible to prepare a mildly hallucinogenic drug of ergot-infested barley, and that a modest quantity of ergot, easily harvested from the nearby barley fields, could suffice for thousands of initiates. This proposal has yet to be examined by experts in pharmacology.

191 E.g. Kritikos and Papadaki (1967: 3: fig. 24).
192 Kritikos and Papadaki (1967: 3: 18, 4: 10). Theophrastus was familiar with several varieties of poppy, such as *Papaver rhoeas* L., *Papaver somniferum*, which is much more potent opium poppy (Thphr. *HP* 9. 12. 4; 9. 8. 2), and *struchnos* (*Datura strmonium* L.) which 'caused madness or ecstasis' (*ekstatikos*; Thphr. *HP* 9.19.1). He also men-tioned a sculptor who took an overdose of the golden thistle, *Skolymus hispanicus*, and became mad or ecstatic, *exestê* (Thphr. *HP* 9. 13. 4), but this word was also used in medical texts and could have alluded to temporary derangement with no cultic connotations.
193 Burkert (1987: figs. 2–4).
194 Cosmopoulos (2015: 19).
195 A. fr. 57 *TGF*; E. *Ba.* 125–135; Arist. *Pol.* 1342ab; Thphr. fr. 87, 88 Wehrli; Iamb. *Myst.* 3. 9; Croissant (1932: 49–61).
196 Str. 10. 3. 9–16.
197 *Salt.* 15; Seaford (2013: 265).
198 Archytas of Tarentum, fourth century, fr. B1 *DK*: '*Rhomboi* . . . which are swung round in mystery rites (*teletai*)'; West (1992: 122); Anderson (1994: 136). *Rhombos* is also important symbolically, since this toy of Dionysus is frequently referred to in the myths of the god's dismemberment: Clem. Al. *Protr.* 2. 17. For uproar and noise see Clinton (2003: 64).
199 In art: Bundrick (2005: 47–48); Pi. fr. 70b Maehler; tambourines and cymbals are associated with Cybele at an early date (West 1992: 124; Roller 1999: 121–123, 155–157) and are even mentioned in the *sumbolon* of the mysteries of Cybele ('I ate from the *tumpanon*, I drank from the cymbal, I carried the *kernos*, I stole into the inner chamber,' Clem. Al. *Protr.* 2. 15; Firm. 18. 1; cf. Eus. *PE* 2. 3. 18; Schol. Pl. *Grg.* 497C). 'Tambourine of an Orphic initiate,' Ὀρφεοτελεστοῦ τύμπανος, is metioned by Philodemus (*Po.* fr. 181 Janko; Graf and Johnston 2007: 146).
200 Seaford (2013: 266–267).
201 *Pol.* 1341a23; West (1992: 105); Rouget (1990: 386–397). *Auloi* were associated with any kind of *mania*, including the florid madness experienced by Ajax and Heracles: S. *Aj.* 610; E. *HF* 871, 879, 897; Menier (2001: 235).
202 Hoffmann (1997: 2); Rouget (1990); see also above in this chapter.
203 Bernabé and Jiménez San Cristóbal (2008: 86–87); cf. Bundrick (2005: 106–116).
204 Crater in Ferrara, attributed to the Group of Polygnotus: Beazley (1978: 1052. 25); Nilsson (1957 fig. 3); Bundrick (2005: 47–48, 159, fig. 94). For detailed discussion see Carpenter (1997: 70–78, figs. 28–29), who defines the scene as illustrating a 'generic ecstatic cult' (Carpenter 1997: 79).
205 Clinton (2003: 67); Dimitrova (2008: 78).
206 Bremmer (2014: 37–48).
207 Seaford (2013: 263–264).
208 D.Chr.12. 33; Ar. *Ra.* 323–336; Burkert (1983: 267, 292); Versnel (1990: 154); Bremmer (2014: 7). Whirling of masked figures dancing, some of them playing musical instruments, is represented on the sculptured veil of Despoina discovered at

Lycosoura (Jost 2003: 157–161, figs. 6.6 and 6.7). On dance and its role in the ecstatic Dionysiac rites, see Delavaud-Roux (1988).

209 Power (2010: 365).

210 Levitin (2006: 191, 267).

211 Pl. *Lg.* 815C cited above; music in mystery rites: *Smp.* 215C; *R* 364B; *R.* 397A-400E, *Lg.* 653C–673A, 700A–701B; Pelosi (2010: 9); Hardie (2004).

212 Arist. *Pol.* 1342b1–5: ὀργιαστικὰ καὶ παθητικά; 1341a20; Bélis (1988: 23); Menier (2001: 237); Bernabé (2016a: 31). For the word ὀργιαστικος here see Motte and Pirenne-Delforge (1992: 135).

213 Pl. *R.* 364B–365A; D.S. 3. 65. 6; Graf and Johnston (2007: 142); Edmonds III (2013: 17, 209); Bremmer (2014: 58).

214 D.S. 4. 7. 4; Str. 10. 3. 9–10; Hardie (2004: 11–13).

215 D. 18. 259.

216 *Or.* 22. 2; cf. S. fr. 837 *TGF*; Pl. *Phdr.* 251A; Riedweg (1987: 63–65); Burkert (1987: 93).

217 See Ustinova (2009: 229–232).

218 Demetr. *Eloc.* 101; Seaford (1981: 254).

219 D. Chr. 12. 33, translation M. Cary; cf. Clinton (2003: 63); Burkert (1987: 89); Burkert (1993: 185); Bérard (1974: 97).

220 For the importance of alternation between light and darkness in the Eleusinian mysteries, see Burkert (1983: 277–278); Parisinou (2000: 60–71); Schefer (2000: 50–51, 67); Riedweg (1987: 47–56); Clinton (2003: 66–67); Clinton (2004). In a second-century AD epitaph, the deceased is described as a 'hierophant from the radiant Anactoron, ἀπ' αἰγλήεντος ἀνακτόρου' (IG II² 3709, who showed 'light-bringing rites (ὄργια φαεσίμβροτα) of Deo,' (IG II² 3661).

221 E. *Ba.* 608–609 and 486; Versnel (1990: 169); Seaford (1981: 256); Seaford (2006: 52–53); Seaford (2005: 604). For the *Frogs* as a rite of passage see Lada-Richards (1999: 45–122).

222 Ar. *Ra.* 343.

223 Karadima-Matsa and Dimitrova (2003); Clinton (2004: 93); Dimitrova (2008: No. 29, 83–84, 88). In Arcadia, mystery rites were celebrated at night in Lycosoura, Pheneus, and Phigalia (Paus. 8. 15. 2; Schol. Lyc. *Alex.* 211; Jost 2003: 150). Mysteries of the Cabiri on Lemnos were nocturnal, as well (Bremmer 2014: 40).

224 Paus. 1. 40. 6; 2. 37. 6; E. *Ba.* 485; Heraclit. fr. B14 *DK*; Plu. *Mor.* 291A; *LSAM* No. 26; Schol. Ar. *Ra.* 343. Cf. Scarpi (2002: 1: 598–599); Parisinou (2000: 71–72, 118–123).

225 Ustinova (2009: 232–255).

226 Clinton (1992: 86), cf. Seaford (1981: 261); Burkert (1983: 280); Schefer (2000: 53, 65).

227 Mocked by Plato in *R.* 365A, when talking about *Orpheotelestai*: they claim that expiations and purifications by sacrifices, intended for the dead and called *teletai*, redeem from the evil, while terrible things await those who did not perform them.

228 Apuleius describes his initiation into the mysteries of Isis as a 'voluntary death,' *Met.* 11. 21.

229 Fr. 178 Sandbach: Οὕτω κατὰ τὴν εἰς τὸ ὅλον μεταβολὴν καὶ μετακόσμησιν ὀλωλέναι τὴν ψυχὴν λέγομεν ἐκεῖ γενομένην· ἐνταῦθα δ' ἀγνοεῖ, πλὴν ὅταν ἐν τῷ τελευτᾶν ἤδη γένηται· τότε δὲ πάσχει πάθος οἷον οἱ τελεταῖς μεγάλαις κατοργιαζόμενοι. διὸ καὶ τὸ ῥῆμα τῷ ῥήματι καὶ τὸ ἔργον τῷ ἔργῳ τοῦ τελευτᾶν καὶ τελεῖσθαι προσέοικε. This passage is immediately followed by the description of the mystery experience cited above in this chapter.

230 *R.* 365A: εἰσὶ δὲ καὶ τελευτήσασιν, ἃς δὴ τελετὰς καλοῦσιν.

231 Hippol. *Haer.* 5. 8. 42–44; Heraclitus' phrase: fr. B25 *DK*; Clinton (1992: 86).

232 Οὐ μόνον εἶναι τὸν θάνατον θνητοῖς οὐ κακὸν ἀλλ' ἀγαθόν (IG II/III² 3661. 5–6), cf. Clinton (1974: 42); Burkert (1987: 21–23).
    For later sources referring to mystic initiations as a 'sequence of simulative birth/rebirth,' and its dramatisation in the *Frogs*, see Lada-Richards (1999: 103–108).

233 Fr. B15 DK: εἰ μὴ γὰρ Διονύσωι πομπὴν ἐποιοῦντο καὶ ὕμνεον ᾆσμα αἰδοίοισιν, ἀναιδέστατα εἴργαστ' ἄν· ὡυτὸς δὲ Ἀίδης καὶ Διόνυσος, ὅτεωι μαίνονται καὶ ληναΐζουσιν. I translate ληναΐζουσι as 'become maenadic' rather than 'celebrate the Lenaea' (as in DK) because this passage seems to belong to the same context as fr. 14 (both cited by Clement, *Protr.* 22 and 34), where *lênai* are listed between *bakchoi* and *mustai*. On this phrase of Heraclitus and mystery cults see Segal (1990: 417).

234 Burkert (1985: 237); Parke (1977: 107).

235 For this crater see Chapter 3.

236 Betegh (2004).

237 Cole (1993: 277); Seaford (1998: 133).

238 Jaccottet (2003: 1: 137); Seaford (2006: 67).

239 *ISM* 3: 35; 80; 44; Pippidi (1964); Boyancé (1961: 117, 1); Jaccottet (2003: 151–155, Nos. 54, 58, 61).

240 *ISM* 3: 47; Jaccottet (2005a: 198–199).

241 A. Avram, comm. to *ISM* 3: 35.

242 Pippidi (1964); Jaccottet (2003: 153; comm. to No. 54); Ustinova (2009: 237).

243 Χαῖρε παθὼν τὸ πάθημα τὸ δ᾽οὔπω πρόσθ᾽ ἐπεπόνθεις; Graf and Johnston (2007: No 3); Bernabé and Jiménez San Cristóbal (2008: L 8, 93–98, 258); Seaford (1981: 254); Segal (1990: 418–419).

244 Graf and Johnston (2007: No 27; cf. 6, 7); Bernabé and Jiménez San Cristóbal (2008: L 13, 10 ab); Bremmer (2014: 76). 'Holy meadows' in other gold leaves: Graf and Johnston (2007: No 3); Bernabé and Jiménez San Cristóbal (2008: L 8).

245 For a different interpretation of *poinê*, as a soul's enclosure in the body, hence the entire life of the *mustês*, see Bernabé and Jiménez San Cristóbal (2008: 106–108).

It seems plausible that the atonement was for an ancestral crime of humanity at large, rather than family or personal transgressions, and was based on the myth of human origin from the ashes of Titans who had consumed the dismembered Diony- sus, as argued by Burkert (1985: 298), Graf and Johnston (2007: 66–93), Bernabé and Jiménez San Cristóbal (2008: 107, 112), and Bremmer (2014: 76). Against this view see Edmonds III (2013: 296–391).

246 Graf and Johnston (2007: No 5–7); Bernabé and Jiménez San Cristóbal (2008: L 9, 10).

247 καὶ γὰρ ἐγὼν ὑμῶν γένος ὄλβιον εὔχομαι εἶμεν | ἀλά με Μο<ῖ>ρα ἐδάμασε καὶ ἀθάνατοι θεοὶ ἄλλοι καὶ ἀστεροβλῆτα κεραυνόν | κύκλō δ᾽ ἐξέπταν βαρυπενθέος ἀργαλέοιο; text and translation: F. Graf. One may speculate that the entity described as having 'flown out' the circle was the initiate's soul, that is visualised as flying in the epic and later poetry (Bremmer 1983).

248 Bernabé and Jiménez San Cristóbal (2008: 117–121, 193).

249 The symbolism of being struck by lightning probably includes an allusion to the incineration of the Titans; see Mendelsohn (1992: 118–122); Graf and Johnston (2007: 125–127); Bernabé and Jiménez San Cristóbal (2008: 111–114); Jenner (2014: 78–80) for the possibility of a combination of the two interpretations.

250 Δεσποίνας δ᾽ὑπὸ κόλπον ἔδυν χθονίας βασλείας: Graf and Johnston (2007: No. 5, 12–13); Seaford (1998: 134); Bernabé and Jiménez San Cristóbal (2008: L 9, 129–132, 306–310). Nursing: Demeter received Demophon in her κόλπος (*Hom. Hymn to Dem.* 231); adoption: Hera formally adopted Heracles by an imitation of the actual birth, letting Heracles fall through her garments (ἐνδύματα) to the ground (D.S. 4. 39. 2); Edmonds (2009: 80).

251 Chapter 8.

252 Bernabé (2009: 107, 121); Bernabé (2016a: 28). R. Turcan includes 'imitation of death' in his list of six core characteristics of the Greco-Roman mystery rites: Turcan (1998: 121); Segal (1990: 414) and Obbink (2011: 297) note the similarity between initiations and funeral rites.

253 Many centuries later, an inscription from the Mithraeum of Santa Prisca in Rome celebrated the worshipper who was 'piously reborn' (*renatus*) or re-created through the rites, Vermaseren and van Essen (1965: 207–210). An Isiac initiate describes himself as re-created, *recreatus* and *reformatus*, Apul. *Met.* 11. 18, 23; 24.

254 Graf and Johnston (2007: No 26); Bernabé and Jiménez San Cristóbal (2008: L 7).

255 Brelich (1969); Burkert (1987: 8); Lada-Richards (1999: 59); Casadio and Johnston (2009a: 6); Obbink (2011: 297–298); Jenner (2014: 100–101).

256 Furthermore, neurobiological evidence demonstrates that genuine stress resulting from exposure to terrifying initiations, in particular death-related scenes, serves as a strong 'natural motivator for religiosity,' alleviating the very emotions that were prominent during the traumatic experience, and anxiety in general (Atran 2002: 175–181).

257 Similarities between mystic initiations and near-death experiences have been noted by several scholars (Couloubaritsis 1994: 73; Bonnechere 2003a: 214–215; Seaford 2005: 605; Seaford 2006: 53); I discuss this subject in detail in Ustinova (2013).

258 The term coined by R. A. Moody (Moody 1976). For a recent overview see Holden, Greyson, and James (2009).

259 *Mor.* 590A–592E; discussed above; Paus. 9. 39. 5–14; Bonnechere (2003b: 183–193); Bonnechere (2010: 62–70).

260 Blackmore (1993: 19–22); Fox (2003: 1–3, 98–103); Kellehear (2009); Sartori (2014: 70–84). S. Willetts kindly drew my attention to the book by P. Sartori.

261 Blackmore (1993); Jansen (1996); Geyson (2000); Dieguez and Blanke (2011: 250). An overview of explanatory models of near-death experiences: Greyson, Kelly, and Kelly (2009); Sartori (2014: 11–126). For the theological approaches see Fox (2003: 55–97).

262 Zingone and Alvarado (2009: 36); cf. Gabbard and Twemlow (1984: 126); Lukoff (2011: 307).

263 Noyes Jr. et al. (2009: 41–57); Kellehear (2009: 146).

264 Greyson (2000: 320); cf. Moody (1976); Sabom (1982); Siegel (1980); Blackmore (1993); Morse and Perry (1992); Zingone and Alvarado (2009).
    A small minority of survivors report negative to deeply distressing experiences, which include panic and threatening visions (Sartori 2014: 15–23; most researchers estimate their rate between 15% and 20%). In many cases, distressing near-death experiences ultimately transform and lead to achievement of peacefulness. Disturbing near-death experiences manifest the same pattern comprising out-of-body flight, contrast of light and darkness, meetings with various beings, and ineffability. Emotional unrest of these people at the beginning of their experience may be related to the uneasiness of the initial stages of the vortex, loss of control, and feeling of emptiness (Bush 2009).

265 Noyes Jr. et al. (2009).

266 Nieto (1997); Green (2001); Noyes Jr. et al. (2009: 57–59).

267 Siegel (1980).

268 Holden, Greyson, and James (2009: 2–3); Kellehear (2009).
    An excellent example of the awareness of such experiences in the nineteenth century is Leo Tolstoy's depiction of Andrei Bolkonsky's wound in *War and Peace*, volume 1, part 2, chapters 16 and 19: Prince Andrei, wounded at Austerlitz and bleeding, is portrayed lying on his back and beholding the 'high endless sky.' He feels bliss and happiness, thinks that there is nothing but this sky and peace of mind, thanks god for that, and loses consciousness. When he returns to his senses, and finds himself in Napoleon's presence, he can think only of the worthlessness of life and death.

269 Ὑστερόποτμοι or δευτερόποτμοι. Hsch. s.v. *hysteropotmoi*; Plu. *Mor.* 264; S. *El.* 62–64; Garland (1985: 100); Ogden (2001: 261); Ustinova (2009: 218–229).

270 The book is mentioned by Procl. *in R.* 16. 113 (fr. 68 B1 *DK*); Plu. *Mor.* 564D; Detienne (1963: 84).
271 Chariton *Callirhoe* 1. 6–9: ἐλάμβανε παλιγγενεσίαν.
272 Diog. Laert. 8. 61; 67; *DK* 111, 112; cf. Kingsley (1995: 41, 228); Ogden (2001: 118); Todoua (2005: 77–80); van der Eijk (2009). On Empedocles see below, Chapter 8.
273 Pl. *R.* 614A–621D (Annas 1981: 349–353; Annas 1982: 129–139; Morgan 2000: 208–210); Plu. *Mor.* 563B–568A (Gagné 2015).
274 Frutiger (1930: 260–265); Halliwell (1988: 169); Bremmer (2002: 91–92); Boyancé (1966: 99–113); Morgan (1990: 152); Bernabé (2012: 121–126).
275 Gabbard and Twemlow (1984: 142); Blackmore (1993: 9).
276 Morgan (1990: 150).
277 Noyes Jr. et al. (2009: 48).
278 Procl. *In R.* 6. 114–116; fr. 8 Wehrli; commentary: Festugière (1970: 58–70).
279 See Fox (2003: 121–141) for a discussion of the core near-death experience from the perspective of research on mystical experience and its cross-cultural characteristics.
280 Ustinova (2009: 29–32, with refs.).
281 Drab (1981); Blackmore (1991); Zingone and Alvarado (2009: 19).
282 *Mor.* 590B: μεθιέναι τὴν ψυχήν.
283 Vogliano (1937: 1. 20. 18–32); Colomo (2004).
284 *Phdr.* 250B.
285 *Mor.* 382D, cited above.
286 Morse and Perry (1992: 9); Noyes Jr. et al. (2009: 44–45).
287 Ring (2009: vii).
288 Blackmore (1993: 7); Sabom (1982: 16); Siegel (1980: 924).
289 Morse and Perry (1992: 70–76).
290 Moody (1976: 58–64); Blackmore (1993: 146); Becker (1981); Gabbard and Twemlow (1984: 125); Greyson (2000).
291 Morse and Perry (1992: 80); Zingone and Alvarado (2009: 20).
292 Morse and Perry (1992: 79, 9).
293 Morse and Perry (1992: 29–60, statistics: 220–225).
294 μυστήρια [πολὺ ἀ]ληθέστερα μεμύημαι: Vogliano (1937: 1. 20. 18–32); Colomo (2004).
295 The word *arrhêtos*, applied to mystery rites quite often and meaning 'ineffable' or 'unspeakable,' implied 'one that cannot be expressed in words,' rather than 'one prohibited to be put into words' (Brisson 1987: 96–97; Périllié 2015: 201).

References

Anderson, R. 2004. *Emotion and Experience in Classical Athenian Religion: Studies in Athenian Ritual and Belief.* Ph.D. dissertation, Cambridge University.
Anderson, W. A. 1994. *Music and Musicians in Ancient Greece.* Ithaca: Cornell University Press.
Annas, J. 1981. *An Introduction to Plato's Republic.* Oxford: Oxford University Press.
Annas, J. 1982. "Plato's myths of judgement." *Phronesis* 27:119–143.
Atkinson, J. M. 1992. "Shamanisms today." *Annual Review of Anthropology* 21:307–330.
Atran, S. 2002. *In God We Trust: The Evolutionary Landscape of Religion.* Oxford: Oxford University Press.
Balme, M. 2001. *Menander: The Plays and Fragments.* Oxford: Oxford University Press.
Beazley, J. D. 1978. *Attic Black-Figure Vase-Painters.* Oxford: Clarendon Press.
Beck, R. 2000. "Ritual, myth, doctrine, and initiation in the Mysteries of Mithras: New evidence from a cult vessel." *JRS* 90:144–179.
Beck, R. 2006. *The Religion of the Mithras Cult in the Roman Empire: Mysteries of the Unconquered Sun.* Oxford: Oxford University Press.

Becker, C. B. 1981. "The centrality of near-death experiences in Chinese Pure Land Buddhism." *Anabiosis: The Journal of Near-Death Studies* 1 (2):154–171.

Bélis, A. 1988. "Musique at transe dans le cortège dionysiaqie." In *Transe et théâtre*, edited by P. Ghiron-Bistagne, 9–26. Montpellier: Groupe interdisciplinaire du théâtre antique Université Paul Valéry – Montpellier III.

Bérard, C. 1974. *Anodoi: Essai sur l'imagerie des passages chthoniens.* Rome: Institut suisse de Rome.

Bernabé, A. 2009. "Imago inferorum orphica." In *Mystic Cults in Magna Graecia*, edited by G. Casadio and P. A. Johnston, 95–130. Austin: University of Texas Press.

Bernabé, A. 2012. "*Ho Platôn parôidei ta Orpheôs:* Plato's transposition of Orphic netherworld imagery." In *Greek Religion: Philosophy and Salvation*, edited by V. Adluri, 101–137. Berlin: De Gruyter.

Bernabé, A. 2016a. "Aristotle and the mysteries." In *Greek Philosophy and Mystery Cults*, edited by M. J. Martín-Velasco and M. J. García Blanco, 27–42. Newcastle upon Tyne: Cambridge Scholars Publishing.

Bernabé, A. 2016b. "Two Orphic images in Euripides: *Hippolytus* 952–957 and *Cretans* 472 Kannicht." *TC* 8 (2):183–204.

Bernabé, A. and A. I. Jiménez San Cristóbal. 2008. *Instructions for the Netherworld: The Orphic Gold Tablets.* Leiden: Brill.

Betegh, G. 2004. *The Derveni Papyrus: Cosmology, Theology and Interpretation.* Cambridge: Cambridge University Press.

Bianchi, U. 1976. *The Greek Mysteries.* Leiden: Brill.

Bianchi, U. 2004. "Mystéres d'Eleusis. Dionysisme. Orphisme." In *Les civilisations méditerranéens et le sacré*, edited by J. Ries, A. Motte, and N. Spineto, 255–282. Turnhout: Brepols.

Blackmore, S. 1991. "Near-death experiences: In or out of the body." *The Skeptical Inquirer* 16:34–45.

Blackmore, S. 1993. *Dying to Live: Near-Death Experiences.* Buffalo, NY: Prometheus Books.

Boardman, J. 1975. "Herakles, Peisistratos and Eleusis." *JHS* 95:1–22.

Bonnechere, P. 2003a. *Trophonios de Lébadée.* Leiden: Brill.

Bonnechere, P. 2003b. "Trophonios of Lebadea. Mystery aspects of an oracular cult in Boeotia." In *Greek Mysteries: The Archaeology and Ritual of Ancient Greek Secret Cults*, edited by M. B. Cosmopoulos, 169–192. London-New York: Routledge.

Bonnechere, P. 2010. "Notes trophoniaques, IV: avancées, retours, mises au point." *LEC* 78:57–72.

Borgeaud, P. 2013. "Les mystères." In *Panthée: Religious Transformations in the Graeco-Roman Empire*, edited by L. Bricault and C. Bonnet, 131–144. Leiden: Brill.

Bottini, A., ed. 2005. *Il rito segreto: Misteri in Grecia e a Roma.* Milan: Electa.

Bourguignon, E., ed. 1973. *Religion: Altered States of Consciousness, and Social Change.* Columbus: Ohio State University Press.

Bourguignon, E. 1976. *Possession.* San Francisco: Chandler & Sharp.

Bowden, H. 2010. *Mystery Cults of the Ancient World.* Princeton: Princeton University Press.

Boyancé, P. 1937. *Le culte des Muses chez les philosophes grecs.* Paris: de Boccard.

Boyancé, P. 1961. "L'antre dans les mystères de Dionysos." *RPAA* 33:113–126.

Boyancé, P. 1966. "L'influence pythagoricienne sur Platon." In *Filosofia e scienze in Magna Grecia: Atti del Quinto convengo di studi sulla Magna Grecia*, 74–113. Naples: Instituto per la Storia e l'Archeologia della Magna Grecia.

Brelich, A. 1969. *Paides e parthenoi.* Rome: Ateneo.

Bremmer, J. N. 1983. *The Early Greek Concept of the Soul*. Princeton: Princeton University Press.

Bremmer, J. N. 1984. "Greek maenadism reconsidered." *ZPE* 55:267–286.

Bremmer, J. N. 1995. "Religious secrets and secrecy in Classical Greece." In *Secrecy and Concealment: Studies in the History of Mediterranean and Near Eastern Religions*, edited by G. G. Stroumsa and H. G. Kippenberg, 61–78. Leiden: Brill.

Bremmer, J. N. 2002. *The Rise and Fall of the Afterlife*. London-New York: Routledge.

Bremmer, J. N. 2014. *Initiation Into the Mysteries of the Ancient World*. Berlin-Boston: De Gruyter.

Brisson, L. 1987. "Usages et fonctions du secret dans le pythagorisme ancien." In *Le secret*, edited by P. Dujardin, 87–101. Lyon: C.N.R.S. et Presses universitaires de Lyon.

Bundrick, S. D. 2005. *Music and Image in Classical Athens*. Cambridge: Cambridge University Press.

Burkert, W. 1983. *Homo Necans*. Berkeley-Los Angeles: University of California Press.

Burkert, W. 1985. *Greek Religion*. Cambridge, MA: Harvard University Press.

Burkert, W. 1987. *Ancient Mystery Cults*. Cambridge, MA: Harvard University Press.

Burkert, W. 1993. "Concordia Discors: The literary and the archaeological evidence on the sanctuary of Samothrace." In *Greek Sanctuaries*, edited by N. Marinatos and R. Hägg, 178–191. London-New York: Routledge.

Burkert, W. 2009. "Pleading for hell: Postulates, fantasies, and the senselessness of punishment." *Numen* 56:141–160.

Bush, N. E. 2009. "Distressing Western near-death experiences." In *The Handbook of Near-Death Experiences*, edited by J. M. Holden, B. Greyson, and D. James, 63–86. Santa Barbara: Praeger.

Buxton, R.G.A. 1980. "Blindness and limits: Sophocles and the logic of myth." *JHS* 100:22–37.

Cairns, D. 2013. "A short history of shudders." In *Unveiling Emotions II. Emotions in Greece and Rome: Texts, Images, Material Culture*, edited by A. Chaniotis and P. Ducrey, 85–107. Stuttgart: Franz Steiner.

Calame, C. 1992. *The Poetics of Eros in Ancient Greece*. Princeton: Princeton University Press.

Campbell, L. A. 1968. *Mithraic Iconography and Ideology*. Leiden: Brill.

Cardeña, E. and S. Krippner. 2010. "The cultural context of hypnosis." In *Handbook of Clinical Hypnosis*, edited by S. J. Lynn, J. W. Rhue and I. Kirsch, 743–771. Washington, DC: American Psychological Association.

Carpenter, T. H. 1997. *Dionysian Imagery in Fifth-Century Athens*. Oxford: Oxford University Press.

Casadio, G. and P. A. Johnston. 2009a. "Introduction." In *Mystic Cults in Magna Graecia*, edited by G. Casadio and P. A. Johnston, 1–29. Austin: University of Texas Press.

Casadio, G. and P. A. Johnston, eds. 2009b. *Mystic Cults in Magna Graecia*. Austin: University of Texas Press.

Cavanaugh, M. B. 1996. *Eleusis and Athens, Documents in Finance, Religion and Politics*. Atlanta: Scholars Press.

Chantraine, P. 1983–1984. *Dictionnaire étymologique de la langue grecque*. Paris: Klincksieck.

Clinton, K. 1974. *The Sacred Officials of the Eleusinian Mysteries*. Philadelphia: American Philosophical Society.

Clinton, K. 1992. *Myth and Cult: The Iconography of the Eleusinian Mysteries*. Stockholm: Paul Åströms Förlag.

Clinton, K. 1993. "The sanctuary of Demeter and Kore at Eleusis." In *Greek Sanctuaries*, edited by N. Marinatos and R. Hägg, 110–124. London-New York: Paul Åströms Förlag.

Clinton, K. 2003. "Stages of initiation in the Eleusinian and Samothracian Mysteries." In *Greek Mysteries: The Archaeology and Ritual of Ancient Greek Secret Cults*, edited by M. B. Cosmopoulos, 50–78. London-New York: Routledge.

Clinton, K. 2004. "Epiphany in the Eleusinia mysteries." *ICS* 29:85–101.

Cohen, E. 2007. *The Mind Possessed: The Cognition of Spirit Possession in Afro-Brazilian Religious Tradition*. Oxford: Oxford University Press.

Cole, S. G. 1980. "New evidence for the mysteries of Dionysos." *GRBS* 21 (3):223–238.

Cole, S. G. 1984. *Theoi Megaloi: The Cult of the Great Gods at Samothrace*. Leiden: Brill.

Cole, S. G. 1993. "Voices from beyond the grave: Dionysus and the dead." In *Masks of Dionysus*, edited by T. H. Carpenter and C. A. Faraone, 276–295. Ithaca: Cornell University Press.

Cole, S. G. 2003. "Landscapes of Dionysos and Elysian Fields." In *Greek Mysteries: The Archaeology and Ritual of Ancient Greek Secret Cults*, edited by M. B. Cosmopoulos, 193–217. London-New York: Routledge.

Colomo, D. 2004. "Heracles and the Eleusinian Mysteries: P.Mil.Vogl. I 20, 18–32 revisited." *ZPE* 148:87–98.

Cosmopoulos, M. B., ed. 2003. *Greek Mysteries: The Archaeology and Ritual of Ancient Greek Secret Cults*. London-New York: Routledge.

Cosmopoulos, M. B. 2015. *Bronze Age Eleusis and the Origins of the Eleusinian Mysteries*. Cambridge: Cambridge University Press.

Couloubaritsis, L. 1994. "Initiation et pédanterie." In *Mythe et philosophie dans les Nuées d'Aristophane*, edited by L. Couloubaritsis and S. Byl, 69–85. Bruxelles: Ousia.

Crapanzano, V. and V. Garrison, eds. 1977. *Case Studies in Spirit Possession*. New York: Wiley.

Croissant, J. 1932. *Aristote et les mystères*. Liège-Paris: Droz.

Cumont, F. 1933. "La grande inscription bacchique du Metropolitan Museum." *AJA* 37 (2):232–263.

Delatte, A. 1934. *Les conceptions de l'enthousiasme chez les philosophes présocratiques*. Paris: Les Belles Lettres.

Delatte, A. 1954. "Le cycéon, breuvage rituel des mystères d'Éleusis." *Bulletin de la Classe des Lettres de l' Académie royale de Belgique* 40:690–752.

Delavaud-Roux, M.-H. 1988. "La danse au service du culte de Dionysos dans l'antiquité grecque." In *Transe et théâtre*, edited by P. Ghiron-Bistagne, 30–53. Montpellier: Groupe interdisciplinaire du théâtre antique Université Paul Valéry – Montpellier III.

des Places, E. 1981. "Platon et la langue des mystères." In *Études platoniciennes 1929–1979*, 83–98. Leiden: Brill.

Detienne, M. 1963. *La notion de daïmôn dans le pythagorisme ancien*. Paris: Les Belles Lettres.

de Vries, G. J. 1969. *A Commentary on the Phaedrus of Plato*. Amsterdam: Hakkert.

Dieguez, S. and O. Blanke. 2011. "Altered states of bodily consciousness." In *Altering Consciousness: Multidisciplinary Perspectives*, edited by E. Cardeña and M. Winkelman, vol. 2, 237–262. Santa Barbara: Praeger.

Dignas, B. 2002. "Priestly authority in the cult of the Corybantes at Erythrae." *EA* 34:29–43.

Dimitrova, N. M. 2008. *Theoroi and Initiates in Samothrace, Hesperia Suppl. 17*. Princeton: Princeton University Press.

Dodd, D. B., and C. A. Faraone, eds. 2003. *Initiation in Ancient Greek Rituals and Narratives*. London-New York: Routledge.

Dodds, E. R. 1940. "Maenadism in the Bacchae." *HThR* 40:155–176.

Dodds, E. R. 1973. *The Greeks and the Irrational*. Berkeley-Los Angeles: University of California Press.

Dowden, K. 1980. "Grades in the Eleusinian mysteries." *RHR* 197:409–427.

Drab, K. 1981. "The tunnel experience: Reality or hallucination?" *Anabiosis: The Journal of Near-Death Studies* 1:126–152.

Duchemin, J. 1955. *Pindare, poète et prophète*. Paris: Les Belles Lettres.

Dunand, F. 2000. *Isis Mère des Dieux*. Paris: Errance.

Edmonds III, R. G. 2013. *Redefining Ancient Orphism: A Study in Greek Religion*. Cambridge: Cambridge University Press.

Edmonds, R. G. 2009. "Who are you? Mythic narrative and identity in the 'Orphic' gold tablets." In *Mystic Cults in Magna Graecia*, edited by G. Casadio and P. A. Johnston, 73–94. Austin: Texas University Press.

Eidinow, E. 2016. *Envy, Poison, and Death: Women on Trial in Classical Athens*. Oxford: Oxford University Press.

Fachner, J. C. 2011. "Time is the key: Music and altered states of consciousness." In *Altering Consciousness: Multidisciplinary Perspectives*, edited by E. Cardeña and M. Winkelman, vol. 1, 355–376. Santa Barbara: Praeger.

Faraone, C. A. 2013. "Gender differentiation and role models in the worship of Dionysus: The Thracian and Thessalian patterns." In *Redefining Dionysos*, edited by A. Bernabé, M. Herrero de Jáuregui, A. I. Jiménez San Cristóbal, and R. Martín Hernández, 120–143. Berlin-New York: De Gruyter.

Festugière, A. J. 1970. *Proclus: Commentaire sur la République*. Paris: Vrin.

Fox, M. 2003. *Religion, Spirituality and the Near-Death Experience*. London: Routledge.

Frede, D. 2012. "Die Rede des Socrates: Eros als Verlangen nach Unsterblichkeit." In *Platon: Symposium*, edited by C. Horn, 141–158. Berlin: De Gruyter.

Frisk, H. 1973–79. *Griechisches etymologisches Wörterbuch*. Heidelberg: C. Winter.

Frutiger, P. 1930. *Les mythes de Platon*. Paris: Alcan.

Gabbard, G. O. and S. W. Twemlow. 1984. *With the Eyes of the Mind: An Empirical Analysis of Out-of-Body States*. New York: Praeger.

Gagné, R. 2015. "La catabase aérienne de Thespésios: le statut du récit." *EC* 83 (1–4):313–329.

Garland, R. 1985. *The Greek Way of Death*. London: Duckworth.

Geyson, B. 2000. "Dissociation in people who have near-death experiences: Out of their bodies or out of their minds?" *The Lancet* 355:460–463.

Gilovich, T. and K. Savitsky. 2002. "Like goes with like: The role of representativeness in erroneous and pseudo-scientific beliefs." In *Heuristics and Biases: The Psychology of Intuitive Judgement*, edited by T. Gilovich, D. Griffin, and D. Kahneman, 617–624. Cambridge: Cambridge University Press.

Goff, B. E. 2004. *Citizen Bacchae: Women's Ritual Practice in Ancient Greece*. Berkeley.

Gómez Iglesias, M. R. 2016. "The echoes of Eleusis: Love and initiation in the Platonic philosophy." In *Greek Philosophy and Mystery Cults*, edited by M. J. Martín-Velasco and M. J. García Blanco, 61–102. Newcastle upon Tyne: Cambridge Scholars Publishing.

Gomme, A. W. and F. H. Sandbach. 1973. *Menander: A Commentary*. Oxford: Clarendon Press.

Graf, F. 1985. *Nordionische Kulte*. Rome: Schweizerisches Institut in Rom.

Graf, F. 1993. "Dionysian and Orphic eschatology. New texts and old questions." In *Masks of Dionysos*, edited by T. H. Carpenter and C. A. Faraone, 233–258. Ithaca: Cornell University Press.

Graf, F. 2003. "Initiation: A concept with a troubled history." In *Initiation in Ancient Greek Rituals and Narratives: New Critical Perspectives*, edited by D. B. Dodd and C. A. Faraone, 3–24. London-New York: Routledge.

Graf, F. 2010. "'The blessings of madness': Dionysos, madness, and scholarship." *Archiv für Religionsgeschichte* 12:167–180.

Graf, F., and S. I. Johnston. 2007. *Ritual Texts for the Afterlife: Orpheus and the Bacchic Gold Leaves.* London-New York: Routledge.

Gragg, D. L. 2004. "Old and New in Roman Religion: A Cognitive Account." In *Theorizing Religions Past: Archaeology, History, and Cognition*, edited by H. Whitehouse and L. H. Martin, 69–86. Walnut Creek: AltaMira Press.

Green, C. 1968. *Out-of-the-Body Experiences.* London: Hamish Hamilton.

Green, J. T. 2001. "The near-death experience as a shamanic initiation: A case study." *Journal of Near-Death Studies* 19 (4):209–225.

Greyson, B. 2000. "Near-death experiences." In *Varieties of Anomalous Experience: Examining the Scientific Evidence*, edited by E. Cardeña, S. J. Lynn, and S. Krippner, 315–352. Washington, DC: American Psychological Association.

Greyson, B., E. W. Kelly, and E. F. Kelly. 2009. "Explanatory models for near-death experiences." In *The Handbook of Near-Death Experiences*, edited by J. M. Holden, B. Greyson, and D. James, 213–234. Santa Barbara: Praeger.

Guidorizzi, G. 2010. *Ai confini dell' anima: I Greci e la follia.* Milano: Raffaelo Cortina.

Hackforth, R. 1972. *Plato's Phaedrus: Translated With an Introduction and Commentary.* Cambridge: Cambridge University Press.

Halliwell, S. 1988. *Plato: Republic 10, With Translation and Commentary.* Warminster: Aris & Phillips.

Halliwell, S. 2011. *Between Ecstasy and Truth: Interpretations of Greek Poetics From Homer to Longinus.* Oxford: Oxford University Press.

Hardie, A. 2004. "Muses and mysteries." In *Music and the Muses: The Culture of 'Mousikê' in the Classical Athenian City*, edited by P. Murray and P. Wilson, 11–37. Oxford: Oxford University Press.

Henrichs, A. 1978. "Greek menadism from Olympias to Messalina." *HSCPh* 82:120–160.

Henrichs, A. 2003. "*Hieroi logoi* and *hierai bibloi*: The (un)written margins of the sacred in Ancient Greece." *HSCPh* 88:205–240.

Herrmann, P. 2002. "Eine 'pierre errante' in Samos: Kultgesetz der Korybanten." *Chiron* 32:157–171.

Hoessly, F. 2001. *Katharsis: Reinigung als Heilverfahren: Studien zum Ritual der archaischen und klassischen Zeit sowie zum Corpus Hippocraticum.* Göttingen: Vandenhoeck & Ruprecht.

Hoffmann, H. 1997. *Sotades: Symbols of Immortality on Greek Vases.* Oxford: Oxford University Press.

Holden, J. M., B. Greyson, and D. James. 2009. "The field of near-death studies: Past, present, and future." In *The Handbook of Near-Death Experiences*, edited by J. M. Holden, B. Greyson, and D. James, 1–16. Santa Barbara: Praeger.

Inwood, B. 2001. *The Poem of Empedocles.* Toronto: University of Toronto Press.

Jaccottet, A.-F. 2003. *Choisir Dionysos: Les associations dionysiaques ou la face cachée du dionysisme.* Zurich: Akanthus.

Jaccottet, A.-F. 2005a. "Du thiase aux mystères. Dionysos entre le 'privé' et 'l'officiel.'" *Kernos* Suppl. 15:191–205.

Jaccottet, A.-F. 2005b. "Un dieu, plusieurs mystères? Les différents visages des mystères dionysiaques." In *Religions orientales – culti misterici*, edited by C. Bonnet, J. Rüpke, and P. Scarpi, 219–230. Stuttgart: Franz Steiner.

Janko, R. 1997. "The physicist as hierophant: Aristophanes, Socrates and the authorship of the Derveni Papyrus." *ZPE* 118:61–97.

Jansen, K. 1996. "Neuroscience, ketamine, and the near-death experience. The role of glutamate and the NMDA receptor." In *The Near-Death Experience: A Reader*, edited by L. W. Bailey, 265–282. New York-London: Routledge.

Jeanmaire, H. 1970. *Dionysos: Histoire du culte de Bacchus*. Paris: Payot.

Jenner, E. 2014. *The Gold Leaves (Being an Account and Translation From the Ancient Greek of the So-Called 'Orphic' Gold Tablets)*. Pokeno: Atuanui Press.

Jiménez San Cristóbal, A. I. 2009. "The meaning of *bacchos* and *baccheuein* in Orphism." In *Mystic Cults in Magna Graecia*, edited by G. Casadio and P. A. Johnston, 46–60. Austin: Texas University Press.

Jost, M. 2003. "Mystery cults in Arcadia." In *Greek Mysteries: The Archaeology and Ritual of Ancient Greek Secret Cults*, edited by M. B. Cosmopoulos, 143–168. New York-London: Routledge.

Karadima-Matsa, C. and N. Dimitrova. 2003. "Epitaph for an initiate at Samothrace and Eleusis." *Chiron* 33:335–345.

Kellehear, A. 2009. "Census of non-Western near-death experiences to 2005: Observations and critical reflections." In *The Handbook of Near-Death Experiences*, edited by J. M. Holden, B. Greyson, and D. James, 135–158. Santa Barbara: Praeger.

Kerényi, C. 1967. *Eleusis: Archetypal Image of Mother and Daughter*. London: Routledge & Kegan Paul.

Kerényi, C. 1976. *Dionysos*. Princeton: Princeton University Press.

Kingsley, P. 1995. *Ancient Philosophy, Mystery, and Magic: Empedocles and Pythagorean Tradition*. Oxford: Oxford University Press.

Kleinman, A. 1980. *Patients and Healers in the Context of Culture: An Exploration of the Borderline Between Anthropology, Medicine, and Psychiatry*. Berkeley-Los Angeles: University of California Press.

Kraut, R. 1997. *Aristotle: Politics. Books VII and VIII*. Oxford: Oxford University Press.

Kritikos, P. G. and S. P. Papadaki. 1967. "The history of the poppy and of opium and their expansion in antiquity in the eastern Mediterranean area." *Bulletin on Narcotics* 19 (3; 4):17–38; 5–10.

Lada-Richards, I. 1999. *Initiating Dionysus: Ritual and Theatre in Aristophanes' Frogs*. Oxford: Oxford University Press.

Larson, J. 2016. *Understanding Greek Religion: A Cognitive Approach*. London-New York: Routledge.

Lehmann, P. W. 1969. *Samothrace: The Hieron*. New York: Pantheon Books.

Levitin, D. 2006. *This Is Your Brain on Music: Understanding a Human Obsession*. London: Atlantic.

Linforth, I. M. 1941. *The Arts of Orpheus*. Berkeley-Los Angeles: University of California Press.

Linforth, I. M. 1946a. "The Corybantic rites in Plato." *University of California Publications in Classical Philology* 13 (5):121–162.

Linforth, I. M. 1946b. "Telestic madness in Plato. Phaedrus 244DE." *University of California Publications in Classical Philology* 13 (6):163–172.

Ludwig, A. M. 1968. "Altered states of consciousness." In *Trance and Possession States*, edited by R. Prince, 69–95. Montreal: R. M. Bucke Memorial Society.

Lukoff, D. 2011. "Visionary spirituality and mental disorders." In *Altering Consciousness: Multidisciplinary Perspectives. Vol. 2. Biological and Psychological Perspectives*, edited by E. Cardeña and M. Winkelman, 301–326. Santa Barbara: Praeger.

Martin, L. H. 2009. "The Amor and Psyche relief in the Mithraeum of Capua Vetere: An exceptional case of Graeco-Roman syncretism or an ordinary instance of human cognition." In *Mystic Cults in Magna Graecia*, edited by G. Casadio and P. A. Johnston, 277–289. Austin: Texas University Press.

McCauley, R. N., and E. T. Lawson. 2002. *Bringing Ritual to Mind: Psychological Foundations of Cultural Forms*. Cambridge: Cambridge University Press.

McNamara, P. 2009. *The Neuroscience of Religious Experience*. Cambridge: Cambridge University Press.

Mendelsohn, D. 1992. "Synkeraunoô: Dithyrambic language and Dionysiac cult." *CJ* 87 (1):105–124.

Menier, T. 2001. "L'étrangerité dionysiaque." In *Chanter les dieux. Musique et religion dans l'antiquité grecque et romaine*, edited by P. Brulé and C. Vendries, 233–242. Rennes: Presses universitaires de Rennes.

Merkelbach, R. 1984. *Mithras: ein persisch-römischer Mysterienkult*. Königsheim: Hain.

Meyer, M. W. 1987. *The Ancient Mysteries: A Sourcebook*. San Francisco: Harper.

Modarressi, T. 1968. "The zar cult in South Iran." In *Trance and Possession States*, edited by R. Prince, 149–156. Montreal: R. M. Bucke Memorial Society.

Moody, R. A. 1976. *Life After Life: The Investigation of a Phenomenon – Survival of Bodily Death*. New York: Bantam Books.

Morgan, K. A. 2000. *Myth and Philosophy From the Presocratics to Plato*. Cambridge: Cambridge University Press.

Morgan, M. L. 1990. *Platonic Piety: Philosophy and Ritual in Fourth-Century Athens*. New Haven: Yale University Press.

Morse, M. and P. Perry. 1992. *Transformed by the Light: The Powerful Effect of Near-Death Experiences on People's Lives*. London: Platkus.

Most, G. W. 2013. "Heraclitus on religion." *Rhizomata* 1 (2):153–167.

Motte, A. and V. Pirenne-Delforge. 1992. "Le mot et les rites. Aperçu des significations de ὄργια et de quelques dérivés." *Kernos* 5:119–140.

Moulinier, L. 1952. *Le pur et l'impur dans la pensée des Grecs*. Paris: Klincksieck.

Mylonas, G. E. 1961. *Eleusis and the Eleusinian Mysteries*. Princeton: Princeton University Press.

Nervegna, S. 2010. "Menander's *Theophoroumene* between Greece and Rome." *AJPh* 131:23–68.

Nieto, J. C. 1997. *Religious Experience and Mysticism: Otherness as Experience of Transcendence*. Lanham: University Press of America.

Nilsson, M. P. 1957. *The Dionysiac Mysteries of the Hellenistic and Roman Age*. Lund: Gleerup.

North, J. A. 2000. *Roman Religion*. Oxford: Oxford University Press.

Noyes Jr., R., P. Fenwick, J. M. Holden, and S. R. Christian. 2009. "Aftereffects of pleasurable Western adult near-death experiences." In *The Handbook of Near-Death Experiences*, edited by J. M. Holden, B. Greyson, and D. James, 41–62. Santa Barbara: Praeger.

Obbink, D. 2011. "Poetry and performance in the Orphic gold leaves." In *The "Orphic" Gold Tablets and the Greek Religion*, edited by R. E. Edmonds, 291–309. Cambridge: Cambridge University Press.

Ogden, D. 2001. *Greek and Roman Necromancy*. Princeton: Princeton University Press.

Ott, J. 1993. *Pharmacotheon: Entheogenic Drugs, Their Plant Sources and History*. Kennewick: Natural Products Co.

Pachis, P. 2009. "Imaginistic modes of religiosity and the study of the cults of Graeco-Roman world." In *Imagistic Tradition in the Graeco-Roman World: A Cognitive Modeling of History of Religious Research*, edited by L. H. Martin and P. Pachis, 15–34. Thessaloniki: Equinox.

Padel, R. 1995. *Whom Gods Destroy: Elements of Greek and Tragic Madness*. Princeton: Princeton University Press.

Parisinou, E. 2000. *The Light of the Gods: The Role of Light in Archaic and Classical Greek Cult*. London: Duckworth.

Parke, H. W. 1977. *Festivals of the Athenians*. London: Thames & Hudson.

Parker, R. 1983. *Miasma: Pollution and Purification in Early Greek Religion*. Oxford: Oxford University Press.

Parker, R. 2011. *On Greek Religion*. Ithaca: Cornell University Press.

Pelosi, F. 2010. *Plato on Music, Soul and Body*. Cambridge: Cambridge University Press.

Périllié, J.-L. 2015. *Mystères socratiques et traditions orales de l'eudémonisme dans les dialogues de Platon*. Sankt Augustin: Academia.

Persinger, M. A. 1987. *Neuropsychological Bases of God Beliefs*. New York: Praeger.

Pippidi, D. M. 1964. "Grottes dionysiaques à Callatis." *BCH* 88:151–158.

Power, T. 2010. *The Culture of Kithardoidia*. Washington, DC: Center for Hellenic Studies.

Price, S. 1999. *Religions of the Ancient Greeks*. Cambridge: Cambridge University Press.

Quattordio Moreschini, A. 1986. "Per la etimologia di korúbantes/kúrbantes, sacerdoti di Cibele." *Aion* 8:207–217.

Reale, G. and J. Burnett. 2001. *Platone Simposio*. Milan: Rusconi.

Riedweg, C. 1987. *Mysterienterminologie bei Platon, Philon und Klemens von Alexandria*. Berlin-New York: De Gruyter.

Riedweg, C. 1998. "Initiation-Tod-Unterwelt." In *Ansichten griechischer Rituale: Geburtstag-Symposium für Walter Burkert*, edited by F. Graf. Stuttgart: Teubner.

Riedweg, C. 2002. "Poésie orphique et rituel initiatique. Eléments d'un 'discours sacré' dans les lamelles d'or." *RHR* 219 (4):459–481.

Rinella, M. A. 2010. *Pharmakon: Plato, Drug Culture, and Identity in Ancient Athens*. Lanham: Lexington Books.

Ring, K. 2009. "Foreword." In *The Handbook of Near-Death Experiences*, edited by J. M. Holden, B. Greyson, and D. James, viii–xi. Santa Barbara: Praeger.

Rist, J. M. 1977. *Plotinus: The Road to Reality*. Cambridge: Cambridge University Press.

Roller, L. E. 1999. *In Search of God the Mother*. Berkeley-Los Angeles: University of California Press.

Rouget, G. 1990. *La musique et la trance*. Paris: Gallimard.

Rowe, C. J. 1986. *Plato: Phaedrus, Edited With Translation and Commentary*. Warminster: Aris & Phillips.

Rowe, C. J. 1998. *Plato: Symposium, Edited With Introduction, Translation and Commentary*. Warminster: Aris & Phillips.

Sabom, M. 1982. *Recollections of Death: A Medical Investigation*. New York: Simon & Schuster.

Sacks, O. 2007. *Musicophilia: Tales of Music and the Brain*. London: Picador.

Sargant, W. 1973. *The Mind Possessed: A Physiology of Possession, Mysticism and Faith Healing*. London: Heinemann.

Sartori, P. 2014. *The Wisdom of Near-Death Experiences*. London: Watkins Publishing Limited.

Saunders, L. W. 1977. "Variants in zar experience in an Egyptian village." In *Case Studies in Spirit Possession*, edited by V. Crapanzano and V. Garrison, 149–156. New York-London: Wiley.

Scarpi, P. 2002. *Le religioni dei misteri*. Milan: A. Mondadori.

Schachter, A. 1981–94. *Cults of Boeotia*. BICS Suppl. 38. 1–4. London: Institute of Classical Studies.

Schefer, C. 2000. "'Nur für Eingeweihte!' Heraklit und die Mysterien." *A&A* 46:46–75.

Schuddeboom, F. L. 2009. *Greek Religious Terminology – Telete and Orgia*. Leiden: Brill.

Schlesier, R. 2011. "Der bakchische Gott." In *A Different God?*, edited by R. Schlesier, 173–202. Berlin-Boston: De Gruyter.

Seaford, R. 1981. "Dionysiac drama and the Dionysiac mysteries." *CQ* 31:252–275.

Seaford, R. 1996. *Euripides: Bacchae, With an Introduction, Translation and Commentary*. Warminster: Aris & Phillips.

Seaford, R. 1998. "In the mirror of Dionysos." In *The Sacred and the Feminine in Ancient Greece*, edited by S. Blundell and M. Williamson, 128–146. London: Routledge.

Seaford, R. 2005. "Mystic light in Aeschylus' *Bassarai*." *CQ* 55 (2):602–606.

Seaford, R. 2006. *Dionysos*. London-New York: Routledge.

Seaford, R. 2013. "The politics of the mystic chorus." In *Choruses, Ancient and Modern*, edited by J. Billings, F. Budelmann, and F. Macintosh, 261–280. Oxford: Oxford University Press.

Segal, C. 1990. "Dionysus and the gold tablets from Pelinna." *GRBS* 31 (4):411–419.

Sfameni Gasparro, G. 1985. *Soteriology and Mystic Aspects in the Cult of Cybele and Attis*. Leiden: Brill.

Sfameni Gasparro, G. 2011. "Mysteries and Oriental cults. A problem in the history of religions." In *The Religious History of the Roman Empire: Pagans, Jews, and Christians*, edited by J. A. North and S.R.F. Price, 276–324. Oxford: Oxford University Press.

Siegel, R. K. 1980. "The psychology of life after death." *American Psychologist* 35 (10):911–931.

Sifakis, G. M. 2001. *Aristotle on the Function of Tragic Poetry*. Herakleion: Crete University Press.

Simms, R. M. 1990. "M*yesis, telete*, and *mysteria*." *GRBS* 31:183–195.

Snell, B. 1960. *The Discovery of the Mind: The Greek Origins of the European Thought*. New York: Harper & Row.

Sourvinou-Inwood, C. 2003. "Festivals and mysteries. Aspects of the Eleusinian cult." In *Greek Mysteries: The Archaeology and Ritual of Ancient Greek Secret Cults*, edited by M. B. Cosmopoulos, 25–49. London-New York: Routledge.

Todoua, M. 2005. "Empédocle: empêche-vents ou dompteur des mauvais génies? Réflexions autour du fr. 111 Diels-Kranz." *BAGB*:49–81.

Trépanier, S. 2004. *Empedocles: An Interpretation*. New York-London: Routledge.

Turcan, R. 1981. *Mithra et le mithriacisme*. Paris: Presses Universitaires de France.

Turcan, R. 1986. "Bacchoi ou Bacchants? De la dissidence des vivants à la ségrégation des morts." In *L'association dionysiaque dans les sociétés anciennes*, 227–246. Rome: L'École française de Rome.

Turcan, R. 1998. "Initiation." In *Reallexikon für Antike und Christentum*, edited by E. Dassmann, 87–159. Stuttgart: Hiersemann.

Tzifopoulos, Y. 2010. *Paradise Earned: The Bacchic-Orphic Gold Lamellae of Crete*. Cambridge, MA: Harvard University Press.

Ustinova, Y. 1992–1998. "Corybantism: The nature and role of an ecstatic cult in the Greek polis." *Horos* 10–12:503–520.

Ustinova, Y. 2005. "Lege et consuetudine: Private cult associations in the Greek law." *Kernos* Suppl. 5:267–288.

Ustinova, Y. 2009. *Caves and the Ancient Greek Mind: Descending Underground in the Search for Ultimate Truth*. Oxford: Oxford University Press.

Ustinova, Y. 2012. "Madness into memory: Mania and mnêmê in Greek culture." *SCI* 31:109–132.

Ustinova, Y. 2013. "To live in joy and die with hope: Experiential aspects of ancient Greek mystery rites." *BICS* 56 (2):105–123.

van der Eijk, P. J. 2009. "The woman not breathing." In *Heraclides of Pontus*, edited by W. W. Fortenbaugh and E. Pender, 237–250. New Brunswick: Transaction Publishers.

Velardi, R. 1989. *Enthousiasmòs. Possessione rituale e teoria della communicazione poetica in Platone*. Rome: Ed. dell'Ateneo.

Vermaseren, M. J. 1956. *Corpus inscriptionum et monumentorum religionis Mithriacae*. Hague: Nijhoff.

Vermaseren, M. J. 1977. *Cybele and Attis: The Myth and the Cult*. London: Thames & Hudson.

Vermaseren, M. J. and C. C. van Essen. 1965. *The Excavations in the Mithraeum of the Church of Santa Prisca in Rome*. Leiden: Brill.

Versnel, H. S. 1990. *Ter Unus. Isis, Dionysos, Hermes: Three Studies in Henotheism*. Leiden: Brill.

Villanueva Puig, M.-C. 1998. "Le cas du thiase dionysiaque." *Ktèma* 23:365–374.

Vogliano, A. 1937. *Papiri della Università di Milano*. Milan: Istituto Editoriale Cisalpino.

Voutiras, E. 1996. "Un culte domestique des Corybantes." *Kernos* 9:243–256.

Waldner, K. 2013. "Individuality in ancient mystery cults." In *The Individual in the Religions of the Ancient Mediterranean*, edited by J. Rüpke, 215–242. Oxford: Oxford University Press.

Wallis, R. T. 1972. *Neoplatonism*. London: Duckworth.

Wasson, R. G., A. Hofmann, and C.A.P. Ruch. 1998. *The Road to Eleusis: Unveiling the Secret of the Mysteries*. Los Angeles: William Dailey Rare Books Ltd.

West, M. L. 1982. "The Orphics of Olbia." *ZPE* 45:17–29.

West, M. L. 1983. *The Orphic Poems*. Oxford: Oxford University Press.

West, M. L. 1992. *Ancient Greek Music*. Oxford: Oxford University Press.

West, M. L. 2000. "Music therapy in antiquity." In *Music as Medicine: The History of Music Therapy Since Antiquity*, edited by P. Horden, 51–68. Aldershot: Ashgate.

Whitehouse, H. 2004. *Modes of Religiosity: A Cognitive Theory of Religious Transmission*. Walnut Creek: AltaMira Press.

Witt, R. E. 1971. *Isis in the Ancient World*. Baltimore: Johns Hopkins University Press.

Wright, M. R. 1981. *Empedocles: The Extant Fragments*. New Haven: Yale University Press.

Wulff, D. M. 2000. "Mystical experience." In *Varieties of Anomalous Experience: Examining the Scientific Evidence*, edited by E. Cardeña, S. J. Lynn, and S. Krippner, 397–440. Washington, DC: American Psychological Association.

Xygalatas, D., U. Schjoedt, J. Bulbilia, I. Konvalinka, E.-M. Jegindø, P. Reddish, A. W. Geertz, and A. Roepstoff. 2013. "Autobiographical memory in a fire-walking ritual." *Journal of Cognition and Culture* 13:1–16.

Yunis, H. 2011. *Plato: Phaedrus*. Cambridge: Cambridge University Press.

Zingone, N. L. and C. S. Alvarado. 2009. "Pleasurable Western adult near-death experiences: Features, circumstances, and incidence." In *The Handbook of Near-Death Experiences*, edited by J. M. Holden, B. Greyson, and D. James, 17–40. Santa Barbara: Praeger.

Zuntz, G. 1971. *Persephone*. Oxford: Clarendon Press.

3   *Bakcheia*

As early as in the *Iliad*, Dionysus is described as 'mad' (*mainomenos*). The scholium explains the word as referring either to the ability of the god to make others mad, or to his own madness.[1] In fact, both insanity and ecstatic frenzy were attributed to Dionysus in myth and art. According to the myth, the raving god wandered to the mountain of Nysa, which was located in different places from Thrace to Egypt by various authors.[2] Dionysus' madness is attributed to Hera;[3] he is also said to have been purified by Rhea in Phrygia, where he was initiated in her mysteries.[4] In vase painting Dionysus is often portrayed dancing ecstatically, playing musical instruments with his head uplifted, or tearing animals in two.[5]

The mad god's other name was Bacchus, and his worshippers were often called *bakchoi* and *bakchai*.[6] These terms, attested in the seventh century, predate the god's name, which appeared only in the fifth century, implying that the god adopted the designation of the mortal devotees engaged in the activity which was attributed to his power.[7] In fact, Dionysus is rarely called Bacchus, the epiclesis Bacchius being much more common. Thus, Dionysus Bacchius is the god of *bakchoi*, and Bacchus alone means 'the ultimate bacchant.'[8] However, people participating in Bacchic rites and calling themselves *bakchoi* and *bakchai* were hardly interested in the etymology of the god's title: from their perspective, they simply identified with him,[9] and this self-identification of the mortal devotees with a god is unique in Greek religion.[10] We will return to this subject later in this chapter.

Dionysus could both madden and free: in Corinth and Sicyon, he was worshipped as *Bakcheios* (bacchant) and *Lusios* (deliverer) in the same sanctuaries, the two epithets together constituting an 'analytic staging of *mania*,' to cite M. Detienne's elucidation of the unity of the apparently contradicting aspects of the god.[11] Dionysiac frenzy was versatile, bringing about blessedness or disaster, in accordance to the god's (actually, the believer's) disposition. *Mania* inflicted by Dionysus, often called *bakcheia*,[12] was often collective, an epidemic that befell a whole community, but Dionysiac madness could also strike a single person or a small group.

In Greek myth and cult, Dionysus is often represented as 'the god who comes.'[13] This god, whose name is first recorded on Linear B tablets, was indeed a stranger in the milieu of warrior aristocrats: he is mentioned no more than four times in the entire Homeric epos, created for the audience whose ethos was focused on power and military virtue.[14] Arrogant kings, such as Lycurgus and Pentheus, opposed the deceitful god of ecstasy and vineyards and paid dearly for their toughness. Aetiological myths presenting Dionysus as a foreigner may have helped to ease the tension between vine-tending peasants and aristocracy whose interest in wine ended in its consumption, and provide an explanation for the ritual reversal of normality in Dionysus' cult and the ferocity of the god's devotees.[15] Dionysus' arrival from abroad is symbolic of the god's status as an 'outsider' rather than his being an actual newcomer to Greece.[16]

Dionysus' alterity probably also derives from the fact that his votaries were chiefly women, seen by Greek men as 'the second sex.'[17] Men were not absolutely excluded from ecstatic Dionysiac rites: silens and satyrs were featured on Attic vases accompanying the maenads in their revels, and in real life Plato felt at ease talking of the philosopher's *bakcheia*,[18] implying therefore that a male devotee could know Bacchic ecstasy. Nevertheless, the mythological ithyphallic males of Dionysus' retinue, on the one hand, and the effeminate mad Dionysus clad in women's clothes,[19] on the other hand, were both contradictory to the ideal clear-headed warlike male. This visualisation of Dionysus and his entourage appears to reflect the deep suspicion held by Greek males towards the god of ecstasy, and the association of this state predominantly – although not exclusively – with women.[20]

Dionysus and individual madmen in myths

Dionysus did not hurt those who had not offended him or his devotees, and he could even take away one's mind as a charitable act: when Ino planned to sacrifice Phrixus and Helle, Dionysus made them mad, and led them to a wilderness, where their mother Nephele opportunely saved her children by sending them the golden ram.[21]

Dionysiac *mania* possessing an individual could ultimately be beneficial to an entire community: Eurypylus was driven insane by merely looking at an image of Dionysus kept in a chest, and liberated the land of Patrae from a dreadful tradition of human sacrifice by bringing to the city 'the foreign deity,' that is, the image of Dionysus who caused his malady. The hero was thus cured of his insanity, and the city's cruel cultic practices mollified, an event that was commemorated at the festival of Dionysus celebrated in Patrae.[22] This myth highlights two features of Dionysus known throughout the Greek world: he was perceived as a foreign god, and he caused insanity. The standard story of the maddening god ends in an original twist: two tragic situations, Eurypylus' derangement and the city's misery, are resolved by transporting the awesome image of Dionysus to Patrae. Thus the god of *mania* – present in his image – and a madman together brought peace of mind to the suffering citizens.

When he or his followers were wronged, Dionysus was ruthless. The earliest piece of Dionysus' mythical biography is related in the *Iliad*: Lycurgus, the model transgressor 'hated by all the gods,' offended the nurses of 'mad Dionysus,' striking them with his ox-goad and forcing the infant god to find a shelter in the sea; for these misdoings Lycurgus was made blind by Zeus.[23] Attic dramatists returned to the terrible story of Lycurgus more than once.[24] Lycurgus' resistance to Dionysus, subsequent madness and death were dramatised by Aeschylus in his tetralogy *Lycurgeia*, especially in the *Edonians*: the Thracian king who prevented Dionysus and his train from passing through his kingdom was driven mad, mistook his son for a vine and killed him, only to regain his sanity and realise the horror of his deeds; his land became barren, and ultimately Lycurgus was torn into pieces by horses on Mt Pangeus.[25] Sophocles refers to Lycurgus' attempts at hindering dancing women possessed by Dionysus, actions which were punished with madness and imprisonment in a cave.[26] Later authors narrate that Dionysus punished Lycurgus with madness for an attempt to stop the growing of vines in his realm, and made the wretched king kill his own son in an attack of frenzy.[27] According to another version, Lycurgus attacked and killed maenads, chased Dionysus, was eventually captured by the god and finally crucified for his misdeeds.[28]

Lycurgus' half-brother Boutes was also struck with madness by Dionysus for offending the god's devotees: in a fit of frenzy, Boutes threw himself into a well.[29] Antiope was another victim of Dionysus' wrath: she was badly mistreated by Dirce, and after her sons had avenged their mother's humiliation, Dionysus punished Antiope with madness and the urge to wander through the country, but ultimately allowed her to be cured.[30] The reason for Dionysus' anger is hinted at in the fragments of the lost Euripides' tragedy *Antiope*: Dirce was one of his bacchants.[31]

No less famous than Lycurgus were Pentheus king of Thebes and his mother Agave, whose horrifying fate was dramatised by Euripides in the *Bacchae*, as well as by Aeschylus in the lost tragedies *Xanthriae* and *Pentheus*.[32] Dionysus was humiliated by his relatives: his aunt Agave spread a rumour that Dionysus' mother Semele had an affair with a mortal rather than with Zeus, and his cousin Pentheus tried to prevent the women of Thebes from participating in Bacchic rites, when the god returned to his mother's city and induced the people to worship him. Even the miracles performed by Dionysus did not persuade the haughty king who ridiculed the god as an imposter and charlatan, though Agave with her sisters and other women did not resist the god of ecstasy, and willingly participated in his rites. Pentheus was persuaded to spy on the bacchants, wearing female garments, and was easily spotted by his wretched mother, who in the state of Bacchic possession[33] mistook her son for a lion whelp and tore him asunder. Having returned to Thebes carrying her son's disembodied head, Agave recovered her senses, and went into exile. Thus, the proud relatives who slandered Dionysus and his mother were horrendously punished by the god.

Euripides has Dionysus offer Pentheus several chances to acknowledge his divinity, but the king is too arrogant to heed even to his grandfather Cadmus and the wise Tiresias. Pentheus was insane before his madness became obvious to all, for only a madman could decline the advice of his seniors and stubbornly refuse recognition to a god.[34] In due course, Dionysus ruthlessly made Pentheus' frenzy visible by forcing him to rush to the mountains after the bacchants.[35] In the *Bacchae*, the king's *mania* is depicted realistically, including such details as his subjective bizarre feelings of double vision, hallucinations, and delusions of supernatural force,[36] which gradually developed into the characteristic behaviour of a bac-chant, oblivious of his real situation.[37] Then, when Pentheus abandoned himself to the Bacchic frenzy, the god pronounced him sane: 'Your previous mental state was not sound, but now you have the thoughts you ought to have.'[38] Pentheus' real madness was therefore his insolent reluctance to recognise the laws of human existence; when finally he renounced his adherence to rationality and followed the call of the ecstatic god, he became sober and wise – but too late. Pentheus was doomed, for he failed to accept the boundaries of his mortality, rejecting the basic principle known to every Greek: forgetting that he was just a mortal, the king dared to challenge a god, which was utter madness. Quite expectedly, Pentheus was punished with death, but it was preceded by the intricate humiliation of losing his mind and yielding to the will of his foe.

The Bacchic possession of Agave was of a different order: she and her sisters acted like the other women of Thebes, but only for Agave was the participation in the Bacchic rites fatal. The contrast between the guilty sisters of Semele and the rest of the bacchants, who were innocent and returned home undamaged, is most remarkable and will be discussed shortly. The god made his point clear: his foes were destroyed by their madness.

Dionysus and destructive collective *mania* in myth

Although Dionysus inflicted madness upon many individuals, his favourite way of penalising the mortals was by striking whole communities or groups of people with insanity. The popular story of the suicidal frenzy of the pirates, who humil-iated Dionysus by taking him as prisoner, was immortalised by Execias.[39] The myth of Icarius and Erigone served to account for the rite performed in Athens on the third day of the Anthesteria, when girls swung on trees which could later be decorated with hanging figures and masks.[40] Dionysus arrived in Attica, where wine was still unknown, and was welcomed there by Icarius, whom he thanked by giving him a goat-skin full of wine. Icarius shared this gift with his neighbours, who became drunk, suspected Icarius of poisoning them and beat him to death. Icarius' daughter Erigone found her father's body under a tree, and in despair hung herself on it. Dionysus revenged this double death by striking the maidens of Athens with suicidal madness, and the epidemic of hanging was stopped only after the Pythia had instructed the Athenians to institute a festival in honour of Icarius and Erigone.[41]

In another myth, Coresus, Dionysus' priest in Calydon, was rejected by Callirhoë; when the young man prayed to the statue of the god, the god avenged the disgrace of his servant by immediately striking all the Calydonians with frenzy, and sending upon them a deadly epidemic. Dionysus could only be placated by the sacrifice of Callirhoë, who had to be immolated by Coresus the priest. Over-powered by his love for the girl, Coresus killed himself, causing Callirhoë to regret her cruelty and take her own life.[42] In this version, recorded by Pausanias, the myth over-dramatises the situation, making Dionysus responsible not only for the legitimate punishment of the insolent girl, but also for the death of his faithful servant. In any case, in Calydon the whole community was believed to have been driven mad by the god avenging his priest's humiliation.

On numerous occasions, Dionysiac *mania* seized groups of women. The three daughters of Minyas, the founder of Orchomenus, resisted Dionysus and were maddened by the god; while in his grip, they seized and devoured the son of one of the sisters, Leucippe. Dionysus gave the Minyads, similarly to Pentheus, a chance to repent and recognise his power, but was ruthless when rejected twice.[43] The story was probably dramatised by Aeschylus in the *Xantriae*.[44]

The horrible frenzy of the Proetids and women of Argos, who devoured their own children, was often ascribed to Dionysus.[45] Bacchylides is one of the earliest authors to tell the story of the daughters of Proetus, the primaeval king of a city in the Argolis,[46] where Hera was the most prominent deity: the girls boasted that their father's palace was greater than Hera's temple. In this version, Hera drove the Proetids from the palace they were proud of, bonding their mind to a strong overmastering frenzy.[47] The mad Proetids fled to Arcadia, where centuries later their cave was shown.[48] They were cured by Artemis, to whom their father prayed after they wandered in the wilderness for thirteen months.[49] In a fragment of the Hesiodic *Catalogue* referring to the Proetids, the girls imagined that they were cows, and their affliction is called *makhlosunê*, libidinous frenzy, rather than simple *mania*,[50] which aggravated the situation, given the fact that the princesses were still virgins. In fact, in another version of the myth it was Aphrodite rather than Hera who made two daughters of Proetus ran naked through the entire Peloponnesus;[51] Apollodorus politely referred to the Proetids' indecency, saying that they roamed 'in utter disorder.'[52]

In the version current in Hesiod's time and adopted by Diodorus, it was Dionysus who inflicted the madness on all the Argive women: 'Melampous, who was a seer, healed the women of Argos of madness inflicted by Dionysus' wrath,' and received for that two-thirds of the Argolis.[53] In fact, the story that all the women of the country, and not only the daughter of the king, were frenzied, is rather widespread, and attested to since the fifth century.[54] According to Apollodorus, whose account is probably based on that of Hesiod, Melampous took with him young men, and the band chased the Proetids from the mountains in a sort of frenzied dance,[55] a homoeopathic treatment resembling the Corybantic rites and based on prolonged rapid movement. It is noteworthy that during the chase Iphinoe, the elder sister, died, but the other two sisters were cured: chasing away insanity was dangerous, and the victims of possession could lose their life during the treatment. As mentioned above, another early tradition does not refer to Melampous and his cure of the Proetids by either chase or purifications, and attributes the relief to Artemis. Various versions of the healing of the Proetids probably reflect the existence of several traditional healing methods and Peloponnesian cults associated with them.[56] Such components of the story as ecstatic behaviour and the disfiguration of the king's maiden daughters of marriageable age who were eager for sex, their association with animals (cows, particularly connected with Hera) and chasing by a band of young men may indicate connections of the myth to pristine initiation rituals leading to (collective) marriage.[57] The stay in a mountain cave is especially indicative of initiations, since transition rites in Greece were quite often performed in caves.[58] The wandering of the Proetids is reminiscent of maenadic frenzy, and this resemblance might prompt the attribution of their madness to Dionysus at an early date.[59]

In the myth of the Proetids, *mania* of the kings' daughters epitomised the dissolution of normal order. Ritual ecstatic behaviour culminating in marriage, once considered an element of a socially approved rite, began to be perceived as a curse, pollution, and a shameful sickness in the Archaic versions of the myth. Thus, *mania* was turned into a punishment with madness by Hera the goddess of marriage, to be cured by Artemis the goddess of girls' initiations. In any case, in all versions the *mania* of the Proetids is negatively charged, and the cure of female frenzy restores the antithesis to madness, namely the normal social order and the safety of marriage and male dominance.

The list of groups of women driven mad by Dionysus is quite long: the daughters of Eleuther at Eleutherae in Attica were struck with madness for slandering a vision (*phasma*) of Dionysus;[60] as were the women of Chios and Lacedaemon, who were struck by Bacchic frenzy.[61] In this series of myths, the stories of mad violence caused by the wrath of Dionysus function as foundation myths explicating the existing tradition of milder rituals: D. Obbink calls them 'inverted charter myths.'[62]

Greek gods could punish mortals by various plagues, not necessarily madness.[63] Offending communities could be disciplined by means of drought, epidemics, earthquake, and other catastrophes. Dionysus used insanity almost exclusively, and in this respect was unique: his preference for *mania* as penalty reflects the association of this god with madness *par excellence*.

Bakchai and bakchoi in myth, poetry, and art

In contrast to destructive or self-destructive rage with which Dionysus punished mortals who dared to oppose him, frenzy of those who willingly bowed to his power was usually beneficial and could bring about much happiness, but ecstasy enthused by the god was still called and perceived as *mania*. Female followers of Dionysus, in myth and in real life, were often dubbed maenads, *mainades*, literally 'mad' or 'frenzied women,' the word deriving from the same root as the noun *mania* and the verb *mainomai*, 'to rage, be mad.'[64] Other terms for female ecstatic worshippers of Dionysus vary in different areas: *lênai* ('belonging to the wine-press') are attested to in many places;[65] *thuiades* 'frantic dancers' belonged to Delphi, *bassarides* were so called because of the fox skins they wore, and *klôdônes* and *mimallones* were Macedonian words for maenads.[66] The essence of the image is laconically formulated by Timotheus of Miletus, active in the late fifth–early fourth century: 'Frantic dancer, inspired by Phoebus, mad woman, raging rabidly.'[67]

Homer was the first to refer to maenads. At the end of the *Iliad*, upon receiving the news of her husband's death Andromache rushed through the palace 'like a maenad.' This word does not occur elsewhere in Homer, but the poet seems to be familiar with 'frenzied' women associated with Dionysus, and the nurses of 'mad' or 'raging' Dionysus were probably envisaged as ecstatic, as well.[68] The earliest fully fledged reference to a maenad is in the Homeric hymn to Demeter, where the goddess, mad with happiness when she received her child back, 'rushed like a maenad on a mountain shadowed by a forest.'[69] Here, a woman's insane behaviour is linked to running in a mountain forest to create an easily recognisable image of the maenad.

Dionysiac madness was prominent in tragedy before Euripides. The plot of Aeschylus' *Pentheus* anticipated that of Euripides' *Bacchae*.[70] Especially noteworthy is Aeschylus' tetralogy *Edonians, Bassarae, Youths (Neaniskoi)*, and *Lycurgus*, referring to aspects of the Dionysiac frenzy and placing the events in Thrace. In the *Edonians*, the arrival of Dionysus, associated with the Thracian goddess Cotytto, is depicted as involving much noise and playing cymbals and pipes that 'wake *mania*.' The 'soundscape' of Dionysiac frenzy is 'heavy with terror' (*barutarbês*), and in addition to maddening music includes also horrifying voices, subterranean thunder, and echoes of bulls' bellowing. Even the royal palace becomes '*entheos*' and its roof 'participates in *bakcheia*'; and the god or his attendant is called *ho gunnis*, 'man-woman,' or 'sissy.'[71] In *Xantriae*, Dionysiac frenzy is visited upon either Pentheus or the Minyads and compared to a scorpion's sting that tears one apart.[72] All these fragmentary pieces find their place in the complete picture that the *Bacchae* offer.

Even if not murderous for those who joyfully surrender to the god, in myth and drama Bacchic *mania* is disturbing and menacing. In the *Bacchae*, its destructive force is tremendous: killing Pentheus was only the zenith of a wild hunt leading to *ômophagia*, 'the joy of eating raw meat.'[73] Preceding the dismembering (*sparagmos*) of the human victim, cattle is butchered;[74] goat-killing is also referred to, and at the end of the play the murdered king is perceived by his murderous mother as a slaughtered lion whelp.[75] Dionysus is hailed by the chorus as a bull, snake, or lion, thus envisaged in an animal guise:[76] was it the god being killed by his worshippers during *sparagmos* of cattle, snakes, or other animals? And were the god-fighting Pentheus and Lycurgus symbolically equated to Dionysus?[77]

In any case, during the ecstatic Bacchic rites described in the play, normal social order is inverted in many ways. The overwhelming array of sacrifice in the *Bacchae* extends from moderately abnormal *sparagmos* of cattle to Pentheus' much more aberrant intention to 'sacrifice by killing women in the valley of Cithaeron,'[78] which he did not perform; to the blatantly deviant sacrificial murder of the royal son by his mother;[79] to the even more unthinkable wish of mad Agave to partake in her son's flesh in a sacrificial feast,[80] which too did not transpire. In this grim progression, every stage becomes more distant from normality than the preceding one, and wishes not carried out highlight the madness of the characters uttering them.

During this change in social order, gender conventions are reversed. Women rush out of their homes, roaming and dancing freely in the mountains, hunting like men and tearing apart wild beasts instead of sacrificing domestic animals in a proper ceremony – perhaps re-enacting the killing of the god himself. At the same time, males – and Dionysus among them – wear female clothes, and men are defeated by women in battle, thus making the reversal of normality bi-directional.[81] Transvestism could also advance the process of abandoning one's own personality and becoming *entheos*.[82]

The tale of the Minyads, together with Pentheus' pursuit of the maenads, and Lycurgus' and Boutes' chasing of the god's (ecstatic) nurses seem to constitute a pattern:[83] the pursuer of the women struck with Bacchic madness is cruelly punished with insanity leading to terrible destruction. These myths probably serve as an explanation of the troubling memories of uncanny sacrifices of human victims or their substitutes by ecstatic bands of Dionysus' worshipers. Many of these tales include a chase and conflict between men and women, including battles between the sexes in which women triumph – a clear reversal of normality.[84] 'The polar tension between divine madness and human order . . . [is] acted out in a single ritual':[85] the victim and the perpetrator are almost interchangeable, and the victim often takes on the appearance of the god, whose rites involve his own symbolical sacrifice.

Furthermore, *sparagmos* could be perceived not only as dismembering of the victim by the bacchants, but also as a feeling of being pulled to pieces experienced by the bacchants themselves. Aeschylus' fragment cited above describes Lyssa's feelings while possessed by Dionysus: 'From the feet upwards, I am torn apart (literally, 'I experience *sparagmos*') to the top of my head; a spur in my tongue, I say scorpion's sting.'[86] This terrible image of the goddess of rage who is torn into pieces from within must have been inspired by reports of human bacchants, whose sensation of being consumed by the frenzy which Dionysus instilled was probably very disturbing.

Bacchae, *lênai*, or maenads, clad in animal skins, crowned with ivy and bearing *thyrsi*, symbols of Bacchic possession, as well as the boisterous male companions of Dionysus, are attested to not only in myth and drama. Silens and grotesque dancers make their appearance on Corinthian and Attic sympotic vases in the first decades of the sixth century. Drinking and dancing naked, and usually ithyphallic, satyrs were depicted on contemporary Boeotian ware and interpreted as symbolic of a *kômos*, a band of revellers.[87] From the middle of the century, the *thiasos* replaces the *kômos*, and satyrs are frequently depicted dancing together with females or chasing them, in immediate proximity to Dionysus.[88] These female figures are often unidentified, but as early as in mid-sixth century, a crater by Lydus already featured Dionysus with satyrs and female companions carrying huge serpents and wearing fawn skins (*nebrides*).[89] From 540 onwards it became clear that these female figures were indeed maenads, as they began to be frequently depicted wearing animal skins, either of fawns, *nebrides*, or of felines, *pardalides*.[90] In the third quarter of the sixth century the Amasis Painter portrayed satyrs treading grapes and dancing female figures holding drinking vessels, ivy, as well as killed hares.[91] Flat-nosed satyrs were usually represented with erect phalli, animal ears and horse tails, or with a loin cloth to which leather phalli and animal tails were attached. These figures of mixed nature, half-human and half-beastly, may have represented masked participants in various Dionysiac festivals, ecstatic, theatrical, or telestic, emulating mythological figures or expressing their temporally changed identity by the masks they wore.[92] In any case, the appearance of Dionysus' ecstatic retinue in art in the mid-sixth century at the latest implies that the motif had already been well-known to the public for some time.[93]

During the last third of the sixth century, the repertoire of Attic Dionysiac vases comprised mainly *thiasoi* of dancing maenads and satyrs, and maenads riding animals.[94] The sheer number of vases featuring Dionysiac scenes burgeoned during that period.[95] At the end of the sixth century, the standard complex of maenadic characteristics on red-figure pottery included a wild landscape as a background, the figures wearing animal skins (usually of wild felines),[96] *thyrsi*,[97] handling snakes or other animals, holding wine cups, dancing and playing music, and finally having erotic encounters with satyrs.[98] Maenads are frequently shown with their long sleeves unfolded, hiding their hands, and resembling wings, which indicates that the brooches holding the sleeves in the right place were lost.[99] The wing-sleeves motif, depiction of the maenads as barefooted, their hair left loose – all these signs indicated a halt in decency and propriety, deviation from the social norm, and liminality, easily recognisable by every Greek.[100]

Quite often, the maenads struggle against the harassing satyrs; fighting or succumbing to advancing males, the maenads epitomise a type of sexual behaviour totally opposite to that of Athenian citizen women.[101] Some vases feature the aftermath of *bakcheia*, such as the utmost exhaustion of the maenads.[102]

The alterity and sexual ambiguity of both maenads and satyrs is sometimes emphasised by additional means. For instance, maenads wearing a hunter's *chlamus* depicted along with infibulated satyrs on a rhyton by the Sotades Painter were supposedly perceived as transvestite, engaging in the male activity of hunting, and dangerously aggressive women juxtaposed with sexless men.[103] An Attic cylix features a semi-nude maenad, wearing culottes with an artificial phallus attached, dancing in front of seated Dionysus: could the maenad's ambiguous monstrosity be rendered plainer than by portraying her as a hermaphrodite?[104] Bestiality of the satyrs is highlighted by their grotesquely huge phalli, ridiculous rather than hypervirile, excessive sexual energy and especially by presenting them engaged in sexual activities with animals:[105] they personify an antinomy to an image of a good or at least conventionally self-indulging citizen. In addition, satyrs are sometimes represented cross-dressed as maenads, as another indication of the blurred gender boundaries in the Dionysiac inverted universe.[106] The Bacchic ambiance is often far from being playful: sexual violence and resistance to it, hunting and tearing animals apart, indicated by the way they are handled, imply anxiety and fearful apprehension.

Overt maenadic violence appears on some Attic pieces of the late fifth century, articulating the tendency that was hinted at earlier. On one pyxis, seated Dionysus watches maenads dancing frenetically, one of them carrying on her shoulder a clearly terrified baby, and a pair of maenads tearing apart an animal kid.[107] On a hydria attributed to the Louvre Painter, Dionysus and Ariadne are surrounded by a macabre scene, portraying as it seems the punishment of Dionysus' foes, as well as maenads either holding a human head, carrying a child on her shoulders, as if it were an animal kid, or brandishing a part of an animal in her hand.[108] The god himself could participate in *sparagmos*: an Attic stamnos features transvestite bearded ecstatic Dionysus, clad in female garb and tearing a gazelle in half.[109]

A group of fifth-century Attic vases known as 'Lenaea vases' feature women in twisted ecstatic dance around a mask of Dionysus on a pillar clad in multi-coloured garb, obviously an archaic type of the god's image.[110] In some cases, ecstatic women are represented together with a young animal, apparently the intended victim of *sparagmos*.[111] These women are usually interpreted as participating in a maenadic ritual, at the Lenaea or the Anthesteria.[112] Whatever the particular occasion or occasions represented on these vessels, they all feature 'the experience of coming face to face with the god . . . and it is this that is the peculiarly maenadic experience.'[113] Since these vases were created mostly for the Western market, the cult scene must have been 'readable' for customers outside Athens,[114] which means that conventions of the Dionysiac iconography were very similar throughout the Greek world.

The Derveni crater, dated to ca. 370, offers a masterful depiction of various aspects of Bacchic ecstasy:[115] a scene of the sexual encounter of Dionysus and Ariadne is surrounded by maenads roaming, dancing, and collapsing in one another's embrace, asleep in exhaustion, in addition to maenads tearing apart a small animal.[116] Most maenads are portrayed with their backs arched, their bodies twisted, their chins lifted – the set of characteristics that implies alteration of their consciousness.[117] Two maenads, one falling asleep and the other one handling snakes, are portrayed seated on the vessel's shoulder.[118] The maenad carrying a baby on her shoulder and holding it by the leg is extremely agitated; the posture is similar to that of the maenads carrying infants on late fifth-century vases, and to more common depictions of maenads carrying animal kids.[119]

The emphasis on the ecstatic nature of the *thiasos* is quite pronounced during the second half of the sixth century, especially in the red-figure pottery which appeared after 530.[120] Dionysiac, and in particular maenadic scenes are most common on Attic pottery between 460 and 400.[121] While nearly all Bacchic celebrants on Attic vases may be interpreted as mythological or theatrical depictions, the astounding realism of their frenzied movement, uplifted heads and contorted limbs disclose a keen understanding of the ecstatic state that could only result from the artists' real-life observations.[122] These postures could hardly be invented: psychiatrists consider them as characteristic of dissociative disorders, and modern artists employ them in depictions of individuals in state of possession.[123]

Archaic Attic vases featuring maenads predate the bulk of written evidence on the maenadic *mania*,[124] and many of these vessels were produced for export. The iconographic evidence attests to the familiarity of Attic painters and the general public in other places with *bakcheia*, and maenadism in particular, during the sixth century at the latest, and reflects contemporary ideas on the various aspects of the Dionysiac *mania*.[125]

Bakcheia and gender

In one of the three Homeric hymns to Dionysus, the god is called *gunaimanes*, 'he who drives women mad.'[126] Although in myths many men were punished by Dionysus with insanity, the god was still dubbed 'maker of maenads.'[127] In the ecstatic cult of Dionysus, gender asymmetry is quite obvious, but its diverse modalities and extent are still controversial.

There is much debate on the divergence between literary sources on *bakcheia* which refer almost exclusively to female maenads, and iconographic evidence which attests to a massive male presence in Dionysus' retinue. However, only female members of the Dionysiac *thiasos* are routinely represented in self-abandon, indicated by their twisted poses and heads tossed back and inhuman violence (*sparagmos*), followed by exhaustion and drowsiness. Male participants may be tipsy, sexually excited, semi-bestial, and dancing or moving rapidly, but very rarely display signs of alteration of consciousness. The only male who is rather often portrayed as ecstatic, sometimes even participating in *sparagmos* of animals and babies, is Dionysus himself – the maddener of women.

This contrast is explicated by some as reflecting the difference between real-life ritual, in which female maenads were prominent, and the imaginary mythical past, where the satyrs belonged.[128] Another approach is diachronic and functional, sharply separating the roles of the two sexes: it is argued that during the Archaic and Classical ages, women were prone to the Dionysiac *mania*, while men worshipped the god in bands of revellers, *kômoi*, and men and women started to participate together in the Bacchic rites only during the Hellenistic period.[129] Hellenistic and Roman epigraphic evidence is indeed dominated by male and mixed Dionysiac associations.[130] However, although some Dionysiac rituals were restricted to maenads, male bacchants were present in the cult of Dionysus at a very early stage: female *bakchai* were identified with the (mythological) maenads, whereas male *bakchoi* became satyrs.[131] It is supposed that although male bacchants participated in ecstatic rites during the Classical age, they remained in the shadow of the ideal female *thiasoi*, disguised as satyrs, masks hiding their citizen identity. The adherents of this approach suggest to 'read between the lines' of literary texts in order to assess male involvement in *bakcheia*, assuming that the Classical image of exclusively female bacchants was the only way for the male-dominated society to comprehend the disturbing reality and come to terms with it.[132]

However, the existence of male bacchants was not always concealed or discretely alluded to: evidence on male participation in ecstatic Bacchic rituals during the Archaic and Classical periods is sometimes explicit. In the *Ion*, Xuthus recalls his participation in the *thiasoi* of Bacchus' maenads in Delphi.[133] In the *Bacchae*, Tiresias and Cadmus, bearing *thyrsi* and with *nebrides* on their shoulders, readily join in Dionysiac dances, stating that the god wants honour from everyone, and at the end of the play return 'from the Bacchae.'[134] Nevertheless, male bacchants in literature and art seem to be less prone to *bakcheia* than women. Euripides' Tiresias and Cadmus wear Bacchic costumes and carry rods, follow the protocol of the ecstatic *orgia*, and remain almost sane: they only rejoice in forgetting their old age and know that despite their agedness, dancing in the mountains will not require any effort on their part.[135] On some Athenian vases, decently dressed men appear next to women holding *thyrsi*: they are not yet ecstatic, but seem to be preparing the paraphernalia necessary for an ecstatic celebration.[136] During the later period, even males are occasionally shown ecstatic: for instance, on a crater dated between 400 and 300 and featuring satyrs and maenads, a satyr is depicted with his head tossed back, hand raised and entire body bowed.[137]

There is no lack of historical allusions to male worshipers experiencing *bakcheia*. Heraclitus' list of unholy celebrants of mysteries comprised bacchants of both sexes, *bakchoi* and *lênai*.[138] Male bacchants appear in Herodotus' story of the Scythian king Scyles, who joined ecstatic Dionysiac rites conducted in the streets of Olbia.[139] Another male citizen of Olbia, bearing the Dionysiac name Lenaeus, was greeted with a maenadic cry *euai!* in an inscription on a mirror dated ca. 500, implying that in this northern city, men were involved in ecstatic Bacchic cults at an early date.[140] One more example is perhaps the group of Anacreon, whose poem attests to transvestite comastic celebrations; these revellers were even illustrated on inscribed Attic vases.[141] Demosthenes' account of *teletai* organised by Aeschines' mother in Athens[142] attests to male participation in ecstatic rites comprising Dionysiac elements. Demosthenes consistently uses male forms of adjectives and participles, implying that at least some devotees were men, although their leader was a woman. Ecstatic assemblies of the Corybantes, which were also associated with *bakcheia*, attracted aristocratic Athenians.[143]

The fact that male involvement in *bakcheia* was limited is fairly firmly established. The roles of female and male participants in these rites were perhaps divergent, and while maenads and *thuiades* of the Classical age often represent the women of the city, men engaged in ecstatic rites only privately.[144] One can venture a supposition that it was precisely because of the association of Bacchic ecstasy with the maenads that the men shunned the rites which were considered effeminate. When men joined rites of that nature, because of either piety, or emotional attraction, or both reasons, they often preferred rites which were not simply and overtly Bacchic, but focused on other deities, such as the Corybantes and Sabazius, and featured some initiatory traits.

In sum, the fifth and fourth centuries saw some Greek males participating in Bacchic rites, and they did not strive to conceal their participation in ecstatic celebrations. During the centuries that followed, men appeared in numerous inscriptions of voluntary associations worshipping Dionysus, yet the nature of their cults, when specified or at least alluded to, was only seldom ecstatic,[145] and unequivocal accounts of Bacchic frenzy refer mostly to female worshippers. Although the exact proportion of male and female bacchants will never be known, men clearly constituted a minority among them. Some suggestions concerning this imbalance will be discussed shortly.

The historicity of the savage rites

Another age-long controversy deals with the actual nature of Bacchic rites: to what degree were Greek women in the historical past ecstatic, or did they merely pretend to submit to *mania*?[146] Diodorus of Sicily assumed that the maenads of his times celebrated ecstatic Bacchic rites (*bakcheuein*) in imitation of the maenads 'of old':

> And the Boeotians and other Greeks and the Thracians, in memory of the campaign in India have established sacrifices every other year to Dionysus, and believe that at that time the god reveals himself to human beings. Consequently in many Greek cities every other year Bacchic bands of women gather, and it is lawful for the maidens to carry the thyrsus and to join in the *enthousiasmos*, crying out "Euai!" and honouring the god; while the married women, forming in groups, offer sacrifices to the god and become bacchic and, in general, extol with hymns the presence of Dionysus, in this manner imitating the maenads who, as history records, were of old the companions of the god.[147]

In fact, imitation of mythological maenadic behaviour is the most natural approach which historical maenads could assume: religious rites re-enacting a certain action in its commemoration are too numerous to list them here. Imitation not only does not preclude striving to feel like the commemorated individuals, but on the contrary, encourages or even requires that. Abandonment of the ordinary self and temporary adoption of a different self is the core of ecstasy, and Diodorus' description of his contemporaries entering a state of *bakcheia* by means of mimesis of maenads 'of old' provides a fascinating allusion to a most effective type of driving behaviour. Combined with the use of appropriate attributes, such as the Bacchic rods mentioned in the text, screaming, and running, mental re-creation of the images of ecstatic women facilitated the merger with the prototype and corresponding behaviour.

Diodorus distinguishes between the unmarried and married women. Although both gather into Bacchic bands, the behaviour of the maidens is described with the word *sunenthousiazein*, 'join in the *enthousiasmos*,' whereas the activity of the matrons is called 'becoming Bacchic,' *bakcheuein*. Both verbs imply alteration of consciousness and sensation of 'engoddedness,' the only difference being that *bakcheuein* indicates the name of the god.

Was it simply the shyness of Greek girls and exaggerated care for their modesty that are behind the rare distinction between married and unmarried bacchants? Or perhaps this differentiation was only one of the many expressions of suspicion and anxiety of Greek males facing unchaperoned female citizens? The suggestion that sexual liberty was part of the Bacchic cult is based mostly on scenes depicting the sexual reunion of maenads and satyrs in art, and remains controversial.[148] While the chastity of the maenads is emphasised time and again in the *Bacchae*,[149] the same dramatist in another tragedy puts forward a possibility that a man fathered a son during maenadic celebrations in the vicinity of Delphi.[150] Did sexual promiscuity belong, in the opinion of Euripides and his contemporaries, in the mythical past? In any case, there are no indications, mythological or historical, of the maenads' inebriation – in fact, although they are often painted holding wine vessels, there are no hints even at their consumption of wine. Given initiatory connotations apparent in some myths of virgin princesses struck with madness, it is possible that unmarried girls had to stop short of some parts of the celebrations – in imitation of their immediate mythological prototypes.[151] Following this logic, one cannot rule out secret elements in the Bacchic celebrations of the married women – and in fact telestic overtones are quite usual in the references to Dionysiac ecstatic rites.

Plutarch attributed genuine alteration of consciousness to Delphic maenads whose adventure took place in the fourth century:

> female devotees of Dionysus whom they call *thuiades* were in a state of *mania* and wandering at night accidentally arrived at Amphissa. Since they were very weary and did not return to their mind . . . they remained in the market place . . . falling asleep.[152]

The slumber of the *thuiades* was protected by the women of Amphissa, who ran to the marketplace and guarded the sleeping strangers from a possible harassment by the soldiers stationed in the city. This anecdote praises the sisterly concern of the women of Amphissa and their pious care of the devotees of Dionysus – the god could be ruthless to those who wronged his followers, and the whole city could be penalised. Details regarding the state of mind of the *thuiades* are told in passing, but they account for their lack of orientation when in a state of trance, and the following exhaustion and deep sleep: these women were clearly experiencing *mania*.[153]

Pausanias explains that all the women who were frenzied (*mainontai*) in Dionysus' honour were called *thuiades* in Delphi, and in their madness they roamed on the heights of Parnassus, above the clouds.[154] They were headed by a leader, called *archêis*, whose office had been formally established by Plutarch's time.[155] The noun *thuias* derives from the verb *thuô*, 'to move frantically.'[156] Mythic predecessors of the historical *thuiades* were depicted on one of the gambles of the fourth-century Apollo's temple at Delphi, and their nocturnal frenzied dances are mentioned by Sophocles, hence these rites must have come into existence before the Classical period.[157] The antiquity of these rites is further corroborated by the existence of the month of Thyios, named for the festivals of the *thuiades*, in some calendars of the Peloponnesus and Thessaly.[158] Mountain roaming (*oreibasia*) of the women of Delphi survived till Roman times and took place every other year (*trietêris*) in the winter. The bacchants going to the mountain peaks in the winter exposed themselves to no small risk: Plutarch says that they were caught by a snowstorm once and had to be rescued.[159] On their way to the peaks of Parnassus, the *thuiades* stopped in the Corycian cave, belonging to the nymphs, whose proverbial ability to madden mortals is discussed in Chapter 5. Thus, exclusively female ecstatic rites in Dionysus' honour appear to have been celebrated on the Parnassus for hundreds of years, and they did not become 'routinised' and formal even at Plutarch's time. However, these women are definitely not the heroic maenads of Euripides: they were exhausted rather than supernaturally unaffected by fatigue, fell asleep in a marketplace instead of taking towns by force, and needed to be rescued by males instead of being self-sufficient: in their *bakcheia*, the *thuiades* perform extraordinary feats, but they are not super-human.[160]

Quite remarkably, the Athenians sent a delegation of women to the Delphic festival of Dionysus, tradition which supposedly existed in the fifth century.[161] Every second year a group of Athenian women was requested by the city to endure a tough experience of mountain roaming, away from their homes and guardian males. Nothing is known about the principles that determined how particular women were chosen for this mission, but two corollaries are certain. First, under the harsh circumstances of the winter in the mountains, at least some Athenian *thuiades* experienced alteration of consciousness and could give an account of their adventure after returning home. Second, these delegations were organised by the polis, and the women represented the Athenian civic community: they were neither private individuals nor a marginal group. All in all, Athenians of the Classical period received first-hand information on *bakcheia*, and the polis as such sponsored ecstatic activities.

In some places the female worshippers of Dionysus were exposed to extreme suffering and pain. The Minyad story is told by Plutarch as an aetiological myth explaining the local rite of the pursuit of the maenads by a priest of Dionysus at the festival of Agrionia.[162] In Hellenistic Boeotia festivals of Agrionia including female participation were celebrated in several places and are attested to epigraphically.[163] In Strabo's days, mountain roaming associated with possession was still common in the Greek world; as an example, the geographer refers to Prusa in Phrygia.[164] Ritual violence towards women is attested in Argolis, where in Pausanias' time women were flogged during a festival of Dionysus on alternative years, 'just as Spartan boys in honour of Orthia.'[165]

Pentheus' tragic end and the myth of the Minyads hint at the possibility that the bacchants killed and devoured not only animals, but humans as well. In another myth, dramatised by Aeschylus in his *Bassarae*, Thracian maenadic companions of Dionysus known as *bassarides* tore Orpheus into pieces, allegedly because of his misogyny.[166] Later tradition depicts them as biting one another and devouring one another's flesh when possessed by Dionysus, their cannibalism halted only by killing the guilty women.[167] In vase paintings, from the late sixth century onwards, scenes of *sparagmos* portraying maenads and Dionysus himself brandishing parts of animal or human bodies, are not infrequent; the absence of *ômophagia* follows an artistic convention preventing depictions of eating.[168] These vases present mythological or theatrical scenes, but as argued above, their realism is probably based on the painters' personal familiarity with the subject.

Several ancient authors believed that in the past, killing human victims in Dionysus' honour occurred not only in myth, but also in real life. Tearing to pieces (*sparagmos*) and eating raw meat (*ômophagia*), the peak of ecstatic Bacchic rites, are referred to by Plutarch.[169] In at least one case, a priest of Dionysus performed a ritual killing of a woman descending from the Minyads during the festival of Agrionia in Orchomenus: a zealous priest slew a woman, seemingly while re-enacting the culmination of the cruel ritual which was performed by his distant forefathers and politely avoided among the civilised Boeotians of Plutarch's days.[170] The same author, citing a fourth-century authority, narrates that before the battle of Salamis, following the demand of a seer, Themistocles sacrificed three noble Persian youths to Dionysus Ômêstes.[171] Even if this story is dismissed as a fourth-century invention, the choice of the god who had no particular connection to naval warfare is telling: Dionysus Ômêstes was worshipped on Lesbos, where human sacrifices to Dionysus are attested to by at least two independent sources.[172] Theophrastus believed that Bacchic rites in the past involved cannibalism,[173] and Pausanias related a tale of sacrificing boys at Potniae in Dionysus' honour in Boeotia, until the human victim was replaced by a goat.[174] On Tenedos, the human sacrifice to Dionysus was substituted by a calf: a cow that was in calf was treated like a woman, and as soon as she had calved the people of Tenedos sacrificed the newborn to Dionysus the Man-slayer (*Anthrôporrhaistês*), after which the killer was pelted with stones and driven away until he reached the sea.[175] In this case, the man who performed the sacrifice was treated as a polluted murderer, resembling in this respect Agave, who left her city after having unwittingly killed her son.[176] Thus, even when human sacrifice became obsolete, its memory persisted. It is possible to question the Greek memory of the past and maintain that it was construed to match later ideas, but without a doubt, in the opinion of some educated Greeks from the fourth century onwards, *sparagmos* was an extremely disturbing experience, reminding them of human sacrifice.

There is no way to know whether the act of ritually tearing apart men actually took place in Bacchic cults some time in prehistory, but it is important that it was deemed possible: dreadful violence remained associated with Bacchic rituals, notably with the Bacchic *mania*. Partaking in the raw meat of the victim meant partaking in the vitality of another being, the animal's meat being symbolic of human and maybe even divine flesh. Furthermore, devouring raw meat had perceptible connotations, symbolising a state of primaeval barbarity and even bestiality.[177] The key elements of *sparagmos* are contradictory to the regular sacrificial practice: the killed animal was wild rather than domesticated, it was torn apart instead of being properly slaughtered, and its meat was eaten raw rather than cooked. Once again, the dominance of women in these practices underscored the overall abnormality of maenadic behaviour. As such, it was congruent with other elements of the ecstatic Bacchic ritual, articulating the reversion of the social order – with the ultimate aim of endorsing the excising authority by reminding the community of the horrors of its antithesis.

Inscriptions of the Hellenistic period also refer to Dionysiac frenzy. A third-second century epigram from Miletus commemorates 'the holy priestess' of the citizen *bakchai*, who led them to the mountains and performed other rites 'on behalf of the polis' (*pro poleôs*).[178] The final line of the Bacchic priestess' epigram, affirming that she 'knows her share in the beautiful,' seems to allude to the association of ecstatic rites with mystery initiations.[179] A fourth-century sacred law from Lesbos attesting to nocturnal celebrations (*pannuchis*) restricted to women who handled *thyrsi*, is also likely to refer to maenadic rites.[180]

Another Milesian inscription, dated to 276/5, records the existence of priests and priestesses leading *thiasoi*, public and private; the priestess of the polis enjoyed the right 'to throw in the *ômophagion*' and assemble her *thiasos* before the priestess of the other, presumably private, *thiasos*.[181] The enigmatic expression 'to throw in the *ômophagion*' probably means 'to throw the piece of raw meat into the crowd of celebrants.'[182] It is impossible to know whether a still palpitating animal or an already dead victim was to be divided into pieces and eaten raw,[183] but there is no reason to downplay the savagery of this act, substituting dismembering and raw-eating by the more polite 'handling of raw meat' to make it suitable for civilised Greek ladies.[184] Would drenching in bull's blood during the Roman *tauroctonia* be more palatable? The feeling that *ômophagia* is too ferocious and inappropriate appears to reflect the sensibilities of modern scholars rather than those of ancient bacchants.[185] The effect of awesome rites was attained precisely owing to the mixture of excitement and dread that are at the core of Bacchic rapture.[186]

In conjunction with *ômophagia*, other Dionysiac celebrations are also mentioned in the Milesian sacred law, including perhaps mystery rites.[187] The two inscriptions demonstrate that in Hellenistic Miletus, state festivals in honour of Dionysus, that could hardly be secret, as well as mystery and ecstatic rites, were conducted by the same priests and priestesses. The reason for issuing the new regulations remains obscure, but it may be supposed that informal priests and priestesses might have been endowed with charisma and the ability to dominate ecstatic rites that the sacred officials of the polis lacked, and the regulations were necessary to affirm the status of the priests of the state.[188] It is significant that only female priestesses were deemed capable of throwing in the *ômophagion*, which demonstrates that the polis acknowledged the leading role of women in the ecstatic Dionysiac worship.

An inscription from Magnesia engraved in the Imperial period but containing a text traceable to the third century BC at the latest, narrates a fascinating story of a prodigy – an image of Dionysus discovered inside a broken tree, – an embassy to Delphi following this sign, and the Pythia's command to establish the cult of Dionysus in the city.[189] In order to do so, the people of Magnesia were instructed to erect temples 'for the joy of *thyrsi*' (*thursocharoi*), and bring maenads of the bloodline of Ino, Cadmus' daughter, from Thebes. The pious Magnesians brought three maenads and founded three *thiasoi* – the names of the maenads and the *thiasoi* are recorded on the stone. Most significantly, maenadic *orgia* were supported by the supreme authority of the Delphic oracle, which means that these rites were considered indisputably beneficial for the enquiring city.[190] On the back side of the stele the person who erected it and 'inscribed the ancient oracle' refers to himself as *archaios mustês*, 'long-standing initiate.' Thus, the tradition of maenadism and attribution of its origin to Thebes and the family of Cadmus is juxtaposed in this inscription with mystery initiations.

In addition, the prophetic aspect of the cult of Dionysus was not negligible. Euripides has the wise Tiresias observe that 'the ecstatic and the manic (*maniôdes*) have mantic powers (*mantikê*) in large measure. When the god enters someone in force, he causes him in madness to predict the future.'[191] Euripides appears to mean *mania* and prophecy in general, rather than Bacchic frenzy and oracular sanctuaries of Dionysus.[192] However, Tiresias' observation regarding Dionysiac prophecy remains true: in the only oracular shrine of Dionysus in Greece, at Amphicleia in Phocis, prophecy was given by a divinely inspired priest in a state of possession (*katochos*); on Mt Pangaeum in Thrace a priestess uttered prophecies, 'like in Delphi,' that is, in an ecstatic state. Other Bacchic rites, described as *orgia*, were also celebrated in Amphicleia.[193] In the *Bacchae*, the chorus of maenads even foresees the future on the scene,[194] prophecy and frenzy enthused by Dionysus were tightly tied together.

The unity of these divergent kinds of *mania* is forcefully expressed in Timotheus' line cited above: 'frantic dancer, inspired by Phoebus, mad woman, raging rabidly.'[195] It cannot be accidental that in Delphi, where Apollo reigned – and gave prophecy – for nine months, leaving his abode to Dionysus for the winter, the *thuiades* became active exactly when the Pythia was silent. Like the two divine half-brothers who shared the same temple but never met there, the *thuiades* and the Pythia represent two distinct types of possession – different, but sharing nevertheless a common realm, of becoming 'engodded.' In this respect, it may be noteworthy that the Pythia was chosen from the women of the area of Delphi,[196] who seem to have had much practice in alteration of their consciousness. Nothing is known about the criteria for the selection of Apollo's mouthpiece, but I wonder whether abilities of certain Delphic matrons as bacchants did not influence the choice in their favour. In any case, on multiple occasions the Pythia urged introduction of Bacchic rites and interfered with their performance.[197]

Two important questions can be addressed only to a certain extent. First, the geographical and chronological distribution of ecstatic Bacchic rites. There is historical and epigraphic evidence on maenadic activities in Boeotia beginning from the Classical period, and epigraphic data on such activities in Hellenistic Ionia; in addition, myths about maenads in the Peloponnesus reflected perhaps some reality. Athenians who sent their *thuiades* to Delphi must have been familiar with the experience. Male and female ecstatic worshippers of Dionysus were a common sight in Ephesus at about 500, as were male bacchants who were active in Olbia in the fifth century. Images of maenads on the Lenaea vases, purchased in Magna Graecia, were probably meaningful to the public there. These testimonies demonstrate that ecstatic Bacchic experiences were attested to in the Archaic period and widespread in the Classical Greek world; although there is no data on each and every Greek polis, it can be surmised that the extant evidence reflects the real state of affairs only partially, and ecstatic Bacchic rites were celebrated in many Greek cities.

The second question deals with the actual proportion of the population that was personally involved in these celebrations, and is even more difficult to answer. Clearly the *thuiades* represented a small segment of Athenian women, but we have no way of knowing how many of the women of Delphi participated in *oreibasia*. In Olbia, Scyles belonged to a group, but there were other citizens who did not join it. On the other hand, the intervention of the polis in Magnesia and in Miletus indicates that a considerable number of citizens were involved in ecstatic Dionysiac rites. It can only be guessed what happened in each place at a given time, but it is probable that a substantial number of citizen women, and sometimes even men, participated in Bacchic rites.

These considerations demonstrate that the definition of ecstatic cults of Dionysus as 'private' or even 'sectarian,' in contrast to 'public' Dionysiac agricultural festivals,[198] is imprecise and misleading. The dichotomy between private and public spheres is a modern invention rather than a reality of ancient Greek life.[199] However, even in modern terms, delegations of Athenian women travelling to Delphi, Boeotian, and Delphic biennial celebrations, Bacchic *thiasoi* of Magnesia, and many other Dionysiac rites and pertaining regulations can hardly be defined as private initiatives. Secrecy is not necessarily incompatible with polis cults, the Eleusinian mysteries and the Thesmophoria offering excellent examples. In contrast, voluntary participation was indeed characteristic of Bacchic mystery rites, and Dionysiac initiations and ecstatic rites often merged. Thus, ecstatic Dionysiac rites were not private or public in essence: as we have seen, a whole spectrum, from clearly public ceremonies to voluntary organisations, existed during the Classical period. During the Archaic age, the emphasis seems to have been on community or polis rites, whereas during the Hellenistic period voluntary Dionysiac organisations blossomed alongside polis cults.

To summarise: Bacchic *mania* is attested to not only in myth and art, but also in historical and epigraphic testimonies. A 'reduced' view of maenadism, which allows for such elements as *oreibasia* and ecstatic rites, but cleanses Bacchic *mania* of excessive violence, is accepted nowadays by the majority of scholars.[200] I doubt the assertion that *ômophagia* was improbable in Classical context, but for the time being it is sufficient to conclude that maenadic rites comprised women wandering in the mountains and a spectrum of alteration of consciousness. Furthermore, *bakcheia* was often associated with aspects of initiatory rituals[201] and in some cases with oracle-giving.

The dynamics of the *thiasos*

As we have already seen, in myth and art Dionysus Bacchus was constantly accompanied by a retinue of maenads and satyrs, and in real life he was worshipped by congregations of mortals who called themselves *bakchoi* and *bakchai*; groups of both mortal and immortal revelling followers of Dionysus were known as *thiasoi*.[202] Dionysus' entourage is unique: no other Greek god was represented with a permanent cortege and worshipped by bands of people who identified themselves with the mythical followers of the god and with the god himself.[203] This is not a mere poetic image: ecstatic bacchants approached the divine, becoming 'engodded' (*entheoi*). Having Bacchus inside themselves and feeling temporarily like a god rather than mortal was madness and bliss, a state both frightening and exciting: this was *bakcheia*.

At the beginning of the *Bacchae*, the chorus of Dionysus' Asian followers, his mythic *thiasos*, praises the blessed man who is 'happy in his knowledge of the god's mysteries, lives pure life, and joins his soul to the *thiasos*, performing Bacchic rites in the mountains.'[204] Most notably, these lines highlight the collective nature of alteration of consciousness experienced during Bacchic rites: the activity of the bacchants is defined as *thiaseuein psuchan*, the blessed bacchant literally 'participates in the *thiasos* as regards to his soul,' or 'congregationalises his soul,' to cite E. R. Dodds' rendition of this phrase.[205] Bacchic *thiasos* of ecstatic devotees is essentially a community of souls that leave behind their daily routine to merge in the god-enthused joy. Abandoning one's personality would be considered alteration of consciousness for us and *mania* for the Greeks, and the experience of the thrilling unity within the *thiasos* was perceived as unity with the god.[206]

In the *thiasos*, the individual temporarily abandons his – or usually her – own desires, subdued by the common will of the group. Maenads portrayed in the *Bacchae* act in unison, their group cohesion ensuing from group arousal, perceived as collective possession by the god.[207] The *thiasos* is often compared to a group of animals, a flock of birds or a pack of hunting hounds.[208] The maenads merge with the environment, 'sharing their Bacchic frenzy with the mountain and beasts,'[209] and abandoning not only their personality, but their human nature altogether: submissive housewives become predators. The somatic features of the bacchants remain recognisable, but their souls are seized by the god: the bodies of the bacchants are instruments allowing their souls to 'participate in the *thiasos*.' This mental transformation was signified by wearing animal skins, which were symbolic of two aspects: becoming maenads, women turned into animals (and even suckled animal kids); as animals, they could even feel hunted, as Agave clearly did, crying 'We are hunted!'[210] In addition, these animals were often thought of as violent: the maenads were clad in *pardalides*, the skins of predators, more often than *nebrides*, the skins of successfully hunted animals.[211]

Furthermore, the bestiality of the maenads and their fierce violence are paralleled by the animal features of their male counterparts, the satyrs and silens, and their unrestricted sexual aggression. Other gods also contribute to the frenzy of bacchants of both sexes: ever-excited satyrs and silens were under the spell of Eros, while Euripides' maenads were 'Lyssa's hunting dogs,' and in Aeschylus' *Xanthriae* the goddess of wolfish rage 'inspired the bacchants.'[212] Euripides seems to be uncertain about the relation between Lyssa's frenzy and Dionysiac madness: the two states are contrasted more than once, but they also merge not unfrequently, when Lyssa is associated with the maenads, and Heracles' murderous rage is defined as *bakcheia*.[213]

Maenadic experiences described by Plutarch in the passages cited above lasted for many hours, at least a day and a night and the morrow; in the *Bacchae*, the women of Thebes left the city for a day and a night, and returned only the next day. The onset of the maenadic madness seems to have been sudden: Dionysus states that he 'stung with madnesses' the women of Thebes, who left their looms and rushed to the mountains.[214] The herdsman begins his detailed account from the morning when they got up from their sleep on fir branches in the forest, bedecking themselves with fawn skins and snakes, and breast-feeding animal cubs; this pastoral picture changed instantly when the women attacked the grazing cattle.[215] It is noteworthy that in the play the violence of the maenads is sometimes provoked by non-bacchants: always led by Agave, they tear apart the cattle after the herdsmen attempt to capture her, and they do the same to Pentheus after he has been spotted spying on them.[216] However, the maenads plundered two townships without any obvious reason, just because they happened to pass in the vicinity.[217] Ominously, the bacchants stole the infants of the townsmen, for an unspecified purpose – perhaps for another *sparagmos*, on their way to the slaughter of a full-grown victim.[218]

The spectators are not told what occurred between the attack on the two towns and the fight with their male citizens, in which the maenads were victorious, and the ill-considered attempt of Pentheus to view the Bacchic rites. It is clear that at a certain point their violence recessed: immediately before the most portentous scene in the tragedy, the maenads 'sat employing their hands in pleasant tasks . . . singing Bacchic songs to each other.'[219] Then a sudden change happened: having heard the Dionysus' command, as a flock of birds they leapt over a torrent, 'maddened by the god's breath,' and began hurling stones at Pentheus and uprooting the tree on which he was perched; Agave did not recognise her son pleading for his life: 'her mouth dripped foam and her eyes rolled: she was not in her right mind but possessed by the Bacchic god.'[220] Agave's violent madness persisted for quite a long time, sufficient to tear a man asunder. Then, still possessed by the god, together with other maenads, she marched to Thebes, carrying a Bacchic wand with the head of the her son fixed on it, and engaged there in several conversations, first with the chorus and then with her father. All during this macabre parade Agave was 'exultant,' proud of her catch and other great deeds she has committed.[221]

Upon her return to Thebes, Agave is met by a chorus of bacchants, this time the foreign followers of Dionysus who came to Greece as his retinue, rather than Theban women who were on the Cithaeron.[222] The chorus perceives the actual world and is aware of Pentheus' death and Agave's misery, whereas Agave still lives in an alternative reality, holding her son's head and thinking it is a lion's head, and displaying common symptoms of madness, such as rolling eyes.[223] The contrast between the sane chorus and the insane mother is very important: apparently no longer violent, Agave is still possessed by the god – while the dancing Asian bacchants are not ecstatic, but only jubilant, and Euripides describes them as *kômos*,[224] 'band of revellers,' rather than *thiasos*, the term he applied to the raging Theban maenads.

Only during the dialogue with her father Cadmus, who knew the dreadful truth, does Agave begin to return to her senses, and this process is presented in detail.[225]

A(GAVE)	What part of this causes you disgrace or pain?
C(ADMOS)	First turn your eye to the heavens.
A.	There! What did you mean that I look at?
C.	Does it seem the same to you or altered?

A.   It is brighter than before and clearer.

C.   Does your mind still feel giddy?

A.   I don't know what you mean. But I am coming somehow to my senses
        and have abandoned my former state of mind.

C.   Will you hear me and answer truly?

A.   Yes: I have forgotten what we said before, father.

C.   To what household did you come at your marriage?

A.   You married me to Echion, one of the Sown Men, they say.

C.   Well, what son was born in that house to your husband?

A.   Pentheus, his father's son and mine.

C.   Whose head do you have in your hands then?

A.   The hunters told me it's a lion's.

C.   Look at it properly: the effort of doing so is slight.

        . . . .

A.   No, in my misery I hold Pentheus' head! . . . Who killed him?

C.   You killed him, you and your sisters.

        . . . .

A.   But how did we get there?

C.   You were out of your wits, and the whole city was possessed by
        Bacchus.[226]

For the present discussion, the fascinating details of Agave's insanity are of particular importance. At the beginning of the conversation with her father, the
poor woman feels as if a veil has been removed from her eyes. Agave's altered
mental state is further articulated not only by her own words ('I am coming somehow to my senses and have abandoned my former state of mind'[227]), but also by
her complete oblivion of her deeds as a maenad.

This conversation is perhaps an example of 'therapy by words' which was
applied in Greece to people suffering from dissociation.[228] One certainly doubts
that maenadic women returning home from the wilderness were met by
empathic wise and sober relatives and restored to reality as gently as Agave
was. However, the situation depicted in the *Bacchae* is certainly exceptional in
its horror, and the use of a sophisticated technique must have created a remarkable effect on the scene.

The realism of this scene invites a vital question: can the *Bacchae* serve as
evidence for real-life behaviour? With some caveats, my answer is positive, based
on the following four foundations. To start with, there are historical accounts
supporting the claim that bands of Greek women possessed by Dionysus rushed
away from their homes to mountain forests. In addition, epigraphic evidence demonstrates that some frightening Bacchic rites were performed in Hellenistic cities
after Euripides' time. Moreover, even if Euripides presented a paradigm rather
than pure reality, it is important as a reflection of the beliefs held by the Athenian
public on the subject of ecstatic activities.[229] Finally, as we'll see shortly, Euripides'
depiction of the dynamics of maenadic experience makes sense from the point of
view of modern research on alterations of consciousness. However, the play

obviously does not seek to give the future generations an accurate account of Bacchic experiences: as a work of art, it had to be persuasive in the eyes of its audience, and it represents ideal *thiasoi* which performed all the actions characteristic of Bacchic behaviour in a *nec plus ultra* form. Plutarch's maenads are not reported to have killed men or cattle, and even the bacchants portrayed on the vases usually carry smaller animals and snakes rather than body parts of cows – or humans.[230] In sum, the play appears to be modelled on real-life observations that could be exaggerated or otherwise modified to suit the dramatist's aims; it cannot be discarded as a fantasy belonging to a fairy-tale world, but is to be treated very carefully in order to distil from it information on the world of reality.[231]

Judging by the *Bacchae*, maenadic experience comprises a long sequence of actions and changing states of mind of women who abandon, both their everyday mind-set, and their individuality: all during the Bacchic experience, the participants' personal traits are obliterated and each worshipper in the *thiasos* acts in total harmony with the others, as part of a band. Wandering in the wilderness lasted for many hours and included a night of slumber under the sky: obviously, the tension of possession could not be maintained at the same level throughout the day; characteristically, the maenads rested and roamed in the wild together, as a group, sharing the same mood and wishes. The state of *bakcheia* includes many abrupt mood changes: in a blink of the eye, blissfully calm maenads pass to horrible fierceness. They did not necessarily foam at the mouth like Agave, this feature belonging to the set of standard symptoms of madness.[232] However, such details as mountains bursting with milk and wine, or the voice of Dionysus, find their place in the realm of hallucination, visual as well as auditory.[233] Almost super-human physical strength, needed to uproot trees and tear apart large living beings, is characteristic of excited states.[234] The band's unbridled aggression, immune to armed resistance, is shown to develop stage by stage: presumably in reality, not every *thiasos* began by killing animals, continued to the destruction of two towns and culminated in slaughtering a man, but gradual ascension of the destructive force is typical of collective violence.[235] Heroic belligerence of the maenads seems to be an integral part of their image and of the inversion of the normality they epitomise.[236] Finally, the scene of recognition contains details manifest in experiences of individuals returning from altered to a baseline state of consciousness, such as blurred vision and amnesia.[237]

Even in the ideal *thiasos* of the *Bacchae*, and notwithstanding their professed dissolution in the band, the behaviour of the maenads is not absolutely identical. The *thiasos* has a leader, Agave, who incites the other women to assault the cattle or Pentheus.[238] It is noteworthy that when the voice of Dionysus was heard in the absolute stillness of the glad, all the maenads but Cadmus' daughters remained deaf to the divine call; having recognised the command of the god, Agave and her sisters ran to fulfil it, and were followed by all the other bacchants, maddened by Dionysus. Thus, the *thiasos* was led by a person endowed by greater receptiveness to possession and proclivity for ecstatic frenzy. Iconographic evidence attests to the awareness of the differences in the depth of the ecstatic surrender between the individuals. Two motives are especially expressive, of a maenad supporting another one, who is visibly much more exhausted, and of maenads in different postures, some of them twisted, while the others are more relaxed.[239] As noted by Plato, the contrast between the genuine *bakcheia* of the few and mere acting of the many was clear to perspicacious observers in antiquity.[240]

This difference between the majority of participants in various Bacchic rites and those who were able to attain ecstatic frenzy is to be kept in mind when trying to determine to what extent polis festivals, such as the Lenaea in Athens and the Agrionia in Boeotia,[241] included genuine ecstatic behaviour rather than role-playing. The reality was probably nuanced: between true madness and sheer pretence there were many grades of arousal. A real-life *thiasos* cold not present a perfect unity, and in that respect differed from the ideal one depicted by Euripides.

Bakcheia from a comparative viewpoint

Much opposition has been expressed to interpretations of *bakcheia* as an instance of cross-cultural ecstatic behaviour: supposedly, this Greek phenomenon has to be studied only inside its unique cultural milieu.[242] However, as observed in the Introduction, various forms of ecstatic possession are too widespread worldwide to leave one the luxury to disregard the etic nature of this phenomenon, although every comparison must be carefully evaluated.

Dionysus' vengeful insanity struck men and women alike, but its benign form was reserved mostly for women. This gender imbalance may reflect the proclivity of women in patriarchal societies to channel their suppressed psychological tension to ecstatic rites. H. Jeanmaire compared maenadic rites and ecstatic sessions held by Egyptian women at the eve of the twentieth century. These comprised music, dismembering a sacrificial ram and drinking its hot blood, followed by blissful recomposure and return to everyday life with a feeling of 'having fulfilled a sort of hygienic prescription.'[243] Feelings of relief and contended delight are indeed sung by the chorus in the *Bacchae*: 'Blessed is he that out of the sea escapes the storm and wins the harbour; blessed he who triumphs over trouble.'[244]

As another parallel to *ômophagia* H. Jeanmaire cites Moroccan groups known as *thâifa*, to which people of both sexes belonged. The *thâifa* assimilated themselves to predators and annually chased animals, mostly of medium size but sometimes even bovines, tore them apart with their bare hands and teeth, and devoured raw meat.[245] It is noteworthy that the Greek maenads wore skins of leopards and foxes and ostensibly hunted with their own hands, and are called 'hounds' by Euripides, therefore identified with predators.

Oreibasia was not over with at the end of pagan antiquity, and in the twentieth century and nowadays, during the May festival of Anastenaria ('sighers') celebrated in Northern Greece, women and girls dance with the men of their villages, and then rush in a state of trance to the mountains, carrying icons of St. Constantine, who as they feel commanded them to follow him. They cross mountain gorges and return home unharmed; they are also able, having attained this trance after hours of ecstatic dancing, to walk barefoot on glowing red coals. During the several days of the festival, they have very little food and sleep, but they hear monotonous music almost continuously. Nowadays as in the past, the Orthodox Church opposes the tradition of Anastenaria as pagan superstition.[246] Thus, untrained women who grew up in patriarchal communities were, and still are, able to survive mountain roaming and perform extraordinary deeds while in a trance-like state, acts they would never dream of when in a regular state of mind.

Anthropological and historical parallels, most notably Italian tarantism, demonstrate that ecstatic dancing is contagious and easily turns even reluctant observers into dancers, whirling against their will.[247] The victims of the irresistible drive ascribed to daemonic possession, men and women alike, danced to exhaustion and experienced alterations of consciousness, which involved extraordinary endurance and visions.[248] Outbreaks of compulsive dancing in Germany begun in the eleventh century, claiming the lives of dozens of people who danced themselves to death. It is noteworthy that dancing epidemics often followed periods of acute distress, such as deluges, hunger, and other plagues, and are interpreted as reaction to extreme conditions in a society where beliefs in possession by the devil or evil spirits were very common. As a result of cultural contagion, in regions where people believed in the dancing curse and in conditions of deep psychological distress, some of them became more suggestible than usual, and entered a trance involving compulsive dancing.[249] In the second half of the sixteenth century, dancing possession reappeared in Germany periodically and reached its maximum intensity towards a specific day, for instance, St. John's or St. Vitus' Day. Thus, states of possession became controlled, and the peak of the dancing period turned into an annual ecstatic festival.[250] The possibility of public abandon and loss of restraint, allowing the release of suppressed misery, had a restorative effect on the participants; to cite G. Rouget, it was 'hysteriotherapy.'[251]

The evolution of St. Vitus' dance from purely spontaneous outbreaks of dancing epidemics into a periodic festival probably hints at the possible manner in which maenadism developed. Cultural contagion may have been responsible for the impulsive eruptions of abnormal behaviour among women, who joined together in the most anti-patriarchal action imaginable in a patriarchal society, leaving home and running away from the protective oppression of men, sometimes even taking on certain aspects of animal behaviour. Such outbursts of female protest, attributed to possession by a supernatural being or beings, are attested elsewhere, from early modern European nuns to contemporary Jakun women of Malaysia.[252] This was 'the way to be mad' for women normally controlled by men, in the Greek and Jakun culture alike.[253] Under social and cultural conditions that had triggered its initial appearance, Greek maenadism probably evolved from occasional epidemics to periodic festivals: spontaneous outbreaks of *mania* were mitigated, but even in the institutionalised form, Dionysiac frenzy was still considered potentially dangerous. If this suggestion is correct, Dionysiac *mania* exemplifies the possibility of socially dreaded pathology evolving into socially acceptable cultic behaviour, ritually resolving – to a certain extant – the problem which triggered the malady.[254] No wonder that the word *mania* encapsulated both meanings, disease as well as beneficial state of mind: this ambiguity was present at all the stages in the history of *bakcheia*.

I don't claim that there is any continuity or connection between ancient Greek and modern rites, Greek, Moroccan, or Italian. The comparisons cited above serve to illustrate three points. First, they demonstrate that in several modern communities around the Mediterranean, women participated or still participate in ecstatic rites involving eating raw meat and mountain-roaming: maenadism does not need to be artificially cleansed of 'excessive savagery' in order to fit into our picture of the civilised world of the ancient Greek city.

In addition, the effect of participation in the ecstatic rites is beneficial: after the fierce outburst and period of consciousness alteration, the devotees returned to their routine refreshed. By channelling strain, especially prominent in subdued women in patriarchal societies, collective ecstasy resolves psychological tension and brings about feelings of peace and satisfaction. In Greece, the complex of recurrent fits of compulsive dancing in the wilderness appears to have been considered as periodic visitations – epidemics – by Dionysus, the god who makes his presence evident through possession.

Finally, ritual reversal affirms the norm: the inverted gender roles of the bacchants emphasise the perpetuity of traditional gender roles in the male-dominated society.[255] On the one hand, women roaming in the wild, hunting men and – according to myth – even fighting and killing them and destroying towns, and on the other hand, men wearing female clothing: this behaviour emphasised the norms and delineated their limits. To conclude: temporary *mania* served to sustain normal restrained behaviour, of women in particular, and was therefore not only tolerated, but even encouraged by the communities: women safely remained 'the second sex.'[256]

Aspects of physiology and psychology of *bakcheia*

Bakcheia involves enormous physical efforts, which could be conceived as superhuman, but are actually attested in humans in altered states of consciousness. It is not surprising that women, who were able to uproot trees in the highlands, endure the winter cold without any preparation, and supposedly without supplies, were so fatigued that they could fall asleep in the middle of a foreign city. Exhaustion from excessive movement is one of the methods of manipulation of consciousness.[257] When coupled with hunger and dehydration, exertion could easily bring about alteration of consciousness, including audial and visual hallucinations, abnormal physical resilience, etc.[258]

Other driving behaviours could enhance the effects of exertion. Crying simultaneously '*eis oros*' ('to the mountain') and *euhoi*, and the use of 'mind-altering' musical instruments, such as the tambourine and *aulos*, could bring about ecstatic states.[259] An Attic cylix features a cartoon-like image: first a satyr playing an *aulos* to a seated demure maenad, then two satyrs mesmerising a maenad with their dance, and finally (the same) maenad is depicted raving, a panther's skin on her shoulders: music and frenetic dance have worked, and the maenad has become ecstatic.[260] This sequence is dubbed 'initiation of a maenad,'[261] and in fact can be regarded as a *thronôsis* of the maenad. It demonstrates graphically the overlap between Bacchic ecstatic and initiatory ceremonies, which ensues from quite a number of written sources.

The nocturnal setting of many Bacchic celebrations and the flickering torch lights in the dark were also effective means of consciousness manipulation.[262] The typically maenadic head tossing, often portrayed in art, is not only a visible symbol of alteration of consciousness, but also a method of its induction. Bacchic women in Delphi were called *thuiades*, frantic dancers: intensive physical activities, roaming in the wild and frantic dancing in particular, are effectively used for the manipulation of consciousness.[263]

Another important factor is the human ability to imitate the behaviour of others unintentionally, often not even being aware of this simulation. This ability is to a considerable extent developed due to mirror neurons, which make us empathise with the emotions and sensations of other people: in a word, these neurons blur the border between the self and others. Normally, the inhibitory circuit suppresses unwanted simulation, but even in people with undamaged inhibition the mirror-neuron system sometimes takes over, and we clench our fists while watching a dramatic episode in a movie, for example.[264] In a state of intense arousal, when control and inhibition are low, one's consciousness merges with that of the group: this is the transformation that Euripides called *thiaseuein psuchan*, when the bacchant 'congregationalises her (or his) soul.'[265]

In this context, modern research on the nocebo effect is noteworthy. This effect is the opposite of placebo: it causes sickness or even death by mere expectation of a contact with a certain agent or substance, especially as a response to a shared exposure of a group to a stressful social context. It is important to emphasise that a 'real' causal agent is not needed for a group to react in a similar negative way to a nocebo: for example, a large number of employees in an office can fall ill following exposure to a perfectly harmless, but strange smell. Such sociogenic outbreaks are now considered to be more common than estimated previously.[266] Given the profusion of driving agents and anticipation of the trieteric festival, an epidemic of temporary *mania* among the women in a Greek city is not surprising.

Furthermore, maenadic behaviour was probably learnt, and as observed in the Introduction, learning can render consciousness manipulation relatively accessible. According to Diodorus, teenage girls – 'maidens' – participated in maenadic rites.[267] The Ferrara crater features two girls imitating the movements of adult women, perhaps their mothers; E. Keuls describes them as 'apprentice mad-women.'[268]

Alteration of consciousness of the participants in the Bacchic rites was expressed in a number of symptoms. The factors just mentioned triggered endorphin release, which could cause the feeling of happiness and induced hallucinations, including gustatory (the taste of milk and honey) and olfactory (sweet smell), referred to by Euripides in the *Bacchae*.[269] Auditory hallucinations are perhaps hinted at by such epithets of Dionysus as *Bromios* (Thunderer), or in contrast by the total silence 'heard' by the bacchants.[270] Visual hallucinations experienced by the bacchants ranged from images of vines to apparitions of the bull-like god, discussed in detail above.

In the state of Bacchic *mania*, perception was changed: on the scene, Pentheus saw two suns, and Agave mistook her son for a lion whelp, her father having to exert much effort to return her to the world of actuality; in real life, the women of Delphi described by Plutarch were absorbed in their *mania* and entirely indifferent to their environment. The transvestism and reversed gender behaviour of Dionysus and his retinue may reflect the change in the attitude of the ecstatic worshippers to their own gender: in the state of *mania*, gender differences became unimportant.[271] Gender ambiguity could be conceptualised as (anti)-social by observers and *post factum* by experiencers themselves – while possessed by the god, they lived the feeling of totality and did not really care about their gender roles. Modern research demonstrates that alteration of consciousness changes, sometime dramatically, the attitude to the world both within and outside of the experiencer. Furthermore, collective suffering and physical pain, from the cold, wounds, and exhaustion, are known to provide psychological relief and increase the identification of a participant in extreme rites with the group.[272]

In addition, studies of hypnotic analgesia and dramatic improvements in strength and endurance of hypnotic patients[273] may be important for the understanding of maenadic behaviour. Hypnosis, and in particular self-hypnosis, can be introduced when the subject is most vigorously active, and produces undeniable alterations of consciousness.[274] Given the collective mutually enhancing *mania* of the maenads, their insensibility to pain and ability to perform fascinating, almost super-human, physical feats can be explained as resulting from the alteration of their consciousness. Again, the maenads' belief in fact that they were possessed was of major importance. As J. F. Kihlstrom observes, 'there is enough research on the "self-fulfilling prophecy" to lend credence to the idea that a person's belief that he or she is stronger might actually lead to enhanced performance on tasks of strength and endurance.'[275]

Interaction between ecstatic behaviour and stress has been extensively studied during the recent years. Violent forms of spirit possession are interpreted by some experts in medical anthropology as 'resistance,' a form of reaction to extremely stressful situations.[276] Even in its mild forms, such as Pentecostal worship, ecstatic behaviour has a moderating influence on stress levels and adaptation.[277]

The bacchants are time and again described as blessed and joyful. Their happiness results from abandonment of their normal identity, meaning liberation from social demands, memories, and troubles, as well as a suspension of intelligent control. Alteration of consciousness allows acute sensation of timelessness, a minute of joy that is eternal.[278] These are perhaps the reasons for worshipping Dionysus as the Liberator, *Lusios*, and especially for the feeling of heavenly bliss experienced by the bacchants.

At the beginning of this chapter I argued that Dionysus Bacchius was the god of *bakchoi*, and ecstatic behaviour of humans preceded the concept of the god of ecstasy. The findings of the whole chapter square well with the insights of R. N. McCauley and E. T. Lawson on the psychological foundations of ecstatic cults:

> new rituals [involving extremely high levels of sensory pageantry] erupt, . . .
> and they are inevitably propelled away from the first attractor. Construing

the resulting rituals in terms of special agent form is how the conceptual scheme *accommodates* rituals with such high levels of sensory pageantry.[279]

In ancient Greece, widely spread and genuine psychological motivations brought about ecstatic phenomena that were subsequently associated with the cult of Dionysus, who began to be called Bacchius. Similar developments in many other societies were persecuted and oppressed. In Greece, the opposition to the uncontrollable behaviour of the bacchants was limited and did not succeed in subduing their disorderly celebrations or in splitting the polis communities: *bakcheia* belonged to the mainstream.

Conclusions

The clue to Bacchic *mania* is in the realisation that the destructive and beneficial effects of ecstatic possession intermingle, and it seems that in antiquity this was intuitively grasped, reflected in myth, and presented on the stage by Euripides in the *Bacchae*. This tragedy discloses the playwright's understanding that ecstatic states are inherent to human nature and it is sheer folly to suppress them; Pentheus was mad when he acted so, and began to think soundly only when he dropped his resistance – too late for himself. In contrast, the women of Thebes, as well as Cadmus and Tiresias who willingly submitted to the Dionysiac possession, suffered no harm. To quote R. S. Kraemer: 'It is insane to be sane, sane to be insane.'[280] Mortals who eagerly surrender to the divinely inflicted madness will find in it the greatest joy and return to normality relieved of their grief; those unwilling to succumb will be maddened, but with disastrous consequences: Dionysus is 'most terrible and most gentle to men.'[281]

Collective ecstatic *mania* was inherently dangerous, at least in two respects. First of all, in the state of the possession norms of social control were suspended, and horrible acts of violence might be committed. This state would be threatening enough by itself, but the accompanying blurring of reality and imagery could bring about fatal consequences. In myth and in real life, people possessed by Dionysus tore apart animals; in myth bacchants tore apart human beings as well. No wonder that maenadism and especially the uncanny rites of *ômophagia* troubled the Greeks who vindicated contemporary practices as a commemoration of past events: destructive energies that exploded in women butchering animals with their bare hands must have been frightening. Dionysiac *mania*, involving a break away from reality and radically abnormal, even violent behaviour, filled people with awe.

Another expression of the suspension of normal order was the inversion of gender roles. Male authority was threatened by women leaving their homes and abandoning themselves to experiences that at least in some places remained beyond the reach of men. Male suspicions and horrors gave rise to a whole series of images of mad women, whose derangement was expressed in their aggressiveness, physical force, and refusal to submit to male sexual demands. These creatures were portrayed as liminal and semi-bestial. However, by attributing terrible atrocities to the maenads, the myth brought *ad extremum* not only a male dread of ecstatic women,[282] but also a female fear of loss of control and acceptance of the role women were allotted: 'good' women always returned demurely to their traditional duties. The more frightening and morally deficient Bacchic *mania* looked to the Greeks of both sexes, the more understandable is the tendency to emphasise in myth and cult Dionysus' alterity as a foreigner of ambiguous gender, indifferent to traditional virtues.

Bacchic madness was perceived as ordained by Dionysus, and therefore inescapable. Most importantly, returning to their homes, many people felt relief and divine bliss, and valued the importance of ecstatic experiences for the maintenance of inner peace and harmony: the Bacchic god was a purifier and a liberator, *Katharsios* and *Lusios*.[283] Bacchic *mania* was therefore indispensable for the maintenance of the proper order of things in the society.[284] Furthermore, Bacchic ecstatic rites and mystery initiations, along with other Dionysiac rites celebrated by a community, were often interconnected. The irresistible and wholesome tradition of *bakcheia* was therefore maintained for hundreds of years, and combined aspects of community celebrations with voluntary cults based on personal initiative.

It has been suggested that the cultic recognition of Dionysus allowed the channelling of the destructive *mania* which was Dionysus' punishment, into 'white *mania*' from which the bacchant returned undamaged.[285] I find no such dichotomy. Dionysus was perceived as the god of insanity, which was not necessarily negative, unlike that caused by Lyssa. However, Bacchic *mania* was certainly of divine origin, and as such potentially threatening – as everything divine that was dangerous to humans, for instance the sight of Dionysus' immortal father to his mortal mother. Ambiguity is the essence of Bacchic *mania*: being not like regular humans is becoming either divine or bestial or both at the same time. This state is risky and exhilarating, liberation is frightening and joyful: the opposites are always linked together. The threats of *mania* could be controlled and prevented. To those who are pure – that is, who eagerly accepted the god and his rites and let the ecstatic current carry them – *bakcheia* brought happiness;[286] to those who impiously resisted the god, his rites were fatal. When experienced correctly, Bacchic *mania* bestowed harmony and joy upon individuals and cities.

Whatever social and therapeutic benefits *bakcheia* endowed, for the Greeks it was an experience of *enthousiasmos*, aiming at attaining unity with the god;[287] we would define it as an alteration of consciousness bringing about mystical experience. This quality is most essential in the Bacchic *mania*, and it is shared by the *bakchai* and *bakchoi* who participated in ecstatic rites in the mountains or in the streets, and *bakchai* and *bakchoi* who underwent secret *teletai*. The fundamental equivalence of experience was keenly apprehended by the Greeks and alluded to on multiple occasions. However, ecstatic *bakcheia* differed from mystery initiations in three respects.[288] The association with violence, not necessarily actual, always lurked in the consciousness of the bacchants; the majority of ecstatic celebrants were women; and ecstatic rites appear to promise happiness and relief in this life only, whereas mystery rites also ensured bliss after death. The happiness of a bacchant was transient; the happiness of an initiate was for eternity.

Notes

1   *Il.* 6. 132 with scholia; Eumelus *Europia* fr. 27 West. Another reference to his madness is by Aeschulus (*TGF* fr. 20); Kirk (1990: 174).
2   This mountain seems to be symbolic of actual mountains where the devotees of Bacchus celebrated their rites, Dodds (1944: 139).
3   Eur. *Cyc.* 2–3; Plato *Leg.* 672B.
4   Eumelus *Europia* fr. 27 West; Schol. (D) *Il.* 6. 132. Later the two events were combined, and Dionysus' madness inflicted by Hera was considered cleansed by Rhea: Apollod. 3. 5. 1; Graf (2010: 171–173).
5   E.g. the famous cylix by the Brygos Painter, featuring Dionysus playing a lyre, with his mouth open and his head thrown back (Beazley 1963: 371. 14; Carpenter 1997: 83; Bundrick 2005: fig. 62), as well as other vases (Beazley 1963: 298, 406. 2, 585. 34, 592. 33, analysed in Carpenter 1993). T. H. Carpenter argues that these are scenes of pathology rather than ecstasy; I accept the interpretation by Bérard and Bron (1984) of these and similar images of Dionysus as 'the prince of maenads.'
6   Chantraine (1983–1984: s.v. *bakchos*). The origin of the word *bakchos* is unclear.
7   Santamaría (2013: 38–42, with refs.). The first occurrence of Bacchos as the god's name: S. *OT* 211.
8   Graf (1985: 286); Santamaría (2013: 44).
9   Cole (1980: 229).
10 The parallel of Zeus called *megistos kouros* by Cretan *kouroi*, cited by F. Graf and M. A. Santamaría, is partial: *kouros* has never become Zeus' name.
11 Paus. 2. 2. 6; 2. 7. 6; cf. Ath. 3. 78C on the two masks of Dionysus on Naxos, one depicting him as Baccheus and the other one as Meilichius (soothing); Detienne (1989: 25). On Dionysus as liberator see Seaford (2006: 29).
12 For *mania* and *bakcheia* used 'indistinctively and often in a coordinated way' see Cole (1980: 49, with examples).
13 The concept of Dionysus as 'der kommende Gott' put forward by W. Otto (1933) and widely accepted nowadays (Detienne 1986; Versnel 1990: 133), although some elements of the Bacchic cult may have been imported to Greece (Burkert 1985: 162). For Dionysus' arrivals in myth see Detienne (1986); Montiglio (2005: 73–83); for the god's rites of advent: Sourvinou-Inwood (2005: 151–161).
14 *Il.* 6. 132; 14. 325; *Od.* 11. 325; 24. 74; Demeter is also rare in Homer, supposedly because of the non-heroic role of both gods (Kirk 1990: 173). For Dionysus in the Mycenaean culture, see Burkert (1985: 31, 162); Wathelet (1991: 62).
15 The bloodthirsty Artemis Orthia in Sparta was also deemed foreign, Paus. 3. 16. 7–11; Detienne (1986: 59). For Dionysus as the god of the margins see Seaford (1994: 238–251).
16 Although two groups of maenads appear in Euripides' *Bacchae*, the Theban and the Lydian – the latter seemingly foreign – there is no difference in attire or behaviour between the two groups: the barbarians act exactly like the Greeks.
17 Cartledge (2002: 79).
18 *Smp.* 218B; for male bacchants see below.
19 Dionysus represented on Attic vases as ecstatic or mad, with Thracian attributes: Beazley (1963: 298, 406. 2); Carpenter (1997: 37–38); the god's effeminacy and transvestism: Bremmer (1999); Buxton (2013: 229–232).
20 Dionysus as a paradox and Dionysiac ambiguities: Versnel (1990: 96–205).
21 E. *Phrixus* 2 *TGF* 77; Hyg. *Fab.* 3
22 Paus. 7. 19–20; Seaford (1994: 252–255).
23 *Il.* 6. 130–140; Jeanmaire (1970: 61–67); Gantz (1993: 1: 113–114); Faraone (2013: 123–126).
24 Jouan (1992: 72).

25 *TGF* fr. 57–67; 124–126; West (1990: 26–32); Jouan (1992: 72–76); Xanthaki-Karamanou (2012). This version is retold by Apollod. 3. 5. 1. On the iconography of this myth see Kefalidou (2009: 95–96); Topper (2015).

26 S. *Ant.* 955–62. In this version, the Thracian king Lycurgus approaches other Thracian kings and priests who, after their human existence above the earth has culminated, continued to live as daemons in underground caves: Ustinova (2009b: 100–105).

27 Hyg. *Fab.* 132.

28 D.S. 1. 20; 3. 65.

29 D.S. 5. 50; van Hooff (1990: 97).

30 Paus. 9. 17. 6; 10. 32. 11.

31 *TGF* 203; Hyg. *Fab.* 8. 7.

32 *TGH* frs. 168–172; 183; later sources: Apollod. 3. 5. 2; Hyg. *Fab.* 184, 240, 254; Paus. 1. 20. 3; 2. 2. 7; 9. 2. 4; 9. 5. 4; Theocritus (Molinos Tejada 1992; Gantz 1993: 2: 481–483).

33 E. *Ba.* 1124.

34 E. *Ba.* 326, 504, 887.

35 E. *Ba.* 850.

36 E. *Ba.* 918–922, 945.

37 E. *Ba.* 925–964.

38 E. *Ba.* 947–948: τὰς δὲ πρὶν φρένας οὐκ εἶχες ὑγιεῖς, νῦν δ' ἔχεις οἵας σε δεῖ (translation D. Kovacs).

39 *h. Bacch.*1–59; Apollod. 3. 5. 3; Execias' cylix: Beazley (1978: 146. 21).

40 Parke (1977: 118–119).

41 Hyg. *Fab.* 130; Apollod. 3. 14. 7; Jeanmaire (1970: 165–166). A maiden who hung herself was the focus of a Dionysiac festival in Delphi (Plu. *Mor.* 293DE). Virgins at large were considered prone to suicidal acts, as attested by the Hippocratic tract *Girls*, recommending early marriage as the most efficient preventive measure.

42 Paus. 7. 21. 1–5.

43 Ael. V H 3. 42; Plu. *Mor.* 299E–300A; Ant. Lib. 10; Bonnechere (1994: 186–188).

44 *TGF* fr. 168–172; Detienne (1986: 64–66); Jouan (1992: 77–78); Gantz (1993: 2: 736–737); Acker (2002: 101–111).

45 Apollod. 2. 2. 2; 3. 5. 2.

46 For the myth and its versions associating Proetus with several cities, see Burkert (1983: 168–173); Graf (1985: 77–78); Dowden (1989: 71–95); Bonnechere (1994: 136–139, 192–194); Montiglio (2005: 16–19); Kowalzig (2007: 269–283).

47 B. 11. 45–46: παραπλῆγι φρένας καρτερᾷ ζεύξασ' ἀνάγκᾳ. In the version of Acusilaus, ca. 500, it is explained that they had slighted the ancient image of the goddess (Apollod. 2. 2. 2; Acus. FGH 2F28; Bremmer 2013: 10).

48 Paus. 8. 18. 7.

49 B.11. 92–112; O'Brien-Moore (1924: 102–105).

50 Fr. 132, 133 Merkelbach-West; Vian (1965: 25); Henrichs (1974). Μαχλοσύνη was explicated as a common kind of *mania* in women, Phot., Suda, s.v. *makhlosunê*.

51 Ael. *VH* 3. 42.

52 Μετ' ἀκοσμίας ἁπάσης, Apollod. 2. 2. 2.

53 Hes. fr. 131 Merkelbach-West; D.S. 4. 68; this version is supposedly a later development, based on the association of woman's frenzy with Dionysus, Jeanmaire (1970: 203–205); Burkert (1983: 170).

54 Hdt. 9. 34; Paus. 2. 18. 4; Apollod. 2. 2. 2; Dowden (1989: 75–85).

55 Apollod. 2. 2. 2; Vian (1965: 29).

56 In particular the cult of Artemis *Hemera* ('tame' or 'gentle'), whose sanctuary was equipped with a pool that could provide water for purifications (Dowden 1989: 81, 91–92).

57 Dowden (1989: 88–89); Bonnechere (1994: 136–139); Montiglio (2005: 17); Kowalzig (2007: 274).
58 Dowden (1989: 91); caves and initiations: Ustinova (2009b: 226–254, esp. 245–246 on age transition rites).
59 Kowalzig (2007: 277: 'the girls acquired Dionysiac language once the two legends mixed in a fifth-century context').
60 Suid., s.v. melan; Detienne (1986: 77).
61 Ael. VH 3. 42; Harp. s.v. Homeridai; Dowden (1989: 83–84); Edmonds III (2013: 314–315).
62 Obbink (1993: 70).
63 For a list see Mattes (1970).
64 For a survey of the research on the subject see Villanueva Puig (2009: 27–33).
65 Seaford (1994: 262).
66 Plu. Alex. 2; Jeanmaire (1970: 158).
67 Fr. 2b Page θυιάδα φοιβάδα μαινάδα λυσσάδα.
68 Μαινάδι ἴση; Il. 22. 460; Richardson (1993: 156); Schlesier (2011: 182–185). Rushing Andromache is described as 'frenzied' (mainomenê) in another song (6. 389–390). Nurses: Il. 6. 132–137; Schlesier (2011: 176–182).
69 Line 386: ἤϊξ' ἠΰτε μαινὰς ὄρος κάτα δάσκιον ὕλης; Richardson (1974: 281).
70 TGF fr. 183.
71 TGF fr. 57, 58, 61; Xanthaki-Karamanou (2012: 326–332); Bacchic 'soundscape': Yerucham (2016).
72 TGF 169. The title Ξάντριαι derives from ξαίνουσι, either 'to tear asunder' (Leucippe's child or Pentheus, according to Philostratus, Images 3. 18) or 'to card wool' (as the Minyads persisted, notwithstanding Dionysus' command, Ael. HM 3. 42).
73 E. Ba. 138: ὠμοφάγος χάρις; Roux (1972: 68).
74 E. Ba. 734; 1125.
75 E. Ba. 138.
76 E. Ba. 1017–1019; the god was born with bull horns and crowned with snakes: Ba. 100–101; he looks like a bull to Pentheus: Ba. 920; Jaccottet (2003: 230). Dionysiac rites and snake-handling: Bremmer (1984: 268). Dionysus as a bull: Plu. Mor. 299B (in Elea); Jaccottet (2003: 1: 102–103).
77 Harrison (1928: 478); Dodds (1940: 166); Jeanmaire (1970: 251–254); Burkert (1983: 177); Hoffmann (1997: 101); Bonnechere (1994: 215–216). Strabo reports Lycurgus to have been identified with Dionysus (10. 3. 16). Dismemberment of Dionysus was first referred to by Callimachus, but was probably much more ancient, and a late source attests to Lenaean songs about 'Dionysus' sparagmos' (Clem. Al. Protr. 1. 2; Seaford 1994: 284; Lada-Richards 1999: 96). R. Seaford links the murder of Dionysus with the frequent association of maenads with lamentation (Seaford 1994: 322–323). One wonders whether it was the rite of sparagmos that prompted the Orphic idea of dismemberment of Dionysus-Zagreus (Bonnechere 1994: 215). For reassessment of the evidence on this myth see Henrichs (2011).
78 E. Ba. 794.
79 E. Ba. 1114.
80 E. Ba. 1184, 1241; Henrichs (2000: 188).
81 E. Ba. 748–768; Kraemer (1979: 68); Jaccottet (2003: 229–232).
82 Seaford (1994: 272–273).
83 Dodds (1944: xxvii).
84 Dowden (1989: 84). Mad women chased by a man or a group of men are reminiscent of the purification of the Proetids by Melampous and a band of young warriors, discussed above in this chapter.
85 Burkert (1983: 175).

86 *TGF* fr. 169: ἐκ ποδῶν δ' ἄνω | ὑπέρχεται σπαραγμὸς εἰς ἄκρον κάρα, | κέντημα γλώσσης (or Λύσσης), σκορπίου βέλος λέγω.
87 Isler-Kerényi (2007: 27–43).
88 Villanueva Puig (2009: 79–101); Isler-Kerényi (2007: 49–52). For the identification of pre–late sixth-century companions of silens as nymphs rather than maenads see Hedreen (1994).
89 The crater: Beazley (1978: 108. 5). Villanueva Puig (2009: 101–108, figs. 19–20); Hedreen (1994: 52), Carpenter (1997: 52–57), and Isler-Kerényi (2007: 98) doubt the identification of these characters as maenads, suggesting that they could be nymphs holding snakes.
90 As for instance on an amphora from Louvre, Isler-Kerényi (2007: 112, figs. 51–52); Beazley (1978: 297. 12); and an amphora by Lydus from the British Museum, Isler-Kerényi (2007: 127, fig. 63), Beazley (1978: Addenda 30. 109. 29). These figures are identified as maenads by J. D. Beazley, M. W. Edwards and M.-C. Villanueva Puig (Edwards 1960: 80; Villanueva Puig 2009: 108). T. H. Carpenter and C. Isler-Kerényi who regard them as nymphs wearing animal skins seem to be too cautious.
    For the distinction between *nebrides* and *pardalides* see Edwards (1960).
91 Amphorae in Antikenmuseum Basel (Beazley 1978: Addenda 43. 151); Isler-Kerényi 2007: 132, figs. 67–68) and in Cabinet des Médailles in Paris (Beazley 1978: Addenda 43. 152. 25); Isler-Kerényi (2007: 134, fig. 70). Here again, Isler-Kerényi, emphasising the role of female characters as 'mediators between males as the god of wine, is reluctant to identify them as maenads, whereas Villanueva Puig (2009: 109–173) interprets most of them as maenadic figures.
92 Burkert (1985: 166); Bérard (1992: 16); Bérard and Bron (1984). For a discussion 'how satyric is the centaur, how centauric is the satyr, and which poses the greater threat for humankind,' see Osborne (1994: 55).
93 Osborne (1997: 197–198).
94 Villanueva Puig (2009: 175–187). Carpenter (1997: 52–57) insists on the identification of these figures as nymphs, or female attendants of Dionysus whose nature is unclear.
95 See the statistics of Osborne (1997: 198–199).
96 Edwards (1960: 83).
97 For their sudden appearance in the art, see Edwards (1960: 84).
98 Villanueva Puig (2009: 58–77, figs. 1–11); the most conspicuous examples are the amphora by the Cleophrades Painter in Munich (Beazley 1963: 182. 6), the cylix by Brygos Painter in Munich (Beazley 1963: 371. 15), and cylices by Macron (Beazley 1963: 563. 52–53), to mention only a few. Cf. Goff (2004: 266–269).
99 Kefalidou (2009: 92).
100 Maenads' hair depicted loose in art: Beazley (1963: 381. 176, 182. 6); Villanueva Puig (2013: 270–271); in tragedy: E. *Ba.* 150; 665; Bremmer (1984: 277).
101 Villanueva Puig (2009: 214).
102 Beazley (1963: 1247. 1); Villanueva Puig (2013: 276, fig. 7).
103 Hoffmann (1997: 22–23, figs. 5–6); Beazley (1963: 764. 10).
104 Beazley (1963: 1519. 13); Bérard and Bron (1986: 141).
105 A scene of erotic frenzy with sphinxes is especially striking (Beazley 1963: 1700); Lissarrague (1990).
106 Miller (1999: 249, fig. 28, 29).
107 Beazley (1963: 1328. 92); Villanueva Puig (2013: 281, fig. 11).
108 Beazley (1963: 134. 3); Villanueva Puig (2013: 276, fig. 12); Barr-Sharrar (2008: 96–97, fig. 85).
109 Beazley (1963: 298).
110 Frontisi-Ducroux (1991); Versnel (1990: 146); Carpenter (1997: 80–82); Seaford (1994: 264–265).
111 As for instance on a lekythos from Eleusis, Beazley (1978: 504. 18); Villanueva Puig (2013: 266).

112 See the revue of current views in Frontisi-Ducroux (1986: 165); Frontisi-Ducroux (1991: 223–236) is reluctant to associate the scenes with a particular festival, but regards them as reflecting real cultic practices.

113 Osborne (1997: 208); Carpenter (1997: 60) insists that the women are nymphs.

114 Isler-Kerényi (2007: 228).

115 Barr-Sharrar (2008); Villanueva Puig (2013).

116 Barr-Sharrar (2008: pl. 2; 3).

117 Barr-Sharrar (2008: 143).

118 Barr-Sharrar (2008: figs. 155, 158).

119 Barr-Sharrar (2008: fig. 108); a late fourth-century gold earring from the Bolshaya Bliznitza tumulus in the area of the Cimmerian Bosporus features a maenad carrying a human child on her shoulder (Barr-Sharrar 2008: fig. 109).

120 Villanueva Puig (2009: 208).

121 Lawler (1927).

122 Lawler (1927: 79); Osborne (1997: 195); Kefalidou (2009: 93); Goff (2004: 274).

123 Jeanmaire (1970: 159); Barasch (1991).
     G. Hedreen (1994: 58–59) deconstructs complex images of ecstatic group celebrations into separate 'realistic elements' and argues that since the elements could be invented rather than be 'real and historical,' the images were invented, as well, and real-life maenads did not exist in Classical Greece. However, the value of an image of interacting personages goes far beyond the mere sum of particular features, and in order to be able to create the image Attic artists had to be acquainted with real-life models. Hedreen (1994: 69) supposes that the imagery of silens and maenads in the late sixth century came from drama rather than from ecstatic ritual. The question is where did it arrive from to drama? Why were animal skins and snakes introduced? And why did the nymphs, who were represented playfully consenting to silens' sexual demands before that time, switch to exclusive allegiance to Dionysus? If Bacchic ritual is a fantasy, did the word *bakcheia* derive from fantasy, as well? These and many other questions are left unanswered. Hedreen's hypothesis that female companions of Dionysus on Attic pottery were no more than mythological or theatrical characters, remains unconvincing (cf. Osborne 1997: 197).

124 Villanueva Puig (2009: 207).

125 Osborne (1997: 195). Even if these women were semi-divine attendants of Dionysus rather than mortal women, as argued by Carpenter (1997: 62) – and Carpenter's position seems hyper-cautious – realistic representation of ecstatic females in the retinue of Dionysus presupposes familiarity of the artists with real-life ecstatic phenomena. Ecstatic figures of both sexes involved in presumably Dionysiac ritual are represented on the Ferrara crater, which features mortals even in the opinion of Carpenter (1997: 71–78); on this crater see above, Chapter 2.

126 *h. Bacch.* 1. 17; Nonnus uses the same epithet in 16. 229, 252, and θηλυμανής in 17. 184 and 36. 469.

127 The rendering of *gynaimanes* by Rayor (2004: 15).

128 Jeanmaire (1970: 278).

129 Nilsson (1957: 8–10); Kraemer (1979: 72); Henrichs (1978); Henrichs (1982: 139); Henrichs (1984b); Faraone (2013).

130 Jaccottet (2003: 1: 94–95).

131 Bérard (1992); Bérard and Bron (1986: 23).

132 Jaccottet (2003: 1: 95–97).

133 E. *Ion* 550–551.

134 E. *Ba.* 195–206, 249–251, 1224–1225, 114–119.

135 E. *Ba.* 187–188, 195–206; Buxton (2013: 226–227). An epode (lines 135–166) is interpreted by some as indicating that the male leader of the Bacchic rites who falls on the ground, joyfully eating raw flesh, is a mortal (Dodds 1940: 170; Kraemer 1979: 71; Burkert 1985: 292), or a maenad possessed by the god (Villanueva Puig 2013:

274), rather than the god himself, as argued by Henrichs (1984b). Unfortunately, this passage is corrupted, metrically problematic and unequivocal, therefore insufficient to assume that the *Bacchae* features ecstatic male celebrants in addition to Pentheus, whose *bakcheia* is a sinister punishment. For a discussion of this passage see: Dodds (1944: 85–88); Henrichs (1984b); Seaford (1996: 164–165).

136 Bérard and Bron (1986: 23–36, figs. 9–12).

137 By Painter of Louvre G521: Beazley (1963: 1442. 2).

138 Heraclit., fr. 14 *DK* (νυκτιπόλοις, μάγοις, βάκχοις, λήναις, μύσταις); above, Chapter 2.

139 Hdt. 4. 79, above, Chapter 2.

140 Graf and Johnston (2007: 187); Bremmer (2014: 71).

141 Anacr. fr. 43 Page; Slater (1978).

142 D. 18. 259–260, cited and discussed above, Chapter 2.

143 Above, Chapter 2.
     Plato repeatedly refers to *bakcheia* of men and male *bakchoi*, in particular in his dictum 'Many bear the Bacchic rod, but few are bacchants' (*Phd.* 69D; *Smp.* 218B), but he probably refers to the participants in mystery cults; see Chapter 8.

144 Parker (1983: 287).

145 Jaccottet (2003: 1: 97–99).

146 For perspectives on this issue, see Henrichs (1982: n. 53); Osborne (1997: 187–190); Versnel (1990: 134–155).

147 D.S. 4. 3. 2–3: καὶ τοὺς μὲν Βοιωτοὺς καὶ τοὺς ἄλλους Ἕλληνας καὶ Θρᾷκας ἀπομνημονεύοντας τῆς κατὰ τὴν Ἰνδικὴν στρατείας καταδεῖξαι τὰς τριετηρίδας θυσίας Διονύσῳ, καὶ τὸν θεὸν νομίζειν κατὰ τὸν χρόνον τοῦτον ποιεῖσθαι τὰς παρὰ τοῖς ἀνθρώποις ἐπιφανείας. διὸ καὶ παρὰ πολλαῖς τῶν Ἑλληνίδων πόλεων διὰ τριῶν ἐτῶν βακχεῖά τε γυναικῶν ἀθροίζεσθαι, καὶ ταῖς παρθένοις νόμιμον εἶναι θυρσοφορεῖν καὶ συνενθουσιάζειν εὐαζούσαις καὶ τιμώσαις τὸν θεόν· τὰς δὲ γυναῖκας κατὰ συστήματα θυσιάζειν τῷ θεῷ καὶ βακχεύειν καὶ καθόλου τὴν παρουσίαν ὑμνεῖν τοῦ Διονύσου, μιμουμένας τὰς ἱστορουμένας τὸ παλαιὸν παρεδρεύειν τῷ θεῷ μαινάδας (translation C. H. Oldfather, modified). Henrichs (1978: 144) considers maenadic rituals of the historical tomes as 'mimetic, or commemorative,' inferring that they only pretended to be ecstatic.

148 Bérard (1992). In contrast, E. C. Keuls (1984) interprets scenes of sexual chase and rape of maenads by satyrs as promoting conjugal love; her argumentation, based on juxtaposition of scenes of sexual pursuit and conjugal encounters on a few vases and identification of satyrs coming upon sleeping maenads with Dionysus and Ariadne on Naxos, fails to convince.

149 E.g. *Ba.* 314–318; Kraemer (1979: 68).

150 E. *Ion* 550–560.

151 Porres Caballero (2013: 165); on Bacchic madness and girls' initiations see above in this chapter.

152 *Mor.* 249E: αἱ περὶ τὸν Διόνυσον γυναῖκες, ἃς Θυιάδας ὀνομάζουσιν, ἐκμανεῖσαι καὶ περιπλανηθεῖσαι νυκτὸς ἔλαθον ἐν Ἀμφίσσῃ γενόμεναι· κατάκοποι δ' οὖσαι καὶ μηδέπω τοῦ φρονεῖν παρόντος αὐταῖς ἐν τῇ ἀγορᾷ προέμεναι . . . ἔκειντο καθεύδουσαι. Dodds (1944: xiv); Jeanmaire (1970: 178–180); Villanueva Puig (1986).

153 Villanueva Puig (2009: 45).

154 Paus. 10. 6. 4; 10. 32. 7.

155 Plu. *Mor.* 364E.

156 Chantraine (1983–1984: s.v. *thuô*); Harrison (1960: 65).

157 Paus. 10. 19. 4; S. *Ant.* 1151–1152 (Θυίασιν, αἵ σε μαινόμεναι πάννυχοι χορεύουσι); cf. Plu. *Mor.* 365A; Villanueva Puig (1986: 38–40); Villanueva Puig (2013: 284–286); Sourvinou-Inwood (2005: 211–212). Trieteric celebrations of *Bromios'* rites is mentioned in Aristonous' fourth-century paean: Henrichs (1978: 137).

158 Cole (2010: 329).

159 D. S. 4. 3. 3; Plu. *Mor.* 953D.

160 Goff (2004: 276); Parker (2011: 243).
161 Paus. 10. 4. 3; Henrichs (1978); Seaford (1994: 264); Villanueva Puig (2013: 285).
     Biennial Dionysiac festivals of unspecified nature are attested elsewhere: Dodds
     (1940: 155).
162 Hsch, s.v. *agriania; agrianeaion;* Plu. *Mor.* 299E–300A; 717A; Burkert (1983: 173–
     175); Graf (1985: 80); Seaford (1996: 37); Bonnechere (1994: 197–201); Bernabé
     (2014).
163 In Chaeronea, Orchomenus, perhaps in Haliartus and Tanagra, as well. In Thebes
     Agrionia was the agonistic part of the festival of Dionysus, Schachter (1981–94: 1:
     185–192).
164 Str. 10. 3. 23: τὰς ὀρειβασίας τῶν περὶ τὸ θεῖον σπουδαζόντων καὶ αὐτῶν τῶν θεῶν
     καὶ τοὺς ἐνθουσιασμοὺς . . . μυθεύουσι ('they tell stories about mountain roaming
     of those who venerate the gods and of the gods themselves, and about divine posses-
     sion'); 12. 4. 5.
165 Paus. 8. 23. 1.
166 *TGF* fr. 23–25; West (1983: 36–46); Jouan (1992: 74); other versions: Paus. 9. 30.7–8;
     Conon *FGH* 26 fr. 1. 45.
167 Porph. *Abst.* 2. 8; Detienne (1977: 63).
168 See above and Halm-Tisserant (2004: 123–126), plates 1–6; Villanueva Puig (2013:
     278).
169 *Mor.* 417C; cf. Seaford (1996: 36–37); Henrichs (1978).
170 *Mor.* 299E–300A; Hughes (1991: 131–132).
171 *Them.* 13; Phaenias fr. 25 Wehrli; Burkert (1966: 113, opting for the historical prob-
     ability of the episode); Graf (1985: 76); Hughes (1991: 111–115, arguing against its
     historicity); Bonnechere (1994: 288–291, undecided).
172 Alcaeus fr. 129 Lobel-Page referring specifically to Dionysus *Ômêstes;* Dosiades, *FGH* 4
     fr. 7; Graf (1985: 74–80); Hughes (1991: 121); Bonnechere (1994: 223). Ael. *VH* 13. 2
     narrates a Lesbian tale of a priest of Dionysus, whose children played in the sanctuary,
     and one son unintentionally killed another one on the god's altar. Other sources attest
     to Dionysus' epiclesis *Omadios,* 'eating raw flesh,' on Tenedos and Chios (Porhyr. *Abst.*
     2.55; Dodds 1944: xix; Henrichs 1969: 236; Graf 1985: 74–80; Seaford 1994: 294).
173 Thphr. fr. 3, in Porhyr. *Abst.* 2.8.
     Seidensticker (1979) convincingly argues that the second half of the *Bacchae* cor-
     responds step-by-step to the stages of the sacrificial ritual, and that by evoking the
     sacrifice-pattern Euripides consciously demonstrated 'the essence of tragedy as ritu-
     alised sacrifice.' Continuing this line of argument: since the slaughtered victim was a
     man, Euripides probably was one of those who thought that originally Dionysus had
     received at his festival a human sacrifice.
174 Paus. 9. 8. 2; the sacrifice of Callirhoë demanded by Dionysus, which had to be per-
     formed by the god's priest, hints at a similar phenomenon (Paus. 7. 21. 1–5, see
     above).
175 Ael. *NA* 12. 34; Dodds (1944: xix); Hughes (1991: 85–86).
176 For human victims sacrificed to Dionysus as *pharmakoi* see Seaford (1994: 311–318).
177 Bremmer (1984: 276); Bonnechere (1994: 225); Vernant in Detienne and Vernant
     (1989: 38–39).
178 SEG 17. 503; Henrichs (1969: 225–226); Jaccottet (2003: 2: No 149, 1: 74).
179 καλῶμ μοῖραν ἐπισταμένῃ; Henrichs (1969: 238); Versnel (1990: 152); see also
     above, Chapter 2.
180 LSCG 127.
181 LSAM 48. 3–4: μὴ ἐξεῖναι ὠμοφάγιον ἐμβαλεῖν μηθενὶ πρότερον [ἢ ἡ ἱέ]ρεια ὑπὲρ
     τῆς πόλεως ἐμβάλῃ; μὴ ἐξεῖναι δὲ μηδὲ [συν]αγαγεῖν τὸν θίασον μηθενὶ πρότερον
     τοῦ δημοσίου. For a discussion of this inscription see Haussollier (1919); Henrichs
     (1969); Villanueva Puig (1998); Jaccottet (2003: 2: No 150, 1: 74–75); Connelly
     (2007: 179–181).

182 ὠμοφάγιον ἐμβαλεῖν; see Dodds (1940: 164); Dodds (1944: xvi); Henrichs (1978: 150); Seaford (1996: 37); Halm-Tisserant (2004: 128–129); Villanueva Puig (2009: 44). Jeanmaire (1970: 265–266) cites Dionysus' epiclesis *Aigobolos* in Potniae (Paus. 9. 8. 2), which is perhaps to be understood as 'goat-thrower,' rather than 'goat-shooter.'

183 Jeanmaire (1970: 265); Goff (2004: 272).

184 Detienne (1977: 90); Henrichs (1982: 144); Seaford (1996: 37); Villanueva Puig (2009: 44); Porres Caballero (2013: 179). Versnel (1990: 143) is uncertain as to our ability to assess the degree to which these accounts reflect reality. E. R. Dodds (1944: xvii) compares the Milesian rite to the modern Arab practice, when a priest throws a victim from a terrace to the ecstatic crowd below. This comparison is rejected by Henrichs (1982: 145), who argues that 'nothing in the available evidence suggests that historical maenads indulged in *sparagmos* or *omophagia*,' and that *ômophagia* in Miletus was a particular type of sacrifice to Dionysus (Henrichs 1978: 148–151).

185 The efforts to 'mitigate' the image of the Greeks are reminiscent of the attempts to question the fact that Greek ladies went to theatres, brilliantly refuted by M. A. Katz (1998) in the article entitled 'Did the women of ancient Athens attend the theatre in the eighteenth century?'

186 See Bonnechere (1994: 214–215) on *ômophagia* as the peak of the Bacchic rites, which was practiced by Greek men, and especially women.

187 Lines 21 and 14–15.

188 Ustinova (2005: 188).

189 *IMagn*. 215; Parke and Wormell (1956: 2 No. 338; 1: 334–335); Jeanmaire (1970: 197–198); Henrichs (1969: 240); Henrichs (1978: 124–133); Henrichs (1982: 153, n. 149); Jaccottet (2003: 2: No 146; 1: 77–78); Connelly (2007: 254–255).

190 Whether this oracle was authentic is insignificant for the present discussion: what matters is that the maenadic rites were believed to have been authorised by Delphi.

191 τὸ γὰρ βακχεύσιμον | καὶ τὸ μανιῶδες μαντικὴν πολλὴν ἔχει· | ὅταν γὰρ ὁ θεὸς ἐς τὸ σῶμ' ἔλθηι πολύς, | λέγειν τὸ μέλλον τοὺς μεμηνότας ποιεῖ, E. *Ba*. 298–301, translation D. Kovacs.
It is suggested that the word μουσόμαντις in Aeschylus' *Edonians* (*TGF* fr. 60) refers to Dionysus (Jouan 1992: 84), rather than to Orpheus (West 1990: 29).

192 Dodds (1944: 108–109); Seaford (1996: 177); Roux (1972: 352–353).

193 Amphicleia: Paus. 10. 33. 11. In Thrace, the god had two prophetic sanctuaries, on Mt Pangaeum (Hdt. 7. 111), and in Rhodopi (Perdizet 1910: 42), and he is referred to as a prophet in Thracian contexts: E. *Hec*. 1267, *Rh*. 972.

194 *Ba*. 982. Plutarch cited these verses twice, and understood them as referring to liberation of inspiration and ideas that remain unperceived by the sober mind: *Mor*. 432E and 716B; Dodds (1944: 108–109).

195 Fr. 2b Page.

196 Chapter 1.

197 Jeanmaire (1970: 197).

198 For instance, by Kraemer (1979: 67); Versnel (1990: 186, 189).

199 For a discussion of private and public in Greek religion, see *Kernos* Suppl. 5 (2005). For criticism of H. Versnel's and A. Henrichs' approaches, see Osborne (1997: 190–193).

200 Bremmer (1984); Versnel (1990); Villanueva Puig (2013), adopting a position halfway between the researchers who opt for the historicity of the entire maenadic complex, including *ômophagia*, such as E. R. Dodds and H. Jeanmaire, on the one hand, and, those who claim that 'it cannot be demonstrated that "madness" understood as an abnormal psychological state was an authentic quality of the historical maenad, despite her name,' such as A. Henrichs (Henrichs 1982: 146), on the other hand. The position of Porres Caballero (2013: 170) is that 'we should admit that these women had, at least, an altered state of mind,' in which she is however reluctant to

recognise 'a real possession.' For an analysis of approaches to Dionysiac violence in modern European culture, see Henrichs (1984a).
201 Acker (2002: *passim*, esp. 121–148), arguing that maenadic rites were sort of female initiations, seems to go too far: notwithstanding their quasi-secrecy, frequent appellation (*teletai* or *orgiai*) and celebration away from the polis, in the absence of the change of the status of the celebrants, maenadic rites resist the categorisation as 'initiations.'
202 The word *thiasos* had other meanings as well: it could designate a voluntary association of worshippers of gods other than Dionysus, or subdivisions of phratries in Attica: Arnaoutoglou (2003: 60–70). For the historiography of the Dionysiac *thiasos*, see Jaccottet (2003: 1: 17–29).
203 Burkert (1985: 162).
204 E. Ba. 67–72: ὦ μάκαρ, ὅστις εὐδαίμων τελετὰς θεῶν εἰ | δὼς βιοτὰν ἁγιστεύει καὶ θιασεύεται ψυ|χὰν ἐν ὄρεσσι βακχεύ|ων ὁσίοις καθαρμοῖσιν.
205 Dodds (1944: 75).
206 Dodds (1944: 75–76); Sfameni Gasparro (2011: 301).
207 E. Ba. 677–764; Seaford (2006: 33).
208 E. Ba. 748, 731, 977.
209 E. Ba. 726–727, πᾶν δὲ συνεβάκχευ' ὄρος καὶ θῆρες. These verses may also refer to the overwhelming power of Dionysus to dominate the environment: in the *Edonians* (*TGF* fr. 58), he took control of the royal palace, 'the house is possessed by the god, the roof is Bacchic' (ἐνθουσιᾷ δὴ δῶμα, βακχεύει στέγη).
210 E. Ba. 732.
211 Edwards (1960: 83), cf. Winnington-Ingram (1948: 107).
212 E. Ba. 977; *TGF* fr. 169: ἐπιθειαζούσα ταῖς Βάκχαις, Phot., Sud., s.v. *oktôpous*; O'Brien-Moore (1924: 80). Lyssa's frenzy is contrasted to Dionysiac madness.
213 Contrast: *HF* 889–892; Heracles' *bakcheia*: *HF* 1087; 1119; 1122. See also below, Chapter 4.
214 E. Ba. 116–119; 32–33: ᾤστρησ' ἐγὼ μανίαις.
215 E. Ba. 677–775.
216 E. Ba. 731–734; 1080–1136.
217 E. Ba. 748–768.
218 Villanueva Puig (2009: 57).
219 E. Ba. 1053–1057, translation D. Kovacs.
220 E. Ba. 1122–1124: ἡ δ' ἀφρὸν ἐξιεῖσα . . . οὐ φρονοῦσ' ἃ χρὴ φρονεῖν, ἐκ Βακχίου κατείχετ' (translation D. Kovacs).
221 E. Ba. 1198–1199.
222 E. Ba. 1153–1215.
223 E. Ba. 1166–1176; fiercely rolling and bloodshed eyes of madmen in tragedy: E. *HF* 932–933; *Or.* 219–220; 253–254; *Ba.* 1123; S. *Aj.* 447.
224 E. Ba. 1167.
225 E. Ba. 1260–1295.
226 E. Ba. 1260–1295 (translation D. Kovacs):
{Αγ.} τί δ' οὐ καλῶς τῶνδ' ἢ τί λυπηρῶς ἔχει;
{Κα.} πρῶτον μὲν ἐς τόνδ' αἰθέρ' ὄμμα σὸν μέθες.
{Αγ.} ἰδού· τί μοι τόνδ' ἐξυπεῖπας εἰσορᾶν;
{Κα.} ἔθ' αὐτὸς ἤ σοι μεταβολὰς ἔχειν δοκεῖ;
{Αγ.} λαμπρότερος ἢ πρὶν καὶ διειπετέστερος.
{Κα.} τὸ δὲ πτοηθὲν τόδ' ἔτι σῇ ψυχῇι πάρα;
{Αγ.} οὐκ οἶδα τοὔπος τοῦτο· γίγνομαι δέ πως
ἔννους, μετασταθεῖσα τῶν πάρος φρενῶν.
{Κα.} κλύοις ἂν οὖν τι κἀποκρίναι' ἂν σαφῶς;
{Αγ.} ὡς ἐκλέλησμαί γ' ἃ πάρος εἴπομεν, πάτερ.
{Κα.} ἐς ποῖον ἦλθες οἶκον ὑμεναίων μέτα;

{Αγ.} Σπαρτῶι μ' ἔδωκας, ὡς λέγουσ', Ἐχίονι.
{Κα.} τίς οὖν ἐν οἴκοις παῖς ἐγένετο σῶι πόσει;
{Αγ.} Πενθεύς, ἐμῆι τε καὶ πατρὸς κοινωνίαι.
{Κα.} τίνος πρόσωπον δῆτ' ἐν ἀγκάλαις ἔχεις;
{Αγ.} λέοντος, ὥ γ' ἔφασκον αἱ θηρώμεναι.
{Κα.} σκέψαι νυν ὀρθῶς· βραχὺς ὁ μόχθος εἰσιδεῖν.
. . .
{Αγ.} οὔκ, ἀλλὰ Πενθέως ἡ τάλαιν' ἔχω κάρα.
. . .
{Αγ.} τίς ἔκτανέν νιν;
{Κα.} σύ νιν κατέκτας καὶ κασίγνηται σέθεν.
{Αγ.} ποῦ δ' ὤλετ'; ἢ κατ' οἶκον, ἢ ποίοις τόποις;
. . .
{Αγ.} ἡμεῖς δ' ἐκεῖσε τίνι τρόπωι κατήραμεν;
{Κα.} ἐμάνητε, πᾶσά τ' ἐξεβακχεύθη πόλις.

227 E. *Ba.* 1269–1270.
228 This exchange between a father and an offspring recovering from an attack of insanity is perhaps an elaboration of an earlier scene, in Euripides' *Heracles* (*HF* 1089–1428). The accuracy of Euripides' psychological observations and their compatibility to modern treatment methods have been discerned by E. R. Dodds (1944: 215–217, comm. to lines 1264–1277). On the basis of clinical data and psychiatric theory, G. Devereux (1970) convincingly demonstrated 'the clinical plausibility' of the scene. This interpretation has been accepted by a number of scholars: Roux (1972: 609); Seaford (1996: 247–248); Riley (2008: 39–40); and Shalev (2012). Gill (1985: 315) and V. Leiniekes (1996: 120–121) regard the scene rather as a form of verbal cure, an example of the art of persuasion. For Euripides' keen interest in medicine see Craik (2001).
     G. Devereux supposes that during his stay in Macedonia Euripides observed real-life insight-and-recall psychotherapy, and compares it to anthropologically attested shamanic techniques of treatment, based on this principle. In fact, Socrates praised Thracian – but not Macedonian – healers for their therapeutic approach based on 'treatment of the soul' (Pl. *Chrm.* 156D–157B; Ustinova 2009a: 267). However, even if this claim was based on an opinion current among the Greeks, Socrates explicitly spoke about cure of bodily ailments, rather than mental disorders. Therefore, borrowing this technique from barbarians remains undocumented.
229 The idea that the depiction of the Dionysiac ecstasy by Euripides was prompted by his stay in semi-barbarous Macedonia where he witnessed the fierce rites in their primitive form, has been rejected by Dodds (1940: 170), who demonstrates that Euripides depicted Bacchic rites before his residence in Macedonia: in *Helen* (1301–1367), staged in 412, and in the *Cretans* (*TGF* fr. 472), presumably an early play (Bernabé 2016a). Macedonian experiences may have inspired Euripides to engage with the subject profoundly, as he did in the *Bacchae*, but they were not his only or main source of information on ecstatic *mania* (Dodds 1940: 176).
230 Plates in Halm-Tisserant (2004) represent *sparagmos* of humans (pl. 3. 2; 6. 3) and cattle (pl. 2: 1–2), but these are exceptions; in most cases, the maenads are depicted with small deer, or even less impressive animals, such as hares (Jeanmaire 1970: 253).
231 See Villanueva Puig (2009: 50) for a similar approach.
232 Agave: E. *Ba.* 1122–1124; other examples: E. *HF* 934; *IT* 307–308.
233 Kefalidou (2009: 93–94) suggests that a lion depicted next to a maenad in the scene of dismemberment of Pentheus on a hydria in Berlin and a hare in a similar proximity to a maenad on a cup originating from the circle of the Nicosthenes Painter (Bažant and Berger-Doer 1994: 312, Nos. 40, 41), are visual signs of what was going on in the women's heads and alludes to a myth preceding the versions of Aeschylus

(*Eum.* 25–26) who compares Pentheus to a hare, and Euripides' *Bacchae* by about a hundred years; these scenes are, to her knowledge, the first time when delusion was represented on a Greek vase. Konstantinou (forthcoming) contends that wavy or 'zigzagged-shaped' rocks in some Dionysiac scenes represent 'dancing' mountains, reflecting 'blurred sensory perception of space.'

234 Cf. Paus. 10. 32. 6 on a cave sacred to Apollo at Aulae that contained an image of the god bestowing strength: the men sacred to the god leaped from rocks and uprooted trees.

235 And can still be witnessed nowadays: Reicher (2000).

236 Paus. 2. 20. 4: maenads fought with Dionysus in his expedition against Argos; Simon (1978: 252).

237 Dodds (1944: 216, comm. to line 1272); Devereux (1970: 37).

238 E. *Ba.* 731; 1106.

239 To the examples of the amphora by the Cleophrades Painter (Beazley 1963: 182. 6) and the Derveni crater, cited above, one may add a lekythos by the Eretria Painter, dated to 430–420, featuring seven maenads, two of them serenely holding their rods, one reclining, one playing a tambourine, one absolutely ecstatic, as if lifted by some inner force, and a group of two, a calmer maenad holding in her arms a collapsing one (Beazley 1963: 1248. 1; Cook 1960: 182, plate 47).

240 Pl. *Phd.* 69D. Jiménez San Cristóbal (2009: 48–52) maintains that the expression 'marks an inclusive opposition . . . , among the many thyrsus-bearers, only a few are or will become bacchi.'

241 Agrionia: Hsch, s.v. *agriania*; Plu. *Mor.* 299E–300A; 717A.

242 Henrichs (1982). For renewed assertion of the importance of comparative approach see Osborne (1997: 195).

243 Jeanmaire (1970: 128–131).

244 E. *Ba.* 902–903, translation D. Kovacs; Winnington-Ingram (1948: 114–115).

245 Jeanmaire (1970: 259–260).

246 Jeanmaire (1970: 183–185); Sifakis (2001: 79–81); Karanika (2005: 32–35); Xygalatas (2011); Xygalatas (2014). The controversy about the origins of the Anastenaria is irrelevant for the present discussion.

Fire-walking is attested in the earlier Mediterranean world, in Cilicia (Str. 12. 2. 7; Dupont-Sommer and Robert 1964: 53–64) and in Italy (Str. 5. 2. 9 ; Pl. *NH* 7. 2. 19; Rissanen 2012).

247 Rouget (1990: 93–98, 296–308); Karanika (2005: 25–30).

248 Dodds (1940: 159–161); Dodds (1944: xv); Waller (2009).

249 Waller (2009).

250 Dodds (1944: xvi); Waller (2009).

251 Rouget (1990: 305).

252 Bartholomew and Wessely (2002).

253 Hacking (2002: 55); Wiley and Allen (2009: 366–368).

254 Contrary to the opinion of Porres Caballero (2013: 167).

255 Simon (1978: 251–257); Kraemer (1979: 68); Bremmer (1984: 285); Goff (2004: 276–279); Parker (2011: 243).

256 Kraemer's suggestion that Dionysiac ecstasy was a retreat for 'unsuccessful' women, i.e. childless or unmarried, and the comparison of maenadism to *zar* and *bori* (Kraemer 1979: 73–77) seem to be misleading, because we have no hint at the problematic status of the maenads, or illnesses of particular participants: all the women were supposedly possessed by Dionysus. For *zar* and *bori* and their affinity with the Corybantic rites, see Chapter 2.

257 See Introduction.

258 Henrichs (1982: 147), claiming that 'the peculiar religious identity of the maenads had more to do with sweat and physical exhaustion than with an abnormal state of mind,' seems to disregard the connection between the physical and mental states of the humans.

259 Bremmer (1984: 277); Bélis (1988); Menier (2001: 236); Yerucham (2016). On mind-altering effects of music see above, Introduction and Chapter 2.
260 Beazley (1963: 865. 2). For the role of *auloi* in inducing Bacchic ecstasy see Menier (2001: 234).
261 Bérard and Bron (1986: 141); Hoffmann (1997: 29).
262 On alteration of light and darkness as a method of consciousness manipulation, see Chapter 2.
263 On Bacchic dance and trance see Delavaud-Roux (1988), including a detailed analysis of elements of Bacchic dancing, such as whirled movement, leaps, and twisting.
264 Ramachandran (2011: 117–125).
265 E. *Ba.* 72.
266 Hahn (1998); Bartholomew and Wessely (2002).
267 D.S. 4. 3. 2–3, cited above in this chapter.
268 Keuls (1984: 143); Versnel (1990: 143); the crater: Beazley (1978: 1052. 25), discussed above, Chapter 2.
269 Bremmer (1984: 281–282).
270 E. *Ba.* 1084–1085; Villanueva Puig (2013: 267).
271 Hoffmann (1997: 29); Miller (1999: 245–247).
272 Fischer and Xygalatas (2014).
273 Kihlstrom (1994: 210–218).
274 Kihlstrom (1994: 210).
275 Kihlstrom (1994: 215).
276 Good (1994: 58).
277 Lynn et al. (2011).
278 Introduction.
279 McCauley and Lawson (2002: 190), italics in the original.
280 Kraemer (1979: 67).
281 E. *Ba.* 861.
282 Bremmer (1984: 273).
283 *Lusios*: Paus. 2. 2. 6 (Corinth); 2. 7. 6 (Sicyon); 9. 16. 6 (Thebes); *Katharsios*: S. *Ant.* 1143.
284 Therefore I disagree with M. Detienne who regards Dionysiac ecstatic cults as an 'anti-system' and 'subversion,' directed against the traditional cults and values (Detienne 1977: 62–65).
285 Jaccottet (2005: 195).
286 E. *Ba.* 72–76, see the text above in this chapter.
287 Osborne (1997: 209).
288 Cf. Sfameni Gasparro (1985: 18) for the lack of 'structure' characteristic of mystery initiations, in the Bacchic rites.

References

Acker, C. 2002. *Dionysos en transe: la voix des femmes*. Paris: L'Harmattan.
Arnaoutoglou, I. N. 2003. *Thusias heneka kai sunousias: Private Religious Associations in Hellenistic Athens*. Athens: Academy of Athens.
Barasch, M. 1991. *Imago Hominis: Studies in the Language of Art*. Vienna: IRSA.
Barr-Sharrar, B. 2008. *The Derveni Krater*. Princeton: American School of Classical Studies at Athens.
Bartholomew, R. E. and S. Wessely. 2002. "Protean nature of mass sociogenic illness. From possessed nuns to chemical and biological terrorism fears." *British Journal of Psychiatry* 180 (4): 300–306.

Bažant, J. and G. Berger-Doer. 1994. "Pentheus." In *LIMC*, 306–312.

Beazley, J. D. 1963. *Attic Red-Figure Vase-Painters*. Oxford: Clarendon Press.

Beazley, J. D. 1978. *Attic Black-Figure Vase-Painters*. Oxford: Clarendon Press.

Bélis, A. 1988. "Musique at transe dans le cortège dionysiaqie." In *Transe et théâtre*, edited by P. Ghiron-Bistagne, 9–26. Montpellier: Groupe interdisciplinaire du théâtre antique Université Paul Valéry – Montpellier III.

Bérard, C. 1992. "Phantasmatique érotique dans l'orgiasme dionysiaque." *Kernos* 5:13–26.

Bérard, C. and C. Bron. 1984. "Le jeu du satyre." In *La cité des images*, 127–145. Paris: Nathan.

Bérard, C. and C. Bron. 1986. "Bacchos au coeur de la cité. Le thiase dionysiaque dans l'espace politique." In *L'association dionysiaque dans les sociétés anciennes*, 13–30. Rome: L'École française de Rome.

Bernabé, A. 2014. "Metamorphosis metamorphoseos: Dionysus and the daughters of Minyas." In *Metamorfosi tra scienza e letteratura*, edited by F. Citti, L. Pasetti, and D. Pellacani, 1–13. Firenze: Olschki.

Bernabé, A. 2016. "Two Orphic Images in Euripides: *Hippolytus* 952–957 and *Cretans* 472 Kannicht." *TC* 8 (2):183–204.

Bonnechere, P. 1994. *Le sacrifice humain en Grèce ancienne*. Athènes-Liège: Centre International d'Étude de la Religion Grecque Antique.

Bremmer, J. N. 1984. "Greek maenadism reconsidered." *ZPE* 55:267–286.

Bremmer, J. N. 1999. "Transvestite Dionysus." In *Rites of Passage in Ancient Greece: Literature, Religion, Society*, edited by M. W. Padilla, 183–200. London-Toronto: Bucknell University Press.

Bremmer, J. N. 2013. "The agency of Greek and Roman statues." *OAth* 6:7–21.

Bremmer, J. N. 2014. *Initiation Into the Mysteries of the Ancient World*. Berlin-Boston: De Gruyter.

Bundrick, S. D. 2005. *Music and Image in Classical Athens*. Cambridge: Cambridge University Press.

Burkert, W. 1966. "Greek tragedy and sacrificial ritual." *GRBS* 7:87–121.

Burkert, W. 1983. *Homo Necans*. Berkeley-Los Angeles: University of California Press.

Burkert, W. 1985. *Greek Religion*. Cambridge, MA: Harvard University Press.

Buxton, R. 2013. *Myths and Tragedies in Their Ancient Greek Contexts*. Oxford: Oxford University Press.

Carpenter, T. H. 1993. "On the beardless Dionysus." In *Masks of Dionysus*, edited by T. H. Carpenter and C. A. Faraone, 185–206. Ithaca: Cornell University Press.

Carpenter, T. H. 1997. *Dionysian Imagery in Fifth-Century Athens*. Oxford: Oxford University Press.

Cartledge, P. 2002. *The Greeks: A Portrait of Self and Others*. Oxford: Oxford University Press.

Chantraine, P. 1983–1984. *Dictionnaire étymologique de la langue grecque*. Paris: Klincksieck.

Cole, S. G. 1980. "New evidence for the mysteries of Dionysos." *GRBS* 21 (3):223–238.

Cole, S. G. 2010. "Finding Dionysus." In *Greek Religion*, edited by D. Ogden, 327–341. Oxford: Oxford University Press.

Connelly, J. B. 2007. *Portrait of a Priestess: Women and Ritual in Ancient Greece*. Princeton: Princeton University Press.

Cook, R. M. 1960. *Greek Painted Pottery*. Methuen: London.

Craik, E. M. 2001. "Medical references in Euripides." *BICS* 45:81–95.

Delavaud-Roux, M.-H. 1988. "La danse au service du culte de Dionysos dans l'antiquité grecque." In *Transe et théâtre*, edited by P. Ghiron-Bistagne, 30–53. Montpellier: Groupe interdisciplinaire du théâtre antique Université Paul Valéry – Montpellier III.

Detienne, M. 1977. *Dionysos mis à mort*. Paris: Gallimard.

Detienne, M. 1986. "Dionysos et ses parousies: un dieu épidémique." In *L'association dionysiaque dans les sociétés anciennes*, 53–83. Rome: L'École française de Rome.

Detienne, M. 1989. *Dionysus at Large*. Cambridge, MA: Harvard University Press.

Detienne, M., and J.-P. Vernant. 1989. *The Cuisine of Sacrifice Among the Greeks*. Chicago: The University of Chicago Press.

Devereux, G. 1970. "The psychotherapy scene in Euripides' *Bacchae*." *JHS* 90:35–48.

Dodds, E. R. 1940. "Maenadism in the Bacchae." *HThR* 40:155–176.

Dodds, E. R. 1944. *Euripides: Bacchae, Edited With Introduction and Commentary*. Oxford: Clarendon Press.

Dowden, K. 1989. *Death and the Maiden: Girls' Initiation Rites in Greek Mythology*. London-New York: Routledge.

Dupont-Sommer, R. and L. Robert. 1964. *La déesse de Hiérapolis Castabala (Cilicie)*. Paris: Adrien Maisonneuve.

Edmonds III, R. G. 2013. *Redefining Ancient Orphism: A Study in Greek Religion*. Cambridge: Cambridge University Press.

Edwards, M. W. 1960. "Representation of maenads on archaic red-figure vesels." *JHS* 80:78–87.

Faraone, C. A. 2013. "Gender differentiation and role models in the worship of Dionysus: The Thracian and Thessalian patterns." In *Redefining Dionysos*, edited by A. Bernabé, M. Herrero de Jáuregui, A. I. Jiménez San Cristóbal, and R. Martín Hernández, 120–143. Berlin-New York: De Gruyter.

Fischer, R. and D. Xygalatas. 2014. "Extreme rituals as social technologies." *Journal of Cognition and Culture* 14:245–355.

Frontisi-Ducroux, F. 1986. "Images du ménadisme féminin: les vases des 'Lénéennes.'" In *L'association dionysiaque dans les sociétés anciennes*, 165–176. Rome: L'École française de Rome.

Frontisi-Ducroux, F. 1991. *Le dieu-masque: Une figure du Dionysos d'Athènes*. Paris: La Découverte.

Gantz, T. 1993. *Early Greek Myth*. 2 vols. Baltimore: The Johns Hopkins University Press.

Gill, C. 1985. "Ancient psychotherapy." *JHI* 46:307–325.

Goff, B. E. 2004. *Citizen Bacchae: Women's Ritual Practice in Ancient Greece*. Berkeley: University of California Press.

Good, B. J. 1994. *Medicine, Rationality, and Experience: An Anthropological Perspective*. Cambridge: Cambridge University Press.

Graf, F. 1985. *Nordionische Kulte*. Rome: Schweizerisches Institut in Rom.

Graf, F. 2010. "'The blessings of madness.' Dionysos, madness, and scholarship." *Archiv für Religionsgeschichte* 12:167–180.

Graf, F. and S. I. Johnston. 2007. *Ritual Texts for the Afterlife: Orpheus and the Bacchic Gold Leaves*. London-New York: Routledge.

Hacking, I. 2002. *Mad Travelers: Reflections on the Reality of Transient Mental Illnesses*. Cambridge, MA: Harvard University Press.

Hahn, R. A. 1998. "The nocebo phenomenon: Concept, evidence, and implications for public health." In *Understanding and Applying Medical Anthropology*, edited by P. Brown, 138–146. Mountain View: Mayfield.

Halm-Tisserant, M. 2004. "Le sparagmos, un rite de magie fécondante." *Kernos* 17:119–142.

Harrison, E. L. 1960. "Notes on Homeric psychology." *Phoenix* 14:63–80.

Harrison, J. E. 1928. *Prolegomena to the Study of Greek Religion.* Cambridge: Cambridge University Press.

Haussollier, B. 1919. "Bacchantes milésiennes." *BCH* 32:256–261.

Hedreen, G. 1994. "Silens, nymphs, and maenads." *JHS* 114:47–69.

Henrichs, A. 1969. "Die Maenaden von Milet." *ZPE* 4:223–241.

Henrichs, A. 1974. "Die Proitiden im hesiodischen Katalog." *ZPE* 15:297–301.

Henrichs, A. 1978. "Greek menadism from Olympias to Messalina." *HSCPh* 82:120–160.

Henrichs, A. 1982. "Changing Dionysiac identities." In *Jewish and Christian Self-Definition*, edited by B. M. Meyer and E. P. Sanders, 137–160. London: SCM Press.

Henrichs, A. 1984a. "Loss of self, suffering, violence: The modern view of Dionysus from Nietzsche to Girard." *HSCPh* 88:205–240.

Henrichs, A. 1984b. "Male intruders among the maenads: The so-called male celebrant." In *MNEMAI: Classical Studies in Memory of Karl K. Hulley*, edited by H. D. Evjen, 69–92. Chico: Scholars Press.

Henrichs, A. 2000. "Drama and *dromena*: Bloodshed, violence, and sacrificial metaphor in Euripides." *HSCPh* 100:173–188.

Henrichs, A. 2011. "Dionysos dismembered and restored to life: The earliest evidence (*OF* I-II)." In *Tracing Orpheus: Studies of Orphic Fragments in Honour of Alberto Bernabé*, edited by M. Herrero de Jáuregui, A. I. Jiménez San Cristóbal, and E. R. Luján Martínez, 61–68. Berlin-Boston: De Gruyter.

Hoffmann, H. 1997. *Sotades: Symbols of Immortality on Greek Vases.* Oxford: Oxford University Press.

Hughes, D. D. 1991. *Human Sacrifice in Ancient Greece.* London-New York: Routledge.

Isler-Kerényi, C. 2007. *Dionysos in Archaic Greece: An Understanding Through Images.* Leiden: Brill.

Jaccottet, A.-F. 2003. *Choisir Dionysos: Les associations dionysiaques ou la face cachée du dionysisme.* Zurich: Akanthus.

Jaccottet, A.-F. 2005. "Du thiase aux mystères. Dionysos entre le 'privé' et 'l'officiel.'" *Kernos* Suppl. 15:191–205.

Jeanmaire, H. 1970. *Dionysos: Histoire du culte de Bacchus.* Paris: Payot.

Jiménez San Cristóbal, A. I. 2009. "The meaning of *bacchos* and *baccheuein* in Orphism." In *Mystic Cults in Magna Graecia*, edited by G. Casadio and P. A. Johnston, 46–60. Austin: Texas University Press.

Jouan, F. 1992. "Dionysos chez Eschyle." *Kernos* 5:71–86.

Karanika, A. 2005. "Ecstatsis in healing: Practices in Southern Italy and Greece from antiquity to the present." In *Performing Ecstasies: Music, Dance, and Ritual in the Mediterranean*, edited by L. Del Guidica and N. van Deusen, 25–36. Ottawa: Institute of Mediaeval Music.

Katz, M. A. 1998. "Did the women of ancient Athens attend the theater in the eighteenth century?" *CPh* 93:105–124.

Kefalidou, E. 2009. "The iconography of madness in Attic vase-painting." In *Athenian Potters and Painters*, edited by J. H. Oakley and O. Palagia, 90–99. Oxford: Oxbow Books.

Keuls, E. 1984. "Male-female interaction in fifth-century Dionysiac ritual as shown in Attic vase painting." *ZPE* 55:287–296.

Kihlstrom, J. F. 1994. "Altering states of consciousness." In *Learning, Remembering, Believing: Enhancing Human Performance*, edited by D. Druckman and R. A. Bjork, 207–248, 351–364. Washington, DC: The National Academies Press.

Kirk, G. S. 1990. *The Iliad: A Commentary. Books 5–8.* Cambridge: Cambridge University Press.

Konstantinou, A. forthcoming. "'To the mountain': The ritual space of maenadism in the Athenian imaginary." In *Ascending and Descending the Acropolis: Sacred Travel in Ancient Attica and Its Borderland*, edited by W. Friese, S. Handberg, and T. M. Kristensen. Aarhus: Danish Institute at Athens.

Kowalzig, B. 2007. *Singing for the Gods: Performances of Myth and Ritual in Archaic and Classical Greece.* Oxford: Oxford University Press.

Kraemer, R. S. 1979. "Ecstasy and possession: The attraction of women to the cult of Dionysus." *HThR* 72:55–80.

Lada-Richards, I. 1999. *Initiating Dionysus: Ritual and Theatre in Aristophanes' Frogs.* Oxford: Oxford University Press.

Lawler, L. B. 1927. "The maenads: A contribution to the study of the dance in ancient Greece." *Memoirs of the American Academy in Rome* 6:69–112.

Leiniekes, V. 1996. *The City of Dionysos: A Study of Euripides' Bakchai.* Stuttgart: Teubner.

Lissarrague, F. 1990. "The sexual life of satyrs." In *Before Sexuality: The Construction of Erotic Experience in the Ancient Greek World*, edited by D. M. Halperin, J. J. Winkler, and F. I. Zeitlin, 53–82. Princeton: Princeton University Press.

Lynn, C. D., J. Paris, C. A. Frye, and L. M. Schell. 2011. "Glossolalia is associated with differences in biomarkers of arousal and stress among Apostolic Pentecostals." *Religion, Brain and Behavior* 1 (3):173–191.

Mattes, J. 1970. *Der Wahnsinn im griechischen Mythos und in der Dichtung bis zum Drama des fünften Jahrhunderts.* Heidelberg: Winter.

McCauley, R. N. and E. T. Lawson. 2002. *Bringing Ritual to Mind: Psychological Foundations of Cultural Forms.* Cambridge: Cambridge University Press.

Menier, T. 2001. "L'étrangerité dionysiaque." In *Chanter les dieux. Musique et religion dans l'antiquité grecque et romaine*, edited by P. Brulé and C. Vendries, 233–242. Rennes: Presses universitaires de Rennes.

Miller, M. C. 1999. "Reexamining transvestism in Archaic and Classical Athens: The Zewadski stamnos." *AJA* 103 (2):223–253.

Molinos Tejada, M. T. 1992. "Sur *Les Bacchantes* de Théocrite." *Kernos* 5:109–117.

Montiglio, S. 2005. *Wandering in Ancient Greek Culture.* Chicago: The University of Chicago Press.

Nilsson, M. P. 1957. *The Dionysiac Mysteries of the Hellenistic and Roman Age.* Lund: Gleerup.

Obbink, D. 1993. "Dionysus poured out: Ancient and modern theories of sacrifice and cultural formation." In *Masks of Dionysus*, edited by T. H. Carpenter and C. A. Faraone, 65–86. Ithaca: Cornell University Press.

O'Brien-Moore, A. 1924. *Madness in Ancient Literature.* Weimar: Wagner.

Osborne, R. 1994. "Framing the centaur: Reading fifth-century architectural sculpture." In *Art and Text in Ancient Greek Culture*, edited by S. Goldhill, 52–84. Cambridge: Cambridge University Press.

Osborne, R. 1997. "The ecstasy and the tragedy: Varieties of religious experience in art, drama, and society." In *Greek Tragedy and the Historian*, edited by C. Pelling, 187–211. Oxford: Oxford University Press.

Otto, W. F. 1933. *Dionysos: Mythos und Kultus.* Frankfurt am Main: Klostermann.

Parke, H. W. 1977. *Festivals of the Athenians.* London: Thames & Hudson.

Parke, H. W. and D.E.W. Wormell. 1956. *The Delphic Oracle*. 2 vols. Oxford: Blackwell.

Parker, R. 1983. *Miasma: Pollution and Purification in Early Greek Religion*. Oxford: Oxford University Press.

Parker, R. 2011. *On Greek Religion*. Ithaca: Cornell University Press.

Perdizet, P. 1910. *Cultes et mythes du Pangée*. Paris-Nancy: Berger-Levrault.

Porres Caballero, S. 2013. "Maenadic ecstasy in Greece: Fact or fiction?" In *Redefining Dionysus*, edited by A. Bernabé, M. Herrero de Jáuregui, A. I. Jiménez San Cristóbal, and R. Martín Hernández, 159–184. Berlin: De Gruyter.

Ramachandran, V. S. 2011. *The Tell-Tale Brain: Unlocking the Mystery of Human Nature*. London: Heinemann.

Rayor, D. J. 2004. *The Homeric Hymns*. Berkeley-Los Angeles: University of California Press.

Reicher, S. 2000. "Crowd behavior." In *Encyclopedia of Psychology*, edited by A. E. Kazdin, 374–377. Washington, DC: American Psychological Association.

Richardson, N. J. 1974. *The Homeric Hymn to Demeter*. Oxford: Clarendon Press.

Richardson, N. J. 1993. *The Iliad: A Commentary. Books 21–24*. Cambridge: Cambridge University Press.

Riley, K. 2008. *The Reception and Performance of Euripides' Heracles*. Oxford: Oxford University Press.

Rissanen, M. 2012. "The *Hirpi Sorani* and the wolf cults of Central Italy." *Arctos* 46:115–135.

Rouget, G. 1990. *La musique et la trance*. Paris: Gallimard.

Roux, J. 1972. *Euripide, Les Bacchantes, II: Commentaire*. Paris: Les Belles Lettres.

Santamaría, M. A. 2013. "The term *bacchos* and Dionysos Bacchios." In *Redefining Dionysos*, edited by A. Bernabé, M. Herrero de Jáuregui, A. I. Jiménez San Cristóbal, and R. Martín Hernández, 38–57. Berlin: De Gruyter.

Schachter, A. 1981–94. *Cults of Boeotia*. 4 vols., BICS Suppl. 38, 1–4. London: Institute of Classical Studies.

Schlesier, R. 2011. "Der bakchische Gott." In *A Different God?* edited by R. Schlesier, 173–202. Berlin-Boston: De Gruyter.

Seaford, R. 1994. *Reciprocity and Ritual: Homer and Tragedy in the Developing City-State*. Oxford: Oxford University Press.

Seaford, R. 1996. *Euripides: Bacchae, With an Introduction, Translation and Commentary*. Warminster: Aris & Phillips.

Seaford, R. 2006. *Dionysos*. London-New York: Routledge.

Seidensticker, B. 1979. "Sacrificial ritual in the *Bacchae*." In *Arktouros: Hellenic Studies Presented to B. M. W. Knox on the Occasion of His 65th Birthday*, edited by G. W. Bowersock, W. Burkert, and M.C.J. Putnam, 181–190. Berlin-New York: De Gruyter.

Sfameni Gasparro, G. 1985. *Soteriology and Mystic Aspects in the Cult of Cybele and Attis*. Leiden: Brill.

Sfameni Gasparro, G. 2011. "Mysteries and Oriental cults: A problem in the history of religions." In *The Religious History of the Roman Empire: Pagans, Jews, and Christians*, edited by J. A. North and S.R.F. Price, 276–324. Oxford: Oxford University Press.

Shalev, D. 2012. "Diagnostics of altered mental states: From Euripides' Bacchae to medieval Arabic texts." *SCI* 31:161–183.

Sifakis, G. M. 2001. *Aristotle on the Function of Tragic Poetry*. Herakleion: Crete University Press.

Simon, B. 1978. *Mind and Madness in Ancient Greece: The Classical Roots of Modern Psychiatry*. Ithaca: Cornell University Press.

Slater, W. J. 1978. "Artemon and Anacreon: No text without context." *Phoenix* 32 (3):185–194.

Sourvinou-Inwood, C. 2005. *Hylas, the Nymphs, Dionysus and Others*. Stockholm: Paul Aaström.

Topper, K. R. 2015. "Dionysos comes to Thrace: The metaphor of corrupted sacrifice and the introduction of Dionysian cult in images of Lykourgos's madness." *Arethusa* 48: 139–171.

Ustinova, Y. 2005. "Lege et consuetudine: Private cult associations in the Greek law." *Kernos* Suppl. 5:267–288.

Ustinova, Y. 2009a. "Apollo Iatros: A Greek god of Pontic origin." In *Die Griechen und ihre Nachbarn am Nordrand des Schwarzen Meeres*, edited by K. Stähler and D. Metzler, 245–298. Münster: Ugarit-Verlag.

Ustinova, Y. 2009b. *Caves and the Ancient Greek Mind: Descending Underground in the Search for Ultimate Truth*. Oxford: Oxford University Press.

van Hooff, A.J.L. 1990. *From Autothanasia to Suicide: Self-killing in Classical Antiquity*. London: Routledge.

Versnel, H. S. 1990. *Ter Unus. Isis, Dionysos, Hermes: Three Studies in Henotheism*. Leiden: Brill.

Vian, F. 1965. "Mélampous et les Proities." *RÉA* 67:23–30.

Villanueva Puig, M.-C. 1986. "À propos des thyiades de Delphes." In *L'association dionysiaque dans les sociétés anciennes*, 31–51. Rome: L'École française de Rome.

Villanueva Puig, M.-C. 1998. "Le cas du thiase dionysiaque." *Ktèma* 23:365–374.

Villanueva Puig, M.-C. 2009. *Ménades. Recherche sur la genèse iconographique du thiase féminin de Dionysos*. Paris: Les Belles Lettres.

Villanueva Puig, M.-C. 2013. "Un cas de possession ritualisée: le ménadisme." In *Perception et construction du divine dans l'Antiquité*, edited by P. Borgeaud and D. Fabiano, 261–292. Geneva: Droz.

Waller, J. 2009. "A forgotten plague: Making sense of dancing mania." *The Lancet* 373 (9664):624–625.

Wathelet, P. 1991. "Dionysos chez Homère ou la folie divine." *Kernos* 4:61–82.

West, M. L. 1983. "Tragica VI." *BICS* 30:63–72.

West, M. L. 1990. *Studies in Aeschylus*. Oxford: Oxford University Press.

Wiley, A. S. and J. S. Allen. 2009. *Medical Anthropology: A Biocultural Approach*. Oxford: Oxford University Press.

Winnington-Ingram, R. P. 1948. *Euripides and Dionysus*. Cambridge: Cambridge University Press.

Xanthaki-Karamanou, G. 2012. "The 'Dionysiac' plays of Aeschylus and Euripides' Bacchae: Reaffirming traditional cult in late fifth century." In *Crisis on Stage*, edited by A. Markantonatos and B. Zimmermann, 323–342. Berlin: De Gruyter.

Xygalatas, D. 2011. "Ethnography, historiography, and the making of history in the tradition of the Anastenaria." *History and Anthropology* 22 (1):57–74.

Xygalatas, D. 2014. *The Burning Saints: Cognition and Culture in the Fire-Walking Rituals of the Anastenaria*. London: Routledge.

Yerucham, A. 2016. "Cultic soundscapes in Euripides' Bacchae." *RCCM* 14:138–154.

4 *Mania* on the battlefield and on the march

An uncanny relationship connected Dionysus Bacchius to two very different gods, Pan and Lyssa, who shared several common features, notably the ability to drive mortals mad and a semi-bestial nature. As we have seen, Lyssa the goddess of wolfish rage, could 'inspire the bacchants';[1] however, she was most prominent as the deity who inspired gruesome combat fury. The goat-like Pan resembled the silens, and was the god of *paneia*, panic, which is inexplicable fear, above all in military contexts.[2] In the fifth-century Homeric hymn praising his accomplishments, Pan is said to be especially pleasing to Dionysus Bacchius, most probably because the two gods shared more than one expertise, primarily *mania* and music.[3] Ferocity and drunkenness, terror and twisted perception – these human reactions, associated with Dionysus Bacchius *par excellence*, were usually attributed to the will of other gods, when manifested in a military environment.

Warfare often involves abnormal behaviour, including aggressive insanity and irrational uncontrolled reactions. Warriors' rage, expressed on the battlefield, was praised and supported by their community, seeking military victories at any price. However, fighting was often harmful not only to the body, but also to the mind of the soldiers, who returned home stressed, dysfunctional, or insane, and became dangerous or useless to the society which had sent them to the war. Thus, madness inherent to heroic inspiration was beneficial – although not mentioned by Socrates in his list of the blessings of *mania* – and therefore sung by the poets, while the psychological injuries caused in combat presented a menace to the society. In addition, battlefield alterations of consciousness included visions that encouraged the desperate, and the enemy's panic was a divine gift which could ensure one's victory: battlefield *mania* had many faces. In this chapter, I will discuss madness of valour and fear and the ambiguity of these states, as seen by the Greeks and by modern psychologists.

Combat fury: Lyssa

Before the gates of Thebes, mortally wounded Tydeus was given the head of Melanippus, whom he had just killed; Tydeus, wounded though he was, split open the head and sucked the brains out of it, an action that nauseated Athena and made her abandon the decision to make Tydeus immortal. This scene appears in the *Thebais* and is depicted in the fifth-century art.[4] Tydeus is not the only Greek hero who committed acts of inconceivable brutality. Achilles' unquenchable hatred for Hector could only be satisfied by the merciless mutilation of Hector's corpse: this savage cruelty, which is described as madness, appalled the gods.[5]

Mythological heroes have dreamt of cutting off their enemy's heads on several occasions,[6] and at times have been compared to animals devouring their prey.[7] Achilles and his Myrmidons are portrayed as exceptionally fierce: ready for the battle, Achilles' soldiers are like 'raw-eating wolves' (*lukoi ômophagoi*), and Hecuba calls Achilles *omêstês*, 'one who devours raw meat.'[8] The last words that Hector hears before his death convey the wish of Achilles to cut Hector's flesh and eat it raw.[9] Given the fact that Homer regarded cannibalism as *mania*, and raw-eating as primitive,[10] nothing can epitomise bestial warrior madness more powerfully than the drive to devour human flesh. In addition, the lesser Ajax is portrayed severing the head of his foe and throwing it like a ball, so that it falls at Hector's feet,[11] and Peneleus proudly carried his enemy's severed head on a spear 'like a poppy-head.'[12] Scenes of decapitation and mutilation of bodies are quite common in the *Iliad*, and are depicted by the poet as a repugnant, but inescapable part of warfare.[13]

The word usage and images of the epic are immediately reminiscent of the expressions used in references to Bacchic rites, in drama, and in other contexts, which have been analysed in the previous chapter, such as Dionysus' worship as *Omêstês*, description of the maenads as 'Lyssa's swift dogs,'[14] and the emphasis on their non-human energy and ferocity. A Bacchic counterpart to Peneleus brandishing an enemy's head on the spear is Agave parading with her son's head on a *thyrsus*; soldiers compared to a pack of wolves are mirrored in the *thiasos* of maenadic hunting hounds. In addition, a Hellenistic source attests warlike dances (*purrhichê*) performed by dancers carrying Bacchic rods and torches instead of spears, and in the fifth and fourth centuries satyrs too became involved in *purrhichê*.[15] One cannot escape the impression that in many respects, the mad warrior was the male equivalent of the maenad, the 'mad woman.' Even after Homer, warriors are still described as mad: in Aeschylus' *Seven against Thebes*, Tydeus rages (*margos*), eager for battle and Hippomedon, 'possessed by Ares, raves in Bacchic ecstasy like a *thuias*, his look causing terror.'[16] The hero in the grip of the god of battle fare is unequivocally compared to a maenad seized by Dionysus: the resemblance of the states of possession by these gods cannot be underscored in stronger terms.

The great warriors of Homer were not simply fearless and merciless on the battlefield, they actually went berserk.[17] While engaged in fighting, Hector is represented as mad (*mainetai*),[18] as both he and Achilles are driven by *lussa*, rabid, literally wolfish, fury, the word deriving from *lukos*, wolf.[19] Diomedes rages, seized by *lussa* as well,[20] and even describes his spear as 'raging.'[21] Patroclus, a less prominent hero, is also associated with *mania*: his 'hands rage' when he enters a battle.[22] Achilles' *lussa* is expressed by limitless courage and lust of glory: in the combat, 'strong *lussa* always held his heart, and he was enraged to win glory.'[23] Mad fury in battle is almost synonymic to ultimate valour: only the greatest heroes fight, impelled by the gods in outbursts of rabid rage: all the rest are sane, less brave – and less admirable.[24]

The words applied by Homer in the depictions of raging heroes are not metaphors: in his fury, Hector foams at the mouth, his face distorts, his eyes become fiery,[25] and he is described by his opponent as a 'rabid dog.'[26] These portrayals resemble the stereotype image of the madman's behaviour in Attic tragedy: throughout the fifth century, fiercely rolling and bloodshot eyes and a foaming mouth are constant signs of madness.[27] Flashing eyes, contorted faces, and a frenzy of raging people are not mere literary *topoi*: in their martial fury, the berserks contorted their faces and bodies frighteningly[28] – and that is exactly what the most eminent Homeric heroes did.

The horrible frenzy of Aeschylus' Argive warriors is presented as negative by the besieged Thebans, and the *lussa* of Homer's heroes is usually referred to by their opponents in fight.[29] However, it is precisely the fear caused to the enemies that makes battle frenzy a warrior's prized asset. It was in the grip of *lussa* that Achilles fought most fiercely, eager to win glory.[30] Forgetful of danger and mercy, endowed with abnormal force, non-human in their violence, male maenads were most deadly for their enemies – and consequently a precious resource for their own community.

As mentioned in the Introduction, Lyssa had a talking role in several tragedies, and was portrayed on vases as a fear-provoking semi-bestial female with canine heads emerging from her human head.[31] In Euripides' *Heracles*, Hera wished to throw the hero into the depth of misery, making him slay his family in a fit of frenzy. However, the deity who directly caused Heracles' murderous madness was Lyssa, rather than Hera herself, though she was quite able to drive people mad on her own, as the list of her victims demonstrates.[32] This is hardly incidental: Lyssa seems to have been chosen because the derangement she inflicted led to uncontrolled violence and slaughter.

Lussa, rabies, was well-known as an animal disease, and Pausanias was sure that Actaeon's dogs, that tore him apart, were rabid.[33] Since it takes between a month and three months before a human bitten by a rabid dog develops the symptoms of the disease, it is improbable that the connection between canine rabies and human hydrophobia was known in Archaic Greece – in fact, even Aristotle was convinced that *lussa* could infect only animals.[34] It is however feasible that unbounded murderous violence was associated with rabies, and given a canine name by analogy: the symptoms of rabid dogs, such as unstoppable running, a foaming mouth, insensitivity to pain, and mostly horrible violence, were evident in soldiers in the grip of battlefield madness. This association, combined with the comparison of groups of young males to packs of ferocious wolves or dogs, attested in several Indo-European cultures (to be discussed shortly), probably prompted the concept of *lussa*, murderous bestial rage of individual warriors and combat units.[35] This phenomenon was personified as Lyssa, the goddess of mad violence and fearlessness, primarily – but not exclusively – in the battlefield.

Not only mortal heroes were frenzied during combat: Homer describes Ares as 'mad' (*mainomenos*) more than once.[36] When Ares takes possession of a warrior, the mortal is filled with force.[37] Most significantly, Odysseus makes a gnomic remark that 'Ares raves randomly' (or 'blindly'),[38] meaning that frenzy is inherent to the behaviour of the war-god, hence to the war.[39] Ares remains mad (*mainomenos*) in later poetry, as well: for Aeschylus, he is 'mad, inspiring to frenzy, slaying the people, defiling the holiness.'[40] In modern research, Ares is often represented as the embodiment of hateful brutality,[41] yet his image is much more complex:[42] Ares incarnates the war as it is, where violent excitement, scorn of danger, and savage aggression are not only culturally acceptable, but necessary for annihilating the enemy and thus socially desirable. Ares' fury is the divine prototype of the madness of great warriors, best praised if called 'equal to Ares.'[43] Similarly, many of these warriors, 'dear to Ares,' were possessed by mad fury on the battlefield.

Madness during the combat is intricately associated with the hero's *menos*, physical and mental energy. Excessive *menos* can be destructive no less than *mania*: Andromache bitterly predicts to Hector that his own *menos* will destroy him.[44] Diomedes is depicted as mad (*mainetai*) beyond measure, while nobody can match his *menos*,[45] and the proximity of the two words seems to indicate that Homer is aware of the semantic connection between *menos* and *mania*. *Menos* is the most common Homeric designation for intrepid courage and zeal, as well as mind, spiritual force, rage, and anger; very often, it is conceived of as an external force, a power with which the gods impassion mortals.[46] Etymologically, it is cognate to *mania*, and both words are related to the Indo-European *men-*, meaning 'active mental force.'[47] *Mênis*, the first word in the *Iliad* – and in Western literature – designating numinous anger, of Achilles or of the gods, is perhaps another continuation of the same stem.[48]

This etymology suggests that Proto-Indo-Europeans were aware of the phenomenon of battlefield madness, and associated fearlessness with frenzied rage. Decades ago, G. Dumézil noticed that prominent warriors displayed a bestial nature:[49] in Indo-European cultural and linguistic evidence, heroic *furor*, transporting the warrior beyond himself and turning him into an animal, allows exploits of which he would not be capable in his regular state of mind.[50] Eating raw flesh, of their enemies or of animals, was attributed to heroes of the past in many Indo-European cultures, and in particular the Germanic legends.[51] In several Indo-European cultures, bands of young men known as *Männerbünde* were attributed *Kampfwut*, mad fearlessness and inhuman force, and associated with wolves, dogs, or bears.[52] Ancient rites involving the warrior's transformation into a wolf are echoed in Greek myths, as well as historically attested cults and customs, associated with lycanthropy, mainly of initiatory character, marking the transition from a youth to a warrior – who requires wolfish stamina and bloodthirst to become worthy of praise.[53]

Some of the ancient soldiers may have feigned loss of control and the accompanying frenzy, and we will never know how many warriors in each generation actually experienced *furor bersercicus*.[54] The crucial point is that mad courage and relentlessness, connected to canine violence, were expected from young Indo-European warriors belonging to different cultures and praised as a virtue to be emulated. These warriors formed the elite units of the past.[55]

Indo-European reckless raging warriors took pride in fighting naked, disdaining human garb and assimilating to wild beasts – and Greek eighth-century statuettes often portray warriors naked but for their helmet and belt, even with a shield hurled backwards in a typical berserk gesture.[56] Whatever the reasons for other representations of naked male body in Greece, the lack of a cuirass and the position of the shield of naked warriors are telling.

A hero may easily lose control of his surging *menos*, and his excessive force might look to the outsider like rabid madness. Indo-European mythology reflects the ambiguity of combat valour: seized by martial frenzy, Cuchulainn, a great Celtic hero, was about to attack his own army; the Roman Horatius killed his sister on his way from the battle with the Curiatii.[57] *Mania* is inseparable from heroic vigour and potentially dangerous to society, but since elite units are the core and the pride of every army, ancient communities had to comply with the ambiguity between the desirable berserk fury and feared aggressive insanity.

Attribution of fearlessness to divine intervention persisted in post-Homeric poetry: Ares remains 'mad' for Aeschylus.[58] The life legend of Tyrtaeus, who began as a despised Athenian and ended up by saving Sparta as a military leader, is doubtlessly unhistorical – but the pattern which lies at its base is revealing.[59] Fourth-century sources refer to the leading role of the Athenian Tyrtaeus in winning the Second Messenian War, and later authors give an account of the Spartans' frustration as they asked the Pythia for council, and were advised to bring in an Athenian.[60] Several details immediately stand out: the lame and lowly Tyrtaeus was 'simple-minded' or even 'mad,'[61] but when this living joke arrived in Sparta, the god who gave the oracle made him a victorious general. Tyrtaeus' military method is conspicuous: he 'became inspired' (*epipnous*), and the soldiers, instilled with *enthousiasmos*, rushed into battle.[62] Whatever the historicity of this legend, it comprises several crucial notions: super-human powers that endorse the poet, his liminality and inspirational madness induced by divine will, as well as poetry enthused by the god and the contagion of madness, which is passed on from the insane poet to soldiers who become insane, forget their fear – and triumph. In this story, martial *mania* springs from its musico-poetic counterpart, and this link underscores the flexibility and interconnectedness of different kinds of *mania* in the world view of the Greeks.

Tyrtaeus of Sparta was not the only poet who incited military spirit: another famous inspired singer who was a leader of a warrior band is Orpheus, who in Conon's account was killed while performing rites (*orgiazein*) of armed men in a hall of initiations (*teletai*).[63] Hector boasted of his knowledge of warfare, stressing that he knows how to 'sing and dance' (*melpesthai*) for Ares in a close fight,[64] and this expertise was considered no less crucial than the ability to wield the shield or attack chariots. In other Indo-European cultures, famous warriors are often poets and musicians, as well.[65] T. M. Compton demonstrates that the common ground shared by poetry and military valour was their attribution to divine inspiration conceived as madness: 'As violence was dependent on a special kind of war madness, so poetry also was dependent on madness.'[66]

Music and dance were essential in manipulating the consciousness of military units or groups of soldiers. Flute players are depicted marching before the hoplite cohort on the mid-seventh century Chigi vase.[67] Pyrrhic dancing doubtlessly belonged to a very ancient tradition, prominent in several important festivals of Classical Athens, such as the Panathenaea and the City Dionysia. Even if its military value in the fifth century is unclear, symbolically it was part of a series of rites creating civic cohesion.[68] During the Classical period, armed dances, among them *purrhichê*, were not only an important stage of male transition rites and a rehearsal of real-life attacks,[69] but also a way to bring about an intense feeling of oneness in the dancers.[70] On Crete and in Boeotia armed dances were supposed to inspire valour, and the boys of Thespiae learnt dancing in palaestra, 'for the fact that they acquired courage through their music, as well as through the care of their bodies, and they practiced the movements they made when wearing armour to musical accompaniment.'[71] In earlier times, when war dances were probably performed before battle, their ardour could easily lead to a fighting frenzy.[72] In any case, the ubiquity of war dances in Greece is indicative of a symbolic connection of dancing and martial excitement.[73] Thus, the Greeks appear to have used time-honoured techniques of consciousness manipulation, such as rhythmic music, singing and dancing, for creating emotional bonds between soldiers, attuning them for a common action, diminishing apprehension, and supporting optimism.[74]

Another method of priming for battle was alcohol consumption, known to depress self-protecting instincts and induce courage, as well as cruel aggression. Belligerent inebriation was often quite literal: the Greeks did not fight sober,[75] and sometimes they were quite drunk.[76]

During or after the battle, inebriation with violence could come. In the fifth century, it was probably common knowledge that bloodshed could drive the murderer crazy. In *Heracles*, when the protagonist commits terrible atrocities, killing his wife and children, his father asks him whether he is being maddened by the fresh corpses of those whom he had just slain.[77] In the context of the play, Amphitryon misses the point, but he puts forward a suggestion that is intended to look probable to the audience: successful slaughter may destroy the mind of the killer, even if he is victorious. In *Eurypylus*, when Sophocles depicts the Argive soldiers laughing while trampling over dead bodies, he apparently means that they are not simply enjoying their revenge, but have temporarily lost their minds[78] – yet the dramatist clearly does not consider this horrible behaviour inconceivable. The word *maschalismos*, denoting the nauseating practice of cutting off the dead enemy's extremities and hanging them upon their necks, occurs only in drama: the question is whether this act could have been depicted so vividly if it were absolutely unprecedented.[79]

Homer sang the glory of great heroes, and since their valour was associated with their *lussa*, the poet freely used terms implying frenzy in his combat scenes. In historical times, the tactics of the hoplite phalanx emphasised cooperation between soldiers rather than personal rage.[80] However, the terrible head-to-head collisions of the soldiers required tremendous mental efforts, fuelled with wrath bordering on fury.[81] Centuries after Homer, soldiers could still fight while possessed by rabid rage, *lussa*. A Spartan dishonoured at Thermopylae, who wished to restore his good name, rushed into the battle in a frenzy (*lussôn*) at Plataea.[82] Similar cases must have been known to Aristotle, who attributed reckless courage in battle to madness: 'we should call a man mad (*mainomenos*), or else insensitive to pain, if he feared nothing.'[83]

Usually however, the fury of an individual hero was replaced by the rage of many or all the soldiers. When Xenophon's army won a spectacular victory, he and his people 'feared that some *lussa* had fallen on us, as if on dogs.'[84] In two passages on bravery, Aristotle attributed formidable fearlessness to the Celts, explaining that they owed their daring to a 'passion' (*thumos*), supposedly a national trait that they cultivated; the philosopher's admiration of the barbarians' excessive boldness is mixed with contempt for their lack of ignorance and madness.[85] The two authors, referring to the Greeks and barbarians, associated limitless courage and battlefield fury with an exceptional mental state, which invited comparisons to beasts and caused aversion and admiration simultaneously.

R. Garland argues convincingly that the most famous battle in the Greek history, the battle of Marathon, was won due to the exceptional elation of the Athenians, which looked like madness.[86] In Herodotus' account,

> Their battle being arrayed and the omens of sacrifice favouring, straightway the Athenians were let go and charged the Persians at a run. There was between the armies a space no less than eight furlongs. When the Persians saw them come running they prepared to receive them, imputing to the Athenians *mania* and utter self-destruction, seeing that they were so few and charging them at speed. . . . But the Athenians, closing all together with the Persians, fought in memorable fashion; for they were the first Greeks . . . who charged their enemies at a run, and the first who endured the sight of Median garments and men clad therein; till then the Greeks were frightened by the very name of the Medes.[87]

Herodotus could hardly know how the Persians assessed the behaviour of the Greeks. However, he was able to learn from the surviving Marathonian heroes and their sons that the Athenian soldiers felt possessed by *mania*: they were fearless to such a degree that their onslaught looked suicidal, they ran almost a kilometre and a half in full armour, and boldly withstood the horrifying sight of the Persian formation. The combination of humanly impossible physical feats[88] and heroic valour was viable owing to martial rage, defined by Herodotus – or his sources – as *mania*. We will see shortly that this frenzy was accompanied by visions experienced by many Athenians who claimed to have seen either supporting or adversary super-human warriors on the battlefield.[89] Thus, at the moment of tremendous danger, thousands of extremely stressed Athenians probably underwent an alteration of consciousness that neutralised their fear, endowed them with tremendous force, and gave rise to hallucinations.

Warrior's *lussa* could not be switched off easily, and bloodthirsty savagery remained inseparable from great martial exploits. Although some extremes, such as the mutilation of the enemy's corpses, began to be regarded as inappropriate in Classical Greece, defacement of bodies was well-known, although considered impious and characteristic of barbarians. After the battle of Plataea in 479, Pausanias refused to cut off the head of the Persian Mardonius, as a revenge for the decapitation of Leonidas' corpse by the Persians a year earlier, but the idea, put forward by an aristocrat from Aegina, was hardly unheard of.[90] After the battle of Cunaxa, Greek mercenaries disfigured the bodies of their fallen enemies in order to inspire terror in their foes.[91] Soldiers appear dancing and holding severed heads in fifth-century art.[92] It is very possible that Tyrtaeus' graphic description of an old soldier, lying dead 'and clutching his bloodied genitals, his nakedness exposed,' refers to mutilation.[93] Even cannibalistic dreams were not unknown: in 398/7, at the preparatory stage of Cinadon's conspiracy, helots, perioeci, and Spartans of lower class were unable to conceal their desire 'to eat the Spartans raw.'[94]

Extreme cruelty is attested to on multiple occasions. Enemies seeking refuge could be burnt alive, as the Argives who were burnt by the Spartans in 494, or stoned to death, as the Corinthians slaughtered by the Athenians in 460.[95] Prisoners of war could be drowned: first tied with ropes, and then pushed under the water with spears,[96] as was the fate of sailors on two triremes detained by the Athenians in 405.[97] In 413, having captured Mycalessus, the Thracians under Athenian command massacred all the inhabitants, with their women and children, and every other living thing, including beasts of burden; the collective responsibility of the Athenians for the acts of the Thracians whom they led to this city seems evident.[98] In 511, the Crotoniates in their wrath (*orgê*) did not take prisoners, but slew all the Sybarites who tried to escape.[99] This fury was of course inspired by each soldier's personal hatred of the enemy and the excitement of the battle, enhanced by secretion of adrenalin and steroids that occurs in humans under extreme stress.[100] Battlefield rage allowed fighters to vent their anger and tension,[101] yet it also belonged to the age-long tradition, reflected in the *Iliad*. In Archaic and Classical Greece, battlefield phenomena involving limitless brutality, indicative of rabid fury, persisted and are attested to frequently.

In sum, in early Archaic Greece (like many other Indo-European cultures) reckless martial fury made a warrior more useful to his community and was therefore supported, cultivated, and rewarded with 'unwilting glory,' as well as mundane privileges. While Homer and Aeschylus are still in the realm of poetic images, their creations merge into a picture of a society which accepted fury on the battlefield as an attribute of a valiant warrior. With changes in combat tactics during the Classical period, the warrior's rage transformed, but did not disappear: the battlefield fury of an intrepid fighter was still conductive to madness and praised as heroic, highly valued by society.[102] The *Kampfwut* of the Indo-European warriors remained an asset on Greek battlefields.

Psychological injuries and combat stress: Phobos[103]

Even the most valiant Homeric heroes knew fear – Hector flew in fear from Achilles, and Achilles in his turn was frightened by the flooding of the river Scamander.[104] A rational perception of danger fear could inflate to exorbitant dimensions of fear. Today, uncontrollable incapacitating fear is considered one of the symptoms of combat stress.[105] Delirious rage on the battlefield may lead to a horrible anti-climax, but even non-heroic exposure to combat situations could result in mental disorders, ranging from depression to bouts of feral insanity. Dysfunctional reactions to combat stress range from immediate (e.g. dissociative fugue, panic attack), through acute (e.g. acute stress disorder or ASD), to late or chronic (e.g. post-traumatic stress disorder or PTSD) stress reactions, and include exacerbation of previous psychopathology.[106] Not only the fear of being killed or wounded may lead to a breakdown, but revulsion to killing another human also has a very powerful effect.[107] It has been demonstrated that general trauma intensity, including physical distance between adversaries, is crucial in determining the possibility of long-term psychiatric consequences: the closer the engagement the higher the potential risk for developing a psychiatric disorder.[108] Ancient battle techniques were mostly based on close combat: the killer often looked into the eyes of the person he was killing.[109] From this point of view, an ancient soldier was even more exposed than a modern one to psychiatric collapse:[110] the danger of mutilation and death were always present, but in addition the experience of witnessing the death of a person one had just killed might become traumatic by itself.

In ancient Greece, one may surmise that the psychological risk of being in battle was balanced by seasonal cessation of intensive warfare, pro-war education, campaigning in groups of people who have known each other since their childhood, and other cultural and social factors that defined soldiering as part of the male identity.[111] However, the unceasing war efforts of Greek cities probably resulted in a high rate of acute and chronic psychiatric casualties.

The Greeks knew how horrible the sight of the battlefield was: Tyrtaeus wrote that 'no man is good in war unless he can bear the sight of blood and death.'[112] The brutality of the 'killing zone' was nightmarish.[113] Xenophon describes the final sights of the battle of Coronea:

> Now that the fighting was at an end, a weird spectacle met the eye, as one surveyed the scene of the conflict – the earth stained with blood, friend and foe lying dead side by side, shields smashed to pieces, spears snapped in two, daggers bared of their sheaths, some on the ground, some embedded in the bodies, some yet gripped by the hand.[114]

Apparently, not everyone could stand the dreadful spectre of imminent death. The power of paralyzing fear was masterfully depicted by Homer: his heroes could be stricken or frozen with horror or burst into tears at the sight of the enemy.[115] Such fear, that is almost always fatal, is depicted in horrifying detail: for instance, Alcathous' limbs were bound by Poseidon, so that he could not flee, 'and stood motionless like a pillar or a tree.'[116] In Homer, overpowering stupefaction is often attributed to divine intervention: a man who could not move on the battlefield seemed possessed.[117] Thus, even the glorious heroes could be paralyzed by Zeus, who 'stirred fear (*phobos*) in mighty Ajax' making him first freeze in astonishment, and then retreat slowly.'[118]

The stress of the combat and anticipation of destruction could bring about hallucinations and severe psychiatric injuries. For instance, an inscription referring to a battle fought by the Athenians, in all probability the battle of Coronea (447), ascribes the defeat to the intervention of a hero who helped the Boeotians: 'one of the half-gods came against you and wrought your undoing.'[119] In his account of the battle of Marathon, Herodotus relates the marvellous story of Epizelus, who fought valiantly and suddenly saw an apparition (*phasma*) of a tall hoplite with an enormous beard; the phantom passed Epizelus by, but killed the soldier next to him. Although Epizelus was not injured at all, he lost his sight forever.[120] Herodotus' narration is based on accounts going back to Epizelus' own story. Epizelus earned such fame that he was even portrayed on a painting of the battle of Marathon in the *Stoa Poikilê*, a hall in Athens adorned by Polygnotus.[121] The identification of the supernatural visitation and even the historical accuracy of Epizelus' story are less important than the fact that a soldier could lose his sight following a vision on the battlefield, and the fifth-century Athenians accepted the account as credible.[122]

The god Phobos is the son of Ares, and the common noun *phobos* could designate fear, primitive and uncontrolled.[123] Homer's greatest heroes, such as Hector, Diomedes, and Patroclus, are called 'devisers' of *phobos*.[124] Mythical and historic heroes are said to have sacrificed to this god before the battles.[125] The Spartans propitiated Phobos, the god of fear, because this nation of intrepid soldiers knew well that their enemies' terror would win the battle for them no less than their own valour.[126] In the fifth century, the people of Selinous thanked Phobos, alongside Zeus and Athena, for saving their city and granting them victory.[127]

Later historians still credited the gods with causing self-destructive fear and confusion during battles.[128] Xenophon describes the behaviour of the Argives at Corinth in 393, which the Spartans used to their advantage:

> For to have a crowd of enemies delivered into their hands, frightened, shocked, presenting their unprotected sides, no one rallying to his own defence, but all rendering all possible assistance toward their own destruction, – how could one help regarding this as divine? On that day, at all events, so many fell within a short time that men accustomed to see heaps of corn, wood, or stones, beheld then heaps of dead bodies.[129]

Dread caused by the sight of the enemy, loud chattering of teeth, losing control of the bowels, and the clanging armour of the shuddering soldiers occurred all too often, and even experienced officers were not immune to terror.[130] Spartans put an emphasis on the prophylactics of fear by educating their youths to resist terror no less than physical hardships and pain, and cultivating the shamefulness of cowardice.[131] The Spartan phalanx was especially notorious for its demeanour, 'at once awesome and terrifying' for their adversaries.[132] When thanking Phobos for salvation, the Greeks knew very well what they gained owing to the enemy's fright.

Paralyzing fear, uncontrollable emotional responses, and desertion are indeed 'constant companions in any war.'[133] In addition to social pressure, cities issued laws penalising cowardice: the laws of Athens punished desertion; in Sparta the laws against cowards were even harsher.[134] Gorgias stresses the irrationality of succumbing to fear, an act that ruins one's reputation forever.[135] The soldier's conundrum between the possibility of being wounded or killed while remaining with the army *versus* the certainty of disgrace if he fled the battlefield is implicit in Gorgias' depiction of the total loss of self-command due to terror.

The cult of Phobos underscores the significance of virtually freezing the enemy in overpowering fear and goes hand in hand with the notion of Lyssa as 'Gorgon . . . with the petrifying gaze.'[136] Lyssa's power to derange people's minds worked in two directions: it instilled wolfish rage in the warriors of one side and robbed the other side of the ability to fight. Exact assessments of the range of 'mentally overwhelming experiences of the war,'[137] be it bestial rage or irrational stupor, are certainly impossible, and there is no doubt that individual behaviour displayed the full range from berserk fury to immobile trepidation – Homer already knew that. *Lussa's* effects belonged to the extremes of this range, and both were *mania* for the Greeks.

Panic

Usually represented as a horned semi-goat, Pan belongs to the countryside; primitive – or bucolic – Arcadia, the land of herdsmen, was his domain.[138] The son of Hermes and accomplished musician, he may be playful, and like satyrs with whom he shares his semi-bestial nature, is often portrayed playing shepherd's pipes.[139] In the Homeric hymn in his honour, the newly-born baby Pan is said to have been so monstrous that his nurses fled away. The adult god was indeed frightening, haunting men who ventured into wild forests and meadows. Pan is proverbial as a god who deranges mortals, instilling in them panic (*panika deimata* or *paneia*) – terror, confusion, or excitement.[140] Participating in Dionysus' military campaign, Pan invented a stratagem of terrorising the enemy with echo: panic confusion was attributed to divine origin.[141] The Peripatetic philosopher Clearchus of Soli, whose interest in special states of the human psyche is exemplified in his writings on near-death experiences and hypnosis, penned a treatise entitled *On Panic*; we can only guess what aspect of possession by Pan attracted Clearchus' attention.[142]

The fear of wilderness was already associated with phantoms in antiquity: in the fourth century, Apollodorus of Athens suggested that people who heard an echo sounding in a forest or a mountain and were unable to discern its source attributed it to the deities of the savage nature, the nymphs and Pan playing his syrinx and flute in a cave.[143] When a sound or vision seemed inexplicable – and alone in a wild landscape, many experiences were bound to seem so – they frightened and were ascribed a supernatural origin. Photius puts it bluntly: 'Pan is the source of visions.'[144]

A natural soundscape, as we will see shortly, was sometimes perceived as Pan's or the nymphs' commands.[145] Sounds are often misinterpreted: even under normal circumstances, people easily imagine speech when in reality they hear a medley of noises. In his discussion of acoustic projection, J. Banks demonstrates that 'rhymes produced by even non-vocal sounds may . . . occasionally come to resemble those of speech.'[146] Our mind 'projects meaning' into ambiguous imagery; for instance, it shapes clouds into familiar patterns.[147] The same psychological mechanism combines indistinct sounds into words or phrases. These combinations are endogenous and subjective, but as psychological experiments demonstrate, when the listeners were prompted in advance what meanings they were to anticipate, an illusion of exogeny was created, and the listeners sensed the meaning as objective and external.[148] These findings explain the mechanism behind auditory illusions of hearing divine voices, in particular in unfamiliar or stressful environments.

Panic is contagious and may affect crowds, but its roots are in the individual's surrender to the grip of mysterious awe. The reason for the association of the god of savage nature with madness is rather apparent: withdrawal to the wilderness and isolation from society disturbs the human mind and incites phantoms and irrational fears.[149] Disorientation, a subjective feeling of being unsure about one's location, normally causes anxiety and when taken to the extreme, can lead to delusion and increased suggestibility, i.e. alterations of consciousness.[150] The correlation between being alone in a deserted place and derangement caused by fear was known to Hippocratic physicians.[151] In a word, loneliness leads to insanity, and Pan's terror epitomises this association.

Panic *mania* could be individual or collective. A common perpetrator of madness, Pan was one of the first suspects as a supernatural being who drove a person out of his or her wits. Although the terms 'panolepsy' and 'panolept' appear only after the second century AD,[152] the notion of seizure by Pan is doubtlessly much more ancient. In the theatre, Glauce's agony seemed to have been caused by Pan, and the love-smitten Phaedra was described as *entheos*, 'engodded' by Pan, or other gods.[153] A person could swear in Pan's name, beseeching the god to drive him mad if the oath had been false.[154]

The visions that Pan instilled in men were usually frightening, and Pan's domain extended from phantoms imagined by lonely individuals in the wilderness to terror experienced by large groups in the most intimidating circumstances people could imagine, war. Ungrounded panic on the battlefield or in the army camp was quite common: 'In all armies, and most of all in the largest, terrors and fears (*phoboi kai deimata*) are apt to arise, especially at night and when they are marching through a hostile country,' says Thucydides.[155] An example of suicidal behaviour resulting from this form of panic is given by Pausanias: some men of the army of Mardonius who tried to pillage the sanctuary of the Cabiri were immediately struck with madness, and flung themselves to their death, leaping either into the sea or from the precipices.[156] The story, even if invented at some stage by the Boeotians, was presumably very ancient, and attests to the conviction that an army under strain could be seized by mass madness.[157]

Pan was particularly dreaded at wartime: in the *Rhesus*, the ungrounded fear of the Trojans at night is immediately attributed to Pan: the soldiers, in Hector's words, were stirred by Pan's whip, which causes them to tremble.[158] The whip of the herdsmen's immortal patron strikes humans instead of animals, and drives people to insanity as surely as the strikes of a mortal herdsman would cause his flock to obey his will.[159] No wonder that the semi-bestial Pan was believed to madden men and animals alike: Suda's explanation of panic fear is that 'this occurs during military campaigns, when suddenly confusion affects horses and soldiers, for no visible reason.'[160]

Cases of *paneia* during exposure to combat are described by Greek historians.[161] An extreme case of panic happened in 279, when panic terror drove the Gauls out of their minds after the defeat at Delphi:

> The barbarians . . . putting to the sword those who, disabled by wounds or sickness, could not go with them . . . encamped . . . and during the night there fell on them a 'panic. . . .' It was when the evening was turning to night, the confusion fell on the army, and at first only a few became mad, and these imagined that they heard the trampling of horses at a gallop, and the attack of advancing enemies; but after a little time the delusion spread to all. So rushing to arms they divided into two parties, killing and being killed, neither understanding their mother tongue nor recognising one another's forms or the shape of their shields. Both parties alike under the present delusion thought that their opponents were Greek, men and armour, and that the language they spoke was Greek, so that a great mutual slaughter was wrought among the Gauls by the madness sent by the god.[162]

Although we cannot know the details of this event, which is laden with signs of divine wrath and may have been exaggerated, the reaction of the Gauls could be interpreted as the cognitive disorganisation found in acute post-traumatic reactions.[163] The tremendous psychological strain of killing their own comrades, together with the despair of defeat, exhaustion, an unfamiliar location and late hour, created circumstances which required only a spark to ignite a full-fledged attack of collective mental disorder. Pausanias explains this episode from his point of view, saying that 'causeless terrors (*deimata*) are said to come from Pan.'[164]

Other cases of disarray and terror on the battlefield, especially those involving mysterious sounds, were attributed to Pan's intervention. When the army of the Thirty Tyrants was caught in a snowstorm, 'an uproar called panic' forced them to retreat without fighting.[165] Panic attacks usually occurred in darkness and on the land, but sometimes on the sea or during daytime; they might strike during a battle, but were most usual on the march: Polybius reports several cases of panic occurring on the land and on the sea.[166] Obviously, at war times the disastrous panic of one side meant jubilation for the other side: Pan who was believed to have inflicted delirium on the Gauls was the saviour of the Greeks at Delphi.

Since sheer terror is *mania*, Dionysus, the god of *mania par excellence*, was also credited with an ability to drive men mad on the battlefield: he could evoke the 'drunkenness of fear' in the soldiers, and make them scatter before they touched their arms.[167] It is probably because of that reason that Pan is called Dionysus' *strategos* and the two gods are represented as combatants by Polyaenus.[168]

Greek military leaders had to deal with the psychological aftermath of warfare, and some of them even managed to prevent outbursts of ungrounded terror among their soldiers. Aeneas the Tactician, writing in the mid-fourth century,[169] penned a chapter on *paneia*, where he discussed the confusions and fears that arise in military contexts, among both civilians and soldiers.[170] He was aware of the fact that 'such fears usually occur after a defeat in a battle, sometimes in daytime but more often at night,'[171] and advised commanders either to shout 'Paean' (addressing Apollo in his capability as a healer)[172] or just say to the soldiers that it was mere panic, thus implying that the phenomenon was a mental disorder to be treated by an appeal to a healing god. Aeneas also suggested more mundane methods designed to prevent groundless fears in a military camp.

Since panic fear was easily transmitted, it was recommended that in case of a panic attack in the camp, the soldiers remain in their small tents, and the disorder be confined.[173] In the fourth century, Euphratas, a Spartan governor in Thrace, forced his soldiers to remain seated in their beds, rather than running in confusion throughout the camp: those who ran were treated as enemies. The fear of being killed kept the soldiers in their place.[174] Another Spartan, Clearchus, handled night panic in the camp by talking to the soldiers in order to make them understand that their fears were groundless, and commanded them to get ready in the morning, as if they were preparing for a battle.[175] Since panic arises from mental tension and anticipation of a disaster, keeping the minds of the soldiers occupied with their routine duties would seem to be an excellent way to prevent them from over-extending their imagination. When the situation was particularly desperate, Xenophon was sure that the soldiers should be made to think 'not of what they are going to suffer but of what they are going to do.'[176]

The recommendations for neutralising panic attacks disclose the understanding of their nature: it was believed to ensue from thinking about dangers, and could be prevented or stopped by addressing the soldiers' thoughts. Showing the soldiers that their fears were groundless, comforting them by prayer, or making them focus on the practicalities of combatting were ways to calm their minds, based on the conviction that *paneia* grew from within. Isolating the soldiers into small groups reflects the realisation that panic was contagious: once it appeared in the mind of one person, other mentally depleted people would catch it immediately, if exposed. Thus, the exposure had to be prevented at all costs.

The reason behind the association of the god of flocks and savage nature with wartime ungrounded terror seems to ensue from the initial basic quality of *paneia*: it was an uncontrollable fear of the unknown, in a strange environment where apprehension of danger brought about feeling of danger that seemed real. Panic fear usually lacks definite causes: an unexplained ambiguity triggers hallucinations, making victims of panic imagine non-existing horrors. The same happened in cities under siege, and armies on the march, especially at night and after a defeat, when people naturally dread the worst. Disorientation during combat was also a considerable factor causing anxiety and uncontrollable fear. In addition, both hunting, initially associated with Pan, and warfare caused fatigue and strain, as well as hunger and thirst. All these conditions together arouse physiological changes that often encourage hallucinations, in antiquity and nowadays. A cry of a single soldier scared by a phantom could easily cause a chain reaction among his fearful comrades, culminating in total disarray. The physical and mental condition of an exhausted soldier who mistakes his comrades-in-arms for enemies resembles the state of an exhausted hunter or traveller, strained by every rustling leaf and seeing the frightening face of the semi-bestial god in every tree trunk or strange rock. Thus, strained nerves in an environment perceived as hostile, combined with extreme fatigue, resulted in a similar effect, overwhelming fear without specific reason.[177] *Paneia* was numinous, and regarded as divine: a great misfortune for one side and a stroke of luck for the other one.

Battlefield epiphanies

Visions occurring as a result of all the factors just mentioned and believed to be enthused by the god of savage nature could also be benign. Pan's intervention in 490, before the battle of Marathon, while the Persians were invading Attica, is one of the most famous cases of epiphany in Greek history. The messenger Pheidippides was sent to Lacedaemon to summon help; the Spartans replied that they would be ready to leave for Attica only several days later – devastating news for Pheidippides and the Athenians.[178] In the wild hills of Arcadia, Pan's land *par excellence*, Pheidippides suddenly met Pan, who shouted his name. The god reminded the Athenian runner of his benevolence towards his compatriots in the past, present, and future, and requested proper respect. When told about this epiphany, the Athenians immediately regretted their neglect, and founded a temple of Pan beneath the Acropolis, establishing a yearly festival as well.[179] Pan's help against the Persians was gratefully acknowledged by the Athenians, and Miltiades in particular.[180]

Hallucinations occur frequently under extreme physical and psychological stress. It should not be surprising that the runner, covering about 300 kilometres in just two days, with little sleep, probably dehydrated and surely hypoglycaemic, had hallucinations. In the Arcadian wilderness, Pan's domain *par excellence*, perhaps in twilight or darkness, after hours of effort and realising the probability of an imminent disaster, Pheidippides was eager to feel the god's presence and support, and his overloaded brain could easily produce the audio-visual phantasm of Pan talking to him.[181] R. Garland's analysis is illuminating:

> Pheidippides was the medium by which the Athenians reckoned on receiving outside assistance in the form of an ally or *summachos* who would enable them to snatch victory from the jaws of defeat. And this, of course, is the identical role which the runner would have performed if the mission had met with success in the way that was originally intended.[182]

Thus, Pheidippides was desperate to bring help – and he brought it.

Pan's epiphany to Pheidippides was 'a multi-sensory phenomenon,'[183] reminiscent of encounters of inquirers or temple officials with oracular gods, discussed in

Chapter 2. In oracular sanctuaries, the consciousness of individuals intending to meet the god was rendered malleable by means of fasting, purifications, sojourns in isolated or dark chambers, etc., and the séances of divination were prepared according to the procedure developed in each sanctuary. Pan's epiphany was spontaneous, but its numinosity ensued from the similar sensation of the experiencer, who firmly believed that he had seen and heard a god, and of his countrymen, who were immediately convinced that the event had really occurred. As a result, Pheidippides' alteration of consciousness was a blessing for himself – he became famous overnight – and the Athenians, who were endowed with the belief that a god was with them at a juncture in their history when many thought that only a miracle could save the city.

Combat epiphanies could be associated with figures other than Pan, and be reported by groups rather than individuals.[184] Military epiphanies, which occurred to people who were undoubtedly awake – in contrast to visitations in dreams which are of a different nature – would be defined as hallucinations by contemporary researchers. The difference between a dream and an epiphany 'proper' is sometimes underscored in the ancient sources: daytime *phasmata* were less common than dreams and therefore valued higher.[185] Wartime apparitions fascinated ancient writers, who dedicated books to these phenomena, and boosted the patriotic feelings of the citizens of many poleis who commemorated them in inscriptions.[186] Numerous accounts of such epiphanies are all variations of the same pattern: a hero or a god appearing in the midst of the battle to support the warriors or even fight himself, thus granting victory to an army. There is no doubt that the soldiers were primed by their education, first and foremost by the Homeric stories,[187] and secretly dreamt to receive divine help, like the epic heroes of the past. This longing for help, based on traditional beliefs and heightened by apprehension, resulted in the substantial number of recorded combat epiphanies.

During the Persian Wars, apparitions reportedly occurred during three battles: at Marathon, Theseus and a less known hero, Echetlaeus, attacked the Persians; at Delphi two giant soldiers pursued and killed the enemies. At Salamis, Athenian sailors were helped by no less than three phantoms: the sons of Aeacus, the hero Cychreus in the form of a serpent, and an unnamed woman who 'cried commands loud enough for all the Greek fleet to hear.'[188] Furthermore, when before the battle people who stayed in Attica saw a phantom looking like a cloud of dust raised above Eleusis by 30000 men and heard mystic singing of Iacchus, both prodigies were interpreted as signs of divine support.[189] In addition, Spartans possibly claimed to have experienced an epiphany of the Dioscuri at Plataea.[190] During the Peloponnesian war, Zeus Ammon appeared to Lysander.[191] At Leuctra, the Messenian hero Aristomenes helped the Thebans against the Spartans.[192] On the sea, apparitions of mysterious lights were often interpreted as epiphanies of the Dioscuri: for instance, before the battle of Aegospotami in 405 they shined for the Spartans, and inspired them for the battle.[193] In 344 a torch 'like those carried by the *mustai*' in the Eleusinian mysteries, appeared in front of Timoleon's fleet sailing to Sicily, and was interpreted as a manifestation of Persephone's goodwill, a sign representing the goddess.[194] In 279 Apollo was seen supporting the defenders of

Delphi against the Celts, and the grateful people of Cos returned the favour by 'thank-offerings to the god for the epiphany that has taken place' and erected a stele with the decree on this matter.[195] In addition, on the first day of this fight, phantoms (*phasmata*) of four supporting heroes appeared before the Greeks.[196] Demeter in the guise of a woman supposedly killed Pyrrhus of Epirus, Hermes led the youths of Tanagra into a battle, and Parthenos supported the Greeks of Chersonesus in their fight against the barbarians.[197]

Contrary to anticipated or prepared cultic appearances of deities, these phenomena are categorised as 'crisis epiphanies.'[198] In all these cases, as well as in many others, supporting apparitions were perceived by large numbers of extremely stressed soldiers, facing the probability of the demise of their entire community. Sometimes, as for instance at Salamis, it can be shown that the combatants suffered from general exhaustion and lack of sleep.[199] Psychological factors and expectations determine the nature of hallucinated objects, and a shared expectation may generate a vision common to a group.[200] Experienced by individuals or groups, the sensation of being supported by a mysterious being is known as 'the sensed presence,' attested to in ancient and modern history, and probably developed as an adaptive reaction to life-threatening situations: the sensation of mysterious assistance was a source of comfort and courage to people struggling for their lives.[201] This phenomenon played an important role in Greek culture, where battlefield epiphanies were incorporated in the artistic, religious, and literary discourse.[202]

Conclusions

Warriors' *mania*, expressed in intrepid courage and a blatant disregard of pain, as well as bestial cruelty to the enemy, was known in Archaic Greece, valued as a praised social asset, and feared because of its destructive force. Battlefield madness had to be harnessed and channelled in the desirable direction, outside the community. Unlimited fearlessness and a propensity to slaughter aroused awe, and had to be controlled. Martial frenzy was instilled by various methods, and music was prominent as a primer to violence. Heroic figures were often endowed with poetic inspiration: *mania* could be mercurial. During the Classical period, rabid fury (*lussa*) of individual soldiers gave way to extreme violence displayed by entire units, but the phenomenon of the raging warrior did not disappear.

The opposite of *lussa* was dread, also experienced during combat. It could be personified and even worshipped as Phobos: instilling uncontrollable fear in the enemy was a sure way to victory. Usually, sheer terror, irrational and irresistible, was called *paneia*, panic, and belonged to the realm of Pan, whose expertise in *mania* matched that of Dionysus. The agony expressed by the terrified enemy was reason enough for the lucky adversary to be pleased, and therefore on the battlefield, Lyssa, Pan, and Phobos could be praised allies: in fact, using echoing as a means to terrify the enemy, Pan won battles for Dionysus himself.

In a society which regarded military service as the primary duty of every citizen, combat-related long- and short-term psychological distress was quite common, and irrespective of their bravery, many soldiers were repeatedly haunted by mental injuries, closely resembling those known today, such as PTSD. Many Greek authors mentioned mental stress produced by warfare, referring mostly to disorders occurring on the battlefield or immediately after the combat, and describing conditions of enduring distress following combat trauma. Thus, martial *mania*, be it heroic fury or shameful fear, could persist after the battle and affect the life of the individual and his community.

Battlefield visions could also provide the soldiers with hope and a sense of support. Quite often they were attributed to Pan, the god of hallucinations, in particular auditory phantasms. Whatever the source of wartime epiphanies reported by Greek authors, they were positive experiences: contrary to hallucinations which provoked panic, these apparitions inspired the fighters. In contrast to other alterations of consciousness on the battlefield, epiphanies had never been considered as manifestations of derangement, and were firmly believed and immortalised for the benefit of the generations to come.

Lussa and *paneia* were the two contrasting extremes of the warrior's behaviour on the battlefield. Both phenomena were instilled by gods with animal traits, regarded as *mania*, and could be experienced either individually or in groups. It is noteworthy that Lyssa and Pan were not foreign to the realm of Dionysus: aberration of perception and bestial or super-human behaviour were considered cognate to *bakcheia*.

Lyssa and Ares are among the Greek gods who caused *mania* that could be both a curse and a blessing. Moreover, these two gods could rage and abandon themselves to ecstasy. Together with Dionysus, they present a sharp contrast to the ways of most other gods, who remained clear-headed and aloof while they took away the mind of the mortals. The fascinating ambiguity of these gods, both mad and maddening, leads to the very core of the Greek concept of *mania*. Terrifying as it was, possession by Ares or Lyssa was advantageous in combat, and therefore highly valued.

Notes

1 *TGF* fr. 169: ἐπιθειαζούσα ταῖς Βάκχαις; above, Chapter 3.
2 For Pan's mixanthropy see Aston (2011: 272–277); hybrid aspects associated with terrifying presence and the ability to drive insane shared with Dionysus: Aston (2011: 182).
3 H.*Pan* 46; Thomas (2011: 169); Borgeaud (1979: 169–170).
4 Apollod. 3. 6. 8; *Thebais* (Schol. in *Il*. 5. 126, Pherecyd. fr. 97 *FGH*); a pediment relief from Pyrgi, ca 465 (de Grummond 2006: 55, fig. iv.3; this relief was kindly indicated to me by Afroditi Angelopoulou); the Attic Rosi crater (Beazley 1947; Vermeule 1979: 133).
5 Hom. *Il*. 24. 114–116; 24. 135–136; Segal (1971: 33–47).
6 Hom. *Il*. 17. 39; 126; 18. 335; Eur. *Rhes*. 254; Vermeule (1979: 107); Ustinova (2002: 109).
7 Hom. *Il*. 3. 21–26; 11. 121. 299; 17. 62–65, 540–542; Griffin (1980: 19).
8 Hom. *Il*. 16. 156–157; 24. 207; Eck (2012: 148–152). In fact, Achilles was brought up on eating entrails of wild animals raw: Griffin (1980: 20).

9 Hom. *Il.* 22. 345–348;

10 *Od.* 9. 350; Eck (2012: 152–156); Detienne and Vernant (1989: 38); and above, the Introduction.

11 Hom. *Il.* 23. 202–205.

12 Hom. *Il.* 14. 494–500; 16. 339–341.

13 Segal (1971, esp. 20–21); on decapitation: Eck (2012: 156–158).

14 E. *Ba.* 977: θοαὶ Λύσσας κύνες.

15 Ath. 13. 631AB; Pl. *Lg.* 815C; Slater (1993: 200–205); Ceccarelli (2004: 110–111).

16 A. *Th.* 380, 483, 498–499: ἔνθεος δ' Ἄρει βακχᾶι πρὸς ἀλκήν, θυιὰς ὥς, φόβον βλέπων. On *thuiades* see above, Chapter 3.

17 Hershkowitz (1998: 133–134, 142–145); van Wees (2004: 164); Eck (2012: 136–148).

18 Hom. *Il.* 8. 355; 9. 238;15. 605; 21. 5.

19 Hom. *Il.* 8. 299; 9. 305; 9. 238–239; 13. 53; 21. 542–543; Lincoln (1975).

20 Μαργαίνει, *Il.* 5. 881; λυσσώδης : *Il.* 13. 53 The verb 'rages,' μαίνεται, is also used in descriptions of his behaviour, Hom. *Il.* 5. 185; 6. 101.

21 *Il.* 8. 111: μαίνεται.

22 *Il.* 16. 245: χεῖρες μαίνονθ.'

23 Hom. *Il.* 21. 542–543: λύσσα δέ οἱ κῆρ αἰὲν ἔχε κρατερή, μενέαινε δὲ κῦδος ἀρέσθαι.

24 van Wees (2004: 162).

25 Hom. *Il.* 15. 605–609; 8. 349; 16. 607; 19. 17; Griffin (1980: 35).

26 *Il.* 8. 299.

27 Introduction.

28 Speidel (2002: 260).

29 Hershkowitz (1998: 142).

30 *Il.* 542–543.

31 Introduction.

32 Dionysus (Apollod. 3.5.1), Io (A. *Supp.* 564; *PV* 567; Dowden 1989: 117–145), Ino (fr. 70 Merkelbach-West; A. *TGF* fr. 1–4; Paus. 1. 44. 7; Hyg. *Fab.* 2. 4) and the Proetids (B. 11. 45–46; Apollod. 2. 2. 2; Acus. *FGH* 2F28; Paus. 8. 18. 7; see also Chapter 3 and the Introduction.

33 Paus. 9. 2. 4, talking of *nosos lussa,* 'disease of *lussa.*'

34 Arist. *HA* 604a5. However, three centuries after Aristotle, Celsus was aware of the connection between a bite by a rabid animal and hydrophobia, and attributed it to venom (*virus*) transmitted through the saliva: *De medicina* 5. 27. 2

35 Cf. Gilovich and Savitsky (2002) on representativeness and association.

36 Hom. *Il.* 5. 717; 831; 15. 128; Eck (2012: 168–169).

37 *Il.* 17. 210–212.

38 ἐπιμὶξ δέ τε μαίνεται ὁ Ἄρης, Hom. *Od.* 11. 537.

39 Griffin (1980: 35); Hershkowitz (1998: 134); Heubeck and Hoekstra (1989: 109).

40 μαινομένοις δ' ἐπιπνεῖ λαοδάμας μιαίνων εὐσέβειαν Ἄρης, A. *Th.* 343, translation H. W. Smyth.

41 Burkert (1985: 169).

42 Deacy (2000: 285–298).

43 Hom. *Il.* 5. 576; 13. 295; 20. 46; comparisons of Hector to Ares: *Il.* 8. 349; 15. 605.

44 Hom. *Il.* 6. 407.

45 Hom. *Il.* 6. 100–101: ὅδε λίην μαίνεται, οὐδέ τίς οἱ δύναται μένος ἰσοφαρίζειν; Hershkowitz (1998: 142).

46 Hom. *Il.* 5. 125; Deacy (2000: 144); Zaborowski (2002: 308–309). On *menos*, see: Redfield (1975: 171–174); Bremmer (1983: 57–60); Padel (1992: 24–26).

47 Beekes (2010: s.v. *menos*); Frisk (1973–1979: s.v. *menos*); Chantraine (1983–1984: s.v. *mainomai*). For the Indo-European *men-*, see above, Introduction.

48 Considine (1985); Considine (1986); *mênis* in poetry: Loraux (1989: 226–231). P. Considine's suggestion is accepted by Hershkowitz (1998: 154). Notwithstanding

'semantically obvious connection with *menos*' (Beekes 2010: s.v. *mênis*), H. Frisk, P. Chantraine, and R. Beekes define the etymology of this word as unknown (Frisk 1973–1979 s.v. *mênis*; Chantraine 1983–1984: s.v. *mênis*; Beekes 2010: s.v. *mênis*).

49 Dumézil (1985: 207–211).
50 Dumézil (1942: 16–26); Dumézil (1985: 23).
51 Griffin (1980: 20–21); e.g. Achilles, and above in this chapter.
52 Wikander (1938); Dumézil (1970: 141); McCone (1987); Speidel (2002); Ustinova (2002); Liberman (2005); West (2007: 449–451).
53 Ustinova (2002: 108).
54 Liberman (2005: 409).
55 Speidel (2002: 277); Liberman (2005: 402); Woodard (2013: 238–268).
56 Speidel (2002: 262); on naked *berseker* see also Liberman (2005: 403); West (2007: 449). Ritual nudity was associated with rites of passage (Lada-Richards 1999: 75–78) and is significant that raging warriors were usually young.
57 Compton (2006: 212, 329).
58 *Th.* 343 cited above.
59 Compton (2006: 119–129); Power (2010: 404–405).
60 Pl. *Lg.* 629A; Lycurg. *In Leocr.* 106; Paus. 4. 15. 6; Compton (2006: 120).
61 νοῦν τε ἥκιστα ἔχειν (Paus. 4. 15. 6); παρακόπτειν (D. L. 2. 43).
62 Schol. in *Leg.* 629A; Plu. *Cleom.* 2. 3; D.S. 8. 27. Compton (2006: 124).
63 Conon *FGH* 26 fr. 1. 45, as interpreted by Graf (1987); Compton (2006: 178–180).
64 Hom. *Il.* 7. 241.
65 Compton (2006: 210–213, 233–252).
66 Compton (2006: 249).
67 Hurwit (2002).
68 Ceccarelli (2004: 117).
69 Pl. *Lg.* 815A; Lonsdale (1993: 137–168); Delavaud-Roux (1993), with multiple illustrations and analysis of the movements; Ceccarelli (2004).
70 For cognitive aspects of Greek dancing, and in particular its bonding role, see Larson (2016: 148–156).
71 Ath. 14. 629C, citing Amphion of Thespiae (*FGH* 387 fr.1); translation S. Douglas Olson. Crete: Ephor. *FGH* 70 F149 (Str. 10. 4. 20); West (1992: 36).
72 Speidel (2002: 285–286).
73 War dances of both the barbarians and the Greeks are described in detail by Xenophon, listing those of the Thracians, Mysians, Paphlagonians, Aenianians, Magnesians, and Arcadians (*Anab.* 6. 1. 5–13). For the variety of war dances performed by the Greeks see Poursat (1968); Delavaud-Roux (1993: 38–39, 170–173).
74 Music as a means of manipulating emotions and affective states: above, the Introduction; Atran (2002: 172).
75 E.g. X. *HG* 6. 4. 8; Hanson (2000: 126–131).
76 Plu. *Dio.* 30. 3; cf. Arist. *EE* 1229a20 on intoxication that makes men fearless.
77 E. *HF* 966–967.
78 S. fr. 210 *TGF*, ll.47–48; Tritle (2004: 331).
79 A. *Ch.* 439; Soph. *El.* 445; Eck (2012: 163–166).
80 Hanson (2000: 190).
81 Hanson (2000: 135–193).
82 Hdt. 9. 71.
83 Arist. *EN* 1115b25, translation H. Rackham: εἴη δ' ἄν τις μαινόμενος ἢ ἀνάλγητος, εἰ μηδὲν φοβοῖτο. Cf. Ahonen (2014: 81).
84 X. *An.* 5. 7. 26: ἔδεισαν δὲ μὴ λύττα τις ὥσπερ κυσὶν ἡμῖν ἐμπεπτώκοι.
85 Arist. *EE* 1229b25; *EN* 1115b29.
86 Garland (1992: 52–53).
87 Hdt. 6.112: Ὡς δέ σφι διετέτακτο καὶ τὰ σφάγια ἐγίνετο καλά, ἐνθαῦτα ὡς ἀπείθησαν οἱ Ἀθηναῖοι, δρόμῳ ἵεντο ἐς τοὺς βαρβάρους· ἦσαν δὲ στάδιοι οὐκ ἐλάσσονες τὸ

μεταίχμιον αὐτῶν ἦ ὀκτώ. Οἱ δὲ Πέρσαι ὁρῶντες δρόμῳ ἐπιόντας παρεσκευάζοντο ὡς δεξόμενοι, μανίην τε τοῖσι Ἀθηναίοισι ἐπέφερον καὶ πάγχυ ὀλεθρίην, ὁρῶντες αὐτοὺς ἐόντας ὀλίγους, καὶ τούτους δρόμῳ ἐπειγομένους . . . Ἀθηναῖοι δὲ ἐπείτε ἀθρόοι προσέμειξαν τοῖσι βαρβάροισι, ἐμάχοντο ἀξίως λόγου. Πρῶτοι μὲν γὰρ Ἑλλήνων πάντων . . . δρόμῳ ἐς πολεμίους ἐχρήσαντο, πρῶτοι δὲ ἀνέσχοντο ἐσθῆτά τε Μηδικὴν ὁρῶντες καὶ [τοὺς] ἄνδρας ταύτην ἐσθημένους· τέως δὲ ἦν τοῖσι Ἕλλησι καὶ τὸ οὔνομα τὸ Μήδων φόβος ἀκοῦσαι (translation A. D. Godley, modified).

88 Garland (1992: 53).
89 Below in this chapter.
90 Hdt. 9. 78–79.
91 X. An. 3. 4. 5. Stripping the dead enemies of weapons and clothing was the norm, and leaving them their tunics was considered a particularly generous gesture (X. *HG* 2. 4. 19).
92 For instance, on an Attic black-figure lekythos by Beldam Painter: Haspels (1936: 269; Appendix XVII. No. 67).
93 Tyrt. fr. 10: 21–25 West; Tritle (1997: 124); van Wees (2004: 136).
94 X. *HG* 3. 3. 6.
95 Hdt. 6. 79–80; Th. 1. 106.
96 van Wees (2004: 216).
97 X. *HG* 3. 1. 32 Extreme hysteria of this year caused the Athenians to commit many outrages, including cutting off the right hand of every prisoner taken alive, X. *HG* 3. 1. 31.
98 Th. 7. 29; Hornblower (1991–2008): 3: 598; Raaflaub (2014: 32).
99 D.S. 12. 10. 1
100 Shay (1994: 92).
101 Tritle (1997: 133).
102 Speidel (2002: 285) maintains that 'fighting madness, individual and in groups, is in the nature of the mankind and has often been harnessed for military purposes.'
103 The following section draws on the article co-authored with E. Cardeña: Ustinova and Cardeña (2014). I am grateful to Etzel Cardeña for the pleasure of working together on this paper and for the permission to use it in this book.
104 *Il.* 22. 137; 21. 249; on fear as emotion see Konstan (2006: 129–155).
105 Solomon (1993: 28).
106 Cardeña et al. (2012). On PTSD in ancient Greece see Ustinova and Cardeña (2014).
107 Marlowe (1986: 7–24).
108 Gabriel (2007: 15); Meagher (2006: 11–13).
109 van Wees (2004: 151).
110 Hanson (2000: 101); Gabriel (2007: 14–15).
111 Crowley (2012).
112 Tyrt. fr. 12 West, 10–11.
113 Raaflaub (2014: 22).
114 X. *Ages.* 2. 14, translation E. C. Marchant.
115 E.g. *Il.* 13. 85–88, 279–283, 394, 434–436; 16. 403; 17. 694; van Wees (2004: 162); Loraux (1989: 96–97); the most detailed analysis of the depictions of fear in Homer is Zaborowski (2002).
116 *Il.* 13. 436: ὥς τε στήλην ἠ δένδρεον . . . ἀτρέμας ἑσταότα.
117 *Il.* 16. 804–806; 13. 434–436; Hershkowitz (1998: 156).
118 *Il.* 11: 545–549: Αἴανθ' . . . ἐν φόβον ὦρσε· στῆ δὲ ταφών . . . ἐντροπαλιζόμενος ὀλίγον γόνυ γουνὸς ἀμείβων.
119 ἀλλά τις ὑμᾶς ἡμιθέων θείαν [–]ν ἀντιάσας ἔβλαψεν, Pritchett (1974–1979: 3: 26); Harris (2013: 295).
120 Hdt. 6. 117; Suid. s.v. *Hippias* (2) and *Polyzelos*.
121 *Ael.* 7. 38; Harrison (1972: 353–378); Krentz (2010: 16–17). Several researchers identify Epizelus' condition as psychogenic, resulting from the stress of the battle and

culminating in conversion blindness (Sekunda 2002: 69; Krentz 2010: 157; Meagher 2006: 16; van Wees 2004: 151; Tritle 2000. The idea was first put forward by Moss 1967: 713). For a detailed discussion see Ustinova and Cardeña (2014).

122 Later tradition even identified Epizelus' vision of the warrior with Pan, who appeared to Pheidippides before the battle (Suid. s.v. *Hippias*; Gartziou-Tatti 2013: 100). I discuss Pheidippides' hallucination below. At the moment, it is only to be indicated that Pan was deemed to support the Athenians, so the identification of a giant fighting on the Persian side with an ally of the Greeks is hardly possible.

123 Hom. *Il.* 4. 440; Hes. *Thgn.* 933; Chantraine (1983–1984: s.v. *phebomai*); Patera (2013: 114).

124 Μήστωρ φόβοιο: Hom. *Il.* 12. 39; 6. 278; 23. 16.

125 Plu. *Alex.* 31. 9; *Thes.* 27. 2; A. *Sept.* 42; Patera (2013: 113–115) on the cult of Phobos.

126 Plu. *Cleom.* 9 and Richer (2012: 107–122).

127 *IG* 14. 268 (*Syll.*³ 1122). See also Patera (2013) on fear of scorn or defeat as a positive emotion.

128 For examples of such fear see Raaflaub (2014: 22–24).

129 X. *HG* 4. 4. 14: τὸ γὰρ ἐγχειρισθῆναι αὐτοῖς πολεμίων πλῆθος πεφοβημένον, ἐκπεπληγμένον, τὰ γυμνὰ παρέχον, ἐπὶ τὸ μάχεσθαι οὐδένα τρεπόμενον, εἰς δὲ τὸ ἀπόλλυσθαι πάντας πάντα ὑπηρετοῦντας, πῶς οὐκ ἄν τις θεῖον ἡγήσαιτο; τότε γοῦν οὕτως ἐν ὀλίγῳ πολλοὶ ἔπεσον ὥστε εἰθισμένοι ὁρᾶν οἱ ἄνθρωποι σωροὺς σίτου, ξύλων, λίθων, τότε ἐθεάσαντο σωροὺς νεκρῶν (translation C. L. Brownson, modified).

130 Polyaen. 3. 9. 4; Th. 5. 10; Plu. *Arat.* 29. 5–6; Ar. *Pax* 241; Hanson (2000: 101–102).
     In the *Humours*, one of the early Hippocratic texts, the author assumes that various stressful situations, by means of sight and hearing, affect the intellect (*gnômê*) and cause the body (*sôma*) to react: for instance, fear produces shaking legs and pallor (*Hum.* 9; Pigeaud 1989: 42–43).

131 Rawlings (2007: 210–217); Patera (2013: 115–116).

132 X. *Ages.* 2. 7; Plu. *Lys.* 22. 2.

133 Gabriel (1987: 62); for cowardice and desertion in Greece see Christ (2006: 88–111).

134 Aeschin. 3. 175; *Plu. Ages.* 30. 3; Lys. 13. 12; 14. 11; Christ (2006: 118–124); Balot (2010: 88–108); Crowley (2012: 105–107).

135 *The Encomium of Helen*; for a detailed discussion see Ustinova and Cardeña (2014).

136 Γοργὼν . . . Λύσσα μαρμαρωπός, E. *FH* 882–883, translation M.R. Halleran.

137 Sargant (1973: 3).

138 Jost (1985: 456–458).

139 Boardman (1997); Pan's music: E. *Ba.* 951; Paus. 8. 38. 11; his double nature: Pl. *Cra.* 408D; bestiality: Jost (1985: 464–467).

140 Suid, s.v. *panikon deima*; Borgeaud (1979: 137–148); for the term *paneia* see p. 138.

141 Polyean. 1. 2.

142 Ath. 389; Lewy (1938); above, Chapter 2.

143 *FGH* 244 fr. 135.

144 S.v. *Panos skotos*.

145 For the nymphs see Chapter 5.

146 Banks (2012: 26).

147 Banks (2012: 38).

148 Banks (2012: 31–32).

149 Meillier (1975: 131); Borgeaud (1979: 151); Lavagne (1988: 66).

150 Montello and Moyes (2012: 387–388).

151 Hp. *Int.* 48.

152 Borgeaud (1979: 163).

153 E. *Med.* 1173; *Hipp.* 142.

154 Theoc. 5. 15–16; Men. *Dysc.* 309–331; Borgeaud (1979: 155).

155 Th. 7. 80, translation C. F. Smith, slightly modified; cf. Hdt. 7. 43.
156 Paus. 9. 25. 9: τούτοις παραφρονῆσαί τε συνέπεσεν αὐτίκα καὶ ἀπώλοντο ἐς θάλασσάν τε καὶ ἀπὸ τῶν κρημνῶν ἑαυτοὺς ῥίπτοντες.
157 An inscription commemorating an epiphany of Zeus to the people of Panamara in 39, describes the adversary Parthians as frightened by the god's thunderbolts and disoriented by the deep fog, and consequently jumping off the cliffs, as if maddened by the Furies, and successfully defeated by the Greeks, encouraged by the god's help (*IStratonikeia* 10; Petridou 2015: 139–140).
158 E. *Rh.* 36–37: Πανὸς τρομερᾶι μάστιγι; Borgeaud (1979).
159 The notion of pangs of madness is immediately reminiscent of the 'stings' of the gadfly's barb (*oistros*) bringing insanity upon Io; see Chapter 2. For terms designating insanity and based on different verbs designating striking, see above, Introduction, and Byl (2004).
160 τοῦτο γίνεται ἐπὶ τῶν στρατοπέδων, ἡνίκα αἰφνίδιον οἵ τε ἵπποι καὶ οἱ ἄνθρωποι ἐκταραχθῶσι, μηδεμιᾶς αἰτίας προφανείσης, Suid. s.v. *panikôi deimati*.
161 X. *HG* 4. 4. 11–12; Polyaen. 3. 9. 4; 3. 9. 10; Plb. 5. 96. 3; 5. 110. 1; 20. 6. 12; Onasander 6. 5; Borgeaud (1979: 137–148).
162 Paus. 10. 23. 6–9: οἱ δὲ βάρβαροι . . . ἑαυτῶν τοὺς ἀδυνάτους τραύματα ἕπεσθαι καὶ ἀρρωστίαν φονεύουσιν . . . ἐστρατοπεδεύσαντο . . . , ἐν δὲ τῇ νυκτὶ φόβος σφίσιν ἐμπίπτει Πανικός· . . . ἐνέπεσε μὲν ἐς τὸ στράτευμα ἡ ταραχὴ περὶ βαθεῖαν τὴν ἑσπέραν, καὶ ὀλίγοι τὸ κατ᾽ ἀρχὰς ἐγένοντο οἱ παραχθέντες ἐκ τοῦ νοῦ, ἐδόξαζόν τε οὗτοι κτύπου τε ἐπελαυνομένων ἵππων καὶ ἐφόδου πολεμίων <αἰσθάνεσθαι>· μετὰ δὲ οὐ πολὺ καὶ ἐς ἅπαντας διέδρα ἡ ἄγνοια. ἀναλαβόντες οὖν τὰ ὅπλα καὶ διαστάντες ἔκτεινόν τε ἀλλήλους καὶ ἀνὰ μέρος ἐκτείνοντο, οὔτε γλώσσης τῆς ἐπιχωρίου συνιέντες οὔτε τὰς ἀλλήλων μορφὰς οὔτε τῶν θυρεῶν καθορῶντες τὰ σχήματα· ἀλλὰ ἀμφοτέραις ταῖς τάξεσιν ὁμοίως ὑπὸ τῆς ἐν τῷ παρόντι ἀγνοίας οἵ τε ἄνδρες οἱ ἀνθεστηκότες εἶναί σφισιν Ἕλληνες καὶ αὐτοὶ καὶ τὰ ὅπλα ἐφαίνοντο καὶ Ἑλλάδα ἀφιέναι τὴν φωνήν, ἥ τε ἐκ τοῦ θεοῦ μανία πλεῖστον ἐξειργάσατο ὑπ᾽ ἀλλήλων τοῖς Γαλάταις τὸν φόνον (translation W.H.S. Jones).
163 Ustinova and Cardeña (2014: 742).
164 Paus. 10. 23. 7: . . . Πανικός· τὰ γὰρ ἀπὸ αἰτίας οὐδεμιᾶς δείματα ἐκ τούτου φασὶ γίνεσθαι.
165 DS 14. 32. 3: θορύβου τοῦ καλουμένου Πανικοῦ; X. *HG* 2. 4. 2–3.
166 Polyb. 5. 96. 3; 20. 6. 12; 5. 110. 1.
167 Pl. *Lg.* 639B: μέθῃ τοῦ φόβου; E. *Ba.* 303–304; D. C. 54. 34. 5.
168 Polyaen. 1. 2.
169 Whitehead (1990: 10).
170 Aen. Tact. 27.
171 Aen. Tact. 27. 4.
172 Paean as a healing or purificatory song: Rutherford (2001: 15); paean in military contexts, before and after battle: Rutherford (2001: 42–47).
173 Suid, s.v. *panikôi deimati*; unfortunately, the source of this advice cannot be identified.
174 Aen. Tact. 27. 7.
175 X. *HG* 2. 2. 19–21.
176 *An.* 3. 1. 41.
177 Borgeaud (1979: 183).
178 For the plausibility of the apparition happening during Pheidippides' run back from Sparta see Garland (1992: 49).
179 Hdt. 6. 105; Paus. 1. 28. 4; 8. 54. 6; Herman (2011: 128); Borgeaud (1979: 195–197).
180 *AP* 16. 232 (attributed to Semonides of Ceos); 16. 269; Mastrapas (2013: 113); Gartziou-Tatti (2013: 98).
181 Herodotus (6. 105) uses the word περιπίπτει, 'fell in,' and refers to Pheidippides hearing Pan's words, but Pausanias (8. 54. 6) mentions the god's 'appearance': φανῆναι τὸν Πᾶνα (Hornblower 2001: 143; Scott 2005: 369; Petridou 2015: 13–14).

182　Garland (1992: 51).
183　Platt (2015: 495).
184　Pritchett (1974–1979: 3: 19–46); Wheeler (2004); Herman (2011); Petridou (2015: 113–141).
185　E.g. *IG* XIV. 1014: οὐκ ὄναρ, 'not during sleep': Versnel (1987: 50). However, both visions and dreams could be regarded as divine epiphanies, and quite often the nature of epiphanies remains unclear: Versnel (1987). The word *phasma* was often used to describe dreams: Petridou (2015: 66).
186　Pritchett (1974–1979: 3: 12); Parker (2011: 10–11).
187　Petridou (2015: 109–113) includes the Trojan apparitions in her discussion of 'epiphanies in crisis,' thus underscoring the fact that people believed in the veracity of these stories.
188　Hdt. 8. 84, translation A. D. Godley; other apparitions at Salamis: Plu. *Themist.* 15. 1; Paus. 1. 36. 1; Theseus: Plu. *Thes.* 35. 8; Paus. 1. 15. 3; Echetlaeus: Paus. 1. 32. 5; Delphi: Hdt. 8. 38; a list of twenty-two occurrences attested to in Greek sources: Wheeler (2004).
189　Hdt. 8. 65.
190　Hornblower (2001).
191　Either in waking reality (Paus. 3. 18. 3) or in a dream (Plu. *Lys.* 20. 4–6); Petridou (2015: 138–139).
192　Paus. 4. 32. 4.
193　Paus. 10. 9. 7; Plu. *Lys.* 12. The Dioscuri were envisaged as accompanying the Spartans to battles: Hdt. 5. 75; Hornblower (2001: 141).
194　Plu. *Tim.* 8; Platt (2015: 496).
195　καὶ τῶι θεῶι χαριστήρια ἀποδιδοὺς τάς τε ἐπιφανείας τὰς γεγενημένας ἕνεκεν; *Syll.*³ 398; Herman (2011: 137).
196　Paus. 1. 4. 4; 10. 23. 3; Pritchett (1974–1979: 3, 30–32).
197　Demeter: Paus. 1. 13. 7; Hermes: Paus. 9. 22. 2; Parthenos: *IOSPE* I² 343; 352.
198　Platt (2015: 494); Petridou (2015: 18–19, 107).
199　Wheeler (2004: 8).
200　Thus, several people surviving together after a shipwreck and sharing the same expectancies (mental set) may 'see' a non-existent ship projected against the empty sea and insist on its reality: West (1997: 502).
201　Herman (2011: 153).
202　Herman (2011: 154).

References

Ahonen, M. 2014. *Mental Disorders in Ancient Philosophy*. Heidelberg-New York: Springer.

Aston, E. 2011. *Mixanthrôpoi: Anymal-Human Hybrid Deities in Greek Religion*, vol. 25, *Kernos Supplément*. Liège: Centre International d'Étude de la Religion Grecque Antique.

Atran, S. 2002. *In God We Trust: The Evolutionary Landscape of Religion*. Oxford: Oxford University Press.

Balot, R. K. 2010. "Democratizing courage in classical Athens." In *War, Democracy and Culture in Classical Athens*, edited by D. M. Pritchard, 88–108. Cambridge: Cambridge University Press.

Banks, J. 2012. *Rorschach Audio: Art and Illusion for Sound*. London: Disinformation.

Beazley, J. D. 1947. "The Rosi Krater." *JHS* 67:1–9.

Beekes, R. 2010. *Etymological Dictionary of Greek*. Leiden: Brill.

Boardman, J. 1997. "Pan." In *LIMC* 8:923–941.

Borgeaud, P. 1979. *Recherches sur le dieu Pan*. Rome: Institut suisse de Rome.

Bremmer, J. N. 1983. *The Early Greek Concept of the Soul.* Princeton: Princeton University Press.

Burkert, W. 1985. *Greek Religion.* Cambridge, MA: Harvard University Press.

Byl, S. 2004. "Le délire, symptôme cnidien ou coaque?" In *La médicine grecque antique,* edited by J. Jouanna and J. Leclant, 45–52. Paris: de Boccard.

Cardeña, E., L. Butler, S. Reijman, and D. Spiegel. 2012. "Disorders of extreme stress." In *Handbook of Psychology: Clinical Psychology,* edited by I. B. Weiner, G. Stricker, and T. A. Widiger, 497–548. New York: Wiley.

Ceccarelli, P. 2004. "Dancing the pyrrhichê in Athens." In *Music and the Muses: The Culture of 'Mousikê' in the Classical Athenian City,* edited by P. Murray and P. Wilson, 91–117. Oxford: Oxford University Press.

Chantraine, P. 1983–1984. *Dictionnaire étymologique de la langue grecque.* Paris: Klincksieck.

Christ, M. R. 2006. *The Bad Citizen in Classical Athens.* Cambridge: Cambridge University Press.

Compton, T. M. 2006. *Victim of the Muses: Poet as Scapegoat, Warrior and Hero in Greco-Roman and Indo-European Myth and History.* Washington, DC: Center for Hellenic Studies.

Considine, P. 1985. "The Indo-European origin of Greek *mênis* 'wrath.'" *TPhS* 83:144–170.

Considine, P. 1986. "The etymology of MHNIΣ." In *Studies in Honour of T. B. L. Webster,* edited by J. H. Betts, J. T. Hooker, and J. R. Green. Bristol: Bristol Classical Press.

Crowley, J. 2012. *The Psychology of the Athenian Hoplite: The Culture of Combat in Classical Athens.* Cambridge: Cambridge University Press.

Deacy, S. 2000. "Athena and Ares. War, violence and warlike deities." In *War and Violence in Ancient Greece,* edited by H. van Wees, 285–298. Swansea: Classical Press of Wales.

de Grummond, N. T. 2006. *Etruscan Myth, Sacred History, and Legend.* Philadelphia: University of Pennsylvania Museum of Archaeology and Anthropology.

Delavaud-Roux, M.-H. 1993. *Les danses armées en Grèce antique.* Aix-en-Provence: Publications de l'Université de Provence.

Detienne, M. and J.-P. Vernant. 1989. *The Cuisine of Sacrifice Among the Greeks.* Chicago: The University of Chicago Press.

Dowden, K. 1989. *Death and the Maiden: Girls' Initiation Rites in Greek Mythology.* London-New York: Routledge.

Dumézil, G. 1942. *Horace et les Curiaces.* Paris: Gallimard.

Dumézil, G. 1970. *The Destiny of the Warrior.* Chicago: The University of Chicago Press.

Dumézil, G. 1985. *Heur et malheur du guerrier.* Paris: Flammarion.

Eck, B. 2012. *La Mort rouge. Homicide, guerre et souillure en Grèce ancienne.* Paris: Les Belles Lettres.

Frisk, H. 1973–79. *Griechisches etymologisches Wörterbuch.* Heidelberg: C. Winter.

Gabriel, R. A. 1987. *No More Heroes: Madness and Psychiatry in War.* New York: Hill and Wang.

Gabriel, R. A. 2007. *Soldiers' Lives Through History: The Ancient World.* Westport: Greenwood Press.

Garland, R. 1992. *Introducing New Gods: The Politics of Athenian Religion.* Ithaca: Cornell University Press.

Gartziou-Tatti, A. 2013. "Gods, heroes and the battle of Marathon." In *Marathon – 2,500 Years (BICS Suppl. 124),* edited by C. Carey and M. Edwards, 91–110. London: The Institute of Classical Studies University of London.

Gilovich, T. and K. Savitsky. 2002. "Like goes with like: The role of representativeness in erroneous and pseudo-scientific beliefs." In *Heuristics and Biases: The Psychology of Intuitive Judgement*, edited by T. Gilovich, D. Griffin, and D. Kahneman, 617–624. Cambridge: Cambridge University Press.

Graf, F. 1987. "Orpheus: A poet among men." In *Interpretation of Greek Mythology*, edited by J. Bremmer, 80–106. London: Routledge.

Griffin, J. 1980. *Homer on Life and Death*. Oxford: Clarendon Press.

Hanson, V. D. 2000. *The Western Way of War*. Berkeley-Los Angeles: University of California Press.

Harris, W. V. 2013. "Greek and Roman hallucinations." In *Mental Disorders in the Classical World*, edited by W. V. Harris, 285–306. Leiden: Brill.

Harrison, E. B. 1972. "The South frieze of the Nike temple and the Marathonian painting in the painted Stoa." *AJA* 76:353–378.

Haspels, C.H.E. 1936. *Attic Black-Figured Lekythoi*. Paris: de Boccard.

Herman, G. 2011. "Greek epiphanies and the sensed presence." *Historia* 60:127–157.

Hershkowitz, D. 1998. *The Madness of Epic: Reading Insanity From Homer to Statius*. Oxford: Oxford University Press.

Heubeck, A. and A. Hoekstra. 1989. *A Commentary on Homer's Odyssey: Books IX-XVI*. Oxford: Oxford University Press.

Hornblower, S. 1991–2008. *A Commentary on Thucydides*. Oxford: Oxford University Press.

Hornblower, S. 2001. "Epic and epiphanies: Herodotus and the 'New Simonides.'" In *The New Simonides: Contexts of Praise and Desire*, edited by D. Boedeker and D. Sider, 135–147. Oxford: Oxford University Press.

Hurwit, J. M. 2002. "Reading the Chigi Vase." *Hesperia* 22:1–22.

Jost, M. 1985. *Sanctuaires et cultes d'Arcadie*. Paris: Vrin.

Konstan, D. 2006. *The Emotions of the Ancient Greeks: Studies in Aristotle and Classical Literature*. Toronto: University of Toronto Press.

Krentz, P. 2010. *The Battle of Marathon*. New Haven: Yale University Press.

Lada-Richards, I. 1999. *Initiating Dionysus: Ritual and Theatre in Aristophanes' Frogs*. Oxford: Oxford University Press.

Larson, J. 2016. *Understanding Greek Religion: A Cognitive Approach*. London-New York: Routledge.

Lavagne, H. 1988. *Operosa antra. Recherches sur la grotte à Rome de Sylla à Hadrien*. Rome: de Boccard.

Lewy, H. 1938. "Aristotle and the Jewish sage according to Clearchus of Soli." *HThR* 31:205–235.

Liberman, A. 2005. "Berserks in history and legend." *Russian History* 32:401–411.

Lincoln, B. 1975. "Homeric *lussa*: Wolfish rage." *Indogermanische Forschungen* 80:98–105.

Lonsdale, S. H. 1993. *Dance and Ritual Play in Greek Religion*. Baltimore: Johns Hopkins University Press.

Loraux, N. 1989. *Les expériences de Tirésias*. Paris: Gallimard.

Marlowe, D. 1986. "The human dimension of battle and combat breakdown." In *Military Psychiatry: A Comparative Perspective*, edited by R. A. Gabriel, 7–24. New York-Westport, CT: Greenwood Press.

Mastrapas, A. 2013. "The battle of Marathon and the introduction of Pan's worship to Athens: The political dimension of a legend through written evidence and archaeological finds." In *Marathon – 2,500 Years* (BICS Suppl. 124), edited by C. Carey and M. Edwards, 111–122. London: Wiley

McCone, K. R. 1987. "Hund, Wolf und Krieger bei den Indogermanen." In *Studien zum indogermanischen Wortschatz*, edited by W. Meid, 101–154. Innsbruck: Institut für Sprachwissenschaft der Universität Innsbruck.

Meagher, R. E. 2006. *Herakles Gone Mad: Rethinking Heroism in an Age of Endless War*. Northampton: Olive Branch Press.

Meillier, C. 1975. "L'épiphanie du dieu Pan au livre II de Daphnis et Chloé." *REG* 88:121–132.

Montello, D. R. and H. Moyes. 2012. "Why dark zones are sacred: Turning to behavioral and cognitive science for answers." In *Sacred Darkness: A Global Perspective on the Ritual Use of Caves*, edited by H. Moyes, 385–396. Boulder: University Press of Colorado.

Moss, G. C. 1967. "Mental disorder in antiquity." In *Disease in Antiquity*, edited by D. Brothwell and A. T. Sandison, 709–722. Springfield: Charles Thomas.

Padel, R. 1992. *In and Out of the Mind: Greek Images of the Tragic Self*. Princeton: Princeton University Press.

Parker, R. 2011. *On Greek Religion*. Ithaca: Cornell University Press.

Patera, M. 2013. "Reflections on the discourse of fear in Greek sources." In *Unveiling Emotions II. Emotions in Greece and Rome: Texts, Images, Material Culture*, edited by A. Chaniotis and P. Ducrey, 109–134. Stuttgart: Franz Steiner.

Petridou, G. 2015. *Divine Epiphany in Greek Literature and Culture*. Oxford: Oxford University Press.

Pigeaud, J. 1989. *La maladie de l'âme: étude sur la relation de l'âme et du corps dans la tradition médico-philosophique antique*. Paris: Les Belles Lettres.

Platt, V. 2015. "Epiphany." In *The Oxford Handbook of Greek Religion*, edited by E. Eidinow and J. Kindt, 491–504. Oxford: Oxford University Press.

Poursat, J.-C. 1968. "Les représentations de danse armée dans la céramique attique." *BCH* 92:550–615.

Power, T. 2010. *The Culture of Kithardoidia*. Washington, DC: Center for Hellenic Studies.

Pritchett, W. K. 1974–1979. *The Greek State at War*. Berkeley-Los Angeles: University of California Press.

Raaflaub, K. A. 2014. "War and the city: The brutality of war and its impact on the community." In *Combat Trauma and the Ancient Greeks*, edited by P. Meineck and D. Konstan, 15–46. New York: Palgrave Macmillan.

Rawlings, L. 2007. *The Ancient Greeks at War*. Manchester: Manchester University Press.

Redfield, J. M. 1975. *Nature and Culture in the Iliad: The Tragedy of Hector*. Chicago: The University of Chicago Press.

Richer, N. 2012. *La religion des Spartiates*. Paris: Les Belles Lettres.

Rutherford, I. 2001. *Pindar's Paeans*. Oxford: Oxford University Press.

Sargant, W. 1973. *The Mind Possessed: A Physiology of Possession, Mysticism and Faith Healing*. London: Heinemann.

Scott, L. 2005. *Historical Commentary on Herodotus Book 6*. Leiden: Brill.

Segal, C. 1971. *The Theme of the Mutilation of the Corpse in the Iliad*. Leiden: Brill.

Sekunda, N. 2002. *Marathon 490 BC*. Oxford: Osprey.

Shay, J. 1994. *Achilles in Vietnam: Combat Trauma and the Undoing of Character*. New York: Atheneum.

Slater, W. J. 1993. "Three problems in the history of drama." *Phoenix* 47 (3):189–212.

Solomon, Z. 1993. *Combat Stress Reaction: The Enduring Toll of War*. New York: Plenum Press.

Speidel, M. 2002. "Berserks: A history of Indo-European 'mad warriors.'" *Journal of World History* 13:253–290.

Thomas, O. 2011. "The Homeric hymn to Pan." In *The Homeic Hymns: Interpretative Essays*, edited by A. Faulkner, 151–172. Oxford: Oxford University Press.

Tritle, L. A. 1997. "Hector's body: Mutilation of the dead in ancient Greece and Vietnam." *Ancient History Bulletin* 11:123–136.

Tritle, L. A. 2000. *From Melos to My Lai: War and Survival*. London: Routledge.

Tritle, L. A. 2004. "Xenophon's portrait of Clearchus: A study in post-traumatic stress disorder." In *Xenophon and His World*, edited by C. Tuplin, 325–339. Stuttgart: Franz Steiner.

Ustinova, Y. 2002. "Lycanthropy in Sarmatian warrior societies: The Kobyakovo torque." *Ancient West and East* 1:102–123.

Ustinova, Y. and E. Cardeña. 2014. "Combat stress disorders and their treatment in ancient Greece." *Psychological Trauma: Theory, Research, Practice, and Policy* 6 (6):739–748.

van Wees, H. 2004. *Greek Warfare: Myths and Realities*. London: Duckworth.

Vermeule, E. 1979. *Aspects of Death in Early Greek Art and Poetry*. Berkeley-Los Angeles: University of California Press.

Versnel, H. S. 1987. "What did ancient man see when he saw a god? Some reflections on Greco-Roman epiphany." In *Effigies Dei: Essays on the History of Religions*, edited by D. van der Plas, 42–55. Leiden: Brill.

West, L. J. 1997. "Perception." In *Encyclopaedia Britannica*, 25: 481–502.

West, M. L. 1992. *Ancient Greek Music*. Oxford: Oxford University Press.

West, M. L. 2007. *Indo-European Poetry and Myth*. Oxford: Oxford University Press.

Wheeler, G. 2004. "Battlefield epiphanies in ancient Greece: A survey." *Digressus* 4:1–14.

Whitehead, D. 1990. *Aeneias the Tactician: How to Survive Under Siege. Translated With Introduction and Commentary*. Oxford: Oxford University Press.

Wikander, S. 1938. *Der arische Männerbund*. Lund: Ohlsson.

Woodard, R. D. 2013. *Myth, Ritual, and the Warrior in Roman and Indo-European Antiquity*. Cambridge: Cambridge University Press.

Zaborowski, R. 2002. *La crainte et le courage dans l'Iliade et l'Odyssée*. Warsaw: Stakroos.

5 Nympholepsy

The nymphs and Pan and were able to seize people and make them possessed, nympholeptic, or panoleptic. Both states were numinous: like other types of divine possession, they produced temporary elevation above the normal human mental condition. Frightening and weird, nympholepsy and panolepsy conferred mantic abilities and inspired hallucinations that had noetic quality.[1]

Nympholepsy, panolepsy, and vatic abilities

The nymphs were divine or semi-divine youthful and mischievous residents of water-springs, mountains, caves, and groves. The Homeric hymn to Aphrodite defines them as neither mortal nor immortal, living a long life, eating heavenly food and happily dancing and making love to silens.[2] From the fifth century on, they are often depicted together with Pan, especially on votive offerings discovered in numerous caves sacred to these deities of wild nature.[3] This position in between mortals and immortals, as well as their association with places not civilised by men, hence excluded from the mundane normality, rendered the nymphs particularly liminal and ambiguous.[4]

The nymphs were also believed to be endowed with vatic powers:[5] a Parnassian nymph whose name was Daphnis (laurel) was the first prophetess of Gaia's oracle at Delphi.[6] Myths attribute nymphs as mothers to a number of prominent prophetic personages, both legendary and quasi-historical, such as the Sibyl, Mopsos son of Ampyx, Idmon, Tiresias, and Epimenides.[7] A nymph was the mother of the Erythraean Sibyl, who was buried in a grotto sacred to the nymphs.[8]

Among other sacred sites, the nymphs owned a *manteion* in Illyria and the Corycian cave, the seat of a famous lot oracle.[9] The cave was named after a nymph named Coryca, Apollo's beloved and the mother of his son.[10] During the Classical period, when the Corycian nymphs were consistently associated with Apollo, the cave was perhaps an annex to the sanctuary at Delphi, intended for humbler people who left numerous but cheap offerings.[11] An inscription discovered there was left by a woman who 'was seized as she listened to the nymphs and Pan,'[12] that is, experienced auditory hallucinations, was found in the Corycian cave, thus confirming at least one case of inspiration by the nymphs. It is most likely that other cases of nympholepsy occurred in the cave, without leaving documentary evidence.

Pan, as we have already seen, shuns the urban environment and is usually worshipped in the wild, together with the nymphs. Pan is also able to seize or invade human beings, making them panoleptic, possessed by the god.[13] Panolepsy brings about divine inspiration, which confers mantic abilities. According to myth, Pan was Apollo's instructor in prophecy.[14] In his native Arcadia, Pan was the foremost oracular deity,[15] possessing a cavern on Mount Lycaeum, which was active as an oracle.[16] Another Arcadian oracle of the same god was located in Lycosoura 'in the days of old,' where his prophetess was a nymph, Erato.[17] In Menander's comedy *The Bad-Tempered Man* (*Dyscolus*), a character pretends to vaticinate instead of Pan in a cave sacred to this god and the nymphs. The scene suggests that Pan's prophecy was delivered in the form of inspired utterances.[18] Pan's involvement in divination seems to result from the association of this activity with *mania*, and attribution of this state to the deities of the wilderness, Pan together with the nymphs.

Mythology hints at the connection of vatic abilities enthused by the nymphs with alteration of consciousness. The most ancient and perhaps the most noteworthy piece of evidence on the prophetic powers of the nymphs is a passage in the *Homeric Hymn to Hermes*, where Apollo is said to have ceded to Hermes an oracle, belonging to three winged virgins.[19] From these august teachers of divination the great oracular god Apollo learnt the mantic art, when still a boy. The three prophetic maidens were most probably the Parnassian nymphs, who resided in the Corycian cave.[20] They are depicted as living on Mt Parnassus and flying in search of honey: as soon as they eat honeycomb, they are filled with prophetic enthusiasm and start telling the truth. When deprived of the divine food, they give untruthful responses. The Parnassian bee-nymphs who needed honey to attain the prophetic inspiration seem to belong to a very archaic tradition linking divination to consumption of a sacred intoxicating substance.[21] Poetry belonged to the same realm as prophecy, as both were under Apollo's patronage, and vatic utterings were often rendered in verse.[22] Altered states of consciousness, required for inspired prophecy-giving, may resemble inebriation, which explains why the prophetic nymphs were so intimately associated with honey, the symbol of intoxication.

No wonder that prophetic inspiration and poetic rapture, as well as other kinds of *mania*, were often ascribed to nympholepsy.[23] Hesychius describes nympholepts as 'those possessed by the nymphs; they are seers and inspired.'[24] Numerous references to prophetic nympholepts demonstrate that this definition followed a rich and ancient tradition. Bacis, a famous Boeotian prophet (*chrêsmologos*), was considered a nympholept.[25] A sage and a prophet, Melesagoras of Eleusis claimed that he acquired his talents 'because the nymphs seized him.'[26] Socrates asserts that, if seized by the nymphs, he would abandon prose speech for hexametres, like these mythical or semi-mythical figures.[27] In the cave of the Sphragidian nymphs on Mt Cithaeron many local inhabitants became nympholepts, possessed and endowed with oracular powers. The Sphragidian cave itself was once an oracular shrine, where predictions were given by the nymphs.[28]

The involvement of the nymphs and Pan in music, and especially in choral dancing, is noteworthy.[29] Pan was a dance-lover, *philochoros*, the *choregos* (chorus leader) of the nymphs 'accustomed to choral dancing,' and the dancing nymphs are depicted together with Pan playing a syrinx on countless votive reliefs discovered in caves sacred to them.[30] The charm of these divine pleasures is enormous, and may be dangerous for a mere mortal. A fifth-century hymn inscribed on a stele in Epidaurus acclaims musical talents of Pan and the nymphs:

> Pan, leader of the naiad nymphs, I sing, glory of the golden choruses, lord of lively song; from his far-sounding syrinx he pours inspired charm (literally, Siren's song); to the melody he steps lightly, leaping through the well-shaded caves, playing and displaying his protean body, graceful dancer, fair in face, resplendent with blond beard. The echo of your panic melody reaches as far as starry Olympus, pervading the gathering of the Olympian gods with an immortal song. All of the earth and sea compound your grace; you are the mainstay of all, O Pan, Pan.[31]

In this hymn, Pan's all-encompassing power is in his music, which is endowed with magic abilities. His song is *entheos*, inspired, or 'engodded' – which raises an interesting question about the source of the god's 'engoddedness.' Pan's music is the Siren's tune, it enchants and enraptures, depriving the mortals of free will; it is irresistible and treacherous. His tune is called 'the muse,'[32] associating the melody created by the shepherds' god with the highest musical achievement. The auditory illusion, the 'panic' echo, is accompanied by instable vision, and thus Pan is described as protean.

The music created by Pan is bewitching, and together with the nymphs he can easily engulf the mortals in his dreamlike world of sound and movement. For a human, especially when he is lonely in a mountain forest, the vertigo of the nymphs' whirling dances and Pan's music is charming, possessing, and can lead to euphoria – or disaster.

In the *Phaedrus*, Plato makes use of the image of inspired nympholept, when in a delightful grove on the bank of Ilissus, away from the city and its bustle, his Socrates notices that something supernatural is happening to him: 'Truly the place seems filled with a divine presence; so do not be surprised if I often seem to be possessed by the nymphs (*numpholêptos*) as my discourse progresses, for I am already almost uttering dithyrambs.'[33] Time and again, Socrates defines his state as *enthousiasmos*, possession by the nymphs.[34] The charm of the place is meaningful: Plato underscores the harmony between the beautiful *topos* and the *logos* focused on beauty that Socrates begins there.[35] It is notable that although feeling possessed, Socrates continues his speech, with additional rhetoric fluency, and attributes his skills to the nymphs.[36] Even given Socrates' playful self-irony, these passages reflect a three-fold association: an enchanting uninhabited place, nymphs, and the inspiration they arouse, not necessarily fully driving the inspired person out of his mind, but rather causing elation and enhancing creativity. In a state of nympholepsy a sensitive individual was inspired to the point of creating poetry, and could attain 'insight or understanding' that were beyond his capabilities in an ordinary state of mind.[37]

Nympholepts and their caves

A fascinating case of possession by the nymphs in the late fifth–early fourth century is attested to by inscriptions from the cave at Vari in Attica:[38] Archedamus of Thera, who dedicated several ex-votos at the cave, calls himself *numpholēptos* in one of them.[39] Archedamus received instructions (*phradeis*) from the nymphs, which means that he had the power to communicate with the immortals: 'Archedamus of Thera, the nympholept, at the instruction of the nymphs worked out this cavern.'[40] His encounters with the nymphs appear to have been varied: several inscriptions refer to the nymphs in plural, while one ex-voto, unfortunately only partially readable, commemorates construction of a home 'for the nymph.'[41]

As W. R. Connor observes, 'for all their crudeness, these inscriptions show some signs of the elevation of language and the tendency towards hexameter verse.'[42] Archedamus' aesthetic aspirations went further, and he embellished the cave and planted a garden near its entrance – a gentle gesture of reverence to the natural charm of the place, and perhaps a hint at the erotic attraction of the nymphs, to be celebrated in the set of the caressing greenery.[43] He even portrayed himself on a wall of the cave as a stonecutter, equipped with the instruments necessary for the work – a fascinating expression of reverence, and perhaps of a wish to remain forever in his beloved cave. Near this image, proud of his accomplishments, he inscribed his name twice.[44]

Pan and Apollo were worshipped in the cave alongside the nymphs, as rock reliefs and inscriptions testify.[45] The inner part of the cave, separated by a massive rock as well as by a man-made threshold, is dominated by a rudely cut and mutilated enthroned figure, and by an oval object, both carved out of the rock. These are most probably representations of a nymph and of an *omphalos*.[46] The *omphalos* is a recognised symbol of the oracular centre at Delphi, and represents the prophetic function of Archedamus' cave, as *omphaloi* are found in other prophetic caves, such as the grotto at Claros. A source of flowing water must have been in the cave in antiquity, underscoring the association between water, prophecy, and the cult of the nymphs.[47] Archedamus appears to have been enchanted by the nymphs whom he imagined as abiding in the cave, and spent there countless days tending and adorning it. He conveyed his devotion in inscriptions that reveal an effort at poetic expression. Archedamus' communication with the nymphs had in his opinion a prophetic aspect, therefore Apollo, himself a frequent visitor of caves,[48] was offered worship alongside the nymphs and their regular companion, Pan.

We can speculate how the altered state of consciousness described by Archedamus as nympholepsy was reached. A stay in the darkness and the silence of the cave was perhaps sufficient; if a person entered it with some faint source of light, the powerful figure of the seated nymph, stalactites, and other natural features, could inspire fantastic visions. Mental images passing through the mind during such a sojourn could readily be interpreted as utterings of the nymphs and/or prophetic revelations. The beauty of the nymphs and their profound connection to vegetation and blossom may have prompted Archedamus the idea to embellish their cave.

Similar to the case of Archedamus is that of Pantalces, whose name is mentioned in two inscriptions in a cave near Pharsalus in Thessaly.[49] In antiquity, a water source issued from the back of this narrow cavern. Since the Archaic period, the cave, situated in a picturesque place and commanding an impressive view, had been sacred to the nymphs.[50] Pantalces' inscriptions are dated paleographically, the shorter dedication is from the fifth century, and the longer one was engraved at a slightly later date.[51] The first inscription attests to a dedication of 'this endeavour' and a laurel tree 'to the goddesses.'[52] This was presumably the beginning of Pantalces' long project of embellishing the cave, which included cutting a stairway allowing access to the cave and planting a garden. This landscaping development continued for several decades, judging by the difference between the letter forms of the two inscriptions. The second inscription[53] is a 20-line long hexametre poem, mentioning the nymphs, Pan, Hermes, Apollo, Heracles, Chiron, Asclepius, and Hygiea, and listing 'sacred things' offered to the gods, such as painted tablets, statues, and other gifts. Each of the gods and heroes bestowed upon Pantalces various blessings: he received wisdom and poetic talent from Chiron, Apollo and his son Asclepius endowed him with health and splendid life, whereas Pan gave him laughter and merriment – a hint at Pantalces' hilarious panolepsy[54] – along with 'self-restraint in hubris.'[55] Pantalces was as devoted to the care of his cave as Archedamus: having 'built up the stones' with the force Heracles gave him, he tended the flora with his own hands and looked after other parts of the precinct.[56]

The inscription hints at the possible epiphany of the nymphs, describing their arrival and commands: 'the nymphs made Pantalces a good man, and lighting upon this place, made him its guardian, the man who planted all this and toiled with his hands, and gave him in return prosperous life for all the days.'[57] The verb *epibainein* chosen by Pantalces is employed by Homer in the scenes of divine descents to the earth.[58] These verses convey the sensation of a vision of the nymphs coming from above to the terrace in front of the cave's mouth, similar to the airborne female figures depicted on Sotades' vessel, to which I will return shortly. In his hallucination, Pantalces could hear the nymphs' voices, quite like Archedamus did. It is noteworthy that Pantalces does not allude to a similar apparition of any other gods or heroes whom he mentioned: these deities were perhaps associated with the cave by the local lore, and Pantalces may have felt their presence during his long sojourns in the sanctuary and imagine their positive influence on his life, but only the nymphs are probably portrayed as visiting the site.

At the end of his dedication, Pantalces invites everyone to come to the cave, sacrifice to Pan, pray, and enjoy themselves, because 'here is the place of forgetfulness of all the misfortunes,'[59] hinting as it seems at the Homeric verse referring to a drug 'ridding the mind of all evils.'[60] This is the genuine reason that convinced

Pantalces to cultivate this cave: it was his retreat from every hardship, a place where he felt good, laughing as Pan taught him, happily forgetting himself. He kindly invited everyone to join him.

Pantalces' inscriptions attest to a profound change of mind, *metanoia* that may be compared to conversion. Ardent personal devotion, obsessive commitment to a place, an independent decision to embellish it – all these are exceptional acts in Greece. Three of Pantalces' remarks hint at the misery he felt before he found the cave: he describes the cave as a place to forget the troubles, thanks to the nymphs he became a good man, and thanks to Pan he acquired the gift described by an exceptional phrase that I render as 'self-restraint in hubris.'[61] These statements probably imply that before the blessed experience in the cave he had many troubles which he wished to forget, and saw himself as not 'good' and insolent. The cognitive anthropologist S. Atran asserts that 'linked feelings of guilt, anxiety, and social alienation are often conspicuous factors in religious possession, conversion, and mystical experience.'[62] In Pantalces' case, the guilt he felt for not being a good man and the numinous experience of the epiphany, seem to have led to his *metanoia*, i.e. adopting an idiosyncratic way of life, different from that of other people, and extreme intensification of piety. Pantalces found a niche where he felt comfortable – by a curious twist, it was a cave. Owing to his encounters with the divine, Pantalces felt privileged and elated above the ordinary human destiny: the subtle 'heroic undercurrent' in the tone of the poem ensues from his profound belief in being chosen by the nymphs and the other gods.[63]

A cave Nymphaeum near Kafizin on Cyprus yielded hundreds of sherds with dedications inscribed in Greek and in the local script.[64] While an association (*koinônia*) of men gathered there in the late third century and ameliorated the cave, most dedications were inscribed by one Onesagoras, who seems to have been the leading figure, his name appearing in more than 250 inscriptions.[65] Onesagoras worshipped a single nymph, rather than a plurality,[66] and addressed her as 'his own sister' or daughter.[67] In one inscription he even seems to take the liberty of styling himself as the nymph's suitor.[68] Many vases that he dedicated at the cave bear not only inscriptions, but also drawings of a bearded head, possibly his own.[69] It seems that devotees of the nymphs show an unusual propensity to leave their own images in the caves of the nymphs they worshipped. Onesagoras practiced some sort of divination, as appears to be implied by the strange word *manziarchêsas* meaning 'having performed the role of *mantiarchos*.'[70] He does not explicitly ascribe his vatic abilities to nympholepsy, but the intensity and intimacy of his connection to the nymph point toward this correlation.[71]

In contrast to the caves of Archedamus and Pantalces, which were visited by worshippers before and after these two nympholepts, the cult in Onesagoras' cave existed for only seven years, and faded after his demise.[72] This is a unique expression of the exceptionally personal contact between the nympholept, his nymph, and the place where he met up with her phantom. Similar devotion is reflected in a third-century AD epitaph from Cos, in which a man called himself 'servant of the nymphs,'[73] and beyond his name, loyalty to the nymphs is the only biographical fact that he or people close to him wished to commemorate. In the third century, a neighbour of Pantalces from Thessaly also founded a hilltop 'home' for the fine-looking Naïades.[74]

These cases of exclusive devotion to the nymphs are too numerous to be accidental: there must have been a particular reason that made all these men serve their nymphs with such zeal that is reminiscent or close to conversion. Some of these people probably found in their exceptional faithfulness a shelter from distress, and were driven to their experience of nympholepsy by previous dissatisfaction.

A comprehensive explanation, which squares well with the assumption of background emotional turbulence and marginality suffered by some nympholepts, is perhaps provided by Aristotle. He looks for the constituents of happiness and writes: 'Or does happiness come . . . by a sort of elevation of mind inspired by some divine power, as in the case of persons possessed by a nymph (*numpholêptoi*) or a god?'[75] The pleasure of madness, presumably delightful hallucinations, are discussed by Aristotle in other contexts, as well,[76] but the feelings of joyful bliss and ecstatic delight seem to have been associated with nympholepsy in particular, and people who experienced these sensations, like Socrates on the bank of Ilissus or Archedamus and Pantalces in their caves, tended to attribute their happiness to visitations by the nymphs. This feeling of euphoria could be excited by the aesthetic appeal of natural environments personified by the delightful nymphs.[77]

The recurring cases of male nympholepts worshipping the nymphs in caves suggest a hypothetic interpretation of a unique mid-fifth century vessel, which can perhaps be added to our corpus of evidence on nympholepts. The vase, shaped as a knucklebone, features thirteen beautiful young women, ten of them levitating, on its four sides. Attributed to Sotades and now at the British Museum, it was purchased on Aegina in the 1830s.[78] One side has an opening of irregular shape, representing as it seems the mouth of a cave, with an emaciated bearded man, his hair unkempt, emerging from it and extending his right hand in the direction of three young women, who hold hands and approach him in a dance. The man's left hand is raised, as if pointing at the levitating figures, his mouth is half-open and his brows raised high on his forehead, indicating amazement: the painting seems to portray Pantalces stunned by the apparition of the nymphs.

The levitating female figures have been interpreted as the Aurae or Aeolae in front of Aeolus leaving the cave, or even as Aristophanes' Clouds approaching Socrates; H. Hoffmann regards the man as a shaman facilitating the mystical flight of *psuchai*.[79] In my opinion, the *astragalos*-shaped vessel, with its aperture imitating the mouth of a cave, evokes the caves of the nymphs that served as seats of lot oracles, where knucklebones were used for divination.[80] The three female figures that step on the earth in front of the man are immediately reminiscent of the dancing nymphs, represented on numerous votive plaques discovered in cave Nymphaea.[81] The bony man, wearing no more than an *exomis*, his ribs clearly showing on his bare torso, is a nympholept who has spent much of his time in a cave, who is portrayed within his vision of visitation by an airborne ensemble of flying nymphs; he is stunned, his gaze is that of surprise and utter astonishment.[82] Lacking any hint at authority, he cannot be a mentor or a guide of the women.

The flight of the nymphs is masterfully depicted by means of their postures, especially the position of the feet, and the form of the wing-like long sleeves covering their hands. The flight underscores the dreamlike quality of the scene: in different cultures, visions, such as of Fata Morgana, Constantine's cross, the riders of Mons, and Madonna of Fatima, which are the most famous examples, appear in the sky, so it is not surprising that the chorus of the nymphs descends to the dreamer from above. Curiously, two other known *astragalos*-shaped pieces also feature winged flying characters, Nike and Eros: do they convey the emotional combination of elation caused by intense desire, and hope for good luck and conquest of the beloved?[83] In any case, if my suggestion is right, the knucklebone-shaped vessel by Sotades features a troglodyte nympholept and his hallucination of an encounter with the nymphs.

All the nympholepts are male, and their sensation of ecstasy probably had sexual connotations. *Numphê*, the Greek word designating nymphs *qua* supernatural beings, also means 'bride,' which is most probably not accidental. In the Homeric hymn in her honour, Aphrodite suggests that her son be considered an offspring of a mortal by a nymph, one of those who promiscuously 'mingle in love' with silens in 'the pleasant caves.' In the *Iliad*, nymphs bear children to mortals, following accidental meetings in the countryside.[84] We have just seen that several mantic individuals are attributed nymphs as mothers.[85] Could some nympholepts, in their enchanting caves, have visions of erotic encounters with a nymph?[86]

Greek mythology offers examples of unions of goddesses with mortals: Aphrodite bore Aeneas to Anchises, Thetis was given in marriage to Peleus, and Eos was a serial snatcher of mortal lovers, such as Cleitus, Cephalus, Tithonus, and Orion.[87] This is a very awkward situation, since the sexual relationship between a man and a woman, based by definition on asymmetry and male dominance, is reversed, and an immortal higher being, *qua* female, is subdued to a mortal male: an unbearable shame for a goddess.[88] These myths attest to the persistence of the male dream of a love affair with a supernatural beauty; the more deviant such sexual conquest was in the context of a patriarchal society, the more desirable it became. If love affairs with goddesses were popular because they allowed a channel for male fantasies, these very fantasies could engulf a man in a cave of the nymphs.[89]

Greek myths of love affairs between mortals and nymphs, as well as the phenomenon of nympholepsy, probably gave rise to the traditional story of the marriage of Numa Pompilius, a legendary king of Rome, to the nymph Egeria. In Plutarch's version, Numa wandered alone in groves and meadows, shunning the company of men, not because of distress, but since

> he had tasted the joy of more august companionship and had been honoured with a celestial marriage; the goddess (*daimôn*) Egeria loved him and bestowed herself upon him, and it was his communion with her that gave him a life of blessedness and a wisdom more than human.[90]

The *daimôn* is also defined as a nymph in other sources.[91] Egeria is probably a native Italic water goddess, one of the Camenae, identified with the nymphs or the Muses at an early date.[92] All the major elements of Greek nympholepsy are present in this legend: a tendency towards solitude and spending time in the nature, bizarre behaviour resembling a mental disorder, an erotic relationship with a nymph, and blessedness and enlightenment resulting from the intercourse with her.

Erotic dreams of the nymphs, perceived as an encounter that took place in real life, is immortalised in an early second-century BC inscription from Aquae Flavianae (Algeria), left by a Roman centurion and discussed by V. Platt:[93]

> I wished to carry out Dacian slaughters: I did so.
> I wished to sit in the chair of peace: I sat in it.
> I wished to march along in glorious triumph: I did.
> I wished for the full rewards of the *primus pilus*: I had them.
> I wished to see naked nymphs: I saw them.

Irresistible seductresses of semi-divine status living in woods and rivers and water sources populate the mythologies of many Indo-European peoples, such as the Slavic Vilas and Rusalkas and the Indian Apsaras; all these beauties are dangerous, prone to madden men who happen to their domain.[94] It is easily understandable why the semi-divine creatures are female, seducing lonely males. In patriarchal societies men were free to walk away from the inhabited places, while women, married and unmarried alike, were guarded close to home, and if they ventured out of the inhabited places, they rarely did that on their own. The association of male erotic fantasies with a wild environment is natural: away from the constraints of human communities, men of various cultures were more prone to daydreaming of otherwise unattainable sexual experiences. Nymphs could easily impersonate it, and shifting from daydreaming to hallucination left a man with a sensation of the reality of his vision. Linking of erotic longing with the strangeness or charm of the natural environment could bring about a feeling of illumination or transformation. It is certainly not accidental that Socrates started his laudation of *erôs* when feeling *numpholêptos*.[95]

However, the happiness of a nympholept could go too far and end in a tragedy. The asymmetry in status between male and female sexual partners implied that the mortal male had to pay dearly for the subordination of the divine female during the intimacy: the reversal of the norm regarding penetration as social domination had to be compensated for. Greek myths of liaisons between goddesses and young men almost always end in either sexual incapacitation, total destruction, or dependency of the men, who never return to the human society.[96]

The story of Hylas, Heracles' lover who followed a chorus of dancing nymphs and fell under their power, disappearing forever in a spring,[97] draws a pattern: 'too much happiness'[98] – or too much love of a nymph – could be dangerous. A similar story was told in Bithynia of a handsome lad named Bormus, who vanished, becoming a nympholept.[99] An inscription from Halicarnassus, dated to the late second century, relates a local myth of the nymph Salmacis, who lived in a cave beneath a stream and received there 'in her kindly arms' a beautiful adolescent (*kouros*) Hermaphroditus, raising him to become an extraordinary (*panexokhos*) man.[100] The epigraphic version is benign, and even claims that Hermaphroditus became the local cultural hero and the founder of the institution of marriage. However, Ovid recounts a different and uncanny version having the love-sick nymph seize the boy and merge with him in an eternal union: the two come out of the spring as one person of neither sex; since then, every man who immerses in the spring is emasculated.[101] A human boy or an offspring of two gods, Hermaphroditus is 'received' or 'seized' by the nymph, and through the contact with her, gentle or violent, his nature is profoundly transformed.

Callimachus' epigram portrays a goat-shepherd who became 'sacred' (*hieros*) after a nymph had seized him.[102] His fate is unclear: had he died or disappeared?[103] Or perhaps lost his mind, becoming 'sacred' in the same sense that epilepsy was the 'sacred' disease? In any case, his transformation, vanishing, or transportation to the super-human level of sanctity, was equivalent to death and attributed to the nymphs.[104] The belief underlying this motif appears to be that a male who had been submitted to the power of a nymph could not remain the same: his former self was annulled, replaced by a being of a different status, or disappeared from the world of the mortals altogether. These tales do not antedate the Hellenistic period, but the tradition they reflect was most probably much more ancient.[105] It certainly appears, although in a different key, in the fourth century, in Menander's *Dyscolus*: when the misanthropic protagonist falls down a well, his cook remarks that 'the nymphs took revenge on him.'[106] In a play that is set in front and inside Pan's cave, and in which the nymphs, together with Pan, interfere with the events, this comment can only imply that the propensity of the nymphs to pull their victims into water reservoirs was notorious.[107] In addition, Indo-European ancestry of incredibly beautiful creatures stealing children, men, and men's wits, allows to suppose that the Greek myths of vanishing nympholepts belong to an age-long tradition.[108]

The nymphs were considered dangerously seductive from Homer's time. The retention of Odysseus by the nymph Calypso on her enchanted island is perhaps the first attested story of a nympholept, although this word does not occur in the epos. Calypso, 'the fair-tressed nymph,' lived in a well-tended cave on an island, far away from the places inhabited by the Greeks; this goddess, who had access to nectar and ambrosia, kept Odysseus by force as her bedfellow,[109] and intended to endow him with immortality, eternal youth, and a happy existence free of earthly cares.[110] All the elements of the nympholeptic complex are present here: a faraway beautiful cave as a nymph's dwelling, her sexual relationship with a mortal man, and blessings promised to him in exchange for estrangement from his community. However, in contrast to later nympholepts, Odysseus was not happy to serve as the goddess' plaything, and preserved his memory and desire to return home.

I suppose the myths of men snatched by the nymphs reflect on aspects of real-life nympholepts' behaviour. How much time did Archedamus and Pantalces spend in their caves? Without doubt, many days. Addicted to their encounters with the nymphs, these men returned to caves, embellishing them and adding dedications. We will never know how many other men returned to the places where they experienced an epiphany of a nymph in the hope of being endowed with the same sensation again. The majority of these men did not leave inscriptions or dedications behind, bringing with them humble perishable presents such as flowers or fruit trays, normally reserved for the nymphs. Numerous offerings and dedicatory plaques to the nymphs and Pan have been discovered in caves; most of them give no explanation of the reason why a person took the trouble to offer a gift to a deity, but the sheer number of presents attests to the importance of the nymphs, and it would not be a wild guess that some offerings were brought by nympholepts. In a word, the preserved evidence on Archedamus', Pantalces', and Onesagoras' obsession most probably attests to the outstanding cases, while numerous other nympholepts remain anonymous. However, their compulsive drive to return to the place where they met their nymphs was noticed by their contemporaries, giving rise to the myths of nympholepts who failed to come back from their mysterious lovers.

In his idyll on Hylas, Theocritus calls the nymphs 'terrible goddesses' (*deinai theai*), and the scholiast explains that they are so called because of the 'the fear they produce and bring upon them, wherefore they are called nympholepts.'[111] Homer's Calypso is also defined as a 'terrible goddess.'[112] Whom did the nymphs terrify? Presumably not the nympholepts who were for the most part delighted to stay in their illusory world, but rather those regular people who were shocked by the changes in the nympholept's ways – or his disappearance – and could not comprehend his madness and happiness.

Nymphs were believed to be able to seize and drive mad even animals: Aristotle clarifies the meaning of the word designating the frenzy of horses, *numphian:* 'nympholepsy, during which possession occurs when someone plays the flute, and [it] casts down its eyes. And if someone mounts it, it races until held back, but still casts down its eyes while raging madly'[113] (the verb in the original passage derives from the noun *lussa*[114]). This intriguing passage juxtaposes the power of the nymphs to seize living beings, the bewitching effects of *aulos*, the instrument known to madden people,[115] and *lussa*, bestial fury or rage. The nymphs seem to have been particularly cruel to horses: human nympholepts did not rage.

Thus, too close contact with the nymphs was menacing, and nympholepsy could be ambiguous. However, in contrast to *paneia*, which was often experienced by large groups while caused by one god, nympholepsy could be inflicted by a group of nymphs, while its subject was always individual.[116] Furthermore, possession by the nymphs seems to be enchanting and gentle: nympholepts were never depicted as frantic, but only elated, and even when driven to his demise, Hylas was imagined as lovingly embraced by a nymph.

Conclusions

Pan and the nymphs share the same wild environment, hence personify the idea of separation from civilisation. Withdrawal from the society results in hallucinations and visions that may propel people to prophesy, experience otherworldly happiness – or may terrify and drive them out of their wits. The sensation of being singled out by a nymph, probably with erotic undertones, could give rise to a compulsive drive to return to the place where a man experienced the epiphany.

Isolation from the world inside deep caves becomes almost total, which consequently often serve as environment-inducing altered states of consciousness. Silence and darkness cause sensory deprivation, and with the lack of external stimuli, the waking human mind tends to concentrate within itself and produces images that do not reflect the environment – in a word, the person begins to hallucinate.[117] Intensive discharge of imagery can be caused even by reduction in information input, for instance, a sojourn in a cave where silence is disturbed from time to time by the sound of dripping water or the dominant darkness is interrupted by a flickering light of a candle, while tactile and olfactory sensations become uncannily prominent. Caves invite visions, which are easily ascribed to supernatural agents, and caves were deemed Pan's and the nymphs' favourite places. By extension, other caves, including smaller ones where the effects of the cave environment were limited, but the feeling of awe and contrast with the rest of the world remained dominant, were still perceived as numinous and liminal places.[118] In addition, the cave environment modifies sound, and the connection between the auditory hallucinations and Pan the god of echo and noise-making is not surprising.[119] Thus, caves of various shapes became sacred to Pan and the nymphs, and people, some of them probably following an odd numinous experience, left there numerous votives to these gods.[120]

Although nymphs were often envisaged as dwelling in caves, they belonged to uncultivated landscapes in general. Born and bred to live in human society, when separated from it in an untamed landscape, men felt a spectrum of emotions from fear to bucolic delight, and ascribed these sensations to the gods of the countryside. It is noteworthy that the mythologies of many Indo-European peoples, divine or semi-divine seductresses of irresistible beauty were associated with forests and water sources. Loneliness in such places liberated fantasies, arousing a flow of imagery, sometimes even erotic dreams, which could become overwhelming. These visions were identified as the nymphs, or their counterparts in other cultures – images of attractive, elusive and dangerous super-human females.

Alone in the wilderness, which is the domain of Pan and the nymphs, and an unnatural environment for the human beings who are born to live in the society of other men, people easily hallucinated. In particular, rustles in the cave and the medley of noises in the wilderness provoked acoustic projection,[121] shaping natural sounds into messages from the gods. In Greek terms, people are exposed to seizures by these deities, and become nympholepts and panolepts. Being in the grip of the god was awesome and precarious. On the one hand, Pan might inflict destructive madness on individuals or whole armies, and the nymphs could put an end to the earthly life of the one they chose. On the other hand, possession by the nymphs or Pan might bring about divine *mania*, bestowing visions of epiphany, vatic abilities, poetic inclinations, or sensations of extreme happiness. The experience can even be transformative, changing or profoundly influencing the person's way of life and perception of himself, as the cases of some nympholepts illustrate.

Notes

1 Borgeaud (1979: 137–176); Ustinova (2009: 55–68).
2 *h. Ven.* 259–260; Porph. *De antro* 6, 8; Edwards (1985: 11–19); Larson (2001: 3–11); Sourvinou-Inwood (2005: 103–106); West (2007: 286–288).
3 Pasquier (1977); Sporn (2013).
4 Pache (2011: 4–5).
5 Herter (1937: 1552–1553); Larson (2001: 11–20); Ustinova (2009: 58–60).
6 Paus. 10. 5. 5
7 Hyg. *Fab.* 14; Apollod. 3. 6. 7; Plu. *Sol.* 12; Paus. 10. 12. 3.
8 Paus. 10. 12. 3–6; *IErythr.* 224, 225, 226, second century AD; Buresch (1892: 17–21); Reinach (1891: 280–282); Corssen (1913: 1–4); Graf (1985: 335–337).
9 D.C. 41. 45; Amandry (1984); Larson (1995: 348); Borgeaud (1979: 160).
10 Paus. 10. 6. 3.
11 Such as relief plaques, terracotta statuettes, pottery, coins, and several hundred finger rings: Amandry (1984: 401); Larson (1995: 348).
12 *SEG* 3. 406: Νυμφῶν [καὶ] Πανὸς κλύουσα . . . ἐλήφ[θη].
13 Eurip. *Hipp.* 141–150; *Med.* 1167–1177; Borgeaud (1988: 103). The word *panolêptos* is very rare: Borgeaud (1988: 107).
14 Apollod. 1. 4. 1. For the connection between Pan and Apollo, see Schörner and Goette (2004: 115–116).
15 D.H. 1. 32; Borgeaud (1979: 164); Jost (1985: 491).
16 Porph. *Antr.* 20, Schol. in Theoc. *Idyll.* 1. 123. Jost (1985: 180, 183, 474–475); Bouché-Leclercq (1879–1882: 3, 383).
17 Paus. 8. 37. 11; Jost (1985: 459).
18 Verses 571–572; Gomme and Sandbach (1973: 134, 223); Larson (2001: 245–246); cf. Wickens (1986: 1: 182–183, 2: 245–269).
19 Verses 550–567; Scheiberg (1979); Larson (1995); Larson (2001: 12).
20 Halliday (1913: 211); Dietrich (1978: 6); Amandry (1984: 411); Fontenrose (1974: 427); Larson (1995).
21 See Chapter 6.
22 Scheiberg (1979: 17–19).
23 Pl. *Phdr.* 238CD; Poll. 1. 19; Iamb. *Myst.* 3. 10.
24 Hsch. s.v. *numpholêptoi:* οἱ κατεχόμενοι Νύμφαις. μάντεις δέ εἰσι καὶ ἐπιθειαστικοί.
25 Paus. 4. 27. 4, 10. 12. 11. On Bacis see also Hdt. 8. 20, 77, 96; 9. 43; Paus. 9. 17. 5, 10. 32. 8; Ar. *Pax* 1071 with scholia; *Av.* 962. Beginning with Aristotle (*Pr.* 954A), ancient authors talk about multiple Bacides (Plu. *Mor.* 399A; Schol. in Ar. *Eq.* 123). The multiplicity of Bacides could have been influenced by the multiplicity of the Sibyls (Aune 1983: 38; Parke 1988: 180; Connor 1988: 161; Rohde 1925: 314; Dillery 2005: 180).
26 Max. Tyr. 38. 3; Bouché-Leclercq (1879–1882: 2, 104); Connor (1988: 160).
27 Pl. *Phdr.* 238C–241E; Motte (1963).
28 Plu. *Arist.* 11; Paus. 9. 3. 9; Larson (2001: 19–20).
29 Lonsdale (1993: 261).
30 A. *Pers.* 448; *h. Pan* 3; Lonsdale (1993: 262–275); Sporn (2013: 204).
31 IG IV² I. 130: Πᾶνα τὸν Νυμφαγέτα[ν], | Ναΐδων μέλημ' ἀείδω, | χρυσέων χορῶν ἄγαλμα, | κωτίλας ἄνακτα [μ]οίσας. | εὐθρόου σύριγγος εὖ[χο]ς, | ἔνθεον Σειρῆνα χεύη· | ἐς μέλος δὲ κοῦφα βαίνων | εὐσκίων πήδα κατ' ἄντρων, | παμφυὲς νωμῶν δέμας, | εὐχόρευτος εὐπρόσωπος, | ἐνπρέπων ξανθῶι γενείωι. | ἐς δ' Ὄλυνπον ἀστερωπὸν | ἔρχεται πανῳδὸς ἀχώ, | θεῶν Ὀλυμπίων ὅμιλον | ἀμβρόται ῥαίνοισα μοίσαι. | χθὼν δὲ πᾶσα καὶ θάλασσα | κίρναται τεὰν χάριν· σὺ | γὰρ πέλεις ἔρισμα πάντων, | ὦ ἰὴ Πὰν Πάν. Translation S. H. Londsdale, modified.
32 See below, Chapter 6, on the word *moisa* or *mousa*.

33 *Phdr.* 238D: τῷ ὄντι γὰρ θεῖος ἔοικεν ὁ τόπος εἶναι, ὥστε ἐὰν ἄρα πολλάκις νυμφόληπτος προϊόντος τοῦ λόγου γένωμαι, μὴ θαυμάσῃς· τὰ νῦν γὰρ οὐκέτι πόρρω διθυράμβων φθέγγομαι (translation H. N. Fowler, slightly modified).

34 *Phdr.* 241E, 263D.

35 *Phdr.* 241E Motte (1963); Motte (1963: 406–410); Fabiano (2013: 171).

36 *Phdr.* 263D; Connor (1988: 159).

37 Connor (1988: 158); Pache (2011: 6).

38 The most recent and complete publication of the site: Schörner and Goette (2004). Cf. Ustinova (2009: 61–64).

39 IG I³ 977–980; Schörner and Goette (2004: 42–59, 123–125); Bultrighini (2015: 52–75); Purvis (2003: 33–64).

40 IG I³ 980: Ἀρχέδημος ὁ Θ | ηραῖος ὁ νυμφ | όληπτος φραδ | αῖσι Νυμφῶν τ’ | ἄντρον ἐξηργ | άξατο (translation W. R. Connor). For φραδαῖσι see Purvis (2003: 56).

41 IG I³ 977B; for a discussion of the reading of this inscription, see Purvis (2003: 46–48).

42 Connor (1988: 173).

43 Flowers and vegetation in Greek cults: Motte (1963: 468–470).

44 Purvis (2003: 43). Cf. Connelly (2007: 163) on the reasons behind dedications of statues of priests in sanctuaries where they served.

45 IG I³ 976, 981; Weller (1903), with plans and figures; Dunham (1903); Edwards (1985: 22); Connor (1988: 166–174, 179–189); Wickens (1986: 90–121).

46 Connor (1988: 186). On mantic symbolism of enthroned deities see Bonnechere (2001: 38–41).

47 Connor (1988: 185).

48 Ustinova (2009: 109–155).

49 SEG 1. 247; 248; 2. 357; Peek (1938); Decourt (1995: 88–94, Nos. 72–73); Connor (1988: 162–163); Larson (2001: 16–20); Wagman (2011). The most recent detailed study of the complex: Wagman (2016).

50 The site and the finds, mostly fragments of terracotta figurines, are discussed in Wagman (2016).

51 SEG 1. 247; 248. Both inscriptions are not dated. Having visited the site twice and carefully studied both inscriptions *in situ*, Peek (1938: 25) evaluates the gap as several decades. He is followed by van Straten (1981: 79), Connor (1988: 163), and Larson (2001: 16). In contrast, on the basis of palaeograhical considerations, the first inscription is dated by some scholars to the fifth century (SEG 1. 247), or even as the first half of the fifth century (Decourt 1995: 90 and Wagman 2016: 57). The editors of SEG (1. 248), Decourt (1995: 90) and Wagman (2016: 66, 60), date the second inscription to the fourth century, a hundred years later than the first one, suggesting to regard the two texts as independent documents.

R. Wagman's interpretation of the poem as a tribute to the cult founder raises several difficult questions: Why does the author of the poem fail to indicate his own identity? Or the occasion for Pentalces' supposed commemoration? The discrepancy between the inscriptions may find its explanation in the fact that the short one was written and carved by Pantalces himself when he was relatively young, while the long text was carved by a young stonecutter, by the order of aging Pantalces: this will allow for a considerable difference in characters. The text of the poem could also be ordered by Pantalces, exactly like the contemporary poetic dedication to the nymphs from Thessaly which is signed by its creator (Peek 1974). In fact, Archedamus continued to carve his inscriptions for a 'period of years' (Purvis 2003: 39). Following the opinion of the majority of scholars who studied the two inscriptions (Peek 1938; Hiller von Gaertingen 1937: 57–58; van Straten 1981: 79; Connor 1988: 163; Larson 2001: 16; Purvis 2003: 17, 39; Pache 2011: 52), I consider them as commemorating the life efforts of the same person, inscribed on his own initiative.

52 Decourt (1995: No. 72); Wagman (2016: 57–62, fig. 45: Παντάλκες| ἀνέθεκε| θεαῖς τόδ᾽ ἔργον| τὰν δὲ δάφν[αν]. . .). Since the end of the inscription is barely visible, it is unclear whether Pantalces is the only dedicant, or the tree was planted by another person. For the amendments see *SEG* 2. 357; Decourt (1995: 89–90).

53 Discussion: Peek (1938: 23–27); Decourt (1995: No 73); Wagman (2016: 66–93, fig. 47).

54 In Aristophanes, the nymphs and Pan 'bestow laughter' on the chorus: Ar. *Th.* 979–980.

55 Ἀπόλλων δὲ δίδωσι καὶ υἱὸς τοῦ[δ]ε καὶ Ἑρμῆς| αἰῶν᾽ εἰς τὸν ἅπαντα ὑγίειαν καὶ βίον ἐσθλόν,| Πὰν δὲ γέλωτα καὶ εὐφροσύνην ὕβριν τε δικαίαν | Χίρων δ᾽ αὐτῶι δῶκε σοφόν τ᾽ ἔμεν[αι] καὶ ἀοιδόν. Cf. Socrates' prayer to Pan and other gods of the grove, asking them to grant him inner beauty and accompanying outward blessings (Pl. *Phdr.* 279BC). Pantalces' panolepsy and nympholepsy: Connor (1988: 163).

56 Bonnechere (2001: 34–37). Wagman (2016: 21–26) offers a tentative reconstruction of the sacred garden.

57 ἄνδρα δ᾽ ἐποιήσα(ν)τ᾽<α> ἀγαθὸν Παντάλκεα Νύμφαι | τῶν δ᾽ ἐπιβαινέμεναι χώρων καὶ ἐπίσσκοπον εἶναι,| ὅσπερ ταῦτ᾽ ἐφύτευσε καὶ [ἐ]ξεπονήσατο χερσσίν | ἀντίδοσαν δ᾽ αὐτῶι βίον ἄφθονον ἤματα πάντα.

58 *Il.* 14. 226; *Od.* 5. 50; Decourt (1995: 93); Pache (2011: 54). Wagman (2016: 79) contends that the phrase is to be read as an 'ordinary genitive construction,' 'the nymphs who tread these places.'

59 ἀναβαίνετ[ε], θύετε Πανί,| εὔχεσθε, εὐφραίνεσθε· κακῶν [ἐπίλη]σις ἀπάν[των] ἐνθάδ᾽ ἔνεστ.᾽ I accept [ἐπίλη]σις suggested by W. Peek (1938), rather than ἔξαρσις of *SEG* 1. 248; Decourt (1995: 91) is undecided.

60 *Od.* 4. 221: κακῶν ἐπίληθον ἁπάντω (translation R. Merrill). J. and L. Robert (1958: No. 108) and Decourt (1995: 93) interpret εὐφραίνεσθε in a completely terrestrial sense, as implying a pleasure of a meal following the sacrifice. This overtone is quite possible, but it does not appear to be the main implication of these verses: a picnic is not sufficient to banish every sorrow.

61 Decourt (1995: 91–92) translates εὐφροσύνην ὕβριν τε δικαίαν as 'ardeur maîtresse d'elle-même' and states that they are unparalleled; Borgeaud (1979: 219) suggests 'juste démesure' for ὕβρις δικαία; cf. the commentary Wagman (2016: 82).

62 Atran (2002: 168).

63 Decourt (1995: 92); Wagman (2016: 85–86).

64 Mitford (1980); Masson (1981); *SEG* 30. 1608.

65 Pache (2011: 57).

66 Robert and Robert (1981: No. 636); Larson (2001: 257).

67 ἡ αὐτοῦ ἀδελφή: Mitford (1980: No. 48, 194, 213d; daughter: No. 353, 293; discussion: 261).

68 Mitford (1980: No. 251): [Νύμφηι ἐπ]ηκ[όωι] | [ἱς τὸν μν]ηστῆρ[α]?; Connor (1988: 164). Mitford (1980: 261) does not believe that Onesagoras, however possessive, felt 'passion' for the nymph.

69 Larson (2001: 16); Pache (2011: 66).

70 The term is attested for the sanctuary of Apollo at Pyla: Mitford (1980: No. 258); J. and L. Robert, *Bull.* 10 (1981–84) No. 636; Masson (1981: 641); Connor (1988: 164). On *mantiarchos* on Cyprus see: Masson (1966: 20–21); Robert (1978); Georgoudi (1998: 344).

71 Connor (1988: 164); Ustinova (2009: 64).

72 Mitford (1980: 261): Onesagoras' 'impact upon the cult . . . is overwhelming'; Larson (2001: 18).

73 Νυ(ν)φῶν λατρίς, Mitford (1980: 261).

74 Peek (1974).

75 Arist. *EE* 1214a24: ἤτοι καθάπερ οἱ νυμφόληπτοι καὶ θεόληπτοι τῶν ἀνθρώπων, ἐπιπνοίᾳ δαιμονίου τινὸς ὥσπερ ἐνθουσιάζοντες (translation H. Rackham).

76 See the Introduction.

77 For theophanic powers of *daimonioi topoi* see Motte (1963: 26–37).

78 The vase (BM E804; Beazley 1963: 765: 20; Addenda 286) is discussed in detail by Hoffmann (1997: 106–112, with figs. 60–63).

79 For an overview of the literature and argumentation for his opinion see Hoffmann (1997: 110–112).

80 Amandry (1984: 410); Larson (1995: 347); Ustinova (2009: 66).

81 Amandry (1984: 404–410); Lavagne (1988: 73–80); Larson (2001: 230–231); Barber (2013: 23).

82 Representation of Bacchic delusion on vases has been convincingly argued for Kefalidou (2009), cited in Chapter 3.

83 But for the *astragalos* by Sotades, three other vessels are known and listed by Hoffmann (1997: 171), one knucklebone by the Syriskos Painter (Beazley 1963: 264: 67), featuring Nike, Eros, and lion and a *kalos*-inscription, and the other one, at the Metropolitan museum, featuring winged Eros playing a lyre (Richter 1953: 88; fig. 69g). On erotic connotations of knucklebones see Calame (1992: 15), and below, Chapter 7.

84 *h. Ven.* 259–263; *Il.* 6. 21–26; 14. 442; 20. 383; Larson (2001: 32, 78).

85 See above in this chapter.

86 Larson (2001: 18–19) gives a positive answer to this question, emphasising the fact that 'possession may be understood in sexual terms,' and that in the case of possession of a mortal male by an immortal female we deal with sex-role reversal; cf. Borgeaud (2015: 100). Fabiano (2013: 191) doubts the presence of the erotic aspect in nympholepsy.

87 Hom. *Od.* 5. 121; 15. 250; Hes. *Th.* 984–986; Apollod. 1. 4. 4–5; Larson (2001: 7); Pache (2011: 71–91).

88 *h. Ven.* 247–249; Hom. *Od.* 5. 118–120; Konstan (1994: 181–182).

89 Larson (2001: 66).

90 *Numa* 4: εὐδαίμων ἀνὴρ καὶ τὰ θεῖα πεπνυμένος γέγονεν (translation B. Perrin).

91 *Numa* 8. Livy (1. 19) only indicates that Numa invented the affair with the goddess in order to instil awe in his compatriots.

92 West (2007: 288); Wiseman (2004: 51).

93 Platt (2016): *Optaui Dacos tenere caecos: tenui | [opt]aui in sella pacis residere: sedi | optaui claros sequi triumphos: factum | optaui primi commoda plena pili: hab[ui] | optaui nudas uidere nymphas:uidi* (translation V. Platt).

94 Barber (2013); West (2007: 280–292).

95 Pl. *Phdr.* 238D.

96 Stehle (1989).

97 Theocr. 13; A.R. 1. 1222–1239 are the main literary sources. For a detailed analysis of the corpus of ancient sources on this myth, see Sourvinou-Inwood (2005: 67–99).

98 To use the title of a short story collection by Alice Munro.

99 *Nymphis*: 432 fr. 5b *FGH*; Ath. 14. 619F–620A; nympholept: Hsch. s.v. *Bôrmon*; Sourvinou-Inwood (2005: 129).

100 Isager (1998: column 1, lines 16–23).

101 *Met.* 285–388; other references to the effeminising effects of the water from Salmacis: Vitr. 2. 7. 11–12; Str. 14. 2. 16; Sourvinou-Inwood (2004); Sourvinou-Inwood (2005: 110–111).

102 ἥρπασε Νύμφη, *Anth. Pal.* 7. 518; Connor (1988: 165); Pache (2011: 176). It is suggested that several epitaphs, dated to the Imperial period, referring to deceased children or young women as abducted by a nymph, are associated with this belief: Larson (2001: 14, 70); Nock (1972: 2: 924). In later Classical mythology nymphs and nereids carried away mortal women as well, for instance Dryope (Ant. Lib. 32; Nock 1972: 2: 925; Sourvinou-Inwood 2005: 105). In modern Greek folklore, the descendants of the ancient nymphs and nereids known as *neraïdes* are believed to apprehend men and women, sometimes dancing them to death (Larson 2001: 70).

103 'A poetic metaphor of the poet's death': van Groningen (1958: 311).
104 Borgeaud (1979: 161–162); Larson (2001: 66, 70).
105 Although the tales of Hylas and Bormus are located in non-Greek Bithynia, they appear to be constructed of 'Greek mythological schemata' (Sourvinou-Inwood 2005: 325).
106 Men. *Dys.* 643–644.
107 Lonsdale (1993: 268–271), emphasising the humorous twist: in the comic setting, the nymphs get hold of an old creature instead of a beautiful young man.
108 West (2007: 303); the motif: Barber (2013: 22–25).
109 *Od.* 5. 57, 120, 156–157; Calypso called nymph: *Od.* 5. 14, 30, 57, 149, 153, 196, 230.
110 *Od.* 5. 136: ἀθάνατον καὶ ἀγήραον; 208–209; divine food: 5. 93.
111 Schol. Theoc. 13.44: δειναὶ θεαὶ: παρόσον φόβον ἔσθ' ὅτε αὐτοῖς ἐγγεννῶσί τε καὶ ἐπάγουσιν, ὅθεν καὶ νυμφολήπτους τινάς φαμεν; cf. *Od.* 7. 246; 255; 10. 136; Borgeaud (1979: 162).
112 *Deinê theos*: *Od.* 7. 246; 12. 449; Larson (2001: 27); Pache (2011: 96–108).
113 Τὸ δὲ νυμφιᾶν καλούμενον, ἐν ᾧ συμβαίνει κατέχεσθαι ὅταν αὐλῇ τις, καὶ κατωπιᾶν· καὶ ὅταν ἀναβῇ τις, τροχάζει, ἕως ἂν μέλλῃ τις κατασχεῖν· κατηφεῖ δ' ἀεί καὶ ὅταν λυττήσῃ. Arist. HA 604b10–14.
114 For *lussa*, see the Introduction and Chapter 4.
115 For flute-arousing ecstasy and rendering maenads *entheoi*, see above, Chapter 3.
116 Contrary to the view of Pache (2011: 43) who interprets the fact that many people became nympholepts at the Sphragidian cave as a 'communal form of nympholepsy.' That nympholepsy was common among the inhabitants of an area around a famous cave is to be expected, but the evidence at our disposal does not even hint at a collective experience.
117 See the Introduction. I argue this subject in detail elsewhere: Ustinova (2009: 32–41).
118 Ustinova (2009: 55–67); liminality and ambiguity of caves in Greek myth: Buxton (1994: 104–109).
119 Yioutsos (2014).
120 Edwards (1985); Wickens (1986); Ustinova (2009: 55).
121 Banks (2012) and above, Chapter 4.

References

Amandry, P. 1984. "Le culte des nymphes et de Pan à l'antre Corycien." *BCH* Suppl. 9:395–425.

Atran, S. 2002. *In God We Trust: The Evolutionary Landscape of Religion*. Oxford: Oxford University Press.

Aune, D. E. 1983. *Prophecy in Early Christianity and the Ancient Mediterranean World*. Grand Rapids: Eerdmans.

Banks, J. 2012. *Rorschach Audio: Art and Illusion for Sound*. London: Disinformation.

Barber, E. W. 2013. *The Dancing Goddesses: Folklore, Archaeology, and the Origins of European Dance*. New York: W. W. Norton.

Beazley, J. D. 1963. *Attic Red-Figure Vase-Painters*. Oxford: Clarendon Press.

Bonnechere, P. 2001. "Prairies et jardins grecs de la Grèce de Platon à l'Angleterre d'Alexander Pope." *Kernos* Suppl. 11:29–50.

Borgeaud, P. 1979. *Recherches sur le dieu Pan*. Rome: Institut suisse de Rome.

Borgeaud, P. 1988. *The Cult of Pan in Ancient Greece*. Chicago-London: The University of Chicago Press.

Borgeaud, P. 2015. *Exercices de mythologie*. Geneva: Labor et fides.

Bouché-Leclercq, A. 1879–1882. *Histoire de la divination dans l'Antiquité*. 4 vols. Paris: E. Leroux.

Bultrighini, I. 2015. *Demi attici della Paralia*. Lanciano: Carabba.

Buresch, K. 1892. "Die sibyllinische Quellgrotte in Erythrae." *MDAI(A)* 17:16–36.

Buxton, R. 1994. *Imaginary Greece: The Context of Mythology*. Cambridge: Cambridge University Press.

Calame, C. 1992. *The Poetics of Eros in Ancient Greece*. Princeton: Princeton University Press.

Connelly, J. B. 2007. *Portrait of a Priestess: Women and Ritual in Ancient Greece*. Princeton: Princeton University Press.

Connor, W. R. 1988. "Seized by the nymphs: Nympholepsy and symbolic expression in Classical Greece." *ClAnt* 7 (2):155–189.

Corssen, P. 1913. "Die erythraeische Sibylle." *MDAI(A)* 38:1–22.

Decourt, J.-C. 1995. *Inscriptions de Thessalie 1. Les cités de la valée de l'Énipeus*. Paris: de Boccard.

Dietrich, B. C. 1978. "Reflections on the origins of the oracular Apollo." *BICS* 25:1–18.

Dillery, J. 2005. "Chresmologues and *manteis*: Independent diviners and the problem of authority." In *Mantikê: Studies in Ancient Divination*, edited by S. I. Johnston and P. T. Struck, 167–231. Leiden: Brill.

Dunham, M. I. 1903. "The cave at Vari: Inscriptions." *AJA* 7:289–300.

Edwards, C. M. 1985. *Votive Reliefs to Pan and the Nymphs*. Ph.D. thesis, New York University.

Fabiano, D. 2013. "La nympholepsie entre possession et paysage." In *Perception et construction du divin dans l'Antiquité*, edited by P. Borgeaud and D. Fabiano, 165–195. Geneva: Droz.

Fontenrose, J. 1974. *Python*. New York: Biblo and Tannen.

Georgoudi, S. 1998. "Les porte-parole des dieux: réflexions sur le personel des oracles grecs." In *Sibille e languaggi oracolari*, edited by I. Chirassi Colombo and T. Seppilli, 315–365. Pisa-Rome: Istituti Editoriali e Poligrafici Internazionali.

Gomme, A. W. and F. H. Sandbach. 1973. *Menander: A Commentary*. Oxford: Clarendon Press.

Graf, F. 1985. *Nordionische Kulte*. Rome: Schweizerisches Institut in Rom.

Halliday, W. R. 1913. *Greek Divination: A Study of Its Methods and Principles*. London: Macmillan.

Herter, H. 1937. "Nymphen." In *RE*, 1527–1581.

Hiller von Gaertingen, F. 1937. "Theräische Studien." *ArchEph* 1:48–60.

Hoffmann, H. 1997. *Sotades: Symbols of Immortality on Greek Vases*. Oxford: Oxford University Press.

Isager, S. 1998. "The pride of Halicarnassus. Edition princeps of an inscription from Sakmakis." *ZPE* 123:1–23.

Jost, M. 1985. *Sanctuaires et cultes d'Arcadie*. Paris: Vrin.

Kefalidou, E. 2009. "The iconography of madness in Attic vase-painting." In *Athenian Potters and Painters*, edited by J. H. Oakley and O. Palagia, 90–99. Oxford: Oxbow Books.

Konstan, D. 1994. *Sexual Symmetry: Love in the Ancient Novel and Related Genres*. Princeton: Princeton University Press.

Larson, J. 1995. "The Corycian Nymphs and Bee Maidens of the Homeric Hymn to Hermes." *GRBS* 36 (4):341–357.

Larson, J. 2001. *Greek Nymphs*. Oxford: Oxford University Press.

Lavagne, H. 1988. *Operosa antra. Recherches sur la grotte à Rome de Sylla à Hadrien*. Rome: de Boccard.

Lonsdale, S. H. 1993. *Dance and Ritual Play in Greek Religion*. Baltimore: Johns Hopkins University Press.

Masson, O. 1966. "Kypriaka." *BCH* 90:1–31.

Masson, O. 1981. "A propos des inscriptions chypriotes de Kafizin." *BCH* 105:623–649.

Mitford, T. B. 1980. *The Nymphaeum of Kafizin: The Inscribed Pottery, Kadmos*, Suppl. II. Berlin-New York: De Gruyter.

Motte, A. 1963. "Le pré sacré de Pan et des Nymphes dans la Phèdre de Platon." *AC* 32:460–476.

Nock, A. D. 1972. *Essays on Religion and the Ancient World*. Oxford: Oxford University Press.

Pache, C. O. 2011. *A Moment's Ornament: The Poetics of Nympholepsy in Ancient Greece*. Oxford: Oxford University Press.

Parke, H. W. 1988. *Sibyls and Sibylline Prophecy in Classical Antiquity*. London-New York: Routledge.

Pasquier, A. 1977. "Pan et les nymphs à l'antre corycien." *BCH* Suppl. 4:365–387.

Peek, W. 1938. "Metrische Inschriften." In *Mnemosynon Theodor Wiegand*, edited by J. F. Crome, 14–43. Munich: Bruckmann.

Peek, W. 1974. "Ein Weihgedicht für die Nymphen und drei andere Inschriften aus Atrax." *ZPE* 14:19–28.

Platt, V. 2016. "Sight and the gods: On the desire to see naked nymphs." In *Sight and the Ancient Senses*, edited by M. Squire, 169–189. London: Routledge.

Purvis, A. 2003. *Singular Dedications: Founders and Innovators of Private Cults in Classical Greece*. London: Routledge.

Reinach, S. 1891. "La sancuaire de la Sibylle d'Érythrée." *REG* 4:276–286.

Richter, G.M.A. 1953. *Handbook of the Greek Collection*. Cambridge, MA: Harvard University Press.

Robert, L. 1978. "Sur un Apollon oraculaire à Chypre" *CRAI* 122:338–344.

Robert, J. and Robert, L. 1958. "Bulletin épigraphique." *REG* 71:169–421.

Robert, J. and Robert, L. 1981. "Bulletin épigraphique." *REG* 94:362–485.

Rohde, E. 1925. *Psyche*. London: Routledge & Kegan Paul.

Scheiberg, S. 1979. "The Bee Maidens of the Homeric *Hymn to Hermes*." *HSPh* 83:1–28.

Schörner, G., and H. R. Goette. 2004. *Die Pan-Grotte von Vari*. Mainz: von Zabern.

Sourvinou-Inwood, C. 2004. "Hermaphroditos and Salmakis: The voice of Halikarnassos." In *The Salmakis Inscription and Hellenistic Halikarnassos*, edited by S. Isager and P. Pedersen, 59–84. Odense: University Press of Southern Denmark.

Sourvinou-Inwood, C. 2005. *Hylas, the Nymphs, Dionysus and Others*. Stockholm: Paul Aaström.

Sporn, K. 2013. "Mapping Greek sacred caves: Sources, features, cults." In *Stable Places and Changing Perceptions: Cave Archaeology in Greece*, BAR 2558, edited by F. Mavridis and J.M. Jensen, 202–216. Oxford: Archaeopress.

Stehle, E. 1989. "Sappho's gaze: Fantasies of a goddess and young man." In *Sexuality in Greek and Roman Society*, edited by D. Konstan and M. Nussbaum, 88–125. Providence: Brown University.

Ustinova, Y. 2009. *Caves and the Ancient Greek Mind: Descending Underground in the Search for Ultimate Truth*. Oxford: Oxford University Press.

van Groningen, B. A. 1958. "Quelques problèmes de la poésie bucolique grecque." *Mnemosyne IV.* 11:292–317.

van Straten, F. T. 1981. "Gifts for the gods." In *Faith, Hope and Worship: Aspect of Religious Mentality in the Ancient World*, edited by H.S. Versnel, 65–105. Leiden: Brill.

Wagman, R. M. 2011. "Building for the nymphs." *CQ* 61 (2):748–751.

Wagman, R. M. 2016. *The Cave of the Nymphs at Pharsalus: Studies on a Thessalian Country Shrine*. Leiden: Brill.

Weller, Ch. 1903. "The Cave at Vari." *AJA* 7:263–288.

West, M. L. 2007. *Indo-European Poetry and Myth*. Oxford: Oxford University Press.

Wickens, J. M. 1986. *The Archaeology and History of Cave Use in Attica, Greece, From Late Prehistoric Through Roman Times*. Ph.D. thesis, Indiana University.

Wiseman, T. P. 2004. *The Myths of Rome*. Exeter: University of Exeter Press.

Yioutsos, N. P. 2014. "Pan rituals in ancient Greece: A multi-sensory body experience." In *Archaeoacoustics: The Archaeology of Sound*, edited by L. C. Eneix and E.B.W. Zubrow, 57–67. Myakka City: The OTS Foundation.

6   Poetic *mania*

Poetic *mania* is Socrates' third kind of divine madness:

> And a third kind of possession and madness comes from the Muses. This takes hold upon a gentle and pure soul, arouses it and inspires it to songs and other poetry, and thus by adorning countless deeds of the ancients educates later generations. But he without the divine madness comes to the doors of the Muses, confident that he will be a good poet by art, meets with no success, and the poetry of the sane man vanishes into nothingness before that of the inspired madman.[1]

Greek Muses are unique; there are no corresponding figures in other Indo-European traditions.[2] The word *mousa* has a double meaning: as an appellative, it designates song or music, while as a proper name it indicates the divine patron of these activities.[3]

The Muses, memory, and inspiration[4]

The Muses are the daughters of Mnemosyne, Memory.[5] Hesychius indicates that *Mousai* may be also called *mnêstêres*, mindful, while on Chios, Muses were known as Memories, *Mneiai*.[6] It is the Muse or Muses who inspire the poet to recollect and sing. Invocations of the Muses and scenes of the poet's investiture in the epic, depicting visitations of the poets by the goddesses, are not only literary conventions, but attest to an earnest sensation of an outside source which stimulates the creative process: divine will was needed for a mortal poet to be able to know what a regular mortal could not know, and to utter this knowledge in the enjoyable form of a sweet song.[7]

The word *Mousa* probably derives from the root *men-*, meaning 'mental force,' and designating three spheres, perceiving, remembering, and frenzy.[8] In fact, more than a century ago it was suggested that the etymology of the word *mousa* was related to *mainomai*[9] and that the activities of the Muses included *mania* and *mantikê*. This would imply that the Greek usage preserved the polyvalent undivided semantic field of the Indo-European root.[10] Is this in fact the case?

'Memory,' as conferred by the Muses upon the poet, is not just factual remembrance. Homer praises the Muses as goddesses who know everything, contrary to mortals who hear rumours and know nothing, and in the same passage, claims that they 'called to his mind' all those who came to Troy.[11] Odysseus' reaction to Demodocus' story of the wooden horse is quite noteworthy. Since the bard has never been to Troy, Odysseus assumes that either the Muse or Apollo taught him his song.[12] The poet is recalling what admittedly he cannot know: his 'recollection' does not belong to him, but is rather instilled in his mind by the will of the Muses. The ability to establish mental contact with the world of the beyond, comparable to consulting oracles, is the privilege that Mnemosyne bestows upon the poet.[13] Thus, in epic poetry memory brings the past into the present by means of the '*activation* of consciousness.'[14] This mental procedure acquires a supernatural dimension when the poet recites events which he did not witness, but accessed by means of god-sent inspiration which activated his (cultural) memory.

A combination of knowledge of the past and of poetic talents, in other words, of memory and inspired vision, was indispensable for the composition of epic poetry. For Hesiod, the knowledge of past and future was part of his poetic investiture.[15] In his *Theogony*, the Muses 'breathe into (the poet) the divine voice to celebrate future and past.'[16] Archilochus claimed that as a young boy he received his lyre from the Muses.[17] In E. R. Dodds' words, 'such visions, welling up from the unknown depth of the mind, must once have been felt as something immediately "given", and because of its immediacy more trustworthy than oral tradition.'[18] The moment of inspiration may be envisaged as an initiation into the Muses' mysteries.[19] The poet is therefore compared to seers, who were distinguished by their divinely inspired knowledge of the past, present, and future.[20]

Later poets assume the role of *manteis* in their poetry, and Pindar even refers to himself as 'a prophet of the Muses in verse.'[21] Even if *prophêtês* means 'announcer' rather than 'seer,' Pindar is clearly dependent on the uttering of the Muses.[22] Theognis describes the poet as a messenger, *angelos* of the Muses.[23] In Plato's *Laws*, the poet is compared to the Pythia, as when he is seated on the Muses' tripod, he is no longer in control of his senses (*ouk emphrôn*).[24] According to Plutarch, the Muses were the 'assessors of prophecy' at Delphi.[25] Apollo the divine patron of prophecy and poetry was frequently called *Musagetês*. In the Indo-European world, poetic diction is often associated with special knowledge, attained through alteration of consciousness. In fact, the Latin word *vates* means both inspired poet and prophet, while in Scandinavian and Germanic traditions, poets, such as Suibhne, were often portrayed as mad and/or mantic.[26] Thus, the poet, inspired by the Muses, was believed to receive from them super-human knowledge and the ability to put it into verses.

Music and alteration of consciousness

It is reported that Aeschylus wrote his plays while drunk, and that he began composing tragedies after a visitation by Dionysus in a vineyard. This tradition supposedly reflects his intimate association with Dionysus and the intoxicating inspiration by the god.[27] Archilochus claimed that he knew how to lead the dithyramb when his 'mind is thunderstruck with wine.'[28] Leaping over several thousand years, one can recall star talents of the nineteenth century, such as P. B. Shelley, W. Wordsworth, Lord Byron, J. Keats, S. T. Coleridge, T. Gautier, A. Rimbaud, and C. Baudelaire, all who produced some of their most brilliant works under the influence of wine, opium, laudanum, or hashish.[29] I am not claiming that drugs and alcohol are the principle source of poetic creativity, but it is impossible to ignore the liberating power of drug and alcohol consumption and its contribution to literary achievement, both in the distant past and at present.

Back to antiquity, mead was conceived as belonging to the primaeval past, before the invention of wine, when it was the only fermented beverage drunk by immortals and mortals. The Indo-European root **medhu-* survived in Greek as *methu*, a poetic word for wine, its derivatives meaning drunkenness.[30] Ecstatic intoxication in the Indo-European tradition was the source of poetic creation and prophetic wisdom, as well as a metaphor for these mental states.[31] In Greece honey was a symbol of poetic and prophetic vocation, and myths testify abundantly to the association of bees with the divine patrons of these activities.[32] Poets represent themselves and other poets as bees.[33] Pindar describes his song as 'a bee rushing from story to story.'[34] *The Life of Pindar* cites an anecdote: when the great poet was a boy, he fell asleep on Mt Helicon, in the place where the Muses initiated Hesiod into the art of poetry. As Pindar slept, a bee landed on his mouth and built a honeycomb there.[35] Words flow like honey from the mouth of the poet inspired by the Muses, and the lips of the poet attract bees: a sixth-century epic poet pictures a bee wandering about a bronze statue of Homer, lifting a honeycomb into his divine mouth.[36] Similar stories were told of Sophocles, Plato, Virgil, Lucan, and Ambrose.[37] Honey, and in the past mead, was the symbol of both prophetic and poetic *mania*, the intoxicating power of uttering divinely inspired words.

It is noteworthy that in all these tales bees approach the future poets when they are asleep, and the divine sign becomes manifest immediately following their awakening. 'Hallucinatory states in the borderlands of sleep,' in the psychagogic states between dreaming and waking, are known to produce prolific discharge of apparitions and visions that can even resemble mystical phenomena.[38] The connection between awakening, intoxication, and the onset of creativity is therefore hardly accidental, but rather reflects subjective feelings of the poets and the impressions of people who observed them.

Hesiod's Muses who dwelled on the Helicon are reminiscent of the nymphs who live in the wild and capture mortals who visit their realm.[39] Similarly to the nympholepts, 'those seized by the nymphs,' who were prone to prophecy, Hesiod was chosen by the Muses to sing his poetry: both the prophetic nympholepts and the poets obtained their knowledge, hidden from other mortals, from divine maidens who had summoned them.[40] Plato too depicted inspired poets as seized by the Graces or the Muses.[41] Among later authors, the image of the possessed poet became commonplace: Plutarch described a poet as *mousolêptos*, and Lucian referred to a poet in a matter-of-fact manner as 'inspired and possessed by the Muses.'[42]

The nature of poetic inspiration: Plato

Modern scholars disagree as to the ancient interpretation of the nature of poetic creativity. Some assume that the Greek poets, from Homer on, regarded themselves as divinely inspired.[43] Others maintain that the poets believed their talent to be an enduring gift, and consider the idea of poetic *mania* to be a fifth-century, or Plato's own, invention.[44] There is no doubt that for Plato, 'the poetry of the sane man vanishes into nothingness before that of the inspired madmen.'[45] However, even before him, from the fifth century on, Greek writers were quite explicit about the divine nature of poetry. Good poetry, it was believed, emanated from the gods both because the poet's talent was perceived as an inborn divine gift, and because the creative process had to be initiated and sustained by the will of the Muses. According to Democritus, 'Everything a poet does with enthusiasm and divine *pneuma*, is very good' – the most ancient occurrence of the word *enthousiasmos* in the extant literature.[46] Sophocles is cited as saying to Aeschylus: 'You create what you have to without knowing that,' underscoring the image of 'divinely inspired and mindlessly automatic' dramatist.[47] In the *Frogs*, the grotesque portrait of Aeschylus as a madman rolling his eyes 'in a terrible frenzy'[48] and reflecting the popular opinion on the behaviour of a poet possessed by the Muses is contrasted to the rational and analytical Euripides.[49] The conflict between the two poets represents the opposite views of two schools of thought, two ways of creating poetry: inspired ancient poetry that elates and artful modern poetry that corrupts.[50] Evidently the art *versus* inspiration dichotomy was widely discussed before Plato's day.[51]

Furthermore, the image of the possessed bard had already gained currency in art many decades before Democritus and Plato. The demeanour of bards on some fifth-century vases resembles that of raving maenads. For instance, the *kitharôdos* on the amphora attributed to the Berlin Painter (ca. 490 BC) and on the amphora by the Brygos Painter (ca. 480 BC), as well as Orpheus playing for the Thracians on a mid-fifth century BC crater, are portrayed with uplifted heads abandoning themselves to the Muses like ecstatic maenads raising their heads in the grip of Dionysus.[52] The depiction of musicians in this characteristic posture is attested to in the Aegean since the Bronze age and represents a formulaic expression of extreme physical and/or emotional strain.[53] In the light of this evidence, Democritus and Plato can hardly be credited with the invention of the poetic *mania*. Rather, they articulated the ideas which were initially expressed in epic poetry.

The most thorough explanation of the nature of inspired poetic manticism is given in Plato's *Ion*. Having stated that inspiration (*enthousiasmos*) spreads from the Muse to the poets, and from them to other men, Socrates continues:

> For all the good epic poets utter all those fine poems not from art, but as inspired and possessed, and the good lyric poets likewise; just as the Corybantic worshippers do not dance when in their senses, so the lyric poets do not indite those fine songs in their senses, but when they have started on the

melody and rhythm they begin to be frantic, and it is under possession. . . . For the poets tell us, I believe, that the songs they bring us are the sweets they cull from honey-drooping founts in certain gardens and glades of the Muses – like the bees, and winging the air as these do. . . . For a poet is a light and winged and sacred thing,[54] and is unable ever to indite until he has been inspired and out of his senses, and the mind is no longer in him: every man, whilst he retains possession of that, is powerless to indite a verse or chant an oracle. . . . These fine poems are not human or the work of men, but divine and the work of gods; and that the poets are merely interpreters of the gods, according as each is possessed by one of the heavenly powers.[55]

In Socrates' opinion, good poems are divinely inspired, and poets create them only when 'seized by god.'[56] Socrates compares them to the Corybantic devotees and bacchants, the quintessential ecstatics discussed in Chapter 2. Like prophets, they utter what the gods make them pronounce; they are mediums in a state of possession, messengers of the gods.[57] This contact with the deity is the guarantee of the truthfulness of the poet's creation.[58] Socrates therefore solves the Homeric paradox of the poet 'recalling' what he cannot know: the poet's memory is instilled in him by the deity that uses him as a mouthpiece, thus causing his heightened state – in Socrates' words, his *mania*.

It is crucial to emphasise that *mania* and being 'beside oneself' does not necessarily mean that Plato's inspired poet was 'unable to give any account of what he says' and entirely lacking self-awareness and self-control, as some scholars claim.[59] As we have already seen, *mania* and *enthousiasmos* have their grades, and the state of a poet's consciousness may be altered sufficiently for him and his audience to perceive the change, but nevertheless allow him (some) control of himself and (some) awareness of his surroundings. Socrates' model of poetic creativity is based on a combination of 'controlled expertise . . . and intuitive insight,' the latter perceived as divinely instilled inspiration.[60]

The sharp division between inspired poetry which is sublime and poetry that is mere mimesis, a learnt art, is implied by the position of 'the follower of the Muses,' *mousikos*, and a poet who is one of the mimetic artists in the hierarchy of human souls in the *Phaedrus*: the former is equal to a philosopher and belongs to the highest grade; the latter is allotted the sixth grade out of nine, just above artisans and farmers.[61] The rhapsode is indeed an imitator, a mere interpreter or performer (*hermêneus*), the living instrument communicating to his audience Homer's wisdom.[62] The reason for the dichotomy of the two types of poetry is that, in Plato's opinion, the two types of poetry stem from different sources.[63] To cite M. Finkelberg, in Plato 'inspiration and mimesis act as mutually exclusive.'[64]

A final remark on Plato's views on poetry is in order here. Plato knew what he was talking about from personal experience. There is no reason to doubt the tradition describing his poetic attempts as a young men, and even his intention to compete for a prize with a tragedy.[65] The anecdote that Plato was dissuaded to do so by Socrates right in front of the theatre and burnt his plays immediately, seems to be a picturesque rendering of the simple fact that Plato ultimately devoted himself to philosophy, but even his philosophical dialogues are works of dramatic art written by a person whose sensibility for the music of words is beyond question.[66]

The nature of poetic inspiration: Aristotle

The conviction that inspiration is the heart of good poetry persisted after Plato. Even the usually arch-rational Aristotle assigned to it: 'There is divine inspiration in poetry.'[67] This phrase concludes his discussion of 'enthusiastic (*enthousiaszon-tes*) orators' who 'grip their audience and fill it with enthusiasm (*enthousiasai*)': Aristotle was convinced that their style, with its exaggerations and emotional tension, is appropriate to poetry, as well, because it comprises divine inspiration (*entheon*). The repetition of the word 'enthusiasm' seems to indicate that Aristotle insisted on real excitement among the emotional speakers, their audience – and the poets. This state of mind was certainly no frenzy, but it was apparent and showed that these people were beyond themselves, enough for a Greek speaker to employ a word indicating alteration of consciousness. Thus, Aristotle assumed that poetry involved divine inspiration and extreme excitement. These ideas of Aristotle were shared by his successor Theophrastus, who was convinced that music had three origins, distress, pleasure, and *enthousiasmos*.[68]

In the *Poetics*, discussing the importance of imagining minute details while constructing plots of dramas, Aristotle observes:

> So far as possible one should also work out the plot in gestures, since a natu-ral affinity makes those in the grip of emotions the most convincing, and the truest distress or anger is conveyed by one who actually feels these things. Hence poetry is the work of a gifted person or of a maniac (*manikos*), and of these types, the former imagine, while the latter are ecstatic (*ekstatikoi*).[69]

This passage caused much controversy, both because it does not match the alleged reluctance of Aristotle to admit divine intervention in human affairs, and because the word *ekstatikoi* is often interpreted incorrectly. In fact, Aristotle had never ruled out the concept of divine intervention, and claiming otherwise implies the interpretation of too many passages as psychological observations or metaphors only.[70] He contemplated the idea of divine intervention more than once, saying that the god rules the universe, and declaring the wisest people most beloved by the god and therefore the happiest.[71] Turning to the experience of divine inspiration, Aristotle believed that *enthousiasmos* of nympholepts and theolepts – people possessed by the nymphs or other gods – was inspired by divine powers, *daimonia*, and brought about a feeling of happiness.[72] His opinion on *enthousiôntes* (inspired) soothsayers as predicting involuntarily, and not of their free will,[73] put forward in the same treatise, can only be interpreted as another example of taking inspiration seriously.[74] These passages demonstrate that Aristotle's views on many subjects, including divine inspiration, were compatible to the Platonic position. Although there can be no doubt that he was much more interested in pragmatic issues than in the ethereal inspiration, and his view of poetry and art was 'craft-based,'[75] Aristotle still had to deal with the assertions of prophets and poets and paid a modest tribute to his master.

As to the meaning of *ekstatikos*, in this passage it probably denotes 'deviating from the norm,' and a straightforward connection to English 'ecstasy' is misleading.[76] *Ekstatikos* is carried away, indifferent to everything but his creation, concentrating on the images he begets in his mind – therefore his behaviour looks abnormal. This is a state of mind, and it is transient, irrespective of being god-sent or natural. It can be productive only if experienced by a person whose permanent characteristics comprise inborn talents – *euphuês*. In addition, art and skills are needed, and the discussion of the practical aspects of the poetic creation is the subject of this and the following chapters of the *Poetics*.

Visualisation is one of these techniques (and is found indispensable by many modern writers reflecting on their craft).[77] It is debated whether at the beginning of the cited passage Aristotle refers to the gestures of the author or of the actors.[78] At this point in the treatise it is the poet rather than actors who is in the focus of Aristotle's attention, and he recommends that the poet gesticulates while working on his compositions, since this is a good method of switching identity and becoming one with the tragic hero. Eventually the author would be able to instruct the actors how to behave on the stage when they 'enter the role.' This technique of the poet's self-identification with his characters was known so well that is was parodied in comedy.[79] Aristophanes' Euripides creates characters who are beggars while wearing old rags, and he has a whole collection of pitiful garbs, belonging to different personages.[80] His Agathocles dresses in female outfits when writing women's roles and explains that:

> I change my clothing according as I change my mentality (*gnômê*). A man who is a poet must adopt habits that match the plays he's committed to composing. For example, if one is writing plays about women, one's body must participate in their habits.[81]

Aristotle's recommendation is in fact a re-statement of an established practice.

Aristotle mentions violent emotions and total self-identification with the passions of the characters that are necessary for successful creation. This means temporary abandonment of the dramatist's own self and becoming a different person, precisely the core of an ecstatic experience. This technique is most telling from two perspectives. Psychologically, gesticulating can work as a driving behaviour, pushing the poet to creative elation, stepping out of reality (*ekstasis* in the literal meaning of the word[82]), which involves drifting away from the baseline state of consciousness. From the point of view of a bystander, a poet gesticulating and grimacing while composing his verses looked like madman, the resemblance of the god-sent and deranging *mania* always lurking in the background.

Aristotle used neither hyperbolae nor metaphors, but exact words to convey his conviction that poets must attain total merging with their characters: he meant self-abandonment and designated it with the words *manikos* and *ekstatikos*, associated immediately by his audience with a range of divergent alterations of consciousness. In Greek, these words did not necessarily mean wild frenzy, and we should not read this connotation into the text. Aristotle contends that god-given inborn talents are not sufficient by themselves, and are to be incited by poetic inspiration which is cognate to *mania* and allows leaving behind the poet's real self and identification with the characters.[83] Both the talent and inspiration are to be used skilfully, and art is the third requirement needed to create a successful work of poetry.

Aristotle's views on poetic genius were still influential in the times of Seneca who writes:

> For whether we believe with the Greek poet that 'sometimes it is a pleasure also to rave' (*aliquando et insanire iucundum est*), or with Plato that 'the sane mind knocks in vain at the door of poetry' (*frustra poeticas fores compos sui pepulit*), or with Aristotle that 'no great genius has ever existed without some touch of madness' (*nullum magnum ingenium sine mixtura dementiae fuit*) – be that as it may, the lofty utterance that rises above the attempts of others is impossible unless the mind is excited. When it has scorned the vulgar and the commonplace, and has soared far aloft fired by divine inspiration, then alone it chants a strain too lofty for mortal lips. So long as it is left to itself, it is impossible for it to reach any sublime and difficult height; it must forsake the common track and be driven to frenzy and champ a bit and run away with its rider (*mordeat frenos et rectorem rapiat suum eoque ferat*) and rush to a height that it would have feared to climb by itself.[84]

This view on the poet's inspiration is congruous with modern studies of the creative process, showing that 'although the initial inspiration appears to come to the poet as if from some source other than himself, the subsequent composition of the poem depends on conscious effort and hard work.'[85] Those who claim that according to Plato, 'transmission excludes interpretation,'[86] disregard a very important and prolonged stage in any creative process, including composing – and performing – music and poetry: perfecting the creation, which may take far more time than a relatively short-lived period of inspiration. There is no reason to deny Plato, Aristotle, and their contemporaries awareness of the difference between these two stages.[87]

Modern poets and musicians and their inspiration

Comparison between South Slavic and Greek epic traditions demonstrates that oral epic is subdivided into poetry drawing mainly on the authority of tradition and the one announcing divine inspiration as its source of authority. The former usually give rise to short songs; the latter – poems monumental both in length and in design. Creators of monumental poems of complex structure often feel and declare themselves divinely inspired.[88] In particular, during oral performances the rhythm and sounds of words create a 'propelling force' that is perceived by the

improvising bard as coming from an outside (supernatural) source. Rhythm, especially when accompanied by music, contributes to 'dislocation of consciousness':
the poet's self merges with the stream of his song, and feels as if he were enthused
with the song by a divine agent.[89]

The psychological state of the poet is shared by the audience.[90] The involvement
of the audience in the creative act requiring enhanced mental imagery can also be
interpreted as enthusiasm. Not only bards, but also poets who do not improvise in
front of the audience but create their verses alone, feel carried away by a flow of
sounds, rhythms, associations, and visual images. Since at any given moment the
human mind is capable of focusing on only a small segment of information,[91] total
absorption in creation means that time, space, and other realities of the outside
world are disregarded, and the poet's subjective feeling is that of an existence in his
personal isolated world. In conjunction with the feeling of joy and bliss when a
poem has been created, these subjective sensations are interpreted as poetic inspiration, illumination by an external force, or madness. In any case, they are fragile,
elusive, and easily vanish at minor intrusions from the outside.

R. Kipling sums up this process in his autobiography: 'When your Daemon is
in charge do not try to think consciously. Drift, wait and obey. . . . Walk delicately,
lest he should withdraw.'[92] The same is true of many great musicians. For instance,
W. A. Mozart highlights the delicacy of inspiration: 'Then my soul is on fire with
inspiration, if however nothing occurs to distract my attention.'[93] It is noteworthy
that a modern poet may perceive inspiration as a voice; P. Reverdy wrote that in
a state of inspiration 'thousand voices are silent, and only one speaks, and everything that it says is only a faraway echo of everything that is silent.'[94] This solitary
voice in total silence almost invites its perception as an outside intrusion.

Musicians, even dilettanti, report such phenomena quite often. The psychiatrist and amateur musician O. Sacks recalls several episodes during which he was
haunted by music that he heard within his mind.[95] R. Wagner, M. Ravel, H.
Berlioz, and I. Stravinsky left accounts of creating long parts of their compositions
in a semi-hallucinatory hypnagogic state or in dreams; all they had to do was just
write them down.[96] R. Strauss and G. Puccini attributed their creative ability to
the higher forces, and described the stages leading to experiencing inspiration:
from ardent desire to prayer and expectation, which open the path for some force
to be transmitted into the composer's consciousness from the outside.[97]

J. Brahms reportedly perceived his inspiration as a union with the god, illumination coming from an external source, and a trance state which was difficult to endure:

> I immediately feel vibrations that thrill my whole being. . . . These are the
> Spirit illuminating the soul-power within, and in this exalted state, I see
> clearly what is obscure in in my ordinary moods; then I feel capable of draw-
> ing inspiration from above, as Beethoven did. Above all, I realize at such
> moments the tremendous significance of Jesus' supreme revelation, 'I and
> my Father are one.'. . . Straightaway the ideas flow in upon me, directly
> from God, and not only do I see distinct themes in my mind's eye, but they
> are clothed in the right forms, harmonies and orchestration. . . . Measure

by measure, the finished product is revealed to me when I'm in those rare, inspired moods. . . . I have to be in a semi-trance condition to get such results – a condition when the conscious mind is in temporary abeyance and the sub-conscious is in control, for it is through the subconscious mind, which is a part of Omnipotence, that the inspiration comes. I have to be careful, how-ever, not to lose consciousness, otherwise the ideas fade away.[98]

In Brahms' and Puccini's view, the true inspiration emanates from God, but in order for inspiration to result in a musical masterpiece, it has to be supplemented by the mastery of composition technique, which requires ability and laborious study.[99]

In contrast to artists who were conscious of their inspiration, E. Grieg admitted that he sensed this mood without being able to define it.[100] The moment of inspi-ration is difficult to describe, but a poet knows immediately when it comes. P. Valéry says:

Sometimes I have observed this moment when a sensation arrives at the mind; it is as a gleam of light, not so much illuminating as dazzling. . . . There is an activity, a special sensation; soon you will go into the dark-room and the picture will be seen to emerge. I do not affirm that this is well described, for it is extremely hard to describe.[101]

G. Puccini emphasised fundamental changes in mental functioning when an artist experiences inspiration:

The inspiration from above stimulates the intellect and the emotions. An inspired person sees things in a totally different light from one who is not inspired. Inspiration is an awakening, a quickening of all of man's faculties, and it is manifested in all high artistic achievements. It is an overwhelming, a compelling force. In short, it is a Divine influence.[102]

Poetic rapture brings the poet to the limits of his physical and mental abilities. A. Rimbaud revealed his understanding of the closeness between the vocations of the poet and the prophet, and the suffering on the route to self-expression, which is perceived as an urge beyond the poet's control:

I want to be a poet, and I'm working at turning myself into a seer. You won't understand any of this, and I'm almost incapable of explaining it to you. The idea is to reach the unknown by the derangement of all the senses. It involves enormous suffering, but one must be strong and be a born poet. It's really not my fault.[103]

The great Russian poet A. S. Pushkin gives the following portrayal of the poet:

While still Apollo isn't demanding
Bard at the sacred sacrifice,

Through troubles of the worldly muddling
He wretchedly and blindly shuffles;
His holy lyre is quite silent;
His soul's in the sleeping, soft,
And mid the dwarves of the world-giant,
He, perhaps, is the shortest dwarf.
But when a word of god's commands,
Touches his ear, always attentive,
It starts – the heart of the Bard native –
As a waked eagle ever starts . . .
He runs – the wild, severe, stunned,
Full of confusion, full of noise –
To the deserted waters' shores,
To woods, widespread and humming loud.[104]

This does not imply that the poet, ancient or modern, regards himself as a passive instrument. In the poetic activities we find a delicate interplay of personal and cultural memory, on the one hand, and estrangement from everyday reality, together with mental exaltation and unique insight, on the other. Such characteristics of creative inspiration as its ineffability and irresistibility, changing perception and the very nature of mental processes, experienced by modern poets and composers and identical to the ancient accounts, indicate that we are dealing with a real-life phenomenon, which can be defined as alteration of consciousness.[105]

A final point: the link between creative output and madness that is not a sparkle of inspiration, but a diagnosed psychiatric disease, has been thoroughly discussed during the recent decades. A study of more than a thousand prominent individuals who suffered from various mental illnesses demonstrates that people in 'creative arts' score much higher on various mental disorders than members of other professions, and 'certain types of psychopathology are associated with creative achievement across all professions.' Notably, lifetime depression and anxiety predict significantly higher creative achievement.[106] The role of social expectations, as well as cultural influences, is of course considerable, and the concept of psychiatric diagnosis is extremely controversial.[107] However, there is perhaps a causal link between the tendency towards mental illness and predisposition to creativity. A. Sussman explains the neurological similarities between the two:

> The biological support invokes the frontal lobe of the brain – the main connection between the temporal and parietal lobes, where knowledge and concepts are stored. Unusual activity in the frontal lobe, and in particular the prefrontal cortex, is characteristic of both schizophrenia and manic depression. Hyperactivity in this region may cause a person to draw unusual connections between seemingly unrelated items or ideas, resulting in the delusions of the paranoid schizophrenic or mania. . . . It is not hard to see how these symptoms might be loosely analogous to creative processes – drawing unusual connections or thinking in a unique way are hallmarks of the artistic mind. But the traits of creativity are not only descriptively similar

to some of the side-effects of mental illness – the neurological brain states are actually the same.[108]

A. Sussman also argues that not only the same brain region, but also the same neurotransmitters are involved both in both creativity and schizophrenia.[109] In addition, a manic-depressive artist during the period of mania 'may feel unfettered from societal expectations and norms, more confident in his most farfetched ideas. At the same time, the energy of mania can help the artist focus and complete an enormous amount in a short period of time.'[110] As a result, the work of an artist on the verge of mental illness or actually suffering from it may be novel, exciting, and thought-provoking – some people would call it crazy. Since the artist's self-expression is part of his or her inner world, medication of the illness may lead to uttermost misery, and silence the talent.[111]

In summary, phenomenological similarity between mental disorders and alterations of consciousness was and still remains conspicuous. Therefore, in antiquity as at the present, creative artists, poets and musicians in particular, seem mad to their environment. Furthermore, in many cases this observation contains some truth: madness may be real, and its torture and prizes interconnected. When the neurologist A. Sussman emphasises that 'the benefits of mental illness'[112] are so considerable that quite often treatment of a mentally ill artist may be more harmful to him or her than the illness, it is impossible not to recall the ancient concept of the dual *mania*, encapsulating both madness and inspiration.

Enthusiastic audiences

The Muses affect not only the mind of the poet, they enchant his audience. Homer's Eumaeus the swineherd utters the idea in a concise form:

> Just as when a man gazes upon a minstrel who sings to mortals songs of longing that the gods have taught him, and their desire to hear him has no end, whenever he sings, even so he charmed me when he sat in my hall.[113]

Homer uses the word *thelgein*, 'to bewitch,' to portray a god-inspired bard mesmerising his public, as well as the Sirens enchanting sailors with their songs.[114] The same verb occurs in the depiction of the drugs administered by Circe to animals and humans in order to manipulate their behaviour: songs and drugs are irresistible, and most significantly, they alter people's state of mind.[115] In Hesiod's *Theogony*, when a poet, who is a servant of the Muses, sings the deeds of ancient heroes, the listener 'forgets his sorrows at once and does not remember his anguish at all; for quickly the gifts of the goddesses have turned it aside.'[116] In the words of C. Segal, early love poetry 'seeks to create a verbal equivalent to the magnetic, quasi-magical compulsion which the ancient poets called *thelxis*, "enchantment," or *peithô*, "persuasion."'[117] Eros or Aphrodite combined forces with the Muses to overwhelm the singing poet, as well as his or her audience.[118] This captivation means that people attending a performance by a good bard partially lost their contact with reality or were spellbound to a degree that they forgot their own circumstances.[119] The mind-expanding impact of music some-times combined with the mind-altering effects of the wine: musical recitals were often part of a social gathering where wine was consumed.[120]

Music was believed to heighten the listeners' emotions, drive them to temporal insanity,[121] or alternatively, cure mental disorders.[122] Orpheus epitomises the power of music over the souls, and his spellbinding performance is depicted on a series of fifth-century vases.[123] Other Archaic figures combining the accomplish-ments of poets, prophets, purifiers, and healers, such as Abaris and Epimenides, are discussed in Chapter 8. Lyric poetry combined words with gesture and music, and possessed 'incantatory quality,' and choral music in particular emerged from a ritual context and always preserved its sacral dimension: in a Homeric hymn to Apollo, a singing chorus 'charms the tribes of men.'[124]

Incantations had magic power, and those who knew how to employ that power were believed to be endowed with super-human abilities.[125] In fact, musical charms were popular not only with common people. Pindar compared incantatory magic of music to that of medicine.[126] The Pythagoreans apparently treated bodies and souls with respectively medical and musical *katharsis*.[127] The master himself is reported to have played the lyre in order to put his followers into a calm mood, which means that the Pythagoreans were familiar with the influence of music on the soul.[128] In this respect, they followed an ancient tradition which persisted well into the historic ages. In the fourth century, women in South Italy were afflicted with a strange madness: hearing a mysterious call, they left their homes and rushed out of the cities; having consulted an oracle and following its advice to sing a paean twelve times a day for sixty days, the people of Locri and Rhegium suc-ceeded in curing their womenfolk.[129] The paeans were addressed to Apollo, but in addition to the faith in the god's help the effect resulted from the almost continu-ous exposure to music. During two months they had heard 720 paeans! Traditional methods of musical therapy were approved by prominent intellectuals: Socrates admired the power of Thracian chants, and Theophrastus recommended music as treatment for 'body and soul.'[130] In Sparta, Muses were considered the deities who helped in cases of mental disturbances or other illnesses. When such misfortunes occurred, the Spartans sent for poets, such as Terpander, Thales of Gortyn, Tyr-taeus, and Alcman.[131] Nowadays, music as a form of therapy is making an impres-sive comeback.[132]

Good poetry continued to captivate the audience centuries after Homer and Hesiod. Particularly interesting is the New Music, a style of performance that emerged in the last quarter of the fifth century, of which Phrynis and Timotheus were the most prominent representatives.[133] Performances by Timotheus were characterised by their powerful emotional impact. In addition to masterful use of overwhelming images created by an irresistibly exciting flow of words, this trend introduced a bold innovation, and combinations of different modes.[134] No wonder the 'New Musicians' made extensive use of *aulos*, famous for its mind-altering effect.[135] Despite the denunciation by the conservatives, from the Spartan authori-ties to Plato and Aristotle, the 'new wave' music, numbing the mind and stimulat-ing the senses with the pyrotechnics of its *polukhordia* (multiple notes) and *poluphthongia* (multiple voices), gained tremendous popularity.[136]

In the fourth century, Timocles says that during a tragedy performance 'the mind, forgetting its own cares, and entertained at someone else's suffering, ends up pleasured, and learning something to boot.'[137] Of course neither theatre-goers nor the audience of the bards were 'mad,' but their state of mind was changed substantially. This elation above the baseline state was perceived as otherworldly and attributed to the divine or daemonic forces.

Plato's Socrates was sensitive to the communication between the Muse, the poet, the performer, and the audience, emphasising it by using the word *entheos* and its cognates three times in one sentence: 'The Muse inspires men herself, and then by means of these inspired persons the inspiration spreads to others, and holds them in a connected chain.'[138] In Socrates' opinion, the audience belongs to the 'third ring' of those affected by the Muse, who passes the force of poetic inspiration, like magnetic attraction through a chain, to the creators of original work, and from them to the rhapsodes, and further to the spectators.[139] Plato attributed to poetry psychagogic powers, and referred to the experience of bewitchment by musical creations – even if he did not always approve of their influence on the public.[140]

Aristotle echoes these ideas in the *Politics* when he dwells on the effects of different musical modes on the listeners' souls and states that many kinds of music render them 'enthusiastic' (*enthousiastikai*) or that they 'violently arouse their souls.'[141] He also explains how the passionate musical modes influence the audience:

> For any experience that occurs violently in some souls is found in all, though with different degrees of intensity – for example pity and fear, and also religious excitement (*enthousiasmos*); for some persons are very liable to this form of emotion, and under the influence of sacred music we see these people, when they use tunes that violently arouse the soul, being thrown into a state as if they had received medicinal treatment and taken a purge (*katharsis*); the same experience then must come also to the compassionate and the timid and the other emotional people generally in such degree as befalls each individual of these classes, and all must undergo a purgation and a pleasant feeling of relief.[142]

Two points are most noteworthy. Firstly, in Aristotle's view, music causes a change in the state of mind of the listeners, which he describes in terms common to the discourse on ecstatic cults, discussed above. Secondly, this passage on pity, fear and medical purge (*katharsis*) is immediately followed by discussion of theatrical music which is, in Aristotle opinion, of a similar kind.[143] This juxtaposition calls to mind his famous statement that tragedy 'brings about catharsis of such sufferings through pity and fear.'[144] A discussion of the thorny question whether this phrase may be interpreted in a direct sense, as referring to alleviating the distress of grieving souls, is beyond the scope of this chapter.[145] At the moment, it is sufficient to assume that that in Aristotle's view, the state of mind of many of the theatre audience was profoundly changed and the effect of the changes resembled that of ecstatic cultic ceremonies; they were beneficial for the public in general and could particularly help those suffering from various grievances (although there is no doubt that tragic catharsis is much more than mere evacuation of excessive or negative energy).[146]

This understanding is endorsed by additional passages in the *Poetics* referring to the irresistible spell of drama over its spectators. For instance, emotional peaks in a play are described as 'gripping' or 'stunning' (*ekplêktikoi*),[147] another word denoting overwhelming sensations. Aristotle emphasises the impact of a good plot, which can 'conjure the souls' (*psuchagôgein*) of the audience. The visual effects of a play, as well as the appearance and performance of the actors, could also be 'mesmerising' (*psuchagôgikon*).[148] In Aristotle's days, this word, normally referring to necromantic magic, was employed by Isocrates while describing the spellbinding potency of poetry and music.[149]

Aristotle did not invent the psychagogic powers of the theatre,[150] which are attested by other sources. The whole audience allegedly cried at the *Conquest of Miletus* by Phrynichus, and many pregnant women reportedly had abortions, frightened by the sight of the August goddesses in Aeschylus' *Eumenides*; even bloodthirsty tyrants, such as Alexander of Pherae, shed tears in the theatre.[151] The public at Greek theatrical performances was captivated to the extent that the spectators temporarily withdraw from their own reality; they entered the world of the characters, sharing their passions and experiencing genuine empathy.[152] Similar sensations, as we have seen, were experienced by the audience of epic poets.

How far is Aristotle's spellbinding dramatist from Plato's image of the poet as magnet, enchanting the souls of performers and spectators? In my opinion, they are very close, and both did not think up the overpowering emotions aroused by a good performance, but rather pondered the state of affairs known to everyone, adopted the age-long tradition of ideas about the bewitching and therapeutic powers of music and poetry, developed these ideas systematically and articulated the results of their enquiries.

Conclusions

Poets and their audience believed that their inspiration was possession by the Muses, Apollo, and other gods, and even if this viewpoint gradually became a literary convention, it was rooted in actual human experience. Homer and Hesiod voiced an ancient Indo-European *topos* which became a Greek cultural norm, but this norm was sustained because individuals belonging to the Greek culture felt it was true.[153] I argue that the tradition claiming that poets were enthused by gods was doubtlessly ancient and influential. In addition, the subjective feeling of poets, that their verses are prompted by a capricious external entity, was no less important. The traditional and the experiential strand were intertwined and brought about the concept of divinely inspired poet.[154] It was not a metaphor, but a real experience, felt, lived and transmitted. Plato and Aristotle were aware of the importance of inspiration, sensed as coming from a supernatural external source.

The inspiration of a good poet was contagious: his audience was also elated, forgetful of their worries under the spell of the Muses. Musical performances of the poets captivated their audiences, as Homer and Hesiod were proud to state. Plato's Socrates believed that musical communication was transmitted from the Muse to the poets, and thence to the audience, thus allowing even the listeners a part in the divine sparkle initially ignited by the Muses. Aristotle discussed *enthousiasmos* stimulated by poetry and music, in the theatre and elsewhere, and examined its effects on the souls of the spectators.

Were the inspired poets and their audiences actually mad from the point of view of the majority of Greeks? Neither the poets nor the listeners resembled the violent and horribly suicidal Spartan king Cleomenes, a madman *par excellence*.[155] Temporarily, they were rather like Thrasyllus, happy in his unreal world and immune to other people's actuality.[156] The artist's and his spectator's absorption in the world of fantasy and sounds, oblivion of surrounding reality, unusually acute sense of beauty, emotional rapture, and profound comprehension were so distanced from the regular attitude of most people, including the poets themselves, that this state of mind was attributed to divine inspiration and defined it as *mania*. Then again, the association of poetic and musical activities with *enthousiasmos* and *mania* demonstrates that these concepts were very broad and could encompass the capricious states of intense creativity and transient elation. Socrates' image of the chain of inspiration underscores the idea that deviation from the baseline state of mind had its grades, and all of them could be perceived as *enthousiasmos*.

Notes

1 Pl. *Phdr.* 245A: τρίτη δὲ ἀπὸ Μουσῶν κατοκωχή τε καὶ μανία, λαβοῦσα ἀπαλὴν καὶ ἄβατον ψυχήν, ἐγείρουσα καὶ ἐκβακχεύουσα κατά τε ᾠδὰς καὶ κατὰ τὴν ἄλλην ποίησιν, μυρία τῶν παλαιῶν ἔργα κοσμοῦσα τοὺς ἐπιγιγνομένους παιδεύει· ὃς δ' ἂν ἄνευ μανίας Μουσῶν ἐπὶ ποιητικὰς θύρας ἀφίκηται, πεισθεὶς ὡς ἄρα ἐκ τέχνης ἱκανὸς ποιητὴς ἐσόμενος, ἀτελὴς αὐτός τε καὶ ἡ ποίησις ὑπὸ τῆς τῶν μαινομένων ἡ τοῦ σωφρονοῦντος ἠφανίσθη (translation H. N. Fowler).

2 West (2007: 94); Harriott (1969: 10). For the Muses, see Harriott (1969: 10–33). However, the idea of an inspired poet was pervasive in various Indo-European cultures: González (2013: 181).

3 Detienne (1996: 40).

4 Portions of this chapter draw on my article: Ustinova (2012).

5 Hes. *Th.* 53–62, 915–917; *h. Merc.* 428; Pi. *N.* 7.12; *I.* 6.74; Notopoulos (1938); Murray (1981: 92); Harriott (1969: 18–21); Simondon (1982: 103–112). For the relationship between the memories of the poet and those of his audience, and the psychology of memorisation, see Havelock (1963: 146). For the sacral domain of memory in the Greek culture, see Vernant (1983: 75–105).

6 Hsch. s.v. μναμονόοι· Μοῦσαι. μνηστῆρρες; Plu., *Mor.* 743D. Paus. 9.29.3 cites the names of the Muses in Ascra: Melete, Mneme, and Aoide. For the early origins of this cult see van Groningen (1948); Camilloni (1998: 28–29); Detienne (1996: 41, 151, n. 151); for reservations see Simondon (1982: 104–105). For the meaning of the verb μνάομαι and the emphasis on 'recalling' rather than 'mentioning' see Benveniste (1954); Detienne (1996: 150 n. 3).

7 Hom. *Il.* 1.1, 2.484–492, 11.218–219, 14.508–509, 16.112–113; *Od.* 1.1–8; cf. *Od.* 8.73, 487–491; Hes. *Th.* 30; Emp. *DK* fr. B3; Pi. *N.* 7.11–16; Duchemin (1955:

296–299); Minton (1960); Lanata (1963: 4–5, 8–11, 26–28); Maehler (1963: 37–39); Harriott (1969: 42–43); Finkelberg (1998: 68–73); González (2013: 183–266). Requesting the aid of the Muses is also appropriate at the beginning of an inspired speech in prose: Pl. *Phdr.* 237A, with Hackforth (1972: 37); Mattéi (2003: 91–96).

8 Watkins (1995: 73); Gamkrelidze and Ivanov (1995: 1: 152, 713); West (2007: 32); Setti (1958: 129–130); Lanata (1963: 3); Frisk (1973–1979, s.v. *mousa*); Chantraine (1983–1984: s.v. *mousa*); Walde (2000: 511); Assaël (2003); Griffith (2009: 73); González (2013: 223). Some authorities maintain that the etymology of the word *mousa* is contentious: Duchemin (1955: 26); Murray (1981: 89 n. 16); Simondon (1982: 106); cf. Camilloni (1998: 5–8, 20, 36–37).

9 Bie (1894–1897: 3238); Compton (2006: 173, n. 37).

10 Chadwick (1942: 13); Sperduti (1950: 217).

11 *Il.* 2.491–492: εἰ μὴ Ὀλυμπιάδες Μοῦσαι Διὸς αἰγιόχοιο | θυγατέρες μνησαίαθ᾽ ὅσοι ὑπὸ Ἴλιον ἦλθον. Cf. *Od.* 8.44–45; 73; 479–481; Lanata (1963: 3–7); Snell (1960: 136); Murray (1981: 90–91); Simondon (1982: 108).

12 *Od.* 8.488, cf. Webster (1939: 175).

13 Vernant (1983: 80); Simondon (1982: 114); Bakker (1997: 78).

14 Bakker (2002: 69, italics in the original).

15 On memory as inspired vision see Vernant (1983: 76); cf. Murray (1981: 93); Maehler (1963: 19); Detienne (2007: 68).

16 *Th.* 36–39; Murray (1981: 95).

17 Lefkowitz (2012: 33–34, 162); Kivilo (2010: 95–96); Griffith (2009: 73) regards this as a parody of Hesiod's poetic initiation; Petridou (2015: 219–220) puts the emphasis on the epiphany of the Muses.

18 Dodds (1959: 100, n. 116).

19 Hes. *Th.* 36–39; Ar. *Ra.* 356; Lada-Richards (2002: 88–89); Hardie (2004: 13); Ustinova (2009b: 169). For initiation imagery in Pindar see Duchemin (1955: 39–41); Garner (1992).

20 Chadwick (1942: 2–3); Morrison (1981: 93); Havelock (1963: 105); Garner (1992); Vernant (1983: 76).

21 ἀοίδιμον Πιερίδων προφάταν, fr. 52f Maehler; Dillery (2005: 185); Bowra (1964: 6–8). In fr. 150 Maehler (μαντεύεο, Μοῖσα, προφατεύσω δ᾽ ἐγώ) Pindar asks the Muse to prophesy, and states that he will serve as her prophet or announcer. Cf. Duchemin (1955: 32–33); Simondon (1982: 110–111); Griffith (2009: 73).

22 To quote C.M. Bowra, Pindar knows that 'he must receive their messages and then make them understood by putting them into proper shape' (Bowra 1964: 4).

23 Thgn. 1.769; Murray (1981: 97).

24 Pl. *Lg.* 719c.

25 Plu. *Mor.* 402c; Cornford (1952: 77); Ustinova (2009b: 131 n. 481).

26 West (2007: 28–29); Compton (2006: 173, 209, 233–241, 247, 254–255); Sperduti (1950: 218–219); Setti (1958: 135).

   In German mythology, Mimir (Memory), a wisdom figure, had a well under the roots of the world tree; its spring water was in fact mead, and through drinking it Odin, the war god-magician-poet, was endowed with the poetic gift. In this myth, memory, intoxication, and madness are closely interwoven (Compton 2006: 255–256).

27 Ath. 10.428F; Plu. *Mor.* 715e; Paus. 1. 21. 2; A. fr. T. 117 *TGF*; Lada-Richards 1999: 243–245; Lefkowitz (2012: 71); Compton (2006: 131); cf. Sperduti (1950: 222); contra Harriott (1969: 91); Tigerstedt (1970: 174), interpreting these passages literally.

28 οἴνωι συγκεραυνωθεὶς φρένας, fr. 120 West; Lada-Richards (1999: 243); Compton (2006: 45).

29 Cousins (2011: 284–287), with further examples.

30 **medhu-* is Proto-Indo-European 'beverage made from honey,' surviving as *mádhu,* 'honey' and 'sweet intoxicating beverage,' in Sanskrit and many later Indo-European languages; for the root and the beverage see Gamkrelidze and Ivanov (1995: 2: 517–518).

Unfermented honey could also be intoxicating if the bees fed on some common plants, such as Mediterranean oleander (*Nerium*); famous cases of intoxication with such honey are attested to by Xenophon (*An.* 4. 8. 20–21; [Arist.] *Mir.* 831b) and Strabo (12. 3. 8). Pliny reports that properly aged *meli maenomenon* was valued as mead (*HN* 21.77). In Turkey, 'mad honey' was added to other beverages, and *miel fou* was even imported to Europe in the eighteenth century to be added to wine. Modern toxicological research have identified the compound responsible (grayanotoxin) and established that the experiences following consumption of 'mad honey' range from dizziness to psychedelic optical effects to delirium, and in big dozes it may be fatal (Mayor 1995; Kelhoffer 2005: 65–68). Mediterranean 'mad honey' reinforced perhaps the Indo-European image of honey as intoxicating.

31 Compton (2006: 260–263).

32 Dietrich (1978: 6); Ustinova (2009b: 58–59); Bonnechere (2003: 230). Cf. Porph. *Antr.* 15–19 on honey as a purifying agent, and Arist. *HA* 1. 1. 488a 16–18 on the divine in the nature of bees. See also above, Chapter 5, on honey and the nymphs.

33 Scheiberg (1979: 24, with refs.).

34 Pi. *P.* 10. 45. Other biographers recount Pindar's dreams about the honeycomb (Lefkowitz 2012: 62).

35 *Anth. Pal.* 2. 385–87; Lefkowitz (2012: 7); the place: Hes. *Th.* 22. Other biographers recount Pindar's dreams about the honeycomb (Lefkowitz 2012: 62).

36 Hes. *Th.* 85; *Ant. Pal.* 2. 342–343; Lefkowitz (2012: 28).

37 Cook (1895: 8); Lefkowitz (2012: 85, 176). In Theocritus (*Idyll.* 7. 78) the bees feed honey to the shepherd-poet Comatas.

38 Sacks (2007: 14, 280).

39 It is suggested that similar to the nymphs, the Muses were originally water deities (Walde 2000; Otto 1956: 30; Duchemin 1955: 52), worshipped near water streams (Camilloni 1998: 25–28). In this connection, it should be observed that in Greece, water was considered an important instrument in the mechanism of prophecy-giving (Ustinova 2009b: 131).

40 Snell (1960: 138); on nympholepts see Ustinova (2009b: 61–64, 169–170) and above, Chapter 5.

41 Χάρισιν καὶ Μούσαις ἐφάπτεται , Pl. *Lg.* 682a; Delatte (1934: 7, 57–58, 68); Tigerstedt (1970: 164); Motte (2004: 250–251). For the association of the Muses and the Charites see Simondon (1982: 129).

42 *Mor.* 452b; Lucianus *Hist. Conscr.* 8; Otto (1956: 31).

43 Chadwick (1942); Sikes (1931: 68); Moutsopoulos (1959: 17–22); Vicaire (1963: 75); Duchemin (1955: 31); Webster (1939: 174); Sperduti (1950); Bowra (1964: 13–14); Vernant (1983: 76); Velardi (1989: 99–113); Detienne (1996); Finkelberg (1998: 1–20); Lada-Richards (2002); Guidorizzi (2010: 85–93).

44 Harriott (1969: 50, 78–91); Tigerstedt (1970); Havelock (1963: 155–157); Morgan (2010: 49); for the controversy on the applicability of Plato's remarks to pre-Platonic views of poetry see Murray (1981). E. R. Dodds (1973: 82) emphasises the association of poetic *mania* with Dionysus, and tends to date its emergence earlier than the fifth century. An altogether opposite point of view is that the cultural transformations of the seventh and sixth centuries brought about secularisation and rationalisation of the attitude to poetic creativity (Spentzou 2002: 6).

45 Pl. *Phdr.* 245a, see above; Linforth (1946); Cornford (1952: 66); Padel (1995: 84).

46 ποιητὴς δὲ ἄσσα μὲν ἂν γράφηι μετ᾽ ἐνθουσιασμοῦ καὶ ἱεροῦ πνεύματος, καλὰ κάρτα ἐστίν Democr. DK B18; Delatte (1934: 28–79); Vicaire (1963: 75); Lanata (1963: 256–258); Smith (1965: 420); Harriott (1969: 86–87); Russell (1981: 72–73). Cf. Democr. fr. B21 DK where Homer is described as φύσεως λαχὼν θεαζούσης, endowed either with divine nature (Velardi 1989: 102), or with nature sensitive to divine inspiration (Brancacci 2007: 201). These views of Democritus were known to Roman

authors, and cited by Horace and Cicero (Hor. *Ars* 295–297; Cic. *Div*. 1. 38. 80 = fr. B17*DK*): Brancacci (2007: 202–205); Rütten (1992: 78–79).

47 γὰρ εἰ τὰ δέοντα ποιεῖ᾽ φησίν ᾽ἀλλ᾽ οὐκ εἰδώς γε,᾽ Plu. fr. 130 Sandbach (A. fr. T117c *TGF*); Lefkowitz (2012: 71).

48 Ar. *Ra*. 816–817: μανίας ὑπὸ δεινῆς; Lada-Richards (2002: 85); Naddaf (2013: 303).

49 Ar. *Ra*. 973–974; 945; Lucas (1968: 178); Finkelberg (1998: 8).

50 Finkelberg (1998: 9–10).

51 Wright (2010: 166–167).

52 *Kitharôdos*: Beazley (1963: 197, 383); Anderson (1994: pl. 1, 4); Bundrick (2005: fig. 3, 8); Orpheus: Beazley (1963: 1103); Bundrick (2005: 122, fig. 74); for the maenads see above, Chapter 3.

53 Somville (1992); Kefalidou (2009: 94).

54 For comparisons of the poet to a bee, see above.

55 Pl. *Ion* 533E–534E: πάντες γὰρ οἵ τε τῶν ἐπῶν ποιηταὶ οἱ ἀγαθοὶ οὐκ ἐκ τέχνης ἀλλ᾽ ἔνθεοι ὄντες καὶ κατεχόμενοι πάντα ταῦτα τὰ καλὰ λέγουσι ποιήματα, καὶ οἱ μελοποιοὶ οἱ ἀγαθοὶ ὡσαύτως, ὥσπερ οἱ κορυβαντιῶντες οὐκ ἔμφρονες ὄντες ὀρχοῦνται, οὕτω καὶ οἱ μελοποιοὶ οὐκ ἔμφρονες ὄντες τὰ καλὰ μέλη ταῦτα ποιοῦσιν, ἀλλ᾽ ἐπειδὰν ἐμβῶσιν εἰς τὴν ἁρμονίαν καὶ εἰς τὸν ῥυθμόν, βακχεύουσι καὶ κατεχόμενοι . . . λέγουσι γὰρ δήπουθεν πρὸς ἡμᾶς οἱ ποιηταὶ ὅτι ἀπὸ κρηνῶν μελιρρύτων ἐκ Μουσῶν κήπων τινῶν καὶ ναπῶν δρεπόμενοι τὰ μέλη ἡμῖν φέρουσιν ὥσπερ αἱ μέλitται, καὶ αὐτοὶ οὕτω πετόμενοι . . . κοῦφον γὰρ χρῆμα ποιητής ἐστιν καὶ πτηνὸν καὶ ἱερόν, καὶ οὐ πρότερον οἷός τε ποιεῖν πρὶν ἂν ἔνθεός τε γένηται καὶ ἔκφρων καὶ ὁ νοῦς μηκέτι ἐν αὐτῷ ἐνῇ· ἕως δ᾽ ἂν τουτὶ ἔχῃ τὸ κτῆμα, ἀδύνατος πᾶς ποιεῖν ἄνθρωπός ἐστιν καὶ χρησμῳδεῖν . . . ὅτι οὐκ ἀνθρώπινά ἐστιν τὰ καλὰ ταῦτα ποιήματα οὐδὲ ἀνθρώπων, ἀλλὰ θεῖα καὶ θεῶν, οἱ δὲ ποιηταὶ οὐδὲν ἀλλ᾽ ἢ ἑρμηνῆς εἰσιν τῶν θεῶν, κατεχόμενοι ἐξ ὅτου ἂν ἕκαστος κατέχηται (translation W.R.M. Lamb, slightly modified). For the interpretation of these passages see: Flashar (1958 54–77); Murray (1996: 112–125); Cavarero (2002: 52–54); Capuccino (2011); Gonzalez (2011). Even if these words are taken 'half-seriously,' as suggested by S. Stern-Gillet (Stern-Gillet 2004: 178; Russell 1981: 76), who emphasises Socrates' sarcastic attitude to the poet's knowledge, there is no doubt that 'Plato's poet can achieve greatness only intermittently and through the agency of some divine being' (Stern-Gillet 2004: 182, 194).

56 Pl. *Ion* 536B.

57 Pl. *Apol*. 22B; *Lg*. 719C, and see above.

58 Vicaire (1963: 80).

59 E.g. Collobert (2011: 42–43).

60 Halliwell (2011: 164–179, quotation p. 164).

61 Pl. *Phdr*. 248DE.

62 Capuccino (2011).

63 Finkelberg (1998: 1–7). Plato refers to 'greatest music' and 'finest tragedy' on multiple occasions (*Phd*. 61A; *Phrd*. 248D, 259D, etc.) and presupposes the love of poetry in his audience (Capra 2014: 10). Therefore, the claim that Plato regarded every poetry, inspired or not, as 'flawed reproduction' (Collobert 2011: 55–63) is untenable. To be sure, most kinds of poetry are banned from the education in the ideal state designed in the *Republic*, and contrasted to philosophy which is focused on truth; in this dialogue, he does not even mention divine inspiration of poets. Clearly, Plato is self-contradicting on this matter – as in fact on many other subjects (Halliwell 2011: 204). For an overview of works dealing with the 'schizophrenic' contradiction between Platonic praise and rebuttal of poetry, as well as those attempting to reconcile between the two, see Asmis (1992); Capra (2014: 91–92); Halliwell (2011: 155–207).

64 Finkelberg (1998: 7).

65 D. L. 3. 5; Ael. *VH* 2. 30; anecdotal nature of Diogenes' biography of Plato: Tigerstedt (1977: 39).

66 Kahn (1996: 36).

67 ἔνθεον γὰρ ἡ ποίησις, Arist. *Rh*. 1408b17.

68 Fr. 90 Wimmer: μουσικῆς ἀρχὰς τρεῖς εἶναι, λύπην, ἡδονήν, ἐνθουσιασμόν. Plutarch, having quoted Theophrastus, also equated the spontaneous change of tone and style in the speech of inspired orators and actors, and likened singing and dancing and leaping of people excited with joy to the Bacchic frenzy (Plu. *Mor*. 623A).

69 Arist. *Po*. 1455a32–34: ὅσα δὲ δυνατὸν καὶ τοῖς σχήμασιν συναπεργαζόμενον· πιθανώτατοι γὰρ ἀπὸ τῆς αὐτῆς φύσεως οἱ ἐν τοῖς πάθεσίν εἰσιν, καὶ χειμαίνει ὁ χειμαζόμενος καὶ χαλεπαίνει ὁ ὀργιζόμενος ἀληθινώτατα. διὸ εὐφυοῦς ἡ ποιητική ἐστιν ἢ μανικοῦ· τούτων γὰρ οἱ μὲν εὔπλαστοι οἱ δὲ ἐκστατικοί εἰσιν (translation W. F. Fyfe, modified). The last phrase as I cite it is the reading of the Greek manuscripts, retained by most editors (Bywater 1909; Lucas 1968; Dupont-Roc and Lallot 1980; Gallavotti 1974). Some scholars (Russell and Winterbottom 1972: 113; Russell 1981: 77–78; Tarán and Gutas 2012: 274; Halliwell 1987: 50, 145) amend μᾶλλον ἢ and read the phrase as a statement that poetry exists due to a talented man rather than to madman. Their argument is circular: the text is to be amended because Aristotle does not mention *manikos* in his discussion of the sources of poetry and is usually unfavourable to *enthousiasmos* and *manikos*, so the passage where he does the opposite is to be purged. D. A. Russell's translation brings Aristotle's alleged intolerance for ecstasy *ad nec plus ultra*: 'That is why poetry is the work of a genius rather than of a madman; for the genius is by nature adaptable, while the madman is degenerate' (Russell and Winterbottom 1972: 113). For the refutation of the amendment see Lucas (1968: 177); Dupont-Roc and Lallot (1980: 284–285); Janko (1987: 118).

70 As for instance Halliwell (1998: 85).

71 *EE* 1148a30; *EN* 1179a25; Lucas (1968: 178); Croissant (1932: 21).

72 *EE* 1214a24, cited in Chapter 5; for the *daimonion* in this passage to be understood along Platonic lines, see Décarie (1978: 47).

73 *EE* 1225a22, cited in Chapter 1.

74 And not as 'a purely psychological, not religious' points, as Halliwell (1998: 85).

75 Halliwell (1998: 84).

76 Lucas (1968: 177). Bywater (1909: 244) demonstrates that the word *ekstatikoi* in Aristotle could describe 'extreme form of emotionalism,' as well as mental pathology.

77 Examples of such modern artists are cited by Bywater (1909: 241); Lucas (1968: 176–177).

78 On the ambiguity see: Lucas (1968: 175); Janko (1987: 117); Tarán and Gutas (2012: 273); Munteanu (2012: 80). I follow the authorities (Lucas 1968: 175; Janko 1987: 117, Bywater 1909: 241, and Halliwell 1987: 146) opting in favour of the poet as the person who gesticulates.

79 Janko (1987: 117).

80 Ar. *Ach*. 412–444.

81 Ar. *Th*. 148–152, translation A. H. Sommerstein.

82 It is a paradox that Halliwell (1987: 146) acknowledges that the gesticulating poet is 'working himself in the process into the emotional states which he intends to portray in his characters,' but nevertheless is reluctant to accept that Aristotle called such poets ecstatics, and amends the text of this passage.

83 This juxtaposition of *manikoi* and *euphueis* (talented) was further developed in the Aristotelian *Problems* 30, (954a32), in particular, Maracus of Syracuse is said to be a better poet when in the state of ecstasy (ἐκσταίη) (954a38).

84 *De tranquilitate animi* 17. 10, transl. J. W. Basore.

85 Murray (1981: 88); Stern-Gillet (2004: 196); Bowra (1955: 1–25, esp. 19). On stages in the creative process see Hadamard (1945); Rugg (1963). Cf. Ustinova (2009b: 177–178), and below, Chapter 8, on illumination and rational development of scientific ideas.

86 Collobert (2011: 46).

87 It is suggested that the *Ion* is focused on rhapsodes who perform or interpret poetic work of others, being (living) mediums of (dead) mediums of the gods (Gonzalez 2011). If indeed this is so, the basic principle of creative work based on short-lived inspiration and long work, still holds.

88 Finkelberg (1990).

89 Bakker (1997: 138).

90 Bakker (1997: 55–56) and above.

91 Bakker (1997: 44–46).

92 Rugg (1963: 45).

93 Hadamard (1945: 16).

94 I cite Reverdy after Elie (2003: 243).

95 Sacks (2007: 279–281).

96 Sacks (2007: 282–284).

97 Abell (1955: 108, 116–117, 122).

98 Abell (1955: 5–6).

99 Abell (1955: 6–7, 117).

100 Abell (1955: 162).

101 Hadamard (1945: 17).

102 Abell (1955: 117).

103 Robb (2000: 79–80).

104 *The Poet* (1827), Pushkin (1949: 3: 21):

> Пока не требует поэта | К священной жертве Аполлон, |В заботах суетного света | Он малодушно погружен; |Молчит его святая лира; | Душа вкушает хладный сон, |И меж детей ничтожных мира, |Быть может, всех ничтожней он. |Но лишь божественный глагол |До слуха чуткого коснется, |Душа поэта встрепенется, |Как пробудившийся орел . . . |Бежит он, дикий и суровый, | И звуков и смятенья полн, | На берега пустынных волн, |В широкошумные дубровы. . . .
>
> (translation Y. Bonver)

105 Farthing (1992: 210–211); see also the Introduction.

106 Ludwig (1992: 351); Jamison (1993: 73–87, 101–148).

107 Introduction.

108 Sussman (2007: 22).

109 Sussman (2007: 23).

110 Sussman (2007: 23); Jamison (1993: 2).

111 Sussman (2007: 24).

112 Sussman (2007: 24). Rothenberg (1990) argues against the existence of links between creativity and mental disease.

113 *Od.* 17. 517–521: ὡς δ᾽ ὅτ᾽ ἀοιδὸν ἀνὴρ ποτιδέρκεται, ὅς τε θεῶν ἒξ | ἀείδῃ δεδαὼς ἔπε᾽ ἱμερόεντα βροτοῖσι, | τοῦ δ᾽ ἄμοτον μεμάασιν ἀκουέμεν, ὁππότ᾽ ἀείδῃ· | ὣς ἐμὲ κεῖνος ἔθελγε παρήμενος ἐν μεγάροισι (translation G. E. Dimock).

114 *Od.* 12. 40, 44; Russo, Fernández-Galiano, and Heubeck (1992: 43–44); Halliwell (2011: 47–48).

115 *Od.* 10. 213, 29, 318; Heubeck and Hoekstra (1989: 55–56, 119–120).

116 Hes. *Th.* 102–13, translation G. W. Most; Griffith (2009: 93).

117 Segal (1974: 139).

118 On possession by Eros see Chapter 7; on the combination of rhythmic, phonetic, and ritual effects in Sappho's poetry see Segal (1974).

119 Walsh (1984: 36) suggests that by the degree of alteration of their condition the audience would know how good the singer was.

120 Griffith (2009: 91).

121 Str. 10.3.9–19; Pl. *Grg.* 501e–502d.

122 Linforth (1941); Jeanmaire (1970: 131–138); Rouget (1990: 278–308); Pelosi (2010: 26–27). Musical therapy for mental disorders is attested on other cultures, the most famous example being the treatment of Saul's possession by David's music: *1 Sam*. 16. 14–17; Rouget (1990: 291–293).

123 West (1983: 3–7); Bundrick (2005: 121–124, fig. 74–76).

124 *h. Ap. Del*. 161: θέλγουσι δὲ φῦλ᾽ ἀνθρώπων; Segal (1974: 139–144); Power (2010: 401).

125 West (1992: 32–33). For paean and a healing or apotropaic song-dance see Rutherford (2001: 7, 11, 15, 86). It is hardly surprising that its performance was normally accompanied by *aulos* (Rutherford 2001: 79), the most 'enchanting' among Greek instruments.

126 *Nem*. 8. 49–50; Segal (1974: 142).

127 Aristox. fr. 26 Wehrli; Iamb. *VP* 110; Burkert (1972: 212); West (2000: 55–57); Figari (2006: 135–137).

128 Porph. *VP* 32; Iamb. *VP* 110; West (2000: 249); Boyancé (1937: 100–131); Dodds (1973: 154); Detienne (1963: 47–48); Hermann (2004: 105); Hoessly (2001: 181–188).

129 Aristox. fr. 117 Wehrli (Apollon. *Mir*. 40); West (2000: 55).

130 Socrates: Linforth (1941: 170); Vicaire (1963: 82). For Socrates' praise of spells, see Pl. *Chrm*. 156b; Laín Entralgo (1970: 109–126); van der Ben (1985: 11–19); Ustinova (2009a: 267–274); Theophrastus: fr. 88 Wimmer.

131 Ael. *VH* 12. 50. Thales (or Thaletas), a Cretan musician, is said to have put an end to an epidemic in Sparta in accordance with a Delphic oracle (Plu. *Mor*. 1146BC; Paus. 1. 14. 1; Parke and Wormell 1956: 2: 92, No. 223). Furthermore, Thales and Terpander were believed to promote civic concord with the musical harmony their music created (Power 2010: 394–399; West 1992: 334–335).

132 Sacks (2007: 214–223, 248–258, 335–348); Thaut and Wheeler (2010).

133 West (1992: 356–372).

134 Csapo (2004); Csapo and Wilson (2009); Power (2010: 500–507); Budelmann and Leven (2014: 191–192).

135 Csapo (2004: 217); on *aulos* see Chapters 3.

136 West (1992: 369–372); Csapo and Wilson (2009: 290–292); Power (2010: 504).

137 Timoc. fr. 6 PCG, cited by Ath. 6. 223B: πρὸς ἀλλοτρίῳ τε ψυχαγωγηθεὶς πάθει, μεθ᾽ ἡδονῆς ἀπῆλθε παιδευθεὶς ἅμα (translation Rusten et al. 2011: 518); cf. Diano (1961: 125–129); Sorabji (2000: 292); Munteanu (2012: 133–134).

138 *Ion* 533E: οὕτω δὲ καὶ ἡ Μοῦσα ἐνθέους μὲν ποιεῖ αὐτή, διὰ δὲ τῶν ἐνθέων τούτων ἄλλων ἐνθουσιαζόντων ὁρμαθὸς ἐξαρτᾶται (translation W.R.M. Lamb). See Capuccino (2011: 88) and Gonzalez (2011: 96) on 'chains of *enthousiazontes*' in the *Ion*, although they do not allow for 'horizontal movements,' between poets and rhapsodes and audience. Cf. (Bakker 1997: 55–56). Cf. Delatte (1934: 58–59); Duchemin (1955: 21–53).

139 *Ion* 526B.

140 E.g. *R*. 607B–608A; discussed in detail by Halliwell (2011: 198–207).

141 *Pol*. 1341a10–11.

142 *Pol*. 1342a5–15: ὃ γὰρ περὶ ἐνίας συμβαίνει πάθος ψυχὰς ἰσχυρῶς, τοῦτο ἐν πάσαις ὑπάρχει, τῷ δὲ ἧττον διαφέρει καὶ τῷ μᾶλλον, οἷον ἔλεος καὶ φόβος, ἔτι δ᾽ ἐνθουσιασμός· καὶ γὰρ ὑπὸ ταύτης τῆς κινήσεως κατοκώχιμοί τινές εἰσιν, ἐκ τῶν δ᾽ ἱερῶν μελῶν ὁρῶμεν τούτους, ὅταν χρήσωνται τοῖς ἐξοργιάζουσι τὴν ψυχὴν μέλεσι, καθισταμένους ὥσπερ ἰατρείας τυχόντας καὶ καθάρσεως· ταὐτὸ δὴ τοῦτο ἀναγκαῖον πάσχειν καὶ τοὺς ἐλεήμονας καὶ τοὺς φοβητικοὺς καὶ τοὺς ὅλως παθητικούς, τοὺς δ᾽ ἄλλους καθ᾽ ὅσον ἐπιβάλλει τῶν τοιούτων ἑκάστῳ, καὶ πᾶσι γίγνεσθαί τινα κάθαρσιν καὶ κουφίζεσθαι μεθ᾽ ἡδονῆς (translation H. Rackham, modified). For this passage see Newman (1902: 3: 563–566).

143 *Pol*. 1242a15–25.

144 Arist. *Po.* 1449b25: δι' ἐλέου καὶ φόβου περαίνουσα τὴν τῶν τοιούτων παθημάτων κάθαρσιν. The scholarly debate on this phrase is enormous; for an overview see Halliwell (1998: 350–356); Halliwell (2011: 236–260). To some scholars it looks so perplexing that they argue that it is a later interpolation, distorting the Aristotelian thought. For a refutation of these suggestions see Halliwell (2011: 260–265).

145 The interpretation of Aristotle's phrase as referring to tragedy as 'a treatment of an oppressed person, which seeks . . . to arouse [the oppressive element] and to draw it out' was first put forward by J. Bernays in 1857 (Barnes, Schofield, and Sorabji 1979: 3: 160, originally published as *Grundzüge der verlorenen Abhandlung des Aristotletes über der Tragödie*, Breslau 1857). Bernays' interpretation is endorsed (with modifications) in Croissant (1932: 60); Moulinier (1952: 410–413); Flashar (1956); Belfiore (1992: 291–300), Sorabji (2000: 24, 288–293), Calame (2009), and questioned (for a plethora of reasons) in Vickers (1973: 609–616); Janko (1987: xvii), Sifakis (2001: 74–75); Halliwell (2011: 236–237), among others. Sorabji (2000: 294–297) demonstrates that later thinkers, such as Neoplatonists and neo-Pythagoreans, believed in purging of emotions by catharsis. Even if 'pity and fear' are 'pitiful and fearful incidents of the drama itself' (Nehamas 1992: 307), rather than the emotions of the audience, Aristotle's view on the catharsis still emphasises its effect on the emotions of the spectators and their understanding of the world (Nussbaum 1992: 287). In fact, Bernays' view is hardly that the best audience for a tragedy is that of 'disturbed and unbalanced' spectators, as Janko claims, or that catharsis was 'a mere end-result of evacuative "relief"' (S. Halliwell's words), but rather that the 'disturbed and unbalanced' can benefit from the cathartic effect of the tragedy.

146 Kraut (1997: 211); Halliwell (2011: 252–260).

147 *Po.* 1454a4, 1460b23; Halliwell (2011: 229–230).

148 *Po.* 1450a33; 1450b 16–20; Halliwell (1998: 336–343); Halliwell (2011: 223–227).

149 *Isoc.*2. 48–49; 9. 10–11; Munteanu (2012: 80–90).

150 Halliwell (2011: 259).

151 Hdt. 6. 21; *Vita Aeschyli* 9; Plu. *Mor.* 334A.

152 Cf. Lada (1993).

153 González (2013: 177–179).

154 Cf. Simon (1978: 150): 'Greek culture . . . stood in awe of the creative process much as it stood in awe of overt madness. Both gave some sense of an external agent at work.'

155 Hdt. 6. 75, discussed in the Introduction.

156 Heraclides Ponticus (fr. 56 Wehrli), discussed in the Introduction.

References

Abell, A. M. 1955. *Talks With Great Composers*. London: Spiritualist Press.

Anderson, W. A. 1994. *Music and Musicians in Ancient Greece*. Ithaca: Cornell University Press.

Asmis, E. 1992. "Plato on poetic creativity." In *The Cambridge Companion to Plato*, edited by R. Kraut, 338–364. Cambridge: Cambridge University Press.

Assaël, J. 2003. "Poétique des étymologies de ΜΟΥΣΑ (MOUSA), la Muse." *Noesis* 4:11–53.

Bakker, E. J. 1997. *Poetry in Speech: Orality and Homeric Discourse*. Ithaca: Cornell University Press.

Bakker, E. J. 2002. "Remembering the god's arrival." *Arethusa* 35 (1):63–81.

Barnes, J., M. Schofield, and R. Sorabji. 1979. *Articles on Aristotle*. London: Duckworth.

Beazley, J. D. 1963. *Attic Red-Figure Vase-Painters*. Oxford: Clarendon Press.

Belfiore, E. S. 1992. *Tragic Pleasures: Aristotle on Plot and Emotion.* Princeton: Princeton University Press.

Benveniste, E. 1954. "Formes et sens de *mnaomai.*" In *Sprachgeschichte und Woerterbedeutung: Festschrift A. Debrunner,* 13–18. Bern: Francke Verlag.

Bie, O. 1894–97. "Musen." In *Ausführliches Lexikon der griechischen und römischen Mythologie,* edited by W. H. Roscher, 3238–3295. Leipzig: Teubner.

Bonnechere, P. 2003. *Trophonios de Lébadée.* Leiden: Brill.

Bowra, C. M. 1955. *Inspiration and Poetry.* New York: Macmillan.

Bowra, C. M. 1964. *Pindar.* Oxford: Clarendon Press.

Boyancé, P. 1937. *Le culte des Muses chez les philosophes grecs.* Paris: de Boccard.

Brancacci, A. 2007. "Democritus' *Mousika.*" In *Democritus: Science, the Arts, and the Care of the Soul,* edited by A. Brancacci and P.-M. Morel, 181–206. Leiden: Brill.

Budelmann, F. and P. Leven. 2014. "Timotheus' poetics of blending: A cognitive approach to the language of the New Music." *CPh* 109:191–210.

Bundrick, S. D. 2005. *Music and Image in Classical Athens.* Cambridge: Cambridge University Press.

Burkert, W. 1972. *Lore and Science in Ancient Pythagoreanism.* Cambridge, MA: Harvard University Press.

Bywater, I. 1909. *Aristotle: On the Art of Poetry.* Oxford: Oxford University Press.

Calame, C. 2009. "Émotions et performance poétique: la 'katharsis' érotique dans la poésie mélique des cités grecques." In *Violentes émotions. Approches comparatistes,* edited by P. Borgeaud and A.-C. Rendu Loisel, 29–55. Geneva: Droz.

Camilloni, M. T. 1998. *Le Muse.* Rome: Editori Riuniti.

Capra, A. 2014. *Plato's Four Muses: The Phaedrus and the Poetics of Philosophy.* Washington, DC: Center for Hellenic Studies.

Capuccino, C. 2011. "Plato's *Ion* and the ethics of praise." In *Plato and the Poets,* edited by P. Destrée and F.-G. Herrmann, 63–92. Leiden: Brill.

Cavarero, A. 2002. "The envied Muse: Plato versus Homer." In *Cultivating the Muse: Struggles for Power and Inspiration in Classical Literature,* edited by E. Spentzou and D. Fowler, 47–67. Oxford: Oxford University Press.

Chadwick, N. K. 1942. *Poetry and Prophecy.* Cambridge: Cambridge University Press.

Chantraine, P. 1983–1984. *Dictionnaire étymologique de la langue grecque.* Paris: Klincksieck.

Collobert, C. 2011. "Poetry as flawed reproduction: Possession and mimesis." In *Plato and the Poets,* edited by P. Destrée and F.-G. Herrmann, 41–62. Leiden: Brill.

Compton, T. M. 2006. *Victim of the Muses: Poet as Scapegoat, Warrior and Hero in Greco-Roman and Indo-European Myth and History.* Washington, DC: Center for Hellenic Studies.

Cook, A. B. 1895. "The bee in Greek mythology." *JHS* 15:1–24.

Cornford, F. M. 1952. *Principium Sapientiae: The Origins of Greek Philosophical Thought.* Cambridge: Cambridge University Press.

Cousins, W. E. 2011. "Colored inklings: Altered states of consciousness and literature." In *Altering Consciousness: Multidisciplinary Perspectives. Vol. 1. History, Culture, and the Humanities,* edited by E. Cardeña and M. Winkelman, 277–300. Santa Barbara: Praeger.

Croissant, J. 1932. *Aristote et les mystères.* Liège-Paris: Droz.

Csapo, E. 2004. "The politics of the new music." In *Music and the Muses: The Culture of 'Mousikê' in the Classical Athenian City,* edited by P. Murray and P. Wilson, 207–248. Oxford: Oxford University Press.

Csapo, E. and P. Wilson. 2009. "Timotheus the new musician." In *The Cambridge Companion to Greek Lyric*, edited by F. Budelmann, 277–293. Cambridge: Cambridge University Press.

Décarie, V. 1978. *Aristote. Éthique à Eudème*. Paris: Vrin.

Delatte, A. 1934. *Les conceptions de l'enthousiasme chez les philosophes présocratiques*. Paris: Les Belles Lettres.

Detienne, M. 1963. *La notion de daïmôn dans le pythagorisme ancien*. Paris: Les Belles Lettres.

Detienne, M. 1996. *The Masters of Truth in Archaic Greece*. New York: Zone Books.

Detienne, M. 2007. *The Greeks and Us*. Cambridge: Polity Press.

Diano, C. 1961. "Euripide auteur de catharsis tragique." *Numen* 8:117–141.

Dietrich, B. C. 1978. "Reflections on the origins of the oracular Apollo." *BICS* 25:1–18.

Dillery, J. 2005. "Chresmologues and *manteis*: Independent diviners and the problem of authority." In *Mantikê: Studies in Ancient Divination*, edited by S. I. Johnston and P. T. Struck, 167–231. Leiden: Brill.

Dodds, E. R. 1959. *Plato: Gorgias. A Revised Text With Introduction and Commentary*. Oxford: Clarendon Press.

Dodds, E. R. 1973. *The Greeks and the Irrational*. Berkeley-Los Angeles: University of California Press.

Duchemin, J. 1955. *Pindare, poète et prophète*. Paris: Les Belles Lettres.

Dupont-Roc, R. and J. Lallot. 1980. *Aristote. La poétique*. Paris: Seuil.

Elie, M. 2003. "Fortunes et infortunes de l'inspiration du génie." *Noesis* 4:233–250.

Farthing, G. W. 1992. *The Psychology of Consciousness*. Englewood Cliffs: Prentice-Hall.

Figari, J. 2006. "Musique et médicine dans la philosophie présocratique." In *Musique et antiquité*, edited by O. Mortir-Waldschmidt, 121–145. Paris: Les Belles Lettres.

Finkelberg, M. 1990. "A creative oral poet and the Muse." *AJPh* 111:293–303.

Finkelberg, M. 1998. *The Birth of Literary Fiction in Ancient Greece*. Oxford: Oxford University Press.

Flashar, H. 1956. "Die medizinischen Grundlagen der Lehre von der Wirkung der Dichtung in der griechischen Poetik." *Hermes* 84:12–48.

Flashar, H. 1958. *Der Dialog Ion als Zeugnis platonischer Philosophie*. Berlin: Akademie-Verlag.

Frisk, H. 1973–79. *Griechisches etymologisches Wörterbuch*. Heidelberg: C. Winter.

Gallavotti, C. 1974. *Aristotele. Dell'arte poetica*. Milan: Arnoldo Mondadori Editore.

Gamkrelidze, T. V. and V. V. Ivanov. 1995. *Indo-European and the Indo-Europeans*. Berlin-New York: De Gruyter.

Garner, R. 1992. "Mules, mysteries, and song in Pindar's *Olympian* 6." *ClAnt* 11 (1):45–67.

Gonzalez, F. J. 2011. "The hermeneutics of madness: Poet and philosopher in Plato's *Ion* and *Phaedrus*." In *Plato and the Poets*, edited by P. Destrée and F.-G. Herrmann, 93–110. Leiden: Brill.

González, J. M. 2013. *The Epic Rhapsode and His Craft*. Washington, DC: Center for Hellenic Studies.

Griffith, M. 2009. "Greek lyric and the place of humans in the world." In *The Cambridge Companion to Greek Lyric*, edited by F. Budelmann, 72–94. Cambridge: Cambridge University Press.

Guidorizzi, G. 2010. *Ai confini dell' anima. I Greci e la follia*. Milano: Raffaelo Cortina.

Hackforth, R. 1972. *Plato's Phaedrus: Translated With an Introduction and Commentary*. Cambridge: Cambridge University Press.

Hadamard, J. 1945. *The Psychology of Invention in the Mathematical Field*. Princeton: Princeton University Press.

Halliwell, S. 1987. *The Poetics of Aristotle: Translation and Commentary*. London: Duckworth.

Halliwell, S. 1998. *Aristotle's Poetics*. Chapel Hill: University of North Carolina Press.

Halliwell, S. 2011. *Between Ecstasy and Truth: Interpretations of Greek Poetics From Homer to Longinus*. Oxford: Oxford University Press.

Hardie, A. 2004. "Muses and mysteries." In *Music and the Muses: The Culture of 'Mousikê' in the Classical Athenian City*, edited by P. Murray and P. Wilson, 11–37. Oxford: Oxford University Press.

Harriott, R. 1969. *Poetry and Criticism Before Plato*. London: Methuen.

Havelock, E. A. 1963. *Preface to Plato*. Cambridge, MA: Harvard University Press.

Hermann, A. 2004. *To Think Like God: Pythagoras and Parmenides. The Origins of Philosophy*. Las Vegas: Parmenides Press.

Heubeck, A. and A. Hoekstra. 1989. *A Commentary on Homer's Odyssey: Books IX-XVI*. Oxford: Oxford University Press.

Hoessly, F. 2001. *Katharsis: Reinigung als Heilverfahren. Studien zum Ritual der archaischen und klassischen Zeit sowie zum Corpus Hippocraticum*. Göttingen: Vandenhoeck & Ruprecht.

Jamison, K. R. 1993. *Touched With Fire: Manic-Depressive Illness and the Artistic Temperament*. New York: The Free Press.

Janko, R. 1987. *Aristotle: Poetics*. Indianapolis-Cambridge: Hackett.

Jeanmaire, H. 1970. *Dionysos. Histoire du culte de Bacchus*. Paris: Payot.

Kahn, C. H. 1996. *Plato and the Socratic Dialogue*. Cambridge: Cambridge University Press.

Kefalidou, E. 2009. "The iconography of madness in Attic vase-painting." In *Athenian Potters and Painters*, edited by J. H. Oakley and O. Palagia, 90–99. Oxford: Oxbow Books.

Kelhoffer, J. A. 2005. "John the Baptist's 'wild honey' and 'honey in antiquity.'" *GRBS* 45:59–73.

Kivilo, M. 2010. *Early Greek Poets' Lives: The Shaping of the Tradition*. Leiden: Brill.

Kraut, R. 1997. *Aristotle: Politics. Books VII and VIII*. Oxford: Oxford University Press.

Lada, I. 1993. "'Emphatic understanding': Emotion and cognition in classical dramatic audience-response." *PCPhS* 39:93–140.

Lada-Richards, I. 1999. *Initiating Dionysus: Ritual and Theatre in Aristophanes' Frogs*. Oxford: Oxford University Press.

Lada-Richards, I. 2002. "Reinscribing the Muse: Greek drama and the discourse of inspired creativity." In *Cultivating the Muse: Struggles for Power and Inspiration in Classical Literature*, edited by E. Spentzou and D. Fowler, 69–91. Oxford: Oxford University Press.

Laín Entralgo, P. 1970. *The Therapy of the Word in Classical Antiquity*. Translated by L. J. Rather and J. M. Sharp. New Haven: Yale University Press.

Lanata, J. 1963. *Poetica pre-platonica. Testimonianze e frammenti*. Firenze: La Nuova Italia.

Lefkowitz, M. R. 2012. *The Lives of the Greek Poets*. Baltimore: Johns Hopkins University Press.

Linforth, I. M. 1941. *The Arts of Orpheus*. Berkeley-Los Angeles: University of California Press.

Linforth, I. M. 1946. "Telestic madness in Plato. Phaedrus 244DE." *University of California Publications in Classical Philology* 13 (6):163–172.

Lucas, D. W. 1968. *Aristotle: Poetics*. Oxford: Clarendon Press.

Ludwig, A. M. 1992. "Creative achievement and psychopathology: Comparison among professions." *American Journal of Psychotherapy* 46 (3):330–356.

Maehler, H. 1963. *Die Auffassung des Dichterberufs im frühen Griechentum bis zur Zeit Pindars*. Goettingen: Vandenhoeck und Ruprecht.

Mattéi, J.-F. 2003. "L'inspiration de la poésie et de la philosophie chez Platon." *Noesis* 4:73–96.

Mayor, A. 1995. "Mad honey!" *Archaeology*, November/December 48:32–40.

Minton, W. W. 1960. "Homer's invocations of the Muses: Traditional patterns." *TAPA* 91:293–309.

Morgan, K. A. 2010. "Inspiration, recollection, and *mimesis* in Plato's *Phaedrus*." In *Ancient Models of Mind: Studies in Human and Divine Rationality*, edited by A. Nightingale and D. Sedley, 45–63. Cambridge: Cambridge University Press.

Morrison, J. S. 1981. "The Classical World." In *Divination and Oracles*, edited by M. Loewe and C. Blacker, 87–114. London: Allen & Unwin.

Motte, A. 2004. "Le sacré dans la nature et dans l'homme: la perception du devin chez les Grecs." In *Les civilisations méditerranéens et le sacré*, edited by J. Ries, A. Motte, and N. Spineto, 229–254. Turnhout: Brepols.

Moulinier, L. 1952. *Le pur et l'impur dans la pensée des Grecs*. Paris: Klincksieck.

Moutsopoulos, E. 1959. *La musique dans l'oeuvre de Platon*. Paris: Presses Universitaires de France.

Munteanu, D. L. 2012. *Tragic Pathos: Pity and Fear in Greek Philosophy and Tragedy*, Cambridge: Cambridge University Press.

Murray, P. 1981. "Poetic inspiration in early Greece." *JHS* 101:87–100.

Murray, P. 1996. *Plato on Poetry: Ion; Republic 376e-398b9; Republic 595–608b10*. Cambridge: Cambridge University Press.

Naddaf, G. 2013. "Philosophic and poetic inspiration in the *Republic*." In *Dialogues on Plato's Politeia (Republic)*, edited by N. Notomi and L. Brisson, 301–306. Sankt Augustin: Academia.

Nehamas, A. 1992. "Pity and fear in the *Rhetoric* and the *Poetics*." In *Essays on Aristotle's Poetics*, edited by A. O. Rorty, 291–314. Princeton: Princeton University Press.

Newman, W. L. 1902. *The Politics of Aristotle*. Oxford: Clarendon Press.

Notopoulos, J. A. 1938. "Mnemosyne in oral literature." *TAPA* 69:465–493.

Nussbaum, M. C. 1992. "Tragedy and self-sufficiency: Plato and Aristotle on pity and fear." In *Essays on Aristotle's Poetics*, edited by A. O. Rorty, 261–290. Princeton: Princeton University Press.

Otto, W. 1956. *Die Musen und die goettliche Ursprung des Singens und Sagens*. Darmstadt: Wissenschaftliche Buchergesellschaft.

Padel, R. 1995. *Whom Gods Destroy: Elements of Greek and Tragic Madness*. Princeton: Princeton University Press.

Parke, H. W. and D. E. W. Wormell. 1956. *The Delphic Oracle*. 2 vols. Oxford: Blackwell.

Pelosi, F. 2010. *Plato on Music, Soul and Body*. Cambridge: Cambridge University Press.

Petridou, G. 2015. *Divine Epiphany in Greek Literature and Culture*. Oxford: Oxford University Press.

Power, T. 2010. *The Culture of Kithardoidia*. Washington, DC: Center for Hellenic Studies.

Pushkin, A. S. 1949. *Polnoeye sobraniye sochineniy v desyati tomakh (Complete Works in Ten Volumes)*. Moscow-Leningrad: Izdatel'stvo Akademii Nauk.

Robb, G. 2000. *Rimbaud*. New York: Norton.

Rothenberg, A. 1990. *Creativity and Madness*. Baltimore: Johns Hopkins University Press.

Rouget, G. 1990. *La musique et la trance*. Paris: Gallimard.

Rugg, H. 1963. *Imagination*. New York: Harper & Row.

Russell, D. A. 1981. *Criticism in Antiquity*. London: Duckworth.

Russell, D. A. and M. Winterbottom. 1972. *Ancient Literary Criticism*. Oxford: Clarendon Press.

Russo, J., M. Fernández-Galiano, and A. Heubeck. 1992. *A Commentary on Homer's Odyssey, Books XVII-XXIV*. Oxford: Oxford University Press.

Rusten, J., J. Henderson, D. Konstan, G.R. Rosen, and N.W. Slater. 2011. *The Birth of Comedy: Texts, Documents, and Art From Athenian Comic Competitions, 486–280*. Baltimore: Johns Hopkins University Press.

Rutherford, I. 2001. *Pindar's Paeans*. Oxford: Oxford University Press.

Rütten, T. 1992. *Demokrit-lachender Philosoph und sanguinischer Melancholiker*. Leiden: Brill.

Sacks, O. 2007. *Musicophilia: Tales of Music and the Brain*. London: Picador.

Scheiberg, S. 1979. "The bee maidens of the Homeric *Hymn to Hermes*." *HSPh* 83:1–28.

Segal, C. 1974. "Eros and incantation: Sappho and oral poetry." *Arethusa* 7 (2):139–160.

Setti, A. 1958. "La memoria e il canto. Saggio di poetica arcaica greca." *Studi italiani di filologia classica* 30:129–171.

Sifakis, G. M. 2001. *Aristotle on the Function of Tragic Poetry*. Herakleion: Crete University Press.

Sikes, E. E. 1931. *The Greek View of Poetry*. London: Methuen.

Simon, B. 1978. *Mind and Madness in Ancient Greece: The Classical Roots of Modern Psychiatry*. Ithaca: Cornell University Press.

Simondon, M. 1982. *La mémoire et l'oublie dans la pensée grecque jusqu'à la fin du Ve siècle avant J.-C.* Paris: Le Belles Lettres.

Smith, W. D. 1965. "So-called possession in pre-Christian Greece." *TAPhA* 96:403–426.

Snell, B. 1960. *The Discovery of the Mind: The Greek Origins of the European Thought*. New York: Harper & Row.

Somville, P. 1992. "Le signe d'extase et la musique." *Kernos* 5:173–181.

Sorabji, R. 2000. *Emotion and Peace of Mind, From Stoic Agitation to Christian Temptation*. Oxford: Oxford University Press.

Spentzou, E. 2002. "Secularizing the Muse." In *Cultivating the Muse: Struggles for Power and Inspiration in Classical Literature*, edited by E. Spentzou and D. Fowler, 1–28. Oxford: Oxford University Press.

Sperduti, A. 1950. "The divine nature of poetry in Antiquity." *TAPA* 81:209–240.

Stern-Gillet, S. 2004. "On (mis)interpreting Plato's *Ion*." *Phronesis* 49 (2):169–201.

Sussman, A. 2007. "Mental illness and creativity: A neurological view of the 'tortured artist.'" *Stanford Journal of Neuroscience* 1 (1):21–24.

Tarán, L. and D. Gutas. 2012. *Aristotle, Poetics: Editio Maior of the Greek Text With Historical Introductions and Philological Commentaries*. Leiden: Brill.

Thaut, M. H. and B. L. Wheeler. 2010. "Music therapy." In *Music and Emotion: Theory, Research, Applications*, edited by P.N. Juslin and J.A. Sloboda, 791–817. Oxford: Oxford University Press.

Tigerstedt, E. N. 1970. "Furor poeticus: Poetic inspiration in Greek literature before Democritus and Plato." *Journal of the History of Ideas* 31 (2):163–178.

Tigerstedt, E. N. 1977. *Interpreting Plato*. Stockholm: Almqvist & Wiksell.

Ustinova, Y. 2009a. "Apollo Iatros: A Greek god of Pontic origin." In *Die Griechen und ihre Nachbarn am Nordrand des Schwarzen Meeres*, edited by K. Stähler and D. Metzler, 245–298. Münster: Ugarit-Verlag.

Ustinova, Y. 2009b. *Caves and the Ancient Greek Mind: Descending Underground in the Search for Ultimate Truth*. Oxford: Oxford University Press.

Ustinova, Y. 2012. "Madness into memory: Mania and mnêmê in Greek culture." *SCI* 31:109–132.

van der Ben, N. 1985. *The Charmides of Plato: Problems and Interpretations*. Amsterdam: B.R. Grüner.

van Groningen, B. A. 1948. "Les trois Muses de l'Hélicon." *AC* 17:287–296.

Velardi, R. 1989. *Enthousiasmòs. Possessione rituale e teoria della communicazione poetica in Platone.* Rome: Ed. dell'Ateneo.

Vernant, J.-P. 1983. *Myth and Thought Among the Greeks.* London: Routledge & Kegan Paul.

Vicaire, P. 1963. "Le Grecs et le mystère d'inspiration poétique." *BAGB*:68–85.

Vickers, B. 1973. *Towards Greek Tragedy: Drama, Myth, Society.* London: Longman.

Walde, C. 2000. "Musen." In *Der Neue Pauly* 8:511–512.

Walsh, G. B. 1984. *The Varieties of Enchantment: Early Greek Views of the Nature and Function of Poetry.* Chapel Hill: The University of North Carolina Press.

Watkins, C. 1995. *How to Kill a Dragon: Aspects of Indo-European Poetics.* Oxford: Oxford University Press.

Webster, T.B.L. 1939. "Greek theories of art and literature down to 400 B.C." *CQ* 33:166–179.

West, M. L. 1983. *The Orphic Poems.* Oxford: Oxford University Press.

West, M. L. 1992. *Ancient Greek Music.* Oxford: Oxford University Press.

West, M. L. 2000. "Music therapy in antiquity." In *Music as Medicine: The History of Music Therapy Since Antiquity*, edited by P. Horden, 51–68. Aldershot: Ashgate.

West, M. L. 2007. *Indo-European Poetry and Myth.* Oxford: Oxford University Press.

Wright, M. 2010. "The tragedian as critic: Euripides and early Greek poetics." *JHS* 130:165–184.

7   Erotic *mania*

Erôs is sometimes interpreted as love, which is misleading: it is infatuation, sexual desire bordering on passion, quite distant from the conjugal bonds that are usually based on a much less ardent *philia*.[1] Prodicus, one of the prominent fifth-century thinkers, tried to characterise erôs quantitatively. He defines erôs as 'desire doubled,' and *mania* as 'erôs doubled.'[2] Thus, by definition erôs is immoderate and transient: a passion cannot endure. An excess of erôs can only be *mania*, and there is ample evidence that most Greeks would support this opinion.

Erotic *mania* is one of the main topics of the *Phaedrus*, and its discussion is dramatically broken into two parts: at the beginning, Socrates claims that genuine love is sheer madness. He considers erôs an irrational desire, which overcomes the sane judgment and makes people behave in a manner contrary to their own good and the good of the beloved.[3] Later on, though, in his palinode, Socrates announces that whatever he said against erôs was not true – and praises those types of *mania* that are sent by gods to the humans as blessings.[4] Plato must have had good reasons to portray Socrates as changing his opinion in such a striking fashion. This chapter will begin with Plato's views on erotic *mania*, and proceed to two main questions: What did other Greeks think on this topic, and which components of Socrates' opinion on erôs corresponded to the views held by less eccentric people?

Plato on the erotic *mania*

In the *Phaedrus*, Socrates first listens to his young friend Phaedrus reading the speech composed by the orator Lysias who claimed that true lovers were mad, and that their passion was less desirable than the mild affection of non-lovers:

> They [lovers] confess that they are insane, rather than in their right mind, and that they know they are foolish, but cannot control themselves; and so how could they, when they have come to their senses, think those acts are good which they determined upon in such a condition?[5]

Mad erôs of genuine lovers jeopardises the very foundations of the society, undermining the reliability of the lover as a citizen, argues Lysias. Socrates not only concurs, but adds his own arguments, putting an emphasis on the danger to the individuals, both the lover and the beloved. It is plain that he believes that 'sense and sanity' are contrasted to '*erôs* and *mania*' and 'the lover (*erastês*) is 'necessarily without reason,' while non-lover 'is in possession of his reason.'[6] The images Socrates employs are powerful: *erôs* of an older man in love with a youth is an *oistros*, gadfly's sting, the word used to describe Io's torture.[7] Furthermore, the lover's attraction to *erômenos*, the beloved, is like a wolf's attraction to a lamb, or craving for food to fill one's stomach.[8] Therefore, a boy who does not escape from an *erastês* surrenders to one who is 'faithless, irritable, jealous, and disagreeable, harmful to his property, harmful to his physical condition, and most harmful by far to the cultivation of his soul.'[9]

Till this moment, Socrates was in the grip of the nymphs, mischievous creatures prone to lead people astray.[10] Yet at a certain moment Socrates is depicted as awakened from his enchanted misunderstanding: his *daimonion* gave him a sign, he then heard a voice demanding that he repent, and being a seer (*mantis*), Socrates immediately understood his offence and began a speech of refutation.[11] In Socrates' – and Plato's – view, the *daimonion* has never failed to guide him to the truth, so Socrates' palinode is presented as divinely inspired and absolutely reliable.

He renounces his own words, offers the examples of the god-given *mania* listed in the Introduction, and states his further intentions:

> Let him show in addition that love is not sent from heaven for the advantage of lover and beloved alike, and we will grant him the prize of victory. We, on our part, must prove that such madness [i.e. erotic madness] is given by the gods for our greatest happiness; and our proof will not be believed by the merely clever, but will be accepted by the truly wise.[12]

In contrast to his earlier argument that love means lack of self-control and is therefore a vile sort of madness, in the palinode Socrates strives to demonstrate that *erôs* is divine. If the lover preserves the dignity of the beloved and reveres his beauty and soul, erotic *mania* is a gift from the gods.[13] This self-control was not invented by Socrates, but was actually exercised by virtuous people.[14]

Socrates also argues that the beloved, *erômenos*, becomes an image of the divine for the lover, *erastês*, who thus ends up admiring the eternal and divine, overwhelmed by the elated desire and moved towards the truth.[15] The lover's madness is alluded to in multiple ways: he 'shudders,' overwhelmed by a steam of beauty, 'boils,' while filled with joy in the beloved's presence. His state is constantly changing, his soul palpitating, stung all over. He worships the beloved as a god.[16] The lover is compared to a maenad, and becomes possessed by a god, 'to the extent a mortal can be possessed'; he is 'disturbed' or 'astonished.'[17] In its most refined form, when purified by the tumult of mixed perplexity and fury (*lutta*), the maddened (*emmanês*) soul reaches the greatest delight when it beholds the beauty of the beloved:

> the whole soul, stung in every part, rages with pain; and then again, remembering the beautiful one, it rejoices. So, because of these two mingled sensations, it is greatly troubled by its strange condition; it is perplexed and

maddened, and in its madness it cannot sleep at night or stay in any one place by day, but it is filled with longing and hastens wherever it hopes to see the beautiful one. And when it sees him . . . this pleasure which it enjoys is the sweetest of pleasures at the time.[18]

The overwhelming accumulation of words designating different aspects of painful madness (*oistros, lutta, mania*) leaves no room for doubt as to the complete madness of the lover. However, physical sensations of frenzy such as shuddering, sweat, and heat, allow the soul to mature,[19] and if only it does not indulge its lust, this hierarchy of sensations, all of them different degrees of madness, culminates in an initiation into the true mysteries of *erôs*.[20] Erotic madness leads the lover from the contemplation of beauty to the contemplation of the divine, and is therefore one of the greatest goods for the mortals.[21] This characteristically Platonic leap from madness to revelation and back to reason makes erotic rapture a way to attain transcendent reality.

Finally, Socrates arrives at a dialectic thesis that *erôs* can be both good and evil, depending on its nature. Having put forward the idea of the duality of madness, discussed in the Introduction, Socrates concludes:

> So our two discourses conceived of madness as naturally one principle within us, and one discourse, cutting off the left-hand part, continued to divide this until it found among its parts a sort of left-handed love, which is very justly reviled, but the other discourse, leading us to the right-hand part of madness, found a love having the same name as the first, but divine, which it held up to view and praised as the author of our greatest blessings.[22]

Thus, towards the end of this dialogue Plato has Socrates arrive at a synthesis of his two claims and maintain that there are two forms of *erôs*, and the correct attitude should take into account this duality: human carnal *erôs* puts the lover's virtue to test, while divine *erôs* is the supreme good.[23] Socrates pretends to regard his palinode as 'playful,'[24] but pronounces himself 'a seer (*mantis*), not a very good one, but . . . good enough for my own purposes.'[25] It is one of Plato's 'paradoxes of simultaneous levity and gravity':[26] he treats the point with utter seriousness, and attributes the source of this speech to divine inspiration.

Plato discusses these ideas in the *Republic* and *Symposium*, supposedly predating the *Phaedrus*.[27] In the *Republic* he argues that there is no pleasure more acute and more insane (*manikôtera*) than sexual desire; love is a search of pleasure that drives man beside himself, and in the ideal city is to be restricted to non-physical love only, a pure desire of beauty. As to physical love, self-restraint is the virtue that allows a wise person to curb his passion.[28] The most fundamental experience of beauty, according to Plato, is the pleasure a man takes in seeing a handsome youth, and from this we can infer that aesthetic education in the *Republic* is still focused on the beauty of the male body.[29] In this respect, Socrates' confession in the *Charmides* is most telling: when he caught a glimpse of a beautiful youth's naked body inside his cloak, he was 'on fire and not in his right mind'; however, consumed by desire as a fawn by a lion, Socrates immediately recovered his self-control.[30] Even a wise man's *erôs* is ignited by sight, but the true philosopher, passionate as he may be (and as Plato doubtlessly was himself) is able to master his carnal desire.[31]

Furthermore, moderate and prudent desire can be beneficial for the society. In the *Symposium*, Diotima contends that every *erôs* is a form of longing for immortality. In its most primitive physical form, *erôs* bestows worldly immortality on animals and humans, allowing them to have offspring; a higher form of immortality is eternal fame, for instance that of Achilles and Alcestis; even loftier is the yearning for virtue and justice exemplified by wise lawgivers, such as Lycurgus and Solon.[32] However, the highest form of *erôs* is the love of beauty that is conductive to true immortality,[33] and its essence is initiation into the mystery of the divine:

> When a man by the right method of boy-loving ascends from these particulars and begins to descry that beauty, he is almost able to lay hold of the final secret. . . . From personal beauty he proceeds to beautiful observances, from observance to beautiful learning, and from learning at last to that particular study which is concerned with the beautiful itself and that alone; so that at the end he comes to know the very essence of beauty. In that state of life among all others . . . a man finds it truly worthwhile to live, as he contemplates essential beauty.[34]

This has to be done by proper means, and contemplation of divine beauty allows one to attain supreme virtue, win the friendship of gods and become immortal.[35] In the *Symposium*, the lover's trajectory to the divine by means of revelation through contemplation of beauty is not explicitly defined as madness. It is, however, compared to mystery initiations, and to the philosopher's revelatory route to ultimate truth, experiences that Plato associates with *mania*.[36] The great mystery of love is disclosed to Socrates by Diotima of Mantinea, the seer respected by Zeus.[37] Socrates' conception of *erôs* is clearly different from that of other interlocutors and exalted above their worldly understanding of erotic attraction. Thus, Plato's perspective in the *Symposium* is close to that expressed in the *Phaedrus*:[38] true love is cognate to *mania*, and when experienced correctly and in accordance with virtue, it is the greatest gift allowing mortals to approach immortality and the ultimate knowledge. This great mystery is revealed to the chosen individuals by means of divine inspiration, 'engoddedness' with *erôs*.[39]

As I argue in Chapter 8, in the *Republic* and the *Symposium*, erotic desire for the truth or for the ideal Forms that leads to the birth of virtue or supreme knowledge is a way to designate the mystical state. This is not the moderate self-controlling *orthos erôs* of the educator to the educated, or of a lawgiver to justice, which can hardly be called *mania*, but the overwhelming passion, and the more it transcends the normal human limits, the greater blessing it endows on the person who experiences it.

J. P. Harris looks at the dichotomy 'lover'–'non-lover' from the cognitive viewpoint. In Socrates' initial speech, the lover is represented as ill (*nosein*), meaning of course mental illness, while the non-lover is healthy, in his sound mind (*sôphronein*).[40] There is more in this opposition. If we take into consideration the palinode, the non-lover's sanity is contrasted to two phenomena, both designated as *mania*. The juxtaposition of the two kinds of *mania* discloses the congruity of their nature – both are the absence of conventional reason – and at the same time Socrates argues that the two are profoundly different from each other. Briefly stated, according to Plato's theory of *mania*, derangement and enthusiasm are cognitively the same, but phenomenologically, they belong to different worlds, the mentally sick being sub-human and the engodded super-human.

In sum, Plato sees erotic *mania* as ambiguous. It is a folly when physical lust prevails, since this madness is human, although caused by the god of love. The majority of the humankind who are not initiated into the mysteries of wisdom knows only the erotic *mania* of the vulgar carnal kind, bringing shame and down-right destruction. Erotic *mania* is commended when immaculate, distanced from the corporeal consummation, and aimed at the apprehension of the good and the transcendent. This madness is divine, it leads to a mystical union of the soul with the ideal Forms and brings about the highest knowledge a mortal can attain, but is reserved for the tiny minority of the virtuous and wise.[41] Thus, Socrates expounds his authentic views throughout the *Phaedrus*,[42] but at the beginning of the dialogue he talks about the majority of the humanity, for whom erotic *mania* is an evil; in the palinode he discusses the possibilities open to the select few, and at the end sums up his argument. Convinced that for the majority of humankind true *erôs* was *mania*, toward the end of his life Plato banned it from his ideal state.[43]

Greeks on *erôs* as *mania*

Socrates' initial position in the *Phaedrus*, that *erôs* is sickness and madness, reflects common opinion, unsurprisingly adopted by the down-to-earth Socrates of Xenophon.[44] Sophocles' chorus, a mouthpiece of conventional views, sings to Eros: 'The one that has you is mad.'[45] In Euripides' words, 'to the mortals, *erôs* means madness.'[46] Thus, every person in the grip of Eros is mad, but even madness has its degrees, and some are more mad than others. For instance, Ibycus is characterised as 'the most erotomaniacal about the youths' by Suda, whether because of the profoundness of his passion or because of his general weakness for beautiful boys, which was notorious.[47]

Poets could call passionate love *mania*. Since the Archaic age, love was often thought of as an irresistible force, and poets from the Archaic to the Hellenistic period have complained about the lover's absolute powerlessness.[48] Anacreon is most emphatic, depicting how merely looking at the beloved fills him with desire – and madness: 'I desire Cleoboulus; I am mad about Cleoboulus; I gaze at Cleoboulus.'[49] Theocritus describes falling in love as madness: 'in madness,' his Atalanta hurled herself 'in depth of love,' and even Aphrodite was overcome by *lussa*, rage or fury, when falling in love.[50] Lovesickness may cause another kind of madness, which resembles passive depression and is no less self-destructive than overt frenzy. Infatuated with love, Theocritus' heroine became mad (*emanên*) and depressed to the point of taking to bed and refusing food.[51] Eros strikes one's mind, *phrenes*: Sappho compares his power to 'shake one's mind' to a violent storm that uproots oak trees.[52] Archilochus complains that Eros steals his senses.[53] Thus, desire profoundly shakes one's personality, it is painful, and even if transitory like a tempest, can ruin one's mind.[54]

In the seventh century Alcman called Eros *margos*, 'madman,' while portraying him as a playful child;[55] Theognis said that he had been 'nourished by *maniai*.'[56] Eros is again described as *margos* in the third century by Apollonius of Rhodes, and the scholiast explains that the mischievous god was 'doing follies.'[57] The infantile god is naughty, and his toys, in Anacreon's words, are 'madnesses and confusion.'[58] Eros suddenly takes possession of an individual who was quite sane a moment before, and the burden of desire hurts.[59] In a word, for Anacreon, being in love is synonymous to being mad: 'Again I'm in love and I'm not in love; I'm mad and I'm not mad.'[60]

The most famous Sappho's poem, greatly admired in antiquity, allows a unique glimpse into the subjective feelings of the poet in love.[61] Sappho describes her reaction at seeing the beloved girl with a man:

> . . . such exchange
> makes my heart pound with alarm
> Let me so much as glimpse you, my voice
> fails me completely
> My tongue is broken; a subtle flame
> instantly courses beneath my skin.
> No vision is left in my eyes. A whirring
> fills my ears.
> Cold sweat flows. Trembling
> shakes my entire frame. I grow
> paler than grass and feel as though
> I have nearly died.[62]

This passionate sensation, conveyed 'from the inside,' involves a range of physiological and psychological symptoms, and lasts only when Sappho is observing her beloved. She seems to herself 'almost dead,' and actually numb and blind, completely lacking control of her body, clearly living through a deviation from her baseline state of consciousness. G. Devereux interprets the symptoms described in this poem as a 'text-book case' of anxiety attack. Even if this clinically precise reading of the poem is too literal, the totality of ten symptoms, taken together, clearly creates a picture of extreme anxiety and suffering.[63] This poem is often considered as a template for later authors' descriptions of erotic madness, in particular for Plato and Plutarch.[64] Sappho's influence was so remarkable due to the faithfulness of the image she created to the real-life sensations known to genuine lovers: she succeeded in articulating the indescribable agony of passion.

The nearly crude physicality of Sappho's confession was probably not confined to this particular poem. In the first century AD, the anonymous century author of the tract *On the Sublime*, known as [Pseudo]-Longinus, who cited this poem by Sappho, observed that 'in describing erotic passion, Sappho always uses the feelings that result from it in real life. . . . She is extremely skilful at selecting and combining the most remarkable and intense of these feelings.'[65]

According to the tradition, Sappho committed suicide because of her love for Phaon; Menander described her passion for him as a 'stinging desire,' *oistrôn pothos*,[66] using a word that is very prominent in depictions of madness. In *Prometheus Bound*, Io is stung by a gadfly barb,[67] which is a physical cause of madness. The sting of *oistros*, the gadfly's barb, is irritating – and maddening, in the literal sense of the word. In epic, as well as tragedy, it is synonymous with a sudden attack of frenzy.[68] Oistros, like Mania, appeared in art: on a mid-fifth-century crater Oistros is depicted as a youth with snakes coiling in his hair, maddening the bull who had just killed Dirce. The scene is considered an illustration of Euripides' *Antiope*.[69] Thus, even in drama the pangs of desire could destroy one's mind and bring the lover to death.

Dramatic commotions of mind and body were not reserved to lesbian or female passion only. Menelaus' stuporous depression, when yearning for the recently-eloped Helen, is described by Aeschylus in clinical detail, including anguish, grief, silence, indifference to the surroundings, and depression.[70] Archilochus' agony was no more bearable than that of Sappho, and he believed it to be caused by the gods:

> I lie racked by desire, lifeless. By will of the gods, cruel pains penetrate my bones.[71]

Not only Socrates admitted worshipping the beloved as a god. Anacreon is credited with saying that he did not compose hymns to gods, because his beloved were his gods.[72] Maximus of Tyre maintained that Sappho practiced the same 'art of love' as Socrates, both of them feeling madness because of their love, and falling under the spell of the beauty of their beloved, he of males, she of females. In fact, Sappho compares the happy person seated in front of her beloved to no less than a god.[73]

Tragic poets referred to the madness of passionate love more than once. Love-sick Helen was spitefully dubbed 'mad,' *margos*, by Euripides' Clytaemnestra.[74] *Hippolytus* allows a glimpse into the inner world of a woman desperately in love, and depicts the response of the surrounding people to her behaviour. Phaedra calls her adulterous passion 'madness' several times: 'I am mad, a *daimôn* took possession of me and I fell,' and her nurse describes her as 'out of her mind.'[75] This madness is described as 'pollution of mind'; when Phaedra is still keeping her secret and has done no harm, she says: 'My hands are pure, but some pollution is in my mind.'[76] Love tortures Phaedra, and appears as an illness (*nosos*) or possession to the chorus. In fact, she is asked whether one of the deities inflicting madness, Pan or Hecate or the Corybantes, has seized her.[77]

In *Hippolytus*, being in love is compared to Bacchic possession twice.[78] The chorus likens Heracles' bride Iole to an unyoked filly whom Aphrodite yoked by filling her with love and thus making her a bacchant:[79] a powerful image of a woman in love as both bestial and frenzied. Phaedra wishes to dash through wild woods, chasing a hind.[80] The destructive potential of love may be hinted at here. In fact, Socrates ironically compares the love for a boy to the wolf's love of a lamb, and for Theocritus, Aphrodite's love for Adonis was induced by *lussa*, canine fury.[81] In addition, Phaedra's dream of a maenadic purchase of a beautiful living creature may also refer the awesome Bacchic rite of *sparagmos*, animals being torn apart by the bacchants, discussed in Chapter 3. If it is so, Phaedra's dream is a powerful combination of two images of mad love, as Bacchic possession and as passionate destruction.

In addition to Aphrodite and Eros, Pan was also reputed to enthuse humans with uncontrollable sexual desire,[82] even if usually the deeds of the goatish god were grotesque and suited comedy more than other genres. In *Lysistrata*, the first guess of the Athenians was that the pandemic erection of the Spartans was caused by Pan's naughtiness.[83] Menander located his *Dyscolus* in Phyle, an area sacred to Pan and the nymphs, where Pan struck the young hero with mad (*entheastikôs*) love for a local girl.[84] Even in Theocritus' idyll the ambience is comical: an unsuccessful lover asks Pan to 'bring the boy uninvited into his loving arms' – an ignominious act for a young male, – threatening the god with various misfortunes, such as an itch all over his body, in case he does not heed.[85] Pan himself was notoriously *duserôs*, unlucky in love, and therefore it is no wonder that panic sexual desire could be ridiculous.[86] Semi-bestial and often ithyphallic, the god of shepherds and wild nature who did not shun mating with animals[87] embodied the carnal brutality of sexual drive, free of all human constrains.

The belief that passionate love is similar to *mania* was not confined to poetry. As mentioned above, Prodicus defined 'erôs doubled' as *mania*.[88] Gorgias was convinced that *erôs* was 'a human sickness and mistake (*agnoêma*) of soul.'[89] Lysias defines a whole sequence of outrageous acts committed by a person whose *eromenos* left him as 'madness.' As we have just seen, Plato has this orator deliver a long discourse on damages caused by passionate erotic desire.[90] Xenophon describes a person infatuated with sexual desire to the degree of committing adultery as entirely 'possessed by an evil spirit,' *kakodaimonôn*, which means that he was absolutely mad.[91] Later, Plutarch has one of his characters contend that 'no other passion in the world is attended with more violent grief, more excessive joy, or greater ecstasies and fury,' than *erôs*.[92]

Plutarch also describes a case of erotic madness at a third-century royal court.[93] Antiochus the son of king Seleucus fell in love with his stepmother and was so distressed by his desire that he condemned himself to death by abstaining from food, pretending that he had fallen ill. Yet his physician Erasistratus determined the actual cause of the prince's despair by observing his behaviour. Whenever his beloved came in, he displayed all the signs of suffering listed by Sappho: 'stammering speech, fiery flashes, darkened vision, sudden sweats, irregular palpitations of the heart, and finally, as his soul was taken by storm, helplessness, stupor, and pallor.'[94] The physician persuaded Seleucus to abandon his wife to his son, in order to prevent Antiochus' death, and the two married. Even if the list of symptoms of lovesickness is modelled on Sappho's poem, which was familiar to Plutarch, and the romantic story is embellished with fiction, it is not the authenticity of the episode[95] that is important here, but rather the opinion of Plutarch's Hellenistic sources that unsatisfied love could be fatal, and caused a series of pathologies, from suicidal inclinations to stupor.

How mad were ardent lovers, in the opinion of the Greeks? Euripides' Phaedra is aware of her personality, status, and environment every moment of her suffering; she would prefer to be rid of her self-awareness, but she can only think of one way to attain that: to perish.[96] She also knows that she has a choice: 'We learn the good and know it, but we don't make the effort, some because of laziness, others preferring a different pleasure than virtue.'[97] Furthermore, she compares her passion for Hippolytus to the lust of her mother for the Cretan bull, and understands perfectly well that her love is prohibited.[98] In her agony, Phaedra would not be considered as literally mad by most modern spectators.

The question is whether Phaedra was deranged in the opinion of Euripides' contemporaries. Her behaviour seems to the chorus as possession and illness, but the audience was plainly told that although the passion is difficult to resist, she was conscious of the situation. She made her fateful choice, which was immoral in many respects, fully aware of its implications.[99] Likewise, Medea, talking about all the crimes she committed for the sake of her love, does not claim that she was not aware of their gravity.

The lover is indeed divinely inspired due to the presence of the god inside of him, and being in the state of *entheos* appears out of his wits.[100] This state could fluctuate between a baseline state of soundness when a person in love was aware of the circumstances and could control his or her actions, and most intense experiences like the one described by Sappho. Greek authors who refer to overwhelming erotic desire as *mania* are not to be understood as diagnosing ardent lovers with prolonged delirium. However, for some moments the lovers' state of consciousness deviated from the average, therefore the (relatively) lasting condition of being in love which made such occasions possible was quite naturally dubbed *mania*. In addition, the lovers' behaviour was far from the model of moderation required by the social norms, and madness was defined not only 'from within,' by the person experiencing change in his or her state of consciousness, but rather 'from without,' by the judgmental society.

Finally, calling passionate love *mania* was not a poetic *topos*. Detailed accounts of the mental and physical symptoms experienced by lovers, some of them in the first person, leave no doubt that some Greeks, when in love, experienced certain deviations from the baseline state, and were aware of that. This conclusion is endorsed by observations of modern psychologists on qualitative changes brought about by intense love, such as alteration in the sense of time, sensation of merging with the beloved, and boundlessness.[101]

Blessings of the erotic *mania*?

'Filled with *erôs*,' or possessed by Eros, in the state of *mania*, a person might fail to master his or her will for pleasure. When *erôs* was involved, self-control was doubly important, for one had to be aware of the effects of love-making on the well-being of two persons and their social environments, therefore Greek discourse on sexual desire involved much moralising and discussion of boundaries.[102]

The most famous example of the terrible destructive potential of the erotic desire is of course the Trojan War which followed the reckless actions of Paris and Helen. In Gorgias' *Encomium of Helen*, her erotic passion, combined with persuasion and divine intervention, are presented as an irresistible force.[103] In lyric poetry, *erôs* is often pictured as a devastating storm, a woeful sickness, stealing the joys of life. Ibycus' picture of Eros' power is a good example: 'Eros does not allow me any time of rest; . . . shooting from Cypris with cruel madnesses, dark, unabashed, he forcefully shakes our minds to their very bottom.'[104] This image is contrasted to a pastoral picture of a spring blossom on a vine in an 'untouched garden of maidens,'[105] that is, a place of delightful love games. The devastating passion of real desire, naturally for a boy in Ibycus' case, stands out against the mellow sweetness of the scene focused on girls and inviting heterosexual connotations: *erôs* is maddening, while mild attraction to a maiden – hinting perhaps at marriage – is no more than charming.

In tragedy, passionate love is often devastating.[106] In Sophocles' *Antigone*, Eros is reproached: 'You take just men's minds aside into injustice.'[107] In Euripides' *Hippolitus*, the chorus calls Eros 'tyrant over men,' who is able to throw the mortals into an array of calamities by his arrows.[108] Driven by her passion for Jason, Medea has betrayed her home and committed murders: all that, Jason acknowledges, forced by Eros and his 'unescapable arrows'; the chorus knows that Medea was led from her father's house by 'maddened heart.'[109] Euripides employs twice the schema of an innocent woman struck by a deity with irresistible passion to another person as a punishment, and bringing disaster on herself and other people, first in the fragmentary *Cretans* and later in the *Hippolytus*.[110] In the *Cretans*, after Minos had failed to sacrifice to Poseidon the bull as he had vowed, the vengeful god used his wife Pasiphae as an instrument of revenge, enthusing her with lust for the bull, and bringing shame on the royal house.[111] In *Hippolytus*, Pasiphae's daughter, the queen Phaedra, is struck by Aphrodite with an irresistible desire for her husband's son. The play ends with the suicide of the adulteress, who is in fact a victim of the ruthless goddess of love, and in a terrible catastrophe for the whole royal house.[112]

Excessive passion is pictured as undesirable and destructive not only by tragic authors. Aristotle does not have much to say about erotic *mania* and *erôs* in general, but the passages he has penned, along with those produced by other writers who subscribed to his views, demonstrate that he did not find any positive facets in passionate love.[113] Aristotle lists erotic passion in a matter-of-fact manner together with misfortunes that can cause one to commit suicide, such as poverty and pain.[114] Pseudo-Aristotelian *Problems* catalogue mental pathologies caused by the excess of hot black bile: people in this condition become mad (*manikoi*), amorous (*erotikoi*), easily irascible, or talkative.[115] In the same vein, Pausanias observes that the water of the river allegedly washing away people's *erôs* 'is more valuable to the humankind than great wealth,'[116] meaning that *erôs* is to be purged as a plague.

The love of Candaules for his own wife was in Herodotus' opinion abnormal, and cost the king his life: Candaules fell in love, and as a result of his extravagant passion lost his good judgment, since he was 'doomed to disaster.'[117] The tale demonstrates that even excessive marital love was considered ominous, but passion outside of marriage was even worse. Gorgias, arguing that erotic passion was either a divine compulsion or a human sickness, concludes that it is a misfortune falling upon a helpless person – such as Helen who could not resist her desire for Paris.[118]

Examples of perils brought about by *erôs* for beautiful boys are numerous. Xenophon tells a story of a man who was willing to give his life to save a beautiful boy about to be put to death.[119] A man passionately in love could squander all his property, trying to gain the favours of his beloved, as did a metic who sold all he had and brought the proceeds to Alcibiades.[120] Another ardent lover, in Heraclea in Italy, performed absolutely reckless crimes, including a murder, in order to get the heavily guarded object that his beloved wished to have, and later assassinated the local tyrant, who tried to force himself upon the boy.[121] No wonder that *erôs* doubled was *mania* in Prodicus' opinion, and was compared to insanity by Xenophon.[122] Everyone knew that real *erôs* was madness, and this prevalent opinion was eloquently demonstrated in Plato's *Phaedrus*, by Lysias and (the unreformed) Socrates. Even when the word is used metaphorically, the ability of *erôs* to bring about catastrophe is always in the background: in Socrates' view, every excessive desire, even for food and wine, can be called *erôs*.[123] The desire for excellence or gain was *erôs*, according to Pindar, who remarked that when unattained, it caused 'acute madnesses.'[124] Thus, in Aeschylus' days, an '*erôs* to pillage' could prevail over an army. Thucydides explains that the Athenians decided to launch a military expedition to Sicily against all odds, because an '*erôs* to sail fell upon them.'[125] More than once, Aristophanes uses the word *erôs* and its derivatives to depict extreme, usually destructive passions of his heroes – for peace, litigation, or political success.[126]

Given all the suffering erotic *mania* can cause, does it contain a blessing for a regular mortal? In *Hippolytus*, the chorus of respectable women pleads:

> Eros, Eros, you who distill desire
> Upon the eyes and bring sweet joy
> To the souls of those you war against,
> May you never appear to harm me,
> May you never come in discord.
> For the shafts of fire or the stars are not more powerful
> Than those of Aphrodite which Eros, the son of Zeus,
> Lets fly from his hands.[127]

Similarly, in *Medea* the chorus of women maintains that immoderate *erôs* brings misfortune to men, and prays to 'awesome' (*deina*) Aphrodite to act in temperance.[128] In Euripides' *Stenoboea*, Bellerophon observes that *erôtes* are dual, one leading to Hades, while the other one leads to 'moderation and virtue.'[129] In another Euripidean fragment, a personage wishes to be endowed with *erôs* that does not lead to stupidity.[130] Xenophon says that

> whereas those who are possessed of the other gods have a tendency to be sterner of countenance, more terrifying of voice, and more vehement, those

who are inspired by moderate Eros have a more tender look, subdue their voices to more gentle tones, and assume a supremely noble bearing.[131]

The idea of moderate passion contains a contradiction is terms, and it discloses the deep ambiguity of the Classical Greek attitude to *erôs*, with which various authors wrestled, each in his own way. Euripides and Xenophon maintain that there are two *erôtes*, the hateful passion inducing frenzy and causing catastrophes, and the much-preferred mild desire, which does not produce any disasters. At the beginning of *Phaedrus* Plato's Socrates says that real *erôs* is mad and destructive, and only the lukewarm sexual attraction of non-lovers is tolerable. He removes the contradiction in a radical manner, by claiming that temperate desire is good, but it is not real *erôs*. Prudent *erôs* does not exist.

Passionate love is *mania*, and lack of self-restraint is inherent to it. Because of that reason, Lysias and Socrates in his first speech preferred non-lovers to lovers. Thus, erotic *mania* was usually regarded as a curse, but in contrast to Plato's Socrates, ordinary Greeks were worried not by the physicality of *erôs*, which was quite enjoyable and legitimate, but by its excesses. In Greece, sexual appetite and activity were not problematised per se, but it had to be satisfied in socially acceptable ways: legitimate *erôs* 'aimed at beauty without hubris.'[132] When no socially important human being was harmed (slaves obviously did not count), the elation of erotic desire was ethically neutral or even positive.[133] In contrast, passionate desire out of proper social context was a 'pollution of mind' – if only Euripides knew about Mary Douglas' definition of pollution as 'matter out of place'![134]

Conclusions

The 'bittersweet'[135] *erôs* of Sappho appears to have been regarded by Theognis as well as most other Greeks, as bitter rather than sweet, and in any case dangerous and potentially destructive. Most people doubted that erotic *mania* could be tamed, and opted for less ardent but controllable attraction, siding therefore with Plato's Lysias.[136] For them, *erôs* in moderation was gratifying, while passionate desire threatened individuals and even communities.

Plato considered erotic passion as an excellent example of the ambiguous kinds of *mania*, and had Socrates articulate this idea. Together with his contemporaries who enjoyed love in a respectful fashion, Plato's Socrates thought that a lover had to revere the beloved's soul and body: passion out of control was definitely detrimental to the lover and the beloved. Here Plato parted ways from common thought, suggesting that in a wise person, erotic *mania* in conjunction with ascetic discipline is conductive to a (mystical) union with the divine and therefore a blessing. Very few other people would agree with that.

Not a single lover, possessed as he or she was by Eros, is ever described as delirious:[137] lovers' perception is not compromised, and they are able to discern between good and bad. There is no contrast between the commonsensical Lysias' speech and the conscious understanding of passionate Phaedra: people knew what they were doing when they were 'mad with love.' Erotic *mania* considered as *enthousiasmos*, 'engoddedness,'[138] hushed the voice of mind, but did not take one's wits away completely.

A more general corollary follows: to the Greeks, being in a state of *mania* did not necessarily mean being deranged to the extent of losing perception of reality. Subjective feelings of physical and mental commotion and objective abandon of self-restraint were sufficient to define a state as *mania*.

Notes

1 Konstan (1994: 57, 178); Ludwig (2002: 7–9).
2 Fr. B7 *DK*: ἐπιθυμίαν μὲν διπλασιασθεῖσαν ἔρωτα εἶναι, ἔρωτα δὲ διπλασιασθέντα μανίαν γίγνεσθαι; Dover (1974: 127).
3 *Phdr.* 238C–240.
4 *Phdr.* 244A.
5 *Phdr.* 231D καὶ γὰρ αὐτοὶ ὁμολογοῦσι νοσεῖν μᾶλλον ἢ σωφρονεῖν, καὶ εἰδέναι ὅτι κακῶς φρονοῦσιν, ἀλλ' οὐ δύνασθαι αὑτῶν κρατεῖν· ὥστε πῶς ἂν εὖ φρονήσαντες ταῦτα καλῶς ἔχειν ἡγήσαιντο περὶ ὧν οὕτω διακείμενοι βουλεύονται (translation H. N. Fowler).
   Most modern readers judge this speech as cold, prudent, and rhetoric (Hackforth 1972: 27; Rowe 1986: 144–146; Ferrari 1987: 45–59), but Nussbaum (2002: 66) finds Lysias' position sensible.
6 *Phdr.* 241AC.
7 *Phdr.* 240D; on *oistros* see below in this chapter.
8 *Phdr.* 241D.
9 *Phdr.* 241C, translation H. N. Fowler. A similar stance is taken by Socrates in the *Lysis* 205–206; Dover (1989: 51–52).
10 *Phdr.* 241E; on nympholepsy see Chapter 5.
11 *Phdr.* 242C. On Socrates' *daimonion* see below. For the symbolism of Socrates' words and gestures, in particular his unveiling, in the transition from the first to the second speech, see Cairns (2013: 241–247); Ferrari (1987: 1–59). For an analysis of Socrates multiple 'inspirational sources,' see Capra (2014: 30–33).
12 *Phdr.* 245BC: ἀλλὰ τόδε πρὸς ἐκείνῳ δείξας φερέσθω τὰ νικητήρια, ὡς οὐκ ἐπ' ὠφελίᾳ ὁ ἔρως τῷ ἐρῶντι καὶ τῷ ἐρωμένῳ ἐκ θεῶν ἐπιπέμπεται. ἡμῖν δὲ ἀποδεικτέον αὖ τοὐναντίον, ὡς ἐπ' εὐτυχίᾳ τῇ μεγίστῃ παρὰ θεῶν ἡ τοιαύτη μανία δίδοται· ἡ δὲ δὴ ἀπόδειξις ἔσται δεινοῖς μὲν ἄπιστος, σοφοῖς δὲ πιστή (translation H. N. Fowler).
13 *Phdr.* 252A.
14 Nussbaum (2002: 72), citing the examples of Phaedrus and Pausanias in the *Smp.* 178E–179C; 181AB, Hiero in X. *Hier.* 1. 31–32 and Achilles in Aeschylus' *Myrmidons* (*TGF* 135, 136). In fact, Alcibiades' praises of Socrates' exceptional self-control (*Symp.* 216D–217D, esp. 216E) demonstrates that the great ironist was quite serious on this matter. For an analysis of Socrates' repression of pleasure see Ferrari (1987: 95–102, 110).
15 *Phdr.* 250AB; Calame (1992: 189); Price (1989: 67); Morgan (1990: 174–181).
16 *Phdr.* 251BD.
17 *Phdr.* 253A; 250A; 255B; Rowe (1986: 186).
18 *Phdr.* 251DE: ὥστε πᾶσα κεντουμένη κύκλῳ ἡ ψυχὴ οἰστρᾷ καὶ ὀδυνᾶται, μνήμην δ' αὖ ἔχουσα τοῦ καλοῦ γέγηθεν. ἐκ δὲ ἀμφοτέρων μεμειγμένων ἀδημονεῖ τε τῇ ἀτοπίᾳ τοῦ πάθους καὶ ἀποροῦσα λυττᾷ, καὶ ἐμμανὴς οὖσα οὔτε νυκτὸς δύναται καθεύδειν οὔτε μεθ' ἡμέραν οὗ ἂν ᾖ μένειν, θεῖ δὲ ποθοῦσα ὅπου ἂν οἴηται ὄψεσθαι τὸν ἔχοντα τὸ κάλλος· ἰδοῦσα δὲ . . . ἡδονὴν δ' αὖ ταύτην γλυκυτάτην ἐν τῷ παρόντι καρποῦται (translation W.R.M. Lamb).
19 *Phdr.* 251 B; Ferrari (1987: 151–154).

20 *Phdr.* 253C.
21 *Phdr.* 249DE.
22 *Phdr.* 265E–266A: οὕτω καὶ τὸ τῆς παρανοίας ὡς <ἓν> ἐν ἡμῖν πεφυκὸς εἶδος ἡγησαμένω τὼ λόγω, ὁ μὲν τὸ ἐπ' ἀριστερὰ τεμνόμενος μέρος, πάλιν τοῦτο τέμνων οὐκ ἐπανῆκεν πρὶν ἐν αὐτοῖς ἐφευρὼν ὀνομαζόμενον σκαιόν τινα ἔρωτα ἐλοιδόρησεν μάλ' ἐν δίκῃ, ὁ δ' εἰς τὰ ἐν δεξιᾷ τῆς μανίας ἀγαγὼν ἡμᾶς, ὁμώνυμον μὲν ἐκείνῳ, θεῖον δ' αὖ τινα ἔρωτα ἐφευρὼν καὶ προτεινάμενος ἐπήνεσεν ὡς μεγίστων αἴτιον ἡμῖν ἀγαθῶν (translation H. N. Fowler).
23 *Phdr.* 265E–266A; Rowe (1986: 8); Cairns (2013: 234); Harris (2006).
24 *Phdr.* 265C.
25 *Phdr.* 242C, translation H. N. Fowler; Ferrari (1987: 116).
26 Rhodes (2003: 185) on the *Symposium*.
27 The date of the *Phaedrus* being approximately 370 (Hackforth 1972: 7; Rowe 1986: 14; Morgan 1990: 102, 237). Ledger (1989: 224) suggests ca. 380 for the *Republic* and *Symposium* and ca. 365 for the *Phaedrus*.
28 *R*. 3. 402E–403B.
29 Lear (2006: 115); Nussbaum (2002: 70).
30 *Chrm.* 155D.
31 Price (1989: 223); Gómez Iglesias (2016: 71).
32 *Smp.* 208A–209E.
33 *Smp.* 207A.
34 *Smp.* 211B–D: ὅταν δή τις ἀπὸ τῶνδε διὰ τὸ ὀρθῶς παιδεραστεῖν ἐπανιὼν ἐκεῖνο τὸ καλὸν ἄρχηται καθορᾶν, σχεδὸν ἄν τι ἅπτοιτο τοῦ τέλους . . . καὶ ἀπὸ τῶν καλῶν σωμάτων ἐπὶ τὰ καλὰ ἐπιτηδεύματα, καὶ ἀπὸ τῶν ἐπιτηδευμάτων ἐπὶ τὰ καλὰ μαθήματα, καὶ ἀπὸ τῶν μαθημάτων ἐπ' ἐκεῖνο τὸ μάθημα τελευτῆσαι, ὅ ἐστιν οὐκ ἄλλου ἢ αὐτοῦ ἐκείνου τοῦ καλοῦ μάθημα, καὶ γνῷ αὐτὸ τελευτῶν ὃ ἔστι καλόν. ἐνταῦθα τοῦ βίου . . . εἴπερ που ἄλλοθι, βιωτὸν ἀνθρώπῳ, θεωμένῳ αὐτὸ τὸ καλόν (translation W.R.M. Lamb).
35 *Smp.* 212E.
36 Discussed in Chapter 2.
37 For the name and its meaning see below, Chapter 8.
38 Gooch (1992); Gómez Iglesias (2016).
39 Gómez Iglesias (2016: 95).
40 *Phdr.* 231D; 241A; Harris (2006: 391–395).
41 *Phdr.* 256A; Rowe (1990: 243–244). On the body and its desires as impeding philosophical inquiry see Pl. *Phd.* 65A–66D.
42 For the question whether Socrates was inspired by the Muses and Pan (262D, 263D) throughout his speech or only during its part, see Price (1989: 66); de Vries (1969: ad loc.).
43 *Lg.* 835E–842A, esp. 839A.
44 X. *Mem.* 1. 3. 11, cf. 1. 2. 22; 1. 3. 14.
45 S. *Ant.* 781.
46 Fr. 161 *TGF*: τὸ μαίνεσθαι δ' ἄρ' ἦν ἔρως βροτοῖς.
47 *S.v.* Ibycus: γέγονε δὲ ἐρωτομανέστατος περὶ μειράκια; Ath. 13. 301B.
48 Calame (1992: 14–19).
49 PMG fr. 14: Κλεοβούλου μὲν ἔγωγ' ἐρέω, |Κλεοβούλωι δ' ἐπιμαίνομαι, | Κλεόβουλον δὲ διοσκέω.
50 Theoc. 3. 40–42; 47; 11: 10–11.
51 Theoc. 2. 82; Toohey (2004: 269).
52 Fr. 47 Lobel-Page: Ἔρος δ' ἐτίναξέ μοι φρένας, ὡς ἄνεμος κὰτ ὄρος δρύσιν ἐμπέτων.
53 Fr. 191 West: κλέψας . . . φρένας; Sullivan (1996).
54 Calame (1992: 19); Padel (1992: 88–98).
55 PMG fr. 58 = 147 Calame.
56 Thgn. 1231: Ἔρως, μανίαι σε τιθηνήσαντο.

57 Ap. R. 3. 120: μάργος Ἔρως, with schol.: ὁ μαργαίνειν ποιῶν; Calame (1983: 556).
58 Anacr. *PMG* fr. 53: ἀστραγάλαι δ᾽ Ἔρωτός εἰσιν μανίαι τε καὶ κυδοιμοί. On erotic associations of knucklebones see Calame (1992: 15).
59 Thgn. 1322; 1337; Calame (1992: 16).
60 *PMG* fr. 83: ἐρέω τε δηὖτε κοὐκ ἐρέω, καὶ μαίνομαι κοὐ μαίνομαι.
61 Snyder (1997: 28–29); Hutchinson (2001: 168); D'Angour (2013).
62 Sappho fr. 31 Lobel-Page: τό μ᾽ ἦ μὰν |καρδίαν ἐν στήθεσιν ἐπτόαισεν, |ὡς γὰρ ἔς σ᾽ ἴδω βρόχε᾽ ὥς με φώναι- | σ᾽ οὐδ᾽ ἓν ἔτ᾽ εἴκει, |ἀλλ᾽ ἄκαν μὲν γλῶσσα †ἔαγε λέπτον |δ᾽ αὔτικα χρῶι πῦρ | ὑπαδεδρόμηκεν, |ὀππάτεσσι δ᾽ οὐδ᾽ ἓν ὄρημμ᾽, ἐπιρρόμ- |βεισι δ᾽ ἄκουαι, |†ἔκαδε μ᾽ ἴδρως ψῦχρος κακχέεται† τρόμος δὲ |παῖσαν ἄγρει, χλωροτέρα δὲ ποίας |ἔμμι, τεθνάκην δ᾽ ὀλίγω 'πιδεύης |φαίνομ᾽ ἔμ᾽ αὔται· |ἀλλὰ πὰν τόλματον ἐπεὶ †καὶ πένητα† (translation D. Mulroy).
    J.M. Snyder renders χλωροτέρα as 'more moist'; Hutchinson (2001: 175) holds that the adjective connotes pallor.
63 Devereux (1970).
64 Plato in the *Phaedrus* (251A–253A), discussed by Pender (2011: 339). Plutarch mentions this poem twice, in *Mor.* 81A and 763A.
65 *De subl.* 10, translation D. Mulroy.
66 οἰστρῶντι πόθῳ ῥῖψαι πέτρας, fr. 258 Körte-Thierfelder; for this story see Compton (2006: 103–104); Lefkowitz (2012: 43); Kivilo (2010: 179–182).
67 A. *PV* 877–879: 'Once again convulsive pain and frenzy, smiting my brain, inflame me. I am stung by the gadfly's barb, unforged by fire' (ὑπό μ᾽ αὖ σφάκελος καὶ φρενοπλῆγες μανίαι θάλπουσ᾽, οἴστρου δ᾽ ἄρδις χρίει μ᾽ ἄπυρος, translation H. W. Smyth); *PV* 589; *Supp.* 308.
68 Hom. *Od.* 22. 300; Padel (1992: 120–121); Padel (1995: 14–17).
69 Trendall (1989: 91, fig. 211).
70 A. *Ag.* 410–419; Devereux (1968).
71 Fr. 193 West: δύστηνος ἔγκειμαι πόθωι, |ἄψυχος, χαλεπῆισι θεῶν ὀδύνηισιν ἕκητι | πεπαρμένος δι᾽ ὀστέων (translation D. Murloy).
72 Schol. Pind. *Isthm.* 2. 1.
73 *Diss.* 24. 37; 24. 18; Sappho fr. 31 Lobel-Page.
74 E. *El.* 1027.
75 E. *Hipp.* 241: ἐμάνην, ἔπεσον δαίμονος ἄτηι; 239: παρακόπτει φρένας; cf. 248, 232.
76 E. *Hipp.* 317: χεῖρες μὲν ἁγναί, φρὴν δ᾽ ἔχει μίασμά τι.
77 E. *Hipp.* 141–144, 223, 269.
78 Calame (1992: 148–149).
79 E. *Hipp.* 545–554.
80 E. *Hipp.* 215–222.
81 *Phdr.* 241D; Theoc. 3. 47.
82 Borgeaud (1988: 85). On the association of Pan with Aphrodite in ritual and art see Borgeaud (1988: 75).
83 Ar. *Lys.* 998.
84 Men. *Dysc.* 44.
85 Theoc. 7. 103: ἄκλητον τήνοιο φίλας ἐς χεῖρας ἐρείσαις (translation J. Redfield in Borgeaud 1988: 68).
86 Borgeaud (1988: 77).
87 Borgeaud (1988: 80).
88 Fr. B7 *DK*; Dover (1974: 127).
89 *Hel.* 19.
90 Lys. 3. 7; the context allows to take the word *mania* as an exaggeration aiming to persuade the jury; Pl. *Phdr.* 230E–234C, which was perhaps based on Lysias' own views (Yunis 2011: 98).
91 X. *Mem.* 1. 2. 5.

92 Plu. *Mor.* 623C: οὔτε μείζονας ἐκστάσεις καὶ παραφροσύνας.
93 Plu. *Demetr.* 38.
94 Plu. *Demetr.* 38. 4, translation B. Perrin.
95 Amantini, Carena, and Manfredini (1995: 360); Vatin (1970: 86); Toohey (2004: 270) opt for its historicity; Wellmann (1907: 333) doubts it. The image of frustrated lover became a *topos* and was amply used by the ancient novelists, such as Chariton, Xenophon of Ephesus and Heliodorus, and in later poetry, for instance in Apollonius' *Argonautica* (3. 284–298; 755–765): Toohey (2004: 273–276).
96 E. *Hipp.* 248–249, 'it is best to die unaware': ἀλλὰ κρατεῖ μὴ γιγνώσκοντ᾽ ἀπολέσθαι.
97 E. *Hipp.* 380–381: τὰ χρήστ᾽ ἐπιστάμεσθα καὶ γιγνώσκομεν, |οὐκ ἐκπονοῦμεν δ᾽, οἱ μὲν ἀργίας ὕπο, | οἱ δ᾽ ἡδονὴν προθέντες ἀντὶ τοῦ καλοῦ | ἄλλην τιν᾽.
98 E. *Hipp.* 337–338.
99 Knox (1983); Sourvinou-Inwood (1997: 181–182). For Phaedra's inner struggle see: Gill (1990).
100 Price (1989: 64).
101 Cardeña (2011: 280, 289).
102 Nussbaum (2002).
103 *Hel.* 21–22; Helen's sins did not contradict – or perhaps even reinforced – the belief in her divinity, emphasised by Isocrates (*Hel.* 63; Capra (2014): 65–69).
104 *PMG* fr. 5, ἐμοὶ δ᾽ ἔρος . . . |οὐδεμίαν κατάκοιτος ὤραν. . . . |αἴσσων παρὰ Κύπριδος ἀζαλέ | αις μανίαισιν ἐρεμνὸς ἀθαμβὴς | ἐγκρατέως πεδόθεν φυλάσσει | ἡμετέρας φρένας. For a commentary on this fragment, see Cazzatto (2013).
105 Παρθένων κῆπος ἀκήρατος.
106 Thumiger (2013: 30–31).
107 S. *Ant.* 791–792: σὺ καὶ δικαίων ἀδίκους φρένας παρασπᾶς ἐπὶ λώβᾳ.
108 E. *Hipp.* 525–564.
109 E. *Med.* 434: μαινομένᾳ καρδίᾳ.
110 Zeitlin (1985); Sourvinou-Inwood (1997: 178–180).
111 Fr. 471–472 *TGF*, esp. Pasiphae's monologue in fr. 472e.
112 In an earlier version of the play, known from its fragments, Euripides made Phaedra a shameless seductress who acted of her own will, *TGF* fr. 428–447.
113 Price (1989: 236–249).
114 Arist. *EN* 116a12.
115 *Pr.* 30. 1; 954a52.
116 Paus. 7. 23. 3.
117 Hdt. 1. 8.
118 *Hel.* 19.
119 X. *Anab.* 7. 4. 7–11.
120 Plu. *Alc.* 5.
121 Phanias of Eresus, *FHG* fr. 16; cf. Arist. *EE* 1229a20 on the reckless bravery of lovers.
122 Fr. B7 *DK*; X. *Mem.* 3. 9. 7.
123 Pl. *Phdr.* 238AC.
124 Pi. *N.* 11. 49.
125 A. *A.* 341; Th. 6. 24. On *erôs* in Thucydides and in political discourse see Ludwig (2002, esp. 121–169). *Erôs* for military success occurs elsewhere in drama (E. *IA* 808–809) and in public speeches: Isoc. 10. 52; cf. Hornblower (1991–2008: 3: 361).
126 Ar. *Ach.* 22; *V.* 89; *Eq.* 732; Robson (2013).
127 E. *Hipp.* 525–532: Ἔρως Ἔρως, ὁ κατ᾽ ὀμμάτων | στάζων πόθον, εἰσάγων γλυκεῖαν | ψυχᾷ χάριν οὓς ἐπιστρατεύσηι, | μή μοί ποτε σὺν κακῶι φανείης | μηδ᾽ ἄρρυθμος ἔλθοις. | οὔτε γὰρ πυρὸς οὔτ᾽ ἄστρων ὑπέρτερον βέλος | οἷον τὸ τᾶς Ἀφροδίτας ἵησιν ἐκ χερῶν | Ἔρως ὁ Διὸς παῖς (translation J. Morwood).
128 E. *Med.* 627–642.
129 εἰς τὸ σῶφρον ἐπ᾽ ἀρετήν, fr. 661 *TGF*.

130 οὐκ εἰς τὸ μῶρον . . . τρέπων, fr. 331 *TGF*.
131 X. Smp. 1. 9. 10: οἱ μὲν ἐξ ἄλλων πρὸς τὸ γοργότεροί τε ὁρᾶσθαι καὶ φοβερώτερον φθέγγεσθαι καὶ σφοδρότεροι εἶναι φέρονται, οἱ δ᾿ ὑπὸ τοῦ σώφρονος ἔρωτος ἔνθεοι τά τε ὄμματα φιλοφρονεστέρως ἔχουσι καὶ τὴν φωνὴν πραοτέραν ποιοῦνται καὶ τὰ σχήματα εἰς τὸ ἐλευθεριώτερον ἄγουσιν (translation O.J. Todd, modified).
132 Democrit. fr. B73 *DK*; Aeschin. 1. 136; Dover (1974: 205–206).
133 Nussbaum (2002: 58–65).
134 E. *Hipp.* 317 cited above; Douglas (1966).
135 Sappho: γλυκύπικρος, fr. 130 Lobel-Page, cf. 'bitter and sweet,' πικρὸς καὶ γλυκύς in Thgn. 1353; Calame (1992: 16).
136 As did Epicurus, and to a certain extent the Stoics, Nussbaum (2002: 73–80).
137 The word is applied quite often, e.g. by Goff (1990: passim).
138 To cite G. Gordon: 'eros signals the divine' (Gordon 2012: 6).

References

Amantini, L. S., C. Carena, and M. Manfredini. 1995. *Plutarco. Le vite di Demetrio e di Antonio.* Milan: Biblioteca Universale Rizzoli.

Borgeaud, P. 1988. *The Cult of Pan in Ancient Greece.* Chicago-London: The University of Chicago Press.

Cairns, D. 2013. "The imagery of erôs in Plato's Phaedrus." In *Erôs in Ancient Greece*, edited by E. Sanders, C. Thumiger, C. Carey, and N. J. Lowe, 233–250. Oxford: Oxford University Press.

Calame, C. 1983. *Alcman. Introduction, texte critique, témoignages, traduction et commentaire.* Rome: Edizioni dell'Ateneo.

Calame, C. 1992. *The Poetics of Eros in Ancient Greece.* Princeton: Princeton University Press.

Capra, A. 2014. *Plato's Four Muses: The Phaedrus and the Poetics of Philosophy.* Washington, DC: Center for Hellenic Studies.

Cardeña, E. 2011. "Altered consciousness in emotions and psychopathology." In *Altering Consciousness: Multidisciplinary Perspectives*, edited by E. Cardeña and M. Winkelman, vol. 2, 279–300. Santa Barbara: Praeger.

Cazzatto, V. 2013. "Words of erôs in Ibycus Fragment 286 (PMGF)." In *Erôs in Ancient Greece*, edited by E. Sanders, C. Thumiger, C. Carey, and N. J. Lowe, 266–276. Oxford: Oxford University Press.

Compton, T. M. 2006. *Victim of the Muses: Poet as Scapegoat, Warrior and Hero in Greco-Roman and Indo-European Myth and History.* Washington, DC: Center for Hellenic Studies.

D'Angour, A. 2013. "Love's battlefield: Rethinking Sappho fragment 31." In *Erôs in Ancient Greece*, edited by E. Sanders, C. Thumiger, C. Carey and N. J. Lowe, 59–71. Oxford: Oxford University Press.

Devereux, G. 1968. "L'état dépressive et le rêve de Ménélas (A. Ag. 410–19)." *RÉG* 81:xii–xv.

Devereux, G. 1970. "The nature of Sappho's seizure in Fr. 31 LP as evidence of her inversion." *CQ* 20:17–31.

de Vries, G. J. 1969. *A Commentary on the Phaedrus of Plato.* Amsterdam: Hakkert.

Douglas, M. 1966. *Purity and Danger: An Analysis of Concepts of Pollution and Taboo.* London: Routledge & Kegan Paul.

Dover, K. J. 1974. *Greek Popular Morality in the Time of Plato and Aristotle.* Oxford: Clarendon Press.

Dover, K. J. 1989. *Greek Homosexuality*. Cambridge, MA: Harvard University Press.

Ferrari, G.R.F. 1987. *Listening to the Cicadas: A Study in Plato's Phaedrus*. Cambridge: Cambridge University Press.

Gill, C. 1990. "The articulation of the self in Euripides' *Hippolytus*." In *Euripides, Women, and Sexuality*, edited by A. Powell, 76–107. London: Routledge.

Goff, B. E. 1990. *The Noose of Words: Readings of Desire, Violence, and Language in Euripides' Hippolytus*. Cambridge: Cambridge University Press.

Gómez Iglesias, M. R. 2016. "The echoes of Eleusis: Love and initiation in the Platonic philosophy." In *Greek Philosophy and Mystery Cults*, edited by M. J. Martín-Velasco and M. J. García Blanco, 61–102. Newcastle upon Tyne: Cambridge Scholars Publishing.

Gooch, P. W. 1992. "Has Plato changed Socrates' heart in the *Phaedrus*?" In *Understanding the Phaedrus: Proceedings of the II Symposium Platonicum*, edited by L. Rossetti, 309–312. Sankt Augustin: Academia.

Gordon, J. 2012. *Plato's Erotic World: From Cosmic Origins to Human Death*. Cambridge: Cambridge University Press.

Hackforth, R. 1972. *Plato's Phaedrus: Translated With an Introduction and Commentary*. Cambridge: Cambridge University Press.

Harris, J. P. 2006. "Divine madness and human sanity in Plato's *Phaedrus*." *Mouseion* 6:387–406.

Hornblower, S. 1991–2008. *A Commentary on Thucydides*. Oxford: Oxford University Press.

Hutchinson, G. O. 2001. *Greek Lyric Poetry: A Commentary on Selected Larger Pieces*. Oxford: Oxford University Press.

Kivilo, M. 2010. *Early Greek Poets' Lives: The Shaping of the Tradition*. Leiden: Brill.

Knox, B.M.W. 1983. "The *Hippolytus* of Euripides." In *Oxford Readings in Greek Tragedy*, edited by E. Segal, 311–331. Oxford: Oxford University Press.

Konstan, D. 1994. *Sexual Symmetry: Love in the Ancient Novel and Related Genres*. Princeton: Princeton University Press.

Lear, G. R. 2006. "Plato on learning to love beauty." In *The Blackwell Guide to Plato's Republic*, edited by G. Santas. Malden: Blackwell.

Ledger, G. R. 1989. *Re-counting Plato: A Computer Analysis of Plato's Style*. Oxford: Oxford University Press.

Lefkowitz, M. R. 2012. *The Lives of the Greek Poets*. Baltimore: Johns Hopkins University Press.

Ludwig, P. W. 2002. *Eros and Polis: Desire and Community in Greek Political Theory*. Cambridge: Cambridge University Press.

Morgan, M. L. 1990. *Platonic Piety: Philosophy and Ritual in Fourth-Century Athens*. New Haven: Yale University Press.

Nussbaum, M. C. 2002. "Eros and ethic norms: Philosophers respond to a cultural dilemma." In *The Sleep of Reason: Erotic Experience and Sexual Ethics in Ancient Greece and Rome*, edited by M. C. Nussbaum and J. Sihvola, 55–94. Chicago: The University of Chicago Press.

Padel, R. 1992. *In and Out of the Mind: Greek Images of the Tragic Self*. Princeton: Princeton University Press.

Padel, R. 1995. *Whom Gods Destroy: Elements of Greek and Tragic Madness*. Princeton: Princeton University Press.

Pender, E. 2011. "A transfer of energy: Lyric eros in Phaedrus." In *Plato and the Poets*, edited by P. Destrée and F.-G. Herrmann, 327–348. Leiden: Brill.

Price, A. W. 1989. *Love and Friendship in Plato and Aristotle*. Oxford: Oxford University Press.

Rhodes, J. M. 2003. *Eros, Wisdom, and Silence: Plato's Erotic Dialogues*. Columbia: University of Missouri Press.

Robson, J. 2013. "The language(s) of love in Aristophanes." In *Erôs in Ancient Greece*, edited by E. Sanders, C. Thumiger, C. Carey, and N. J. Lowe, 251–266. Oxford: Oxford University Press.

Rowe, C. J. 1986. *Plato: Phaedrus, Edited With Translation and Commentary*. Warminster: Aris & Phillips.

Rowe, C. J. 1990. "Philosophy, love, and madness." In *The Person and the Human Mind*, edited by C. Gill, 227–246. Oxford: Oxford University Press.

Snyder, J. M. 1997. *Lesbian Desire in the Lyrics of Sappho*. New York: Columbia University Press.

Sourvinou-Inwood, C. 1997. "Tragedy and religion: Constructs and readings." In *Greek Tragedy and the Historian*, edited by C.B.P. Pelling, 161–186. Oxford: Oxford University Press.

Sullivan, S. D. 1996. "Disturbances of the mind and heart in early Greek poetry." *AC* 65:31–51.

Thumiger, C. 2013. "Mad erôs and eroticised madness in tragedy." In *Erôs in Ancient Greece*, edited by E. Sanders, C. Thumiger, C. Carey, and N. J. Lowe, 27–40. Oxford: Oxford University Press.

Toohey, P. 2004. *Melancholy, Love, and Time: Boundaries of the Self in Ancient Literature*. Ann Arbor: University of Michigan Press.

Trendall, A. D. 1989. *Red Figure Vases of South Italy and Sicily*. London: Thames & Hudson.

Vatin, C. 1970. *Recherches sur le mariage et la condition de la femme mariée à l'époque hellénistique*. Paris: de Boccard.

Wellmann, M. 1907. "Erasistratos 2." In *RE* 6:333–350.

Yunis, H. 2011. *Plato: Phaedrus*. Cambridge: Cambridge University Press.

Zeitlin, F. I. 1985. "The power of Aphrodite: Eros and the boundaries of the self in the *Hippolytus*." In *Directions in Euripidean Criticism*, edited by P. Burian, 52–111. Durham, NC: Duke University Press.

8 The philosopher's *mania* and his path to truth

Many modern scholars tend to disregard the importance of alterations of consciousness within the activities of ancient thinkers on the simple grounds that their doctrines contained brilliant insights that were formulated in discursive form. While ecstatic activities of some Archaic sages, such as Epimenides or Hermotimus, who are not considered philosophers *sensu stricto*, are recognised, beginning from Pythagoras the very existence of such activities is contested. Parmenides and Empedocles are nowadays in the centre of controversy: some argue that their path to the truth comprised mystical revelations, whereas others regard their allusions to soul journeys as metaphors. Alterations of consciousness experienced by Plato and Socrates remain an almost embarrassing subject, and the evidence attesting to such experiences of the two great thinkers is usually either suppressed, or interpreted as figures of speech.[1] In this chapter, I will examine Socrates' and Plato's association of the search for ultimate truth with *mania*, and review evidence regarding earlier thinkers whose philosophic activities may have involved alterations of consciousness.

To do justice to unreason, no rationalist needs to change sides.[2] As I have already argued elsewhere,[3] there is no intrinsic contradiction between rational deliberate discourse and spontaneous flashes of illumination or inspiration. Among modern philosophers and scientists, more than a few arrived at their seminal ideas in dreams or trance-like reveries. The life of René Descartes, considered the founder of modern philosophy, provides a good example: many of the great philosopher's fundamental ideas emerged first in his dreams, and only later were rendered in distinct logical form.[4] C. F. Gauss, one of the most influential mathematicians in history, gives an account of his years of unsuccessful attempts at proving a theorem:

> Finally, two days ago, I succeeded, not on account on my painful efforts, but by the grace of God. Like a sudden flash of lightning, the riddle happened to be solved. I myself cannot say what was the conducting thread which connected what I previously knew with what made my success possible.[5]

Srinivasa Ramanujan, a mathematical genius of almost supernatural abilities, born in India in the late nineteenth century and later active in Cambridge, explained that 'the fully formed equations were whispered to him in dreams' by the presiding goddess of his native village.[6] O. Loewi, awarded the Nobel Prize for his new concept of brain activity, was struck by the revolutionary idea of chemical transmission while sleeping.[7] D. I. Mendeleyev, the prominent Russian chemist who formulated in 1869 the periodic classification of the elements, first saw his famous table in a dream.[8] Another chemist, A. Kekulé, devised a structural formula for the benzene molecule when he was dozing in front of a fireplace.[9]

J. Hadamard, a prominent mathematician, devoted a book to the *Psychology of Invention in the Mathematical Field*. Having surveyed a hundred leading mathematicians and physicists at about 1900, he arrived at the conclusion that not only he, but other colleagues as well, regarded their solutions as resulting from sudden spontaneous insights.[10] In the most fascinating cases of intuition, the scientist remains unaware of his mind's concentration on a certain problem, and the solution is perceived as illumination coming from the outside, rather than inside of his or her mind. In the words of J. Hadamard,

> we must admit that some parts of the mental process develop so deeply in the unconscious that some parts of it, even important ones, remain hidden from our conscious self. We come very near the phenomena of dual personality such as were observed by psychologists of the nineteenth century.[11]

J. Hadamard also demonstrated that the illumination is usually preceded by 'an incubation stage' and followed by later conscious work.[12]

This sequence of stages in the creative process is not limited to mathematics and physics. Paul Cézanne's describes his artistic endeavour by writing that 'A tender excitement grips me. . . . A sort of liberation. The radiation of the soul, the vision, the mysterious becoming external, reciprocal action between the earth and the sun, the ideal and the real, the colours.'[13] Both Cézanne and Albert Einstein sought the concentration in the quietness of the mind leading to the spark of intuition.[14] It is the thesis of H. Rugg that 'the true locus of the creative imagination is the border state that marks off the conscious from the non-conscious,' which he labels 'transliminal mind.'[15]

Thus, the creative process starts with a perceived difficulty and its definition; suggested solutions may surface under any circumstances, including daydreaming and sudden inexplicable insight; these suggestions are to be developed by reasoning and accepted or rejected as a result of further observation.[16] C. G. Hempel argues that even in modern science, a hypothesis may be freely invented and can come from the most unexpected sources, including mystic inspiration; scientific objectivity is safeguarded by subsequent scrutiny of the proposed ideas.[17] The distinction between 'context of discovery' and 'context of justification' profoundly influenced the discussion of discovery in the twentieth century. This distinction is quite complex, and the emphasis is put on the way an idea or theory is conceived – 'the eureka moment' – and the process of validation of the idea and its logical and experimental support.[18] Karl Popper maintains that 'the act of conceiving or inventing a theory' is not susceptible to logical analysis:

The question how it happens that a new idea occurs to a man – whether it is a musical theme, a dramatic conflict, or a scientific theory – may be of great interest to empirical psychology; but it is irrelevant to the logical analysis of scientific knowledge.[19]

The question how Greek thinkers arrived at their ideas, what they thought about this process, and what their contemporaries thought is 'of great interest' to the students of Greek culture. The distinction between 'context of discovery' and 'context of justification' demonstrates that there is no conflict between revelation or illumination, even when attributed to a deity, and logical deliberation.

Socrates' *mania*

On several occasions, Plato has Socrates compare his search for ultimate knowledge to *mania*. This point is most clear in the *Symposium*: Alcibiades remarks that all those present at the banquet 'partook in the philosopher's *mania* and *bakcheia*' (Bacchic ecstasy), stressing that they are initiated – as opposed to servants and other people who are 'vulgar and ignorant.'[20] The route to pure knowledge is via initiation; this idea is exquisitely elaborated by Diotima, and has already been discussed.[21] Alcibiades' words are neither a joke of a drunken reveller, nor just a metaphor, juxtaposing the acquisition of telestic and philosophic wisdom. Plato asserts that both kinds of wisdom, the telestic and the philosophic, are attained as revelation, rather than by rational deliberation or learning.

Plato took this point so seriously that he had Socrates put it forward himself. In the *Phaedo* and *Phaedrus*, Socrates refers to philosopher's *mania* both implicitly and explicitly. In the *Phaedo*, the idea that the ascetic knowledge attained by the philosopher's soul is a form of preparation for the otherworldly bliss[22] brings together philosophic inquiry and the wisdom attained in mystery rites. He says:

> For as they say concerning mystery rites, many bear the Bacchic rod, but few are bacchants (*bakchoi*), and the latter are, in my opinion, those who have practiced philosophy aright. And in my life, I have left nothing undone, but made every effort to become one of them.[23]

This passage associates philosophy with *bakcheia*, that is, rites with a pronounced ecstatic element. It is a part of a longer passage discussing mysteries in general, but if Plato meant indefinite 'devotees' or 'initiates'[24] he could have used the word *mustai*; instead, he insists on the realm of Dionysus, indicating that by his choice of two terms distinctly belonging to the realm of the god's ecstatic rites, *bakchoi* and 'bearers of Bacchic rods.'

Plato's Socrates speaks on the basis of his personal knowledge, emphasised by his awareness of the imperative necessity to experience correctly the state of *bakcheia* which we can interpret as alteration of consciousness. He declares that throughout his life he strove to become one of the true philosophers, who are true *bakchoi*, which means that in addition to pursuing wisdom and virtue mentioned by Socrates earlier, he attempted to manipulate his consciousness in a correct manner. The stage in the *Phaedo* is the opposite of the joyful symposium where Alcibiades spoke of the philosopher's *bakcheia*: this is Socrates' last conversation with friends who are philosophers themselves. On the threshold of his imminent death Socrates spoke earnestly.[25]

It is important to determine what kind of ecstasy Plato's Alcibiades and Socrates meant when they referred to the philosopher's *bakcheia*. This word does not necessarily imply frenzy: self-abandonment to the god could be quiet and internal. We will see shortly that this was Socrates' own experience, and testimonies by other authors suggest this interpretation, as well. In Herodotus' view, 'Orphic and Bacchic' observances were actually 'Egyptian and Pythagorean':[26] even if inaccurate, this comparison implies that 'Orphic and Bacchic' rites were not necessarily frenetic, and that the 'Pythagorean' practices resembled mystery rites. Euripides associates Hippolytus' peculiar way of life and 'playing *bakchos*' with Orpheus:[27] here again, the emphasis is on Hippolytus' efforts at distancing himself from most people, rather than his participation in wild rites.[28] Golden leaves discovered in Italy, Thessaly, and Crete, containing instructions to initiates into mysteries and featuring the word *bakchos*, appear to belong to a milieu of similar people, deeply convinced that their destiny is unique: in Chapter 2 I argue that they probably experienced alterations of consciousness, but hardly in a frenzied manner. Thus, Socratic *bakcheia* did not have to be turbulent: solitary manipulation of consciousness and self-cultivation in a narrow circle of co-practitioners was sufficient to define a person as *bakchos*.

Furthermore, the main subject of the *Phaedo* is welcoming death which liberates the soul from the bonds of the body and allows its union with the divine: practicing for death is 'training for immortality.'[29] Socrates argues that the sustenance of the body and its desires hinders the pursuit of the truth, and that even when people turn to philosophy,

> if pure knowledge is impossible while the body is with us, one of two things must follow, either it cannot be acquired at all or only when we are dead; for then the soul will be by itself apart from the body, but not before. And while we live, we shall, I think, be nearest to knowledge when we avoid, so far as possible, intercourse and communion with the body.[30]

The route to approaching 'reality' is by silencing the senses and letting the soul be 'alone by itself as far as possible and taking leave of the body'; the philosopher's soul therefore is to 'despise the body and run away from it.'[31] The philosopher's withdrawal, *chôrismos*, was 'a mystical discipline of spiritual ascent,'[32] rather than mere asceticism. Socrates expertly describes out-of-body ecstatic experiences that involve the sensation of one's mind leaving the body and mingling with the eternal reality:

> And does not the purification consist in this which has been mentioned long ago in our discourse, in separating, as far as possible, the soul from the body

and teaching the soul the habit of collecting and bringing itself together from all the parts of the body, and living, so far as it can, both now and hereafter, alone by itself, freed from the body as from fetters?[33]

Learning the technique of separation from the body and concentration of the soul is a long process that requires training and practice. Below I will discuss the out-of-body experiences of Archaic sages: Socrates was probably referring to this ancient tradition, and defined its adepts as *bakchoi* who practiced philosophy in the correct manner.[34] This 'practice of mental withdrawal and concentration' was in E. R. Dodds' eyes the true Platonic or Socratic mysticism.[35]

Earlier in the *Phaedo*, separation of body and soul is defined as the essence of the death.[36] As I have already argued, alteration of consciousness accompanied at times by an out-of-body feeling and intended to serve as a rehearsal of death, constituted the core of the major Greek mystery initiations. This experience was beyond doubt familiar to almost every Athenian. It is clear that Socrates and Plato were quite aware of the gap between experiences of *mustai* and philosophers, on the one hand, and normal cognition based on sensory perception, on the other. This awareness is demonstrated by the association of the philosopher's *chôrismos* with altered states of consciousness experienced during mystery rites, in particular, of Dionysus. Thus, when Alcibiades spoke, as Socrates' devoted and well-informed follower, of 'the philosopher's *mania* and *bakcheia*,' he was quite serious.

In the *Phaedrus*, Plato has Socrates explain one of his main tenets. In the distant past, when blameless and unencumbered by the body, the soul was able to see 'the blessed sight and vision of the most blessed of the mysteries, . . . the sight of simple and calm and happy apparitions.'[37] In contrast, when the soul is entombed in the body, 'by means of inaccurate organs of sense, only a few, and with difficulty' succeed in catching a glimpse of the divine perfection.[38] Presently, according to Socrates, the only mortal who is able to attain the divine, 'the real being,' is the philosopher. Through the recollection, *anamnêsis*, of the pure essence of reality,[39] the limits of human knowledge are transcended: it is a revelation, an escape from the temporal and reunification with the divine.[40]

Plato asserts a striking contrast between the inner contents of *anamnêsis* and the visible bizarre behaviour of the one who experiences it. Socrates says that those few who are able to recognise in this world the visions that they preserve as the memory of the divine reality, are stricken with astonishment and 'no longer aware of themselves.'[41] Most notably, he is aware of the fact that the philosopher, who alone is able to attain the divine essence of things, appears to the multitude, all those who are unable to recognise his godly inspiration, to be 'disturbed' and 'possessed.'[42] Thus, in the *Phaedrus* Socrates states that the core of the divine truth is the soul's recollection of its divine essence, and it is attained in a process that is the philosopher's initiation, by means of *mania*.[43] Plato makes his readers understand that the philosopher's *mania* has two faces, and is experienced in a different way by the philosopher and his surroundings: to uninitiated observers, it appears as sheer madness, while the philosopher himself perceives it as *bakcheia*, an alteration of consciousness leading to revelation. This revelation, interpreted as a recollection of the ideal Forms seen by the philosopher's soul in the past life, is to be checked by reason, and reason alone cannot lead to the transcendental reality; therefore both the philosopher's *mania* and reason are necessary preconditions for his perception of truth.[44]

Socrates is described as subject to a strange condition that attracted general attention.[45] In Plato's *Symposium* two occurrences of this condition are related in detail. The first one had occurred when Socrates, fresh from the bath and accompanied by an acquaintance on his way to a dinner party, remained behind his companion, absorbed in his thoughts, and was found standing in the porch of his host's neighbour. A friend who knew Socrates' ways asked not to disturb him: 'Let him alone; it is a habit he has. Occasionally he turns aside, anywhere at random, and there he stands.' Socrates joined the dinner when the others were half-way through it.[46] Another occurrence happened much earlier, during the siege of Potidaea in 432, and was recalled by Alcibiades: there Socrates became immersed in resolving some problem, and remained motionless on the same spot in the camp during a day and a night.[47] Centuries later Aulus Gellius added an interesting detail concerning this vigil: Socrates remained 'staring in one direction and pensive as if it resulted from some separation of the mind and soul from the body';[48] regrettably, it is unclear whether these notes were made by Socrates' comrades in arms or ensue from observations of other people in a similar condition.

Socrates' asceticism became proverbial to such an extent that Aristophanes used or invented a verb *sôkratein*, 'to endure,' literally 'to behave like Socrates.'[49] Alcibiades recounts that Socrates prevailed over strongest erotic temptations, and when on a military campaign, endured hunger and many other hardships. In particular, in winter frost he went barefoot on the ice.[50] In the words of B. Russel, Socrates 'had achieved the complete mastery of the soul over the body.'[51]

Modern researchers refer to Socrates' hours of detachment as 'catalepsy,'[52] 'fits of abstraction,'[53] 'cataleptic trances,'[54] or even as proof of his 'endurance and courage.'[55] In fact, at Potidaea Socrates was clearly experiencing alteration of consciousness.[56] The awkwardness that these accounts cause many scholars, and their reluctance to admit the mystical nature of Socrates' meditations, ensues from the common opinion associating alteration of consciousness with frantic movement or 'mystic rapture,'[57] which is far from being accurate. The altered state of Socrates' mind and body may be compared with radical detachment attested in mystical traditions worldwide, from India to mediaeval Europe, which comprises disregard of bodily needs, self-sufficiency, and enhanced awareness.[58] Socrates' 'mental tightness'[59] was required for the intense concentration, intellectual discipline referred to by his disciple Plato as necessary for proper philosophising, to which I will return shortly.

Another unusual trait of Socrates was his claim of communicating with a supernatural being. His *daimonion*, 'the sign (*sêmeion*) . . . came to [him] frequently . . . and prevented him' from actions he was about to take. This sign was auditory: on multiple occasions Socrates heard 'a voice,' *phône*.[60] Plato's Socrates talked of his *daimonion* quite freely and assumed it to be god-sent; he had experienced this ever since his childhood.[61] The divine sign fell on Socrates abruptly, without his previous knowledge and effort, quite often, even on quite trivial occasions.[62] An episode narrated by Socrates in the *Euthydemus* allows a glimpse at such an occurrence: he was sitting in the undressing room of a public gymnasium; when he was about to leave, his 'regular spiritual sign,' *sêmeion daimonion*, came to him; a group of people entered the room, and Socrates was able to recognise them, note their movements and talk to them.[63] The visitation of the sign did not interfere with his perception of the surroundings: communication with the *daimonion* must have been brief and in any case did not involve detachment. There is no indication that when his sign came upon Socrates he was 'out of his mind.'[64]

Socrates highly praised his *daimonion*, and Plato ostensibly recognised it as divine and made it play a considerable role in several dialogues, most notably in the *Phaedrus* where it forces Socrates to denounce his speech and offer a palinode instead.[65] In the *Apology*, Socrates declares to the judges that he continues to philosophise as long as he is inspired by the god (*empneô*).[66] His *daimonion* was of primary importance to Socrates, and most probably to his prosecutors; it is quite possible that it was in the focus of accusation in impiety, and cost Socrates his life.[67] In any case, he considered the *daimonion* as his unique gift.[68]

Socrates' appreciation of the crucial role of his *daimonion* is further supported by Diotima's assumption that 'the whole of the *daimonion* is between the divine and the mortal,' it is the means of communication between the god and the man, either awake or asleep, and whoever is an expert in this is *daimonios anêr*, a 'man of *daimonion*.'[69] The status of the *daimonion* as mediator of the god[70] makes one value its visitations as moments of contact with the divine; multiple encounters with it bestow upon Socrates the title of *daimonios anêr*.

Besides Plato, Socrates' communication with the *daimonion* is attested by another contemporary. Xenophon adds that Socrates' 'divine sign' not only dissuaded him from certain actions but also directed him towards certain actions:

> Whereas most people say that the birds or the people they meet dissuade or encourage them, Socrates said what he meant: for he said that the divine sign (*daimonion*) was signalling him. Many of his companions were counselled by him to do this or not to do that in accordance with the warnings of the divine sign: and those who followed his advice prospered, and those who rejected it had cause for regret. And yet who would not admit that he wished to appear neither a fool not a fraud to his companions? But he would have been thought both had he proved to be mistaken when he alleged that his counsel was in accordance with divine revelation (*hypo theou phainomena*).[71]

Xenophon's words seem to echo the opinion of disbelievers who considered Socrates *êlithios*, 'idiot,' which is a rather high degree of senselessness, according to the grades defined by the author of the *Second Alcibiades*.[72] Communicating with the *daimonion* looked strange to some people; many would question Socrates' warnings based on the admonitions of the voice he heard.[73] In fact, a list of those who chose to mistrust the *daimonion*, preserved in the later tradition, appears to develop from the critical discourse of Socrates' contemporaries.[74]

Many Athenians strongly disliked Socrates a long time before his trial, and even more people gladly laughed at his burlesque image at the theatre.[75] Aristophanes applied to Socrates *topoi* common in portrayals of madmen, such as rambling in the streets with his eyes rolling, or irrepressible chattering; he even diagnosed Socrates and his followers with derangement: 'It is not nice to sit beside Socrates and chatter . . . ; wasting time on scratching nonsense and nit-picking is to be out of one's mind.'[76] However, not a single extant comedy hints at any specific symptom of Socrates' madness: not only the *daimonion*, but even trances are not mentioned. The charming traits attributed to Socrates by Aristophanes may have been employed in order to enhance the comic effect, rather than make fun of Socrates' personal character.[77] Nevertheless, Aristophanes' caricature is telling: to most people, all the philosophers looked quite insane; besides, they were all charlatans.[78]

In fact, Plato offers an example of this attitude. His Euthyphro, an intellectual interested in questions of piety and philology, appears in the *Cratylus* as a 'divinely inspired' expert on names, including those of gods and heroes.[79] This learned soothsayer was perhaps as annoying as Socrates, and he knew perfectly well how much the Athenians disliked people like Socrates and himself:

> Why, they even laugh at me and say I'm crazy (*mainomenos*) when I say anything in the assembly about divine things and foretell the future to them. And yet there is not one of the things I have foretold that is not true.[80]

Talking 'about divine things' was exactly what Socrates did in the opinion of his compatriots, and this occupation was considered strange enough to label a man as mad.

Centuries after his execution, Socrates' sensitivity to the divine voice was attributed to the purity of his soul, either alone, or in conjunction with his ascetic way of life.[81] Socrates was deemed to have been able to receive unmediated messages from the divine, as the Neoplatonist Plutarch has his Simmias argue in *On the Sign of Socrates*.[82] Simmias, a character in Plato's *Phaedo*, and hence a person close to Socrates, claims that Socrates' *daimonion* was 'perception of voice rather than vision, or perhaps a mental image of speech'; 'not spoken, but rather voiceless word (*logos*) of a daimon that contacted his intelligence directly,' from without his body, and 'had no need of verbs and nouns.'[83]

Some modern scholars regard the *daimonion's* voice as mere 'reassuring' Socrates' rational reasoning,[84] an ironic way of 'alluding to dissuasive reason,'[85] a source of 'intuitive certainty,' or 'flashes of insight' concerning certain actions, which were 'quintessentially rational.'[86] In fact, we do not have any evidence that Socrates' *daimonion* addressed him in an articulated form:[87] it could prevent him from certain actions or encourage him to act, but this signal did not need to be perceived as verbal. In any case, linguistic consciousness is not the essence of rationality – a sensation may be felt as such and only later verbalised, ascribed to a supernatural agent and grounded by rational deliberation,[88] which is exactly what we see in *Phaedrus*. The sign is experienced by Socrates as something foreign to himself, a divine intrusion.[89] In its essence, Socrates' *daimonion* appears to have been a sudden experience of 'indisputable truth, which is itself in no way either a product or qualified by ratiocination,'[90] but it is not a revelation, and does not disclose any hidden truth.[91] For Socrates, it was a manifestation of divine wisdom and absolutely trustworthy, and his belief in its credibility was ultimately based on his belief in the gods.[92]

Even nowadays, in critical or life-threatening situations sensed presence of a guide is perceived by many mentally healthy people of different faiths as well as non-believers, originating from various cultures and all walks of life; these guides provide a measure of hope and consistently offer correct advice. Those who undergo such apparitions regard them as absolutely trustworthy and often attribute to them their rescue from imminent death.[93] In addition, as discussed in the opening remarks to this chapter, unexpected striking enlightening experiences are sometimes perceived as stemming from an outer source, a deity or its intermediary.[94] It may be surmised that Socrates' *daimonion*, that visited him usually at critical, dangerous, or intellectually challenging junctures in his life, belonged to this kind of real-life psychological experiences.

The question is whether Socrates' communication with the *daimonion* was perceived by his surroundings as abnormality comparable to his trances, and whether he himself would define its visitations as cases of *mania*, similar to the separation of the soul from the body while philosophising. My inclination is to believe that neither society nor Socrates himself equated these two phenomena. Divine incursion was postulated as a reason for one's actions in Homer, and while it was certainly not expected to be as usual in the fifth century as in the epos, it still belonged to the realm of normal religious experience.[95] His *daimonion* was a frequent visitor, but Socrates trusted and acted upon the orders of other manifestations of the divine, for instance those that appeared in his dreams.[96] In Socrates' intellectual world, where human reason was considered as inherently faulty,[97] following a voice perceived as divine would be quite logical – certainly no less natural that the common belief in epiphanies.[98] Socrates' behaviour, perception, and cognition were not actually affected by the *daimonion* which never caused him to look bizarre, as he might have during his trances. Thus, receiving frequent and direct messages from a *daimonion* could be accepted in good faith or doubted, considered detrimental to the polis and judged as a transgression, but it was not regarded as *mania*, certainly not by Socrates and his associates.[99] To the 'average Athenian,' Socrates looked crazy enough just because of his strange lifestyle and way of talking on almost every subject, and visitations of the *daimonion* constituted no more than an additional strange feature demonstrating that Socrates was deranged, along with other people who wasted their time on pointless thinking.

To recapitulate: there are four kinds of testimonies on Socrates' abnormality, ranging from madness to weirdness. First, Plato's Socrates was quite aware of the fact that his behaviour looked bizarre or even mad to the masses, and said that in plain words, which were echoed by his associate, Alcibiades. Second, Plato's Socrates compared his philosophising to Bacchic initiations, and alluded to out-of-body experiences. Third, Socrates' prolonged trance-like meditations could not happen if not in an altered state of consciousness. In these three cases, Socrates' contemporaries probably referred to his behaviour as *mania*, and we can detect elements of a state which we call alteration of consciousness. The fourth one, although perhaps the most famous, does not seem to have troubled Socrates' contemporaries, who could either trust or mistrust his *daimonion*, but never insinuated that receiving its commands was more than a peculiarity.

Plato's mystical experiences

Plato's writings suggest that he knew mystical experiences himself.[100] Excluding the letters, Plato never refers to his experiences in the first person, therefore my assertion that the greatest philosopher of the European tradition attained some of his ideas as a (mystic) revelation is also based on the conviction that a person cannot predicate some of his important tenets on the idea of illumination and author long passages describing mystic states without having experienced them. Whether we dub this experience as 'ecstatic' or 'metaphysical' is insubstantial: the important thing is its difference from regular waking state of consciousness.[101] It should be stressed once again that alteration of consciousness leading to a most profound subjective feeling of illumination – and assumedly dubbed as *mania* by Socrates and Plato – were not necessarily perceived as frenzy or derangement by the surrounding people: limitless bliss could be completely introvert and resemble *bakcheia* only from the viewpoint of the individual experiencing it. I will limit my discussion of this vast topic to several passages that are particularly noteworthy.

In his *Seventh Letter* Plato gives precious details regarding his own views. This remarkable, perhaps autobiographic, document is considered by the majority of experts as authentic or at least authored by one of Plato's disciples shortly after his death.[102] Even if we assume for a moment the latter view, the document remains extremely important, since immediately after the master's demise his views could not be brutally distorted by one of his pupils: it is bound to represent Plato's position quite faithfully. Plato writes:

> There does not exist, nor will ever exist, any treatise of mine dealing with these subjects. For it does not at all admit of verbal expression like other studies, but, as a result of continued application to the subject itself and communion therewith, it is brought to birth in the soul of a sudden, as light that is kindled by a leaping spark, and thereafter it nourishes itself.[103]

This passage was interpreted in a mystical sense by Plotinus who admired it,[104] and by Kant who assaulted its message as charlatanic[105] – but whatever their attitude to mysticism, the two great thinkers recognised the kernel of the text: it reports an illumination.[106] At this point in the *Seventh Letter* Plato claims that some of his tenets cannot be adequately expressed in words, though he prefers oral conversation to written text[107] (but he will write that a few paragraphs later). In fact, in the *Phaedrus*, a text of unquestionable authenticity, Plato has Socrates contend in a similar vein, i.e. that really worthy discourses 'are written in the soul' and cannot be expressed in words, either written or spoken.[108]

Accordingly, Plato does not say much about the nature of the ineffable things, but for two facts: they result from a long pondering on the subject ('communion' with it) and appear in sudden flashes. The instantaneousness of the revelation is especially noteworthy: the same adverb 'abruptly,' *exaiphnês*, characterises the goal (*telos*) of the initiation which is the vision of the divine world in the *Symposium*, and the illumination of the soul in the *Republic*.[109] 'The communion' may perhaps allude to the erotic passion of the soul for the ideas, and the illumination is the state of enhanced sensibility which brings about sensations of elation and heavenly joy.[110] This experience is ineffable, and even *post factum* cannot be adequately put into words.[111]

The route leading to illumination is excruciating, and the experience itself is almost painful. Plato explains that one has to carry out 'a diligent and prolonged investigation,' 'examining names and definitions, visions and sense-perceptions' and employing questions and answers – all that conductive to the ultimate knowledge, which is the true reality and 'bursts out the light of intelligence and reason regarding each object in the mind of him who uses every effort of which mankind is capable.'[112] Thus, true knowledge requires preliminary deliberation, but they are separated by a gap: their nature is different. This position is immediately reminiscent of the accounts of modern thinkers and scientists, cited in the introductory notes to this chapter, who arrived at their seminal ideas as a result of sudden illumination: this spark of truth is possible only after a prolonged and sometimes excruciating contemplation of a problem, an 'incubation period' culminating in the realisation of the solution.

Plato puts forward the claim that the true knowledge cannot be appreciated by the public, and therefore must not be communicated in writing.[113] Esoteric doctrines, 'so-called unwritten views' (*legomena agrapha dogmata*), of his great teacher were known to Aristotle.[114] However, the assertion that an unprepared mind is unable to perceive the true reality[115] is only the second corollary of the revelatory nature of the ultimate knowledge; the first – and most essential – corollary, its ineffability, has already been stated earlier.[116] Accordingly, both oral and written philosophical discourse served in Plato's opinion as a method of educating the soul and rendering it sensitive enough to recover (recall) the truth of which it possesses.[117]

The author of the letter accentuates another point that is stressed in many mystical traditions: a genuine student of philosophy must follow the teacher who is guiding him on the route to truth, and never desist before he reaches the goal – *telos*, a word from the vocabulary of mystery cults – of his studies; only then would he be able to proceed without his teacher. Such a student must 'cleave fast' to philosophy and to a special mode of daily life which allows immersion in philosophy.[118] Certain secret tenets may cause harm to most people:

> But were I to undertake this task [write on the nature of reality] it would not, as I think, prove a good thing for men, save for some few who are able to discover the truth themselves with but little instruction; for all the rest, some it would most unreasonably fill with a mistaken contempt, and others with an overweening and empty aspiration, as though they had learnt something august.[119]

Thus, only as a result of prolonged intellectual efforts and ascetic lifestyle can one approach certain doctrines. The select few who had committed themselves to the attainment of perfection formed the elitist community of people who could comprehend the 'unwritten views.'[120] In his last work, the *Laws*, in the discussion of the education of the wardens, Plato makes the same point with a certain twist, leading however to the same conclusion.

> For even the learners themselves could not be sure that they were learning at the opportune time until each of them had acquired within his soul some knowledge of the subject in question. Accordingly, although it would be wrong to term all these matters 'indescribable,' they should be termed 'imprescribable,' seeing that the prescribing of them beforehand does nothing to elucidate the question under discussion.[121]

Here, Plato still claims that true knowledge can be perceived after one's soul is prepared from within, by its inner work rather than by teaching: only a perceptive soul can be led to further enlightenment. Once again, an idea clearly articulated in the *Seventh Letter* is conveyed in a slightly different form in a text undoubtedly penned by Plato.

Plato's approach to philosophical education is congruent to that of Greek mystery initiations: a person had to be duly primed in order to be exposed to the ultimate revelation. This affinity was highlighted by Plutarch, who compared *epopteia*, that is, the end of a mystery initiation that conveys its fundamental truth, to a lightning flashing through the soul, and to the aim (*telos*) of philosophy in Plato and Aristotle: in both cases, a long preliminary travail was deemed obligatory, but its supreme aim is to prepare one's mind for a revelatory insight.[122] Exactly as a *mustês* could talk to another *mustês* about his or her experience and expect mutual understanding, the 'unsayable' (*aporrhêta*) things were prohibited for discussion solely with the uninitiated: an enlightened philosopher could count on the comprehension of his own kind, and would not attempt to persuade the ignorant with the 'unsayable before the time' (*aprorrhêta*) as Plato insists in the *Laws*.[123] In order to be exposed to Plato's highest knowledge, one needed both dialectical training and experiential education – in order to attain *epopteia* in a mystery rite, one has to acquire the knowledge of the relevant tradition and to 'become fit' psychologically.

The philosopher's mental state as attested in the *Seventh Letter* is not that of a participant in initiation rites: a philosopher attains a state of heightened intellectual ability rather than initiatory *enthousiasmos* (engoddedness), and his arousal results from ascetic discipline and dialectic deliberation rather than rituals.[124] The Platonic philosopher did not need to experience *epopteia* in order to attain bliss – he philosophised, hoping to arrive at his sudden flash of insight. Yet both the true *bakchos* and philosopher experienced the sensation of illumination that was ineffable, and the state of both can properly be described as *mania* in ancient Greek and alteration of consciousness in modern terms. In Plato's opinion, it was pointless to write about this sensation, but it could be referred to orally in a circle of other experiencers, and hinted at in writing.

The authenticity of the *Seventh Letter*, and in particular of the passages forming 'the philosophical digression,' is questioned by those who consider Plato an arch-rationalist,[125] but many stretches in the dialogues that are undeniably the philosopher's own work attest to ideas that square with the *Seventh Letter*. The description of 'the region above the heavens' in the *Phaedrus* is especially remarkable:

> But the region above the heaven was never worthily sung by any earthly poet, nor will it ever be. It is, however, as I shall tell; for I must dare to speak the truth. . . . For the colourless, formless, and intangible truly existing essence, with which all true knowledge is concerned, holds the region and is visible only to the mind, the pilot of the soul. Now the divine intelligence, since it is nurtured on mind and pure knowledge, and the intelligence of every soul which is capable of receiving that which befits it, rejoices in seeing reality for a space of time and by gazing upon truth is nourished and made happy until the revolution brings it again to the same place. In the revolution it beholds absolute justice, temperance, and knowledge, not such knowledge that has a beginning and varies as it is associated with one or another of the things we call realities, but that which abides in the real eternal absolute.[126]

In the *Phaedrus*, the soul which is perfect and winged ascends to the domain of the divine reality, in its erotic longing for the ideal Forms, and experiences there the ultimate joy. By means of this initiation the philosopher becomes divine or akin to divine and attains the highest degree of *eudaimonia* that is possible to the mortal.[127] Such elements as spiritual ascent, erotic union with the eternal, feeling of transcendent timelessness that is also the greatest happiness, and association of the experience with the divine are indicative of a genuine mystical experience.[128] In addition, Plato lists the subjective feelings experienced by those whose souls grow feathered wings: shuddering and palpitations of the soul, as well as fever, irritation, and itching mingled with joy and pleasure.[129] It is noteworthy that souls differ in their ability to rise, and some sink or have their wings broken: the mystic's ascent is notoriously perilous, mystical experience can go terribly wrong, and in many traditions consecutive stages of mystical experience are allowed only after a long apprenticeship.[130]

Hints at alteration of consciousness may be discerned in the *Symposium*, as well. Diotima's characterisation of the notion of beauty as 'the great open sea (or ocean, *pelagos*) of the beautiful' is reminiscent of the oceanic sensation felt by some during the alteration of consciousness, and the image of erotic union in soul and begetting of virtue resulting from contemplating the eternal beauty are indicative of the erotic aspects of mystical experiences, discussed below.[131]

The Platonic philosopher is attributed experiences that are difficult to interpret otherwise than as out-of-body states:

> but really it is only his body that has its place and home in the city; his mind, considering all these things petty and of no account, disdains them and is borne in all directions, as Pindar says, 'both below the earth,' and measuring the surface of the earth, and 'above the sky,' studying the stars, and

investigating the universal nature of every thing that is, each in its entirety, never lowering itself to anything close at hand.[132]

This passage is reminiscent of soul travelling of Archaic sages and philosophers, such as Hermotimus, Aristeas, Parmenides, and Empedocles, discussed below. Plato's recurrent depictions of the soul's ascent and flight attest to his acquaintance with the age-long tradition of self-cultivation and manipulation of consciousness; furthermore, they are too closely connected to the core of Socrates' (and Plato's) world view to be regarded as borrowed images or figures of speech: Plato most probably experienced out-of-body states himself.

Another telling example is Socrates' argument for the superiority of the philosopher and the culmination of true learning in the *Republic* VI:

> Shall we not then be defending him fairly if we say that as a true lover of learning, he was born to fight his way toward reality and not fritter away his time among those many individual subjects that are reckoned to be real; he moves on without losing heart or ceasing from his passion until he grasps the nature of each and every thing through that part of the soul which is fitted to get hold of something of that sort through its kinship with it. Through this, after he has consorted and had intercourse with what really exists, and given birth to intelligence and truth, he may gain knowledge and a true life, and be nourished and so be relieved of his birth pangs, but not before?[133]

By means of this route, a philosopher comes to comprehend Forms of the real beauty and real good.[134] Writing about this passage, T. M. Robinson observes: 'If *Rep.* 490A9-B6 is not mysticism, what is? The notion of *unio mystica* and *unio sexualis* surely underlie words like ἅψασθαι, ἐφάψασθαι, πλησιάσας, and γεννήσας'[135] ('grasp,' 'get hold,' 'has consorted,' and 'has given birth' in the passage above).

The language is indeed explicitly sexual, and the *erôs* for the ideal Forms leads to painful but joyful birth of the true knowledge.[136] The erotic passion is for the truth of 'what really exists,' which is transcendent reality, incomprehensible by regular perception, therefore sexual union is only a feeble worldly metaphor of the ineffable *unio mystica*, immersion or mingling with the eternal reality.[137] The soul is considered 'congenial' to the eternal reality, and suffers until it is begets the truth by means of this mystical union.[138] An enlightened soul can easily afford being ascetic, as Plato suggests, and rid itself of all the unnecessary desires, including erotic attraction:[139] it knows much more acute pleasure, the ultimate bliss of the mystic union. The true knowledge that is 'born' in pain is beyond the knowledge of particularities – and in fact Socrates differentiates the lofty idea of eternal good from the scientific knowledge and stresses its superiority.[140]

Erotic passion for philosophy and truth is a recurrent theme in the *Republic*: the soul that is 'akin to the divine, the immortal and the eternal' experiences 'longing' for the ideal Forms.[141] Furthermore, the extremely dense passage in the *Republic* is paralleled by a very similar sequence of erotic desire, grasping the ideal Form, having intercourse with it, and begetting virtue in the *Symposium*.[142] In the

Republic, this movement is articulated by Socrates; in the *Symposium*, by Diotima –
the two speakers who are barely distinguishable from Plato himself. The entire
experience of the union with the divine as a sexual union appears consistently
enough to regard it as an important part of Plato's own life. The soul's erotic desire
for the divine is the erotic *mania* of the philosopher, on which the *Phaedrus* is
focused and which is discussed in Chapter 7. The cited passages, attributed to
Socrates but penned by Plato, allow the assumption that Plato himself knew the
bliss of *unio mystica* and found the erotic *mania* as the closest possible verbal
expression of this ineffable experience.

Erotic relationship between the soul and the divine is the subject of writings of
Christian, Muslim, and Jewish mystics, who used sexual language of longing and
union, struggling to give accounts of their inherently ineffable mystic unions.[143]
Association of sexual and mystic capacity, including comparison of mystical
enlightenment with orgasm, is quite common around the globe: perhaps the most
famous are St Teresa of Ávila with her accounts of the painful sweetness of ecstasy
and John of the Cross with his poetic depictions of sensual raptures that serve as
a portal to transcendence, but these renderings of *unio mystica* in erotic terms are
by no means exceptional.[144] Bernard of Clairvaux consistently envisaged the
human soul's union with the divine as a 'mystical marriage,' with the Song of
Songs as its metaphor.[145] An influential approach in neuroscience associates the
mechanism of mystical experience with orgasms, the former being an evolutionary
by-product of the latter.[146] Given this proximity, it is no wonder that the use of
sexual imagery to convey mystical experiences is one of the universals of
mysticism.[147]

The role of reason in Plato is to deliberate and to rule the soul,[148] and its passion
and pleasure are to contemplate. The ultimate stage of the latter is the mystical
union of the philosopher's souls with the ideal reality, to which the philosopher
strives: Socrates boldly calls this state the philosopher's *bakcheia*. The philosopher's duty is to contemplate this experience and put into words its parts that can
be verbalised – the most precious revelations, as stated in the *Seventh Letter*, will
remain ineffable.[149] Most significantly, Plato's esotericism cannot be reduced to a
secret code, musical or other, hidden in his writings:[150] it was the route to the
knowledge of reality, attained as a revelation. Plato's esoteric doctrine is more
than the substantive content, which is sometimes exposed in his dialogues; it
comprised both the revelation and the method of reaching it, which he preferred
to convey orally, and only occasionally and briefly discuss in writing.[151]

I am in no way arguing that the entire corpus of Platonic texts ensues from
mystic revelations. Actually, I suppose that most of what Plato and his disciples
did was absolutely rational – as it is certainly right for the modern thinkers and
scientists who reported experiencing moments of enlightenment. What I suggest
is that some of Plato's most cherished core ideas arrived as a result of illumination –
'the spark' referred to in the *Seventh Letter*, and it could not be but ephemeral, a
single moment that makes a long toil worthwhile. The 'spark' was preceded by a
protracted concentration on a problem, and followed by a painful process of conveying the idea to words; this process is attested to in Plato's dialogues, and

underscored in the *Seventh Letter*. The 'context of discovery' comprised therefore mystical insights that were hinted to in Plato's dialogues drawing on them: these texts constitute 'the context of justification.' Thus, states that we label as altera-tions of consciousness, and Plato and his contemporaries perceived as *mania*, were probably experienced by Plato, and played an important role in his search for the eternal truth.

Mania and Archaic sages: Epimenides, Aethalides, and Hermotimus

Alterations of consciousness of several Presocratic thinkers can be assumed quite confidently. Although never designated as *mania*, they allow a glimpse at the activities that could prompt Plato's Socrates to characterise the philosopher's state of mind as *mania*.

Referring to Epimenides of Crete, Plutarch mentions sages of Solon's age, who 'acquired their knowledge of the divine by means of ecstatic and telestic wis-dom.'[152] Epimenides, one of the canonical Seven Sages, an exorcist, a prophet, and a poet, was credited with truthful predictions concerning the future of Athens and Sparta,[153] and famous for his purification of Attica from the pollution caused by the murder of Cylon's supporters.[154] Exorcism was often performed as a mystery initiation, and Epimenides' feats as a purifier may account for his reputation as master of telestic wisdom. Epimenides was also credited with truthful predictions, and with the authorship of several epic poems.[155] Thus, Epimenides enjoyed the fame of being endowed by the gods with a generous three-fold blessing of pro-phetic, telestic, and poetic *mania*.

Epimenides' reputation as a *mantis*, and expert in divinely inspired and hidden wisdom was enhanced by many extraordinary details of his biography. The most intriguing episode is his protracted slumber in a cave: Epimenides was said to have fallen asleep in a cave for forty to sixty years.[156] He claimed that during this sleep in the cave of the Dictaean Zeus he talked to the gods, listened to their conversa-tions and met Truth (*Alêtheia*) and Justice (*Dikê*).[157] Ascetic seclusion in a cave, rewarded with divine illumination, hints at the possibility that the image of this semi-legendary sage absorbed some features of real-life ecstatics. In addition, Epi-menides reportedly tried to found a sanctuary of the nymphs, but was stopped by a direct divine command: a voice instructed him to consecrate the shrine to Zeus.[158]

Epimenides' intimate connection with the nymphs is emphasised in several tales. Either he was the son of a nymph, Balte, or obtained his magic nourishment from the nymphs.[159] This supernatural food separated Epimenides from the rest of humanity: nobody ever saw him eating or relieving himself.[160] He lived for either about a hundred and fifty or two hundred and ninety years.[161] Epimenides is said to have often pretended to (to die and) be reborn,[162] which is perhaps an attempt to describe in a different way the ability of his soul to leave his body and return whenever he wished.[163] In Epimenides, we find a fascinating combination of ecstatic activities, prophecy, and bizarre conduct. These odd ways were perhaps intentionally cultivated, in order to astonish everyone, and to comply with the image an eccentric very different from regular mortals.

Epimenides' life story contains numerous fantastic episodes, but remains nevertheless the biography of a historic personage, a seer, exorcist, and purifier, who practiced ecstatic techniques of catalepsy and catabasis.[164] He is portrayed as an extremely gifted mystic who enhanced his ecstatic states by fasting, and attained them by means of sensory deprivation in the depth of sacred caves.[165] Although Epimenides' prolonged cave sleep seems to have been an elaboration of a traditional rite, he became renown due to his personal talents and feats, even if these were embellished in the legend. Whatever its historicity, in the popular image of Epimenides we find Socrates' precursor, at least in two respects: like Socrates, Epimenides was blessed with the ability to perceive divine signs directly, and he piously acted as commanded by the gods. His long slumber is reminiscent of Socrates' trances: was this legend a popular elaboration of real-life long meditations in the isolation of a cave?

Epimenides shares some key features with several archaic legendary and semi-legendary personages, *maîtres de vérité* whose road to divine truth led through various mystical states.[166] Abaris, a Hyperborean holy man, wandered all over the earth, while in the god's grip (*entheos*), Apollo's arrow in his hand, curing sicknesses and purifying pestilence, and predicting earthquakes.[167] According to Herodotus, in the time of Croesus and Cyrus, Aristeas of Proconnesus, seized by Apollo (*phoibolamptos*), was said to be seen simultaneously in different places, his soul reaching the most remote countries; his soul left his body 'whenever he wished.' A later rationalising version of Aristeas' soul journeys maintains that his body remained in Proconnesus, and remained alive, although looked like a corpse. The *Arimaspeia*, a poem recording these voyages, is attributed to him. According to his legendary biography, 240 years after his first appearance to the world, Aristeas arrived in Metapontum in Italy in the form of a raven, together with Apollo, and the Metapontines set up Aristeas' bronze statue in the marketplace.[168]

Aethalides was said to have been gifted by Hermes so that his soul could travel above the earth or below it, in Hades.[169] Hermotimus of Clazomenae was capable of experiencing out-of-body states at will; during the wanderings of his soul, Hermotimus' body remained motionless at home, and returning to his body after long journeys, his soul would bring knowledge of the future and other mantic gifts.[170] Aethalides, Hermotimus, and Aristeas presumably used similar techniques of attaining states of almost total detachment, allowing prolonged soul flights and visions.

Soul journeys that comprised illumination and acquisition of mantic and magic abilities are attributed to all these figures, and coupled with eccentric behaviour appear to be their most important common characteristic. Their idiosyncrasy is telling: people endowed with rare, seemingly supernatural abilities at discerning the messages of the gods, behaved strangely and might look deranged. Later tradition ascribed to all of them as a group sojourns in hidden places, implying that super-human feats were commonly associated with prolonged seclusion and sensory deprivation.[171]

All in all, it seems that alteration of consciousness endowing its practitioners with super-human wisdom was known in Archaic Greece and continued an age-old tradition. The feats of the Archaic *maîtres de vérité*, whose bizarre behaviour separated them from the contemporary Greeks, were reportedly narrated in their poems. This tradition was most probably known to Plato's Socrates.

Mania and Presocratic philosophers:
Pythagoras, Parmenides, and Empedocles

Pythagoras was credited with meetings with Epimenides;[172] reflecting the belief that these personalities were compatible. The controversy as to whether Pythagoras was a natural philosopher and mathematician, founder of a sect and expert on the fate of the soul after death, or both, still continues.[173] It is noteworthy that the early tradition, including Plato and Aristotle, hardly mentions Pythagoras' own achievements in natural philosophy, but rather pictures him as a charismatic teacher who formulated a new way of life for himself and his followers.[174] The teacher's life was the ultimate proof of the truth of his tenets.[175]

Like Epimenides, Pythagoras and his followers emphasised his super-human traits. From a fairly early time, many considered him divine, or at least the god's progeny.[176] By praising Pythagoras as 'master especially of all kinds of wise works,'[177] Empedocles was alluding not to mundane skills, but rather to miraculous acts that were within the powers of the semi-divine sage, endowed with knowledge of past and future, including his own previous incarnations, and the capacity to apply his knowledge for practical purposes, such as suppressing winds, calming storms,[178] or treating sick souls by means of charms.[179] Pythagoras' extraordinary traits and abilities[180] belong to the sphere in which the earlier *maîtres de vérité* were prominent and which is connected by many modern scholars with shamanic experiences.[181]

Pythagoras' descents into secret chambers and caves were well-known, and his legend contains several reiterations of this motif.[182] In these secluded places, Pythagoras learnt to remain quiet.[183] Like Epimenides, Pythagoras is credited with consuming special foods that freed him of hunger and thirst,[184] or even with abstaining from food and drink entirely during his sojourns in sacred precincts.[185] This tradition indicates awareness of the fact that fasting enhanced the mind-changing effect of subterranean sojourns, and enabled the sojourner to remain silent and motionless in the darkness of the isolated chamber: an ascetic technique of manipulation of consciousness was familiar to the Greeks, from Pythagoras to Hippolytus. Even if some accounts of Pythagoras' catabaseis, as well as other abnormal deeds, are late elaborations of his life legend, they seem to be based on a reliable basis, and Pythagoras' retreats into seclusion were part of his path to wisdom.

Pythagoras' writings did not survive – to the extent that they ever existed, since the great master supposedly deliberately refrained from writing.[186] The Pythagoreans held their teaching in extreme secrecy, and while some important doctrines, such as the immortality of the soul and reincarnation, were familiar to the public,[187] other parts of the Pythagorean creed remained ineffable.[188] Ineffability of doctrines and contempt of writing are immediately reminiscent of Plato's 'unwritten doctrines' and Socrates' attitude to writing; the reason might be the peculiar way of attaining these insights, which led through illumination.

Pythagoras' disciples were to live through various trials, including prolonged silence,[189] and unequivocally accept a set of orally transmitted precepts, *akousmata* or *sumbola*:[190] in a word, they formed a sect.[191] No wonder that Pythagoras' own house was known as 'the house of mysteries':[192] similar to participants in mystery cults, the Pythagorean brotherhood shared common secrets not to be disclosed to uninitiated, and required elaborate initiations.[193]

The early Pythagoreans placed emphasis on revealed wisdom and on dreams as a direct way of contact with the divine and a prominent means of divination.[194] Iamblichus explained that Pythagoras prohibited foods that either prevented men from communion with the gods, or interfered with divination, or defiled the soul and the purity of visions:[195] the Pythagorean teaching was closely affiliated with mystery rites, and valued dreams and visions as crucial ways of reaching divine revelation. The Pythagoreans appear to have mastered methods of yoga-like breath control and used them for manipulation of consciousness. Empedocles admired Pythagoras as

> a man of outstanding knowledge, who possessed the greatest wealth of *prapides* and became especially capable of all wise deeds. For whenever he stretched his *prapides*, easily he contemplated each of the things existing in the tenth and twentieth generation of men.[196]

These verses clearly attest to the alleged ability of Pythagoras to embrace in his thought aeons of time and the wholeness of reality, reminiscent of the talents of the Archaic ecstatics. As we can see both in Homer and in Classical poetry, the word *prapides* had a physical identity and meant an organ in the chest that served as a seat of intellectual and emotional activity.[197] Empedocles appears to have considered the *prapides* as the organ that had to be employed in order to achieve the separation of the soul from the body, probably by means of breath control, which is an essential technique of attaining out-of-body states.[198] It is plausible that the same technique was used by Aristeas, Hermotimus, and Aethalides.

In sum, the ascetic practices of Pythagoras and his disciples, including sensory deprivation and fasting, along with the emphasis on ineffability of the resulting knowledge indicate that alteration of consciousness held a place of honour in their methods of philosophising.

Whereas the tenets of Pythagoras are known from the writings of others, Parmenides, the founder of the Eleatic school, expounds his creed and the way he arrived at it in a hexametre poem.[199] The very choice of epic verse rather than prose is meaningful: in contrast to prose, poetry was inspired by the divinity, hence by definition, as a genre, ensued from a super-human source.[200] In the opening lines of the poem, known as the *proem* (prologue), Parmenides describes his own catabasis as a youth, *kouros*, into the underworld. The mares swiftly bring his chariot along the road of the divinity (*daimôn*), 'that bears the man who knows.'[201] The all-encompassing revelation that awaits him is anticipated by the daughters of the Sun, who escort him: after they 'leave the house of Night for the light,'[202] they unveil, that is, reveal their essence to Parmenides. Having passed the 'yawning abyss,' the youth is kindly greeted by the goddess (*thea*), who reveals to him 'the unshakable heart of the rounded truth,' as opposed to the false beliefs of mortals.[203]

This is a powerful depiction of a spiritual journey.[204] The dense verses of the proem could not be written as an academic exercise in epic stylisation, but convey a rehearsal of a genuine experience, mystical revelation, perceived as a bliss given to the unique few favoured by the goddess: the route followed by the *kouros* is 'far from the pathways of men.'[205] The trip of the youth is reminiscent of ecstatic flights of archaic personages, such as Aethalides, Abaris, Aristeas, and Hermotimus. The direction of Parmenides' journey, to the heavens and enlightenment[206] or into the netherworld, is still discussed.[207] In my opinion, Parmenides journeyed through the netherworld, to light and enlightenment at its end.[208]

Swift movement from darkness into light, a gate opening magically, entrance into a deep chasm, a benevolent supreme being looking out for the traveller at the end of his journey, and an overwhelming joy at comprehending the greatest mystery of the world – all these are basic elements of the mental vortex.[209] This experience is one of the most common in laboratory experiments investigating the effects of various hallucinogens, as well as stress factors,[210] and frequently appears in anthropological accounts of altered states of consciousness as experienced by shamans and other religious practitioners.[211] Its basic characteristics are a tunnel-like perspective, with images appearing on its walls; it often terminates in bright light in the centre of the field of vision, and the light sometimes described as warm or benevolent, or as brightly lit human forms.[212] Tunnels are ubiquitous in hallucinations induced by various means, and even at the instant just before sleep.[213] All the senses are involved in the experience of the vortex: people hear voices and sounds, feel breathless and weightless (therefore floating or flying), their vision may blur, and they may gain the impression of being in a different world. These sensations, which are universal, result from the neurological processes in the human brain.[214]

The *kouros'* chariot is a polyvalent image, consistently occurring in Greek literature, starting from Pindar, via Empedocles and Plato, where it symbolises the soul as the united force of the horses and their charioteer, to the Pythagorean *Golden Verses*.[215] The image of a chariot-ride to enlightenment via the darkness is not limited to the Greek world and is known in Jewish and Islamic mysticism.[216] Comparison to a chariot-ride through the night appears to be the simplest way to convey the sensation of swiftly moving through the darkness, that is, vortex experiences typical of the early stages of altered states of consciousness.[217]

The interpretation of Parmenides' journey as a passage to enlightenment via the netherworld is endorsed by the wording of the goddess' greetings: 'No ill fate has sent you to travel this path, which indeed lies far from the steps of men, but right and justice.'[218] 'Ill fate' is death, and this phrase seems to imply that Parmenides is among the few privileged mortals who pass alive into the realm of the goddess, which means that the author perceived the place where he arrived as the netherworld, but knew that for him, the chosen one, the visit would be beneficial.

Parmenides' radical monism[219] originates in mystical insight. The core of his teaching is that reality is an undifferentiated whole.[220] The diversity of things perceived by the senses of mortals, for Parmenides, is the deceitful Way of Seeming: all change, motion, and differentiation are illusory. The divine Way of Truth is to comprehend reality as unitary, eternal, indivisible, and motionless. Perception is refuted as delusion, and thinking, being, and uttering coalesce. For K. Popper, the core of Parmenides' insight is 'that divine knowledge of reality is rational and therefore truthful, while human opinion of appearance is based upon our senses, which are not only unreliable but totally misleading.'[221] He stresses the extreme discrepancy between Parmenides' teaching and common sense:

> What is shocking in Parmenides' poem (and constitutes a complete break with the old tradition that distinguishes between divine knowledge and human fallible conjecture) is not that the goddess declares our human world of experience to be false and illusory, but that she reveals, and claims to be true – and even proves! – a theory of reality that must seem impossible and even insane to every sane person.[222]

Parmenides was adamant in his insistence that this 'insane' revelation was the only divine and eternal truth. All the mundane experience of his life meant nothing in comparison with the intensity of his insight. Such a paradoxical doctrine, discarding whatever Parmenides could have learnt from his cultural and physical environment, 'is not derived from cold deduction but from direct perception, a mystical experience,' as M. West observes.[223] In more recent publications, P. Kingsley and M. L. Gemelli Marciano view the immediacy and totality of Parmenides' contact with reality as indicating that it was attained in a mystical state.[224]

In his poem, Parmenides appears to struggle with the limits of ordinary language, in order to put into words something that is by its nature beyond words.[225] The ultimate reality of Parmenides is essentially ineffable and is perceived as direct revelation, rather than as a mediated communication. Parmenides' spiritual journey is neither an allegory nor a traditional literary device: the wording of his proem demonstrates that we are reading a *post eventum* description of an ecstatic revelation.[226]

A comparison between Parmenides' 'immovable heart of the truth' and mystic experiences is instructive.[227] The heart of the mystical insight achieved in altered states of consciousness, is that the world of appearances is a construed illusion, and the underlying reality is the eternal loving unchangeable oneness.[228] The mystic is so completely absorbed in the contemplation of the one truth of the world, that he or she obliterates all perception of the physical world. At the peak of mystical experience, at the state of absolute unitary being, no sense of time and space exists, and absolute reality is attained, which is conceptualised as the sensation of union with the God or the Absolute. For people who have experienced mystical revelation, this state, and even the memory of it, carry the sense of greater fundamental reality than the reality generated by their awareness of day-to-day living. The congruity between Parmenides' truth and mystical reality is astonishing.[229]

The goddess instructs Parmenides to verify by rational methods any knowledge acquired by revelation: 'estimate by reasoning (*krinai logô*) the hard-hitting refutation (*poludêris elegchos*) uttered by me.'[230] These verses ostensibly indicate the path to be taken from experiencing a vision to its comprehension and expression: the insight gained in an altered state of consciousness must be re-considered in a normal state of mind, by means of rational judgment.[231] Moreover, it was the awareness of the divine truth that was initially mystical and had to be put into imperfect human words later; as for the critical analysis of the human world of appearances, Parmenides' mundane waking logic was sufficient.[232]

It appears plausible that Parmenides' spiritual endeavour was a part of initiation ceremonies, required for the admission into the Eleatic association. In Parmenides' *proem*, the journey to the realm of the goddess is undertaken by a youth, *kouros*, of an age that was, traditionally, the time for the most significant transition rites in the life of a Greek man.[233] The element of initiations into mystery rites is evident in the unveiling of the hidden ultimate truth to the *kouros*. However, before meeting the goddess, the *kouros* had already been 'the man who knows,' and had travelled the road which 'lies far from the paths of men,'[234] implying that he possessed secret knowledge concealed from ordinary mortals.[235] The *proem* appears to suggest two stages of initiations, the lower stage endowing the select few with the ability to take the mystical road to the goddess, and the higher stage comprising the ultimate revelation. Parmenides seems to refer to the *kouros'* apprenticeship preceding the life-changing mystical experience – much in the same manner as Plato described the process of concentration before a 'spark' can be expected.

The philosopher's journey is pictured in the *proem* as a drive of the initiate to the world of the beyond, where the goddess discloses to him the ultimate truth: images suggested by Parmenides' cultural environment and based on the epic conventions. This literary description serves as a word wrap for a primary mental experience of the ecstatic passage through a dark space to the blissful awareness of the shining 'unchanging living reality,' through which the author lived, perhaps on several occasions.[236]

Parmenides was the head of the Eleatic school which flourished from the sixth century BC till the first centuries AD in the Greek colony Elea, called Velia by the Romans. The association owned a large building with a subterranean chamber, cryptoporticus, which yielded herms with inscriptions referring to heads of the school as *iatroi*, healers or physicians, and *phôlarchoi*, 'lords of the den.'[237] One of the herms represented the great philosopher himself.[238] Although pholarchs are called *iatroi*, the corporation in Elea was not a medical training establishment. It was rather an association of philosophers,[239] a community of followers that probably resembled the Pythagorean sect, religious practitioners, who assumed the role of healers on certain occasions, and used magical techniques, similar to those attributed to Pythagoras and Empedocles.[240]

The building with the cryptoporticus was erected to accommodate the activities of the Ouliads and their pholarchs, 'lords of the den.' The word *phôleos* means 'den,' 'lair,' or 'hole,' usually underground, of snakes, lions, bears, and other animals;[241] *phôleuein* is 'to live or hide in a cave or a hole, to hibernate.'[242] It is probable that pholarchs in Elea adopted the Pythagorean tradition of the philosophers' descent into underground chambers.[243] The Eleatic philosophy was profoundly influenced by Pythagoras,[244] and healing played an essential role in the Pythagorean teaching and practice.[245] It is suggested that the 'den' was founded in the fifth century by Parmenides himself,[246] a Pythagorean by training.[247] In fact, the Pythagorean Ameinias reportedly converted Parmenides to *hêsuchia*, 'contemplative life,' literally 'silence,' that is, the Pythagorean life.[248] Parmenides' *hêsuchia* could imply not only introspective serenity, but also recurrent withdrawals into the quiet of an underground chamber[249] in order to attain divine revelation.

Following Epimenides and Pythagoras, who were granted their super-human knowledge by the gods or daemons during their catabaseis, the Ouliads probably adopted the practice of entering an altered state of consciousness in the darkness and stillness of their den in order to be endowed with divine wisdom and resultant supernatural power.

In conclusion, I would like to emphasise that the interpretation of Parmenides' tenets as ensuing from a mystical revelation is based first and foremost on the reading of Parmenides' own text, and had been put forward by several prominent experts on ancient philosophy before the publication of the Elean archaeological complex. The inscriptions and architectural remains unearthed there allow new perspectives on the context of Parmenides' philosophy, supplementing its text-centred construal with precious details.[250] They allow a tentative reconstruction of techniques applied by Parmenides and his followers in order to attain mystical revelations and meditate on his tenets which contradicted whatever the organs of perception could communicate to them.

While Pythagoras' and Parmenides' behaviour has never been clearly defined as *mania* in the extant tradition, Empedocles' activities are associated with madness, *furor*, and *bakcheia* by two ancient authors. Plutarch in *On the Sign of Socrates* refers to Empedocles' ecstatic activities. The rationalist Galaxidorus attempts to present Socrates as a fellow-rationalist, and praises him for cleansing philosophy of false notions: 'He received philosophy that Pythagoras loaded with visions and tales and superstition . . . and Empedocles rendered even more Bacchic.'[251] Unfortunately, there is a lacuna in the text, and Galaxidorus may have listed other philosophers, as well;[252] Pythagoras' philosophy was probably also 'Bacchic' in his opinion. In any case, it is clear that heightening of the philosophers' Bacchic ecstasy is ascribed to Empedocles' influence. Galaxidorus' main idea, concerning Socrates' knowledge and its sources, is questioned in this dialogue, but his statement on ancient philosophers remains unchallenged; given the importance of Pythagoreanism for Plutarch, in particular in this dialogue,[253] Galaxidorus appears to recite well-known facts.

Empedocles' views on divine *mania* are conveyed by the fifth-century AD medical author Caelius Aurelianus, who adapted the work of Soranus of Ephesus, active in the second-century AD. The author addressed Empedocles' *furor* immediately after having faithfully related Plato's passage from the *Phaedrus* on the four subdivisions of god-sent *mania*. It is reasonable to accept the reference to Empedocles and his adherents as authentic:[254] 'The school of Empedocles holds that one form of madness (*furor*) consists in a purification of the soul, and the other in an alienation of the reason, resulting from a bodily disease or indisposition.'[255]

The 'alienation of reason' is a mental disorder which is discussed in detail in the rest of Caelius Aurelianus' chapter on chronic *mania*, but the 'madness consisting in alienation of the reason' may be juxtaposed with Empedocles' poem *Purifications* and his request from the gods for 'a pure stream' in the opening verses of his poem.[256] This passage, notwithstanding its date, seems to testify to the pre-Platonic association of spiritual quest, as well as philosophic and/or poetic creativity, with *mania*.

Empedocles' accomplishments, the control over weather and the souls, healing, as well as the ability to enter the heaven and the netherworld, are considered by many as characteristically shamanic.[257] However, Empedocles' own poems (or poem) testify better than any other text that this thinker obtained many of his insights as revelations, practiced ecstatic soul travelling, and regarded the transmission of philosophic knowledge as initiation. Empedocles considered the vocations of prophet, bard, healer, and ruler to be the highest point the human soul can reach,[258] and, in all probability regarded himself as an incarnation of all of them, prepared for the ultimate incarnation as a god, and already regarded as such by his fellow-citizens.[259] In particular, the feat of 'bringing back the force of a dead man from Hades' could not be accomplished except through the sorcerer's own descent into the netherworld.[260] If so, Empedocles believed that he had performed catabasis on multiple occasions, whenever he wished, which implies that like Aethalides and other Archaic sages, he and his environment envisaged his soul's travelling – out-of-body experiences, in modern parlance – as voyages to Hades. Soul travelling between the worlds is the most essential ecstatic practice, and Empedocles' own boasting of this gift is a clear testimony to his involvement in alteration of consciousness. Another allusion to such practices is Empedocles' advice to his disciple 'to press (or set to work) his strained *prapides* and contemplate [the ideas of his master] kindly, with pure attention' in order to gain absolute understanding; Empedocles also praised 'the happy man who acquired the wealth of divine *prapides*.'[261] Empedocles probably exercised and recommended techniques of concentration and breath control, following in this respect Pythagoras, whose spiritual achievements, gained owing to 'stretching' of the *prapides*, have already been discussed.

The dichotomy between religion and natural philosophy was apparently foreign to Empedocles.[262] In his vision of the cosmogony, Empedocles depicts a vortex, and insists on this image, using two synonyms, *dinê* and *strophalinx*, both meaning 'whirl, eddy.'[263] The vortex envisaged by Empedocles consists of various objects combining and mingling and exchanging their paths. This picture of endless rotation of shifting shapes immediately evokes numerous accounts of the mental vortex experienced in altered states of consciousness.[264] At the second stage of his cosmogony, namely zoogony, Empedocles draws a nightmarish picture of 'many faces without necks, arms wandered without shoulders, the eyes strayed alone, in need of foreheads' which begin to merge with one another.[265] These apparitions – Aetius in the sixth century AD called them 'phantom-like,' *eidôlophaneis*[266] – are immediately reminiscent of apparitions experienced in the state of trance. Here again, the visualisation is extremely vivid. The vortex and the phantoms are classical examples of mental images appearing during altered states of consciousness. It is clear from their visual intensity that Empedocles' description is not just an intellectual construct or a fantasy. He believes that he had a revelation,[267] and delights in the magnificent picture he saw: 'a wonder to look upon.'[268]

It is suggested that Empedocles' invocations to the Muse ensue from his experience of her epiphany.[269] In principle, 'the whole' cannot be perceived by the humans limited to their life experiences, but a divine being, the Muse, allowed Empedocles access to the very limits of the mortal thought.[270] In Empedocles' fragments, the affinity of the mortal consciousness to the divine mind, *phrên hierê*, which is the real god, is hinted to on several occasions,[271] and most dramatically in his instruction concerning the correct way to arrive at true knowledge: 'but know that clearly, listening to the account from a god.'[272] The philosopher's way to wisdom, alluded to in his admonition to the disciple, appears to be envisaged as his mystery initiation by the Muse who mediates between him and the divine mind.[273] Empedocles' revelations are reminiscent of Parmenides' mystic encounter with the goddess who disclosed to him the eternal truth.[274] The Muse also guided the philosopher-poet in his self-imposed censorship: some things were not suitable 'for creatures of the day to hear,' therefore Empedocles himself urges his disciple to keep the esoteric teaching 'mute in his breast.'[275] Socrates' mystagogue, the wise but mortal Diotima, is preceded by Empedocles' immortal mystagogue, who conducts him to the apprehension of his non-anthropomorphic god. In his turn, Empedocles, like Diotima, promises to initiate his disciple into the mysteries of divine wisdom.[276]

In sum, Empedocles' tenets seem to have been developed in three stages, each corresponding to a different state of the author's mind. First it struck Empedocles as a revelatory vision, most probably in a trance-like state. Later, when in a normal waking state of consciousness, he worked it out into a coherent system.[277] Finally, he expounded his ideas in verse.[278] Empedocles' *mania* is attested to by the contents of his poems and by the appreciation of his philosophising as involving *furor* and *bakcheia* by his later readers.

Shamans and mystics?

Abaris, Hermotimus, Epimenides, and Pythagoras are considered by many scholars following K. Meuli to have been shamanic figures.[279] In contrast, many refute any connection whatsoever between Greek spirituality and shamanism.[280] The comparison of ecstatics to shamans, almost standard in Biblical Studies,[281] is still considered controversial in Classical Studies.

Regarding shamanism, the main division between the classicists is between those who argue that trances, soul travelling, claims at super-human knowledge, and other phenomena attested in Greece feature characteristics associated with shamanism, and those who maintain that ecstatic practices of the Greeks are *sui generis* and have nothing to do with shamanism. The boundaries between the adversaries broadly correspond to the gap between anthropologists who regard shamanism as etic, that is, cross-cultural phenomenon, and those who insist that it is emic, culture-specific, limited to Siberia where it originated.[282] The controversy is not about the term, but about theory and methodology. If shamanism is universal, then data, observations, and conclusions concerning shamanic activities in different cultures can be applied to the study of congruent activities in other cultures, including that of ancient Greece. If it is not so, then classicists have nothing to learn from anthropologists and neuroscientists studying shamanism.

The last two decades saw important developments that are relevant to shamanism and Classics.[283] In 1992, Jane Atkinson wrote about 'shamanisms' in plural, emphasising culture-specific settings as well as the generic quality of the term and the phenomena. Since then the word 'shamanism,' in singular, has made its comeback in a series of overarching studies, covering various activities, such as healing, music, use of psychoactive substances in order to manipulate consciousness, and the modalities of performance. Shamanism is studied in two perspectives: ethnographically and sociologically in contemporary societies, and historically and archaeologically in the societies of the past. Historically, shamanism seems to have appeared with the early *Homo sapiens*, and still occurs mainly in foraging societies; it continued into agricultural societies of the past and present in a heavily transformed version. This cultural and chronological diversity underscores the cross-cultural nature of the concept of shamanism and its heuristic validity, even if the term is a Western construct. Thus, the majority opinion today regards shamanism as etic, worldwide phenomenon.[284]

Another important question is what the core of shamanism is and whether the term may be used in a universal sense, to denote the cross-cultural human propensity to experience altered states of consciousness. In recent decades research suggests that shamanistic experiences are focused on manipulation of consciousness. To use the definition of M. Winkelman, the shaman is 'a technician of consciousness who utilizes those potentials for healing and for personal and social transformations.'[285] This approach is quite established in neuroscience and cognitive science of religion.[286] Two points are crucial. First, not any alteration of consciousness is shamanic: 'the key feature of shamanism is soul flight or out-of-body experience.'[287] Assessment of empirical characteristics of other magico-religious practitioners worldwide reveal clusters that are typical of other categories, different from shamans. Secondly, shamanic practices are not atemporal: variations in cultural context affect their characteristics.

Returning to the Greeks, three inferences are essential. First, the result is neuropsychological research make redundant the question whether Greek ascetic visionaries and mystics owe their techniques, lore, cosmology, or any other part of their practice and teaching to shamanism, with which they were acquainted in its Scythian version, or through Anatolian[288] or even Indian connections.[289] There are other venues of explanation apart from diffusion. 'Traces of shamanism' in ancient Greece do not need to be explicated as 'vestiges of pre-Olympian world.'[290] Nor did the ancient Greeks have to borrow from other cultures their techniques of reaching altered states of consciousness or accounts of ecstatic revelations. Being human, they could not escape encounters with such states which had existed inside their own culture from times immemorial.[291] The conclusion that the Greeks did not need to adopt ecstatic techniques from overseas implies that the diffusionist model should be abandoned. The question to be asked is how ecstatic practices evolved inside the Greek culture.

Second, since shamanism is regarded as a cross-cultural phenomenon, we can legitimately discuss the question whether ancient Greek culture contained shamanic elements. Third, a major misconception of the 'shamanistic' approach is that it associates all altered states of consciousness with shamanism, or even with its Scythian variety. However, shamanism is only one category of alteration of consciousness, and this is important methodologically. When exploring ritual healing, prophetic trances, visions and mystical experiences of the Greeks we should not label all of them as 'shamanistic' only because they involve altered states of consciousness.

Given that the Archaic Greek experts in manipulation of consciousness did not have to learn their ecstatic techniques from foreign cultures, we return to the question whether these techniques can be defined as 'shamanic' or profitably compared with them. If indeed soul flight or out-of-body experience is the core of shamanism, especially when providing insights leading to personal growth and combined with healing, then the activities of Abaris, Epimenides, Hermotimus, and later Pythagoras, Parmenides, and Empedocles contained shamanic elements. Even in these cases, it is important to stress that ancient Greek world view and religious practice were not shamanic, and many characteristics of shamanism, such as control of animal spirits and belief in their ability to transform into animals, communal ritual activities led by the shaman, and extensive involvement in sorcery,[292] are not attested to in the evidence on the Presocratics. As to Socrates and Plato, they seem to have been familiar with the Archaic techniques of consciousness manipulation, but this knowledge alone is not sufficient to ascribe shamanistic traits to these two thinkers. Conversely, as discussed above, in many respects they were close to the mystical tradition, entailing a different cluster of characteristics. Most essential in the mystical assemblage is the experience of fusion with the divine One; in addition, ineffability; cessation of usual notions of time and space; modification of the feeling of the mystic's own body and perception of the environment; abandonment of the self; change of the world view; intense joy and experience of all-embracing love.[293] Not all these characteristics appear in the evidence on Socrates and Plato, who cannot therefore be defined as mystics *sensu stricto*, but seem to have lived through mystical experiences.

Tagging Greek thinkers as 'shamans' or 'mystics' is a simple way to call attention to their engagement in alteration of consciousness, but it is imprecise and may be misleading, prompting associations with clusters of characteristics absent in Greece. However, comparisons – rather than identifications – with shamanism, mysticism, and other cultural phenomena involving alteration of consciousness are essential and fruitful. They sharpen the researcher's eye for details that could otherwise remain unnoticed, and allow evaluation of etic and emic features of the activity in question. In addition, this approach, which may be defined as phenomenological, makes possible cautious inferences from congruent or similar phenomena in other cultures.

For instance, some psychiatrists and scholars, beginning from Ph. Pinel,[294] argue that Greek thinkers who experienced visions and revelations, Socrates in particular, were in a way mentally deranged. The opposite assertion, namely that alterations of consciousness of Greek thinkers did not result from pathological conditions, is corroborated by modern research on shamanism and mysticism: self-cultivation and manipulation of consciousness are practiced by individuals who are quite healthy mentally and physically.[295] Thus, modern research of experiencers of consciousness alterations suggests that in ancient Greece as well, manipulation of consciousness by sages and philosophers did not indicate that they were insane.

Another interesting comparison comes from the world of both Eastern and Western mysticism. Mediaeval Ch'an and Zen Buddhists have left rich literature, including biographies of the great masters, but one of the most essential understandings is that authentic mystical transmission could take place in the community, between a master and a disciple, and remained not only oral, but even wordless. Jesuit spirituality is also 'at its very core, oral,' 'a lamplight transmitted generation to generation, orally, from teacher to disciple.'[296] The peak experience of mystical enlightenment can be attained solely as a result of a routine of renouncement, contemplation, and study.[297] This coexistence of extensive writing and reading with the requirement of personal apprenticeship and self-cultivation, common to several mystical traditions, allows a better understanding of the paradoxical mistrust of written texts on the part of a prolific writer, such as Plato.

Furthermore, comparisons between practices involving manipulation of consciousness in Greece and other societies allow an attempt at rough reconstruction of their history in Greece. In certain historical and social situations the ability of some people to alter their state of consciousness is suppressed, whereas in other societies, ancient Greece among them, it is valued and cultivated. This phenomenon did not spring from naught, it probably continued a long tradition of manipulation of consciousness which had left traces in the culture's mythology. Such figures as Hermes who mediated between the three worlds, of the gods, humans, and the dead, and Orpheus the singer of charms, prophet and traveller to Hades, are only two examples of divine or heroic personages modelled on real-life shamanic individuals.[298] S. West has convincingly demonstrated that the elements interpreted as shamanistic 'derive from ancient Greek poetic tradition itself based on preliterate forms of narrative in the development of which shamanistic performances may well have been of primary importance.'[299]

The sixth century may seem as bringing a proliferation of figures involved in such practices, but the increase in extant sources probably ensues from the growing interest in recording curious facts rather than a growth in the number of spiritual seekers, supposedly following the exposure to the shamanic cultures of the Black Sea area.[300] In the sixth and fifth centuries, soul voyages of the type practiced by Hermotimus and Aethalides were still familiar to the public, but were cleansed of supernatural traits characteristic of Abaris and Aristeas, safely associated with long-gone days. Although Pythagoras' paranormal endeavours were famous, and perhaps exaggerated, Empedocles had to work hard in order to leave to posterity an image of himself as a supernatural being. Parmenides' claims were more limited: he only maintained that he met a divine being in a supernatural way, hinting at initiatory context. All these figures probably made efforts in order to manipulate their consciousness, be that seclusion in an isolated space, breath exercises, or other methods.

In Socrates' case, the deity was replaced by a modest *daimonion*, and the emphasis was moved to the achievements of the philosopher's soul; comparisons to initiations remain a dominant motif, and the words *mania* and *bakcheia* used in Socrates' inner circle indicate the awareness of the nature of a part of his philosophising. With Plato, it is only the philosopher's soul and its passionate attraction to the ineffable divine reality that persist. Most significantly, Socrates' trances and Plato's moments of illumination seem to have been spontaneous rather than based on a traditional technique.

In summary, in the seventh to fourth centuries, alterations of consciousness of Greek thinkers, or the ideas regarding these phenomena, underwent important transformations along two main lines. On the one hand, the technical aspect changed, from traditional sojourns in closed spaces and intentional manipulation of consciousness, perhaps by means of breathing techniques, to trances and out-of-body experiences and spontaneous illuminations. This is not to say that a particular technique was exclusive during a given period: these are tendencies rather than prescribed rules. On the other hand, the source of the divine truth evolved, as well, from non-equivocal identification with a usually named deity, to a daemon or unnamed divinity. Thus, the technique and cultural interpretation of alterations of consciousness of Greek thinkers transformed, but their importance remained crucial, from the Archaic *maîtres de vérité* to Socrates and Plato.

Coda: Democritus the mad philosopher

The Hippocratic corpus contains a series of apocryphal texts concerning Democritus' madness.[301] The entire story is most probably a late Hellenistic invention, to be associated with the Cynic circles,[302] but it is very instructive. The council of Abdera asked Hippocrates to come from Cos and cure Democritus' madness: the man behaved in a bizarre way, he laughed at everything and everyone, investigated 'things in Hades,' saw 'images' in the air, and said that he sometimes 'travelled in the boundless.'[303] The latter idea is perhaps modelled on the images of the Archaic masters of truth whose souls were said to leave their bodies at will, and travel to distant lands.[304] In another letter, Hippocrates summarises further details that he has heard about Democritus, who had neither family nor property, but spent his time 'in caves and in stillness (*hêsuchia*)': once again, the eccentric philosopher is ascribed habits based on the traditional image of a thinker, from Pythagoras to Aristophanes' Socrates.[305] Before Hippocrates had seen him, Democritus was diagnosed as melancholic, and his flight to caves was explained by the philosopher's wish to be free from distraction, rather than by his madness: the Abderites did not understand the reasons of Democritus' behaviour.[306] How could they? In every Greek community solitary existence, that is avoidance of human company, was immediately conspicuous.[307]

Hippocrates' perspicacity was validated by an apparition of Asclepius and Alêtheia (Verity) in his dream: he realised that Democritus' behaviour seemed aberrant to ignorant common people, but in reality resulted from the philosopher's supreme wisdom and unwillingness to take part in mundane human activities.[308] Hippocrates therefore announced to his Abderite friends that Democritus did not need any medical attention, and this conviction was further reinforced when the two great men met. The physician found the philosopher seating in the countryside, pale and emaciated, with cut up animals and books around him, writing a treatise on madness (*peri maniês*);[309] in order to discover the reason of madness, Democritus dissected animals and looked for the location of bile in their bodies.[310] Obviously, nothing could please Hippocrates more than a meeting with a scientist exploring animals in search of one of the humours that were the cornerstone of his medical theory. Democritus explained to Hippocrates how miserable and mad all the regular people were, absorbed in their ridiculous passions, and at the end of their conversation Hippocrates pronounced the 'mad' philosopher 'wisest of men.' At the end of the day, it became clear that not the bile caused real madness but the senselessness of the majority of humans wasting their lives thoughtlessly. Hippocrates was intelligent enough to comprehend that he had been one of these people, constantly busy with unimportant tasks and neglecting his intellectual pursuits: the madman had cured his doctor.[311]

This fable demonstrates that even in late Hellenistic period, the 'vulgar and uninitiated' could deem behaviour of philosophers deviant enough to require medical attention. Similar to the Hellenistic author of pseudo-Aristotelian *Problem* 30, who lists prominent philosophers among the renowned melancholics,[312] the writer of the letters associates *melancholia* with genius: mental disorder and exceptional wisdom looked so similar that they could be easily confused. The intellectual who took the trouble to compose the letters clearly regarded himself as one of the wise who knew that the sublime nature of a philosopher's mad conduct could be correctly apprehended only by his enlightened peers, such as the knowledgeable Hippocrates.

Conclusions

Writing on Pythagoras' theory that the nature of things is Number, F. M. Cornford supposed that this great discovery resulted from an illumination that crowned a long and painful travail, a phase of enhanced mental activity that had to have alternated with phases of observation and contemplation:

> The final act of recognition must be overwhelming, because the truth, in such a moment of insight, is not presented as an intellectual formula, compact and comprehensive. It comes rather as an undefined mass of significance, fused in a glow of intense feeling. It may take years or generations for all the meaning and implications to be drawn out and expressed in words. In

that process the glow of feeling fades out, and it may be forgotten that it was an essential part of the original experience. Certainly the apprehension of beauty – in particular, the beauty of harmonious sound – inspired the theory of Pythagoras, which could never have been framed by mere cold deductions of logical reasoning.[313]

Rational argumentation and the final coherent form of the doctrines of Greek philosophers do not imply that the origin of the proposed tenets was in pure ratiocination. It is only to be expected that for the most part, what Greek philosophers wrote stemmed from logical deliberation: Plato or the Platonic philosopher who penned the *Seventh Letter* required long-term concentration on philosophising before being endowed with a spark of insight; and rendering this insight in a comprehensible form, as well as 'checking by reason' required by Parmenides' goddess, would also be a long endeavour. However, it was the moment of illumination that was the pinnacle of the intellectual efforts and rendered them worthwhile.

Socrates' alteration of consciousness is attested to by his own words (*pace* Plato), testimonies of people who knew him, and the contents of his teaching as related by Plato. Plato's mystical experiences are implicitly alluded to in his writings, and explicitly attested to in the *Seventh Letter*. Parmenides' alteration of consciousness can be inferred from his own description of his experience and his doctrine; Empedocles' visions can be assumed by judging his texts and references to his madness by later writers. Life legends of the Archaic *maîtres de vérité* imply that during that period, sages practiced alterations of consciousness. Socrates is *daimonios anêr* owing to his meetings with the *daimonion*, and in this respect he belongs to the same line as Epimenides, *theios anêr* who talked to the gods, and Parmenides and Empedocles, who encountered only one goddess or Muse.

These thinkers were neither shamans nor mystics, although their activities comprised elements associated with shamanic or mystical clusters. Notwithstanding idiosyncrasies of these colourful figures, a pattern characterising their modes of alteration of consciousness emerges: the Presocratics appear to have intentionally manipulated their consciousness, and therefore were in a position to control it. Socrates and Plato possibly experienced alterations of consciousness but these were spontaneous moments of illumination that could occur in a most unpredictable place. Out-of-body experiences are alluded to persistently almost by all of the discussed personages. The way of verbalisation of visions attained in the state of altered consciousness evolved from epic poems comprising accounts of encounters with deities to oral conversations or written texts rendered in prose, describing revelations in much more abstract form.

Although in the extant evidence Plato's Socrates alone refers to his own philosophising as *mania*, it is only this definition of the spiritual quest that is unique: alterations of consciousness were probably experienced by several thinkers of the Archaic and Classical periods.

Notes

1 For instance, J. Bussanich observes: 'The partial or complete eclipse of the role of faith or revelation in the philosophy of Socrates (and even in Plato) is the result of excessive focus on the philosopher's beliefs or ideas while ignoring the experiences which motivated them' (Bussanich 1999: 38).

2 A paraphrase of Price (1989: 67): 'Plato, the arch-rationalist, is at last doing justice to unreason; but we shall not find him changing sides.' As is clear from this chapter, I disagree with A. W. Price's way to substantiate his conclusion.

3 Ustinova (2009a: 177–178).

4 Cottingham (2000); Clarke (2006: 58–59).

5 Hadamard (1945: 15).

6 Ramachandran and Blakeslee (1998: 195).

7 Mazzarello (2000).

8 Mazzarello (2000).

9 Hempel (1966: 16).

10 Hadamard (1945).

11 Hadamard (1945: 122); Rugg (1963: 39–42).

12 Hadamard (1945: 16, 56–64).

13 Rugg (1963: 30).

14 Rugg (1963: 32).

15 Rugg (1963: 39–42).

16 Rugg (1963: 22); cf. Martindale (1981: 372–373) on 'effortless, non-intellectual nature of creative inspiration' and 'illuminative flash' as a stage in the creative process.

17 Hempel (1966: 3–18).

18 These ideas were put forward by Reichenbach (1938). For a recent overview of the subject see Schickore and Steinle (2006).

19 Popper (1959: 7).

20 Pl. *Symp.* 218B; Morgan (1990: 95–96); Périllié (2015: 99). For a different interpretation of this phrase see Rosen (1968: 13, 303).

21 See Chapter 2. In addition, if ritual initiation requires ritual purity, philosophical initiation entails moral purity – and Socrates' virtuousness is attested by Alcibiades, who confesses his failed attempt to seduce Socrates (*Smp.* 219BC).

 V. Adluri, arguing that 'Platonic philosophy is meant to transform the reader in the manner of an initiation ritual' (Adluri 2006: 408), assumes perhaps an exceedingly radical position, attributing to Plato a wish to transform all or many of his readers: only very few people could, in Plato's opinion, be initiated into the mysteries of wisdom and become true philosophers. I discuss this subject in the next section.

22 *Phd.* 69CD, above, Chapter 2; Morgan (1990: 63–64, 75).

23 *Phd.* 69CD: ὥς φασιν οἱ περὶ τὰς τελετάς, "ναρθηκοφόροι μὲν πολλοί, βάκχοι δέ τε παῦροι·" οὗτοι δ' εἰσὶν κατὰ τὴν ἐμὴν δόξαν οὐκ ἄλλοι ἢ οἱ πεφιλοσοφηκότες ὀρθῶς. ὧν δὴ καὶ ἐγὼ κατά γε τὸ δυνατὸν οὐδὲν ἀπέλιπον ἐν τῷ βίῳ ἀλλὰ παντὶ τρόπῳ προυθυμήθην γενέσθαι. This most important passage is usually treated just as a reference to mystery initiations (e.g. Burnet 1911: 45; Rowe 1993: 151), or even not mentioned in a commentary (e.g. Gallop 1975: 103). Socrates' linking of rational inquiry with ecstatic rites is emphasised by M. L. Morgan (1990: 64), but he regarded it as a comparison, rather than a positive statement. In contrast, K. A. Morgan (2010: 64) finds in the *Phaedo* no more than 'the imagery of religious revelation and initiation,' 'drawing religious and mystical models into a philosophical discussion.'

24 As translated by D. Gallop ('devotees'), C. J. Rowe ('true initiates'), W.R.M. Lamb ('mystics'). R. Hackforth preserves 'Bacchants.'

25 And was far from irony, which Dixsaut (1991: 338–339) finds in the comparison of philosophers with *bakchoi*. For the exaltation of Socrates' audience see Périllié (2015:

54, 57, 69). The capability of Socrates to communicate his elated state of mind to his listeners may be compared with the ability of the inspired poets to their audience, discussed in Chapter 6.

26 Hdt. 2. 81.

27 E. *Hipp.* 952–955.

28 West (1983: 16).

29 Vernant (1983: 110–112).

30 *Phd.* 66 DE: εἰ γὰρ μὴ οἷόν τε μετὰ τοῦ σώματος μηδὲν καθαρῶς γνῶναι, δυοῖν θάτερον, ἢ οὐδαμοῦ ἔστιν κτήσασθαι τὸ εἰδέναι ἢ τελευτήσασιν· τότε γὰρ αὐτὴ καθ' αὑτὴν ἡ ψυχὴ ἔσται χωρὶς τοῦ σώματος, πρότερον δ' οὔ. καὶ ἐν ᾧ ἂν ζῶμεν, οὕτως, ὡς ἔοικεν, ἐγγυτάτω ἐσόμεθα τοῦ εἰδέναι, ἐὰν ὅτι μάλιστα μηδὲν ὁμιλῶμεν τῷ σώματι μηδὲ κοινωνῶμεν (translation H. N. Fowler). See Morgan (1990: 55–79).

31 *Phd.* 65CD. For the expression χαίρειν ἐᾶν, 'bid farewell,' or 'take leave' see Burnet (1911: 27); Hackforth (1972: 46).

   The body is considered as hampering or even corrupting the soul in several key Platonic dialogues: besides the *Phaedrus*, discussed below, one can cite the *Republic* (611C); *Timaeus* (43BC), etc.

32 Robin (1935: 99).

33 *Phd.* 67C: Κάθαρσις δὲ εἶναι ἆρα οὐ τοῦτο συμβαίνει, ὅπερ πάλαι ἐν τῷ λόγῳ λέγεται, τὸ χωρίζειν ὅτι μάλιστα ἀπὸ τοῦ σώματος τὴν ψυχὴν καὶ ἐθίσαι αὐτὴν καθ' αὑτὴν πανταχόθεν ἐκ τοῦ σώματος συναγείρεσθαί τε καὶ ἀθροίζεσθαι, καὶ οἰκεῖν κατὰ τὸ δυνατὸν καὶ ἐν τῷ νῦν παρόντι καὶ ἐν τῷ ἔπειτα μόνην καθ' αὑτήν, ἐκλυομένην ὥσπερ [ἐκ] δεσμῶν ἐκ τοῦ σώματος (translation H.N. Fowler). Socrates insists on these ideas in *Phd.* 81BC, 83A: Detienne (1963: 71).

34 Bussanich (2006: 200).

35 Dodds (1945: 22).

36 *Phd.* 64C.

37 *Phdr.* 250C, cf. 247DE; Riedweg (1987: 37–38, 55); see also Chapter 2.

38 *Phdr.* 250AB. Plato is most probably alluding to the Eleusinian mysteries and their 'shine,' Riedweg (1987: 41, 46–47).

39 *Phdr.* 247DE. On *anamnêsis* see Vlastos (1995); Gulley (1962: 4–23); Ackrill (1973); Gallop (1975: 113–137); Bostock (1986: 60–115); Morgan (1990: 69–71); Bedu-Addo (1991); Scott (1995: 24–52).

40 Vernant (1983: 93–94); Simondon (1982: 312); Adluri (2006: 419); Ustinova (2012: 122).

41 οὐκέτ' αὐτῶν γίγνονται, 250A.

42 *Phdr.* 249D: ἐνθουσιάζων δὲ λέληθεν τοὺς πολλούς. Morgan (2010: 54–55) interprets the word ἐνθουσιάζων as 'divinely occupied': 'rather than being invaded by an out-side force, the mind of the philosopher leaves the mortal world'; 'being inspired is being next to the divine, by means of your memory'; Rowe (1990: 237): 'state. . . . of inspiration.' Carter (1967: 116) stops short of accepting the irrationality of the phi-losopher's madness; in his opinion, the philosopher's madness is possession by love, who is a spirit that 'interprets between gods and men,' but it looks like madness only to the multitude. In reality, 'the knowledge of the Forms can only be got by reason.' Werner (2011: 51) emphasises the passivity of divine madness, when 'the individual becomes a vehicle for divine action.'

43 Morgan 1990: 170–171, 161: Plato 'endorsed philosophy as the highest form of mad-ness'; Morgan 2010: 56: 'Inspiration is recollection'; Carter (1967: 116) suggests an interpretation which identifies recollection with inspiration and enthusiasm. C. Schefer goes even further and suggests that mystical initiation is 'the central idea of the dialogue, emphasised in its title 'The Radiant' (Schefer 1996: 196).

44 Carter (1967: 117–118).

45 Pl. *Symp.* 220D, cf. 174D; Guthrie (1962–67: 3: 402–405); Nieto (1997: 39); Morgan (1990: 94).

46   *Smp*. 174D–175C, translation W.R.M. Lamb.
47   *Smp*. 220D.
48   Gel. 2. 1. 1: *oculis eundem in locum directis cogitabundus, tamquam quodam secessu mentis atque animi facto a corpore.*
49   *Av*. 1281; Dover (1968: li); X. *Mem*. 1. 6. 2
50   Pl. *Symp*. 219B–220C.
51   Russel (1961: 109).
52   Pigeaud (2008: 628–629).
53   Hackforth (1972: 16); Montiglio (2005: 172).
54   Burnet (1911: xlvii); Russel (1961: 107).
55   Rosen (1968: 308–309).
56   Morgan (1990: 93); Bussanich (2006: 210). For an opposite view, namely the claim that Socrates was no mystic, see Vlastos (1991: 97); McPherran (1996a: 295).
57   E.g. Hackforth (1972: 15).
58   Bussanich (1999: 45–46).
        Some meditative practices, in modern West and East, are known to allow maintenance of normal body temperature in extremely frigid conditions, for instance, G-tummo meditation in Tibet (Kozhevnikov et al. 2013); the Dutch record holder Win Hof is known for his ability to withstand cold by using his mind: www.icemanwimhof.com/en-home, viewed on April 2, 2015. E. Cardeña kindly brought this information to my attention.
59   Montiglio (2005: 172).
60   Pl. *Phdr*. 242BC; for various aspects of the subject see Brisson (2005).
61   Pl. *Ap*. 31D; 40BC; 41D; *Tht*. 151A.
62   Pl. *Ap*. 40A; Brisson (2005: 5).
63   *Euthd*. 272E.
64   As argued by Vlastos (1991: 167–171, 280–287). On *daimonion* as not impairing Socrates' consciousness see McPherran (1996b: 180–181); Bussanich (2006: 206).
65   See Chapter 7.
66   *Ap*. 29D; Naddaf (2013: 306); cf. *Phdr*. 265B, *R*. 499BC on divine inspiration.
67   McPherran (1996a: 135); McPherran (2011: 132). For a discussion of the *daimonion* and the motivations behind the prosecution see Brickhouse and Smith (2000).
68   P. *R*. 6. 496C; Brisson (2005: 5).
69   *Smp*. 202E–203A; 219C.
70   Brisson (2005: 3).
71   X. *Mem*. 1. 1. 4–5, translation E.C. Marchant; 4. 8. 1; X. *Ap*. 13. Protropaic function of the *daimonion*: Diog. Laert. 2. 5. 29; Long (2006: 64); Pigeaud (2008: 627–628).
72   [Pl.] *Alc*. 2 140CD.
73   X. *Mem*. 4. 8. 1.
74   [Ps]-Pl. *Thg*. 128D–130A; Cic. *Div*. 1. 54. 123–124. Cicero even refers to a catalogue of Socrates' premonitions by the Stoic Antipater.
75   Havelock (1972), Dover (1968: xxxii–lvii) and Sommerstein (1982: 3) maintain that Aristophanes' Socrates is basically a grotesque, typifying all the crazy intellectuals and other parasites; Strauss (1966) and Nussbaum (1980) contend that notwithstanding comic distortion, Aristophanes still portrayed the individual philosopher Socrates.
76   *Nu*. 362. *Ra*. 1491–1500: χαρίεν οὖν μὴ Σωκράτει |παρακαθήμενον λαλεῖν. . .|. . .καὶ σκαριφησμοῖσι λήρων |διατριβὴν ἀργὸν ποιεῖσθαι,|παραφρονοῦντος ἀνδρός; see Sommerstein (1996: 295). Λαλεῖν, λήρων and παραφρνέω are words used in Hippocratic descriptions of derangement (Byl 1990).
77   Dover (1968: lii–liii).
78   *Nu*. 102.
79   *Cr*. 396D, 399A, 407D, 409D; on Euthyphro's identification see Ademollo (2011: 242); Barney (2001: 57).

80 *Euthph.* 3C, translation H. N. Fowler.
81 Cic. *Div.* 1. 54. 122; Plu. *Mor.* 588DF.
82 For a comprehensive analysis of the text see Nesselrath (2010).
83 Plu. *Mor.* 588D: τὸ Σωκράτους δαιμόνιον οὐκ ὄψις ἀλλὰ φωνῆς τινος αἴσθησις ἢ λόγου νόησις, 588E: λόγον . . . δαίμονος ἄνευ φωνῆς ἐφαπτόμενον αὐτῷ τῷ δηλουμένῳ τοῦ νοοῦντος; 589BC. Simmias: Corlu (1970: 17–18); for a commentary on these passages see Döring (1984); Babut (1984).
84 Vlastos (1991: 280–287); see also his correspondence on this matter: Vlastos et al. (2000).
85 Nussbaum (1980: 234).
86 Long (2006: 67, 72); McPherran (1996a: 187–194); McPherran (1996b: 180).
87 As Long (2006: 67) assumes.
88 As Brickhouse and Smith (2000: 86), and contrary to the argument by Long (2006: 67). One may compare Einstein's account of his non-verbal associative thinking in images, rendered in conventional words only at a late stage (Hadamard 1945: 142).
89 Lampe (2013: 405–406); Brisson (2005: 3).
90 Brickhouse and Smith (2000: 86); Brickhouse and Smith (1994: 190).
91 Brisson (2005: 2).
92 Reeve (2000: 35); Bussanich (1999: 16–17); Bussanich (2006: 206–208).
93 Herman (2011: 128–134).
94 Hadamard (1945: 122).
95 Furthermore, the borderline between one's inner self and external intrusion was not as clear as in modern secular Western culture, as testified to by numerous Socrates' remarks (e.g. *Tht.* 150D–151D; *Chrm.* 172E–173A; Lampe 2013: 406–408). See Lukoff (2011: 314) on the importance of cultural situation for diagnosing a vision as pathology.
96 E.g. *Phd.* 60E–61A. For the divergence in Socrates' attitude to his *daimonion* and dreams see McPherran (1996b: 179).
97 *Phd.* passim, esp. 66B–67B.
98 Graf (2004); Herman (2011).
99 Pigeaud (2008: 649).
100 Hackforth (1972: 15); Havelock (1963: 371); Motte (1963: 426).
101 F. M. Cornford, writing on the final stage of the trajectory to immortality in the *Symposium*, arrives at the following conclusion: 'The eye of the soul directly contemplates reality. We may, and perhaps must, conjecture that the description is based on some experience which Plato had at privileged moments. There is no warrant in tradition for supporting that he ever passed in a condition of trance or ecstasy. The Neoplatonists would have seized eagerly on any such tradition, had it existed in the school. Perhaps Plato's experience should be called metaphysical, rather than religious – a recognition of ultimate truth. On the other hand, it is not purely intellectual, but a conversion of every element in the soul by the last transfiguration of Eros: and at that point the distinction between the metaphysical and the religious may become meaningless' (Cornford 1950: 78). Although some details in Cornford's assessment are arguable, its general assertions are persuasive.
D. S. Werner suggests to interpret the philosopher's *mania* as 'a particular kind of *epistemic state*, in which the soul achieves a rapturous vision of the Forms' (Werner 2011: 48, italics in the original).
102 See the survey of the opinions on the subject in Brisson (1987a: 72). For convincing arguments in support of the letter's authenticity, based on its content, see Aalders (1972); Rhodes (2003: 119–130); Szlezák (1985: 386–405); Brisson (1987a: 138–166); Liatzi (2008: 10–14). A statistical analysis of the Platonic corpus has demonstrated that the *Seventh Letter* is stylometrically very close to the *Laws* and was written by Plato at the same time as the *Philebus*, in the mid- or late-350s (Ledger 1989: 148–151, 208–209). See Brisson (1987a: 19) for a survey of earlier stylometric

research and his own conclusion that the style of the *Letters* corresponds to that of the *Laws*. The *Seventh Letter* as Plato's autobiography: Brisson (2000: 15–14).

　　Scholars who consider it Plato's work or at least Platonic: Howald (1923: 19); Harward (1932: 72–75); Morrow (1935: 61–79); Crombie (1962–1963: 1: 14); Guthrie (1962–67: 4: 65–66); Rosen (1968: xiii–xvii); Solmsen (1969); Gaiser (1980: 18); von Fritz (1966); Brisson (1987a: 20); Sayre (1988: 94); Bussanich (1999: 49); Knab (2006: 50); Naddaf (2013: 304). Edelstein (1966) and Gulley (1971) argue that this text was a forgery written during the first decades after Plato's death; Burnyeat and Frede (2015) regard it as a fake written by a second-century mediocre dramatist.

103 *Ep.* 7. 341C: οὔκουν ἐμόν γε περὶ αὐτῶν ἔστιν σύγγραμμα οὐδὲ μήποτε γένηται· ῥητὸν γὰρ οὐδαμῶς ἐστιν ὡς ἄλλα μαθήματα, ἀλλ᾽ ἐκ πολλῆς συνουσίας γιγνομένης περὶ τὸ πρᾶγμα αὐτὸ καὶ τοῦ συζῆν ἐξαίφνης, οἷον ἀπὸ πυρὸς πηδήσαντος ἐξαφθὲν φῶς, ἐν τῇ ψυχῇ γενόμενον αὐτὸ ἑαυτὸ ἤδη τρέφει (translation R. G. Bury).

104 Plot. 6. 9. 4.

105 Rhodes (2003: 176–177).

106 'Mystica quaedam flamma in animo rite praeparato exsiliens': Novotný (1930: 221); Rhodes (2003: 178); Ferber (2007: 42–51); Motte (1963: 426); Liatzi (2008: 70, 95). *Contra*: Morrow (1935: 76); Harward (1932: 212, 217); Krämer (1990: 42).

107 Sayre (1988: 97): 'this comprehension comes like a flash of insight that cannot be expressed in linguistic form'; Ferber (2007: 47–51); Gonzalez (1995: 185). Brisson (1987a: 150–151) and Krämer (1990: 57) interpret this phrase otherwise.

108 *Phdr.* 277D–278A; Sayre (1988: 98); Gonzalez (1995: 186); Werner (2011: 69). Novotný (1930: 217) stresses in Plato's phrase the ultimate truth 'cannot be expressed in words' rather than 'is not to be expressed in words' ('verbis exprimi non possunt,' non 'verbis ea exprimi non licet').

109 *Smp.* 210E; *R.* 515C, Rosen (1968: xv); des Places (1981: 92–93); Naddaf (2013: 304); Gómez Iglesias (2016: 81).

110 Howald (1923: 44); Novotný (1930: 217, 221).

111 This quality of revelations may be behind Plato's choice of the word *muthos* – and the genre of a myth – on many occasions when he strove to convey the knowledge, *logos*, acquired through numinous experiences: the language of mysticism took much time to evolve, and the form of a traditional story might be convenient, especially when communicating ideas that were associated with the realm of religion and morals. For instance, *muthos* and *logos* are juxtaposed in the *Gorgias* (522E–523A) when Socrates says that his eschatological myth is going to be true. Morgan (1990: 73–75) and Dodds (1959: 376–377) argue that Plato's myths are communications of 'insights which could not be expressed save in symbolic terms.' Cf. Moore (1978: 105–107) on the difficulty of putting mystical experience into words, on the one hand, and the use of symbolic and figurative language by the mystics who made the effort to communicate their experiences, on the other.

112 *Ep.* 7. 344B: ἐξέλαμψε φρόνησις περὶ ἕκαστον καὶ νοῦς, συντείνων ὅτι μάλιστ᾽ εἰς δύναμιν ἀνθρωπίνην (translation R. G. Bury).

113 *Ep.* 7. 344C. Written word inferior to oral uttering: Pl. *Phdr.* 274B–278E; Szlezák (1985: 7–19); Ferrari (1987: 205–222); occasional (or unique) choice of the format of public lecture rather than conversation is attributed to Plato by Aristotle's pupil Arisoxenus (*Harm.* 2. 30–31; Gaiser 1980). For the importance of oral transmission in Plato see Krämer (1959) (English translation of a revised version: Krämer 1990); Gaiser (1980); Szlezák (1985); Szlezák (1993).

114 Arist. *Ph.*209b15, cf. *Met.* 1. 6, 987a–988a, with the comm. by Simplicius, on the 'first principles.' The *Seventh Letter*, taken together with the testimonies of Aristotle and other authorities, gave rise to the theory that Plato had 'unwritten doctrines,' the main tenet put forward by L. Strauss (Strauss 1952: 24) and nowadays associated with the Tübingen school (Krämer 1959; Gaiser 1968; Szlezák 1985; Richard 1986; Périllié 2015). It was refuted by many, notably Vlastos (1963), Ferber (2007), and

Sayre (1993) (see a review of some of the arguments against the approach adopted by the Tübingen school in Richard 1986: 29–35). Even if esoteric teachings were not an all-around alternative philosophic system, as argued by the Tübingen school, the very existence of Plato's oral teachings is difficult to doubt (Robin 1935: 17, 32, 330; Rosen 1968: xv–xxvi; Sayre 1988; Rowe 2003: 23–24, 196–200; Kahn 2001: 58–62). For a bibliographical survey see Ferber (2007: 82–84). I am grateful to Peter Agocs for the discussion of the subject.

115 Which is the essence of esotericism, in contrast to secrecy required by the Pythagoreans: for the difference between esotericism and secrecy see Szlezák (1993: 113–115).

116 Gonzalez (1995: 185).

117 Sayre (1988: 103–104).

118 *Ep.* 7. 340 CD; Sayre (1988: 102).

119 *Ep.* 7. 341E: ἀλλ' οὔτε ἀνθρώποις ἡγοῦμαι τὴν ἐπιχείρησιν περὶ αὐτῶν λεγομένην ἀγαθόν, εἰ μή τισιν ὀλίγοις ὁπόσοι δυνατοὶ ἀνευρεῖν αὐτοὶ διὰ σμικρᾶς ἐνδείξεως, τῶν τε δὴ ἄλλων τοὺς μὲν καταφρονήσεως οὐκ ὀρθῆς ἐμπλήσειεν ἂν οὐδαμῇ ἐμμελῶς, τοὺς δὲ ὑψηλῆς καὶ χαύνης ἐλπίδος, ὡς σέμν' ἄττα μεμαθηκότας (translation R. G. Bury, slightly modified). This statement is reminiscent of the view of the author of the Derveni papyrus, who deplores the fate of seeking superficial knowledge (Betegh 2004: col. 20).

120 See Harmless (2008: 238–239) for 'mystical communities' as religious or quasireligious groups of people attaining spiritual perfection at the price of considerable renunciations.

121 *Lg.* 12. 968E: οὐδὲ γὰρ αὐτοῖς τοῖς μανθάνουσι δῆλα γίγνοιτ' ἂν ὅτι πρὸς καιρὸν μανθάνεται, πρὶν ἐντὸς τῆς ψυχῆς ἑκάστῳ που μαθήματος ἐπιστήμην γεγονέναι. οὕτω δὴ πάντα τὰ περὶ ταῦτα ἀπόρρητα μὲν λεχθέντα οὐκ ἂν ὀρθῶς λέγοιτο, ἀπόρρητα δὲ διὰ τὸ μηδὲν προρρηθέντα δηλοῦν τῶν λεγομένων (translation R. G. Bury). For a different interpretation see Gaiser (1980: 15, 31).

122 Above, Chapter 2; cf. another Plutarch's simile comparing philosophy to mystery initiation: *Mor.* 81DE. Aristophanes also puts an emphasis on the resemblance of philosophical education to mystery initiations, but of course in a burlesque form (*Nu.* 140; 250, 824; Dover 1968: xli).

123 *Lg.* 12. 968E, cited above; the term *aprorrhêta* is translated by R. G. Bury as 'imprescribable.'

124 Howald (1923: 44–45).

125 'The philosophical digression': 342A–345C; survey of the hypercritical approach to the authenticity of the *Seventh Letter*: Brisson (1987a: 145); Sayre (1988).

126 *Phdr.* 247CE: Τὸν δὲ ὑπερουράνιον τόπον οὔτε τις ὕμνησέ πω τῶν τῇδε ποιητὴς οὔτε ποτὲ ὑμνήσει κατ' ἀξίαν. ἔχει δὲ ὧδε – τολμητέον γὰρ οὖν τό γε ἀληθὲς εἰπεῖν . . . – ἡ γὰρ ἀχρώματός τε καὶ ἀσχημάτιστος καὶ ἀναφὴς οὐσία ὄντως οὖσα, ψυχῆς κυβερνήτῃ μόνῳ θεατὴ νῷ, περὶ ἣν τὸ τῆς ἀληθοῦς ἐπιστήμης γένος, τοῦτον ἔχει τὸν τόπον. ἅτ' οὖν θεοῦ διάνοια νῷ τε καὶ ἐπιστήμῃ ἀκηράτῳ τρεφομένη, καὶ ἁπάσης ψυχῆς ὅση ἂν μέλῃ τὸ προσῆκον δέξασθαι, ἰδοῦσα διὰ χρόνου τὸ ὂν ἀγαπᾷ τε καὶ θεωροῦσα τἀληθῆ τρέφεται καὶ εὐπαθεῖ, ἕως ἂν κύκλῳ ἡ περιφορὰ εἰς ταὐτὸν περιενέγκῃ. ἐν δὲ τῇ περιόδῳ καθορᾷ μὲν αὐτὴν δικαιοσύνην, καθορᾷ δὲ σωφροσύνην, καθορᾷ δὲ ἐπιστήμην, οὐχ ᾗ γένεσις πρόσεστιν, οὐδ' ἥ ἐστίν που ἑτέρα ἐν ἑτέρῳ οὖσα ὧν ἡμεῖς νῦν ὄντων καλοῦμεν, ἀλλὰ τὴν ἐν τῷ ὅ ἐστιν ὂν ὄντως ἐπιστήμην οὖσαν (translation H. N. Fowler).

127 *Phdr.* 248BC; Morgan (1990: 174, 187).

128 This passage is reminiscent of numerous texts penned by mystics belonging to different cultural traditions. A quotation from St Edmund of Canterbury who lived in the thirteenth century will suffice: 'The first step in contemplation is for the soul to retreat within itself and there completely to recollect itself. The second step in contemplation is for the soul to see what it is when it is so collected. The third step is for the soul to raise itself beyond itself and to strive to see two things; its Creator, and His

own nature. But the soul can never attain to this until it has learned to subdue every image, corporeal, earthly and celestial, to reject whatever may come to it through sight or hearing or touch or taste or any other bodily sensation, and to tread it down, so that the soul may see what in itself is outside of its body. . . . After this, when you have in this way looked at your Creator and His creatures, put every corporeal image outside your heart, and let your naked intention fly up above all human reasoning and there you shall find such great sweetness and such great secrets that without special grace there is no one who can think of it except only him who has experienced it' (cited in Sargant 1973: 76–77).

129 *Phdr.* 251AE.
130 Bishop (1995). For the tradition of long preparation in the Pythagorean community see below in this chapter.
131 *Smp.* 210D, 212A. On oceanic sensation see the Introduction.
132 *Tht.* 173E–174A: . . . ἀλλὰ τῷ ὄντι τὸ σῶμα μόνον ἐν τῇ πόλει κεῖται αὐτοῦ καὶ ἐπιδημεῖ, ἡ δὲ διάνοια, ταῦτα πάντα ἡγησαμένη σμικρὰ καὶ οὐδέν, ἀτιμάσασα πανταχῇ πέτεται κατὰ Πίνδαρον "τᾶς τε γᾶς ὑπένερθε" καὶ τὰ ἐπίπεδα γεωμετροῦσα, "οὐρανοῦ θ' ὕπερ" ἀστρονομοῦσα, καὶ πᾶσαν πάντη φύσιν ἐρευνωμένη τῶν ὄντων ἑκάστου ὅλου, εἰς τῶν ἐγγὺς οὐδὲν αὐτὴν συγκαθιεῖσα (translation H. N. Fowler) ; cf. Bussanich (2006: 211) on this passage: 'quasi-shamanic picture of the philosopher.'
133 *R.* 490AB: Ἆρ᾽ οὖν δὴ οὐ μετρίως ἀπολογησόμεθα ὅτι πρὸς τὸ ὂν πεφυκὼς εἴη ἁμιλλᾶσθαι ὅ γε ὄντως φιλομαθής, καὶ οὐκ ἐπιμένοι ἐπὶ τοῖς δοξαζομένοις εἶναι πολλοῖς ἑκάστοις, ἀλλ᾽ ἴοι καὶ οὐκ ἀμβλύνοιτο οὐδ᾽ ἀπολήγοι τοῦ ἔρωτος, πρὶν αὐτοῦ ὃ ἔστιν ἑκάστου τῆς φύσεως ἅψασθαι ᾧ προσήκει ψυχῆς ἐφάπτεσθαι τοῦ τοιούτου – προσήκει δὲ συγγενεῖ – ᾧ πλησιάσας καὶ μιγεὶς τῷ ὄντι ὄντως, γεννήσας νοῦν καὶ ἀλήθειαν, γνοίη τε καὶ ἀληθῶς ζῴη καὶ τρέφοιτο καὶ οὕτω λήγοι ὠδῖνος, πρὶν δ᾽ οὒ (translation C. Emlyn-Jones and W. Preddy, modified).

   C. Emlyn-Jones and W. Preddy translate πλησιάσας καὶ μιγείς as 'approached and immersed himself,' which emasculates the potent sexual metaphor of a mystical union leading to the birth of the truth. Cf. 'approached and entered into union' (F. M. Cornford); 'getting near . . . and having intercourse with' (G.M.A. Grube); 'come near and joined with' (J. Sachs).
134 *R.* 507B.
135 Robinson (2000: 143); Robinson (1995: 56).
136 Nettleship (1964: 205). Cf. *Tht.* 148E, 150B, 186A.
137 See also the Introduction.
138 Nettleship (1964: 205).
139 *P.* 559AC.
140 McPherran (2010: 211); Lisi (2007: 213).
141 *R.* 611E; 485AB; 499BC; 501D; Obdrzalek (2013: 215).
142 *Smp.* 211E–212A; Price (1989: 52); Obdrzalek (2013: 217).
143 Streng (1978); Sargant (1973: 76); Robinson (1995: 50); Moore (1978); Nabert (2005: 127–128), and most notably the collection Hanegraaff and Kripal (2008).
144 McGinn (1989: 63–65); Williams (2003); Dupré (1999: 20–21); Maliszewski et al. (2011: 196–199).
145 Harmless (2008: 48–50).
146 Newberg, d'Aquili, and Rause (2001).
147 If in fact one accepts that mysticism is universal, like James (1961); Zaehner (1961); Stace (1960); Lacrosse (2005); to a certain extant McGinn (1991); for the opposite approach, based on the idea of the dominance of cultural context, see Katz (1983); Keller (1978). Harmless (2008) offers a synthesis of the two approaches, regarding mysticism as part of the human nature, and at the same time insisting on situating individual mystics in their historical milieu. The controversy on this subject is one of the main problems in the study of mysticism.

148 *P.* 441E–442C; Obdrzalek (2013: 219–220).
149 For the problem of verbalisation of mystical experiences and their ineffability see
Moore (1978: 102–105); Stace (1960: 28–29); Streng (1978); Harmless (2008: 235–
238). The ineffability of mystical experience is laconically defined by a Jewish philosopher and theologian Franz Rozenzweig: 'Light does not talk but shines' (as quoted
by Wolfson 2010: 107).
150 Musical pattern in Plato's dialogues is suggested by Kennedy (2010); his ideas are
criticized by Walsh (2012), requiring actual secret messages to be revealed in order to
assume the existence of esoteric teaching.
151 Cf. Russel (1961: 141): 'Throughout Plato's philosophy there is the same fusion of
intellect and mysticism as in Pythagoreanism, but at this final culmination mysticism
clearly has the upper hand.'
152 *Sol.* 12: σοφὸς περὶ τὰ θεῖα τὴν ἐνθουσιαστικὴν καὶ τελεστικὴν σοφίαν; for a more
detailed discussion of these figures, see Ustinova (2009a: 178–186).
153 D. L. 1. 112, 114; Pl. *Lg.* 1. 642 D 4; Suid., s.v. *Epimenidês*; Rohde (1925: 332–333);
Svenbro (1993: 136); West (1983: 49).
154 The story of his purification of Attica, is dated to either to 604–601 or to 596–593
(Arist. *Ath.* 1; D. L. 1. 109, Suida, s.v. *Epimenidês*, Plu. *Sol.* 12; Pl. *Lg.* 1. 642 D 4;
Paus. 1. 14. 4; cf. Diels (1891); Demoulin (1901); Burkert (1972: 103, 151); Leclerc
(1992); Dillery (2005: 181); Compton (2006: 174–177); for doubts regarding the
historicity of this event see West (1983: 46).
155 D. L. 1. 112, 114; Pl. *Lg.* 1. 642 D 4; Suda, s.v. *Epimenides*; Rohde (1925: 332–333);
Svenbro (1993: 136). West (1983: 49) suggests that these poems were most probably
composed at a later date, and attributed to Epimenides.
156 This story was current as early as in the sixth century: *DK* A1; D. L. 1. 109; Paus. 1.
14. 4; Plu. *Mor.* 784A.
157 Max. Tyr. 10. 1; 38. 3; Demoulin (1901: 98); Rohde (1925: 96); Halliday (1913: 91);
Burkert (1969: 16).
158 D. L. 1. 114 (Theopomp. *FGH* 115 F69).
159 Plu. *Sol.* 12. Cf. Plu. *Num.* 4 on Numa Pompilius and the nymph Egeria who loved
him and disclosed divine mysteries to him.
160 D. L. 1. 114 (Timaeus *FGH* 566 F4); cf. Rohde (1925: 331); Burkert (1972: 151);
Dodds (1973: 142).
161 D. L. 1. 112; Suda, s.v. *Epimenides*.
162 προσποιηθῆναί τε πολλάκις ἀναβεβιωκέναι, D. L. 1. 114. The idea of multiple reincarnations is reminiscent of Pythagoras' doctrine of metempsychosis: Diels (1891:
396) regards Epimenides' rebirths as 'Pythagorean fabrication,' whereas Burkert
(1972: 151) observes 'parallel development from common origins.'
163 Suid., s.v. *Epimenidês*; Detienne (1963: 70). Suida's wording suggests association with
Aristeas or Hermotimos of Clasomenae, whose out-of-body experiences are discussed
below.
164 Parke (1988: 174); cf. Demoulin (1901: 136–137); Dodds (1973: 141–146); West
(1983: 45).
165 Ustinova (2009a: 178–184).
166 Clearch. fr. 8 Wehrli; Clem.Al. *Strom.* 1. 21. 133; Apollon. *Mir.* 1. 1–6; Detienne
(1963: 69–85); Detienne (1996); Nilsson (1961–1967: 1: 616–620); Pollard (1965:
106–116); Bonnechere (2003: 118–125).
167 Abaris' legend was known in the fifth century to Pindar (Harp. s.v. *Abaris*) and to
Herodotus (4. 36); cf. Pl. *Chrm.* 158CD; Iamb. *VP* 91, 136, 141, Porph. *VP* 29; Rohde
(1925: 300, 328); Corssen (1912); Baudy (1996).
168 Hdt. 4. 13–15; Ath. 13. 605C; Suda, s.v. *Aristeas*, Max. Tyr. *Diss.* 10. 2, 38. 3; Plin.
Nat. 7. 174; 'Testimonia' in Bolton (1962: 206–214); Rohde (1925: 300, 328–329);
Corssen (1912: 44); Meuli (1935: 153); Pollard (1965: 109); Burkert (1972: 143);

Eliade (1970: 36); Bremmer (1983: 25–38); Ivantchik (1993); Selser (1996); West (2004). For a rationalising interpretation of Aristeas' experience, see Bolton (1962: 133, 141), with W. Burkert's criticism (Burkert 1963).

In the first century AD Lucanus (1. 676–695) spoke of a Roman matron who flew over the earth 'possessed by Apollo,' while her body strolled in the streets (Culianu 1983: 37).

169   Pherecydes fr. B8 *DK*.

170   Arist. *Met.* A3. 984b19; Apollon. *Mir.* 1. 3; Plin. *Nat.* 7. 174; Lucianus *Musc. Enc.* 7; this person is called Hermodorus of Clazomenae in Plu. *Mor.* 592C and Proclus *In R.* 2. 113. 24; Rohde (1925: 300, 331); Dodds (1973: 141). It is noteworthy that Hermotimos is named among the earlier incarnations of Pythagoras (D.L. 8. 5). J. Bremmer regards Hermotimos' story as a late invention (Bremmer 2002: 39).

Aristotle supposedly recorded a story of a Greek king, whose soul had left his body for several days, and returned from the invisible world with prophetic knowledge (Arist. fr. 11 Ross).

171   Greg. Nazianz. *Or.* 4. 59: 'Such was the childishness of their Empedocleis and Aristaii and some Empedotimi and Trophonii and a host of similar miserable people. . . . [They] hid themselves in some adyta, because of the same disease and egocentricity, and when it was found out, received less profit from their dishonesty than contempt from the disclosure.' Notwithstanding the theologian's anti-pagan pathos, this remark appears to reflect the popular tradition well-known to his audience and referred to by Sophocles (*El.* 62–64).

172   Iamb. *VP* 91–93, 147, 215.

173   Barnes (1979: 100–114); Hermann (2004: 20); Zhmud (2012: 148, 207–220).

174   E.g. Pl. *R.* 600 AB; Burkert (1972: 215–217); Huffman (2003: 404); Riedweg (2005: 1).

175   Burkert (1972: 147).

176   Arist. fr. 192 Rose (Iamb. *VP* 31), Ael. *Var. Hist.* 2. 26; D. L. 8. 11; Iamb. *VP* 4, 30, 140; Porph. *VP* 28. Corssen (1912: 30–31); Lévy (1927: 7, 10, 44–45); Boyancé (1937: 233–241); Burkert (1972: 141–143, 146–149); Giangiulio (1993); Schefer (1996: 34–38); Riedweg (2005: 71–73); Pythagoras as *daimôn* and *theios anêr*: Detienne (1963: esp. 132–135).

177   Empedocles *DK* B129 (Porph. *Vita Pyth.* 30); Detienne (1963: 79–85); Burkert (1972: 137); Riedweg (2005: 54–55, 77).

178   Porph. *VP* 29; Iamb. *VP* 135; Burkert (1972: 138–144); Hermann (2004: 43); Riedweg (2005: 4–5, with further refs).

179   Porph. *VP* 33; Iamb. *VP* 64, 163. For the use of music for magical purposes by the Pythagoreans, see Boyancé (1937: 100–131); Dodds (1973: 154); Detienne (1963: 47–48); Hermann (2004: 105). For Pythagoras as healer see Lévy (1927: 42); de Vogel (1966: 232–244); Kingsley (1995: 327, 342); Thorn (1995: 213–214).

180   For instance, his golden thigh, as well as his ability to bilocate, employ magical healing skills and chase away pestilences: D. L. 8. 11–12; Ael. *Var. Hist.* 2. 26; 4. 17; Apollonius *Hist. mirab.* 1. 6; Iamb. *VP* 28, 92, 140; Porph. *VP* 29; cf. Corssen (1912: 30–38); Lévy (1926: 12–14; 1927: 40–42); Detienne (1963: 69–70); Burkert (1972: 141–143, 160); Kingsley (1995: 291, 327).

181   Kahn (1960: 32); Detienne (1963: 82); Dodds (1973: 144); Burkert (1972: 140–165); West (1983: 149); Flint et al. (1999: 118); Brisson (1987b: 95); for a denial of such association see Zhmud (2012: 221–230).

182   See Ustinova (2009a: 186–191) for details.

183   Hippol. *Refut.* 1. 2. 18.

184   Porph. *VP* 34. The earliest account of Pythagoras' fasting in a subterranean chamber is Hermippus' narration.

185   Iamb. *VP* 141; Riedweg (2005: 33).

186   Riedweg 1997; Riedweg (2005: 43).

187 Dicaearchus in Porph., *VP* 19; cf. Hdt. 2. 123; D. S. 10. 5. 1; Burkert (1972: 122, 179); Kingsley (1995: 368); Bremmer (1995: 63–70); Bremmer (2002: 12); Brisson (1987b).

188 Iamb. *VP* 31; D. L. 8. 15.

189 D. L. 8. 10; Iamb. *VP* 72–73, cf. Bremmer (1992); Hermann (2004: 53).

190 Burkert (1972: 166–192); Brisson (1987b: 83–84); Kingsley (1995: 319); Hermann (2004: 82–86).

191 Burkert (1982: 18); Riedweg (2005: 98–104); Seaford (2004: 228); Freyburger-Galland, Freyburger, and Tautil (1986: 134–161); Brisson (1987b); Kahn (2001: 11); cf. Hermann (2004: 33–40, 56).

192 Iamb. *VP* 143, Timaeus *FGH* 566 F131.

193 Burkert (1972: 179); Riedweg (2005: 98–104); Morrison (1956: 149–152).

194 D. L. 8. 32.

195 *VP* 106–107; cf. Detienne (1963: 43–45); Thorn (1995: 220).

196 DK fr. B129: ἦν δέ τις ἐν κείνοισιν ἀνὴρ περιώσια εἰδώς,| ὃς δὴ μήκιστον πραπίδων ἐκτήσατο πλοῦτον, | παντοίων τε μάλιστα σοφῶν <τ'> ἐπιήρανος ἔργων· |ὁππότε γὰρ πάσῃσιν ὀρέξαιτο πραπίδεσσιν, |ῥεῖ' ὅ γε τῶν ὄντων πάντων λεύσσεσκεν ἕκαστον | καί τε δέκ' ἀνθρώπων καί τ' εἴκοσιν αἰώνεσσιν. Iamblicus (*VP* 15) and Porphyrius (*VP* 30) cite these words as referring to Pythagoras, and Diogenes Laertius (D. L. 8. 54) explains that Timaeus associated Empedocles' praise with either Pythagoras or Parmenides.

197 In Empedocles' fragments, the word *prapides* is usually interpreted as 'thoughts' or 'wisdom' (Inwood 2001: 256, fr. 99; Wright 1981: 205, fr. 6). It is in fact one of the meanings that is attested in Homer, where the word occurs eleven times (Sullivan 1987). However, in several Homeric passages this word, like *phrenes*, can designate diaphragm or some undefined organ in the chest, a location of intellectual activity and emotion (*Il.* 11. 579; 22. 43; 24. 514), as maintained by the scholiasts to *Il.* 11. 579 and 13. 412 (Sullivan 1987: 183–184, 190). Especially important is *Il.* 11. 579, where a warrior is struck 'in the liver under the *prapides*': there can be no doubt that *prapides* is part of the chest, properly rendered as 'midriff' in English. In later texts (Hes. *Th.* 608; 656; Pi. *Is.* 8. 30; *Pyth.* 4. 281; 5. 67; *Ol.* 2. 94, A. *Supp.* 93; A. 380; 802, E. *Ba.* 427, 999; *And.* 480), the word designates a source and location of intellectual activity (Sullivan 1987: 192).

Physical origin of 'mental terminology' in Homer is present in other words designating 'mental organs,' and finds parallels even in modern word usage: cf. 'lose heart' in English or 'kopflos' in German (Harrison 1960: 65–66).

198 Delatte (1934: 26–27) interprets the expression ὀρέξαιτο πραπίδεσσιν as 'making efforts' or 'exercising his diaphragm'; Gernet (1968: 425); Detienne (1963: 79–81); Vernant (1983: 86–87, 110–111); Kingsley (2002: 401).

199 Fr. B1 DK; For the language and style of the proem see Guthrie (1962–1967: 2: 10); Pellikaan (1974); Gallop (1984: 4); Coxon (1986: 7–11); Granger (2008); Palmer (2009: 51–61); Gemelli Marciano (2013: 65–80). I discuss Parmenides in Ustinova (2004) and Ustinova (2009a: 191–209).

200 See above, Chapter 6.

201 Contrary to the majority opinion, Morrison (1955: 59) and Kingsley (2002: 371) suggest that it is the female divinity rather than the road that bears Parmenides, who therefore is portrayed here as *theoleptos*, seized by the deity. Whatever the correct reading of this phrase, the context of the fragment leaves no doubt about the role of the goddess as the ultimate source of Parmenides' wisdom, and the ecstatic nature of the road leading to it.

202 Line 9; Burkert (1969: 17); West (1983: 109); Palmer (2009: 57–59).

203 Line 29; Morrison (1955: 60); Burkert (1969: 15); Detienne (1996: 130–131); Curd (1999: 18–21). For various readings of this phrase see Diels (1897: 54); Mourelatos

(1970: 154); Tarán (1965: 16–17); Gemelli Marciano (2008: 36–37); Gemelli Marciano (2013: 81).

The gesture of a handclasp is meaningful: it symbolises Parmenides' equality with the goddess and is a pledge of her eagerness to disclose the truth to him (Mansfeld 2005).

204 Coxon (1986: 156); West (1971: 226); Jaeger (1947: 94); Cornford (1952: 118); Guthrie (1962–1967: 2: 11); Claus (1981: 111); Nieto (1997: 36); Gemelli Marciano (2008); cf. Diels (1897: 14); Verdenius (1942: 67); Verdenius (1948); White (2005: 20, 74). Even if reluctant to admit the existence of experiences in Greece, Kirk, Raven, and Schofield (1983: 244) define Parmenides' *proem* as a description of 'a path of thought ('a highway') which leads to a transcendent comprehension both of changeless truth and of mortal opinion.' Tarán (1965: 21–31) assumes that this journey has nothing to do with real experience, and argues that the proem does not depict a religious revelation, but is a part of a literary device. He does not contend that the *Proem* is in the form of a revelation, but suggests that Parmenides chose to present his doctrine in the form of the goddess' monologue in order to render his innovative doctrine more trustworthy. The interpretation of the *proem* as a description of a spiritual journey is opposed also by Bowra (1937); Mourelatos (1970: 45–46); Hermann (2004: 163); Cordero (2004: 23); Granger (2008).

205 Line 27.

206 Jaeger (1947: 93); Fränkel (1975: 365); Mansfeld (1964: 234–247); Diels (1897: 14); Cornford (1952: 118); Guthrie (1962–1967: 2: 11); Claus (1981: 111).

207 Mourelatos (1970: 42–44); Burkert (1969); Furley (1973: 2); Miller (1979: 28); Kingsley (1999: 93–100); Palmer (2009: 55); Gemelli Marciano (2008: 78–81); descent of a shaman to the netherworld: Morrison (1955: 59); a cyclic journey culminating in catabasis to the House of Night: Pellikaan (1974: 60–62). Some remain undecided as to where the *kouros* went: Tarán (1965: 24); Owens (1979); Austin (1986); Curd (1999: 19); cf. Mourelatos (1970: 14–16); Morgan (2000: 78); Hermann (2004: 166).

208 Ustinova (2009a: 201); cf. Cosgrove (2011); Cursaru (2016: 51).

209 I treat this subject in detail in Ustinova (2009a: esp. 29–30).

210 Siegel and Jarvik (1975: 116, 143).

211 Shamans: Harner (1990: 28–30); Siegel and Jarvik (1975: 127); Jewish apocalyptists: *1En.* 14. 8–24; cf. Merkur (1989: 136–137); Carlsson (2004: 36–41).

212 Siegel (1980: 923).

213 Blackmore (1993: 71).

214 Siegel (1980: 923); Drab (1981: 145–146); Lewis-Williams (2002: 145).

215 Pi. *O.* 6. 22; 9. 80; *I.* 2. 1–3; 9. 62; Empedocles fr. B3 *DK*; Pl. *Phdr.* 246A.; *Golden Verses* 69, cf. Hierocles *Comm.* 16); cf. Morrison (1955: 59); Tarán (1965: 31); Fränkel (1975: 351); West (1997: 205); Cordero (2004: 25).

216 Renaud (1987); Stroumsa (1996: 169–183); Piemontese (1987). In particular, Jewish mystical literature of late antiquity contains depictions of mystical visions of *yordei merkabah*, those who 'descend by the chariot.' G. Stroumsa demonstrates that the experience of *yordei merkabah* was the mystical voyage into the netherworld, ending in the vision of the divine world or even of the divinity itself. In this respect, visions of Jewish *yordei merkabah* are congruent to Parmenides' journey through darkness to light. Classical study of the *merkabah* mysticism: Sholem (1965); see also Wolfson (1993).

217 Ustinova (2009a: 28–32).

218 Fr. B1 *DK*; Coxon (1986: 167), cf. Loenen (1959: 72–74).

219 For an overview of the ongoing discussion of the question how strict Parmenides' monism was, see Palmer (2009: 25–32). See Trépanier (2004: 131–144) for a defence of the current consensus on Parmenides' monism.

220 Fr. B2; 8 *DK*, cf. Loenen (1959, 3–124, esp. 82–84).

221 Popper (2001: 97).

222 Popper (2001: 69).

223 West (1971: 222–223); Seaford (2004: 229). Parmenides obtained his understanding of the truth 'by a kind of grace' (Snell 1960: 148), 'the act of disclosure and revelation,' 'nothing less than disclosure of divine grace' (Nieto 1997: 35). For H. Fränkel, the 'radical, even brutal, consistency' of Parmenides' thought proves that the philosopher experienced and realized his conception personally, having achieved 'the *unio mystica* with true Being' (Fränkel 1975: 366–367).

224 Kingsley (2002); Kingsley (1999); Gemelli Marciano (2008); Gemelli Marciano (2013).

225 Coxon (1986: 168); Morgan (2000: 85); Fränkel (1975: 365); Seaford (2004: 229).

226 Detailed argument against the interpretation of the proem as an allegory: Gemelli Marciano (2013: 54–58).

227 In his book on the varieties of mystical experiences, Zaehner (1961: 47, 141) compares Parmenides' transcendence of time and space to the revelations of modern mystics.

228 Blackmore (1993: 149).

229 By different ways of reasoning, P. Kingsley and M. L. Gemelli Marciano (Kingsley 2002; Kingsley 1999; Gemelli Marciano 2008; Gemelli Marciano 2013) arrive at similar conclusions.

230 Fr. B 7 *DK*; cf. Verdenius (1942: 64); Furley (1973: 9–10); Mourelatos (2013: 164–172). Against the traditional reading of this phrase: Gemelli Marciano (2013: 87–88).

231 West (1971: 223); Curd (1999: 20).

232 Fränkel (1975: 367).

233 Verdenius (1948: 119); Morgan (2000: 74). See however Tarán (1965: 16); Cordero (2004: 24) for different interpretations of the word *kouros*.

234 Fr. B1 *DK*; Verdenius 1948: 120; Burkert 1969: 5; Kingsley 1999: 62, 71–75.
   According to Tarán (1965: 30), the wording of the *proem* suggests that the journey was undertaken by the author on multiple occasions (cf. Couloubaritsis 1986: 92; Coxon 1986: 161). If indeed it is so, we have evidence of recurring experiences of an altered state of consciousness. However, Tarán's inference that revelation could not be repeated is at variance with numerous instances of people experiencing recurrence of divine revelations, described in detail as his own frequent experiences by Plotinus (*Enneads* 4. 8. 1. 1–10) and reported in modern neuropsychological research, for instance, of Zen meditation (Austin 1998).

235 A. H. Coxon (1986: 15–16) suggests that this qualification assumes the *kouros'* adherence to an association resembling the Pythagorean community. On mystery cults and Parmenides see Kingsley (1999: 71–74); Seaford (2004: 262–265); Palmer (2009: 58).

236 This understanding of Parmenides' personality is in striking contrast to the view of Parmenides as an ancient counterpart to modern 'armchair philosophers.' Thus, A. H. Coxon interprets the passage through the darkness to illumination as basically the intellectual feat of 'a Pythagorean philosopher at the crisis of his career' (Coxon 1986: 170–171). In J. Owens' view, 'the imagery of the proem, like carefully chosen background music, sets the tone for philosophical reflection' (Owens 1979: 25).

237 The term, as well as the pholarch's functions, are discussed in a number of works: Pugliese Carratelli (1970); Pugliese Carratelli (1963); Pugliese Carratelli (1990); Nutton (1970); Musitelli (1980); Sacco (1981); Kingsley (1995: 225); Ustinova (2004); Ustinova (2009a: 191–199). The building was initially constructed in the Julio-Claudian period, but its upper part was refaced in the time of Hadrian. Publication of the complex: Fabbri and Trotta (1989). On the date of the building see Fabbri and Trotta (1989: 27–28); see also Napoli (1966: 223–225); Nutton (1970: 211–212).

238 *SEG* 38. 1020; cf. *SEG* 39. 1078; *Bull.* 78 (1965) 490; Masson (1988: 176, figs. 1–3); Fabbri and Trotta (1989: 69–75). The inscriptions are dated to ca. 61 BC, 160 BC, and AD 16 (*SEG* 39. 1078, lemma; Fabbri and Trotta 1989: 124–125; Morel 2000: 43). Cf.

Pugliese Carratelli (1963: 386); Nutton (1970: 212); Benedum and Michler (1971: 302); *SEG* 38. 1020.

239   Nutton (1970); Benedum (1971: 929–935); Rawson (1985: 30–31); Morel (2000: 43–44); Pugliese Carratelli (1970: 246).

240   Many years before the discovery of the cryptoporticus, W. Jaeger described Parmenides' philosophical school as a 'community of faithful' and 'a secularized form of . . . a religious conventicle' (Jaeger 1947: 96–97).

241   E.g. Arist. *HA.* passim, esp. 599a–600b, where these words occur many times. See also Musitelli (1980). In a few contexts *phôleos* or *phôleuein* are used metaphorically in reports of unusual human behaviour: Str. 11. 5. 7, 14. 1. 44; J. *BJ* 4. 9. 3; Plu. *Mor.* 733D (Artist. fr. 43 Rose). The meaning of the word *phôleos* in a very short fragment of Callimachus (fr. 68 Pfeiffer) remains an open question, cf. Pugliese Carratelli (1970: 245); Ustinova (2004: 29).

242   Ustinova (2004); Ustinova (2009a: 191–199).

243   Other interpretations of the function of *phôleos* in Elea: Pugliese Carratelli (1970: 245); Sacco (1981: 239). Musitelli (1980: 253–254); McKay (2000: 11); Kingsley (1999).

244   D. L. 9. 21; cf. Kingsley (1995: 323 note 22; 333).

245   Iamb. *VP* 18; Boyancé (1937: 104); Pugliese Carratelli (1963: 386); Kingsley (1995: 331).

246   Burkert (1969: 22); Rawson (1985: 31), cf. Benedum (1971: 929).

247   D. L. 9. 21–23, cf. Tarán (1965: 3); Coxon (1986: 18); Riedweg (2005: 115).

248   Coxon (1986: 38); cf. Hermann (2004: 129).

249   Kingsley (1999: 177–183).

250   Palmer (2009: 61–62) disputes any connection between the inscriptions of the pholarchs and understanding of Parmenides' philosophy; the archaeological evidence from Velia is even not mentioned in J. Palmer's book.

251   Plu. *Mor.* 580C: φασμάτων δὲ καὶ μύθων καὶ δεισιδαιμονίας ἀνάπλεω φιλοσοφίαν ἀπὸ Πυθαγόρου. . . . Ἐμπεδοκλέους δεξάμενος εὖ μάλα βεβακχευμένην. Lacuna: ἀπὸ Πυθαγόρου. . . . Ἐμπεδοκλέους. The meaning of *bebakcheumenê* is mollified in translations to 'complete intoxication' (D. A. Russel) or 'exaltation' (P. H. de Lacy and B. Einarson). On Galaxidorus see: Corlu (1970: 18–19).

252   Nesselrath (2010: 88).

253   Dillon (2010).

254   Delatte (1934: 21–25); Guthrie (1962–1967: 2: 227–228); Hardie (2013: 231).

255   Chron. 1. 5, translation I. E. Drabkin, modified: *Item Empedoclem sequentes alium [furorem] dicunt ex animi purgamento fieri, alium alienatione mentis ex corporis causa sive iniquitate.*

256   *DK* B3.2; Delatte (1934: 23–24); Hardie (2013: 232).

257   D. L. 8. 59–60; 67–70; Philostarat. *Vita Apoll.* 1. 2; Plin. *Nat.* 30. 1. 9; Suda, s.v. *Empedocles*; Iambl. *VP* 135, Clem. Al. *Strom.* 6. 3. 30; Graf (1997: 33–34); Todoua (2005: 58–59); Dodds (1973: 140); Kahn (1960: 33); Flint et al. (1999: 118).

258   *DK* fr. 146–147.

259   *DK* fr. 112, 115; Palmer (2013: 309–312); Gemelli Marciano (2005: 374).

260   *DK* 111; Kingsley (1995: 41, 228); Ogden (2001: 118); Todoua (2005: 77–80); Palmer (2013: 314); Gregory (2013: 177).

261   Fr. B110, 132 *DK*; Detienne (1963: 82); Vernant (1983: 114); see above in this chapter. Here again, *prapides* are 'thinking organs' or 'thoughts,' respectively in Inwood (2001: 258, fr. 100); Wright (1981: 210, fr. 16; 205, fr. 4).

262   The assignment of the surviving fragments attributed to Empedocles to two poems is traditional, but debatable; it is suggested that Empedocles expounded his views on a variety of subjects in one and the same epic (Inwood 2001: 8–19; Trépanier 2004: 6–30). The publication of the Strasbourg papyrus endorses however the traditional view that there were two poems (Martin and Primavesi 1999: 119).

The disparity between Empedocles' philosophic and religious doctrines is recognised by many modern scholars. For the analysis and refutation of this view, Kahn (1960); Kingsley (2002: 341, 355); Inwood (2001: 21–22).

263 *DK* 35.The word *dinê* also occurs in the recently published Strasbourg papyrus of the same Empedocles' poem: Martin and Primavesi (1999: fr. a (ii) 4, 19; d 8).

264 Discussed above in this chapter.

265 Arist., *De caelo* 300b30, Simplicius *De caelo* 587. 1. *DK* 57 (translation G. S. Kirk, J. E. Raven and M. Schofield).

266 Aetius 5. 19. 5, *DK* A72.

267 For Empedocles' doctrine as revelation in form, spirit, and contents, see Kahn (1960: 8).

268 Ustinova (2009a: 209–215).

269 *DK* B3; 131; Hardie (2013: 216–220). For Lucretius, the poetry of Empedocles is the voice of divinely inspired genius (1. 731, 5. 97), cf. Cornford (1952: 64).

270 *DK* B2. 6–9; Palmer (2013: 324–325).

271 E.g. *DK* B132: a man 'attaining the wealth of the divine *prapides*'; *phrên hierê*: *DK* fr. B134. 4–5; Hardie (2013: 225).

272 *DK* B23: ἀλλὰ τορῶς ταῦτ' ἴσθι, θεοῦ πάρα μῦθον ἀκούσας; Hardie (2013: 225); Palmer (2013).

273 Hardie (2013: 239–240).

274 Palmer (2013: 327–328).

275 *DK* 3; 111, Kahn (1960: 8); Kingsley (2002: 347).

276 Kingsley (1995: 367–368); Parker (1995: 499). On elements of 'Orphic-Dionysiac' mysteries (ideas, ritual and language) in Empedocles' poems see Guthrie (1952: 197); Riedweg (1995); Seaford (1986: 10–12).

277 *DK* B17. 26.

278 *DK* 3. For Lucretius, the poetry of Empedocles is the voice of divinely inspired genius (1. 731, 5. 97); Cornford (1952: 64).

279 Moravcsik (1936); Meuli (1935); Gernet (1968: 425–428); Nilsson (1961–1967: 1: 617–618); Pollard (1965: 109); Detienne (1963: 80–82); Motte (1963: 373); Dodds (1973: 141); Vernant (1983: 87); Ginzburg (1991: 209); Kingsley (1994: 190); Baudy (1996); Selser (1996); West (2004); Dillery (2005: 178); Gregory (2013: 133–135, 177). The importance of shamanism for the interpretation of Greek culture was first proposed by H. Diels (Diels 1891) and E. Rohde (Rohde 1925).

280 Bremmer (1983: 24–35); Bremmer (2002: 27–40); Dowden (1979); Dowden (1980); Zhmud (1992: 207–220).

281 Aune (1983: 83, 86–87); Grabbe (1995: 149).

282 The etic approach was launched by M. Eliade (Eliade 1974: 6) and followed by Winkelman (2000: 64); Pearson (2002: esp. 74), to mention only a few names; emic approach is represented by Siikala (1987); McCall (2007). The divergence of opinions is illustrated by the discussion of the paper by Klein et al. (2002), most commentators denouncing the authors' emic approach.

283 The change may be illustrated by a comparison between the papers by Jane Atkinson (Atkinson 1992) and Thomas DuBois (DuBois 2011).

284 DuBois (2009); Pearson (2002).

285 Winkelman (2000: 6).

286 Austin (1998); Newberg (2010); Whitehouse (2004).

287 Winkelman (2011: 159).

288 West (1997: 150).

289 Dowden (1979); Dowden (1980).

290 As done by Butterworth (1966).

291 Winkelman (2000: 7); Iversen (2001: 73).

292 For a 'checklist' of shamanic characteristics see Winkelman (2011: 162); cf. Winkelman (2000: 57–63); Pearson (2002: 65–76).

293 A helpful 'checklist' of the features of mystical ecstasy: Dierkens (2005: 36).
294 Pigeaud (2008: 621–656).
295 See the Introduction.
296 Harmless (2008: 239–245; quotations: 240–241).
297 Harmless (2008: 246–247).
298 Orpheus: West (1983: 4–5, 146–147); Graf (1987).
299 West (2004: 61).
300 West (2004: 62).
301 *Ep.* 10–23; Smith (1990).
302 Composed about the turn of the era (Smith 1990: 28; Littré 1961: 1: 430–431; Anastassiou and Irmer 2006: 195; Pigeaud 1989: 452; Longrigg 1993: 67; Pigeaud 1989: 465; Rütten 1992: 1). Salem (1996: 351) suggests early first century AD. Cynic associations: Stuart (1958: 185–186); Smith (1990: 28–29); Salem (1996: 361–362).
     All the surviving biographies of Hippocrates are fictional, as well: Rubin Pinault (1992: 5). Aelian (*VH* 4. 20; Democr. fr. A16 *DK*), as well as *The Life of Hippocrates According to Soranus*, written between the second and the sixth centuries AD, also mention the summoning of Hippocrates by the Abderites to cure Democritus from madness; Suda and Tzetzes make elderly Hippocrates a student of Democritus (Suid., s.v. *Hippocrates*; fr. A10 *DK*; Rubin Pinault 1992: 7, 11, 18).
303 *Ep.* 1. 1: ἀποδημεῖν . . . λέγει ἐς τὴν ἀπειρίην.
304 Discussed above in this chapter.
305 On philosophers' descent into caves and the practice of stillness, see Ustinova (2009b: 177–217) and above in this chapter.
306 *Ep.* 12, 14; Rütten (1992: 54, 74).
307 In Aristophanes' *Plutus* (903), the Just Man asks if the Sycophant is a farmer, and gets as a reply: 'Do you think I'm melancholic?' (μελαγχολᾶν μ᾽οὕτως οἴει). The phrase is explained by two scholiasts as alluding to the predisposition of farmers to run away to the wilderness: μαίνεσθαι, ὥστε ἀποτρέχειν εἰς τὰς ἐρημίας, ὡς οἱ γεωργοί, cf. O'Brien-Moore (1924: 64). *Melancholia* in Aristophanes: Miller (1945: 82); Langholf (1990: 48); on the concept of *melancholia* see Flashar (1966); Jouanna (2012: 241–258), and the Epilogue below.
308 *Ep.* 15.
309 Could the author of the letters hint at Democritus' interest in divine *mania*, in particular *enthousiasmos* (discussed above, Chapter 3), as Rütten (1992: 78–79) suggests?
310 *Ep.* 17.
311 Salem (1996: 359).
312 For the discussion of *melancholia* see below, Epilogue.
313 Cornford (1950: 25–26).

References

Aalders, G.J.D. 1972. "Political thought in the Platonic epistles." In *Pseudepigrapha I*, edited by K. von Fritz, 145–175. Geneva: Vandoeuvres.

Ackrill, J. L. 1973. "*Anamnesis* in the *Phaedo*: Remarks on 73c-75c." In *Exegesis and Argument: Studies in Greek Philosophy Presented to G. Vlastos*, edited by E. N. Lee, A.P.D. Mourelatos, and R. M. Rorty, 177–195. Assen: Van Gorcum.

Ademollo, F. 2011. *The Cratylus of Plato*. Cambridge: Cambridge University Press.

Adluri, V. 2006. "Initiation into the mysteries: The experience of the irrational in Plato." *Mouseion* 6:407–423.

Anastassiou, A. and D. Irmer. 2006. *Testimonien zum Corpus Hippocraticum*. Göttingen: Vandenhoeck & Ruprecht.

Atkinson, J. M. 1992. "Shamanisms today." *Annual Review of Anthropology* 21:307–330.

Aune, D. E. 1983. *Prophecy in Early Christianity and the Ancient Mediterranean World*. Grand Rapids: Eerdmans.

Austin, J. 1998. *Zen and the Brain: Toward and Understanding of Meditation and Consciousness*. Cambridge, MA-London: MIT Press.

Austin, S. 1986. *Parmenides: Being, Bounds, and Logic*. New Haven: Yale University Press.

Babut, D. 1984. "Le dialogue de Plutarque 'Sur le démon de Socrate.' Essai d'interprétation." *BAGB*:51–76.

Barnes, J. 1979. *The Presocratic Philosophers*. London: Routledge & Kegan Paul.

Barney, R. 2001. *Names and Nature in Plato's Cratylus*. London-New York: Routledge.

Baudy, G. 1996. "Abaris." In *Der Neue Pauly* 1:5–6.

Bedu-Addo, J. T. 1991. "Sense-experience and the argument for recollection in Plato's Phaedo." *Phronesis* 36 (1):27–60.

Benedum, J. 1971. "Uliades, Ulis." In *RE* Suppl., 14:921–931; 931–935.

Benedum, J. and M. Michler. 1971. "Parmenides Uliades und die Medizinschule von Elea." *Clio Medica. Acta Academiae Internationalis Historiae Medicinae* 6 (4):295–306.

Betegh, G. 2004. *The Derveni Papyrus: Cosmology, Theology and Interpretation*. Cambridge: Cambridge University Press.

Bishop, D. H., ed. 1995. *Mysticism and the Mystical Experience: East and West*. London-Toronto: Associated University Presses.

Blackmore, S. 1993. *Dying to Live: Near-Death Experiences*. Buffalo, NY: Prometheus Books.

Bolton, J.D.P. 1962. *Aristeas of Proconnessus*. Oxford: Clarendon Press.

Bonnechere, P. 2003. *Trophonios de Lébadée*. Leiden: Brill.

Bostock, D. 1986. *Plato's Phaedo*. Oxford: Oxford University Press.

Bowra, C. M. 1937. "The proem of Parmenides." *CPh* 32 (2):97–112.

Boyancé, P. 1937. *Le culte des Muses chez les philosophes grecs*. Paris: de Boccard.

Bremmer, J. N. 1983. *The Early Greek Concept of the Soul*. Princeton: Princeton University Press.

Bremmer, J. N. 1992. "Symbols of marginality from early Pythagoreans to late antique monks." *GR* 39 (2):205–214.

Bremmer, J. N. 1995. "Religious secrets and secrecy in Classical Greece." In *Secrecy and Concealment: Studies in the History of Mediterranean and Near Eastern Religions*, edited by G. G. Stroumsa and H. G. Kippenberg, 61–78. Leiden: Brill.

Bremmer, J. N. 2002. *The Rise and Fall of the Afterlife*. London-New York: Routledge.

Brickhouse, T. C. and N. D. Smith. 1994. *Plato's Socrates*. Oxford: Oxford University Press.

Brickhouse, T. C. and N. D. Smith. 2000. "Socrates' gods and his *daimonion*." In *Reason and Religion in Socratic Philosophy*, edited by N. D. Smith and P. B. Woodruff, 74–88. Oxford: Oxford University Press.

Brisson, L. 1987a. *Platon: Lettres*. Paris: Flammarion.

Brisson, L. 1987b. "Usages et fonctions du secret dans le pythagorisme ancien." In *Le secret*, edited by P. Dujardin, 87–101. Lyon: C.N.R.S. et Presses universitaires de Lyon.

Brisson, L. 2000. *Lectures de Platon*. Paris: J. Vrin.

Brisson, L. 2005. "Socrates and the divine sign according to Plato's testimony: Philosophical practice as rooted in religious tradition." In *Socrates' Divine Sign: Religion, Practice and Value in Socratic Philosophy*, edited by P. Destrée and N. D. Smith, 1–12. Kelowna: Academic Printing and Publishing.

Burkert, W. 1963. "Review of: J. D. P. Bolton, Aristeas of Proconnesus. Oxford, 1962." *Gnomon* 35:235–240.

Burkert, W. 1969. "Das Proömium des Parmenides und die Katabasis des Pythagoras." *Phronesis* 14:1–30.

Burkert, W. 1972. *Lore and Science in Ancient Pythagoreanism*. Cambridge, MA: Harvard University Press.

Burkert, W. 1982. "The problem of Orphics and Pythagoreans." In *Jewish and Christian Self-Definition*, edited by B. F. Meyer and E. P. Sanders, 1–22. London: SCM Press.

Burnet, J. 1911. *Plato's Phaedo: Edited With Introduction and Notes*. Oxford: Oxford University Press.

Burnyeat, M. and M. Frede. 2015. *The Pseudo-Platonic Seventh Letter*. Oxford: Oxford University Press.

Bussanich, J. 1999. "Socrates the mystic." In *Traditions of Platonism: Essays Presented to John Dillon*, edited by J. Cleary, 29–51. Alsershot-Brookfield: Ashgate.

Bussanich, J. 2006. "Socrates and religious experience." In *The Blackwell Companion to Socrates*, edited by S. Ahbel-Rappe and R. Kamtekar, 200–213. Oxford: Wiley-Blackwell.

Butterworth, E.A.S. 1966. *Some Traces of the Pre-Olympian World in Greek Literature and Myth*. Berlin: De Gruyter.

Byl, S. 1990. "Le vocabulaire hippocratique dans les comédies d'Aristophane et particulièrement dans les deux dernières." *RPh* 64:151–162.

Carlsson, L. 2004. *Round Trips to Heaven: Otherwordly Travelers in Early Judaism and Christianity*. Stockholm: Almqvist & Wiksell.

Carter, R. E. 1967. "Plato and inspiration." *JHPh* 5 (2):111–121.

Clarke, D. 2006. *Descartes: A Biography*. Cambridge: Cambridge University Press.

Claus, D. B. 1981. *Toward the Soul: An Inquiry Into the Meaning of Psyche Before Plato*. New Haven: Yale University Press.

Compton, T. M. 2006. *Victim of the Muses: Poet as Scapegoat, Warrior and Hero in Greco-Roman and Indo-European Myth and History*. Washington, DC: Center for Hellenic Studies.

Cordero, N.-L. 2004. *By Being, It Is*. Las Vegas: Parmenides Publishing.

Corlu, A. 1970. *Plutarque, Le démon de Socrate: Texte et traduction avec une introduction et des notes*. Paris: Klincksieck.

Cornford, F. M. 1950. *The Unwritten Philosophy and Other Essays*. Cambridge: Cambridge University Press.

Cornford, F. M. 1952. *Principium Sapientiae: The Origins of Greek Philosophical Thought*. Cambridge: Cambridge University Press.

Corssen, P. 1912. "Der Abaris des Heraklides Ponticus." *RhM* 67:21–47.

Cosgrove, M. R. 2011. "The unknown 'Knowing Man': Parmenides B1, 3." *CQ* 61: 28–47.

Cottingham, J. 2000. *Descartes*. Oxford: Blackwell.

Couloubaritsis, L. 1986. *Mythe et philosophie chez Parménide*. Brussels: Ousia.

Coxon, A. H. 1986. *The Fragments of Parmenides*. Assen: Van Gorcum.

Crombie, I. M. 1962–1963. *An Examination of Plato's Doctrines*. London: Routledge & Kegan Paul.

Culianu, I. P. 1983. *Psychanodia I*. Leiden: Brill.

Curd, P. 1999. *The Legacy of Parmenides*. Princeton: Princeton University Press.

Cursaru, G. 2016. "Le Proème de Parménide: anabase et /ou catabase ?" *CEA* 53:39–63.

Delatte, A. 1934. *Les conceptions de l'enthousiasme chez les philosophes présocratiques*. Paris: Les Belles Lettres.

Demoulin, H. 1901. *Épiménide de Crète*. Bruxelles: Lamertin.

des Places, E. 1981. "Platon et la langue des mystères." In *Études platoniciennes 1929–1979*, 83–98. Leiden: Brill.

Detienne, M. 1963. *La notion de daïmôn dans le pythagorisme ancien*. Paris: Les Belles Lettres.

Detienne, M. 1996. *The Masters of Truth in Archaic Greece.* New York: Zone Books.

de Vogel, C. J. 1966. *Pythagoras and Early Pythagoreanism.* Assen: Van Gorcum.

Diels, H. 1891. "Über Epimenides von Kreta." *Sitzungsberiche der Preussischen Akademie der Wissenschaften. Philosophisch-historische Klasse* 1:387–403.

Diels, H. 1897. *Parmenides Lehrgedicht.* Berlin: Reimer.

Dierkens, J. 2005. "Les techniques de méditation et les inductions théurgiques vers les états mystiques." In *Mystique: la passion de l'Un, de l'Antiquité à nos jours,* edited by A. Dierkens and B. Beyer de Ryke, 25–46. Bruxelles: Editions de l'Université de Bruxelles.

Dillery, J. 2005. "Chresmologues and *manteis*: Independent diviners and the problem of authority." In *Mantikê: Studies in Ancient Divination,* edited by S. I. Johnston and P. T. Struck, 167–231. Leiden: Brill.

Dillon, J. 2010. "Pythagoreanism in Plutarch." In *Plutarch: On the Daimonion of Socrates. Human Liberation, Divine Guidance and Philosophy,* edited by H.-G. Nesselrath, 141–144. Tübingen: Mohr Siebeck.

Dixsaut, M. 1991. *Platon: Phédon.* Paris: Flammarion.

Dodds, E. R. 1945. "Plato and the Irrational." *JHS* 65:16–25.

Dodds, E. R. 1959. *Plato: Gorgias. A Revised Text With Introduction and Commentary.* Oxford: Clarendon Press.

Dodds, E. R. 1973. *The Greeks and the Irrational.* Berkeley-Los Angeles: University of California Press.

Döring, K. 1984. "Plutarch und das Daimonion des Sokrates." *Mnemosyne* 37:376–392.

Dover, K. J. 1968. *Aristophanes: Clouds. Edited With Introduction and Commentary.* Oxford: Clarendon Press.

Dowden, K. 1979. "Apollon et l'esprit dans la machine: origines." *RÉG* 92:293–318.

Dowden, K. 1980. "Deux notes sur les Scythes et les Arimaspes." *RÉG* 93:486–492.

Drab, K. 1981. "The tunnel experience: Reality or hallucination?" *Anabiosis: The Journal of Near-Death Studies* 1:126–152.

DuBois, T. A. 2009. *An Introduction to Shamanism.* Cambridge: Cambridge University Press.

DuBois, T. A. 2011. "Trends in contemporary research on shamanism." *Numen* 58:100–128.

Dupré, L. 1999. "Unio mystica: The state and the experience." In *Mystical Union in Judaism, Christianity, and Islam,* edited by M. Idel and B. McGinn, 3–23. New York: Continuum.

Edelstein, L. 1966. *Plato's Seventh Letter.* Leiden: Brill.

Eliade, M. 1970. *Zalmoxis: The Vanishing God.* Chicago: The University of Chicago Press.

Eliade, M. 1974. *Shamanism: Archaic Techniques of Ecstasy.* Princeton: Princeton University Press.

Fabbri, M. and A. Trotta. 1989. *Una scuola-collegio di età augustea.* Rome: Bretschneider.

Ferber, R. 2007. *Warum hat Platon die 'ungeschriebene Lehre' nicht geschrieben?* Munich: Beck.

Ferrari, G.R.F. 1987. *Listening to the Cicadas: A Study in Plato's Phaedrus.* Cambridge: Cambridge University Press.

Flashar, H. 1966. *Melancholie und Melancholiker in den medizinischen Theorien der Antike.* Berlin: De Gruyter.

Flint, V., R. Gordon, G. Luck, and D. Ogden. 1999. *Witchcraft and Magic in Europe: Ancient Greece and Rome.* London: Athlone.

Fränkel, H. 1975. *Early Greek Poetry and Philosophy.* Oxford: Blackwell.

Freyburger-Galland, M.-L., G. Freyburger, and J.-C. Tautil. 1986. *Sectes religieuses en Grèce et à Rome dans l'Antiquité païenne.* Paris: Les Belles Lettres.

Furley, D. J. 1973. "Notes on Parmenides." In *Exegesis and Argument: Studies Presented to G. Vlastos*, edited by E. N. Lee, A.P.D. Morelatos, and R. M. Rorty, 1–15. Assen: Van Gorcum.

Gaiser, K. 1968. *Platons ungeschribene Lehre*. Stuttgart: Klett.

Gaiser, K. 1980. "Plato's enigmatic lecture 'On the Good.'" *Phronesis* 25:5–37.

Gallop, D. 1975. *Plato: Phaedo. Translated With Notes*. Oxford: Clarendon Press.

Gallop, D. 1984. *Parmenides of Elea: Fragments*. Toronto: University of Toronto Press.

Gemelli Marciano, M. L. 2005. "Empedocles' zoogony and embryology." In *The Empedoclean* Κόσμος: *Structure, Process and the Question of Cyclicity*, edited by A. L. Pierris, 373–404. Patras: Institute for Philosophical Research.

Gemelli Marciano, M. L. 2008. "Images and experience: At the roots of Parmenides' *Aletheia*." *AncPhil* 28:21–48.

Gemelli Marciano, M. L. 2013. "Parmenide: suoni, immagini, esperienza. Con alcune considerazioni 'inattuali' zu Zenone." In *Eleatica 2007. Parmenide: suoni, immagini, esperienza*, edited by L. Rossetti and M. Pulpito, 43–126. Sankt Augustin: Academia.

Gernet, L. 1968. *Anthropologie de la Grèce antique*. Paris: F. Maspéro.

Giangiulio, M. 1993. "Sapienza pitagorica e religiosità apollinea. Tra cultura della città e orizzonti panellenici." In *Forme di religiosità e tradizioni sapienziali in Magna Grecia*, edited by A. C. Cassio and P. Poccetti, 9–27. Naples: Istituti editoriali e poligrafici internazionali.

Ginzburg, C. 1991. *Ecstasies: Deciphering the Witches' Sabbath*. London: Penguin.

Gómez Iglesias, M. R. 2016. "The echoes of Eleusis: Love and initiation in the Platonic philosophy." In *Greek Philosophy and Mystery Cults*, edited by M. J. Martín-Velasco and M. J. García Blanco, 61–102. Newcastle upon Tyne: Cambridge Scholars Publishing.

Gonzalez, F. J. 1995. "Self-knowledge, practical knowledge, and insight: Plato's dialectic and the dialogue form." In *The Third Way: New Directions in Platonic Studies*, edited by F. J. Gonzalez, 155–188. Lanham: Rowman & Littlefield.

Grabbe, L. L. 1995. *Priests, Prophets, Diviners, Sages: A Socio-Historical Study of Religious Specialists in Ancient Israel*. Valley Forge: Trinity Press International.

Graf, F. 1987. "Orpheus: A poet among men." In *Interpretation of Greek Mythology*, edited by J. Bremmer, 80–106. London: Routledge.

Graf, F. 1997. *Magic in the Ancient World*. Cambridge, MA: Harvard University Press.

Graf, F. 2004. "Trick or treat? On collective epiphanies in antiquity." *ICS* 29:111–127.

Granger, H. 2008. "The proem of Parmenides' poem." *AncPhil* 28:1–20.

Gregory, A. 2013. *The Presocratics and the Supernatural: Magic, Philosophy and Science in Early Greece*. London: Bloomsbury.

Gulley, N. 1962. *Plato's Theory of Knowledge*. London: Methuen.

Gulley, N. 1971. "The authenticity of the Platonic epistles." In *Pseudepigrapha I*, edited by K. von Fritz, 105–143. Geneva: Vandoeuvres.

Guthrie, W.K.C. 1952. *Orpheus and Greek Religion*. London: Methuen.

Guthrie, W.K.C. 1962–67. *A History of Greek Philosophy*. Cambridge: Cambridge University Press.

Hackforth, R. 1972. *Plato's Phaedrus: Translated With an Introduction and Commentary*. Cambridge: Cambridge University Press.

Hadamard, J. 1945. *The Psychology of Invention in the Mathematical Field*. Princeton: Princeton University Press.

Halliday, W. R. 1913. *Greek Divination: A Study of Its Methods and Principles*. London: Macmillan.

Hanegraaff, W. J. and J. J. Kripal, eds. 2008. *Hiddent Intercourse: Eros and Sexuality in the History of Western Esotericism*. Leiden: Brill.

Hardie, A. 2013. "Empedocles and the Muse of the *agathos logos.*" *AJPh* 134 (2):209–246.

Harmless, W. 2008. *Mystics.* Oxford: Oxford University Press.

Harner, M. 1990. *The Way of the Shaman.* San Francisco: Harper.

Harrison, E. L. 1960. "Notes on Homeric psychology." *Phoenix* 14:63–80.

Harward, J. 1932. *The Platonic Epistles.* Cambridge: Cambridge University Press.

Havelock, E. A. 1963. *Preface to Plato.* Cambridge, MA: Harvard University Press.

Havelock, E. A. 1972. "The Socratic self as it is parodied in Aristophanes' *Clouds.*" *YClS* 22:1–18.

Hempel, C. G. 1966. *Philosophy of Natural Science.* Princeton: Princeton University Press.

Herman, G. 2011. "Greek epiphanies and the sensed presence." *Historia* 60:127–157.

Hermann, A. 2004. *To Think Like God: Pythagoras and Parmenides. The Origins of Philosophy.* Las Vegas: Parmenides Press.

Howald, E. 1923. *Die Briefe Platons.* Zurich: Orell Füssli.

Huffman, C. 2003. "Pythagoreanism." In *A Guide to Greek Thought,* edited by J. Brunschwig and G.E.R. Lloyd, 396–414. Cambridge, MA: Harvard University Press.

Inwood, B. 2001. *The Poem of Empedocles.* Toronto: University of Toronto Press.

Ivantchik, A. I. 1993. "La datation du poème l'Armaspée d'Aristéas de Proconnèse." *AC* 62:35–67.

Iversen, L. 2001. *Drugs: A Very Short Introduction.* Oxford: Oxford University Press.

Jaeger, W. 1947. *The Theology of the Early Greek Philosophers.* Oxford: Clarendon Press.

James, W. 1961. *The Varieties of Religious Experience.* London: Collier-MacMillan.

Jouanna, J. 2012. *Greek Medicine From Hippocrates to Galen: Selected Papers.* Leiden: Brill.

Kahn, C. H. 1960. "Religion and natural philosophy in Empedocles' doctrine of the soul." *AGPh* 42:3–35.

Kahn, C. H. 2001. *Pythagoras and the Pythagoreans: A Brief History.* Indianapolis: Hackett.

Katz, S. T. 1983. *Mysticism and Religious Traditions.* Oxford: Oxford University Press.

Keller, C. A. 1978. "Mystical literature." In *Mysticism and Philosophical Analysis,* edited by S. T. Katz, 75–100. London: Sheldon Press.

Kennedy, J. B. 2010. "Plato's forms, Pythagorean mathematics, and stichometry." *Apeiron* 1:1–32.

Kingsley, P. 1994. "Greeks, Shamans and Magi." *Studia Iranica* 23:187–198.

Kingsley, P. 1995. *Ancient Philosophy, Mystery, and Magic: Empedocles and Pythagorean Tradition.* Oxford: Oxford University Press.

Kingsley, P. 1999. *In the Dark Places of Wisdom.* London: Duckworth.

Kingsley, P. 2002. "Empedocles for the new millennium." *AncPhil* 22:333–413.

Kirk, G. S., J. E. Raven, and M. Schofield. 1983. *The Presocratic Philosophers.* Cambridge: Cambridge University Press.

Klein, C. F., E. Guzmán, E. C. Mandell, and M. Stanfield-Mazzi. 2002. "The role of shamanism in Mesoamerican art." *Current Anthropology* 43 (3):383–419.

Knab, R. 2006. *Platons Siebter Brief: Einleitung, Text, Übersetzung, Kommentar.* Hildesheim: Olms.

Kozhevnikov, M., J. Elliot, J. Shaepgard, and K. Gramann. 2013. "Neurocognitive and somatic components of temperature increases during g-Tummo meditation: Legend and reality." *PLoS ONE* 8 (3):e58244.

Krämer, H. J. 1959. *Arete bei Platon und Aristoteles: Zum Wesen und zur Geschichte der platonischen Ontologie.* Heidelberg: C. Winter.

Krämer, H. J. 1990. *Plato and the Foundations of Metaphysics: A Work on the Theory of the Principles and Unwritten Doctrines of Plato With a Collection of the Fundamental Documents.* Albany: State University of New York Press.

Lacrosse, J. 2005. "De la commensurabilité des discours mystiques en Orient et en Occident. Une comparaison entre Plotin et Çankara." In *Mystique: la passion de l'Un, de l'Antiquité à nos jours*, edited by A. Dierkens and B. Beyer de Ryke, 215–221. Bruxelles: Éditions de l'Université de Bruxelles.

Lampe, K. 2013. "Rationality, eros, and daemonic influence in the Platonic *Theages* and the Academy of Polemo and Crates." *AJPh* 134 (3):383–424.

Langholf, V. 1990. *Medical Theories in Hippocrates: Early Texts and the 'Epidemics.'* Berlin-New York: De Gruyter.

Leclerc, M.-C. 1992. "Épiménide sans paradoxe." *Kernos* 5:221–233.

Ledger, G. R. 1989. *Re-counting Plato: A Computer Analysis of Plato's Style*. Oxford: Oxford University Press.

Lévy, I. 1926. *Rechereches sur les sources de la légende de Pythagore*. Paris: Leroux.

Lévy, I. 1927. *La légende de Pythagore: de Grèce à Palestine*. Paris: Champion.

Lewis-Williams, D. 2002. *The Mind in the Cave*. London: Thames & Hudson.

Liatzi, M. 2008. *Die semiotische Erkenntnistheorie Platons im Siebten Brief*. Munich: C. H. Beck.

Lisi, F. L. 2007. "The form of the good." In *The Ascent to the Good*, edited by F. L. Lisi, 199–227. Sankt Augustin: Academia.

Littré, É. 1961. *Oeuvres complètes d'Hippocrate*. Reprint of the 1827–61 edition. Amsterdam: Hakkert.

Loenen, J.H.M.M. 1959. *Parmenides, Melissus, Gorgias: A Reinterpretation of Eleatic Philosophy*. Assen: van Gorcum.

Long, A. A. 2006. "How does Socrates' divine sign communicate with him?" In *A Companion to Socrates*, edited by S. Ahbel-Rappe and R. Kamtekar, 63–74. Malden, MA-Oxford: Blackwell.

Longrigg, J. 1993. *Greek Rational Medicine: Philosophy and Medicine From Alcmaeon to the Alexandrians*. London: Routledge.

Lukoff, D. 2011. "Visionary spirituality and mental disorders." In *Altering Consciousness: Multidisciplinary Perspectives*, edited by E. Cardeña and M. Winkelman, vol. 2, 301–326. Santa Barbara: Praeger.

Maliszewski, M., B. Vaughan, S. Kripper, G. Holler, and C. Fracasso. 2011. "Altering consciousness through sexual activity." In *Altering Consciousness: Multidisciplinary Perspectives*, edited by E. Cardeña and M. Winkelman, vol. 2, 189–210. Santa Barbara: Praeger.

Mansfeld, J. 1964. *Die Offenbarung des Parmenides und die menschliche Welt*. Assen: van Gorcum.

Mansfeld, J. 2005. "Minima Parmenidea." *Mnemosyne* 68:554–560.

Martin, A. and O. Primavesi. 1999. *L'Empédocle de Strasbourg*. Berlin: De Gruyter.

Martindale, C. 1981. *Cognition and Consciousness*. Homewood, IL: Dorsey Press.

Masson, O. 1988. "Le culte ionien d'Apollon Oulios, d'après des données onomastiques nouvelles." *JS*:173–181.

Mazzarello, P. 2000. "What dreams may come?" *Nature* 408 (November, 30):525.

McCall, G. S. 2007. "Add shamans and stir? A critical review of the shamanism model of forager rock art production." *Journal of Anthropological Archaeology* 26:224–233.

McGinn, B. 1989. "Mystical union in the Western Christian tradition." In *Mystical Union and Monotheistic Faith: An Ecumenical Dialogue*, edited by M. Idel and B. McGinn, 59–86. New York: Macmillan.

McGinn, B. 1991. *The Foundations of Mysticism*. New York: Crossroad.

McKay, A. G. 2000. "Apollo the Healer at Elea/Velia (Lucania)." In *Gods in a Landscape: Papers of Section 14 of the 100th Joint Meeting APA/AIA, Washington DC 1998 (Études classiques 9)*, 11–21. Luxembourg: Publications du Centre universitaire de Luxembourg.

McPherran, M. L. 1996a. *The Religion of Socrates*. University Park: Pennsylvania State University Press.

McPherran, M. L. 1996b. "Socratic reason and Socratic revelation." In *Socrates: Critical Assessments*, edited by W. J. Prior, 167–194. London-New York: Routledge.

McPherran, M. L. 2010. *Plato's Republic: A Critical Guide*. Cambridge: Cambridge University Press.

McPherran, M. L. 2011. "Socratic religion." In *The Cambridge Companion to Socrates*, edited by D. R. Morrison, 111–137. Cambridge: Cambridge University Press.

Merkur, D. 1989. "The visionary practices of Jewish Apocalyptists." *The Psychoanalytic Study of Society* 14:119–148.

Meuli, K. 1935. "Scythica." *Hermes* 70:121–176.

Miller, H. W. 1945. "Aristophanes and medical language." *TAPhA* 76:74–83.

Miller, M. H. 1979. "Parmenides and the disclosure of being." *Apeiron* 13 (1):12–35.

Montiglio, S. 2005. *Wandering in Ancient Greek Culture*. Chicago: The University of Chicago Press.

Moore, P. 1978. "Mystical experience, mystical doctrine, mystical technique." In *Mysticism and Philosophical Analysis*, edited by S. Katz, 101–131. London: Sheldon Press.

Moravcsik, G. 1936. "Abaris, Priester von Apollon." *Körösi Csoma-Archivum* (Budapest), Suppl. 1 (2):104–118.

Morel, J.-P. 2000. "Observations sur les cultes de Velia." In *Les cultes des cités phocéennes* (*Études massaliètes 6*), edited by A. Hermary and H. Tréziny, 33–49. Aix-en-Provence: Edisud.

Morgan, K. A. 2000. *Myth and Philosophy From the Presocratics to Plato*. Cambridge: Cambridge University Press.

Morgan, K. A. 2010. "Inspiration, recollection, and *mimesis* in Plato's *Phaedrus*." In *Ancient Models of Mind: Studies in Human and Divine Rationality*, edited by A. Nightingale and D. Sedley, 45–63. Cambridge: Cambridge University Press.

Morgan, M. L. 1990. *Platonic Piety: Philosophy and Ritual in Fourth-Century Athens*. New Haven: Yale University Press.

Morrison, J. S. 1955. "Parmenides and Er." *JHS* 75:59–68.

Morrison, J. S. 1956. "Pythagoras of Samos." *CQ* 6:135–156.

Morrow, G. R. 1935. *Studies in the Platonic Epistles*. Urbana: The University of Illinois.

Motte, A. 1963. "Le pré sacré de Pan et des Nymphes dans le Phèdre de Platon." *AC* 32:460–476.

Mourelatos, A.P.D. 1970. *The Route of Parmenides*. New Haven: Yale University Press.

Mourelatos, A.P.D. 2013. "Sounds, images, mysticism, and logic in Parmenides." In *Eleatica 2007. Parmenide: suoni, immagini, esperienza*, edited by L. Rossetti and M. Pulpito, 159–177. Sankt Augustin: Academia.

Musitelli, S. 1980. "Ancora sui PHOLARCHOI di Velia." *PP* 35:241–255.

Nabert, N. 2005. "L'amour de Dieu dans la spiritualité cartusienne, l'héritage du XIIIe siècle." In *Mystique: la passion de l'Un, de l'Antiquité à nos jours*, edited by A. Dierkens and B. Beyer de Ryke, 121–129. Bruxelles: Editions de l'Université de Bruxelles.

Naddaf, G. 2013. "Philosophic and poetic inspiration in the *Republic*." In *Dialogues on Plato's Politeia (Republic)*, edited by N. Notomi and L. Brisson, 301–306. Sankt Augustin: Academia.

Napoli, M. 1966. "La ricerca archeologica di Velia." *PP* 21:191–226.

Nesselrath, H.-G., ed. 2010. *Plutarch: On the Daimonion of Socrates. Human Liberation, Divine Guidance and Philosophy*. Tübingen: Mohr Siebeck.

Nettleship, R. L. 1964. *Lectures on the Republic of Plato*. London: Macmillan.

Newberg, A. B. 2010. *Principles of Neurotheology*. Farnham: Ashgate.

Newberg, A. B., E. d'Aquili, and V. Rause. 2001. *Why God Won't Go Away? Brain Science and the Biology of Belief*. New York: Ballantine Books.

Nieto, J. C. 1997. *Religious Experience and Mysticism: Otherness as Experience of Transcendence*. Lanham: University Press of America.

Nilsson, M. P. 1961–1967. *Geschichte der griechischen Religion*. Munich: Beck.

Novotný, F. 1930. *Platonis epistulae commentariis illustratae*. Brno: Filosofická Fakulta.

Nussbaum, M. C. 1980. "Aristophanes and Socrates on learning practical wisdom." *YClS* 26:43–97.

Nutton, V. 1970. "The Medical School of Velia." *PP* 25:211–225.

Obdrzalek, S. 2013. "*Erōs Tyrannos* – Philosophical passion and psychic ordering in the *Republic*." In *Dialogues on Plato's Politeia (Republic)*, edited by N. Notomi and L. Brisson, 215–220. Sankt Augustin: Academia.

O'Brien-Moore, A. 1924. *Madness in Ancient Literature*. Weimar: Wagner.

Ogden, D. 2001. *Greek and Roman Necromancy*. Princeton: Princeton University Press.

Owens, J. 1979. "Knowledge and *katabasis* in Parmenides." *The Monist* 62 (1):15–29.

Palmer, J. 2009. *Parmenides and Presocratic Philosophy*. Oxford: Oxford University Press.

Palmer, J. 2013. "Revelation and reasoning in Kalliopeia's address to Empedocles." *Rhizomata* 1 (2):308–329.

Parke, H. W. 1988. *Sibyls and Sibylline Prophecy in Classical Antiquity*. London-New York: Routledge.

Parker, R. 1995. "Early Orphism." In *The Greek World*, edited by A. Powell, 483–510. London-New York: Routledge.

Pearson, J. L. 2002. *Shamanism and the Ancient Mind: A Cognitive Approach to Archaeology*. Walnut Creek: Altamira Press.

Pellikaan, M. E. 1974. *Hesiod and Parmenides: A New View on Their Cosmogonies and on Parmenides' Proem*. Amsterdam: Hakkert.

Périllié, J.-L. 2015. *Mystères socratiques et traditions orales de l'eudémonisme dans les dialogues de Platon*. Sankt Augustin: Academia.

Piemontese, A. 1987. "Le voyage de Mahomet au paradis et en enfer: une version persane du mirâj." In *Apocalypses et voyages dans l'au-delà*, edited by C. Kappler, 293–320. Paris: Editions du Cerf.

Pigeaud, J. 1989. *La maladie de l'âme: étude sur la relation de l'âme et du corps dans la tradition médico-philosophique antique*. Paris: Les Belles Lettres.

Pigeaud, J. 2008. *Poétique du corps. Aux origines de la médecine*. Paris: Les Belles Lettres.

Pollard, J. 1965. *Seers, Shrines and Sirens*. London: Allen & Unwin.

Popper, K. 1959. *The Logic of Scientific Discovery*. London-New York: Routledge.

Popper, K. 2001. *The World of Parmenides*. London-New York: Routledge.

Price, A. W. 1989. *Love and Friendship in Plato and Aristotle*. Oxford: Oxford University Press.

Pugliese Carratelli, G. 1963. "PHOLARCHOS." *PP* 18:385–386.

Pugliese Carratelli, G. 1970. "Ancora su PHOLARCHOS." *PP* 25:243–248.

Pugliese Carratelli, G. 1990. *Tra Cadmo e Orfeo*. Bologna: Societa editrice il Mulino.

Ramachandran, V. S. and S. Blakeslee. 1998. *Phantoms in the Brain*. London: Fourth Estate.

Rawson, E. 1985. *Intellectual Life in the Late Roman Republic*. Baltimore: Johns Hopkins University Press.

Reeve, C.D.C. 2000. "Socrates the Apollonian?" In *Reason and Religion in Socratic Philosophy*, edited by N. D. Smith and P. B. Woodruff, 24–39. Oxford: Oxford University Press.

Reichenbach, H. 1938. *Experience and Prediction: An Analysis of the Foundations and the Structure of Knowledge*. Chicago: The University of Chicago Press.

Renaud, É. 1987. "Le récit du mirâj: une version arabe de l'ascension du Prophète, dans le Tafsîr de Tabarî." In *Apocalypses et voyages dans l'au-delà*, edited by C. Kappler, 267–292. Paris: Editions du Cerf.

Rhodes, J. M. 2003. *Eros, Wisdom, and Silence: Plato's Erotic Dialogues*. Columbia: University of Missouri Press.

Richard, M.-D. 1986. *L'enseignement oral de Platon*. Paris: Cerf.

Riedweg, C. 1987. *Mysterienterminologie bei Platon, Philon und Klemens von Alexandria*. Berlin-New York: De Gruyter.

Riedweg, C. 1995. "Orphisches bei Empedocles." *A&A* 61:34–59.

Riedweg, C. 1997. "'Pythagoras hinterliess keine einzige Schrift' – ein Irrtum? Anmerkungen zu einer alten Streitfrage." *MH* 54:65–92.

Riedweg, C. 2005. *Pythagoras: His Life, Teaching, and Influence*. Ithaca: Cornell University Press.

Robin, L. 1935. *Platon*. Paris: Alcan.

Robinson, T. M. 1995. *Plato's Psychology*. Toronto: University of Toronto Press.

Robinson, T. M. 2000. "The defining features of mind-body dualism in the writings of Plato." In *Psyche and Soma: Physicians and Metaphysicians on the Mind-body Problem From Antiquity to Enlightenment*, edited by J. P. Wright and P. Potter, 37–56. Oxford: Oxford University Press.

Rohde, E. 1925. *Psyche*. London: Routledge & Kegan Paul.

Rosen, S. 1968. *Plato's Symposium*. New Havens: Yale University Press.

Rowe, C. J. 1990. "Philosophy, love, and madness." In *The Person and the Human Mind*, edited by C. Gill, 227–246. Oxford: Oxford University Press.

Rowe, C. J. 1993. *Plato: Phaedo*. Cambridge: Cambridge University Press.

Rowe, C. J. 2003. *Plato*. London: Bristol Classical Press.

Rubin Pinault, J. 1992. *Hippocratic Lives and Legends*. Leiden: Brill.

Rugg, H. 1963. *Imagination*. New York: Harper & Row.

Russel, B. 1961. *History of Western Philosophy*. London: Allen & Unwin.

Rütten, T. 1992. *Demokrit-lachender Philosoph und sanguinischer Melancholiker*. Leiden: Brill.

Sacco, G. 1981. "Pholeuterios-pholarchos." *RFIC* 109:36–40.

Salem, J. 1996. *Démocrite. Grains de poussière dans un rayoun de soleil*. Paris: Vrin.

Sargant, W. 1973. *The Mind Possessed: A Physiology of Possession, Mysticism and Faith Healing*. London: Heinemann.

Sayre, K. M. 1988. "Plato's dialogues in the light of the *Seventh Letter*." In *Platonic Writings/Platonic Readings*, edited by C. L. Griswold, 93–109. London-New York: Routledge.

Sayre, K. M. 1993. "Review of H. J. Krämer, Plato and the foundations of Metaphysics." *Ancient Philosophy* 13:167–184.

Schefer, C. 1996. *Platon und Apollon*. Sankt Augustin: Academia.

Schickore, J. and F. Steinle, eds. 2006. *Revisiting Discovery and Justification: Historical and Philosophical Perspectives on the Context Distinction*. Dordrecht: Springer.

Scott, D. 1995. *Recollection and Experience: Plato's Theory of Learning and Its Successors*. Cambridge: Cambridge University Press.

Seaford, R. 1986. "Immortality, salvation, and the elements." *HSCPh* 90:1–20.

Seaford, R. 2004. *Money and the Early Greek Mind*. Cambridge: Cambridge University Press.

Selser, C. 1996. "Aristeas." In *Der Neue Pauly* 1:1094.

Sholem, G. 1965. *Jewish Gnosticism, Merkavah Mysticism and Talmudic Tradition*. New York: Jewish Theological Seminary of America.

Siegel, R. K. 1980. "The psychology of life after death." *American Psychologist* 35 (10):911–931.

Siegel, R. K. and M. E. Jarvik. 1975. "Drug-induced hallucinations in animals and man." In *Hallucinations: Behaviour, Experience, and Theory*, edited by R. K. Siegel and L. J. West, 81–161. New York: Wiley.

Siikala, A.-L. 1987. "Siberian and Inner Asian shamanism." In *The Encyclopedia of Religion*, edited by M. Eliade, 208–215. New York: Macmillan.

Simondon, M. 1982. *La mémoire et l'oublie dans la pensée grecque jusqu'à la fin du Ve siècle avant J.-C.* Paris: Le Belles Lettres.

Smith, W. D. 1990. *Hippocrates: Pseudoepigraphic Writings.* Leiden: Brill.

Snell, B. 1960. *The Discovery of the Mind: The Greek Origins of the European Thought.* New York: Harper & Row.

Solmsen, F. 1969. "Review of: L. Edelstein, Plato's seventh letter." *Gnomon* 41:29–34.

Sommerstein, A. H. 1982. *Aristophanes: Clouds: Edited With Translation and Notes.* Warminster: Aris & Phillips.

Sommerstein, A. H. 1996. *Aristophanes: Frogs: Edited With Translation and Notes.* Warminster: Aris & Phillips.

Stace, W. T. 1960. *The Teachings of the Mystics.* New York: New American Library.

Strauss, L. 1952. *Persecution and the Art of Writing.* Chicago: The University of Chicago Press.

Strauss, L. 1966. *Socrates and Aristophanes.* Chicago: The University of Chicago Press.

Streng, F. J. 1978. "Language and mystical awareness." In *Mysticism and Philosophical Analysis*, edited by S. Katz, 141–169. London: Sheldon Press.

Stroumsa, G. G. 1996. *Hidden Wisdom: Esoteric Traditions and the Roots of Christian Mysticism.* Leiden: Brill.

Stuart, Z. 1958. "Democritus and the Cynics." *HSCPh* 63:179–191.

Sullivan, S. D. 1987. "*Prapides* in Homer." *Glotta* 65:182–193.

Svenbro, J. 1993. *Phrasikleia: An Anthropology of Reading in Ancient Greece.* Ithaca: Cornell University Press.

Szlezák, T. A. 1985. *Platon und die Schriftlichkeit der Philosophie.* Berlin-New York: De Gruyter.

Szlezák, T. A. 1993. *Reading Plato.* London-New York: Routledge.

Tarán, L. 1965. *Parmenides: A Text With Translation, Commentary, and Critical Essays.* Princeton: Princeton University Press.

Thorn, J. C. 1995. *The Pythagorean Golden Verses.* Leiden: Brill.

Todoua, M. 2005. "Empédocle: empêche-vents ou dompteur des mauvais génies? Réflexions autour du fr. 111 Diels-Kranz." *BAGB*:49–81.

Trépanier, S. 2004. *Empedocles: An Interpretation.* New York-London: Routledge.

Ustinova, Y. 2004. "Truth lies at the bottom of a cave: Apollo Pholeuterios, the pholarchs of the Eleats, and subterranean oracles." *PP* 59:25–44.

Ustinova, Y. 2009a. *Caves and the Ancient Greek Mind: Descending Underground in the Search for Ultimate Truth.* Oxford: Oxford University Press.

Ustinova, Y. 2009b. "Caves and the ancient Greek oracles." *Time and Mind* 2 (3):265–286.

Ustinova, Y. 2012. "Madness into memory: Mania and mnêmê in Greek culture." *SCI* 31:109–132.

Verdenius, W. J. 1942. *Parmenides: Some Comments on His Poem.* Amsterdam: Hakkert.

Verdenius, W. J. 1948. "Parmenides' conception of light." *Mnemosyne* 2:116–131.

Vernant, J.-P. 1983. *Myth and Thought Among the Greeks.* London: Routledge & Kegan Paul.

Vlastos, G. 1963. "Review of: Krämer, H. J., Arete bei Plato und Aristoteles. Heidelberg, 1959." *Gnomon* 41:641–655.

Vlastos, G. 1991. *Socrates: Ironist and Moral Philosopher.* Cambridge: Cambridge University Press.

Vlastos, G. 1995. "Anamnesis in the *Meno.*" In *Studies in Greek Philosophy*, edited by G. Vlastos, 147–165. Princeton: Princeton University Press. Original edition: *Dialogue* 4 (1965):143–165.

Vlastos, G., T. C. Brickhouse, M. L. McPherran, and N. D. Smith. 2000. "Socrates and his daimonion." In *Reason and Religion in Socratic Philosophy*, edited by N. D. Smith and P. B. Woodruff, 176–204. Oxford: Oxford University Press.

von Fritz, K. 1966. "Die philosophische Stelle im siebten platonischen Brief und die Frage der 'esoterischen' Philosophie Platons." *Phronesis* 11:117–153.

Walsh, S. N. 2012. "Empty esoterisms: Doctrines of secret writing and the politics of a Platonic code." *Polis* 29:62–82.

Werner, D. 2011. "Plato on madness and philosophy." *AncPhil* 31 (1):47–72.

West, M. L. 1971. *Early Greek Philosophy and the Orient.* Oxford: Oxford University Press.

West, M. L. 1983. *The Orphic Poems.* Oxford: Oxford University Press.

West, M. L. 1997. *The East Face of Helicon.* Oxford: Oxford University Press.

West, S. 2004. "Herodotus on Aristeas." In *Pontus and the Outside World*, edited by C. J. Tuplin, 43–68. Leiden: Brill.

White, H. 2005. *What Is What-Is? A Study of Parmenides' Poem.* New York: Peter Lang.

Whitehouse, H. 2004. *Modes of Religiosity: A Cognitive Theory of Religious Transmission.* Walnut Creek: AltaMira Press.

Williams, R. 2003. *Teresa of Avila.* London: Continuum.

Winkelman, M. 2000. *Shamanism: The Neural Ecology of Consciousness and Healing.* Westport: Bergin & Garvey.

Winkelman, M. 2011. "Shamanism and the alteration of consciousness." In *Altering Consciousness: Multidisciplinary Perspectives*, edited by E. Cardeña and M. Winkelman, vol. 1, 159–180. Santa Barbara: Praeger.

Wolfson, E. R. 1993. "Yeridah la-merkavah: Typology of ecstasy and enthronement in early Jewish mysticism." In *Mystics of the Book*, edited by R. A. Herrera, 13–44. New York: P. Lang.

Wolfson, E. R. 2010. "Light does not talk but shines: Apophasis and vision in Rosenzweig's theopoetic temporality." In *New Directions in Jewish Philosophy*, edited by A. W. Hughes and E. R. Wolfson, 87–148. Bloomington: Indiana University Press.

Wright, M. R. 1981. *Empedocles: The Extant Fragments.* New Haven: Yale University Press.

Zaehner, R. C. 1961. *Mysticism Sacred and Profane.* Oxford: Oxford University Press.

Zhmud, L. 1992. "Orphism and Graffiti from Olbia." *Hermes* 120:159–168.

Zhmud, L. 2012. *Pythagoras and the Early Pythagoreans.* Oxford: Oxford University Press.

Epilogue
Perspectives on the divine *mania*

This book, which begins with a quotation from the *Phaedrus*, is about inspiration, Plato's *epipnoia*.[1] Both the Greek term and the Latin *inspiratio*, from which the English word derives, convey the idea of breath, an airy invisible flow, entering a person from the outside, temporarily elevating him or her to an extraordinary level – of creativity, vision, knowledge, physical force, or courage, and sometimes causing profound personality changes, *metanoia*. When the Greeks witnessed a state of mind that was beyond comprehension in terms of regular experiences, they thought of *mania*: such phenomena were ascribed either to pure divine intervention or to an interaction of human and divine forces.

Mania involves a sense of loss of control or being led by an external power. It could be self-induced or forced on an individual, violent or quiet, transitory or lasting, illuminating or depriving one of his or her intellect, absolutely absorbing or allowing contact with the environment, divine or bestial. There is no clear-cut distinction between different kinds of *mania*, nor has one ever existed: prophecy and poetry, oracular and initiatory activities, mystery rites and early philosophy were always interwoven.

The essence of *mania* is that it is a state of consciousness different from the baseline waking state of mind. It is a distortion, first and foremost of perception. Mentally disturbed people, as well as seers, poets, and initiates see and hear what others do not. *Mania* is a state at the limits of the human nature. An individual experiencing it might display abilities beyond the normal human range, but can also become wild like an animal, cause irreversible damage, or be unable to return to the former self. Hence, different types of *mania*, even if believed to be instigated by a god, aroused admiration and fear, mixed in varying proportions. Abnormal and difficult to comprehend, divine *mania* belonged to the category of odd and inexplicable that immediately gives rise to awe and alienation. It is similar to 'the sacred,' paradoxically uniting the holy and unclean, which are isolated from the realm of the regular in many cultures, Greek culture included.[2]

Phenomena associated with divine *mania* were prominent in Greek religion. We have seen abundant examples of men and women of citizen status participating in ecstatic rites, employing various techniques of mind manipulation, or experiencing a spontaneous alteration of consciousness. While in the mythological past some opposition to the Bacchic frenzy probably existed, was limited to a number of aristocratic individuals, and successfully overcome. The uneasiness felt by some Greeks facing high-arousal cults was assuaged by attributing all of them to foreign origins, which was often false.[3] Distancing themselves in myths from the 'invention' of the ecstatic practices, the Greeks cognitively resolved the problem of their self-perception as citizens of the decorous civilised world, who only surrendered to the irresistible will of the foreign gods requiring ecstatic worship. Thus, everyone could enjoy blissful self-abandon to the fascinating rites of the Corybantes, Cybele, Sabazius, and Dionysus. Greek cities of the Classical age occasionally regulated, but never suppressed high-arousal cults.[4]

Inspired prophecy-giving was appropriated by sanctuaries run by poleis, at the expense of non-affiliated seers, but remained at the very core of Classical Greek religious practice and belief, mainly in the major oracular sanctuaries after they had gained renown and become Panhellenic. Greek aristocracy fully endorsed these practices: the oracular centre at Didyma was run by the Branchidae clan during the Archaic period, and the Delphic oracle was upheld by the local upper class.[5] The Eleusinian mystery cult, headed by three aristocratic clans and involving deviation from the baseline state of consciousness, was one of the most important cults of Athens. There are good reasons to believe that other mystery cults were run by local nobility in a similar manner.[6] A few intellectuals, such as Plato and Demosthenes, might have disapproved of a particular kind of mystery initiations, but they were powerless to limit them.[7] Pindar, the arch-conservative poet of noble virtue founded a sanctuary for Cybele and Pan in his own house, and exalted this goddess in hymns listing the mild-altering attributes of her cult.[8]

The attitude of the majority of Greeks towards alteration of consciousness was not just tolerance. P. Garnsey defines toleration as an 'active concept, not to be confused with indifference . . . or passive acquiescence,' which 'implies disapproval or disagreement coupled with an unwillingness to take action against those who are viewed with disfavour in the interest of some moral or political principle.'[9] Thus, in order to discern toleration, we must be able to establish that feelings of 'disfavour' towards a certain phenomenon existed – and in Greece, they did not. Furthermore, many cultic and cultural phenomena involving states of *mania* were not innovations or foreign intrusions, but were venerated as part of the ancestral patrimony handed out from generation to generation: people who experienced divine *mania* or enjoyed its effects, were not 'the other,' but 'we,' or at the very least, 'our wives.' It would therefore be misleading to maintain that different kinds of consciousness alteration were merely tolerated in Greece, similar to foreign cults and dissident philosophical teachings:[10] most practices involving *mania* were viewed as mainstream and actively endorsed by the communities.

In contrast, in the majority of complex societies, ancient and modern, ecstatic behaviour was often regarded as deviant, transgressing social norms, immoral and punishable, or eccentric and undesirable.[11] People involved in rites of madness regularly belonged to underprivileged groups, such as ethnic minorities and former slaves.[12] Ecstatic rites were never prominent in ancient Mediterranean societies. Outside the Greek world, inspired prophecy gained approval on an episodic basis only, in Israel of the monarchical period and in Mari.[13] There are no traces of the existence of mystery initiations in the Near East and in Egypt.[14] Egyptian tradition does not contain evidence on alteration of consciousness, and the silence of innumerable sources left by this civilisation proves at the very least that this phenomenon was banished far away from the main concerns of the elite.[15] In Mesopotamia, ecstatic rites existed, but remained marginal throughout the long history of the area.[16] Transvestite or castrated priests of Ishtar who practiced religious frenzy were held in deep contempt.[17] High-arousal rites appear to be alien to the Hittite world, and Kubaba, the minor goddess of the Hittite pantheon, has not developed there ecstatic features.[18] The Greeks linked Kubaba with the Phrygian Cybele – perhaps erroneously – and attributed to the latter goddess frantic rites, in particular of self-castrated eunuchs.[19] In fact, the tradition of eunuch priests, long regarded as the quintessential symbol of Oriental orgiastic frenzy, is not attested in Asia Minor before the Hellenistic period, and its details remain unclear.[20] The evidence on orgiastic rites in the indigenous cult of Cybele is minimal,[21] and some Greek stereotypes of Phrygian cults are deceptive. Thus, the Greeks called ecstatic music mode 'Phrygian,' although there is no evidence of ecstatic musical performances in Phrygia.[22] In any case, judging by the extant evidence, in late second-early first millennium Phrygia high-arousal rites were far from being as prominent as the Greeks assumed.

In Republican Rome, battlefield fury was promoted or tolerated, and poetic inspiration was well-known, but other practices based on the manipulation of consciousness were by and large judged as negative and marginalised or prohibited. Ecstatic cults, for instance of Cybele or Bacchus, were considered as foreign, potentially subversive, and put up with 'in an emasculated form.'[23] The Lupercalia, the fire-walking of Hirpi Sorani, and a few other high-arousal cults were noticeable, but far from being central to Roman religious practice.[24] The popularity of various ecstatic cults in the Roman Empire is quite a different phenomenon, and whatever its reasons may be, it does not affect the fact that the role of such phenomena in Greece was unique in the first millennium BC Mediterranean, and rare in history in general.

The main problem is not why ecstatic practices were allowed in Archaic and Classical Greece, but why they remained part of normative, rather than fringe, socio-religious activities in the complex polis society. In terms of cognitive historiography, this is a problem in 'cultural epidemiology': ideas shared by a considerable part of the people in the community have effects not only on what people think, but also how they behave.[25] In this book, I have attempted to determine what cultural environment supported the existence of alteration of consciousness as a sustained cultural phenomenon, in other words, what kind of shared ideas brought about social reality in which ecstatic practices belonged to the mainstream.

We have seen that 'the desire to alter consciousness is an innate, human, biologically based drive.'[26] Following J. Konorski's approach to hallucination, cited in the Introduction, I suggest picking up the analogy with neural mechanisms that normally inhibit hallucinations and have to be temporarily switched off for hallucinations to occur. *Mutatis mutandis*, the question is not 'Why do people tend to manipulate their consciousness?' but rather 'Why do societies restrict manipulation of consciousness?' The natural tendency to enjoy alteration of consciousness and trust the accompanying visions is limited or suppressed with the transition from traditional to complex societies, when practices involving alteration of consciousness, which are difficult to regulate, are usually pushed to the periphery or restrained by the elites striving to control the masses. Occasionally societies behave in a different manner. Greece is one of these exceptions.

The reason for this uniqueness is Greek 'theology of diversity,' as R. Osborne dubs it.[27] Greece lacked overall religious authority to be endorsed by the city-states, and of course anything resembling central power. Since religious expertise was considered dispensable, no class or social group of people in charge of other people's cultic behaviour had ever emerged in Greece, creating a strong contrast to other parts of the Mediterranean. In the absence of a priestly caste, canonical tradition, or sacerdotal hierarchy, the authority in religious matters largely stayed with the political power.[28] Writing on Classical Athens, R. Garland observes that

> By and large the Demos had little interest in regulating religious conduct, except when security or public order were compromised or threatened. This policy did not stem from any high-minded metaphysical or legal principle, but reflected firstly the sheer impracticality of enforcing a code of behaviour on behalf of a system which was so disjoined and fragmented, and secondly the varied personalities of the gods themselves, whose interests were frequently in conflict.[29]

The situation in other Greek democracies was hardly different. Before and after the rise of the democracy, landowning aristocracy, in Attica and elsewhere, were busy promoting local cults over which they presided or patronised,[30] and had never been embarrassed by manifestations of *mania* required by the tradition for the proper running of a particular cult. Although some Archaic tyrants attempted at religious reforms, none of them opposed ecstatic religion, and several tyrants even promoted the cult of Dionysus, popular with the wide masses of their supporters.[31] As a consequence of the absence of rigid priestly authority and lack of ability or desire to interfere on the part of political powers, the Greeks made the most of the alterations of consciousness that many of them experienced, and developed mechanisms that allowed them successful exploitation of these phenomena. In other words, the Greek idea of freedom included the licence to manipulate consciousness and enjoy, with proper caution and awe, the resulting psychological and social benefits. The Greek lack of restrictions was exceptional, and it determined the unique social environment, a complex society that did not constrain, disdain, or marginalise alterations of consciousness, but overtly admired and promoted its manifestations. To borrow the concept introduced by J. Sørensen, 'the immunology of cultural systems':[32] the Greek cultural model did not develop 'immunal mechanisms' oppressing alteration of consciousness, and minimising its impact on the society. Plato contemplated this reality and defined the concept of the 'blessings of *mania*,' which offers a very important insight into Greek society and culture.

Plato's conception of alteration of consciousness as a source of creativity and exalted knowledge was destined to have a long history in the European culture. During the Hellenistic period, mental disorder began to be regarded by some intellectuals as a sign of a noble mind – and therefore emulated by many who sought to appear exceptional. Section 30 of the pseudo-Aristotelian book *Problems*,[33] dealing with *melancholia*, begins with the question: 'Why is it that all those who are renowned in philosophy or politics or poetry or the arts are clearly melancholic (*melancholikoi*)?'[34] The author lists great heroes of the past, such as Heracles,[35] Ajax, and Bellerophon, and historical figures, such as Lysander, Empedocles, Socrates, and Plato, along with other sufferers from 'diseases which were caused by this bodily mixture.'[36] The afflictions of the melancholics are ascribed to an excess of black bile in their bodies. Among creative individuals, 'most poets' are affected.[37] Altogether, according to the *Problems*, many melancholics[38] achieve outstanding accomplishments and find 'contentment in song' (*ôdês euthumia*), but are prone to frenzy (*ekstasis*) and suffer from depression and sores:[39]

> Those in whom it [black bile] is abundant and hot are frantic, talented, sensual, and easily moved to passion and desire. . . . And many . . . are affected by diseases such as madness or engoddedness (*enthousiastkoi*), which explains the Sibyls and Bakids and all those who become engodded (*entheoi*), because they are like this not due to a disease but by natural temperament.[40]

This concept of a mental disorder which can be both gift and disease is strongly reminiscent of Socrates' speech on various kinds of *mania* in the *Phaedrus*.[41] The pseudo-Aristotelian section on *melancholia* encapsulates references to pathological frenzy and all the four kinds of desirable or divine madness listed in the passage which opens this book: the prophetic and telestic varieties are explicitly mentioned, poetic inspiration is alluded to as a juxtaposition of talent and enthusiasm,[42] and erotic *mania* is indicated with the description of the melancholics as *erôtikoi* and reference to their prominent desires.

There is, however, an important divergence between Plato and the Peripatetic author: while Socrates' *mania* is a blessing which is given by the gods, in the *Problems* inspiration is of natural origin, ensuing from the effect of black bile on some organisms. A revolutionary natural explanation of brilliance is provided: an exceptional talent results from a special equilibrium within an anomaly caused by the action of the black bile in the body.[43] For the Aristotelian philosopher, *mania* still produces genius, but madness is given an earthly, rather than heavenly, cause.[44]

In the *Problems*, *melancholia* is regarded as the nature (*phusis*) of some people, which endows them with various talents but also causes frightening ailments of body and mind.[45] The condition is inborn, may be life-long or temporary, and its symptoms often include acute somatic diseases and fits of frenzy.[46] This concept became fashionable during the Renaissance, was immortalised by A. Dürer, and only in the twentieth century ceded the title of the most discussed mental disorder to depression.[47] Even today, some neuroscientists and psychiatrists maintain that genius is essentially abnormal, and that illness and anomaly can be inductive to creativity and are signs of talent.[48] In any event, there is no doubt that through the Aristotelian texts, Plato's insight on the ambiguities of *mania*, the source of both anguish and super-human inspiration, had a profound effect on the European culture.

Notes

1 Pl. *Phdr.* 265B.
2 On the overlap between sacred and unclean see Douglas (1966), in a condensed form: Douglas (1975: 45–59).
3 See below in the Epilogue; cf. the chapter entitled 'The invention of mythology' in Borgeaud (1996: 31–56).
4 Chapter 3.
5 Chapter 1.
6 For instance, mysteries of Demeter were celebrated by the Lycomidae in their native Phlya, and involved chanting of hymns attributed to Musaeus and Orpheus: Plu. *Them.* 1. 3; Paus. 1. 22. 7; 4. 1. 5–7; 9. 27. 2; 9. 30. 12.
7 Chapter 2.
8 Such as cymbals, whirlers, and other musical instruments (for their effects see Chapters 2 and 3); Pi. *Dith.* 2, fr. 70B van der Weiden; Pyth. 3. 77–79; Paus. 9. 25. 3; Versnel (1990: 106); Parker (2011: 250). Borgeaud (1996: 138) suggests that Cylele arrived in Thebes via Peloponnesus, where her cult is attested to from the sixth century.
9 Garnsey (1984: 1); Sfameni Gasparro (2008: 15).
10 Toleration was the default choice in the Greek polis society (Garnsey 1984: 6; Wallace 1994; Baslez 2007: 51–85). The reasons for cases of persecution have recently been reassessed by Eidinow (2016).
11 For the concept of religious deviance in see Rüpke (2016, esp. p. 3).
12 Lewis (1989).
13 Chapter 1.
14 Nielsen (2014: 9–12). The absence of evidence on mystery rites in the Near East is indisputable, but the situation in Egypt has been debated; for the discussion see Assmann and Bommas (2002). The dominant view is that the phenomenon is not attested to in pre-Hellenistic Egypt (Dunand 2000; Assmann 2000: 35–37). Those who contend that the phenomenon existed base their view mainly on a single passage in Herodotus, where secret rites (*mustêria*) of Osiris are compared to the Greek Thesmophoria, defined as *teletê* (Hdt. 2. 170–171; Bleeker 1965). Herodotus' inaccuracies in the Egyptian logos, as well as his tendency to identify foreign cultic realia with Greek counterparts, preclude far-reaching conclusions based on his single testimony. However, the divergence ensues mostly from the lack of terminological clarity. Although secret dramatic rites certainly were performed in Egypt (Gillam 2005: 150–155), they cannot be interpreted as mystery initiations (Assmann 2000: 37; Nielsen 2014: 10).
15 Even scholars eager to discern such phenomena reluctantly acknowledge that 'contemplation, meditation, ecstasy, mystical experience: these are terms that scarcely appear in studies on Egyptian religion, which is usually qualified as ritualistic and formalistic. But by their very nature, these are experiences that are difficult to convey in discourse, for they have no outward, tangible manifestations. Recently, Philippe Derchain has shown how, in two obscure passages from the Coffin Texts, we can discern the conditions and signs of contemplation. No doubt close examination of other texts would enlarge our perspectives on the dimension of meditation, which the Egyptians had no reason to be ignorant of and which probably remained unrecognised until now

because of an overly superficial reading of the texts. At the very least, we know that drunkenness played a role in certain festivals, particularly those of Hathor, to produce a state perhaps something like that of a trance' (Dunand and Zivie-Coche 2004: 143).

16 Chapter 1.

17 Wilson (1980: 106–107); Borgeaud (1996: 48–49). A striking example of ridicule and despise towards transgender ecstatics in Mesopotamia: Taylor (2008: 174).

18 Laroche (1960: 127); Naumann (1983: 38); Roller (1999: 41–62, 114); Bryce (2002: 149); Borgeaud (1996: 5–6). Taylor (2008) offers an example of Hittite rites involving drinking from a cymbal or drum and ritual blood-letting, which may be compared to Cybele's rites.

19 Association of the two names: Laroche (1960); Roller (1999: 66); Munn (2008). Distinction between Kubaba and Cybele: Sfameni Gasparro (1985: 3); Graf (1984: 119) (who considers Kubabe as an exclusively Lydian goddess).

20 It is impossible to define when self-castration, in particular in ritual, began to be practiced in Anatolia; the earliest evidence is from the third century BC (Lancelotti 2002: 48–49). *Galloi*, their origin, and assessment of different forms of self-abasement: Lane (1996); Smith (1996); Alvar (2008: 246–261); analysis of the meagre evidence on ecstatic practices in the Anatolian cult of Cybele: Taylor (2008).

21 Or non-existent: Roller (1999: 114); analysis of the meagre evidence on ecstatic practices in the Anatolian cult of Cybele: Taylor (2008). Crucially, the Phrygian Mother had no divine consort: Borgeaud (1996: 34).

22 Naumann (1983: 79–80); Roller (1999: 110). Greek definitions of the Phrygian mode: West (1992: 177); Levick (2013: 41–42). The Phrygian mode in Greece was associated with the *aulos* (West 1992: 91–92, 177), but a double flute was represented on a single Phrygian monument (the early sixth-century relief from Boğazköy), and in conjunction with a lyre, which implies harmonious, rather than ecstatic, music (Naumann 1983: 79–80). Percussion instruments, such as tympana, symbolic of orgiastic music, are not attested to in Phrygia, archaeologically or iconographically: Berndt-Ersöz (2006: 169, 172).

23 Garnsey (1984: 9); North (1979); Beard (2012). See also the Introduction.

24 Str. 5. 2. 9; Pl. *NH* 7. 2. 19; Varr. *LL* 5. 85. For the aversion of both Roman masses and elite towards non-traditional overexcited religious practices, see Scheid (2016: 116–118).

25 Heintz (2014: 221). The concept was put forward by D. Sperber (Sperber 2001: 298) and developed by C. Heintz (2011).

26 Winkelman (2000: 7); cf. Iversen (2001: 73); see the Introduction for a detailed discussion of the subject.

27 Osborne (2015: 16).

28 Garland (1984: 75); Garland (1990); Parker (2011: 40–63).

29 Garland (1996: 91).

30 Frost (1996).

31 Dionysus and the Peisistratids: Andrewes (1969: 113); invention of the dithyramb by Arion when hosted by Periander: Andrewes (1969: 52).

32 Sørensen (2005).

33 For the date of its composition see above, Chapter 8. This section was popular in antiquity, and Cicero and Plutarch cite the opening passage as genuinely Aristotelian (Cic. *Tusc.* 1. 33; Plu. *Lys.* 2; for the probability of association of these passages with Aristotle's own ideas see van der Eijk 1990).

34 [Arist.] *Pr.* 953a (30.1), translation E. S. Forster. On the *Problems* see Forster (1927). For a discussion of V. Rose's suggestion that this chapter derives from Theophrastus' *Peri melancholias* (D. L. 5. 44), see Jacques (1998: 221); Klibansky, Panofsky, and Saxl (1964: 41); van der Eijk (1990); van der Eijk (2005: 139–168) finds similar ideas in other Aristotelian writings.

35 The case of Heracles is particularly remarkable, since the ancient tradition attributed him a peculiar 'disease of Heracles' which combined epilepsy, *mania*, and a horrible skin condition; the author of the *Problems* brings all these symptoms together by providing them a single cause, black bile, and thus creates an integrated image of Heracles, a great sufferer and a great hero at the same time and because of the same reason: von Staden (1992: 148–150). In the first century BC, Nicolaus of Damascus attributed Heracles' murderous fit of anger to either his boiling bile or derangement (*FGH* 90 fr. 13).

36 νοσήματα ἀπὸ τῆς τοιαύτης κράσεως τῷ σώματι, 953a31. For an analysis of this list, see Simon (1978: 231–232).

37 953a29.

38 If their abnormal state (*anômalia*) is balanced, 955a35.

39 954a25–26; in this text, ἔκστασις means insanity in the literal sense: in 953a15–21 Ajax and Heracles killing his children are described as suffering from ἔκστασις.

40 954a29–38: ὅσοις δὲ λίαν πολλὴ καὶ θερμή, μανικοὶ καὶ εὐφυεῖς καὶ ἐρωτικοὶ καὶ εὐκίνητοι πρὸς τοὺς θυμοὺς καὶ τὰς ἐπιθυμίας . . . πολλοὶ δὲ καὶ . . . νοσήμασιν ἁλίσκονται μανικοῖς ἢ ἐνθουσιαστικοῖς, ὅθεν Σίβυλλαι καὶ Βάκιδες καὶ οἱ ἔνθεοι γίνονται πάντες, ὅταν μὴ νοσήματι γένωνται ἀλλὰ φυσικῇ κράσει (translation E. S. Forster, modified).

41 *Phdr.* 244A–245C; Klibansky, Panofsky, and Saxl (1964: 17). The connection between the *Phaedrus* and *Problems* 30 was probably established by M. Ficino in the fifteenth century (Hanegraaff 2010).

42 Furthermore, an example of Maracus the Syracusan, a poet who wrote better verses when ecstatic, is cited immediately after this passage (954a38).

43 Hippocratic physicians dealt with medical and organic aspects of the condition which they considered as disease, characterised by mental and somatic symptoms (e.g. *Aere* 10; *Morb.* 1. 3. 13; *Aph.* 3. 14, 20, 22; *Aph.* 6. 23; *Morb.* 1. 30. 7–11; *Prorrh.* 1. 123). *Melancholia* has an exceptional name, which is considered to derive from the substance' that causes the affliction: *melaina cholê*, black bile. *Locus communis* of classical Greek – and later – literature, medical and non-medical, was that excess of black bile resulted in *melancholia*, and the specific form of the disorder depended on the temperature and other properties of this substance. Yet the illness predates the existence of its alleged cause, black bile (Müri 1953; Kudlien 1967: 77–99; Simon 1978: 234–235; Pigeaud 1989: 123). It is very probable that *melancholia* was a popular term, based on association of anger and madness with darkness and blackness, as well as bitterness (Kudlien 1967: 77–99; Joly 1969; Simon 1978: 234–235; Thivel 1981: 311–315; Sassi 2001: 155; Langholf 1990: 48–50; Pigeaud 1989: 102). In any case, at the beginning of the fifth century black bile came into being, and retained for centuries its respectable status of one of the four humours in the human body (Thivel 1981: 311).

44 Klibansky, Panofsky, and Saxl (1964: 40–41); Sassi (2001: 155).

45 Regarding the gifts of the melancholics, the author of the *Problems* followed the ideas of Aristotle put forward in an indisputably authentic treatise *On Divination in Sleep*, where he contends that because of their proclivity to change, the melancholics (*melancholikoi*) rapidly perceive images (*Div. somn.* 464a25–b2).

46 Aristotle maintained that excess of talent in a father may become madness in his offspring: 'Highly gifted (*euphua*) families often degenerate into maniacs (*manikôtera*), as for example, the descendants of Alcibiades and the elder Dionysius (*R.* 1390b28, translation J. H. Freese).

47 On the long history of melancholy see Jackson (1986); Klibansky, Panofsky, and Saxl (1964); Radden (2000); on melancholy in antiquity: Flashar (1966); Pigeaud (1989: 122–138); van der Eijk (2005: 139–168); Jouanna (2012: 241–258).

48 The question whether this is factually true is hotly contested, see Sussman (2007; Jamison 1993: 87–99), and Chapter 6.

References

Alvar, J. 2008. *Romanising Oriental Gods: Myth, Salvation, and Ethics in the Cults of Cybele, Isis, and Mithras*. Leiden: Brill.

Andrewes, A. 1969. *The Greek Tyrants*. London: Hutchinson's University Library.

Assmann, J. 2000. *Weisheit und Mysterium: Das Bild der Griechen von Ägypten*. Munich: C. H. Beck.

Assmann, J. and M. Bommas, eds. 2002. *Ägyptische Mysterien?* Münster: Wilhelm Fink.

Baslez, M.-F. 2007. *Les persécutions dans l'Antiquité. Victimes, héros, martyrs*. Paris: Centre national de la recherche scientifique.

Beard, M. 2012. "The cult of the 'Great Mother' in Imperial Rome." In *Greek and Roman Festivals*, edited by J. R. Brandt and J. W. Iddeng, 323–362. Oxford: Oxford University Press.

Berndt-Ersöz, S. 2006. *Phrygian Rock-Cut Shrines: Structure, Function, and Cult Practice*. Leiden: Brill.

Bleeker, C. J. 1965. "Initiations in ancient Egypt." *Numen* Suppl. 10:49–58.

Borgeaud, P. 1996. *Mother of the Gods: From Cybele to the Virgin Mary*. Baltimore: Johns Hopkins University Press.

Bryce, T. 2002. *Life and Society in the Hittite World*. Oxford: Oxford University Press.

Douglas, M. 1966. *Purity and Danger: An Analysis of Concepts of Pollution and Taboo*. London: Routledge & Kegan Paul.

Douglas, M. 1975. *Implicit Meanings: Essays in Anthropology*. London-Boston: Routledge.

Dunand, F. 2000. *Isis Mère des Dieux*. Paris: Errance.

Dunand, F. and C. Zivie-Coche. 2004. *Gods and Men in Egypt*. Ithaca: Cornell University Press.

Eidinow, E. 2016. *Envy, Poison, and Death: Women on Trial in Classical Athens*. Oxford: Oxford University Press.

Flashar, H. 1966. *Melancholie und Melancholiker in den medizinischen Theorien der Antike*. Berlin: De Gruyter.

Forster, E. S. 1927. *The Works of Aristotle: Problemata*. Oxford: Clarendon Press.

Frost, F. J. 1996. "Faith, authority, and history in early Athens." In *Religion and Power in the Ancient Greek Worlds*, edited by P. Hellström and B. Alroth, 83–90. Stockholm: Almqvist & Wiksell.

Garland, R. 1984. "Religious authority in archaic and classical Athens." *ABSA* 79:75–123.

Garland, R. 1990. "Priests and power in Classical Athens." In *Pagan Priests*, edited by M. Beard and J. North, 73–91. London: Duckworth.

Garland, R. 1996. "Strategies of religious intimidation and coercion in Classical Athens." In *Religion and Power in the Ancient Greek World*, edited by P. Hellström and B. Alroth, 91–100. Stockholm: Almqvist & Wiksell International.

Garnsey, P. 1984. "Religious toleration in Classical antiquity." In *Persecution and Toleration*, edited by W. J. Sheils, 1–27. Oxford: Blackwell.

Gillam, R. 2005. *Performance and Drama in Ancient Egypt*. London: Duckworth.

Graf, F. 1984. "The arrival of Cybele in the Greek East." In *Proceedings of the VIIth Congress of the International Federation of the Societies of Classical Studies*, edited by J. Harmatta, 116–124. Budapest: Akadémiai Kiadó.

Hanegraaff, W. 2010. "The Platonic frenzies in Marsilio Ficino." In *Myths, Martyrs, and Modernity: Studies in the History of Religions in Honour of Jan N. Bremmer*, edited by J. Dijkstra, J. Kroesen and Y. Kuiper, 553–567. Leiden: Brill.

Heintz, C. 2011. "Cognitive history and cultural epidemiology." In *Past Minds: Studies in Cognitive Historiography*, edited by L. H. Martin and J. Sørensen, 11–28. London: Routledge.

Heintz, C. 2014. "Scaffolding in core cognition." In *Developing Scaffolds in Evolution, Culture, and Cognition*, edited by L. R. Caporael, J. R. Griesemer and W. C. Wimmsatt, 209–228. Cambridge, MA: MIT Press.

Iversen, L. 2001. *Drugs: A Very Short Introduction*. Oxford: Oxford University Press.

Jackson, S. W. 1986. *Melancholia and Depression, From Hippocratic Times to Modern Times*. New Haven: Yale University Press.

Jacques, J.-M. 1998. "La bile noire dans l'antiquité grecque: médicine et littérature." *REA* 100:217–234.

Jamison, K. R. 1993. *Touched With Fire: Manic-Depressive Illness and the Artistic Temperament*. New York: The Free Press.

Joly, R. 1969. "Une nouvelle édition de 'La nature de l'homme.'" AC 38:150–157.

Jouanna, J. 2012. *Greek Medicine From Hippocrates to Galen: Selected Papers*. Leiden: Brill.

Klibansky, R., E. Panofsky, and F. Saxl. 1964. *Saturn and Melancholy*. London: Nelson.

Kudlien, F. 1967. *Der Beginn des medizinischen Denkens bei den Griechen*. Zurich: Artemis.

Lancelotti, M. G. 2002. *Attis. Between Myth and History: King, Priest and God*. Leiden: Brill.

Lane, E. N. 1996. "The name of Cybele's priests the 'Galloi.'" In *Cybele, Attis, and Related Cults: Essays Memory of M. J. Vermaseren*, edited by E. N. Lane, 117–134. Leiden: Brill.

Langholf, V. 1990. *Medical Theories in Hippocrates: Early Texts and the 'Epidemics.'* Berlin-New York: De Gruyter.

Laroche, E. 1960. "Koubaba, déesse anatolienne, et le problème des origines de Cybèle." In *Éléments orientaux dans le religion grecque ancienne: Colloque de Strasboug mai 1958*, 113–128. Paris: Presses Universitaires de France.

Levick, B. 2013. "In the Phrygian mode: a region seen from without." In *Roman Phrygia: Culture and Society*, edited by T. Thonemann, 41–54. Cambridge: Cambridge University Press.

Lewis, I. M. 1989. *Ecstatic Religion: A Study of Shamanism and Spirit Possession*. London-New York: Routledge.

Munn, M. 2008. "Kybele as Kubaba in a Lydo-Phrygian Context." In *Anatolian Interfaces: Hittites, Greeks and Their Neighbours*, edited by B. J. Collins, M. R. Bacharova, and I. C. Rutheford, 159–164. Oxford: Oxbow Books.

Müri, W. 1953. "Melancholie und schwarze Galle." *MH* 10:21–38.

Naumann, F. 1983. *Die Ikonographie der Kybele in der phrygischen und der griechischen Kunst, Istambuler Mitteilunden*. Tübingen: Wasmuth.

Nielsen, I. 2014. *Housing the Chosen: The Architectural Context of Mystery Groups and Religious Associations in the Ancient World*. Turnhout: Brepols.

North, J. A. 1979. "Religious toleration in Rome." *PCPhS* 25:85–103.

Osborne, R. 2015. "Unity vs. diversity." In *The Oxford Handbook of Ancient Greek Religion*, edited by E. Eidinow and J. Kindt, 11–20. Oxford: Oxford University Press.

Parker, R. 2011. *On Greek Religion*. Ithaca: Cornell University Press.

Pigeaud, J. 1989. *La maladie de l'âme: étude sur la relation de l'âme et du corps dans la tradition médico-philosophique antique*. Paris: Les Belles Lettres.

Radden, J., ed. 2000. *The Nature of Melancholy: From Aristotle to Kristeva*. Oxford: Oxford University Press.

Roller, L. E. 1999. *In Search of God the Mother*. Berkeley-Los Angeles: University of California Press.

Rüpke, J. 2016. *Religious Deviance in the Roman World*. Cambridge: Cambridge University Press.

Sassi, M. M. 2001. *The Science of Man in Ancient Greece*. Chicago: The University of Chicago Press.

Scheid, J. 2016. *The Gods, the State, and the Individual*. Philadelphia: University of Pennsylvania Press.

Sfameni Gasparro, G. 1985. *Soteriology and Mystic Aspects in the Cult of Cybele and Attis*. Leiden: Brill.

Sfameni Gasparro, G. 2008. "Religious tolerance and intolerance in the ancient world: A religious-historical problem." *Bandue* 11:11–38.

Simon, B. 1978. *Mind and Madness in Ancient Greece: The Classical Roots of Modern Psychiatry*. Ithaca: Cornell University Press.

Smith, J. O. 1996. "The high priests of the temple of Artemis at Ephesus." In *Cybele, Attis, and Related Cults: Essays Memory of M. J. Vermaseren*, edited by E. A. Lane, 323–336. Leiden: Brill.

Sørensen, J. 2005. "Religion in mind: A review article of the cognitive science of religion." *Numen* 52:465–494.

Sperber, D. 2001. "Conceptual tools for a natural science of society and culture." *Proceedings of the British Academy* 111:297–317.

Sussman, A. 2007. "Mental illness and creativity: A neurological view of the 'tortured artist.'" *Stanford Journal of Neuroscience* 1 (1):21–24.

Taylor, P. 2008. "The GALA and the Gallos." In *Anatolian Interfaces: Hittites, Greeks and Their Neighbours*, edited by B. J. Collins, M. R. Bacharova, and I. C. Rutheford, 173–180. Oxford: Oxbow Books.

Thivel, A. 1981. *Cnide et Cos? Essay sur les doctrines médicales dans la Collection hippocratique*. Paris: Les Belles Lettres.

van der Eijk, P. J. 1990. "Aristoteles über die Melancholie." *Mnemosyne* 43:33–72.

van der Eijk, P. J. 2005. *Medicine and Philosophy in Classical Antiquity: Doctors and Philosophers on Nature, Soul, Health and Disease*. Cambridge: Cambridge University Press.

Versnel, H. S. 1990. *Ter Unus. Isis, Dionysos, Hermes: Three Studies in Henotheism*. Leiden: Brill.

von Staden, H. 1992. "The mind and skin of Heracles: Heroic diseases." *Hautes Études Médiévales et Modernes* 70:131–150.

Wallace, R. W. 1994. "Private lives and public enemies: Freedom of thought in Classical Athens." In *Athenian Identity and Civic Ideology*, edited by A. L. Boegehold and A. C. Scafuro, 127–155. Baltimore: Johns Hopkins University Press.

West, M. L. 1992. *Ancient Greek Music*. Oxford: Oxford University Press.

Wilson, R. R. 1980. *Prophecy and Society in Ancient Israel*. Philadelphia: Fortress.

Winkelman, M. 2000. *Shamanism: The Neural Ecology of Consciousness and Healing*. Westport: Bergin & Garvey.

Index

Made in United States
Orlando, FL
12 March 2024

44658316R00226